MICROECONOMICS

MICROECONOMICS

Miltiades Chacholiades

Georgia State University

Macmillan Publishing Company
New York
Collier Macmillan Publishers
London

Macmillan Publishing Company
866 Third Avenue, New York, New York 10022

Collier Macmillan Canada, Inc.

LIBRARY OF CONGRESS CATALOGING IN PUBLICATION DATA

Chacholiades, Miltiades.
   Microeconomics.

   Includes bibliographies and index.
   1. Microeconomics.   I. Title.
HB172.C46   1986   338.5   85-3118
ISBN 0-02-320560-1

Printing: 2 3 4 5 6 7 8   Year: 6 7 8 9 0 1 2 3 4

ISBN 0-02-320560-1

To Mary

PREFACE

This book deals with contemporary microeconomic theory. Its main objective is to develop in a simple, thorough, and up-to-date manner those tools and principles that are necessary for understanding and analyzing microeconomic problems and issues. In the belief that lots of "curve-bending" cultivates intuition, the book relies heavily on a verbal, diagrammatic approach and avoids the gratuitous use of mathematics. All the arguments and explanations can be grasped by students who are familiar with only the material taught in principles of microeconomics.

Microeconomics is addressed primarily to undergraduate students at the junior or senior level. However, the exposition is pitched at a level that is also appropriate to serve the needs of MBA students and perhaps first-year graduate students of economics. Calculus is used only in appendixes at the end of the book, not in the body of the text.

Microeconomics is a truly intermediate book. It provides a smooth transition not only from the introductory course to intermediate microeconomic theory, but also from intermediate theory to advanced theory. Quick reviews of elementary topics provide the link between the principles course and *Microeconomics*. For instance, Chapters 1 and 2 deal with material that is typically covered in the principles course. The discussion within each chapter begins at a fairly elementary level and progresses gradually to higher and higher plateaus. The same philosophy also governs the discussion from chapter to chapter. For instance, while Chapter 2 discusses how supply and demand interact in the market to determine the equilibrium price, Chapters 15, 16, and 17 deal with such topics as the two-sector model, welfare economics, and capital theory, respectively. The gap between intermediate microeconomics and advanced economic theory is then bridged by optional mathematical appendixes. Thus it is fair to say that *Microeconomics* takes the students at the principles level and gradually elevates them to the realm of advanced theory.

The coverage of traditional topics (such as supply and demand, indifference curves, neoclassical production theory, cost curves, perfect competition, monopoly, oligopoly, monopolistic competition, and theory of distribution) is systematic and complete. The book also includes separate chapters, or sections, on such important topics as the two-sector general equilibrium model, optimization over time, uncertainty, and index numbers; nearly all of these additional topics are optional and can be omitted without interrupting the continuity of the book. Great care is exercised in defining each concept and placing it in the right place. The book has been designed to be as "self-teaching" as possible; all arguments are fully developed in a logical and systematic style. The belief is that a textbook should provide the conceptual framework of the subject matter so that classroom time can be devoted to analysis and applications. Instructors using this book will not have to spend their time filling in gaps in the textbook argument or explaining ideas that the book has glossed over.

Intermediate microeconomics typically illustrates important arguments and propositions by means of graphs. *Microeconomics* is no exception. Graphs are used freely throughout the book. They are carefully drawn and each one illustrates an important argument or principle. To help the student use the graphs effectively, extensive captions are provided at the bottom of all diagrams. Each chapter concludes with a numbered summary and a set of questions dealing with realistic situations to help the students understand the various concepts presented in the text. Occasionally, a question may extend the analysis to a more rigorous level. These more difficult questions are indicated by an asterisk(*).

The discussion is spiced throughout with a rich assortment of empirical and theoretical illustrations. All illustrations meet at least the following criteria: (1) they are relevant to the discussion in the text, illustrating an important point; (2) they are of current interest; and (3) they do not require knowledge of tools and concepts (such as statistics or econometrics) that go beyond the scope of *Microeconomics*. Some illustrations (e.g., pp. 121–122, 198–199, 300–301, 403–405, and 425–426) are of the story-telling type which bring out important social consequences of economic phenomena not captured by supply-and-demand diagrams. Other illustrations (e.g., pp. 7–8, 146–147, 238–240, 298–300, 334–336, 427–428, 451–454, and 536–537) give useful information on current economic problems that apply the concepts discussed in the text to realistic and relevant situations. To avoid disruption of the discussion, most illustrations are placed at the end of each chapter. In a few cases, however, illustrations are woven into the main body of the text.

As mentioned earlier, most chapters are supported by mathematical appendixes that deal with more advanced material. Written in the simplest possible way, each appendix contains several illustrations clarifying the various mathematical techniques used. These appendixes are placed at the end of the book because they represent optional material and can be omitted without interrupting the continuity of the book. They are carefully keyed into the main text to allow easy integration for those who choose to use them.

Microeconomics, or parts of it, can be effectively taught in one semester (or quarter), especially if the students do not have to review the material of Chapter 2. At a minimum, a short course should cover Chapters 3, 4, 6 to 16 plus Section 5.1 but excluding Sections 9.7 to 9.9, 10.6, 10.8 to 10.10, 11.1 to 11.6, 12.9, 13.5, and 16.6. (Surely some of the sections and chapters suggested for exclusion could be retained, depending on circumstances.) Also, depending on the level of mathematical sophistication of the students, some or all appendixes can be assigned at the discretion of the instructor. Other arrangements of the material are also possible.

Furthermore, an *Instructor's Manual* is available to accompany *Microeconomics*. For each chapter the Manual begins with a brief summary of the contents of the chapter; it provides a list of key concepts and terms for review; it gives answers to almost all questions that appear at the end of each chapter; and finally it concludes with a set of additional questions.

I am greatly indebted to many great economists, especially my former teachers Robert L. Bishop, Paul A. Samuelson, and Robert M. Solow, whose influence on me must be evident throughout the book.

Perhaps this book would not have been written if it were not for the enthusiastic response of my students over the years both here at Georgia State University and at New York University. Their insightful comments have helped me refine and improve my presentation and clarify obscure points.

I would like to express my thanks to David Salant, Virginia Polytechnic Institute and State University, who reviewed the entire manuscript and offered numerous suggestions for improvement. I would also like to thank Leonard A. Carlson, Emory University; Larry A. Chenault, Miami University; Arthur T. Denzau, Washington University; Errol Glustoff, University of Tennessee; Hyman Joseph, University of Iowa; Charles R. Link, University of Delaware; Stephen M. Miller, University of Connecticut; David E. Mills, University of Virginia; James W. Moser, Miami University; Patricia Moyers, Texas Tech University; Jon P. Nelson, Pennsylvania State University; Donald Owen, Texas Tech University; Robert Piron, Oberlin College; Michael J. Wasylenko, Syracuse University; and my colleagues Loraine Donaldson, Jorge L. Martinez, Joseph M. Pogodzinski, Rubin Saposnik, Mark E. Schaefer, and Bruce A. Seaman, who read parts of the manuscript and made many helpful comments. Indeed, Bruce Seaman contributed several questions especially for Chapter 11. Needless to say, any remaining deficiencies are all mine.

My editors, Chip Price and Jack Repcheck, have been very understanding, cooperative, and supportive at all phases of the manuscript. My research assistants, Bong Young Hong, Keith Leggett, Chwen-Chi Liu, Rengin Somer, and Chairin Weerastavanee, have also been very helpful throughout the writing of the book.

Thanks are due to Betty R. Hutchins for coordinating the typing of a long book; to Marilyn King, who did most of the typing; and to Mary Ann Smith, LaVerne Williams, Francina Holt, and Marian Mealing, who assisted them. Above all, I wish to thank my wife and daughters (Lea, Marina, and Linda), not only for their numerous suggestions and assistance in preparing the manuscript, but also for their encouragement and understanding during the time I spent writing the book.

M. C.

CONTENTS

xi

7 *Costs of Production* 205

PART FOUR *The Firm and the Industry* 245

8 *The Firm: Its Environment and Goals*   247

9 *Perfect Competition*   267

Part A. Static Equilibrium of the Perfectly Competitive Firm 267

Part B. Static Equilibrium of the Perfectly Competitive Industry 280

Part C. Applications 294

Appendixes 543

Indexes 617

MICROECONOMICS

PART ONE

Basic Economic Concepts

CHAPTER
1

Introduction

The two major branches of economics are *microeconomics* and *macroeconomics*. The prefixes "micro" and "macro" come from the Greek words "μικρός" (*mikros*) and "μακρός" (*makros*), meaning "small" and "large," respectively. Microeconomics deals with the economic behavior of "small" economic units (or microunits), such as households, workers, firms, and industries. Macroeconomics studies the behavior of broad economic aggregates, such as national income, employment, consumption, and investment.

In a sense, the micro-macro distinction is artificial. The actual decisions about production, consumption, investment, and employment are made by the microunits of the economy; thus the basic principles of economic theory are those which examine the behavior of the microunits. Indeed, until 1936, when John Maynard Keynes wrote his epoch-making book, *The General Theory of Employment, Interest and Money*, practically all economics was of the microeconomic variety. This is not true today, of course, because macroeconomics has flourished over the last half century. As it turns out, the micro-macro distinction is justified by the basic differences in the objectives and methods of the two branches.

This book is concerned with microeconomics (or microeconomic theory). Its purpose is to provide you with a kit of economic tools (or analytical devices) that will help you understand economic phenomena, issues, and problems.

1.1 The Economic Problem

Take a look at the U.S. economy. At the present time, it has at its disposal over 100 million workers with different kinds of skills (such as physicians, lawyers, teachers, farmers, nurses, musicians, secretaries, plumbers, automobile mechanics, industrial designers, computer programmers, truck drivers, and airplane pilots), over 3.6 million square miles of land of various qualities (such as land suitable for the production of wheat, corn, grapes, and other agricultural products; land rich in coal, oil, and minerals of all kinds; and land in coastal areas suitable for the construction of beautiful condominiums), and an immense collection of capital goods made available by our modern technology (such as machinery of all sorts, buildings, computers, buses, automobiles, trains, and airplanes). At the same time, about 230 million U.S. residents need a variety of goods and services, such as food, clothing, shelter, transportation, entertainment, and health care. Economics is the study of how the available resources (or factors of production), such as labor, land, and capital goods, are allocated and used for the satisfaction of the needs of the people.

There is an economic problem in the first place because of the fundamental law of scarcity. Even though the United States is the wealthiest nation the world has ever known, it still does not have enough resources to satisfy *all* the needs of *all* its residents. This law of scarcity imposes on society the necessity of choice. Somehow it must be decided which needs of which individuals or groups will actually be met. As a social science, economics studies the social machinery for making those choices and decisions. In this book, we investigate the nature of that machinery, how it operates, and why it produces the results it does.

The economic problem is often broken down into three parts:

1. *What* commodities are to be produced, and in what quantities? For example, should the United States produce automobiles, wheat, corn, computers, operas, movies, nuclear weapons, and how much of each?
2. *How* are these commodities to be produced? That is, what resources should be allocated to the production of automobiles, corn, and all other goods and services, and what technological methods must be used? Should we heat our homes with oil, natural gas, or electricity? Should we cook our food on an electric range or a gas range?
3. *For whom* are those commodities to be produced? That is, who is to enjoy the steak, the Cadillac, the fish, the fur, the concert, and the corn? How is the national output of goods and services, or gross national product (GNP), to be *distributed* among the different residents of the country? Should all residents be treated equally? Are there to be some rich and many poor?

The problems of what, how, and for whom are fundamental and common to all economies, although different societies may have different types of social machinery for solving them. Toward the totalitarian (or authoritarian) extreme, the solution is provided on a centralized basis. Some person (or group of persons) identified with the state has absolute power to determine the answers to what, how, and for whom. Toward the laissez-faire (or individualistic) extreme, the state plays a minimum role. The solution is thoroughly decentralized. Every person participates in the economic process both as a consumer and as either an organizer of production or a supplier of resources. Evidently, the analysis of an individualistic economy is inherently more complex than the analysis of an authoritarian economy. Indeed, the analysis of an individualistic economy will occupy us throughout this book.

1.2 **The Invisible Hand**

Have you ever wondered how that nice cup of coffee you may be drinking every day has come about? You probably know that it may have originated in Brazil. But what you may not know is that a great deal of planning was necessary before you actually could enjoy your cup of coffee. Long before the coffee berries were picked, a decision had to be made concerning the planting of coffee trees. It usually takes five years for a seedling to mature and bear a full crop, but this is not all. The process of making coffee ready for consumption requires all sorts of machines: milling machines to remove the parchment and the silver skin of the coffee beans; separator machines to remove sand, dust, and defective beans; blending machines to mix different types of coffee beans; machines for roasting and grinding coffee beans; canneries for preserving the ground coffee in cans or jars; and percolators or drip pots for finally brewing a delicious cup of coffee. Decisions to produce all these machines had to be made in advance, probably in different parts of the world. Each machine must have required a long sequence of decisions before it became available to coffee producers.

The need to coordinate economic activity in a community of millions of people and a multitude of commodities is infinitely more complex than the production of a single commodity such as coffee. For example, a large city, such as New York, Chicago, Los Angeles, or Atlanta, would probably starve to death within a few days if it were not for the continuous influx of goods from the rest of the nation and indeed the world. Who is coordinating all this economic activity? Who is consciously trying to provide solutions to the fundamental problems of what, how, and for whom? Nobody! Yet no person ever goes to bed at night worrying whether the groceries he or she will need the next day will be available at the neighborhood store. The free-enterprise system makes sure that the needed goods and services are available in the right quantities.

In a free-enterprise system every person pursues his or her own self-interest; but in so doing they solve one of the most complex problems known to man as if they were guided by an "invisible hand." This was the vision of Adam Smith (1937, p. 423) over two centuries ago when he wrote:

> But it is only for the sake of profit that any man employs a capital in the support of industry; and he will always, therefore, endeavour to employ it in the support of that industry of which the produce is likely to be of the greatest value, or to exchange for the greatest quantity either of money or of other goods . . . he is in this, as in many other cases, led by an *invisible hand* to promote an end which was no part of his intention. Nor is it always the worse for the society that it was no part of it. By pursuing his own interest he frequently promotes that of the society more effectually than when he really intends to promote it. (Italics added)

More recently, Paul A. Samuelson expressed an idea similar to that of Adam Smith. According to Samuelson (1980, p. 38):

> A competitive system is an elaborate mechanism for unconscious coordination through a system of prices and markets. It is a communication device for pooling the knowledge and actions of millions of diverse individuals. Without a central intelligence, it solves one of the most complex problems imaginable, involving thousands of unknown variables and relations.
> Nobody designed it. It just evolved, and like human nature, it is changing. But it does meet the first test of any social organization—it can survive.

Both Adam Smith and Paul Samuelson remind us that a decentralized free-enterprise economy, in which each agent, consumer or producer, acts solely out of individual self-interest, need not work chaotically. The price system works like an invisible hand, or signaling device, to coordinate the economic activity of millions of diverse individuals. This is indeed a remarkable result.

The price system is not an end in itself. Its main function is to enable the basic economic processes of production and distribution to operate as efficiently as possible. When the price system works smoothly, economic relations become inconspicuous, taken for granted, as attention turns to the resultant flow of goods and services that go to satisfy human wants. But sometimes the functioning of the price system is interrupted by such interferences as war, natural disaster, and even the policies of the Organization of Petroleum Exporting Countries (OPEC). Occasionally, the price system just goes awry, as in the Great Depression of the 1930s. Such interruptions have grave consequences for the economic welfare of society. It is particularly during such crises that most people become aware of the existence and significance of a well-functioning price system.

This book will equip you with tools that will enable you to become aware of the "invisible hand." You will learn its strengths and weaknesses and how it works to provide solutions to the fundamental questions of what, how, and for whom. Microeconomic theory (or microeconomics) is often called *price theory* because a large part of it deals with the workings of the price system.

1.3 The Nature of Theory

What is a theory? Why is theory needed? How can we tell whether a theory is good or bad? These are important questions that deserve answers, if only tentative ones, right from the start.

Mere observations of real-world phenomena are not enough to explain why and how these phenomena occurred, just as watching a television show does not explain how the hidden mechanism of the television set works. Explanation is provided only by theory. Theory is to a scientist what a gun is to a hunter. A hunter cannot go hunting in the forest without a gun. Similarly, an economist, or any other scientist, cannot hope to gain any insights into the workings of a complex world without the aid of theory.

As Plato noted in his famous simile of the sun (*The Republic,* Book VI), sight differs from the other senses, because in addition to the eye and the object, it also requires light. We see clearly an object that is illuminated by the sun. In twilight, we see confusedly, and in pitch darkness, not at all. If we identify the eye and the object with the human mind and a real-world phenomenon, respectively, then the sun (the source of light) becomes the theory that makes the phenomenon intelligible. Without theory we cannot understand or explain how events are linked together, just as we cannot see objects in pitch darkness.

One often hears laypersons invoking the aphorism, "true in theory but not in practice," when they happen to disagree with some explanation of a certain phenomenon. The truth of the matter is that facts do *not* "speak for themselves," and the nonprofessional's idea of what actually happens in practice is usually another simplified theory which in his or her opinion is better than the original one. The real choice is not between theory and practice, but between good and bad theories.

Because real-world phenomena are very complicated, explanation can be attained at the cost of simplification. *All* theories are abstractions of complex reality. This does not mean that our theories are bad. A map of New York City drawn on a one-to-one scale is useless. Similarly, a theory whose complexity approaches that of the real world offers us absolutely no assistance in our search for the fundamental economic laws that govern the U.S. economy or any other real economy. Unless we explain complex reality by something simpler than itself, we can accomplish very little.

Any theory represents a compromise between reality and manageability. To achieve manageability, it is necessary to carry out certain simplifications—to cut out irrelevant details. But the process of simplification should not be carried too far; important influences should not be disregarded. In addition to being manageable, a theory should also be "realistic" in the sense of incorporating the crucial elements of the phenomena that it purports to explain. Otherwise, the conclusions of the theory need not be relevant to the real world. Theorizing is partly an art and partly a science.

Students are often bothered by seemingly unrealistic assumptions. But as mentioned above, all theory is an abstraction of reality. We just cannot criticize the simplifying assumptions of a theory only on the grounds that they are not exact replicas of reality. A crucial test of a theory is whether it performs well, that is, whether it explains or predicts what it is supposed to explain or predict. For instance, consumers may swear that they do not consistently pursue the goal of utility maximization and that they do not even know what their utility functions or indifference curves look like. Yet the theory that is developed on the basis of the assumption of utility maximization explains and predicts consumer behavior well. It is *as if* consumers were unconsciously seeking to maximize their utility.

1.4 Positive Economics Versus Welfare Economics

Throughout this book it is necessary to keep in mind the fundamental distinction between *positive economics,* which is concerned with what actually *is,* and welfare economics, which deals with what *ought to be.* Positive economics is the science that explains how the economic system actually functions, that is, how society makes decisions about production, exchange, and consumption of goods and services, and how changes in the fundamental data of the economy (factor endowments, factor ownership, tastes, and technology) affect the solution to the economic problem.

Here is an example of positive economics. Can you predict what will happen to the price of television sets after the government imposes a tax of $50 on each set? Based on the theory presented in Chapter 2, all good economists will predict that the price of television sets will rise, but probably by less than $50. The accuracy of this prediction can be tested against the facts. Thus we can patiently observe how the price of television sets behaves after the imposition of the tax, and on the basis of this observation we can either verify or refute the prediction. Admittedly, testing a theory empirically is not always an easy task, because of other extraneous influences that may happen to be at work at the same time. However, this problem is not really different from that which other scientists face. In sum, we may say that in positive economics economists act as detached scientists.

In welfare economics, on the other hand, economists make recommendations for the economy on the basis of personal, subjective judgments of what is good or bad, not merely scientific analysis. For instance, consider the issue of income distribution. Is the current distribution of income in the United States satisfactory or desirable? Would an egalitarian income distribution be preferable? To answer these questions, we must make a subjective judgment, or value judgment, of a purely ethical nature. Such value judgment is ascientific; it cannot be proven right or wrong by means of empirical observations or pure logic. Here the economist expresses his or her opinion, but that opinion is no better than the opinion of any other informed citizen.

In practice, ethical beliefs almost always creep into the economist's analysis because any important economic issue is likely to involve an evaluation of several alternatives. This accounts for a well-known disagreement among economists, which is often dramatized by the following joke: "You put five economists in a conference room and you get six different opinions." What we must remember is that most disagreements among economists can be traced to some difference in ethical beliefs, not positive economics. Again, this is not different from any other discipline. For instance, a physician may explain to a despondent parent that because of an accident his child may never walk again without a delicate operation that could prove fatal in 95 of 100 similar cases. How to perform the operation is a scientific matter, but whether to perform the operation or not is a totally different question—it requires a value judgment.

To emphasize the significance of the distinction between positive propositions and welfare (or normative) propositions, a random sample of 600 U.S.-based econ-

Table 1.1 What Economists Think		
Proposition	**Agree**[a] **(percent)**	**Disagree (percent)**
1. Tariffs and import quotas reduce general economic welfare	97	3
2. Cash payments are superior to transfers-in-kind	92	8
3. A minimum wage increases unemployment among young and unskilled workers	90	10
4. A ceiling on rents reduces the quantity and quality of housing available	98	2
5. Effluent taxes represent a better approach to pollution control than does imposition of pollution ceilings	81	19
6. The fundamental cause of the rise in oil prices of the past three years is the monopoly power of the large oil companies	25	75
7. The government *should* be an employer of last resort and initiate a guaranteed job program	53	47
8. The government *should* index the income tax rate structure for inflation	68	32
9. The distribution of income in the United States *should* be more equal	71	29
10. National defense expenditures *should* be reduced from the present level	66	34
11. The level of government spending *should* be reduced (disregarding expenditures for stabilization)	57	43
12. The economic power of labor unions *should* be significantly curtailed	70	30

Source: Kearl et al. (1979).

[a]The "agree" column is the sum of the columns of "generally agree" and "agree with provisions" in the original responses.

omists were polled and asked to express their views on a variety of economic issues. A total of 211 persons responded. A small sample of the results of the study is illustrated in Table 1.1. The first six propositions are drawn from the domain of positive economics. Here the disagreement among economists is minimal. In contrast, the last six propositions, which contain the word *should,* are drawn from the realm of welfare economics. As expected, there exists substantial disagreement among economists with respect to welfare propositions.

Finally, note that positive economics is not totally free of unresolved questions and disagreements among economists. However, this is as it should be. At the frontiers of any science one always finds unresolved questions and disagreements. Indeed, disagreement of this sort is to the development of science what oil is to an automobile engine. Certainly, the purpose of research is to resolve these unsettled questions and narrow the area of disagreement.

SUMMARY

1. Economics is the study of how the available resources are allocated among alternative uses to satisfy human wants. It is divided into microeconomics and macroeconomics.

2. Microeconomics deals with the behavior of

microunits, such as households, workers, and firms. Macroeconomics studies the behavior of broad aggregates, such as national income and employment.

3. *Law of scarcity:* No nation has (or ever had)

enough resources to satisfy all the needs of all its people.

4. The economic problem is often broken down into three parts: what, how, and for whom. These problems are fundamental and common to all economies. In a totalitarian state, the solution is provided on a centralized basis. In a free-enterprise system, the solution is decentralized.

5. In a free-enterprise system every person pursues his or her own self-interest, but in so doing, they provide the solutions to what, how, and for whom as if they were guided by an invisible hand.

6. Theory is necessary for explanation and prediction. All theories are abstractions of complex reality, but important influences should not be disregarded. The crucial test of a theory is whether it explains or predicts what it is supposed to explain or predict.

7. Positive economics is concerned with what is, or how the economic system actually functions. The accuracy of positive propositions can be tested against the facts.

8. Welfare economics deals with what ought to be. Welfare propositions are based on value judgments, which cannot be proven right or wrong by empirical evidence or pure logic.

FURTHER READING

Friedman, M. (1953). "The Methodology of Positive Economics," in *Essays in Positive Economics*. The University of Chicago Press, Chicago.

Kearl, J. R., C. L. Pope, G. T. Whiting, and L. T. Wimmer (1979). "A Confusion of Economists?" *Papers and Proceedings of the American Economic Association*, pp. 28–37.

Knight, F. H. (1951). *The Economic Organization*. Augustus M. Kelley, Publishers, New York.

Nagel, E. (1963). "Assumptions in Economic Theory," *American Economic Review, Papers and Proceedings*, Vol. 53 (May), pp.211–219.

Robbins, L. (1935). *An Essay on the Nature and Significance of Economic Science*, Macmillan & Company Ltd., London.

Samuelson, P. A. (1952). "Economic Theory and Mathematics: An Appraisal," *American Economic Review,* Vol. 42 (May), pp. 56–66. Reprinted in J. E. Stiglitz (ed.), *The Collected Scientific Papers of Paul A. Samuelson,* Vol. 2. The MIT Press, Cambridge, Mass., 1966.

Samuelson, P. A. (1962). "Comment on Ernest Nagel's 'Assumptions in Economic Theory'," *Papers and Proceedings of the American Economic Association,* December 29, pp.231–236. Reprinted in J. E. Stiglitz (ed.), *The Collected Scientific Papers of Paul A. Samuelson,* Vol. 2. The MIT Press, Cambridge, Mass., 1966.

Samuelson, P. A. (1980). *Economics,* 11th ed., McGraw-Hill Book Company, New York. Chapters 1–3.

Smith, A. (1937). *An Inquiry into the Nature and Causes of the Wealth of Nations*. The Modern Library, Random House, Inc., New York. (Originally published in 1776.)

CHAPTER 2

Supply and Demand[1]

One of the main tasks of microeconomics is to explain why commodities (goods and services) have prices, and why some commodities (such as diamonds) are expensive, whereas others (such as haircuts) are cheap.[2] To explain the formation of prices, economists have developed a simple but most powerful instrument of economic analysis: the model of supply and demand. The basic idea is contained in a proposition that is known as the "law of supply and demand": The price of a commodity is determined where "supply equals demand." The law of supply and demand is a cornerstone of economic analysis. Indeed, some people believe that this fundamental law encompasses the entire science of economics.[3] Such a view is oversimplistic, but it does direct attention to the central role played in economics by the basic tools of supply and demand. A good understanding of the law of supply and demand is an important prerequisite to any serious investigation into the workings of a market system.

The law of supply and demand is the subject matter of this chapter. By necessity, the discussion of the law of supply and demand is not exhaustive. It provides only a bird's-eye view of how the law works and of what might happen if it were suspended. In particular, the first five sections of this chapter give a tentative answer to the following important question: How do the forces of supply and demand interact in the market to determine price? In Sections 2.6 and 2.7 we introduce the useful concepts of elasticity of demand and elasticity of supply, respectively. In Section 2.8 we study the effects of shifts in either the demand curve or the supply curve and conclude with an important application: the effects of commodity taxes. Finally, in Section 2.9 we examine the consequences of price controls—a form of government intervention that in effect suspends the law of supply and demand.

---

[1]This is a review chapter. Students familiar with the model of supply and demand may omit this chapter.

[2]The price of a commodity is the amount of money that must be paid for one unit of it.

[3]The Scottish essayist and historian Thomas Carlyle (1795–1881) is quoted as having said: "It's easy to train economists; just teach a parrot to say supply and demand."

2.1 Usefulness and Scarcity

Commodities are used by consumers to satisfy their needs and wants. They are classified into goods and services. Goods are tangible, such as books, cars, and houses. Services are intangible, such as haircuts, concerts, and operas. Goods and services must be distinguished from "bads" and "disservices." The latter are those things that are a nuisance, such as nuclear waste material and noise pollution.

Most commodities are scarce in relation to the uses to which they can be put. Examples of scarce commodities (often called *economic goods*) are all those things that we purchase every day, such as food, clothes, shoes, and gasoline. Nevertheless, there are also commodities that are not scarce. For example, the air we breathe exists in such natural abundance that everyone's desire for it is fully satisfied. Commodities that are not scarce are known as *free goods*. In this book we are interested primarily in economic goods. If all commodities were free goods, there would be no need to study economics.

Typically, the economic goods that are used by consumers to satisfy their needs (known as *economic consumption goods*) come into existence through *production*. This is a process by which resources (such as labor services, land, buildings, machinery, tools, and raw materials) are used to make (*produce*) those things that people desire. Such resources are known as *factors of production*. In a deeper sense, the scarcity of economic consumption goods reflects the scarcity of the factors of production. No society in the history of the world has ever had enough resources to produce all commodities in sufficiently large amounts to satisfy all the needs of all its members.

Only economic goods have prices. This is so because only economic goods have the two basic attributes that are necessary for the existence of prices: *usefulness* and *scarcity*. For instance, nuclear waste material and garbage cannot command positive prices because they are *not* useful—they are "bads," not "goods." But usefulness alone is not enough. To bear a positive price, a commodity must also be scarce. For example, air is clearly useful to all human beings; yet air cannot command a positive price because it is *not* scarce—it is a free good.

In the marketplace, the abstract forces of usefulness and scarcity manifest themselves in the concrete forms of demand and supply, respectively. Commodities are demanded by buyers because they are useful to them, and sellers cannot supply commodities in unlimited quantities because commodities are scarce. For instance, students purchase pocket calculators because they find them useful in performing calculations. The sellers of pocket calculators cannot supply them in unlimited quantities because they cannot produce them freely—the necessary factors for the production of calculators are scarce. We therefore conclude that prices are determined by supply and demand, where supply reflects the scarcity, and demand the usefulness, of commodities.

2.2 The Market

A market is composed of sellers (suppliers) and buyers (demanders). These persons are in close touch with each other in order to sell or buy some commodity. How the buyers and sellers actually keep in touch with each other is not important. If all buyers and sellers are housed in the same building, they can transact business face to face. If they are scattered around the globe (as is the case with the foreign exchange market in which national currencies are traded), they can keep in constant touch with each other and transact business by telephone, telegraph, or teletype.

Because of the close link among buyers and sellers, *the price of the traded commodity tends to uniformity throughout the market* (ignoring differences due to trans-

portation costs). This result is often referred to as the *law of one price.* The justification for this law follows from the fact that no buyer is willing to pay a price
that is higher than the lowest available price (plus transportation costs). Similarly,
no seller is willing to accept a price that is lower than the highest obtainable price
(less transportation costs). As a consequence, the same price must eventually rule
everywhere in the market (with allowance made for transportation costs).

The law of one price does not actually require each buyer or seller to be in close
touch with all other buyers and sellers. It is sufficient that each market participant
is in touch with only a small subset (group) of all other persons in the market. To
the extent that these subsets overlap, the market will function as a unified entity—
as if each person were in touch with every other person in the market. For instance,
a housewife does not check the prices of all grocery stores in town before she purchases, say, Idaho potatoes. It is reasonable to assume that she is only familiar with
the prices of a few stores in her neighborhood. Yet she knows that the price she
pays does not differ substantially from the prices charged by other stores. Since
households are spread throughout the town, neighborhoods overlap; and the geographically dispersed grocery stores are connected like the links of a chain.

We can strengthen the argument for the law of one price by introducing the
concept of *arbitrage,* which is the simultaneous purchase and sale of a commodity
for the sake of profit. When the price of a commodity differs from one part of the
market to another, a trader (*arbitrager*) can make a profit by buying the commodity
where it is cheap and selling it where it is expensive. This kind of arbitrage tends
to establish a uniform price throughout the market by depressing it where it is
high and raising it where it is low.

It must be evident to anyone who has walked through the showrooms of automobile dealers that real markets do not display a uniform price as predicted by the
law of one price. On the contrary, they exhibit a whole array of prices (for the *same*
commodity). Yet persistent price differentials are usually small. Accordingly, the
law of one price is a fair approximation of reality.

The Perfectly Competitive Market

To learn more about supply, demand, and price formation, we devote the remainder of this chapter to the study of a peculiar market form known as a *perfectly
competitive market.* The latter is a market that satisfies the following important
conditions:

1. *Large numbers:* There must be *many small buyers and many small sellers,* so
   that none of them individually can exert any appreciable influence on the
   price. This condition is clearly satisfied in the case of most agricultural commodities. For instance, there are many small wheat farmers and many small
   buyers of wheat (of a particular grade). Each wheat farmer produces only an
   insignificant percentage of the aggregate output of wheat traded in the United
   States every year. Because of this, the typical wheat farmer knows that no
   change (increase or decrease) in his or her output can have an appreciable
   effect on the price of wheat. In other words, every wheat farmer is a *price
   taker.* The many small buyers of wheat are also price takers. Indeed, price
   taking is common among consumers.

2. *Homogeneity of the product:* The buyers and sellers must deal in a *homogenous*
   good. This means that in the eyes of the buyers all the units of the good offered
   for sale must be of the same quality. For instance, every bushel of wheat (of
   a certain grade) offered for sale in the wheat market must be of the same
   quality as any other bushel of wheat (of the same grade). The implication of

this homogeneity assumption is that there cannot be any price difference between units of the same commodity due to a difference in quality.

3. *Perfect knowledge:* All buyers and sellers must be completely informed about the prices that prevail in all parts of the market. This ensures that the law of one price holds.

The model of the perfectly competitive market is very useful. It is used widely by economists because of its ability to explain and predict behavior in the real world.

2.3 Demand

Having discussed the concept of a market, we now turn to the concepts of supply and demand. In this section we deal with demand.

The Quantity Demanded

What do economists mean by "demand"? Economists often attach several meanings to this term. We discuss two of those meanings here: the *quantity demanded* and the *demand curve.*

Consider a hypothetical market for wheat. The quantity of wheat demanded is the total number of bushels of wheat that all buyers (consumers) wish to purchase, given the price of wheat (so many dollars per bushel). Accordingly, "quantity demanded" refers to a *desired* quantity—the total amount that all consumers together are willing to purchase. This desired quantity is not the same thing as the *actual* quantity bought on the market. The latter may be less than the desired quantity if a sufficient amount is not available.

The desired quantity demanded does not include all those amounts that consumers think they need and can use. It includes only those amounts that consumers are *willing to purchase* at the current price. That is, consumers must be *willing and able* to pay the dollar price. For instance, if a poor family wishes to buy a beautiful house but cannot afford its high price, the family's mere desire has no effect on the number of houses demanded. Desired demand means demand that is backed by purchasing power.

Note also that "quantity demanded" may refer either to a *stock* or to a *flow.* The distinction between stocks and flows is very important in economics. A flow variable has a time dimension; that is, it must be described as so much *per week* or *per month.* A stock variable refers to a quantity that exists at an instant of time. A few examples should make the distinction clear. The number of persons living in the United States on January 1, 1986, is a stock, but the number of births *per week* is a flow. Similarly, my accumulated wealth as of December 31, 1985, is a stock; but my income *per month* is a flow. The total quantity of money in existence on July 1, 1985, is a stock, but the additional (new) money created by the Federal Reserve System *per year* is a flow. In this book we are concerned primarily with flow variables, such as the quantity of wheat demanded by ultimate consumers per period of time (say, 2 million bushels of wheat per day or 14 million bushels per week).

The Market Demand Curve

The quantity demanded is primarily a function of (or depends on) the price of the good. Other things equal (i.e., holding other influences constant), *the quantity demanded increases as the price falls.* This is an important economic hypothesis, which is usually referred to as the *law of demand.*

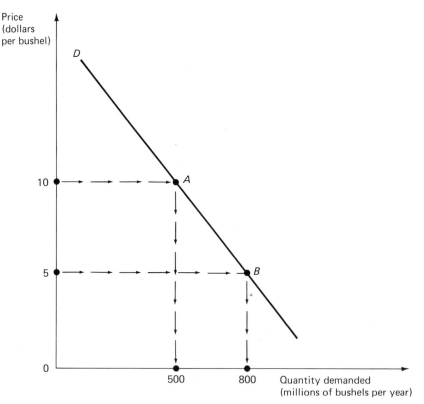

Figure 2.1 The market demand curve. When the price is $10 per bushel, consumers are
willing to purchase 500 million bushels of wheat per year. When the price falls to $5 per
bushel, consumers are willing to increase their purchases to 800 million bushels of wheat
per year. This behavior illustrates the *law of demand.*

The relationship between quantity demanded and price can be represented graphically by a downward-sloping *market demand curve,* as illustrated in Figure 2.1 by
curve *D*. It is conventional—almost universal—to measure price (dollars per unit
of the good) along the vertical axis and quantity demanded per unit of time (millions
of bushels per year) along the horizontal axis.[4] For any given price, the market
demand curve gives the total quantity demanded by all consumers per period of
time, say, per year. For instance, when the price is $10 per bushel, the quantity
demanded is 500 million bushels per year, as shown by the coordinates of point *A*.
As the price falls to $5 per bushel, the quantity demanded increases to 800 million
bushels per year.

In Figure 2.1 the market demand curve is drawn as a straight line. This is done
for convenience only. The important consideration is that the market demand curve
slopes downward from left to right.

What is the economic justification of the law of demand? In other words, why is
it that the quantity demanded increases as the price falls? As the price falls, at

---

[4]The convention of measuring price on the vertical axis and quantity on the horizontal axis is attributable
to the British economist Alfred Marshall (1842–1924). All economists today follow the Marshallian
convention. Nevertheless, Marshall's scheme is opposite to the standard mathematical practice of measuring the dependent variable (quantity demanded) vertically and the independent variable (price)
horizontally.

least some consumers increase their purchases because they find the good cheaper now relative to other goods whose prices have not fallen (or have not fallen as much). For instance, when the price of oil skyrocketed in the 1970s, many consumers switched their homes from oil heating to gas, which suddenly became cheaper relative to oil. Thus an increase in the price of oil reduced the quantity of oil demanded as consumers shifted to gas, which is another way of saying that the demand curve for oil slopes downward.

Another reason for the negative slope of the demand curve is that consumers who were previously unable to buy the good will enter the market when its price falls. This is vividly illustrated by the case of pocket calculators, which have experienced a drastic reduction in price over the last 15 years.

Other Determinants of the Quantity Demanded

The price of a good is not the only variable affecting the demand for it. Several other variables are also important. Included in these other variables are tastes, per capita income, income distribution, prices of related goods, and population size. The market demand curve is drawn on the assumption that all these other variables (except the good's own price) remain constant. When any of these other variables change, the entire market demand curve shifts to a new position, as explained below.

1. *The tastes of consumers:* Suppose that consumers develop a stronger preference for a good. That means that consumers are willing to buy more of it than previously *at each price,* and accordingly the market demand curve shifts to the right. Similarly, when consumers develop a weaker preference for a good, they are willing to buy less of it at each price. Consequently, the market demand curve shifts to the left. As consumers become more energy conscious and eliminate unnecessary driving, the quantity of gasoline demanded de-

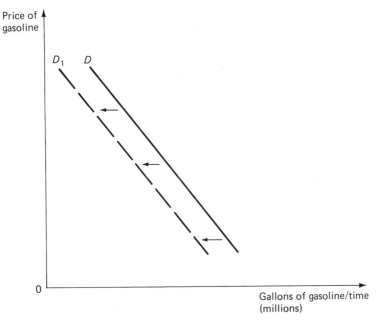

Figure 2.2 A shift of the market demand curve for gasoline. As consumers become more energy-conscious and eliminate unnecessary driving, the quantity of gasoline demanded decreases at every price. Thus market demand curve D shifts to the left, as illustrated by D_1.

creases at every price; thus the entire market demand curve for gasoline shifts to the left. This is illustrated in Figure 2.2 by the shift of the market demand curve from D to D_1.

2. *The average income of consumers:* As per capita income increases while commodity prices remain unchanged, consumers tend to buy more of most goods (known as *normal goods*) and less of some other goods (known as *inferior goods*). For instance, as consumers get richer, they may buy more steaks (normal good) and fewer hamburgers (inferior good). This means that as per capita income increases, the market demand curve for a normal good (steak) shifts to the right while the market demand curve for an inferior good (hamburger) shifts to the left, as illustrated in Figure 2.3.

3. *The distribution of income:* A change in the distribution of income may cause the market demand curve to shift to the right or the left, depending on circumstances. Suppose that Peter's income is increased by $100 and Paul's income is simultaneously reduced by $100. This income redistribution could result, for instance, from an increase in social security benefits to Peter financed by an increase in taxes on Paul's income. How will such income redistribution affect the market demand curve for, say, food?

  If Peter increased his purchases of food by exactly as much as Paul decreased his, the total quantity of food demanded (at the current price) would remain the same—the market demand curve for food would *not* shift. Suppose, however, that Peter (a low-income person) actually increases his purchases of food by more than the amount by which Paul (a high-income person) decreases his. In this case, the total quantity of food demanded will increase—the market demand curve for food will shift to the right. Surely, if at some later date the increases in social security benefits and taxes were canceled, the market demand curve for food would shift to the left; that is, it would shift back to its initial position.

4. *The prices of related goods:* Usually, a need may be satisfied by more than one good. For instance, consumers use beef or pork to satisfy their hunger. Similarly, consumers use wool cloth or cotton cloth to satisfy their need for

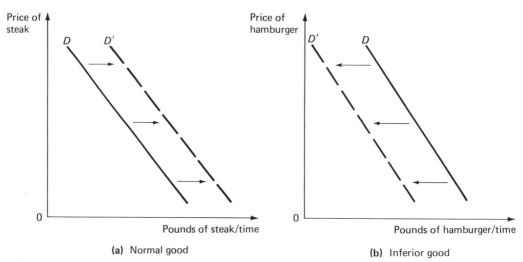

Figure 2.3 Changes in per capita income and the market demand curve. As per capita income increases while the prices of commodities remain unchanged, the market demand curve for steak (normal good) shifts to the right, as illustrated in panel (a), and the market demand curve for hamburger (inferior good) shifts to the left, as illustrated in panel (b).

clothing. Goods such as beef and pork, or wool cloth and cotton cloth, are called *substitutes*—one can be substituted for the other in the satisfaction of the consumers' needs.

The markets of substitutes are related. For instance, when the price of pork (a beef substitute) falls, the market demand curve for beef shifts to the left, because consumers tend to substitute pork for the now more expensive beef. Similarly, when the price of wool cloth rises, the market demand curve for cotton cloth shifts to the right as consumers tend to substitute cotton cloth for the now more expensive wool cloth.

There are also commodities that tend to be used jointly with each other. These commodities are called *complements*. Some examples of complementary goods are autos and tires, coffee and sugar, and tennis balls and tennis rackets. The markets of complementary goods are also related. For instance, as the price of tennis rackets falls, the market demand curve for tennis balls shifts to the right—since more people are playing tennis, more balls are needed.

5. *The size of the population:* As population grows, the demand curves for almost all commodities shift to the right. Obviously, more people need more food, more clothing, more houses, more cars, more gasoline, and more of everything else consumed by the typical family.

2.4 Supply

We continue our discussion of the law of supply and demand in this section by considering the concept of supply.

The Quantity Supplied

The term *quantity supplied* refers to the total amount of a good that sellers are willing to sell in the market, given the price of the good. The quantity supplied is also a *desired* quantity, and it may or may not coincide with the actual quantity sold. For instance, suppose that at the current price, buyers wish to purchase a smaller quantity than the quantity sellers are willing to sell. Then the quantity supplied will exceed the actual quantity sold—sellers cannot force buyers to purchase the larger quantity.

As we have seen, the quantity demanded may refer either to a stock or to a flow. The same is true of the quantity supplied. Thus both the number of genuine Rembrandts supplied and the money supply are stocks. But the millions of bushels of wheat and the millions of tons of coal supplied *per year* are flows.

The Supply Curve

The quantity supplied is a function of many variables. Primarily, however, the quantity supplied is a function of the good's own price. Usually, but not always, the quantity supplied increases as the price rises, other things being equal. In other words, the sellers of a good are usually willing to offer more of it if price is high than if price is low. Even though we shall initially limit our attention to this positive relationship between quantity supplied and price, we must emphasize that there are major exceptions to this simple principle.

The positive relationship between quantity supplied and price can be represented graphically by an upward-sloping *market supply curve,* as illustrated in Figure 2.4 by hypothetical curve S. The vertical axis measures the price (dollars per bushel of wheat), and the horizontal axis measures the quantity supplied per unit of time (millions of bushels of wheat per year). For any given price, the supply curve shows

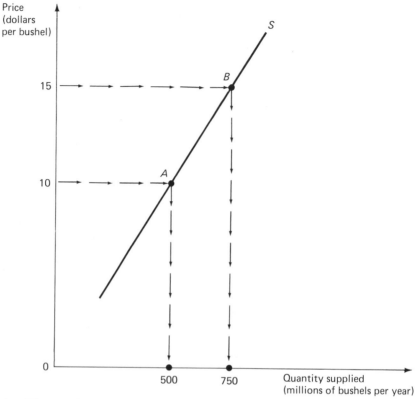

Figure 2.4 The market supply curve. When the price is $10, sellers are willing to sell 500 million bushels of wheat per year. When the price rises to $15, they are willing to increase their sales to 750 million bushels of wheat per year.

the aggregate quantity supplied by all sellers per year. For instance, when the price is $10 per bushel, the quantity supplied is 500 million bushels per year (point *A*), and when the price rises to $15 per bushel, the quantity supplied increases to 750 million bushels per year (point *B*).

Why do supply curves normally slope upward from left to right? To increase the quantity supplied, sellers must increase their production. Typically, producers can increase their output by employing more factors of production, which they can attract from other industries. Normally, these additional factors are more expensive. For instance, to attract more workers, producers may have to pay higher wages. Accordingly, the per unit cost tends to rise as the output of a good expands, and the price must rise to enable producers to cover their higher per unit cost. This is a simplified explanation of why supply curves slope upward.

Other Determinants of the Quantity Supplied

Besides the price of the good, several other variables influence the quantity supplied. The most important of these other variables are the costs of factors of production and the state of technology. The market supply curve is drawn on the assumption that these other variables remain constant. A change in any one of these variables (such as an increase in wages or rents or an improvement in technology) will cause the entire market supply curve to shift to a new position.

For instance, cost-reducing innovations and/or reductions in the costs of factor services will cause the market supply curve to shift downward and to the right, as

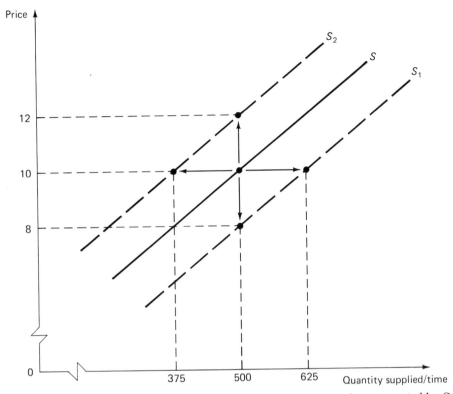

Figure 2.5 Shifts of the supply curve. Initially, the supply curve is represented by S. Any cost-reducing innovations or any reductions in the costs of factor services cause the supply curve to shift downward and to the right, as shown by S_1. Alternatively, any increases in the costs of factor services cause the supply curve to shift upward and to the left, as shown by S_2.

shown in Figure 2.5 by the shift from S to S_1. This means that suppliers become willing either to supply the same quantity (say, 500) at a lower price (i.e., \$8 instead of \$10) or to supply a higher quantity (i.e., 625 instead of 500) at the same price (i.e., \$10).

On the other hand, increases in the costs of factor services cause the market supply curve to shift upward and to the left, as shown in Figure 2.5 by the shift from S to S_2. This means that suppliers become willing either to supply the same quantity (say, 500) at a higher price (i.e., \$12 instead of \$10) or to supply a smaller quantity (i.e., 375 instead of 500) at the same price (i.e., \$10).

The Various Types of Supply: Digression[5]

In general, economists distinguish among three different types of supply curves: the *market-period supply curve,* the *short-run supply curve,* and the *long-run supply curve.* The principal criterion for this important three-way classification is the degree of adjustability of supply decisions.

The market-period supply curve refers to the case of *zero adjustability.* In this case, the output to be sold is already produced and cannot be changed in any way. This is illustrated by an agricultural crop that is harvested only once a year. After

[5]This subsection may be omitted.

the crop is harvested, its quantity cannot be increased. If the commodity is *perishable,* its supply curve will be *vertical,* which in essence means that the producer-suppliers will be willing to sell the already harvested crop at any price that the market will bear. This is shown in Figure 2.6 by vertical line *S.* If the commodity is not perishable and could be stored for any length of time, the supply curve will have some positive slope, as illustrated in Figure 2.6 by line *ABS.* This is quite reasonable because, at progressively lower prices, the producer-suppliers tend to withhold from the market an increasing part of the available stock in the hope of selling it at a higher price later.

The long-run supply curve lies at the other extreme of the spectrum: It implies *total adjustability* in supply decisions. This means that in the *long run* new firms may enter the industry and existing firms may close down if they so choose; in addition, each firm has complete freedom to adjust its productive equipment and capacity. The long-run supply curve summarizes the willingness of all producer-suppliers, both actual and potential, to supply alternative quantities of the good under these conditions of complete adjustability. The long–run supply curve can assume a variety of shapes. We return to this topic in Chapter 10.

In our modern industrial society, production requires the use of specialized equipment that cannot be installed on short order. In the *short run* only those producers who already possess the necessary pieces of equipment can produce output. Potential producers cannot enter the industry. Nevertheless, there is no requirement that each producer who owns the necessary equipment must produce output. A producer will do so only if it is profitable. If the equipment cannot be run profitably, it may be wise to shut down the plant and minimize losses. The *short-run supply curve* summarizes the willingness of the fixed number of active producers to supply alternative quantities of output. The short-run supply curve is always upward sloping—at progressively higher prices the fixed number of producers will be willing to produce larger and larger quantities.

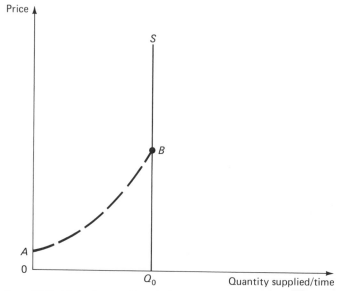

Figure 2.6 The market-period supply curve. The output of a perishable commodity is Q_0. Producer-suppliers are willing to sell this output at any price that the market will bear, as shown by vertical supply curve *S.* If the commodity were not perishable, the supply curve would have some positive slope at low prices, as illustrated by dashed line *AB,* which replaces vertical line segment Q_0B.

For the remainder of this chapter we ignore the distinction between market-period, short-run, and long-run supply curves. In addition, we assume that the typical supply curve slopes upward, even though occasionally we refer to the limiting cases of vertical and horizontal supply curves.

2.5 Equilibrium

Having discussed what factors determine supply and demand, we now turn to the question of how supply and demand interact to determine price in a competitive market.

The Meaning of Equilibrium

The concept of equilibrium is very fundamental in economics and will recur frequently in this book. For this reason, we must know what it means. The word "equilibrium" comes from two Latin words meaning an *equal balance*. In the physical sciences, a body is said to be in equilibrium when the forces acting on it are so well balanced that there is no tendency for it to change position. For instance, a branch of a tree laying on the ground is in equilibrium relative to its surroundings, because it has no tendency for change. However, a branch falling off a tree through the air is not in equilibrium, because the forces acting on it are not balanced and as a result cause it to change its position.

Similarly, an economic variable is said to be in equilibrium when it has no tendency for change, presumably because the economic forces acting on it are balanced. For instance, a price is in equilibrium when the quantity demanded equals (or balances) the quantity supplied. Thus supply and demand may be viewed as two forces pulling in opposite directions, and when they are balanced, the price is in equilibrium and has no tendency to change. That price is known as the *equilibrium price,* and the quantity traded at the equilibrium price is known as the *equilibrium quantity.*

Equilibrium of Supply and Demand[6]

Consider again the wheat market. Figure 2.7 brings together the market-demand and market-supply curves of Figures 2.1 and 2.4, respectively. Equilibrium occurs at point *E*, where demand curve *D* intersects supply curve *S*. At the equilibrium price of $10, the quantity demanded is exactly equal to the quantity supplied (500 million bushels of wheat per year).

Another way of expressing the same idea is to say that when the price is equal to $10, *the market clears*. This means that at the equilibrium price of $10 per bushel, the many buyers and the many sellers in this perfectly competitive market are all able to buy or sell just as much as they wish. Each potential buyer can find a seller, and each seller can find a buyer. Accordingly, no seller or buyer has any incentive to alter his or her behavior, and the equilibrium price ($10) and quantity (500 million bushels per year) have no tendency to change. If not disturbed, equilibrium can last forever.

Note that when the market is in equilibrium, the law of one price necessarily holds. In equilibrium, all market participants pay or receive, as the case may be, the *same* price ($10 per bushel).

The law of one price can be violated only when the market is not in equilibrium.

---

[6]This subsection can be read together with Section A2.1 of the Appendix to Chapter 2.

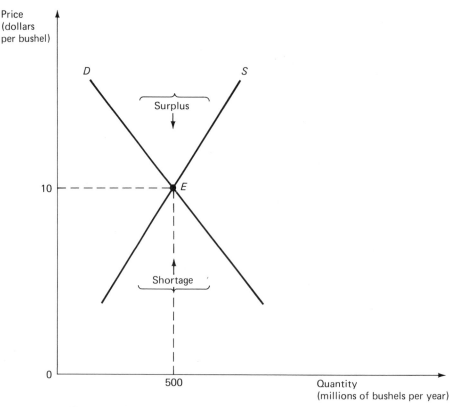

Figure 2.7 *Equilibrium price and quantity.* Equilibrium occurs at point E, where demand curve D intersects supply curve S. At the equilibrium price of $10 per bushel, the quantity demanded (500) is equal to the quantity supplied (500). At prices higher than the equilibrium price of $10, there emerges a *surplus* (or *excess supply*). At prices lower than $10, there emerges a *shortage* (or *excess demand*). Accordingly, the equilibrium is stable—from either side, the price has a tendency to move toward its equilibrium level, as shown by the arrows.

The existence of an array of prices can mean only one thing: that there are further deals to be made, which is an indication that the market has not yet cleared.

Stability of Equilibrium[7]

There is more to the law of supply and demand than the mere equality between the quantity demanded and the quantity supplied. Suppose that a market is not in equilibrium. Is there any guarantee that the market will attain equilibrium? Does every disequilibrium state set in motion forces that automatically bring the market back to equilibrium? The proper study of such questions belongs to *dynamics,* a branch of economics that lies beyond the scope of this book. In this subsection, we merely wish to give an intuitive argument that it is at least plausible for the market to attain equilibrium. Incidentally, when any given state of disequilibrium generates forces that move the market toward equilibrium, that equilibrium is called *stable;* otherwise, the equilibrium is called *unstable.*

Return to the hypothetical wheat market of Figure 2.7. At no price other than the equilibrium price of $10 is the quantity demanded equal to the quantity supplied. For instance, at prices higher than the equilibrium price, the quantity supplied is

[7]This subsection may be read together with Section A2.2 of the Appendix to Chapter 2.

larger than the quantity demanded, and a *surplus* appears in the market. Economists usually refer to this surplus as *excess supply*. In the presence of excess supply, sellers cannot sell all they wish to sell at the current price; at least some of them will wish to sell more than they can actually sell. These dissatisfied sellers will lower their price. Price will continue to fall (as shown by the arrow) until the excess supply disappears, that is, until equilibrium is attained at E.

At prices lower than the equilibrium price, the quantity demanded is larger than the quantity supplied, and a *shortage* develops in the market. Economists usually refer to this shortage as *excess demand*. In the presence of excess demand, buyers cannot buy all they wish to buy at the current price; at least some of them will wish to buy more than they can actually buy. These dissatisfied buyers will raise their prices. Indeed, price will continue to rise (as shown by the arrow) until the excess demand disappears, that is, until equilibrium is attained at E.

We therefore conclude that there are forces that will automatically bring the wheat market of Figure 2.7 back to equilibrium. Indeed, this is always the case when the intersection of a pair of supply and demand curves is such that (1) the quantity supplied is greater than the quantity demanded at all prices higher than the equilibrium price, and (2) the quantity demanded is greater than the quantity supplied at all prices lower than the equilibrium price. These requirements are satisfied when the demand curve is downward sloping and the supply curve is upward sloping.

The perfectly competitive character of the market is crucial to the preceding analysis. The law of supply and demand operates smoothly when the following two conditions are met:

1. Individual buyers and sellers must form their decisions independently of each other.
2. Each disappointed would-be seller must be able to increase his or her sales substantially with a very slight shading of the price; similarly, each disappointed would-be buyer must be able to increase his or her purchases substantially with a very small price increase.

2.6 The Price Elasticity of Demand

As we have seen in Section 2.3, the market demand curve slopes downward from left to right. Accordingly, the quantity demanded increases (decreases) as the good's price falls (rises). The implication of this is that the quantity demanded (or demand) is *responsive* (or sensitive) to a change in price.

In general, the degree of responsiveness of demand to price changes differs from one good to another. For instance, the quantity of salt demanded by consumers is not very much influenced by its price. Thus a rise in the price of salt will not reduce its consumption, principally for two reasons: (1) because there is no good substitute for such a necessity as salt, and (2) because the proportion of a typical consumer's income spent on salt is negligible. On the other hand, a rise in the price of stereo equipment will probably discourage many people from buying such entertainment devices because there are many good substitutes, such as television sets, radios, and theaters.

The degree of responsiveness of demand to price changes is of paramount importance in economics. For instance, the Chrysler Corporation has to know how the public will respond to a change in the price of cars before it inaugurates a rebate program. Or consider a service-station owner who feels that he cannot remain in business unless his sales revenue increases substantially. He cannot naively raise the price of gasoline before he knows how many customers he may lose to his competitors. Levi Strauss, Calvin Klein, and the many producers of phonograph records and other products face similar dilemmas. Federal, state, and local govern-ments cannot formulate sensible policies related to taxation unless they know how sensitive to price changes are the demands of various products, such as liquor and tobacco.

The problem of agriculture is another important example. The demand for many agricultural products is not very responsive to price changes. For this reason, in-creased agricultural output is often an anathema to the farmer, because it causes prices to fall sharply, leading to a *lower income* for the farmer—a problem that constantly concerns all governments around the globe.

The Slope of the Demand Curve

Sometimes students think that the degree of responsiveness of demand to price changes can be measured by the slope of the demand curve. This is not so for two reasons: (1) the *pictorial steepness* of a line has no significance whatever, and (2) the *numerical value* of a slope depends on the units of measurement of quantity and price; that is, it is arbitrary.

Consider the linear demand curve D in Figure 2.8. The vertical (left) scale is 1 inch = $2.50. Assume that we change the vertical scale to 1 inch = $10, as shown by the right scale. Then the demand curve will assume the position indicated by D', which looks much flatter than D. In general, we can make a curve appear as

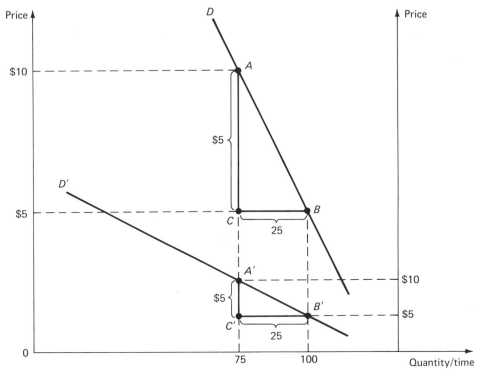

Figure 2.8 The slope of the demand curve. The numerical slope of the linear demand curve D is equal to $-\frac{5}{25}$ ("the rise over the run"). Changing the vertical scale from 1 inch = $2.5 (left scale) to 1 inch = $10 (right scale) causes line D to shift D'. Line D' looks much flatter than D even though its numerical slope continues to be equal to $-\frac{5}{25}$. Points A' and B' on D' correspond to points A and B, respectively, on D. (Distances on Figure 2.8 are not consistent with indicated scales because the original figure was reduced to fit the page.)

steep or as flat as we wish it to be by merely changing the scales of the price and quantity axes.

The slope of linear demand curve D is everywhere the same. To measure it, allow the price to fall from, say, $10 to $5, and the quantity to increase from 75 to 100 units, as shown by points A and B. The numerical slope is given by the ratio (change in price)/(change in quantity), which is $-5/25$. (Recall that the slope of a line is given by "the rise over the run.") Note that the *numerical* slope of a line is not affected by any changes in the horizontal and vertical scales. For example, the numerical slope of D' is exactly equal to the numerical slope of D. Yet the numerical slope of the demand curve does not remain invariant to changes in the units of measurement of quantity or price. Thus a change in the units of measurement of either quantity (say, from quarts to pints) or price (say, from dollars to cents or from dollars to German marks) will cause the *numerical slope* of the demand curve to change. For instance, measuring prices in pounds sterling where, say, £1 = $2, makes the numerical slope of the demand curve of Figure 2.8 equal to $-2.5/25$.

Definition of Elasticity

To measure the degree of responsiveness in the demand for a good to a change in its price, economists use the concept of (price) elasticity of demand, which is defined as follows:

$$\text{elasticity} = \frac{\%\ \text{change in quantity}}{\%\ \text{change in price}}$$
$$= \frac{\text{change in quantity}}{\text{quantity}} \div \frac{\text{change in price}}{\text{price}} \qquad (2.1)$$

Unlike the slope of the demand curve, the elasticity of demand is a *dimensionless* number, because it is a ratio of two percentages (which are independent of units of measurement). Not only does the elasticity coefficient remain invariant to changes in the units of measurement, but it is also meaningful to compare the elasticities of different commodities irrespective of whether the various quantities demanded are measured in such diversified units as bushels of wheat, bottles of wine, gallons of milk, and loaves of bread, or the prices are measured in dollars, yen, marks, or francs.

The Elasticity of Demand and Total Revenue

The *total revenue* received from the sale of a good always equals its price times the quantity sold. For instance, in Figure 2.9, panel (a), the buyers purchase 50 million bushels of wheat per year at the price of $5 per bushel. This means that the total revenue of the suppliers is $250 million per year (i.e., $5 × 50 million). Graphically, this total revenue is given by the area of the rectangle formed by the perpendiculars drawn from point M on the demand curve to the two axes.

When the price falls, the quantity demanded increases. Because price and quantity change in opposite directions, the total revenue (price times quantity) may increase, decrease, or stay the same. The outcome depends on the relationship between the *percentage* increase in quantity and the *percentage* reduction in price. If the percentage increase in quantity exceeds the percentage reduction in price, total revenue increases and demand is said to be *elastic*. If the percentage increase in quantity is smaller than the percentage reduction in price, total revenue decreases and demand is said to be *inelastic*. Finally, in the borderline case where the percentage changes of quantity and price are equal, total revenue stays the same and

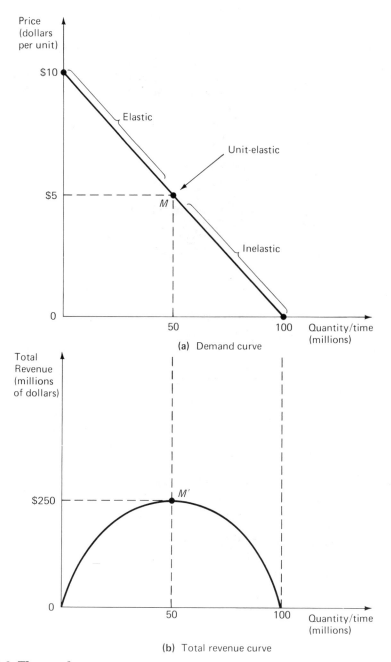

Figure 2.9 The total revenue curve. Each point on the demand curve in panel (a), (such as point *M*) gives a price ($5) and a quantity demanded (50 units). Total revenue equals price times quantity ($5 × 50 = $250). This information is transferred to panel (b) to determine a corresponding point (such as *M'*) on the total revenue curve. In the same way, every other point on the demand curve gives rise to a corresponding point on the total revenue curve. In particular, when the price is $10 the quantity demanded is zero; thus the total revenue is zero and the corresponding point on the total revenue curve is the origin. Similarly, when the price is zero, the quantity demanded is 100; again total revenue is zero and the corresponding point on the total revenue curve lies on the horizontal (quantity) axis. Between the quantities 0 and 100, total revenue first rises until it reaches a maximum (see point *M'*) and then falls. For prices between $5 and $10, demand is elastic; for prices between $0 and $5, demand is inelastic; and for the precise price of $5, demand is unit elastic.

demand is said to be *unit elastic*. (The reader is urged to supply the converse implications for price *increases*.) Referring to the definition of elasticity [equation (2.1)], it becomes apparent that demand is elastic, inelastic, or unit elastic according to whether the numerical value of the elasticity (in absolute terms) is greater than unity, less than unity, or equal to unity, respectively.

Figure 2.9, panel (b), illustrates a *total revenue curve* that corresponds to the demand curve in panel (a). The total revenue curve shows the total expenditure that buyers are willing to make on various hypothetical quantities of the good. Each point on the demand curve determines a corresponding point on the total revenue curve. In particular, when the price is $10, the quantity demanded is zero; hence total revenue is zero, and the relevant point on the total revenue curve is the origin. When the price drops to $5, the quantity demanded increases to 50 (million) and the total revenue increases to $250 (million). Finally, when the price drops to zero, the quantity demanded increases to 100 (million), but the total revenue necessarily falls to zero. Accordingly, as the price falls from $10 to zero, the total revenue first increases until it reaches a maximum (point *M'*), and then decreases.

Demand is elastic over the price region that corresponds to the upward-sloping portion of the total revenue curve, it is inelastic over the price region that corresponds to the downward-sloping portion of the total revenue curve, and it is unit elastic at point *M*, where total revenue is at a maximum (see corresponding point *M'* on the total revenue curve).

Arc Elasticity

We now turn to the question of actually measuring the elasticity of demand. For this purpose, we distinguish between two variants of elasticity: the *point elasticity* of demand (which is defined with respect to a *single point* on the demand curve) and the *arc elasticity* of demand (which applies to the associated change of price and quantity between *two distinct points* on the demand curve). We begin with the measurement of arc elasticity.

Consider points *A* and *B* on the dashed demand curve in Figure 2.10. Suppose that we are initially at point *A*. As the price falls from $10 to $5, the quantity demanded increases from 100 to 200. The total revenue remains constant at $1000 (i.e., $10 × 100 = $5 × 200 = $1000). From this we can infer that the percentage reduction of price must somehow be equal to the percentage increase of quantity giving rise to an elasticity of demand equal to unity. However, the percentage reduction of price is 50 percent (from $10 to $5) and the percentage increase of quantity is 100 percent (from 100 to 200 units). That would suggest an elasticity of 2, which is inconsistent with the constancy of total revenue. Or suppose that we initially start at *B*. As the price rises from $5 to $10 (i.e., by 100 percent), the quantity falls from 200 to 100 (i.e., by 50 percent), with the equally embarrassing implication that the elasticity is 0.5.

The foregoing problems arise because the changes of price and quantity are "large." To avoid these problems, economists calculate the change of price relative to the *average* of the two prices [i.e., ($10 + $5)/2 = $7.50] and the change of quantity relative to the *average* of the two quantities [i.e., (100 + 200)/2 = 150]. When this is done, the percentage changes of price and quantity become equal: $5/$7.50 = 100/150. The numerical value of the elasticity is now restored to unity, exactly as it should be.

Accordingly, the generally accepted formula for calculating the arc elasticity of demand is as follows:

$$\text{arc elasticity} = \frac{\Delta q}{(q_a + q_b)/2} \div \frac{\Delta p}{(p_a + p_b)/2} = \frac{\Delta q}{\Delta p} \frac{p_a + p_b}{q_a + q_b} \tag{2.2}$$

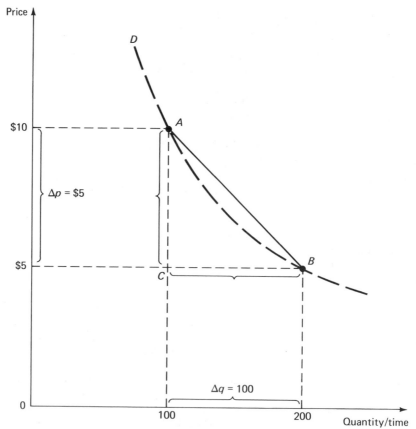

Figure 2.10 The arc elasticity of demand. Total revenue is the same at point A as it is at point B. Hence the elasticity of demand must be unity. However, using alternatively point A's and B's coordinates as the initial price and quantity data, we end up with elasticity coefficients equal to 2 and $\frac{1}{2}$, respectively, which is anomalous. To resolve the difficulty, we must use in formula (2.1) the *average* of the two relevant magnitudes [i.e., ($10 + $5)/2 for price and (100 + 200)/2 for quantity].

where Δq is the change in quantity, Δp the change in price, p_a the price at point A, p_b the price at point B, q_a the quantity at point A, and q_b the quantity at point B.

Because the demand curve slopes downward, price and quantity change in opposite directions. Strictly speaking, therefore, the terms Δq and Δp in formula (2.2) differ in sign, and the elasticity of demand is mathematically *negative*. Nevertheless, the minus sign is almost always ignored and economists speak of the elasticity of demand as if it were a positive number. In this book, we adopt this well-established convention.

Finally, note that arc elasticity depends on the price-quantity coordinates of just two points on the demand curve. Avoid the temptation of thinking that arc elasticity depends on the precise shape of the "arc" over which the elasticity is calculated.

Point Elasticity

The point elasticity of demand is simply the limiting value of the arc elasticity of demand as the arc is allowed to become smaller and smaller in the neighborhood of a certain point. Consider point A on demand curve D in Figure 2.11. If price fell

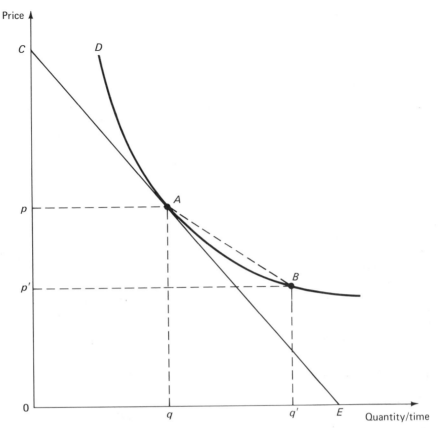

Figure 2.11 The point elasticity of demand. The point elasticity at A is simply the limiting value of the arc elasticity as B moves closer and closer to A. The limiting value of the ratio $\Delta q/\Delta p$ coincides with the reciprocal of the slope of (the tangent CE to) the demand curve at A. The limiting value of the average of p and p' coincides with p, and the limiting value of the average of q and q' coincides with q. Substituting these limiting values into the arc-elasticity formula (2.2), we obtain the point-elasticity formula (2.3).

from p to p', the quantity demanded would increase from q to q', and we would be able to use equation (2.2) to calculate the *arc* elasticity. Now imagine that point B starts moving closer and closer to point A along demand curve D. As this happens, p' and q' will also start moving closer and closer to p and q, respectively. Accordingly, the average of p and p' will tend to p, and the average of q and q' will tend to q. The differences Δp and Δq will tend to zero, but their ratio $\Delta q/\Delta p$. will tend to a definite limiting value which, as it turns out, is the *reciprocal of the slope of tangent CE to demand curve D at point A*. This is seen as follows. Consider again points A and B and form the ratio $\Delta q/\Delta p$, which gives the reciprocal of the slope of dashed line AB. As point B travels along the demand curve toward point A, the slope of line AB moves closer and closer to the slope of the tangent to the demand curve at A. Indeed, it is the reciprocal of the slope of the tangent at A, which coincides with the value of $\Delta q/\Delta p$ when point B coincides with point A. This limiting value of the ratio $\Delta q/\Delta p$ we represent by the symbol dq/dp, where the shift from the difference operator Δ to d indicates that dq and dp are now *infinitesimals,* that is, very, very small. Substituting the limiting values of (1) $\Delta q/\Delta p$, (2) the average of p and p', and

(3) the average of q and q' into the arc-elasticity formula (2.2), we obtain the point elasticity at point A:

$$\text{point elasticity} = \frac{dq}{dp}\frac{p}{q} \tag{2.3}$$

As with the arc elasticity, we again follow the convention of ignoring the minus sign of the point elasticity.

It is important to remember that the point elasticity does not coincide with the slope of the demand curve or with its reciprocal. As formula (2.3) shows, the point elasticity is equal to the reciprocal of the slope of the demand curve (dq/dp) times the factor p/q. This implies that the elasticity changes from one point to another even along a straight-line demand curve, because the ratios p/q differ from point to point.

However, suppose that we are given two linear demand curves that pass through the *same* point A. We can say that the elasticity of the flatter demand curve at A is higher than the elasticity of the steeper curve at A. Similarly, of two parallel, linear demand curves, the one that lies closer to the price axis is more elastic than the other at each price.

The above conclusions should serve as a warning to students who have the irrational feeling that a flat demand curve is always elastic and a steep one is always inelastic. We just cannot tell. In this connection, recall also our earlier observation that the pictorial steepness of a curve is arbitrary and irrelevant.

Graphical Determination of Point Elasticity

It is fairly easy to determine the point elasticity graphically. Consider, for instance, straight-line demand curve CE in Figure 2.12. The reciprocal of the slope of this demand curve is given by the ratio ME/MA, and price and quantity at point A are given by distances MA and $0M$, respectively. Substituting these values into equation (2.3), we obtain

$$\text{point elasticity at } A = \frac{ME}{MA}\frac{MA}{0M} = \frac{ME}{0M}$$

Note that the triangles MEA and KAC are similar and that $0M = KA$. It follows from a well-known property of similar triangles that the ratio $ME/0M$ is equal to the ratios MA/KC and AE/CA. Finally, observing that $MA = 0K$, we have the following important results:

$$\text{point elasticity at } A = \frac{ME}{0M} = \frac{0K}{KC} = \frac{AE}{CA} \tag{2.4}$$

These results are very useful. Indeed, they are the practical rules for evaluating the point elasticity of demand not only at any point on a linear demand curve, but also at any point on *any* demand curve. For instance, to calculate the point elasticity of demand at point A on demand curve D in Figure 2.11, we first draw the tangent to the curve at A (as shown by line CE) and then calculate the elasticity at A as if the tangent were the true demand curve. Accordingly, the elasticity of demand curve D at A is equal to

$$\frac{qE}{0q} = \frac{0p}{pC} = \frac{AE}{CA}$$

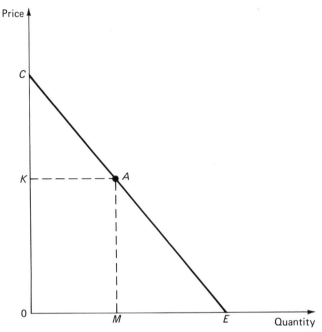

Figure 2.12 Graphical determination of point elasticity. The point elasticity of demand at A is given by any one of the following equal ratios: ME/OM, OK/KC, or AE/CA.

Some Final Remarks

We conclude this section with some additional observations on demand elasticity.

1. Unitary elasticity represents the important dividing line between elastic and inelastic demands. The fact that there are various degrees of elasticity or inelasticity is not as important as the three-way classification into elastic, inelastic, and unit elastic.

2. In general, elasticity differs from one point to another. Nevertheless, there is a class of demand curves that are *constant elastic* (or isoelastic).[8] (An isoelastic demand curve is one that exhibits the *same elasticity at all points* throughout its length.) Economists are interested in the following three special cases of *isoelastic demand curves:*
   (a) *Unit elastic:* In this special case, the constant elasticity is unity. A unit-elastic demand curve is represented graphically by a "rectangular hyperbola," which is a curve that is asymptotic to both axes and has the special property that all price-quantity combinations along it give rise to the same total revenue.
   (b) *Perfectly inelastic:* In this case, the constant elasticity is zero. A perfectly inelastic demand curve is represented graphically by a vertical line. Its economic meaning is that the quantity demanded does not respond to price at all.
   (c) *Perfectly elastic:* In this case, the elasticity of demand is infinite. An infinitely (or perfectly) elastic demand curve is represented graphically by a horizontal line. The simplest way to verify this is to observe that on the basis of equation (2.3), elasticity becomes infinite if, and only if, dq/dp is

[8]The special class of isoelastic demand curves is generated by the formula $qp^e = k$, where q is the quantity, p the price, k a positive constant, and e the constant elasticity.

infinite (for the ratio p/q is always a finite number). It follows, then, that the *reciprocal* of dq/dp, which is the *slope* of the demand curve, must be zero; that is, the demand curve must be horizontal. The commonsense meaning of this is that a negligible price reduction can induce buyers to increase their purchases by huge amounts. Earlier in this chapter we talked of a demand curve that meets these specifications: the demand curve faced by a single supplier in a perfectly competitive market.

Other Elasticities

As we have seen, the quantity demanded is not only a function of the good's own price; it is also a function of many other variables, such as income and prices of other goods. This means that changes in income or prices of other goods cause the quantity demanded to change (i.e., they cause the demand curve to shift).

Economists measure the responsiveness of the quantity demanded to changes in income or prices of other goods by means of elasticities. In particular, the responsiveness of the quantity demanded to income changes is described as the *income elasticity of demand*. Similarly, the responsiveness of the quantity demanded to changes in the price of *another* good is described as the *cross-elasticity of demand*. The precise definitions of these new elasticities are as follows:

$$\text{income elasticity} = \frac{\%\ \text{change in quantity}}{\%\ \text{change in income}}$$

$$\text{cross-elasticity} = \frac{\%\ \text{change in quantity}}{\%\ \text{change in price of other good}}$$

Both the income elasticity and the cross-elasticity of demand can be calculated either as "point" or as "arc" elasticities, following the same general rules as those used for calculating the elasticity of demand.

2.7 The Price Elasticity of Supply

As explained in Section 2.4, the quantity supplied is primarily a function of the commodity's price. The relationship between quantity supplied and price is represented graphically by a supply curve. Supply curves come in various shapes. Usually, they slope upward, implying that price and quantity change in the same direction. For instance, the higher the price of wheat, the more a Kansas farmer will supply.

Like demand curves, supply curves differ from one another with respect to the sensitivity of quantity supplied to price. Economists use the (price) *elasticity of supply* to measure the sensitivity of the quantity supplied to changes in price. This elasticity, like the elasticity of demand, can be calculated either as a point elasticity or as an arc elasticity. The mathematical formulas for calculating the elasticity of supply are exactly the same as those used for calculating the elasticity of demand.

There is no need to repeat any of the analysis of Section 2.6. It is sufficient to summarize briefly some important propositions concerning the elasticity of supply.

1. The elasticity of upward-sloping supply curves is inherently positive.
2. Unlike unitary elasticity of demand, unitary elasticity of supply has no special economic significance. The reason is simple: When both price and quantity change in the same direction, total revenue changes in that same direction also, irrespective of whether the percentage change of price is larger or smaller than the percentage change of quantity.

3. There are two limiting cases of supply curves: vertical (or perfectly inelastic) and horizontal (or infinitely elastic).

A vertical supply curve implies that the quantity supplied is totally unresponsive to price changes. This is illustrated by the case of a perishable commodity that must be sold at any price. The elasticity of supply is zero and supply is said to be *perfectly inelastic*.

A horizontal supply curve represents a most responsive (or *infinitely elastic*) supply. This is illustrated by the supply curve faced by a single consumer in a perfectly competitive market. Typically, the consumer can increase his or her purchases without influencing the supply price. The elasticity of supply of a horizontal curve is infinite, and supply is said to be *infinitely (or perfectly) elastic*.

2.8 Comparative Statics[9]

As explained in Sections 2.3 and 2.4, the market supply and demand curves for a certain good are drawn on the assumption that several variables remain constant. When these variables change, the market supply and demand curves shift to new positions. For instance, the demand curve shifts to a new position whenever any one or more of the variables that lie behind it (such as income or prices of related goods) change. Similarly, the supply curve shifts to a new position whenever any one or more of the variables that lie behind it (such as wage rates or technology) change. How do such shifts of the demand and the supply curves affect the equilibrium price, the equilibrium quantity, and total revenue?

Our approach in analyzing the effects of shifts in either the demand or the supply curve is that of *comparative statics*. Basically, this approach involves a *comparison* between two equilibria: the *initial equilibrium* (i.e., the equilibrium that exists before the shift) and the *final equilibrium* (i.e., the equilibrium that prevails eventually after the shift). The method of comparative statics remains silent on the question of how the market actually moves from one equilibrium to another. The study of the time path followed by price and quantity as they move from the initial to the final equilibrium belongs to *dynamics*. Although comparative statics has obvious shortcomings, it is a very useful approach and offers invaluable insights into the economic process.

Effects of Shifts in the Demand Curve

Consider Figure 2.13. Initially, equilibrium occurs at E, where downward-sloping demand curve D intersects upward-sloping supply curve S. The initial equilibrium price and quantity are P_0 and Q_0, respectively, and the area of rectangle $0Q_0EP_0$ shows the total revenue at that initial equilibrium.

Suppose now that the demand curve shifts to the right, as shown by D_1. Such a shift may be due to an increase in income, a change in tastes, a reduction in the price of a complementary good, or an increase in the price of a substitute good. The precise reason for the shift is not important for our purposes. Immediately after the shift, there emerges a *shortage* (i.e., excess demand) at the initial price P_0. This shortage is given by horizontal distance EF. Disappointed buyers who cannot buy all they want at price P_0 will start raising their bids, and price will start rising (as shown by the arrow). In fact, price will continue to rise until equilibrium is restored at G. Thus eventually price and quantity will assume their new equilibrium levels, P_1 and Q_1, respectively.

The foregoing result is important. It explains many real-world phenomena. For

[9]This section can be read together with Section A2.3 of the Appendix to Chapter 2.

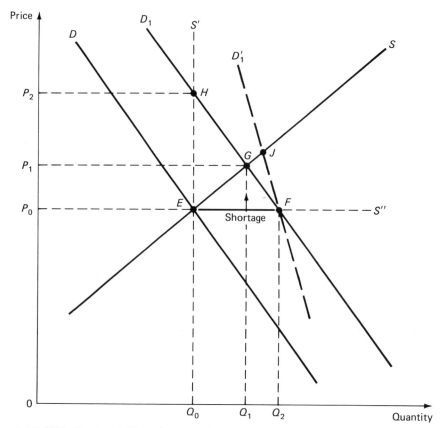

Figure 2.13 *Effects of a shift in demand.* Initially, equilibrium occurs at E, where demand curve D intersects supply curve S. When the demand curve shifts to the right, as illustrated by D_1, equilibrium shifts to G, where both price and quantity are higher relative to E. Had the supply curve been vertical (infinitely inelastic), as shown by S', equilibrium would have shifted to H. Alternatively, had the supply curve been horizontal (infinitely elastic), as shown by S'', equilibrium would have shifted to F.

---

instance, in the summer months most people go on vacation. The demand for gasoline shifts to the right, causing both the price and quantity (gallons per day) of gasoline to rise relative to their respective magnitudes in the winter months. The precise quantitative effects of a rightward shift in the demand curve depend crucially on the elasticity of supply and the elasticity of demand at the initial equilibrium point. We consider the elasticity of supply first.

If the supply curve were perfectly inelastic, as illustrated by vertical line S', equilibrium would have moved from E to H. Price would have increased to P_2, but quantity would have remained constant at Q_0. Alternatively, if the supply curve were perfectly elastic, as illustrated by horizontal line S'', equilibrium would have moved from E to F. Thus quantity would have increased to Q_2, but price would have remained constant at P_0.

Accordingly, for a given shift in the demand curve, the resultant *change in price* is *large* when the *elasticity of supply* is *small*, and the *change in quantity* is *large* when the *elasticity of supply* is *large*. (This conclusion makes a lot of sense because both the old equilibrium point and the new equilibrium point lie on the same supply curve.) Total revenue always increases.

The elasticity of demand is also important. In particular, the *changes in price and quantity* are *large* when the elasticity of demand is small. This is also illustrated in Figure 2.13. Had demand curve D been a little less elastic at E (i.e., a little steeper at E), new demand curve D_1 would have been a little less elastic at F (i.e., a little steeper at F), as shown by dashed demand curve D_1'. Thus equilibrium would have moved from E to J. Note that point J lies on supply curve S beyond point G, implying *larger* changes in price and quantity than point G. In other words, a low elasticity of demand gives rise to a large movement along the unchanging supply curve, which in turn causes large changes in price and quantity.

We therefore conclude that a shift in demand (to the right or to the left) causes a *large change in price* when the *elasticity of demand and* the *elasticity of supply are small*. On the other hand, a shift in demand causes a *large change in quantity* when the *elasticity of demand is small* and the *elasticity of supply is large*.

Effects of Shifts in the Supply Curve

Turn now to shifts in the supply curve. In Figure 2.14, the initial equilibrium at E is disturbed by a rightward shift in the supply curve, as illustrated by S_1. At the initial equilibrium price P_0, there emerges a *surplus* (or *excess supply*) equal to distance EF. Disappointed sellers will put a downward pressure on price by lowering their bids. Price will continue to fall until equilibrium is restored at G, where price

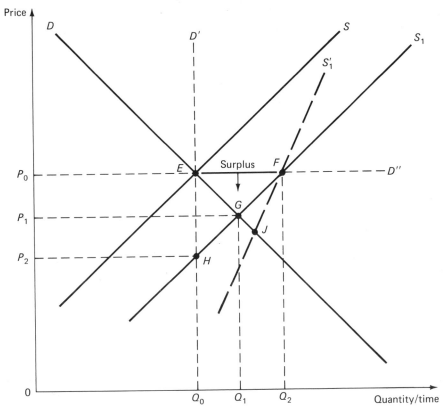

Figure 2.14 Effects of a shift in supply. The initial equilibrium at E (where supply S and demand D intersect) is disturbed by a shift in the supply curve to the right, as shown by S_1. Equilibrium shifts to G, where the price is lower and the quantity is higher relative to E. Had demand been perfectly inelastic (vertical line D'), equilibrium would have shifted to H. Alternatively, had demand been infinitely elastic (horizontal line D''), equilibrium would have shifted to F.

and quantity assume their new equilibrium levels, P_1 and Q_1, respectively. Accordingly, the price *falls* from P_0 to P_1, and the quantity *increases* from Q_0 to Q_1. Thus *price and quantity move in opposite directions,* essentially because both initial equilibrium point E and eventual equilibrium point G lie on the same unchanging demand curve.

The foregoing result can shed light on many real-world phenomena. For instance, it is usually observed that in the summer months more tomatoes are sold than in the winter months. Yet the price of tomatoes is lower in the summer than in the winter. Why? Because in the summer months the supply of tomatoes increases (the supply curve shifts to the right), depressing their price and inducing consumers to buy a larger quantity. The demand curve for tomatoes does not vary from season to season because the tastes and incomes of tomato eaters remain relatively stable.

The elasticity of demand plays a crucial role in the analysis of the effects of shifts in the supply curve. When the elasticity of demand is *low,* a shift in the supply curve will cause a *large change in price* and a *small change in quantity.* On the other hand, when the elasticity of demand is *high,* the *change in price will be small,* but the *change in quantity will be large.* Therefore, low elasticity of demand is responsible for large fluctuations in price, and high elasticity of demand is responsible for large fluctuations in quantity.

Figure 2.14 illustrates the preceding proposition. The supply curve shifts to the right from S to S_1. When the demand curve is perfectly inelastic, as illustrated by (dashed) vertical curve D', price falls substantially from P_0 to P_2 while quantity remains constant at Q_0 (compare points E and H). On the other hand, when the demand curve is perfectly elastic, as illustrated by (dashed) horizontal curve D'', price remains constant at P_0 but quantity increases substantially from Q_0 to Q_2 (compare points E and F).

The effects of shifts in the supply curve depend also on the elasticity of supply. In particular, the *changes in price and quantity are large when the elasticity of supply is low.* Figure 2.14 also illustrates this proposition. Had supply curve S been a little less elastic at E, supply curve S_1 would have been a little less elastic at F, as illustrated by dashed curve S_1'. Thus equilibrium would have moved from E to J. Note that point J lies on demand curve D beyond point G and implies larger changes in price and quantity than point G. In other words, a low elasticity of supply means a large movement along the unchanging demand curve, and thus large changes in price and quantity.

Combining the proposition described above with the similar proposition that we derived in the preceding subsection, we obtain the following important proposition: *Shifts in supply and demand curves cause large fluctuations in price when the elasticities of supply and demand are low.*

As we have seen, a rightward shift of the supply curve causes price and quantity to move in opposite directions. What happens to *total revenue?* The outcome depends again on the elasticity of demand. Thus in Figure 2.14, points E and G both lie on the given and unchanging demand curve D. Consequently, if demand is elastic over "arc" EG, total revenue will increase; if it is inelastic, total revenue will decrease; and if it is unit elastic, total revenue will remain the same.

This conclusion has an important application to the problem of agriculture. As mentioned earlier, increased agricultural output often means *lower income* (i.e., total revenue) for the farmer, because the demand for agricultural products is inelastic.

Shifts in Curves Versus Movements Along Curves

It is important to distinguish between a *shift* in a supply or a demand curve from a *movement along* the same curve. By an "increase of demand" economists usually mean a *shift* in the demand curve to the right, but they could also mean an increase in the quantity demanded brought about by a reduction in price, that is, a *movement along the demand curve*. Similarly, by an "increase in supply" economists typically mean a rightward *shift* in the supply curve, but they could also mean an increase in the quantity supplied brought about by an increase in price, that is, *a movement along the supply curve*.

Imprecise usage of the terms "supply" and "demand" often creates confusion and leads to false statements. For instance, consider the following chain of reasoning:

1. An increase in the demand for housing causes the price of housing to rise.
2. The higher price of housing causes an increase in the supply of housing.
3. The increase in the supply of housing causes the price of housing to fall.
4. So the price of housing may actually fall *below* its initial level.

Can you identify the flaws in the reasoning here? Statement 1 is correct; it refers to a rightward *shift* in the demand curve. Statement 2 is also correct, but only if we interpret the "increase in the supply of housing" to mean a *movement* along the supply curve. Statements 3 and 4 are totally false. They are based on the erroneous view that statement 2 implies a rightward shift in the supply curve.

Effects of Commodity Taxes: Application

The analysis of shifts in supply or demand can be used to shed light on the effects of sales taxes and excise taxes. These are taxes that are levied against many commodities and services by federal, state, or local governments. Typically, countries single out alcohol, gasoline, and tobacco for high rates of taxation. How do such taxes affect the prices paid by consumers? How do they affect the quantities traded?

Legally, taxes may be fixed either on the *ad valorem* basis (i.e., as a fixed percentage of the value of the good traded) or on the *specific* basis (i.e., as a fixed sum of money per physical unit traded). Indeed, in some cases a tax may even be specified on a *compound* basis, that is, as a combination of an ad valorem tax and a specific tax. To keep the analysis as simple as possible, we shall limit our comments to the effects of specific taxes. The effects of both ad valorem and compound taxes are similar to the effects of specific taxes.

A tax drives a wedge between the price paid by the consumer and the price received by the producer. For instance, suppose that a specific tax of 20 cents is levied on each pack of cigarettes. If the price paid by consumers is 80 cents per pack, the price actually received by the sellers must be only 60 cents. The difference of 20 cents accrues to the government in the form of tax revenue. For our present purposes, the significance of this observation is twofold: (1) We must distinguish clearly between the price paid by consumers (buyers) and the price received by producers (sellers), and (2) we can allow our graphical analysis of supply and demand to determine either the price paid by consumers or the price received by producers. Later we can recover the second price by a simple application of the formula

price paid by consumers = price received by producers + tax

Consider Figure 2.15. In the absence of any tax, equilibrium occurs at E, where demand curve D and supply curve S intersect. Suppose that the government disturbs that initial equilibrium by imposing a specific tax equal to vertical distance EF. Does the price paid by smokers (consumers) increase by the amount of the tax? Put differently, how much of the tax is paid by consumers in the form of a higher price, and how much of the tax falls on producers?

To determine directly the price paid by consumers, we must shift the supply curve

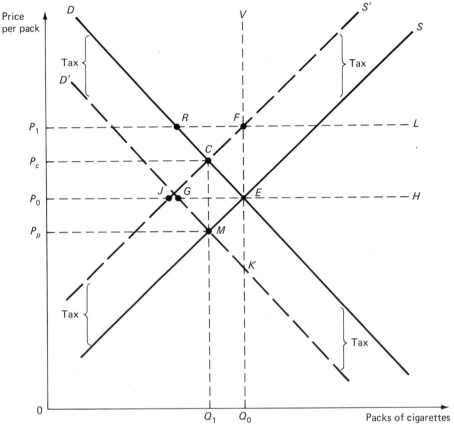

Figure 2.15 Effects of a specific tax. The imposition of a specific tax equal to vertical distance EF causes supply curve S to shift *vertically* upward by the amount of the tax, as shown by S'. Equilibrium moves from E to C. Thus the price paid by consumers *increases* from P_0 to P_c, the price received by producers *falls* from P_0 to P_p, the quantity traded *falls* from Q_0 to Q_1, and the government collects a tax revenue equal to the area of rectangle MCP_cP_p.

upward by the amount of the tax, as shown by dashed supply curve S'. (Note that in this case the vertical axis measures the price paid by consumers.) This is necessary because, after the imposition of the tax, the supply curve must register those prices that consumers have to pay to induce producers to offer alternative quantities, and those prices must be equal to the initial prices (read off supply curve S) plus the tax. For instance, to induce producers to sell quantity Q_0 after the tax is imposed, consumers must pay price P_1, which is equal to initial P_0 plus the tax (given by vertical distance EF). Accordingly, point E on supply curve S must shift to point F on supply curve S'. In general, supply curve S shifts vertically upward by the amount of the specific tax, as shown by supply curve S'.

Accordingly, after the imposition of the tax, equilibrium moves from E to C, where the new supply curve S' intersects demand curve D. The price paid by consumers rises from P_0 to P_c, and the quantity traded falls from Q_0 to Q_1. The price received by producers falls from P_0 to P_p, since $MC = EF = $ tax. Finally, the government collects a tax revenue equal to $CM \times Q_1$, which is given graphically by the area of rectangle MCP_cP_p. The burden of the tax is shared by consumers and producers, with consumers paying $(P_c - P_0)$ and producers absorbing the difference, that is, $(P_0 - P_p)$.

We could reach the same result by alternatively determining the price received by producers. For this purpose, we now measure the price received by producers along the vertical axis. We *shift the demand curve vertically downward by the amount of the tax,* as shown by dashed curve D'. The necessity for this downward shift of the demand curve must be clear: The tax must be subtracted from the prices paid by consumers to determine the net prices that will accrue to producers. Equilibrium shifts now from E to M, where the price received by producers is P_p and the quantity traded is Q_1. The price paid by consumers is again given by P_c. Accordingly, all results correspond to those we derived above by shifting the supply curve instead.

What determines the division of the tax burden between consumers and producers? The elasticities of supply and demand. In particular, we can formulate the following proposition: *The share of tax burden borne by consumers is large (and thus the share borne by producers is small) when (1) the elasticity of demand is low and (2) the elasticity of supply is high.*

Figure 2.15 illustrates this proposition. For simplicity, we consider only the shift of the supply curve. (The vertical axis measures again the price paid by consumers.) As we saw above, the tax causes the supply curve to shift vertically upward from S to S'; thus equilibrium moves from E to C. Had the demand curve been a little more elastic, the price paid by consumers would not have increased to P_c. For example, in the limiting case of an infinitely elastic demand curve illustrated by dashed line H, equilibrium would have moved to G, the price paid by consumers would have remained constant, and the entire tax burden would have fallen on producers. On the other hand, had the demand curve been a little less elastic, the price would have increased above P_c. For instance, in the limiting case of a perfectly inelastic demand curve illustrated by dashed line V, equilibrium would have moved to F, and the price paid by consumers would have increased by the full amount of the tax.

Finally, we can experiment with different supply curves. Return to the pretax equilibrium at E, but assume that the supply curve is infinitely elastic, as illustrated by dashed line H. The tax causes this horizontal supply curve to shift upward, as shown by dashed line L. Equilibrium shifts from E to R, and the price paid by consumers increases by the full amount of the tax. Alternatively, assume that the supply curve is *perfectly inelastic,* as illustrated by vertical line V. Equilibrium now continues to remain at E because a vertical line that shifts vertically upward does not change position. In this case, the price paid by consumers remains constant and the full burden of the tax is borne by producers. This result is sensible because a perfectly inelastic supply curve shows that producers are willing to sell a given quantity at whatever price the market will bear.

2.9 Price Controls

In this concluding section we show how the model of supply and demand can aid in the understanding of issues of public policy. For this purpose we consider briefly the consequences of *price floors* (minimum prices) and *price ceilings* (maximum prices).

Price Floors

Governments often intervene in a market by establishing a *minimum* price (or *price floor*) below which the commodity cannot be sold. A price floor becomes *effective* (or *binding*) only when it is higher than the equilibrium price. Such price floors are usually adopted for agricultural products, because governments are interested in supporting farmers to enjoy a decent standard of living. But the markets for agricultural products are not unique for this kind of government intervention. The labor market is another important example. Based on the notion that everyone should earn decent wages, governments often legislate specific minimum wages. For instance, in 1986 the minimum wage in the United States is $3.35 per hour.

What are the economic consequences of price floors? Consider Figure 2.16. Free-market equilibrium occurs at E. Suppose now that equilibrium price P_0 appears low, and to enable the farmers to enjoy an acceptable standard of living, the government sets a minimum price (price floor) equal to P_1. At this higher price, however, the quantity supplied exceeds the quantity demanded. In particular, at minimum price P_1, there emerges a *surplus* given by horizontal distance AB. The existence of a surplus (excess supply) constitutes the most important difficulty that governments face when they establish price floors.

What can be done with the surplus? In the case of agricultural commodities (such as wheat and corn), the government buys and stores the surplus. But this is not the end of the story. What can the government do with the surplus? If the surplus persists period after period, eventually it must be destroyed or somehow dumped on the market. If it is destroyed, it is apparent that the country wastes scarce resources (by producing and destroying unwanted commodities), not to mention the disturbing moral issue of destroying food when millions of people around the globe go to bed hungry. On the other hand, if the government eventually sells the ac-

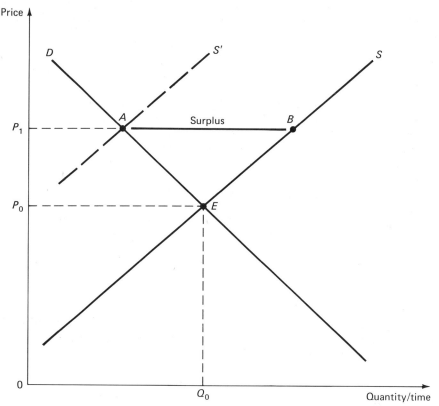

Figure 2.16 Price floor. Free-market equilibrium occurs at E, where demand curve D intersects supply curve S. When the government imposes price floor P_1, which is *higher* than equilibrium price P_0, a surplus (excess supply) develops, as illustrated by horizontal distance AB.

cumulated surpluses on the market, the increased supply will severely depress the price and thus defeat the original purpose of maintaining a high support price for farmers.

To avoid the problem of accumulated surpluses of agricultural commodities, governments often impose *acreage controls*. In effect, the government allows each farmer to use only a fraction of his or her land in order to restrict supply. For instance, suppose that such acreage control causes supply curve S to shift to the left, as shown by dashed curve S'. Such a leftward shift of the supply curve will succeed in raising the price from P_0 to P_1, without any visible surplus. Unfortunately, even this approach inflicts a heavy cost on the economy because of the economic inefficiency that such a scheme introduces into the economic system.

In the case of minimum wages, the problem is slightly different but the result remains the same. Thus at minimum wage P_1, there exists an excess supply of labor equal to distance AB. However, this surplus cannot be stored up. It is lost forever. Further, although it is true that those who are lucky enough to get a job will enjoy a higher income, those unlucky ones who happen to remain unemployed will suffer. An unemployed worker cannot take comfort in the thought that his neighbor has a job that pays a good wage. What is even worse is the fact that those who do remain unemployed are actually the economically needy—unskilled or at best semiskilled workers whom the minimum wage laws are supposed to protect.

The message of the above discussion is clear: The formulation of economic policy is not an easy matter. One of the objectives of economic policy is to induce the economic system to generate those results that are morally and politically acceptable. Yet well-intentioned governments (federal, state, or local) often face hard choices, because every policy involves social costs.

Price Ceilings

For economic, social, or political reasons, governments often fix *maximum* prices (or *price ceilings*). They accomplish this by merely passing a law forbidding any transactions in which the price is higher than the one specified by the law. A price ceiling becomes *effective* (or *binding*) only when it is lower than the corresponding equilibrium price.

Examples of price ceilings are not hard to find. For instance, during World War I and World War II practically all belligerent countries attempted to stop the rising price of foodstuffs by imposing price controls (price ceilings) that were specifically designed to keep the market price below equilibrium.[10] Rent controls (i.e., maximum rents) have been in existence for a long time in New York, London, Paris, and many other cities. In most places, *usury laws* set maximum interest rates on loans.[11] A most recent example of a comprehensive set or program of price ceilings is the *price freeze* that the Nixon administration imposed in 1971 to curb inflation.

What are the economic consequences of price ceilings? Consider Figure 2.17. Free-trade equilibrium occurs at E, where P_0 and Q_0 are the equilibrium price and

---

[10]During a conflict, most resources are diverted from the production of consumption goods to implements of war. However, the demand for peacetime goods is not reduced, because people continue to earn incomes from the production of war goods. In fact, the demand for some consumption goods may even increase because consumers, anticipating prolonged shortages, tend to buy more than they currently need, storing the excess purchases for a rainy day. The result is inflation, that is, rapid rises in the prices of consumption goods.

[11]A positive interest rate has always been an object of suspicion. In ancient times, Aristotle asserted that money is "barren" and condemned the payment of interest on loans. Because of this, many people in the Middle Ages opposed the payment of interest. Indeed, until about the sixteenth century, the Roman Church officially condemned usury as sinful. More recently, Karl Marx (1818–1883) and the communists argued that the payment of interest amounts to sheer exploitation of the working class.

quantity, respectively. Suppose that the government considers price P_0 too high and imposes a price ceiling equal to P_1. Since P_1 is lower than P_0, the price ceiling is effective (or binding). The result is an immediate *shortage* (or excess demand) of the controlled commodity, given by horizontal distance AB. That is, at price P_1, the quantity demanded exceeds the quantity supplied by AB. The existence of a shortage is the most significant economic effect of a price ceiling.

What are the implications of the shortage (excess demand)? Since supply is not enough to satisfy all buyers at the legal price ceiling fixed by the government, *some buyers will not be able to buy all they want*. The immediate consequence of this may be long waiting lines. Indeed, standing in lines is still a way of life in some Eastern European countries, as the recent dramatic events in Poland have reminded us.

When a shortage develops and the price is not allowed to rise, other criteria are usually adopted for the allocation of the limited supply among the many buyers. Thus sellers may allocate scarce supplies according to their preferences. For instance, a butcher may swear that he has no more meat to sell until his favorite customer arrives. Or a landlord may refuse to rent an apartment to couples with children.

Rationing is another method of allocating the limited supply. The government issues ration coupons entitling every person to just so much of the rationed commodity and no more. Of course, the total ration must not be larger than the available supply; otherwise, rationing cannot be successful. With rationing, purchases are not restricted by price; they are restricted by the ration coupons. The distribution of ration coupons reflects the preferences of the government. Whether the actual distribution is equitable depends on each person's point of view.

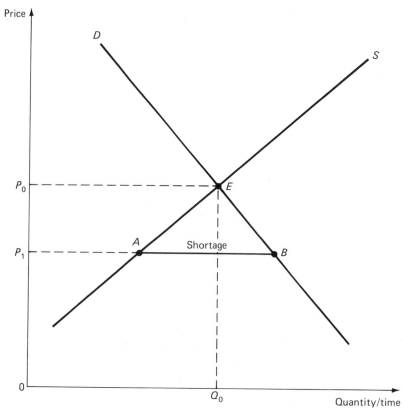

Figure 2.17 Price ceiling. Free-market equilibrium occurs at E. The government imposes a price ceiling equal to P_1, which is *lower* than equilibrium price P_0. The result is a shortage, as illustrated by horizontal distance AB.

An almost inevitable consequence of a price ceiling, with or without rationing, is the development of a *black market,* that is, a market in which commodities (or the coupons that give access to the commodities) are sold illegally at prices above the legal maximum price.

2.10 Selected Empirical Applications

We conclude this chapter with three empirical applications. The first deals with the market for coffee. The second discusses the phenomenon of arbitrage and black-market activities in computers. The third illustrates the effects of price floors by means of Europe's wine lake.

The Market for Coffee

The coffee industry has always been important to the few countries, such as Brazil, that export coffee to the rest of the world. During the 1970s the coffee industry also received considerable attention worldwide because of the dramatic increases in coffee prices.

The short-run supply of coffee has two important characteristics: (1) It is relatively inelastic, mainly because of the long time lag involved in its production—about five years between investment decisions and maximum coffee output, and (2) it is subject to fluctuations caused by occasional frosts in coffee-growing areas. For instance, on July 19, 1975, a hard frost destroyed about half of the 1976 Brazilian coffee crop—about one-fifth of the world supply, because Brazil produces approximately one-third of the world output. (Less severe frosts occurred in 1963, 1969, and 1972.) The 1975 frost led to a quadrupling of the price of coffee within a short period of time, because of the low elasticity of demand for coffee. After the recovery of the Brazilian coffee industry in 1977, consumer prices for coffee fell precipitously.

Coffee consumption in the United States appears to be in a long-term decline. For instance, annual per capita coffee consumption has fallen from 15.7 pounds in 1963 to 9.4 pounds in 1977. However, the roasted coffee market continues to be an important industry, comparable in sales volume to such industries as flour, toys and sporting goods, and women's dresses.

Most studies[12] reveal a low elasticity of demand for coffee, mostly in the range 0.10 to 0.30 (in absolute terms). Three reasons are usually given for the low elasticity coefficient: (1) Coffee plays only a minor role in most consumers' budgets; (2) there are not good substitutes for coffee, although cocoa, soft drinks, and tea can be viewed as imperfect substitutes for coffee; and (3) coffee is potentially addictive (which may be the reason for the absence of good substitutes).

Arbitrage and Black-Market Activities in Computers

At the beginning of 1984, Apple Computer decided to sell $60 million worth of computers to 24 colleges and universities.[13] According to the plan, students and faculty at the participating schools can purchase the new Apple Macintosh for

[12]See C. J. Huang, J. J. Siegfried, and F. Zardoshty, "The Demand for Coffee in the United States, 1963–77," *Quarterly Review of Economics and Business,* Vol. 20 (Summer 1980), pp. 36–49.

[13]The members of the university consortium are Boston College, Brigham Young University, Brown University, Carnegie–Mellon University, City University of New York, Columbia University, Cornell University, Dartmouth College, Drexel University, Harvard University, Northwestern University, Princeton University, Reed College, Rice University, Stanford University, University of Chicago, University of Michigan, University of Notre Dame, University of Pennsylvania, University of Rochester, University of Utah, University of Washington, University of Texas, and Yale University.

between $1000 and $1350. This is a real bargain, in view of the fact that authorized dealers reportedly pay about $1600 and the Mac sells for $2495 retail. It is therefore understandable why the establishment of the university consortium generated fears that many of the machines would be funneled to the black market.

Immediately after Apple Computer announced its plan, classified ads appeared in some college newspapers offering students premiums for the computers. "Sell me a Macintosh at cost plus $200," said one ad in the Dartmouth College student newspaper in Hanover, New Hampshire. Even though the temptation for a quick and sizable profit is apparently too great for cash-strapped students and faculty, there have been few reports of black-market activities as of this writing (May 1984).

Evidently, each participating school has agreed to set up guidelines to discourage reselling. For instance, at the University of Michigan each buyer signs an affidavit that he or she will not lease or sell the computer for at least two years. Also, a small "brand" with the school's name is burned into the back of the computer's plastic case. Finally, the university plans to perform spot surveys of buyers to see if they still own the machines. A violation could potentially result in a claim of $2000 by the school.

Questions:

1. Can black-market activity be stopped?
2. Should Apple Computer maintain two substantially different prices for the same computer?
3. How will the university consortium affect the sales and prices of authorized dealers?

Europe's Wine Lake

To support its farmers, the European Economic Community established a "common agricultural policy." The basic idea of the system is simple: For each agricultural product, the community determines a price floor, known as the *target price,* that it wishes to maintain. The target price is typically set above the perfectly competitive equilibrium level, and the result of this policy is the continuous accumulation of production surpluses. This is illustrated by *Europe's wine lake* (a euphemism for the accumulated surpluses of wine).

Presently (March 1984), Europe's wine lake holds more than 2 million tons (2.7 billion standard bottles) and is still rising. It is estimated that if 1984 is an average season, the Community will produce about 1.4 million tons more grape juice than it needs to satisfy the demand for wine. What can be done to eliminate or substantially reduce the wine lake? *The Economist* (March 3, 1984, pp. 68–70) lists five options of getting rid of the surplus of 1.4 million tons expected in 1984. All options are costly.

1. Make wine and pour it down the drain. This is the most expensive solution. Total cost to the community: $341 million.
2. Persuade the farmers not to pick all the grapes. This would be the cheapest method, but it is not feasible for political and bureaucratic reasons.
3. Make wine and distill it into pure alcohol for industrial products, such as insecticides and shoe polish. This is indeed the present system. Its main problem is that wine alcohol costs about $3000 a ton to make, which is four times as high as the cost of the much purer synthetic alcohol. To make the plan feasible, the Community must provide an enormous subsidy to the making of wine alcohol. Total cost to the community: $338 million.

4. Turn wine alcohol into gasoline. Total cost to the community: $334 million.
5. Use concentrated grape juice, which is rich in sugars, as feed for farm animals such as lambs. If the grape juice could compete with molasses, the main sugary feed for animals, the total cost to the community would be $299 million.

SUMMARY

1. All commodities (goods and services) are useful; they are used by consumers to satisfy their needs. Commodities are divided into economic goods (which are scarce, reflecting the scarcity of factors of production) and free goods. Economic goods have prices (because they are both useful and scarce); free goods do not.

2. *Law of one price:* The price of a commodity tends to uniformity throughout the market (ignoring differences due to transportation costs).

3. Arbitrage is the simultaneous purchase and sale of a commodity for the sake of profit.

4. In a perfectly competitive market many small sellers and buyers deal in a homogeneous commodity. All traders are price takers; each has perfect knowledge of the prices prevailing in all parts of the market.

5. *Law of demand:* As price falls, the quantity demanded increases; that is, the demand curve is downward sloping.

6. The quantity demanded depends not only on the price of the commodity, but also on tastes, per capita income, income distribution, prices of related goods, and population size. When any of these variables change, the market demand curve shifts to a new position.

7. Substitutes are goods (such as beef and pork) that satisfy the same need, and one can be substituted for the other; their markets are related. Complements are goods (such as autos and tires) that tend to be used jointly with each other; their markets are also related.

8. The quantity supplied depends not only on the price of the commodity, but also on the costs of factors of production and the state of technology. When any of the latter variables change, the market supply curve shifts to a new position.

9. The market-period supply curve implies zero adjustability of supply decisions; the short-run supply curve implies imperfect adjustability; and the long-run supply curve implies total adjustability.

10. Market equilibrium occurs at the intersection of the supply and demand curves. At the equilibrium price, the quantity demanded equals (or balances) the quantity supplied.

11. An equilibrium is stable when (a) at all prices higher than the equilibrium price there exists a surplus (excess supply), and (b) at all prices lower than the equilibrium price there exists a shortage (excess demand). These conditions are satisfied when the demand curve is downward sloping and the supply curve is upward sloping.

12. The elasticity of demand (i.e., the percentage change in quantity divided by the percentage change in price) is a dimensionless number that measures the responsiveness of demand to a change in price. The slope of the demand curve is *not* a good indicator of such responsiveness.

13. When price falls, total revenue (price times quantity) increases, decreases, or remains constant according to whether the elasticity of demand is greater than, less than, or equal to unity, respectively.

14. There are two variants of elasticity: (a) the point elasticity (related to a single point) and (b) the arc elasticity (related to two distinct points).

15. There are three important isoelastic demand curves: (a) unit elastic (rectangular hyperbola), (b) perfectly inelastic (vertical), and (c) perfectly elastic (horizontal).

16. Comparative statics involves a comparison between an initial equilibrium and a final equilibrium that is brought about by a shift of the demand or the supply curve.

17. Shifts in supply and demand curves cause large fluctuations in price when the elasticities of supply and demand are low.

18. When the demand curve shifts, price and quantity change in the same direction; but when the supply curve shifts, price and quantity move in opposite directions. The quantity change is large when the elasticity of the curve that shifts is low and the elasticity of the fixed curve is high.

19. A sales tax drives a wedge between the

price paid by consumers and the price received by producers. The share of the tax borne by consumers is large (and that borne by producers is small) when (a) the elasticity of demand is low and (b) the elasticity of supply is high.
20. Effective (or binding) price floors (minimum prices) result in surpluses. In the case of

agricultural products, governments often impose acreage controls to avoid the expected surpluses.
21. Effective price ceilings (maximum prices) result in shortages that lead to the development of black markets. The limited supply is often rationed.

QUESTIONS

1. Suppose that the demand for cantaloupes is

$$P = 160 - 3Q_d$$

where P is the price (in cents) per pound of a cantaloupe and Q_d is the quantity demanded (in millions of pounds) per year. Suppose that the supply curve of cantaloupes is

$$P = 5Q_s$$

where Q_s is the quantity supplied.
  (a) Determine the equilibrium price and quantity of cantaloupes.
  (b) Determine the elasticities of demand and supply at the equilibrium point.
  (c) Suppose that the government puts a price floor of 130 cents per pound of cantaloupes. How big will be the resulting surplus of cantaloupes, and what measures can the government adopt to reduce this surplus?
2. A Greek farmer once said to the author: "No matter what tax the government levies, it falls on the farmer. For example, suppose that the government imposes a tax of 10 drachmas per yard of cloth sold. The cloth sellers simpy raise the price by 10 drachmas per yard and the farmer who purchases the cloth ends up paying the tax."
  (a) Under what supply-demand conditions is the farmer's analysis of the effects of a tax on cloth correct?
  (b) Under what conditions will none of the tax burden fall on the farmer-buyers?
  (c) Suppose that the pretax demand and supply for cloth are governed by the relationships

$$Q_d = 980 - 4P$$
$$Q_s = 20 + 8P$$

where Q_d is the quantity demanded (mil-

lions of yards), Q_s the quantity supplied (millions of yards), and P the price in drachmas (per yard). If the government imposes a tax of 10 drachmas per yard on the sellers of cloth, by how much will the price paid by the farmer-buyers rise?
(*Note:* For simplicity assume that all potential buyers of cloth in Greece are farmers.)
3. Explain why market equilibrium is determined by the *intersection* of the supply curve and the demand curve. What do you understand by the concept of stability of equilibrium?
4. Explain briefly whether the following statements are true or false.
  (a) A straight-line demand curve has a constant elasticity at every point.
  (b) Because the demand for wheat is inelastic, the welfare of the nation can be enhanced by burning 20 percent of each year's output.
  (c) Since 1960 the price of corn has increased while the quantity of corn sold has also increased. From this it must be obvious that the demand for corn slopes upward and to the right.
  (d) When the price of "potatoes" is $10, the quantity demanded is 100. When the price falls to $8 (i.e., when the price falls by $2), the quantity demanded increases to 102 (i.e., the quantity demanded increases by 2). Therefore, the elasticity of demand for potatoes must be unity.
  (e) Any two parallel straight-line demand curves have the same elasticity at each and every level of price.
  (f) If a subsidy of $1 paid to suppliers causes the price paid by consumers to fall by $1, we can conclude that the supply curve is infinitely elastic.
  (g) A tax on cigarettes raises the price paid by smokers, but only initially. As price rises,

demand falls, pulling price down again. The lower price stimulates demand, which makes price go up; and so on. Therefore, the price of cigarettes will continue to oscillate forever.

5. You are given the following data obtained from a hypothetical demand curve:

Price	21	18	15	12	9
Quantity	1	2	3	4	5

(a) Determine total revenue $(p \cdot q)$ at each price.

(b) Over what prices is demand elastic, inelastic, and unit elastic?

(c) Calculate the arc elasticity of demand as price increases from 15 to 18.

6. According to *The Wall Street Journal* (December 15, 1983), tungsten prices have fallen from $171 a ton in 1978 to about $75 in 1983. At a meeting of the Tungsten Committee of the United Nations Conference on Trade and Development, producing countries deplored what they termed the "collapse" of the world market, and they blamed the United States for continuing to sell from its stockpile of the metal despite falling prices. The United States rejected the criticism, explaining that U.S. stockpile releases represented only 1 percent of world consumption "and are therefore insignificant."

(a) Was the criticism of the policy of the United States justified, or were the U.S. stockpile releases so small that they had no appreciable effect on price?

(b) Under what circumstances would the U.S. stockpile releases (about 1 percent of world consumption) have caused the price of tungsten to fall from $171 to $75 a ton?

(c) Suppose that besides the U.S. stockpile releases other factors, such as the world recession, were responsible for the drastic fall in tungsten prices. If the price elasticity of demand for tungsten is 0.50 (in absolute terms), what part of the price reduction was due to the U.S. stockpile releases, and what part was due to other factors?

7. Suppose that the demand for fish depends not only on the price of fish (P_f), but also on the price of beef (P_b). The own-price elasticity of demand for fish is -2.0, and the cross-price elasticity of demand for fish is $+3.0$. The elasticity of supply of fish is zero, and the current price of fish is $5 per pound. Assume that this initial equilibrium is disturbed by a 10 percent rise in the price of beef.

(a) How will the demand curve for fish shift? Draw an approximate graph.

(b) How will the rise in the price of beef affect the equilibrium price of fish? Can you calculate the new equilibrium price of fish?

8. Evaluate the following statements made by Benjamin Zycher (*The Wall Street Journal*, December 20, 1983, p. 30), formerly the top energy-policy specialist for President Reagan's Council of Economic Advisers.

(a) "Price controls do not reduce prices. Controls reduce only reported prices, which exclude time and other resources squandered in efforts to obtain fuel at artificially low ceiling prices."

(b) "Price controls do not help consumers or the poor. By raising true prices . . . controls reduce the total consumption basket."

(c) "There is no reason to believe that allocation of oil by regulatory fiat leads systematically to greater 'equity' or 'fairness' than does the market price mechanism."

*9. Suppose that turnips are traded in a perfectly competitive market. At the current equilibrium, an econometrician estimates that the elasticities of demand and supply are -0.5 and $+2.0$, respectively. Suppose that the initial equilibrium is disturbed by a "small" specific tax (also known as a *per unit tax*). Determine the rates of change of (a) the price paid by consumers, (b) the price received by producers, and (c) the quantity of turnips traded.

FURTHER READING

Baumol, W. J. (1959). *Economic Dynamics,* 2nd ed. The Macmillan Company, New York. Chapter 7.

Behrman, J. R. (1978). *Development, the International Economic Order, and Commodity Agreements.* Addison-Wesley Publishing Company, Inc., Reading, Mass. Chapter 3.

Boulding, K. E. (1966). *Economic Analysis,* 4th ed. Vol. I: *Microeconomics.* Harper & Row, Publishers, Inc., New York. Part I.

Hicks, J. R. (1965). *Capital and Growth.* Oxford University Press, New York. Part 1, especially Chapters 1–11.

Lipsey, R. G., and P. O. Steiner (1981). *Economics,* 6th ed. Harper & Row, Publishers, Inc., New York. Part 2.

Marshall, A. (1959). *Principles of Economics,* 8th ed. Macmillan & Company Ltd., London. Book III, Chapter 4, and Book V, Chapters 1–5.

Samuelson, P. A. (1947). *Foundations of Economic Analysis.* Harvard University Press, Cambridge, Mass. Chapter 2.

Samuelson, P. A. (1980). *Economics,* 11th ed. McGraw-Hill Book Company, New York. Chapters 4, 20, and 21.

Wicksteed, P. H. (1950). *The Commonsense of Political Economy,* Vol. 2. Augustus M. Kelley, Publishers, New York. Chapter 4.

PART TWO

The Theory of Demand

CHAPTER
3

Indifference Curves

In Part One we presented a preliminary view of the law of supply and demand. From that introductory discussion we have learned that in a perfectly competitive market, price is determined by supply and demand. But what economic principles lie behind demand? Behind supply? Only tentative answers to these questions were given in Part One. The time has come to elaborate and extend those ideas.

In this part of the book we concentrate on the *theory of demand;* we look behind the demand curve in an effort to unravel the fundamental principles of demand behavior. The concepts of production and cost, which lie behind the supply curve, are surveyed in Part Three.

There are two important approaches to the theory of demand: the older (cardinal) utility approach and the modern indifference curve approach. The reader is probably more familiar with the cardinal utility approach, which is still part of the principles-of-economics course. However, economists have always felt uncomfortable about cardinal utility, and the notion that marginal utility is diminishing, because utility is not observable in the real world. Our aim in this book is to develop the modern indifference curve approach. The latter is based on the *theory of choice,* which frees the theory of demand from the untenable concept of utility. But to help the reader appreciate the significance and superiority of the new approach, we find it necessary to make repeated references to the basic premises and propositions of the old-fashioned utility model.

We begin our discussion with an elementary introduction to the modern theory of choice (Section 3.1). We then apply the general theory of choice to the particular problem of consumer choice (Section 3.2). Next we show how indifference curves can be derived and examine their basic properties (Section 3.3). In Section 3.4 we provide a brief review of the basic premises of the cardinal utility model, and in Section 3.5 we introduce utility as an ordinal rather than a cardinal measure. We conclude the chapter with an economic interpretation of the shape of indifference curves and the law of diminishing marginal rate of substitution (Section 3.6).

3.1 **The Theory of Choice**[1]

The modern indifference curve approach is based on the theory of choice. Accordingly, the first step in our study must be the examination of the theory of choice. What are its basic premises?

Economic Versus Noneconomic Choices

Every day of our lives, we make many choices. Should I eat a steak or an omelet? Should I watch television or read a book? Should I wear my brown suit or my blue suit? Should I purchase a house or rent an apartment? Some of these choices (such as "Should I wear my brown suit or my blue suit?") are noneconomic in nature; others (such as "Should I purchase a house or rent an apartment?") are economic. The modern theory of choice is a general theory that applies to both economic and noneconomic choices.

In this section we develop the basic procedure of the theory of choice by means of a simple example. Our example will enable us to introduce the fundamental concepts of the theory of choice in their simplest and most obvious form, even though such concepts are capable of the most complicated uses. This is actually the main justification for our approach.

The Universal Set

Consider a traveling salesman (say, a New Yorker) who has to spend a weekend in a strange city (say, Atlanta, Georgia). Suppose that this New Yorker knows only six restaurants in Atlanta and wants to choose one for dinner. His choice must be one among these six restaurants: $a, b, c, d, e,$ and f. How will the salesman make his choice?

The fixed set[2] of six restaurants, that is,

$$S = \{a, b, c, d, e, f\} \tag{3.1}$$

is the frame of reference, or the *universe,* for our present discussion.[3] For this reason we call it the *universal set* and represent it by the symbol S. All other sets that we may consider in our present argument must be subsets of this universal set.

Note that different universal sets must be used for different discussions (or problems). In general, the universal set is selected in such a way as to fit the needs of the problem at hand. In economic choice theory, the universal set is often referred to as the "choice set" or "action set," to draw attention to the nature of the problem, that is, choice among alternatives.

The Attainable Set Versus the Unattainable Set

Return now to the salesman in Atlanta, Georgia. Suppose that after he makes a few telephone calls, he discovers that restaurants $d, e,$ and f are closed for renovation; thus they are not available. Consequently, the salesman must choose a restaurant among the remaining three: $a, b,$ and c.

---

[1]This section is influenced by the delightful book of V. C. Walsh (1970).

[2]A *set* is a collection of *elements,* that is, objects or entities of some sort.

[3]We follow the convention of using lowercase letters to represent *elements* in a set and capital letters to represent sets.

We express such a situation formally by saying that the universal set S is *partitioned* into two *proper* and *disjoint subsets:* the *attainable* (or *feasible*) set

$$A = \{a, b, c\} \tag{3.2}$$

and the *unattainable* (or *nonfeasible*) set

$$A' = \{d, e, f\} \tag{3.3}$$

We say that A is a *subset* of S (or is contained in S) because each element of A is also an element of S. That is, each restaurant in the attainable set A is also in the universal set S. Similarly, the unattainable set A' is a subset of the universal set S, because each restaurant in A' is also in S. However, S is not a subset of either A or A'. That is, not every restaurant in S is in A; similarly, not every restaurant in S is in A'. For this reason, A and A' are called *proper* subsets of S.

Further, subsets A and A' are *disjoint* because they have no element in common (i.e., their *intersection* is the *empty set* $\emptyset$).[4] In other words, A and A' are disjoint because no restaurant belongs to both of them.

Finally, subsets A and A' form a *partition* of S because (1) they are *nonempty* subsets of S, (2) they are *disjoint*, and (3) their union, written $A \cup B$, is the universal set S.[5] In other words, each restaurant in S belongs either to the attainable subset A, or to the unattainable subset A', but not to both.

Strong Ordering

To make further progress, we must now introduce into our discussion a fundamental notion: *ordering*.

As we have seen above, the traveling salesman must choose a restaurant among the three available restaurants. In other words, he must choose an element of the attainable set $A = \{a, b, c\}$. To do so, however, he must first be able to *rank* the elements of the attainable set in some kind of *order of preference*. This preference ranking is known as *ordering*.

More precisely, the salesman must be able to compare any two restaurants in the attainable set, say, restaurants a and b, and tell us unequivocally whether he prefers to have dinner at restaurant a rather than at b, or prefers b to a, or that a and b are equally attractive.

For instance, suppose that the salesman reveals to us that on his scale of preferences restaurant a is definitely preferred to both b and c, and b is definitely preferred to c. Thus restaurant a comes first, b comes second, and c comes third. This is the simplest type of ordering in which each element of the attainable set occupies a unique position in the preference ranking not shared with any other element. This type of ordering is known as *strong ordering*.

There are many familiar examples of strong ordering. For instance, the set of all letters in the alphabet is strongly ordered, as is the set of all positive integers.

Rational Choice in the Presence of Strong Ordering

Assume that the salesman's scale of preferences is strongly ordered, as hypothesized above. What rule will he follow in choosing a restaurant (i.e., making a

---

[4]The intersection of two sets A and B, written $A \cap B$, is the set of all elements that are in both A and B. The empty set, denoted by the symbol $\emptyset$, is that set which has no elements whatever.

[5]The union of two sets A and B, written $A \cup B$, is the set of all elements that are in either A or B (including those which are in both).

decision)? Apparently, the salesman must choose restaurant a, which is the most highly ranked (or ordered) restaurant in the attainable set.

In general, a *rational* decision maker must choose the "most preferred" element in the attainable set, that is, that element that ranks highest in his or her scale of preferences. This important rule is often referred to as the *axiom of rationality*.

Two-Term Consistency and Transitivity

In ranking the elements of the attainable set, we implicitly used two important notions: the notion of *two-term consistency* and the notion of *transitivity*. It is now necessary to make these concepts explicit and study their function and relationship.

Two-term consistency ensures that any two elements in the attainable set are consistently ranked relatively to each other. For instance, the traveling salesman must be able to compare two restaurants at a time and say which he ranks above the other. As we have seen, he prefers a to b and b to c. This means that in the salesman's ranking, a is above b; *thus b can never be above a*. Similarly, b stands higher than c; *thus c can never be above b*.

Two-term consistency is a necessary condition for consistent choices. However, it is not a sufficient condition. Sufficiency requires also *transitivity,* which involves three-term comparisons. For instance, the salesman prefers a to b and b to c. His preferences will be transitive if he also prefers a to c. That is, if there is to be a thread of consistency in his choices, the salesman must *not* also prefer c to a. Accordingly, transitivity ensures consistency by ruling out such "circular" ordering (i.e., ordering without top and bottom).

In the real world, there are many transitive relationships. For instance, if real number n_3 is larger than real number n_2 and n_2 is larger than real number n_1, it follows that n_3 is also larger than n_1. Similarly, if restaurant a is larger (in square feet) than restaurant b and b is larger than c, it follows that a is also larger than c. If Florida is warmer than Georgia and Georgia is warmer than New York, it follows that Florida is also warmer than New York.

However, not all relations are transitive. For instance, if George is in love with Beth and Beth is in love with John, it does *not* follow that George is also in love with John. Similarly, if the Atlanta Braves beat the Houston Astros and the Houston Astros beat the Los Angeles Dodgers, it does not follow that the Atlanta Braves will also beat the Los Angeles Dodgers.

When preferences satisfy the tests of two-way consistency and transitivity, the final choice is simple: Select the element that stands highest in the ranking. As we have seen, the salesman prefers restaurant a to b and b to c, and therefore also prefers a to c. His choice must be restaurant a.

Indifference, Weak Ordering, and Induced Strong Ordering

So far, we have been assuming that the scale of preferences is strongly ordered. Strong ordering simplifies matters substantially, of course, but it is a highly restrictive assumption because it rules out the possibility of *indifference*. (In the theory of consumer choice, strong ordering is not typical.)

Return to the example of the traveling salesman. Recall that his universal set S was partitioned into the attainable set A (consisting of restaurants a, b, and c) and the unattainable set A' (consisting of restaurants d, e, and f). Our simplifying assumption was that the salesman was able to rank the three restaurants in the attainable set in terms of the preference relation. Thus he preferred a to b and b to c, and therefore a to c (because of transitivity).

To understand the concept of indifference, let us first enlarge the universal set. Assume that the traveling salesman has just discovered three additional restaurants in Atlanta, say, x, y, and z. Accordingly, the salesman's universal set consists now of nine restaurants: a, b, c, d, e, f, x, y, and z. Assume further that the three new restaurants, that is, x, y, and z, belong to the attainable set. Thus the attainable set now consists of six restaurants: a, b, c, x, y, and z. The unattainable set consists, as before, of d, e, and f.

Suppose that the salesman ranks restaurant x above y, y above z, and (by transitivity) x above z. However, he is *indifferent* between restaurants a and x, between b and y, and between c and z. When we say that the salesman is "indifferent" between two restaurants, such as a and x, we do not mean that he is lukewarm, disinterested, or unconcerned. Rather, we mean that restaurants a and x are equally attractive to him. In other words, we mean that a and x share the same ranking in the salesman's scale of preferences, or that the preference relation does not hold in either direction. Thus "indifference" is a technical term whose meaning does not necessarily coincide with the everyday usage of the word.

In the presence of indifference, the members of the attainable set can no longer be strongly ordered. For instance, each position in the salesman's ranking is now shared by two restaurants. Thus a and x share the first position, b and y share the second position, and c and z share the third position. This type of ranking that allows the possibility of indifference is called *weak ordering*.

In general, weak ordering is tantamount to a division of the elements of the attainable set into *groups* (or subsets), known as *indifference sets*. The totality of such indifference sets is essentially a *partition* of the attainable set—there are no elements in the attainable set that belong to more than one indifference set, and every element of the attainable set belongs to some indifference set. In our example, the attainable set is partitioned into three indifference sets, I_1, I_2, and I_3, as follows:

$$I_1 = (a, x)$$
$$I_2 = (b, y)$$
$$I_3 = (c, z)$$

Nevertheless, weak ordering is much more than a mere partition of the attainable set into indifference sets. Observe carefully that simple preference holds among the three indifference sets, I_1, I_2, and I_3. Accordingly, even though there is no ordering within each indifference set, *the sequence of indifference sets is strongly ordered.* That is, I_1 is preferred to I_2, I_2 is preferred to I_3, and by transitivity, I_1 is preferred to I_3.

We therefore conclude that by partitioning the attainable set into indifference sets, we can regain the simplicity of strong ordering because simple preference holds among the indifference *sets*. Such a ranking over the sequence of indifference sets is usually referred to as *induced strong ordering*. The purpose of the word "induced" is to provide a warning that the elements of the attainable set cannot be strongly ordered and that strong ordering applies to the sequence of indifference sets only.

Rational Decision in Presence of Indifference

How does a rational decision maker form a choice in the presence of indifference? In particular, how will the traveling salesman choose a restaurant now?

Given that the salesman prefers I_1 to I_2 and I_2 to I_3 (and by transitivity, I_1 to I_3), he will obviously choose indifference set I_1. But how will he choose between restaurants a and x (i.e., between the elements of indifference set I_1)?

Unlike "Buridan's ass," which was unable to choose between two bundles of hay placed at equal distances to right and left and thus died of hunger, human beings do not hesitate to choose under such circumstances. However, choice between two equally preferred elements is best determined by chance rather than deliberate decision. For instance, the salesman's final choice between restaurants a and x may be made on the basis of a toss of a coin.

Note that the indeterminacy disappears when the most preferred set has only one element. This observation actually becomes important in the case of consumer choice, as Chapter 4 shows.

Summary of the Theory of Choice

Here is a brief summary of the procedure of how to solve a problem of choice.

1. Determine the universal (or choice) set.
2. Partition the universal set into the attainable set and the unattainable set.
3. If the elements of the attainable set can be strongly ordered, choose the most highly ordered element.
4. If the elements of the attainable set cannot be strongly ordered, partition the attainable set into a sequence of indifference sets.
5. Order the sequence of indifference sets (induced strong ordering).
6. Choose the most highly ordered indifference *set.*
7. Allow chance to determine one element of the most highly ordered indifference set. The element so selected is the final choice.

3.2 Consumer Choice

We are now ready to apply the principles of the general theory of choice to the specific problem of consumer choice. In this section we can do no more than merely lay the foundations of the modern theory of consumption. In particular, in this section we explore the nature of the problem of consumer choice and introduce explicitly certain axioms of consumer behavior.

The Commodity Space

A typical consumer is concerned with choices among commodities, that is, physical goods and services of all kinds. In general, the consumer chooses among many commodities. However, to illustrate the argument graphically, it is customary to limit the analysis to the case of just two commodities, say X and Y. This restriction makes the analysis somewhat unrealistic, but most of the results obtained from a two-commodity model have general validity and can easily be extended to the general case of many commodities.

For convenience, we also assume that commodities X and Y are *perfectly divisible*. This assumption may appear to violate reality. Many commodities, such as cars and horses, are physically *indivisible*. You just cannot buy (or sell) half a car or half a horse. What is our justification in assuming perfect divisibility? First, some commodities, such as milk and gasoline, are physically divisible. Second, and more important, it makes no difference whether or not a commodity is divisible when we are interested in the *rate (flow)* at which it is consumed per unit of time. For example, in any particular week I cannot purchase one-third of a haircut; I can purchase either one haircut or none at all. Yet if I purchase one haircut every three weeks, I may say that, on the average, I purchase one-third of a haircut per week. In the case of durable consumer goods we may also concentrate on the flow of services they provide per unit of time. For instance, in the case of a car, we may simply consider

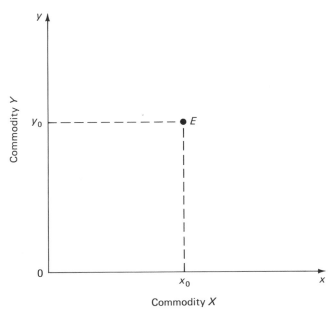

Figure 3.1 The commodity space. Positive amounts of commodities X and Y are measured along the horizontal and vertical axes, respectively. Any commodity bundle can be represented by a point. For instance, bundle (x_0, y_0) is denoted by point E. Conversely, any point in the first quadrant represents a commodity bundle (i.e., a collection of positive amounts of X and Y). The totality of commodity bundles, that is, the entire first quadrant, is known as the commodity space.

the flow of transportation services (i.e., miles traveled) that the car provides per period of time. Even though the car is not a divisible commodity, the number of miles traveled per week is a perfectly divisible flow.

By a *bundle* (or *basket*) of commodities X and Y we merely mean a collection of specific quantities X and Y. For instance, a commodity bundle may consist of x_0 units of commodity X and y_0 units of commodity Y.[6] For convenience, we may refer to this particular bundle by the ordered pair (x_0, y_0), or by a capital letter, such as E. This bundle is actually shown graphically by point E in Figure 3.1.

In general, any bundle of commodities X and Y can be represented graphically by a point in the xy-plane, as illustrated by point E in Figure 3.1. Conversely, any point in the xy-plane represents a particular bundle of X and Y.

The collection of all commodity bundles is known as the *commodity space*. Graphically, the commodity space corresponds to the entire first quadrant of Figure 3.1. The consumer must eventually choose one point (i.e., one commodity bundle) from the commodity space.

The Axioms of Consumer Behavior

Before the consumer can make a rational choice, he or she must be able to rank consistently in order of preference all conceivable bundles of commodities (just like the traveling salesman ranked the available restaurants in order of preference).

---

[6]We find it convenient to use capital letters, such as X and Y, to represent names of commodities. We use corresponding lowercase letters, such as x and y, to represent quantities. Subscripts, such as 0 and 1, to x and y indicate specific quantities of X and Y. For instance, X may represent wheat, x bushels of wheat, and x_0 a specific number of bushels of wheat, such as 100,000 bushels.

This ranking is known as the consumer's *preference function.* What principles govern the preference function? Below we summarize these principles in the form of three axioms (or postulates). These are statements (or assertions) that we accept as true without proof.

1. *Axiom of comparison (or complete-ordering axiom):* Given any two bundles of commodities, say, E and F, the consumer must be able to compare them and state unequivocally one (and only one) of the following three results:
    (a) She prefers E to F, or
    (b) she prefers F to E, or
    (c) she is indifferent between E and F (i.e., she finds E and F equally attractive).
    The axiom of comparison guarantees the existence of two-term consistency, which is a necessary condition for consistent choices.

2. *Axiom of transitivity:* Assume that the consumer is confronted with three bundles, say, E, F, and G. If the consumer prefers E to F and F to G, she must also prefer E to G. Similarly, if the consumer is indifferent between E and F and between F and G, she must also be indifferent between E and G. Further, if she is indifferent between E and F but prefers F to G, she must also prefer E to G. Finally, if she prefers E to F but is indifferent between F and G, she must also prefer E to G.
    The axiom of transitivity involves three-term comparisons. Taken together with the axiom of comparison, the axiom of transitivity implies a thread of

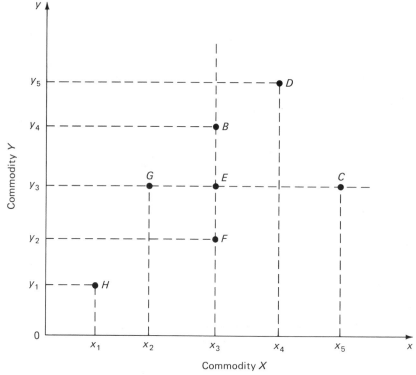

Figure 3.2 The axiom of nonsatiation. The consumer prefers bundle E to bundle F because E has more of commodity Y than F, while both bundles have the same amount of commodity X. Similarly, the consumer prefers E to G, E to H, and F to H. However, the consumer prefers D to E, C to E, and B to E.

consistency in the consumer's choices. The following axiom excludes the possibility that the consumer may be satiated in either commodity.

3. *Axiom of nonsatiation:* Consider two commodity bundles, say, E and F. Assume that bundle E contains at least as much of each commodity as bundle F, and in addition, bundle E contains a larger quantity of at least one commodity than bundle F. Then the consumer must prefer bundle E to bundle F.

The axiom of nonsatiation is illustrated in Figure 3.2. Consider the various commodity bundles represented by points B, C, D, E, F, G, and H. The consumer must prefer E to F because although both bundles have the same amount of commodity X (i.e., x_3), bundle E has a larger amount of commodity Y than bundle F (i.e., $y_3 > y_2$). Similarly, the consumer must prefer E to G because bundle E has a larger quantity of commodity X (i.e., $x_3 > x_2$) while it has the same quantity of commodity Y as bundle G (i.e., y_3). Also, the consumer must prefer bundle F to bundle H because bundle F has more of both commodities than bundle H.

As an exercise, study Figure 3.2 and show that the consumer prefers D to E, B to E, and C to E. Can you predict the consumer's ranking for the following pairs of commodity bundles: C and D, B and C, D and G, and F and G? If not, why not?

Incidentally, note that the consumer's preferences are transitive. As we have seen, the consumer prefers E to F and F to H. Therefore, she must also prefer E to H. That this is so follows from the fact that in comparison with H, bundle E has more of both commodities.

The axiom of nonsatiation means that the consumer is not oversupplied with any commodity. As a consequence, *she prefers more to less.* Although this axiom is not universally valid, we adhere to it throughout the book because it focuses our attention on the economically most meaningful case. In the Appendix to Chapter 3 we show briefly the consequences of dropping the axiom of nonsatiation.

3.3 The Indifference Map[7]

Given the foregoing axioms of consumer behavior, we now proceed to represent graphically the preference ranking of the consumer in terms of an indifference map.

Definition and Derivation of Indifference Curves

As we have seen in Section 3.1, the elements of the attainable set cannot be strongly ordered when indifference is present. Rather, they can be grouped into indifference sets, with each indifference set consisting of those elements that are equally attractive to the decision maker. The resultant sequence of indifference sets can then be strongly ordered.

We now apply the above procedure to the theory of consumption. Recall that all conceivable bundles of commodities are represented by points in the commodity space. Given the axioms of consumer behavior, we can partition the commodity space into a family (or sequence) of indifference sets. Graphically, these indifference sets take the form of *curves*. For this reason we refer to them as *indifference curves*. The entire family of indifference curves is the consumer's *indifference map. An indifference curve is the locus of all points in the commodity space (i.e., all commodity bundles) that are equally attractive to the consumer.* That is, the consumer is indif-

[7]At the end of this section the reader may wish to study Section A3.1 of the Appendix to Chapter 3.

ferent between any two commodity bundles (points) that lie on the same indifference curve.

How can we actually discover an indifference curve? Hypothetically, by asking the consumer to reveal her preferences. For instance, suppose that the consumer reveals to us that she is indifferent between bundles A and B and between bundles B and C. By transitivity she must also be indifferent between bundles A and C. Accordingly, all three bundles must lie on the same indifference curve, as illustrated in Figure 3.3.

Next, recall the assumption that commodities X and Y are perfectly divisible, and assume that the consumer is able to give us all the information we need about her preference ranking. By giving the consumer more and more options (i.e., by asking her to compare more and more pairs of commodity bundles and give us her ranking), we can discover more and more points (or commodity bundles) that are as attractive to her as points A, B, and C. We can then draw a continuous line through all such points. This line is actually an indifference curve, as illustrated in Figure 3.3 by indifference curve I_0.

Following the above procedure, we can discover as many indifference curves as we wish. In other words, by giving more options to the consumer and asking her to reveal her preferences, we can actually discover the entire indifference map.

The indifference map represents the consumer's tastes. A change in tastes corresponds to a shift of the indifference map. Unless stated explicitly otherwise, we assume that the indifference curves do not shift; that is, the consumer's tastes remain constant throughout our analysis.

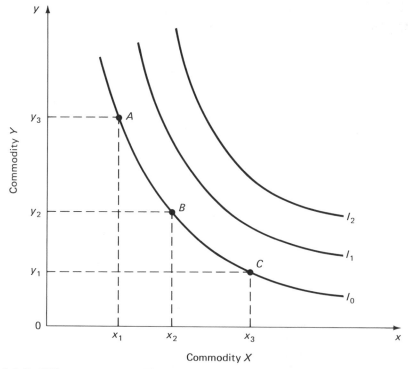

Figure 3.3 Indifference curves. The consumer reveals to us that she is indifferent between bundles A, B, and C. Accordingly, all three bundles lie on the same indifference curve I_0. By drawing a continuous line through all points that are indifferent to A, B, and C, we obtain indifference curve I_0. In a similar manner, we can obtain other indifference curves, such as I_1 and I_2.

Properties of Indifference Curves

Indifference curves have five important properties that are implicit in the drawing of Figure 3.3. These properties are as follows:

1. *One (and only one) indifference curve passes through each point in commodity space.* This property is usually expressed by saying that "indifference curves are everywhere *dense.*"
2. *Indifference curves slope downward* (i.e., they have a *negative slope*).
3. *Indifference curves never intersect one another.*
4. Consider two indifference curves, say I_0 and I_1, and assume that I_1 lies above and to the right of I_0, as shown in Figure 3.3. (We usually express this by saying that I_1 is higher than I_0). *The higher indifference curve (i.e., I_1) represents bundles of commodities that are preferred to the bundles represented by the lower one (i.e., I_0). In short, I_1 is preferred to I_0.*
5. Indifference curves are *convex to the origin.*

The first four properties of indifference curves follow directly from the axioms of consumer behavior. The fifth property ("convex to the origin") is actually an additional assumption.

The first property (i.e., the *density* of indifference curves) follows directly from the axiom of comparison and the assumption that commodities are perfectly divisible. Thus the consumer is always able to rank in order of preference any two bundles of commodities (axiom of comparison). Since each point in the consumption space represents a possible commodity bundle (assumption of perfect divisibility), it follows that each point (i.e., each commodity bundle) must lie on some indifference curve.

An implication of the above property is that we can always draw an indifference curve between any two given indifference curves, irrespective of how close to each other they may lie. (This is similar to a fundamental property of the real number system, namely, that we can always find a real number between any two given real numbers no matter how close to each other they happen to be.) It is, in fact, this basic idea that is expressed by the statement that "indifference curves are everywhere dense."

Turn now to the second property, namely, that indifference curves have a negative slope. This property follows directly from the axiom of nonsatiation. Consider indifference curve I_0 passing through point E in Figure 3.4. (That there exists an indifference curve passing through point E is guaranteed by the first property). The dashed perpendicular lines through point E divide the entire commodity space into four regions. Clearly, any point in region 1 (including the points on the perpendicular lines) is preferred to E because more is preferred to less (axiom of nonsatiation). Similarly, point E is preferred to any point in region 3 (including the points on the perpendicular lines). Accordingly, regions 1 and 3 (including the perpendicular lines) do not contain any points indifferent to point E. By elimination,[8] then, we must conclude that all points indifferent to E must lie in shaded regions 2 and 4. This means that the indifference curve through E must actually pass from region 4 to region 2, as shown by indifference curve I_0; that is, it must have a negative

[8]To prove that there are points in region 4 that are indifferent to E, you may think as follows. Draw line segment ST, as shown in Figure 3.4. Imagine that the consumer travels along line segment ST from S to T. During this trip, the consumer moves from a point (S) that is inferior to E to a point (T) that is superior (i.e., preferred) to E. By continuity, there must exist a point along line segment ST that is indifferent to E, as illustrated by point V. A similar argument can be supplied for points in region 2.

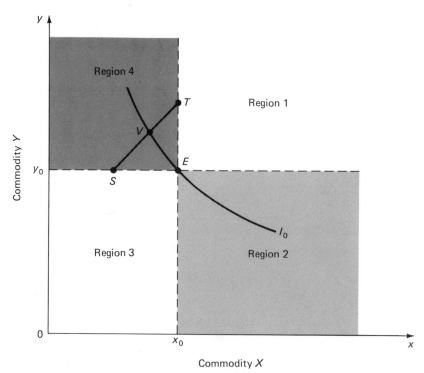

Figure 3.4 The negative slope of indifference curves. All points in region 1 are preferred to point E, and point E is preferred to all points in region 3 (axiom of nonsatiation). Accordingly, the indifference curve through E must pass from shaded region 4 to shaded region 2; that is, it must have a negative slope at E.

slope at point E. Since the above argument holds for any point in the commodity space, we must conclude that indifference curves do slope downward.

We can prove the third property (i.e., that indifference curves never intersect) by showing that intersection leads to a logical contradiction. Consider Figure 3.5, in which we tentatively assume that dashed indifference curve I_2 intersects indifference curve I_1 at point E. Surely, G is indifferent to E, because both G and E lie on indifference curve I_2. Similarly, E is indifferent to F, because both E and F lie on indifference curve I_1. By transitivity, then, G *must be indifferent to F*. However, G contains more of both commodities than F, and thus G *must be preferred to F* (axiom of nonsatiation). Since G cannot be both indifferent to F and preferred to F, we must rule out the possibility of intersection between any two indifference curves.

There is an alternative proof of the property of nonintersection which must be obvious from our discussion of the general theory of choice in Section 3.1. Recall that the division of the elements of the attainable set into indifference sets is essentially a "partition" of the attainable set. Thus each element of the attainable set belongs to one, and only one, indifference set (i.e., the indifference sets are disjoint). The same is true of the indifference curves. A point in the commodity space (i.e., a commodity bundle) must belong to one, and only one, indifference curve. Accordingly, there cannot be any points that are common to two (or more) indifference curves. That is, indifference curves can neither touch nor intersect each other. (The property of nonintersection was anticipated by the first property.)

The fourth property (i.e., that a higher indifference curve is preferred to a lower one) is a direct consequence of the axiom of nonsatiation. Consider indifference curve I_0 passing through point E in Figure 3.4. A higher indifference curve than I_0

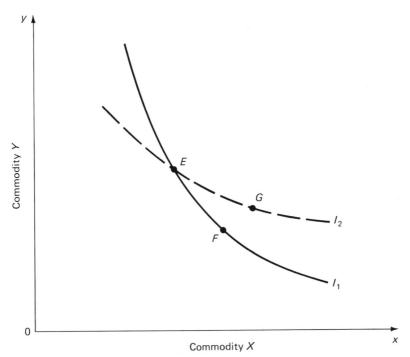

Figure 3.5 The property of nonintersection. Point G is indifferent to E because both G and E lie on indifference curve I_2. Similarly, E is indifferent to F because both E and F lie on indifference curve I_1. By transitivity, then, G *must be indifferent to F.* But G contains more of both commodities than F, and thus G *must be preferred to F* (since more is preferred to less). Because of this logical contradiction, we rule out the possibility of intersection.

must necessarily pass through region 1. Accordingly, a higher indifference curve than I_0 necessarily contains points (i.e., commodity bundles) that are preferred to E. Based on the definition of indifference curves and the axiom of transitivity, we must conclude that every point on any indifference curve that is higher than I_0 must be preferred to every point on I_0.

The last property (i.e., that indifference curves are convex to the origin) does not follow from the axioms of consumer behavior. As we have noted earlier, convexity is an additional assumption. In Section 3.6 we discuss its economic meaning and show that convexity of indifference curves is an eminently reasonable assumption. However, the economic significance and implications of convexity will not be clarified fully until we consider the equilibrium of the consumer in Chapter 4.

3.4 The Cardinal Utility Model: Brief Review

The cardinal utility model attained prominence in economics in the 1870s. The model is attributed to William Stanley Jevons (1835–1882) of Great Britain, Carl Menger (1840–1921) of Austria, and Leon Walras (1834–1910) of France. However, the roots of the model go further back, to the works of Jeremy Bentham (1748–1832), Nassau William Senior (1790–1864), Jules Dupuit (1804–1866), Heinrich Gossen (1810–1854), and many others. In this section we provide a brief review of the fundamental premises of the cardinal utility model.

Basic Assumptions

What are the bare elements of the cardinal utility model? Very crudely put, the model views the consumer (or household) as a "machine" that uses consumption goods and services to produce a psychological output called *utility*. Thus a consumer utilizes food, clothing, housing, and entertainment to produce all those psychological gratifications and satisfactions that accompany such consumption activity.

According to this view, the process of consumption is not essentially different from the process of production. On the contrary, consumption is an integral part of production. Consumption is the last stage of production, with utility being the ultimate output of all economic activity. In essence, all economic goods, including final consumption goods and services, are *intermediate goods;* their ultimate purpose is to satisfy human wants and needs, that is, to produce utility. The production of utility is the ultimate goal of all productive activity.

The founders of the cardinal utility model took it for granted that utility is a *cardinally* measurable quantity, similar to length, weight, and volume. Therefore, they accepted the existence of a unit of measurement of utility called a *util* and postulated that they could determine the precise number of utils produced by the consumption of various quantities of commodities. For the moment we shall go along with this assumption. Imagine that there exists such a thing as a "utilometer" that actually measures utility. One utilometer is attached to each consumer. As a consumer consumes various quantities of goods and services, the utilometer registers the resultant amount of utility.

At this stage the reader may justifiably begin to feel uneasy about the cardinal utility model. What is utility? Is it pleasure? Is it happiness? How can it be measured? There are not any good answers to these questions. For whatever we may actually understand by the term "utility," we must agree on one thing: *Utility is a subjective quantity that is not observable in real life.* Accordingly, we must give up any hope of ever being able to measure it directly. At least to this author's knowledge, nobody has ever been able to invent that fictional utilometer, even though economists have often used indirect methods (such as choice among uncertain prospects) to measure utility up to a linear transformation (see Chapter 5). Nevertheless, as explained in Section 3.5, the assumption of measurability of utility can easily be removed without having to discard the results obtained from it.

In summary, we assume that the consumer utilizes consumption goods and services to produce a psychological output called utility. What is the objective of the consumer? To maximize, subject to the budget constraint, his or her ultimate psychological utility, which is the only true final product in the entire economic process. The principle of utility maximization is the guiding light of consumer behavior.

The Additive Utility Function[9]

The original architects of the cardinal utility model assumed that the utility or satisfaction that a consumer obtains from a good depends only on the quantity of that good which he or she consumes. For instance, the utility that a consumer obtains from the consumption of food depends only on the amount of food consumed per week and nothing else.

Accordingly, the aggregate utility that a consumer obtains from the consumption of a bundle (or "basket") of commodities is equal to the sum total of utilities that the consumer obtains from each commodity separately. That is, the "utilometer" first measures the utility obtained from each commodity independently of the utility obtained from any other commodity, and then it adds up these independently mea-

[9]This section can be read together with Section A4.1 of the Appendix to Chapter 4.

sured utilities to determine the aggregate utility obtained by the consumer from the consumption of all commodities.[10]

This assumption of independent and additive utility is rather restrictive. For instance, it is clearly violated in the case of related goods, that is, substitute goods and complementary goods. For simplicity of exposition, however, we adhere to it in this section. The Appendix to Chapter 4 shows how to remove this untenable assumption. As it turns out, utility theory does not really depend on it.

Total Utility

Because of the simplifying assumption of independent and additive utility, we can use two-dimensional graphs to show the utility obtained from each good as a function of the quantity of the same good consumed by the consumer. This is illustrated by the *total utility curve* of Figure 3.6(a). Along the horizontal axis, we measure the quantity of the good consumed per unit of time, say, the number of pounds of meat consumed by the consumer per week. Along the vertical axis, we measure the *total utility* obtained by the consumer at each rate of consumption of meat. For instance, when the consumer consumes quantity Q_1 (say, 4 pounds of meat per week) he enjoys total utility U_1 (say, 30 utils per week), and when he consumes quantity Q_2 (say, 5 pounds of meat per week), he enjoys total utility U_2 (say, 36 utils per week).

The construction of the total utility curve in Figure 3.6(a) is based on three fundamental assumptions. First, as the rate of consumption increases, total utility increases also, but not proportionately. In particular, *total utility increases at a decreasing rate*. Second, when the rate of consumption increases to Q_3, total utility reaches a maximum (point S). For this reason, quantity Q_3 is often called the *satiation quantity* and point S the *saturation point* (or *satiety point*). Third, any increase in consumption beyond the satiation quantity has a negative effect on total utility. That is, increasing consumption beyond Q_3 (say, beyond the fifteenth pound of meat per week) makes the consumer sick or at least produces a smaller total satisfaction or utility, as shown by the downward-sloping region of the total utility curve just beyond saturation point S. The implications of these assumptions are analyzed below.

Marginal Utility

What is marginal utility? It is the *additional* utility (i.e., the *increase* in total utility) that results from a unit increase in the rate of consumption. For instance, suppose that as a consumer increases his consumption of meat from 4 to 5 pounds per week, his total utility increases from 30 utils to 36 utils. Accordingly, the consumer's total utility increases by 6 utils (i.e., $36 - 30 = 6$), and thus the marginal utility of the fifth pound of meat is 6 utils.

Graphically, marginal utility is given by the slope of the total utility curve at the current rate of consumption. For instance, return to Figure 3.6(a) and suppose that the rate of consumption is Q_1 units per period of time. Then marginal utility is equal to the slope of the total utility curve at point A. We can verify this as

[10]Suppose that a consumer consumes n goods, say $X_1, X_2, \ldots, X_n$, and that $U_i(X_i)$ represents the utility he obtains from the consumption of the ith good. According to the original approach of Jevons, Menger, and Walras, the aggregate utility obtained by the consumer is given by the function

$$U = U_1(X_1) + U_2(X_2) + \cdots + U_n(X_n) \tag{3.4}$$

This function is actually referred to as the *additive* utility function.

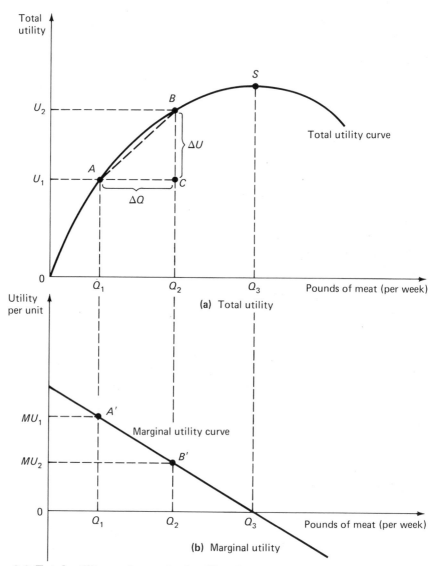

Figure 3.6 Total utility and marginal utility. Panel (a) portrays total utility, and panel (b) marginal utility, at alternative rates of consumption. Thus, when the consumer consumes quantity Q_1, he enjoys total utility U_1 [see point A in panel (a)], and marginal utility MU_1 [see point A' in panel (b)]. Note that MU_1 in panel (b) corresponds to the slope of the total utility curve in panel (a) at point A. As the rate of consumption increases, total utility increases also, but marginal utility diminishes. At satiation quantity Q_3, total utilty is at a maximum and marginal utility is zero. Beyond Q_3 total utility decreases and marginal utility becomes negative.

follows. Suppose that consumption increases from Q_1 to Q_2, causing total utility to increase from U_1 to U_2. By how much did total utility increase per unit increase in consumption? Obviously, the answer is $\Delta U/\Delta Q$, where $\Delta U = U_2 - U_1$, $\Delta Q = Q_2 - Q_1$. But the ratio $\Delta U/\Delta Q$ gives the slope of straight-line segment AB. Now imagine that the increase in the rate of consumption ΔQ becomes progressively smaller, and thus allow point B to travel along the total utility curve toward point A. As point B moves closer and closer to point A, the slope of AB moves closer and closer to the slope of the tangent at A. Consequently, the limiting value of the ratio $\Delta U/\Delta Q$, which represents marginal utility, is equal to the slope of the total utility curve at point A.

Since marginal utility is given by the slope of the total utility curve, it follows that the shape of the total utility curve reflects marginal utility. When the total utility curve is *concave*,[11] as in Figure 3.6(a), marginal utility decreases as consumption increases. Thus, in Figure 3.6(a), the tangent to the total utility curve tends to become flatter and flatter as consumption increases from zero to satiation quantity Q_3.

From the total utility curve of Figure 3.6(a), we have constructed a *marginal utility curve,* as shown in Figure 3.6(b). Thus at each rate of consumption, we calculated the slope of the total utility curve (i.e., marginal utility) and then summarized the results in Figure 3.6(b). Note that the marginal utility curve necessarily has a positive intercept with the vertical axis corresponding to the positive slope of the total utility curve at the origin. In addition, the marginal utility curve intersects the horizontal axis at the satiation quantity Q_3. (At Q_3 the slope of the total utility curve is exactly zero.) Finally, for rates of consumption that are higher than Q_3, the marginal utility curve lies below the horizontal axis; that is, marginal utility becomes *negative*. As it turns out, the marginal utility curve is much more useful than the corresponding total utility curve.

There is an important relationship between the total utility curve of Figure 3.6(a) and the corresponding marginal utility curve of Figure 3.6(b). Thus, as we have already seen, at any rate of consumption, marginal utility is equal to the slope of the total utility curve. Conversely, at any rate of consumption, total utility is equal to the area under the marginal utility curve from zero up to the specified rate of consumption.

Why does the area under the marginal utility curve give total utility? For the simple reason that total utility is the *sum* of marginal utilities. For instance, if the marginal utilities of the first, second, and third units are 10, 9, and 8 utils, respectively, the total utility obtained from the consumption of all three units must be equal to 27 utils (i.e., $10 + 9 + 8 = 27$). This sum of marginal utilities is actually represented graphically in Figure 3.7 by the area of the three shaded rectangles drawn from points A, B, and C.

It may appear from Figure 3.7 that the area under the marginal utility curve is larger than total utility, as evidenced by the three triangular areas, a, b, and c, that are not shaded. This conclusion is false. When consumption increases by *infinitesimal* quantities, not by whole units as portrayed by Figure 3.7, it becomes apparent that total utility corresponds to the *entire* area under the marginal utility curve.[12]

There is a marginal utility curve for each commodity. The entire set of marginal utility curves represents the consumer's tastes or preferences. In the context of the cardinal utility model, a change in consumer tastes means a shift in one or more marginal utility curves.

---

[11]A curve is (strictly) "concave" if it lies *above* a straight line that connects any two points on the curve. For instance, the total utility curve in Figure 3.6(a) lies above dashed chord AB, and since the same property holds for any straight line connecting any two points on the curve, we conclude that the total utility curve of Figure 3.6(a) is concave.

[12]Suppose that total utility is given by the function $U(X)$. Marginal utility is given by its derivative, that is, $U'(X)$. From the fundamental theorem of the differential and integral calculus, it follows that the integral of $U'(X)$ is simply the utility function $U(X)$. But the integral of $U'(X)$ corresponds to the entire area under the marginal utility curve $U'(X)$. [The reader must bear in mind the assumption that $U(0) = 0$.]

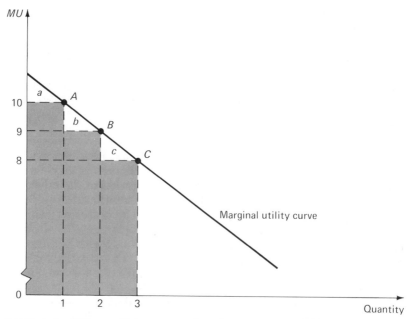

Figure 3.7 Total utility as the area under the marginal utility curve. The marginal utilities of the first, second, and third units are 10, 9, and 8 utils, respectively. Accordingly, the total utility obtained from the first three units of an *indivisible* commodity would be equal to 27 (i.e., 10 + 9 + 8), as shown by the shaded area. If we assume perfect divisibility and allow consumption to increase by infinitesimal quantities, the total utility becomes equal to the entire area under the marginal utility curve, that is, the shaded area plus the triangular areas *a*, *b*, and *c*.

The Law of Diminishing Marginal Utility

The protagonists of the cardinal utility model postulated a fundamental law about the behavior of psychological marginal utility: the *law of diminishing marginal utility*. This law played a crucial role in their theory of consumer behavior. Indeed, the law of diminishing marginal utility is implicit in the construction of Figures 3.6 and 3.7. We now wish to consider the precise content of this law and study its foundations.

Law of diminishing marginal utility: *As the consumer increases his or her rate of consumption of a certain good, the consumer's total (psychological) utility increases, but after a certain point the extra (or marginal) utility obtained from additional units tends to diminish.*

In Figures 3.6 and 3.7, the law of diminishing marginal utility holds from the start. That is, marginal utility starts diminishing from the very first unit consumed. This is not necessary, of course. The law of diminishing marginal utility merely states that marginal utility must tend to fall *beyond a certain rate of consumption*. Thus the law admits the possibility of *increasing* marginal utility at low rates of consumption. For instance, the marginal utility of a second stereo system may be higher than the marginal utility of the first, presumably because two systems enable both parents and children to listen to their respective types of music. However, the marginal utility of a third, fourth, and fifth stero system will be successively smaller.

Is the law of diminishing marginal utility valid? The founders of the cardinal utility model and their followers accepted the law of diminishing utility as a fact of common experience. Through introspection, they assumed the law to be consistent with their own psychological reactions to additional consumption.

No individual want or need, they argued, is insatiable. Even if a commodity, such as air or water, were available in abundant quantities so that we could consume as much as we wished without any sacrifices, *we would still consume only a finite amount*. That finite amount would correspond to our saturation point; that is, our rate of consumption would proceed only up to the point where marginal utility is zero.

However, for rates of consumption lower than the saturation quantity, marginal utility is necessarily positive. Evidently, the marginal utility of each unit actually consumed is positive; otherwise, the consumer would not have consumed it. Additional evidence is provided by the willingness of the consumer to sacrifice something, if he has to, in order to increase his consumption by an extra unit. For instance, a person lost in a desert would probably be willing to sacrifice a great deal for one glass of water. Accordingly, as the rate of consumption increases to the satiation level, marginal utility changes from positive values to zero, which is another way of saying that marginal utility is diminishing.

3.5 Ordinal Utility[13]

In Sections 3.2 and 3.3 we explained how to construct the consumer's preference function (or ranking) and how to represent it graphically by means of an indifference map. During all that discussion, we intentionally avoided the use of the term "utility" because we wished to emphasize that the theory of consumer choice in no way depends on the concept of utility. Indeed, as the next chapter shows, the consumer's indifference map is the only apparatus needed for the development of the theory of demand and the derivation of the downward-sloping demand curve. However, before going any further with the development of the indifference curve approach, we must pause to discuss the concept of *ordinal* utility (as opposed to *cardinal* utility).

Numbering of Indifference Curves

It is well known that the set of all real numbers (in particular, the set of all positive numbers) is strongly ordered. Accordingly, to facilitate the process of consumer choice, economists often use real numbers to represent indifference curves, which, as we have seen, are also strongly ordered.

Thus economists associate each indifference curve with a real number and use that real number as the name (or identification mark) of the indifference curve it represents. In particular, economists associate a higher positive number with a higher indifference curve; thus they can always infer that an indifference curve bearing a higher number is preferred to an indifference curve bearing a lower number. Such inference is tautologically true.

For instance, consider three indifference curves, say I_0, I_1, and I_2. Assume that I_1 is preferred to I_0, I_2 is preferred to I_1, and by transitivity I_2 is preferred to I_0 (see Figure 3.3). We may assign the number 6 to I_0, the number 27 to I_1, and the number 198 to I_2. This assignment of numbers preserves the preference ranking because $6 < 27 < 198$. Of course, we could have selected any other sequence of three numbers as long as the number we assigned to I_2 was higher than the number we assigned to I_1 and the number we assigned to I_1 was higher than the number we assigned to I_0.

Given a consistent numbering (or numerical index), a computer can easily scan

[13]At the end of this section, the reader may wish to study Section A3.2 of the Appendix to Chapter 3.

a sequence of indifference curves, no matter how mixed up it might be, and recon-struct the consumer's preference ranking. This shows how helpful a consistent num-bering is. Indeed, the introduction of a numerical index is a convenient way of summarizing the consumer's ranking and facilitates the use of mathematics in the application of indifference curves.

We can generalize the above procedure by using a continuous function, say, $U = U(x, y)$, that assigns a real number U to a commodity bundle (x, y), with the understanding that a bundle associated with a higher number is preferred to any other bundle that is associated with a lower number. Commodity bundles that are indifferent to one another are, of course, associated with the same number.

It is important to note that the function $U = U(x, y)$ cannot be uniquely specified. Thus, as we saw above, any numbering (or function) that preserves the consumer's preference ranking is quite acceptable. (We pursue this idea a little further in the Appendix to Chapter 3.)

Ordinal Versus Cardinal Utility

It will be recalled that one of the fundamental premises of the neoclassical model of cardinal utility was the assumption that there was an absolute unit of utility (called util) and that the consumer could determine precisely the total number of utils he or she could obtain from the consumption of alternative bundles of com-modities. This was summarized by the *cardinal utility function*. To what extent does the function $U = U(x, y)$ we determined above correspond to the neoclassical cardinal utility function?

To begin with, note that the transition from marginal utility curves to indifference curves coincides with a subtle but fundamental change in the underlying economic model. We no longer have to view the consumer as a machine that uses consumption goods and services (inputs) to produce utility (final output). The consumer merely *chooses* between alternative commodity bundles. Whether the consumer actually derives utility from the consumption of commodities, and how much utility, is a separate matter. The reader should never lose sight of this inconspicuous switch in economic models.

Modern economists use the term "utility" to indicate nothing more than the preference ranking of the consumer. To emphasize this, modern economists employ the term *ordinal utility* rather than "cardinal utility." Ordinal utility derives its name from ordinal numbers, such as first, second, and third, which designate only the *position* occupied by an item in an ordered sequence. Also, modern economists refer to the function $U = U(x, y)$, which summarizes the preference ranking, as the *ordinal utility function*. The latter is *not* the same as the cardinal utility function.

What is the fundamental difference between cardinal magnitudes and ordinal magnitudes? Do not fall into the trap of thinking that a cardinal magnitude, such as temperature, altitude, or time, is measured uniquely, whereas an ordinal mag-nitude, such as brightness, redness, or ordinal utility, is not. For instance, we can measure temperature (a cardinal magnitude) by employing either the Fahrenheit scale or the Celsius scale. Neither scale can claim superiority over the other. How-ever, there exists a very simple rule connecting the two scales. Thus 32° Fahrenheit corresponds to 0° Celsius (freezing point of water), 212° Fahrenheit is 100° Celsius (boiling point of water), and each degree of temperature in the Celsius scale is equivalent to 1.8 degrees in the Fahrenheit scale. Basically, the two scales differ in their choice of *origin* (or zero point) and *unit of measurement* (or unit interval). Similarly, in measuring calendar time we can take as the origin the year Jesus Christ was born or the year Rome was built, and as the unit of measurement the year, week, or day.

Even though cardinal magnitudes cannot be uniquely measured, they have an important property (not shared by ordinal magnitudes): *Irrespective of the choice of origin and unit of measurement, the relative differences among various measurements are always the same.* For instance, the increment of temperature from 68 to 104°F is twice the increment from 32 to 50°F regardless of the scale adopted. Thus $104 - 68 = 2 (50 - 32)$. Converting to the Celsius scale, we have 68°F = 20°C, 104°F = 40°C, 32°F = 0°C, and 50°F = 10°C; therefore, $40 - 20 = 2 (10 - 0)$. Similarly, the time interval from A.D. 1200 to 1800 is three times as large as the time interval from 450 B.C. to 250 B.C., whether we adopt as the origin the year Christ was born or some other year, and as the unit of measurement the year, decade, or century.

In the case of an ordinal magnitude, *there is no scale.* Thus we may say that the kitchen is brighter than the living room, and the living room is brighter than the dining room, but we cannot say that the increase in brightness from the living room to the kitchen is twice as large as the increase in brightness from the dining room to the living room. Similarly, we cannot attribute any economic meaning to the relative differences among various levels of ordinal utility. As we emphasized above, the only meaningful numerical property of specific ordinal utility levels is *order.* For instance, suppose that a consumer prefers commodity bundle A to commodity bundle B, and commodity bundle B to commodity bundle C. Suppose further that we assign the real numbers 40, 10, and 5 to A, B, and C, respectively. We cannot say that A is four times as desirable as B and eight times as desirable as C, or that B is twice as desirable as C. Nor can we say that the increment of utility from B to A is six times as large as the increment of utility from C to B. The only real significance that we can attach to the numbers 40, 10, and 5 is that $40 > 10 > 5$, and nothing else. Recall that we could assign to A, B, and C any other sequence, such as 202, 201, and 1, respectively, as long as the preference ranking was preserved. With the new sequence $(202 > 201 > 1)$ it would appear that the increment of utility from C to B is now 200 times as large as the increment of utility from B to A. Hence we conclude that the relative differences between ordinal utility levels can be changed arbitrarily without violating the consumer's preference ranking.

Furthermore, the reader should never lose sight of the fact that *the consumer's preference ranking must be given before the function $U = U(x, y)$ can be formed.* Pursuing the example above, we should resist the temptation of thinking that bundle A is preferred to bundle B because bundle A is associated with a larger number than bundle B. The fact of the matter is that the opposite is true. Thus *it is because bundle A is preferred to bundle B that a larger number is actually assigned to A, not vice versa.*

Put differently, the function $U = U(x, y)$ is selected *after* the consumer's indifference map is constructed (by asking the consumer to reveal his or her preferences), not before. The fact that we can reconstruct the indifference map from the function $U = U(x, y)$, as shown below, merely means that the function $U = U(x, y)$ was carefully selected to be consistent with that map. The fundamental datum is the indifference map, not the function $U = U(x, y)$.

Why have economists retained the (ordinal) utility function? For various reasons. First, students (and perhaps their instructors) feel more at home with chains of reasoning that are based on utility and the utility function. Second, several well-known results in economics based on the utility function are preserved. Finally, all reasonable preference rankings can be represented by a continuous utility function.[14]

Having clarified the meaning of the terms "utility" and "utility function," we shall feel free to use them in the rest of the book whenever the discussion warrants

---

[14]A rigorous proof of this proposition lies beyond the scope of the present book. For a proof, see Debreu (1959, pp. 72–73.)

their usage. However, the reader should always remember all the qualifications that we have introduced in this section.

Reconstruction of Indifference Map from the Ordinal Utility Function

Given any ordinal utility function $U = U(x, y)$, we can easily reconstruct the consumer's indifference map. Thus to each indifference curve there corresponds a real number, and to each real number there corresponds an indifference curve. To determine an indifference curve, we set U equal to a fixed number, say, U_0. Then the locus of all points that satisfy the equation $U_0 = U(x, y)$ is the corresponding indifference curve. By assigning other values to U, we can construct as many other indifference curves as we please. In other words, we can construct the entire indifference map.

Figure 3.8 illustrates this procedure graphically. First, we represent the ordinal utility function by means of a *utility surface*. A point in the xy-plane represents a collection (or bundle) of given quantities of goods X and Y. For instance, point A' represents x_0 units of X and y_0 units of Y, that is, bundle (x_0, y_0). From every such point, we draw an ordinate in the third dimension. The height of the ordinate corresponds to the amount of *ordinal* utility associated with that particular bundle. For instance, the vertical distance $A'A$ shows the ordinal utility associated with bundle (x_0, y_0). The shaded area is the utility surface, which is merely the locus of all points, such as A, determined in the third dimension. An indifference curve (or contour line) is the locus of all those points in the xy-plane that generate the same

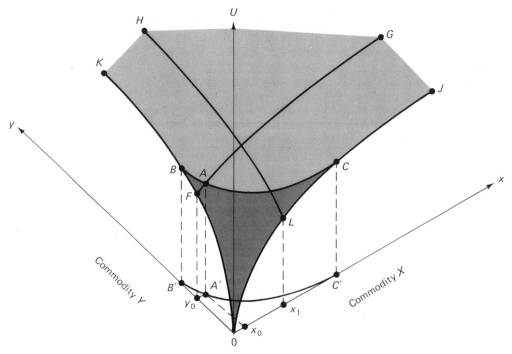

Figure 3.8 The utility surface. Point A' in the xy-plane represents bundle (x_0, y_0). The vertical distance $A'A$ shows the ordinal utility obtained from bundle (x_0, y_0). Point A lies on the utility surface, which is indicated by the shaded area. Curve BAC is the locus of all points on the utility surface whose height is equal to the vertical distance $A'A$. The projection of curve BAC onto the xy-plane, shown by curve $B'A'C'$, is the indifference curve that corresponds to ordinal utility $A'A$.

level of utility, that is, those points that correspond to the same height in the third dimension. Imagine a horizontal plane (i.e., a plane parallel to the xy-plane) intersecting the utility surface at a certain height, say $A'A$, as shown by curve (or cut) BAC. The projection of curve BAC onto the xy-plane, as shown by curve $B'A'C'$, is the indifference curve that corresponds to ordinal utility $A'A$. Other indifference curves can be constructed similarly.[15]

3.6 The Convexity of Indifference Curves

In this section we deal primarily with the economic interpretation of the shape of indifference curves, in particular the assumption that indifference curves are convex to the origin. A further economic justification of the convexity assumption is given in Chapter 4.

The Concept of Commodity Substitution

Let us suppose for a moment that we are traveling along an indifference curve. This trip is, of course, purely imaginary. It will help us, though, unearth certain important economic phenomena that are implied by the shape of indifference curves.

In general, a movement along an indifference curve is equivalent to a change in the consumer's pattern of consumption, a change that preserves the initial level of satisfaction (i.e., ordinal utility). Because the indifference curve is negatively sloped, such a change in the consumer's pattern of consumption involves the *substitution* of one commodity for the other. This is an important economic phenomenon.

Consider, for instance, indifference curve I_0 in Figure 3.9. A movement from point (or bundle) A to point B implies that the consumer increases his consumption of commodity X from 3 units to 5 units as he decreases his consumption of commodity Y from 18 units to 12 units. In other words, the consumer *substitutes* 2 additional units of commodity X for 6 units of commodity Y.

What is the economic meaning of commodity substitution? It is that in order to keep the consumer's level of satisfaction (ordinal utility) unchanged, something must be taken away from the consumer whenever he is given an extra amount of some commodity. Conversely, if some amount of one commodity is taken away from the consumer, he must be compensated for his loss with an extra amount of some other commodity; otherwise, the consumer will be in a less preferred position (i.e., his ordinal utility or satisfaction will be lower). This is a direct consequence of the axiom of nonsatiation.

The Marginal Rate of Substitution

Economists use the concept of the *marginal rate of substitution* to measure the rate at which the consumer can substitute *small* quantities of one commodity for *small* quantities of another commodity as he travels along an indifference curve.

---

[15]The powerful device of indifference curves was first introduced by Francis Y. Edgeworth (1845–1926) and Irving Fisher (1867–1947). However, it was the work of Vilfredo Pareto (1848–1923) that demonstrated how revolutionary the concept of indifference curves actually was. Pareto opened the way toward the construction of a consumer theory that was independent of the need to measure utility cardinally. Pareto's lead was followed quite successfully by Sir John R. Hicks (1904–   ).

The present procedure of deriving the indifference map from the utility function corresponds to the Edgeworth-Fisher-Pareto approach. However, that approach was made to depend on the existence of a unique cardinal utility function, whereas the present approach does not. In fact, as we noted above, the consumer's preference ranking (and thus indifference map) must exist before an ordinal utility function can be found.

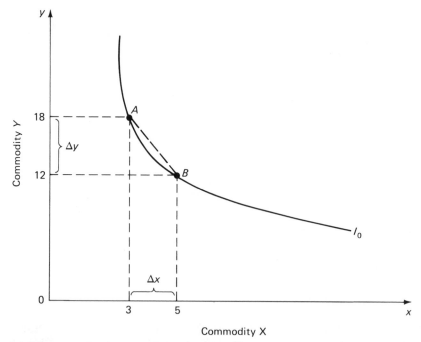

Figure 3.9 The marginal rate of substitution. For the "large" movement from A to B, the marginal rate of substitution is given by the absolute slope of dashed line AB; that is, $MRS_{xy} = \frac{6}{2} = 3$. As point B travels along indifference curve I_0 toward point A, the slope of line AB approaches the slope of the tangent at A. It is the absolute slope of the tangent at A that we define to be "the" marginal rate of substitution of X for Y when the consumer possesses 3 units of X and 18 units of Y.

More precisely, the marginal rate of substitution of commodity X for commodity Y is the maximum amount of Y that the consumer is willing to give up for 1 extra unit of commodity X without changing his satisfaction (ordinal utility).

Actually, we can develop a simple mathematical formula for our new concept. For instance, suppose that the consumer is willing to give up Δy units of commodity Y for Δx additional units of commodity X, where both Δx and Δy are "very small" quantities. How much Y is the consumer willing to sacrifice per additional unit of X? Obviously, the answer is $\Delta y/\Delta x$. Thus the marginal rate of substitution of X for Y, usually designated by the symbol MRS_{xy}, is given by the absolute value[16] of the ratio $\Delta y/\Delta x$. That is,

$$MRS_{xy} = \left| \frac{\Delta y}{\Delta x} \right| \tag{3.5}$$

Graphically, the marginal rate of substitution of X for Y is given by the absolute slope of the indifference curve. Return to Figure 3.9 and consider the "large" movement from A to B along indifference curve I_0. Applying formula (3.5), we easily find that $MRS_{xy} = 6/2 = 3$, which is equal to the absolute slope of straight-line segment AB. Now imagine that point B travels along indifference curve I_0 toward point A. As this happens, the slope of line AB moves closer and closer to the slope of the

---

[16]We must insist on the *absolute value* of the ratio $\Delta y/\Delta x$ because along a downward-sloping indifference curve Δx and Δy have *opposite* signs.

tangent at A. It is this limiting value of the ratio $|\Delta y/\Delta x|$, that is, the absolute slope of the tangent at A, which we define as the marginal rate of substitution of X for Y.

The Law of Diminishing Marginal Rate of Substitution

We are finally in a position to explain the economic meaning of the assumed *convexity* of indifference curves. Consider indifference curve I_0 in Figure 3.10. Follow the imaginary trip from point A all the way to point C. What is meant by the assumption that indifference curves are convex to the origin, as illustrated by curve I_0? Simply this: As we travel from A to C, the marginal rate of substitution of X for Y (i.e., the absolute slope of the indifference curve) tends to become smaller and smaller. Is this a sensible assumption? It most certainly is. Let us see why.

At point A, the consumer is consuming a small amount of X and a large amount of Y. It seems quite reasonable to expect the consumer to be willing to give up a relatively large amount of her plentiful commodity Y for an extra unit of her scarce commodity X. On the other hand, at point C the consumer is consuming a large amount of X and a small amount of Y. Therefore, she must be willing to sacrifice only a very small amount of her scarce commodity Y for an extra unit of her plentiful commodity X. In other words, it seems reasonable to expect the marginal rate of substitution of X for Y to be very high at point A and very low at point C.

In general, as the consumer travels continuously from point A toward point C, her marginal rate of substitution of X for Y tends to diminish. For as her consumption of X increases while her consumption of Y decreases, the consumer becomes progressively more reluctant to sacrifice commodity Y for additional amounts

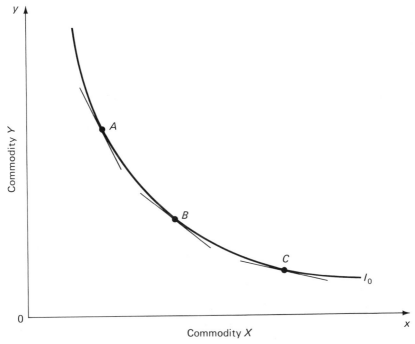

Figure 3.10 The law of diminishing marginal rate of substitution. As the consumer travels continuously from A toward C, his marginal rate of substitution of X for Y tends to diminish. Thus the tangent to indifference curve I_0 at A is steeper than the tangent at B; and the tangent at B is steeper than the tangent at C.

of commodity X. Hence she becomes willing to sacrifice successively smaller quantities of Y for additional units of X. This economic phenomenon is called the *law of diminishing marginal rate of substitution*. It is this law that accounts for the convexity of indifference curves. An additional economic justification for the law of diminishing marginal rate of substitution is given in the next chapter (see Section 4.4.).

Perfect Substitutes and Complements

Figure 3.11 illustrates two limiting shapes of indifference curves. In particular, panel (a) illustrates the case of a straight-line indifference curve and panel (b) the case of an L-shaped indifference curve.

First consider panel (a). As the consumer travels along straight-line indifference curve I_0, her marginal rate of substitution of X for Y remains constant. That is, in this special case, the marginal rate of substitution is completely independent of the relative quantities of X and Y consumed by the consumer. This means that the consumer essentially regards commodities X and Y as *perfect substitutes;* thus she is willing to exchange one for the other at a constant rate, independently of how much she possesses of them already. Examples of commodities that are perfect substitutes are not hard to find. For instance, consider the case of two different brands of milk (or butter), identical in quality and fat content, or the case of nickels and dimes.

The extreme case of commodities that are perfect substitutes does not merit much attention. The consumer does not usually distinguish between such commodities— she regards them to be essentially the same commodity. Indeed, this is a reasonable assumption to adopt for our analysis as well.

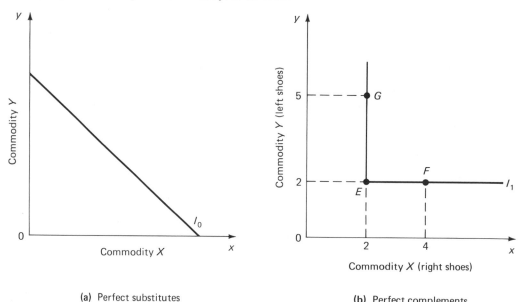

(a) Perfect substitutes   (b) Perfect complements

Figure 3.11 Perfect substitutes and complements. Straight-line indifference curve I_0 in panel (a) illustrates the special case of *perfect substitutes*. In this case the marginal rate of substitution of X for Y remains constant throughout the length of I_0. The L-shaped indifference curve I_1 in panel (b) illustrates the special case of *perfect complements*, that is, commodities, such as left and right shoes, that cannot be substituted for each other at all. The marginal rate of substitution at corner E is indeterminate and implies that one commodity is useless without the other.

At the other extreme of the spectrum is the case of commodities that are *perfect complements*. In this case the two commodities must be used simultaneously; that is, one is useless without the other. In other words, perfect complements are commodities that cannot be substituted for each other at all. Some examples of perfect complements are left and right gloves, and left and right shoes. The extreme case of commodities that are perfect complements is illustrated graphically by L-shaped indifference curves, as shown by indifference curve I_1 in Figure 3.11(b). The meaning of the L shape of these indifference curves is not difficult to understand. For instance, point F (corresponding to two pairs of shoes plus two right shoes) is not any better than point E (which corresponds to just two pairs of shoes) or point G (which corresponds to two pairs of shoes plus three left shoes).

As with perfect substitutes, the case of perfect complements is void of any practical significance. A consumer almost never thinks of left and right shoes, or gloves, as separate commodities. Thus we can shift our attention to "pairs" of shoes, or "pairs" of gloves, as actually done by the consumer.

3.7 Selected Empirical Applications

We conclude this chapter with three empirical applications. The first example illustrates a gradual change in tastes; the second example deals with the observed complementarity between housing and consumer durables, such as furniture, ranges, and refrigerators; and the third example illustrates a consumer choice involving "bads."

The Changing Wine-Drinking Habits of the French

According to the *Economist* (August 27, 1983, p. 49), the French are gradually reducing their wine consumption. During the last two decades, the annual per capita wine consumption in France has dropped by $33\frac{1}{3}$ percent—from 120 liters in the early 1960s to 80 liters presently. This dramatic reduction in per capita wine consumption basically reflects a fundamental change in the preferences of the French people. The reasons for this change in tastes are not very clear. Perhaps the French are slowly realizing that too much wine may be hazardous to their health. What is abundantly clear, however, is that the average Frenchman consumes much less wine now than 20 years ago. Office workers now drink only little wine at lunch. Younger people drink much less wine than their parents. Ambitious people who wish to be exclusive (or to distinguish themselves from the "crowd") turn to other alcoholic beverages, such as gin, vodka, and whiskey. Incidentally, the French imports of gin, vodka, and whiskey are steadily rising.

Problem: Draw indifference curves illustrating the change in the average Frenchman's preferences between wine and "all other goods."

The Complementarity Between Housing and Consumer Durables

During the recession of the early 1980s, mortgage rates remained uncomfortably high, in the range 16 to 17 percent, and the housing market was depressed. As a consequence, the sales of consumer durables, such as furniture, ranges, and refrigerators, were very low. Even though exact figures were not available, industry observers pointed out that hundreds of appliance and furniture businesses went bankrupt during the three-year recession.

But mortgage rates receded in the second half of 1982 to the more acceptable range 12 to 13 percent and the housing market began to revive. In January 1983, new single-family houses were selling at an annual rate of 576,000 units compared with 400,000 new units sold in all of 1982. The housing recovery soon spilled over to consumer durables, as shoppers returned to long-deserted showrooms in search of refrigerators, ranges, dishwashers, furniture, and other major household goods.

The reason for the observed complementarity between housing and consumer durables is simple. On the average, the sale of each new home sparks the sale of two or three major appliances and several pieces of furniture because people cannot live in empty houses. In addition, each new-house sale initiates a sort of musical-chairs game among owners of older homes, which leads to more sales of consumer durables.

The Choice of an Iowa Town to Live with Chemical Waste

The axiom of nonsatiation proclaims that the consumer is not oversupplied with any commodity, and that *he or she prefers more to less.* However, the proposition that more is preferred to less is not a universal law of preference. It applies only to desirable commodities, or *goods;* it does not apply to undesirable commodities, or *bads,* such as nuclear waste, water pollution, air pollution, ordinary household garbage, and so on. (A "good" is defined as a commodity for which more is preferred to less, and a "bad" is a commodity for which less is preferred to more.)

If disposal of undesirable commodities were always free, consumers would discard them easily and costlessly. In that case we would be justified in treating all commodities as if they were goods. But disposal is not always free; as our following example shows, in many cases disposal is a costly activity. Hence we cannot ignore the existence of bads. Consumers often have to choose between commodity bundles that include both goods and bads. For instance, industrial production (a *good*) is often associated with environmental pollution (a *bad*), and consumers must choose either more industrial production *and* pollution, or less industrial production and a cleaner environment.

Since the early 1950s Salisbury Laboratories, a veterinary pharmaceutical company in Charles City, Iowa, had been using an $8\frac{1}{2}$-acre piece of land as a dump site. This area was finally closed in the late 1970s, but according to an article in *The Wall Street Journal* (April 27, 1983, p. 60), buried underground are an estimated 6 million pounds of arsenic, lesser amounts of trichloroethane, and more than a dozen other toxic chemicals. The waste is enough to fill some 50,000 garbage trucks and, ironically, sits atop the underground water supply for much of northeastern Iowa. The potential danger is obvious. Indeed, Iowa environmental officials have called the site a "potential Love Canal." (The reference is to Love Canal in upstate New York, where chemical seepage out of an old dump forced over 200 families to relocate.) Given the potential danger, one would expect the Charles City residents to at least be furious about the unearthed dump site. Yet the disclosure of the chemical contamination was not followed by the usual community outrage. Instead, the residents of Charles City did not express any fears about the dump site. What factors are responsible for the apparent complacency of the residents of Charles City?

First, there is the widespread conviction that the site does not pose any immediate health hazards. This belief is probably based on the responsiveness of Salisbury Laboratories, which has spent $1 million since 1979 to *reduce* the flow of waste into the river. (A complete cleanup would probably cost more than $50 million.) As a result, the flows of orthonitroaniline, arsenic, and trichloroethane have decreased by about 58 percent, 26 percent, and 4 percent, respectively.

More important, the acquiescence of Charles City residents seemed to be related to the city's economic problems. In 1983 the unemployment rate in Floyd County, which includes Charles City, was 19.5 percent—the highest in Iowa—and Salisbury Laboratories is the biggest employer in Charles City. The choice, then, was between industrial production (which provides jobs and incomes, but also potential chemical contamination) and unemployment. Evidently, the residents of Charles City were saying that they preferred industrial production, jobs, and incomes together with the concomitant pollution to high unemployment and a clean environment.

Problem: Draw indifference curves illustrating the choice made by Charles City residents.

SUMMARY

1. The modern theory of demand is based on the theory of choice. The latter theory applies to both economic and noneconomic choices.

2. The universal set (*S*) is partitioned into two proper and disjoint subsets: the attainable set (*A*) and the unattainable set (*A'*).

3. The elements of the attainable set are ranked in order of preference (ordering). To ensure consistent choices, we assume that the preference ranking satisfies two conditions: two-term consistency and transitivity.

4. The consumer's preference function is founded on three axioms: the axiom of comparison (which guarantees two-term consistency), the axiom of transitivity, and the axiom of nonsatiation (more is preferred to less).

5. *Axiom of rationality:* In the presence of strong ordering, a rational decision maker must choose the most preferred element of the attainable set. With weak ordering, a rational decision maker chooses only the most highly ranked indifference set of the attainable set and allows chance to determine one element from the chosen set.

6. An indifference curve is the locus of all points in the commodity space that are equally attractive to the consumer. The entire family of indifference curves (indifference map) represents the consumer's tastes.

7. Indifference curves have five properties: (a) they are everywhere dense (one, and only one, indifference curve passes through each point in the commodity space); (b) they slope downward; (c) they never intersect; (d) they represent different levels of ordinal utility (a higher indifference curve is preferred to a lower one); and (e) they are convex to the origin.

8. To facilitate the process of consumer choice, economists use real numbers to represent indifference curves. A higher indifference curve is always associated with a higher number. This procedure leads to the construction of an ordinal utility function.

9. The ordinal utility function summarizes the consumer's preference ranking; the latter must be given before the ordinal utility function can be formed. The consumer's preference ranking is based on the theory of choice and need not reflect utility. Even if the consumption of commodities were viewed as producing utility, such utility could not be measured cardinally. Relative differences between ordinal utility levels have no significance—they can be changed arbitrarily.

10. The marginal rate of substitution (MRS_{xy}), given by the absolute slope of an indifference curve, shows the number of units of commodity *Y* that the consumer is willing to give up for one extra unit of commodity *X* while remaining at the same level of ordinal utility.

11. *Law of diminishing marginal rate of substitution:* As the consumer travels along an indifference curve substituting commodity *X* for commodity *Y*, the marginal rate of substitution of *X* for *Y* diminishes. This law is implied by the assumed convexity of indifference curves.

12. Straight-line indifference curves (constant marginal rate of substitution) imply that commodities are perfect substitutes. L-shaped indifference curves correspond to commodities that are perfect complements.

QUESTIONS

1. Mrs. Roberts is asked to rank commodity bundles A, B, D,. and E, each combining certain amounts of food and clothing, as follows:

	A	B	D	E
Food	100	30	65	40
Clothing	20	90	30	105

(a) Suppose that Mrs. Roberts says that she is indifferent between A and B and between D and E. Is Mrs. Roberts' behavior consistent with the axioms of consumer behavior?

(b) Would Mrs. Roberts' ranking be consistent if D were replaced by $D' = (90F, 19C)$?

(c) Suppose that Mrs. Roberts is indifferent among A, B, and D. What is her marginal rate of substitution of food for clothing as she moves from B to D and then from D to A?

2. Draw indifference curves reflecting each of the following preference rankings.

(a) "I would rather watch only baseball, or only football, rather than divide my leisure time between them."

(b) "I prefer a mixture of swimming and tennis to being restricted to one of them."

(c) "I hate eating either bread or cheese alone, but I love eating bread with cheese sandwiches."

(d) "I do not care whether I have regular coffee or instant coffee, as long as it is coffee."

3. A consumer is indifferent among commodity bundles A, B, C, D, and E, each consisting of specified quantities of commodities X and Y, as follows:

	A	B	C	D	E
X	50	40	30	20	10
Y	20	30	50	80	120

(a) Plot points A, B, C, D, and E on a graph.

(b) Determine the marginal rate of substitution of Y for X at points A, B, C, D, and E.

(c) Determine also the marginal rate of substitution of X for Y at A, B, C, D, and E.

(d) Verify that $MRS_{xy} = 1/MRS_{yx}$ at each point.

(e) Show that both MRS_{xy} and MRS_{yx} are diminishing.

4. A consumer's preference ranking can be summarized by the ordinal utility function $U = 10xy$, where x represents units of commodity X and y units of commodity Y.

(a) Draw the indifference curve corresponding to $U = 100$.

(b) What is the marginal rate of substitution of X for Y when $x = 5$ and $y = 2$?

(c) Show that the marginal rate of substitution of X for Y is diminishing.

(d) Will this consumer ever consume only X or only Y?

(e) Which of the following utility functions are consistent with the consumer's given preference ranking?

  (i) $U = 10(xy)^5$

  (ii) $U = (10xy)^3 + 2000$

  (iii) $U = 10xy + 20(xy)^2$

  (iv) $U = 10xy + 3x + 5y$

5. Mrs. Jones is willing to give up one bottle of whiskey for 4 pounds of steak. Mrs. Smith is willing to give up 1 pound of steak for four bottles of whiskey.

(a) Are the tastes of Mrs. Smith different from the tastes of Mrs. Jones? Why or why not?

(b) Draw indifference curves to justify the answer you gave to part (a).

6. Economists have substituted the indifference curve approach for the cardinal utility model, partly because utility is not measurable. But indifference curves cannot be measured either. What makes the indifference curve approach superior to the cardinal utility model?

7. Illustrate a change in tastes by means of indifference curves.

8. A consumer's tastes may be influenced by the consumption patterns of other consumers. How can you handle the following situations?

(a) Snob effect (i.e., the desire to be different from others, or exclusive).

(b) Bandwagon effect (i.e., the desire to be like others).

(c) Benevolence (i.e., the wish to see others well off).

(d) Malevolence (i.e., to wish harm for others).

(e) Jealousy.

9. Provide (a) three examples of strong order-

ing, (b) three examples of transitive relations, and (c) three examples of intransitive relations.

10. Give two examples of cardinal scales of magnitude and two examples of ordinal scales.

FURTHER READING

Baumol, W. J. (1977). *Economic Theory and Operations Analysis,* 4th ed., Prentice-Hall, Inc., Englewood Cliffs, N.J. Chapters 9 and 17.

Blaug, M. (1962). *Economic Theory in Retrospect.* Richard D. Irwin, Inc., Homewood, Ill. Chapters 8 and 9.

Debreu, G. (1959). *Theory of Value: An Axiomatic Analysis of Economic Equilibrium,* Cowles Foundation Monograph 17. John Wiley & Sons, Inc., New York.

Hicks, J. R. (1946). *Value and Capital,* 2nd ed. Oxford University Press, London. Chapter 1.

Hicks, J. R. (1956). *A Revision of Demand Theory,* Oxford University Press, London. Part I.

Stigler, G. J. (1950). "The Development of Utility Theory" (I and II), *Journal of Political Economy,* Vol. 58, pp. 307–327, and 373–396.

Walsh, V. C. (1970). *Introduction to Contemporary Microeconomics.* McGraw-Hill Book Company, New York. Parts 1 and 3.

CHAPTER
4

The Modern Theory of Demand

Chapter 3 dealt with the consumer's indifference map and its properties. But how can we use the indifference map to explain and predict the economic behavior of a typical consumer? In particular, how can we determine the equilibrium of the consumer? The consumer's demand curve? Is the law of demand universally valid? If not, under what circumstances is it invalidated? What other insights into the theory of demand can we gain through the use of the indifference map? In this chapter we attempt to answer these and other questions and in so doing, lay the foundations for the modern theory of demand.

In Section 4.1 we deal with the problem of consumer equilibrium and derive an important condition for ordinal utility maximization. The latter condition is compared with the equimarginal principle in Section 4.2. In Section 4.3 we introduce the concept of "corner equilibrium" and explain why consumers do not purchase positive quantities of all available goods and services. In Section 4.4 we explain the economic rationale for the assumed convexity of indifference curves, and in Section 4.5 generalize the analysis to many commodities by means of the simple device of the composite good. The effects of income changes are considered in Section 4.6, and the theory is used in Section 4.7 to evaluate the food stamp program of the United States as well as the subsidy of public education. Section 4.8 continues with the effects of price changes on consumer equilibrium and shows how to derive the consumer's demand curve. The chapter concludes with Section 4.9, which takes up the delicate task of decomposing the total price effect into an income effect and a substitution effect—an analysis that allows us to probe deeply into the foundations of the law of demand.

4.1 Equilibrium of the Consumer

The present section discusses the problem of consumer equilibrium using the modern indifference curve approach.

Statement of the Problem

Consider a consumer who has at his disposal a fixed amount of income per time period. The consumer is confronted with a market for consumption goods and services, the prices of which are already determined; that is, the consumer is a *perfect competitor* (or *price taker*) in the purchase of consumption goods and services. Finally, the tastes of the consumer are summarized by an indifference map. All indifference curves are negatively sloped, nonintersecting, and convex to the origin. How will the consumer allocate his income (or expenditure) among the various goods and services?

The objective of a rational consumer is to divide his fixed income among the various goods and services in such a way as *to maximize his ordinal utility*, that is, *attain the highest possible indifference curve*. Essentially, consumer behavior revolves around this fundamental principle of ordinal utility maximization.

The fixed income and the prevailing fixed commodity prices impose on the consumer a constraint known as the *budget constraint*. Consequently, the consumer maximizes his ordinal utility (i.e., buys that commodity bundle that puts him on the highest possible indifference curve) *subject to his budget constraint.*

The Budget Constraint

The main ingredients of the indifference curve model are two: the indifference map and the budget constraint. In this subsection we express the budget constraint graphically and study its properties.

Consider again a consumer who wishes to spend his fixed income of $500 per week on commodities X and Y whose fixed prices are $p_x = 10 and $p_y = 5, respectively. What commodity bundles (or baskets) are available to him? In other words, what is his feasible or attainable set of commodity bundles?

The Straight-line BL in Figure 4.1 shows all the alternative combinations of X and Y that the consumer can purchase with his entire income. If the consumer spends all his income on X, he can purchase 50 units of X (i.e., $500/$10), as illustrated by point L. At the other extreme, if he spends all his income on Y, he can purchase 100 units of Y (i.e., $500/$5), as illustrated by point B. All other points on straight line BL represent other mixes of X and Y (commodity bundles) that cost $500 exactly. For example, if the consumer spends half of his income on X and half of it on Y, he can purchase 25 units of X and 50 units of Y, as illustrated by point C. Straight line BL is known as the consumer's *budget line* (or budget constraint).

The budget line has several important properties. For convenience, we summarize these properties as follows:

1. Mathematically, the budget line is the locus of all combinations of X and Y (i.e., commodity bundles) that satisfy the equation

$$I = p_x x + p_y y \tag{4.1}$$

    where I is the money income. Equation (4.1), known as the *budget equation,* reflects the notion that all points on the budget line represent commodity bundles that exhaust the consumer's fixed income.

2. *The budget line divides the entire commodity space (i.e., the universal set) into the attainable set and the unattainable set.* For instance, budget line BL divides the commodity space into triangular area $0BL$ (attainable set) and the rest of the space (unattainable set). Given his limited income and the commodity prices, the consumer can choose only among those bundles that lie in triangular area $0BL$, including its boundaries.

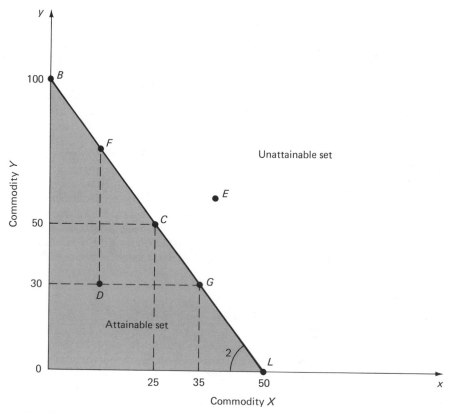

Figure 4.1 The consumer's budget line. The consumer wishes to spend his weekly income of $500 on X and Y whose fixed prices are p_x = $10 and P_y = $5. Budget line BL shows all alternative combinations of X and Y that cost exactly $500; its slope gives the price ratio p_x/p_y. The budget line divides the commodity space into the attainable set and the unattainable set.

_____

We can also express the above idea as follows. Points that lie *outside* the *budget line* (i.e., in the unattainable set), such as point E, cost more than the consumer's limited income; points that lie *inside the budget line,* such as point D, cost *less* than the consumer's income;[1] and points on the budget line cost the entire consumer's income.

The budget line illustrates the fundamental law of scarcity as viewed by the individual consumer. The consumer cannot purchase unlimited quantities of economic goods, because his income is limited. He can choose only among the commodity bundles that belong to the attainable set ($0BL$). The existence of the unattainable set reflects the influence of the law of scarcity.

3. *To determine the budget line graphically, we first find its intercepts with the axes and then join these intercepts by a straight line.* The horizontal and vertical axis intercepts coincide with the maximum number of units of X and Y, respectively, that the consumer can alternatively purchase with his limited income. Thus the horizontal axis intercept is given by the ratio I/p_x, and the

_____

[1]How do we know that bundle D costs less than the consumer's income? Because any bundle along straight-line segment FG, such as C, contains more X and Y than bundle D. Thus D must cost less than C. But the cost of C is just equal to the consumer's income. Accordingly, bundle D must cost less than the consumer's income.

vertical axis intercept by the ratio I/p_y. In Figure 4.1 the intercepts of budget line BL with the horizontal and vertical axes are equal to $I/p_x = \$500/\$10 = 50$ and $I/p_y = \$500/\$5 = 100$, respectively.

The ratios I/p_x and I/p_y express income in terms of X and Y, respectively. At the current prices, the consumer's income can be specified either as I dollars, or I/p_x units of X, or I/p_y units of Y. All three income measures are equivalent.

4. *The absolute slope of the budget line equals the ratio of commodity prices.* Thus

$$\text{absolute slope} = \frac{\text{vertical axis intercept}}{\text{horizontal axis intercept}} = \frac{I/p_y}{I/p_x} = \frac{p_x}{p_y} \qquad (4.2)$$

In Figure 4.1 the absolute slope of budget line BL is equal to $p_x/p_y = \$10/\$5 = 2$.

5. *The absolute slope of the budget line gives the number of units of Y that the consumer must give up in order to purchase an additional unit of X.* In Figure 4.1 the absolute slope of budget line BL is 2, indicating that for each additional unit of X he purchases, the consumer must sacrifice 2 units of Y. This makes sense because at the given prices (i.e., $p_x = \$10$ and $p_y = \$5$), the cost of 2 units of Y equals the cost of 1 unit of X.

The number of units of Y that the consumer must give up for an extra unit of X is known as the *opportunity cost* of X in terms of Y. Accordingly, we may say that the absolute slope of the budget line gives the opportunity cost of X in terms of Y.

6. *The budget line depends only on two elements: the consumer's money income (I) and the commodity prices (p_x, p_y).* When either of these two elements changes, the budget line shifts to a new position, as explained in Sections 4.6 and 4.8.

However, the budget line remains totally unaffected by a particular change: *a proportional increase or decrease in money income and all commodity prices.* Such a change leaves the horizontal and vertical axis intercepts of the budget line the same. For instance, doubling the consumer's income and prices from $I = \$500$, $p_x = \$10$, and $p_y = \$5$ to $I' = \$1000$, $p_x' = \$20$, and $p_y' = \$10$, respectively, does not alter the intercepts: $I/p_x = \$500/\$10 = I'/p_x' = \$1000/\$20 = 50$; and $I/p_y = \$500/\$5 = I'/p_y' = \$1000/\$10 = 100$. When the intercepts remain constant, the entire budget line remains the same.

Maximization of Ordinal Utility

As we noted above, the budget line delineates the attainable set. The consumer must eventually choose a point (or commodity bundle) that belongs to the attainable set. The objective of a rational consumer is to choose the most highly ranked bundle of the attainable set; that is, the consumer must choose that commodity bundle that places him on the highest possible indifference curve. In economic jargon, this is usually expressed by saying that the objective of a rational consumer is to *maximize his ordinal utility*.

Figure 4.2 brings together the consumer's budget line and indifference map. What commodity bundle should the consumer purchase? Apparently, he must purchase bundle $E = (x_e, y_e)$. Among all the points (bundles) that lie in the feasible triangular area $0BL$, only point E enables the consumer to attain indifference curve I_2. This is obviously the best that the consumer can do, because all indifference curves, such as I_3, that are higher than I_2 lie totally in the unattainable set; hence they are out of reach for the consumer. On the other hand, all other feasible bundles, such as F, G, or J (besides E), put the consumer on indifference curves that are inferior to I_2.

The optimum consumption point (E) must necessarily lie *on* the budget line, not

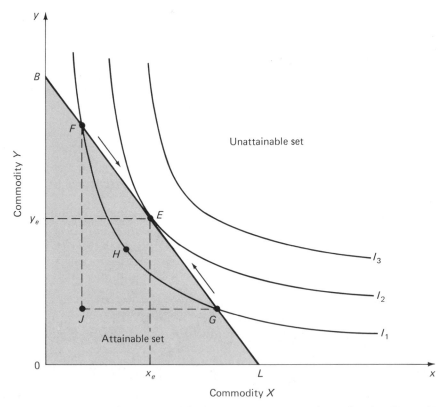

Figure 4.2 Consumer equilibrium. The consumer maximizes his ordinal utility at E, where budget line BL is tangent to indifference curve I_2. From any point along BE, such as point F, the consumer has an incentive to move toward E, as shown by the arrow. Similarly, from any point along EL, such as point G, the consumer also has an incentive to move toward E. Hence equilibrium point E is stable.

---

inside it. This is a consequence of the axiom of nonsatiation, which in effect means that more is preferred to less. For any given bundle inside the budget line, we can identify other bundles on the budget line that are preferred to it. For instance, any bundle along line segment FG is preferred to bundle J. Accordingly, the most preferred bundle in the attainable set must lie on the budget line.

It is evident from Figure 4.2 that at the optimum consumption point (E), *the budget line is tangent to the highest attainable indifference curve* (I_2). Indeed, under our assumptions, this is the fundamental condition for consumer equilibrium (or maximization of ordinal utility).

The tangency at point E implies that the absolute slope of the budget line (i.e., p_x/p_y) is equal to the absolute slope of indifference curve I_2 at E (i.e., the marginal rate of substitution of X for Y at E). Accordingly, the fundamental condition for consumer equilibrium becomes

$$MRS_{xy} = \frac{p_x}{p_y} \tag{4.3}$$

What is the commonsense meaning of the condition for consumer equilibrium? We can discover the significance of equation (4.3) by considering situations in which it is not satisfied. To simplify our discussion, let us assume that the consumer knows that to attain the highest possible indifference curve, he must choose a commodity bundle that lies *on* his budget line (i.e., he must spend his entire income on X and Y). Suppose that he arbitrarily chooses bundle F on indifference curve I_1. Note that at F, indifference curve I_1 is steeper than budget line BL.[2] For concreteness assume that the marginal rate of substitution of X for Y at F (i.e., the absolute slope of I_1 at F) is equal to 3, while the opportunity cost of X in terms of Y (i.e., the absolute slope of budget line BL) is only equal to 2, because, say $p_x = \$10$ and $p_y = \$5$. How does the consumer know that he is *not* maximizing his ordinal utility at F? In what direction should he reallocate his expenditure in order to reach a preferred position?

Starting at F, the consumer can move to a preferred position by transferring dollars from Y to X. The reason is simple. For each extra unit of X he acquires, he *is willing* to give up 3 units of Y without reducing his ordinal utility because the marginal rate of substitution of X for Y is 3. This is the *marginal valuation* that the consumer places on one additional unit of X. What is the cost to the consumer of 1 extra unit of X? It is the opportunity cost of X in terms of Y, indicated by the absolute slope of budget line BL (i.e., 2). Given the prices of X and Y($p_x = \$10$, $p_y = \$5$), the consumer can always acquire 1 extra unit of X by giving up 2 units of Y. Because the marginal valuation of X (3) is larger than its opportunity cost (2), the consumer can increase his ordinal utility be reallocating his expenditure from Y to X.

At every point along line segment BE, the marginal valuation of X exceeds its opportunity cost, and the consumer has a positive inducement to move toward optimum consumption point E, as shown by the arrow. At every point, such as G, along line segment LE, the marginal valuation of X (MRS_{xy}) is lower than the opportunity cost of X (p_x/p_y). The consumer can move to a preferred position by transferring dollars from X to Y, that is, by again moving toward E, as shown by the arrow. We must therefore conclude that only when the marginal rate of substitution of X for Y equals the price ratio p_x/p_y does the consumer have no inducement to reallocate his expenditure between X and Y; that is, only when equation (4.3) is satisfied is he maximizing his ordinal utility.

Proportional Changes in Income and Prices

As we mentioned earlier, proportional increases (or decreases) in money income and all money prices leave the budget line unchanged. An important economic consequence of this observation is that proportional changes in money income and prices have no influence on the equilibrium of the consumer. This means that proportional changes in money income and prices have no effect on the quantities of X and Y demanded by the consumer—a result that is often referred to as the *homogeneity property* of the demand functions.

The homogeneity property rests on the assumption that *the rational consumer can see through the "veil of money."* For him, the significant economic phenomenon is his budget line (or attainable set). Changes in money income and prices can influence the behavior of the rational consumer only through their effect on the budget line. When changes in money income and prices are such that the budget line remains the same, their effect on the consumptive behavior of the rational consumer is nil.

When changes in money income and prices influence the consumptive behavior of the consumer by more than their effect on the budget line warrants, economists say that the consumer suffers from *money illusion*. For instance, if a consumer

---

[2]Along line segment BE all indifference curves are steeper than budget line BL. Similarly, along line segment LE all indifference curves are flatter than budget line BL. If they were not, they would intersect indifference curve I_2.

changes his consumptive behavior following a proportional change in money income and all prices (assuming tastes remain constant), we can rest assured that he is suffering from money illusion. In this book we assume that money illusion is totally absent.

An important consequence of the homogeneity property is that money prices (also referred to as *nominal* or *absolute* prices) are not crucial to our analysis. Indeed, microeconomic theory is not concerned with the determination of absolute money prices and the *price level*. That task is left to macroeconomic theory and monetary theory. In microeconomic theory, only *relative* prices (i.e., price ratios) are important. Thus even though the absolute levels of p_x and p_y are irrelevant to our theory, the price ratio p_x/p_y (i.e., the relative price of X in terms of Y) is very important.

In summary, the significant economic phenomenon is the consumer's budget line, not the absolute money prices and money income. The budget line is perfectly determined when either its intercepts with the axes (i.e., the income measured alternatively in terms of X or Y) are given or one intercept and its slope (i.e., the price ratio p_x/p_y) are known. This is confirmed when we observe that budget equation (4.1) can be written as

$$y = \left(\frac{I}{p_y}\right) - \left(\frac{p_x}{p_y}\right)x \qquad (4.1)'$$

Thus, even though I, p_x, and p_y are sufficient to determine the budget line, they are only incidental phenomena. Of vastly greater economic significance are the ratios I/p_x (income in terms of X), I/p_y *(income in terms Y)*, and p_x/p_y (relative price of X in terms of Y).[3]

4.2 The Equimarginal Principle: Digression

Before proceeding with the development of the modern theory of demand, it is useful to consider the problem of consumer equilibrium within the context of the cardinal utility model. Recall that the objective of a rational consumer is to allocate his expenditure among the various goods in such a way as *to maximize the aggregate amount of psychological utility* that he can obtain from their consumption per week, subject to his fixed income and the prevailing fixed commodity prices.

Utility Maximization

Is there any simple rule that a rational consumer can follow in his search for utility maximization? Most certainly there is: the *equimarginal principle*,[4] which states that the consumer can maximize his utility or satisfaction by allocating his income among the various goods in such a way that *the marginal utility of the last dollar spent on one commodity is exactly equal to the marginal utility of the last dollar spent on any other commodity.*

What is the rationale for the equimarginal principle? A consumer who violates the equimarginal principle is not maximizing his utility because he can always increase total utility by means of an appropriate reallocation of his fixed expenditure among commodities.

Consider a consumer who wishes to allocate his fixed income between two goods, X and Y, whose prices are fixed. Starting from an arbitrary allocation of expenditure

[3]Note also that when we know just two of the three ratios I/p_x, I/p_y, and p_x/p_y, we can easily determine the third from the identity $I/p_y = (I/p_x)(p_x/p_y)$.

[4]The equimarginal principle was first formulated by Gossen in 1854.

between X and Y, calculate the marginal utility of the last dollar spent on each good. Suppose that you find out that the marginal utility of the last dollar spent on X is three utils, while the marginal utility of the last dollar spent on Y is only 1 util. Can the consumer reallocate his expenditure between X and Y in such a way as to increase his aggregate utility? He most certainly can. Let the consumer transfer $1 from Y to X. As he reduces his spending on Y by $1, the consumer *loses* 1 util (i.e., the marginal utility of the last dollar spent on Y). But as he increases his spending on X by $1, he *gains* 3 extra utils (i.e., the marginal utility of the last dollar spent on X). Accordingly, the consumer's aggregate utility increases by 2 utils (i.e., $3 - 1 = 2$).

When the marginal utility of the last dollar spent on X is exactly equal to the marginal utility of the last dollar spent on Y, the consumer can no longer increase his utility by transferring dollars from one good to another, but this is another way of saying that the consumer is maximizing his utility (assuming, of course, that the consumer is spending all his income).

What is the marginal utility of 1 extra dollar spent on X equal to? It is equal to the amount of X bought by $1 times the marginal utility of X (MU_x). For instance, if the price of X is $2 and the marginal utility of an additional unit of X is 6 utils, the marginal utility of an extra dollar spent on X is equal to 3 utils. Thus the extra dollar spent on X buys only one-half of one unit of X; since the marginal utility of a *whole* unit of X is 6 utils, it follows that the additional utility obtained from the consumption of an extra half a unit of X (i.e., the marginal utility of an extra dollar spent on X) must be equal to 3 utils, that is, $\frac{1}{2} \cdot 6 = 3$.

In general, if the price of X is p_x, the marginal utility of an extra dollar spent on X is equal to MU_x/p_x, because one dollar can buy $1/p_x$ units of X. Similarly, the marginal utility of an extra dollar spent on Y is equal to MU_y/p_y, where MU_y is the marginal utility of Y and p_y the price of Y.

Accordingly, we can formulate the equimarginal principle as follows:

$$\frac{MU_x}{p_x} = \frac{MU_y}{p_y} \tag{4.4}$$

When equation (4.4) holds, the consumer is maximizing his utility; that is, equation (4.4) is the condition of consumer equilibrium. Finally, that allocation of expenditure between X and Y that is consistent with equation (4.4) is known as the *consumer equilibrium.*

What is the role of the law of diminishing marginal utility in the attainment of consumer equilibrium? It guarantees that the consumer will indeed be able to arrive at equilibrium condition (4.4) by means of marginal transfers of expenditure from one good to the other, as described above. For instance, suppose that at the initial arbitrary allocation of expenditure between X and Y the consumer finds that $(MU_x/p_x) > (MU_y/p_y)$ and as a result, begins transferring dollars from Y to X. In essence, this means that the consumer increases gradually his consumption of X and decreases gradually his consumption of Y. As this happens, the marginal utility of X (i.e., MU_x) *decreases* gradually, and the marginal utility of Y (i.e., MU_y) *increases* gradually, *because of the law of diminishing marginal utility.* Accordingly, the ratio of MU_x/p_x *falls* gradually, while the ratio of MU_y/p_y *rises* gradually. (Recall that p_x and p_y are fixed.) When the consumer transfers enough dollars from Y to X, the two ratios become equal; that is, equation (4.4) is restored.

We must therefore conclude from the preceding discussion that the equilibrium of the consumer is *stable.* Its *stability is guaranteed by the law of diminishing marginal utility.* Thus if the consumer starts from an arbitrary allocation of expenditure between X and Y, he will soon move to the optimal allocation because of the law of diminishing marginal utility. On the other hand, if the consumer allocates his expenditure between X and Y optimally, he will have no inducement to change his behavior—any transfer of dollars from one good to another will lower his utility.

Graphical Illustration

Figure 4.3 illustrates graphically the preceding analysis. The fixed income of the consumer is given by horizontal distance $00'$. Any point on horizontal line $00'$, such as point A, divides the consumer's expenditures into two parts: $0A$ and $0'A$. Part $0A$ is allocated to good X, and part $0'A$ is allocated to good Y. Along the two vertical axes, we measure the marginal utility per dollar spent on X (left axis) and Y (right axis). Downward-sloping schedule GE gives the marginal utility per dollar spent on X for alternative amounts spent on X. Similarly, "downward-sloping" schedule FE gives the marginal utility per dollar spent on Y. (Keep in mind that the schedule for Y is drawn with 180° rotation and it is read from right to left.)

Suppose now that the consumer allocates arbitrarily the amount $0A$ to X and the amount $0'A$ to Y. What is his aggregate utility equal to? The total utility he obtains from X is given by area $0ADG$. Similarly, the total utility he obtains from Y is given by area $0'ACF$. Thus the consumer's aggregate utility at the initial arbitrary allocation is given by the sum of these two areas; that is, aggregate utility $= 0ADG + 0'ACF$.

Can the consumer increase his utility? He most certainly can. Observe that at the initial arbitrary allocation, the marginal utility per dollar spent on X (i.e., AD)

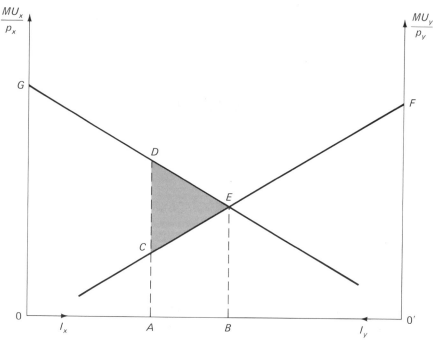

Figure 4.3 Utility maximization. Horizontal distance $00'$ corresponds to the fixed income of the consumer. Point A on line $00'$ divides the consumer's expenditure into two parts: $0A$ allocated to good X, and $0'A$ allocated to good Y. Aggregate utility is, then, equal to $0ADG$ (total utility obtained from X) plus $0'ACF$ (total utility obtained from Y). By transferring AB dollars from Y to X, the consumer can increase his aggregate utility by shaded triangular area CED. The consumers' optimal allocation of expenditure is indicated by intersection E.

is higher than the marginal utility per dollar spent on Y (i.e., AC). Accordingly, the consumer can increase his utility by transferring dollars from Y to X.

Indeed, the consumer can maximize his utility by transferring AB dollars from Y to X. When he does so, his aggregate utility increases by shaded triangular area CED. We can see this as follows. As the consumer reduces his consumption of Y, the total utility he obtains from Y *falls* by area $CABE$. On the other hand, as he increases his consumption of X, the total utility he obtains from X *increases* by area $DABE$. Consequently, the consumer enjoys a net utility gain equal to $DABE - CABE = CED$—that is, the shaded area in the figure.

We therefore conclude that the consumer's optimal allocation of expenditure between X and Y is determined by intersection E, where equilibrium condition (4.4) is satisfied. Further, the total utility obtained from X is given by area $OBEG$, while the total utility obtained from Y is given by area $0'BEF$. Finally, the consumer's maximum aggregate utility is given by the sum $OBEG + 0'BEF$.

Generalization to Many Commodities

The equimarginal principle, that is, the fundamental condition of consumer equilibrium, generalizes easily to many commodities. Suppose that the consumer actually purchases n goods: $X_1, X_2, \ldots, X_n$. The condition of consumer equilibrium now takes the form

$$\frac{MU_1}{p_1} = \frac{MU_2}{p_2} = \cdots = \frac{MU_n}{p_n} \tag{4.5}$$

where MU_i is the marginal utility of good X_i and p_i the price of good X_i, for $i = 1, 2, \ldots, n$.

Indifference Curves Versus Cardinal Utility

Is there any relation between equations (4.3) and (4.4)? Intuitively, it seems clear that when the tastes of a consumer are represented by a utility function, the mathematical condition for utility maximization must be the same whether utility is cardinal or ordinal. Accordingly, we should expect equation (4.3) to be somehow equivalent to (4.4).

This suspicion is actually confirmed when we notice that the marginal rate of substitution is equal to the ratio of marginal utilities. In particular,

$$MRS_{xy} = \frac{MU_x}{MU_y} \tag{4.6}$$

Accepting, for the moment, equation (4.6) as true, we can rewrite equation (4.3) as follows:

$$\frac{MU_x}{MU_y} = \frac{p_x}{p_y} \tag{4.7}$$

As the reader can now demonstrate easily, equations (4.4) and (4.7) are mathematically equivalent.

Nevertheless, the reader should never lose sight of the fact that equation (4.3), or (4.7), was derived with *fewer* assumptions. In particular, we must remember that *we have dropped the heavy burden of cardinal utility and its measurability*.

How can we establish equation (4.6)? A rigorous proof was given in the Appendix to Chapter 3. Here the following heuristic argument is sufficient.

Turn to Figure 4.4 and consider a *small* movement along indifference curve I_0 from, say, A to B.[5] Indeed, it is most helpful to split this movement into two parts: a movement from A to C plus a movement from C to B. As the consumer moves from A to C, his consumption of Y decreases by Δy. As a result, his utility falls. By how much? By $\Delta y \cdot MU_y$. Similarly, as he moves from C to B, his consumption of X increases by Δx. Accordingly his utility increases. By how much? By $\Delta x \cdot MU_x$. In other words, as the consumer moves from A to B, his utility changes twice: It changes first by $\Delta y \cdot MU_y$ and second by $\Delta x \cdot MU_x$. Obviously, the total change in utility is $\Delta y \cdot MU_y + \Delta x \cdot MU_x$. Now recall that points A and B lie on the same indifference curve and therefore the movement from A to B leaves total utility unchanged; that is, the total change in utility is zero. Consequently, we have the equation

$$\Delta y \cdot MU_y + \Delta x \cdot MU_x = 0 \qquad (4.8)$$

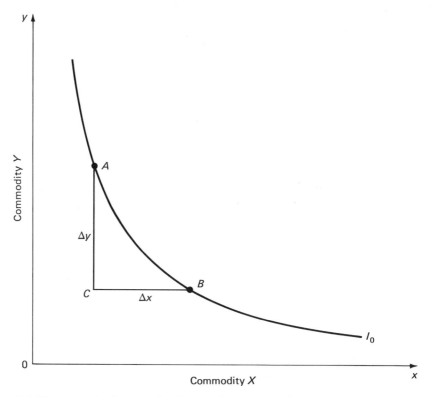

Figure 4.4 The marginal rate of substitution as a ratio of marginal utilities. As the consumer moves from A to C, his utility decreases by $\Delta y \cdot MU_y$; and as he moves from C to B, his utility increases by $\Delta x \cdot MU_x$. Since A and B lie on indifference curve I_0, the total change in utility is zero. That is, $\Delta y \cdot MU_y + \Delta x \cdot MU_x = 0$, or $MRS_{xy} = -\Delta y/\Delta x = MU_x/MU_y$.

---

[5]By necessity, Figure 4.4 illustrates a "large" movement along I_0. The reader should vizualize the "triangle" ABC as corresponding to a very small neighborhood around point A, a neighborhood that is under a powerful magnifying glass.

Finally, equation (4.8) can be rearranged as follows:

$$MRS_{xy} = -\frac{\Delta y}{\Delta x} = \frac{MU_x}{MU_y} \tag{4.9}$$

This proves equation (4.6).

4.3 Corner Equilibrium

The consumer equilibrium illustrated in Figure 4.2 by the *tangency* between budget line *BL* and indifference curve I_2 is often called an *interior solution*. The obvious implication of an interior solution is that the consumer's consumption is *diversified*. At *E*, the consumer purchases something of each of the two commodities. This result, which is often referred to as the *principle of diversification in consumption,* is borne out by everyday experience. Typically, people purchase a basket (bundle) of many different commodities instead of spending their entire income on just one commodity.

In the context of a two-commodity model, an interior solution is satisfactory. Yet in the real world of many commodities, we must recognize the fact that the typical consumer does *not* purchase positive quantities of all the available goods and services. Rather, the typical consumer spends her income on only a *small* number of the available commodities. The reason is that the relative prices (or opportunity costs) of those commodities not purchased by the consumer are very high.[6] Even though you may wish to have a Rolls-Royce, a private airplane, a yacht, or a 10-karat diamond, chances are that your consumption of these, and many more, commodities is zero. Our theory must explain this phenomenon also.

Figure 4.5 illustrates a *corner solution* (as opposed to an interior solution). Convex indifference curve I_1 meets the vertical axis at point *B*. Line BL_1 is *tangent* to indifference curve I_1 at *B*. When the budget line passes through point *B* and is as steep as, or steeper than, line BL_1, equilibrium occurs at "corner" *B*, where the consumer purchases only commodity *Y*. Budget line BL_1 represents the limiting case of a corner solution that satisfies equilibrium condition (4.3). A budget line, such as BL_0, that passes through *B* but is steeper than BL_1 implies that $MRS_{xy} < p_x/p_y$. The last inequality means that the marginal valuation of the first unit of commodity *X* (MRS_{xy}) is lower than its opportunity cost (p_x/p_y); that is, the first unit of *X* is not worth its cost to the consumer.

Alternatively, the consumer would purchase a positive amount of *X* if, and only if, the relative price of *X* were lower than p_1 (absolute slope of BL_1, or MRS_{xy} at *B*). This is illustrated by budget line BL_2, which gives rise to equilibrium at *E* (interior solution). Note that, in general, p_1 depends on income, or the precise location of point *B* along the vertical axis.

4.4 The Economic Rationale for Convexity

In Section 3.6 we gave an intuitive explanation of why indifference curves should be convex to the origin. We now wish to strengthen that argument by providing an economic rationale for convexity. The new exegesis rests on the thesis that *unlike*

---

[6]In some cases, a commodity that is not consumed by a consumer may be a *bad* for him, even though it is a "good" for others. (A commodity is a "bad" when less of it is preferred to more.) Chemotherapy may be a "good" for a cancer patient, but it is certainly a "bad" for a healthy person. The same is true of many other commodities, such as appendectomies and eyeglasses.

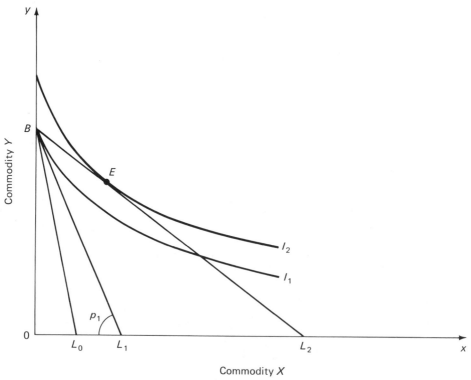

Figure 4.5 Corner solutions. Convex indifference curve I_1 meets the vertical axis at point B. Line BL_1 is tangent to I_1 at B. When the budget line passes through B and is as steep as, or steeper than, tangent BL_1, equilibrium occurs at "corner" B. Budget line BL_1 represents the limiting case of a corner solution that satisfies the equation $MRS_{xy} = p_x/p_y$. Budget line BL_0 (which is steeper than BL_1) gives rise to equilibrium at corner B but implies that $MRS_{xy} < p_x/p_y$. If the budget line were flatter than BL_1, as shown by BL_2, the consumer would consume both commodities (interior solution), as illustrated by point E.

convex indifference curves, nonconvexity gives rise to results that are inconsistent with observed behavior, and because nonconvexity is unacceptable, convexity must be the rule.

When the indifference curves are (strictly) concave, the consumer equilibrium is necessarily a corner solution. This is illustrated in Figure 4.6. Budget line BL is tangent to indifference curve I_2 at point E. Because of the assumed concavity of indifference curves, point E does *not* imply utility maximization. On the contrary, point E represents utility *minimization*. Actually, utility is maximized at point B, a "corner solution." Readers should experiment with different budget lines and convince themselves that all consumer equilibria in Figure 4.6 are corner solutions.[7]

The implication of the corner solution illustrated in Figure 4.6 is that the consumer spends her entire income on commodity Y only. We express this by saying that the consumer *specializes completely* in the consumption of commodity Y. Casual observation reveals that consumers purchase a multitude of different goods and

[7]The argument in the text assumes that the commodity prices are constant, giving rise to a linear budget line. With a budget line that is "more concave" than the indifference curve to which it is tangent, equilibrium will occur at the tangency. A concave budget line arises when the price of each commodity rises with the volume purchased by the consumer.

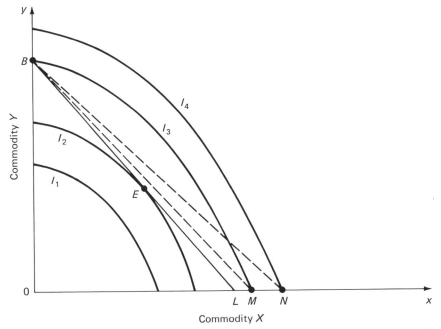

Figure 4.6 Concave indifference curves. The tangency at E coincides with utility *minimization* (*not* maximization). Equilibrium occurs at "corner" B, where budget line BL meets indifference curve I_3. A small reduction in the price of X causes budget line BL to rotate to BN with the result that the consumer shifts from B (where she buys only Y) to N (where she buys only X). Dashed budget line BM gives rise on two equilibria: one at B and another at M.

---

services, a phenomenon that is ruled out by concavity. For this reason, we must reject concave indifference curves.

Note that convex indifference curves can explain both the fact that consumers diversify their consumption (as in Figure 4.2) and also why consumers do *not* purchase positive amounts of *all* goods and services (as in Figure 4.5). Thus convexity is consistent with observed behavior, whereas concavity is not. With convex indifference curves, corner solutions are possible but not inevitable.

Figure 4.6 teaches us two other things. First, concavity may lead to *multiple equilibria*. For instance, budget line BM gives rise to two equilibria: one at B and another at M. Second, a slight change in the market price ratio may lead to a complete metamorphosis of the composition of the commodity basket bought by the consumer. For instance, return to the initial equilibrium at B and consider a reduction in the price of commodity X, which raises the maximum number of units of X that the consumer can purchase with her fixed income from $0L$ to $0N$. The budget line rotates from BL to dashed line BN. Consumer equilibrium shifts to N. This means that with a slight reduction in the price of X, the consumer completely changes her consumption pattern: She switches totally from commodity Y to commodity X. This violates another important empirical result, namely, that consumption patterns are rather stable. These are additional reasons for rejecting concavity.

Figure 4.7 illustrates a more complex case of nonconvex indifference curves. Indifference curve I_1 is not convex; it has a concave region in the middle. Because of this, budget line BL is now tangent to indifference curve I_1 at two points: E and F. The consumer could consume either at tangency E or tangency F. In this case,

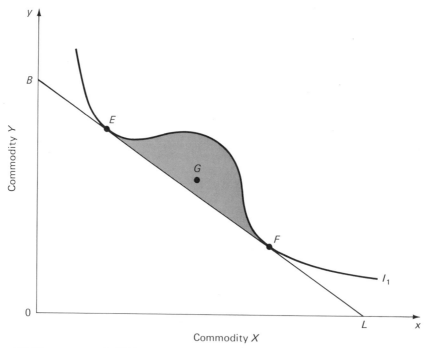

Figure 4.7 Nonconvex indifference curves. Budget line BL is tangent to nonconvex indifference curve I_1 at points E and F (multiple equilibria). Also, the consumer can never be induced to purchase a commodity bundle that lies in the shaded area bounded by indifference curve I_1 and budget line BL.

economic theory alone cannot determine the final equilibrium of the consumer, who may have to flip a coin before she chooses between bundles E and F.

There is another objection to Figure 4.7. The consumer can never choose a commodity bundle that lies in the shaded area bounded by indifference curve I_1 and budget line BL. In other words, there are no combinations of money income and commodity prices that will induce the consumer to purchase some bundle in the shaded area. (As an exercise, the reader should rotate a budget line through point G and show that the consumer can always reach bundles that are preferred to G.) This odd behavior is again due to the nonconvexity of the indifference curve.

We therefore conclude that nonconvexity of indifference curves gives rise to strange consumption behavior patterns that contradict observed behavior. Only convex indifference curves can generate consumption patterns that are consistent with observed behavior. Here, then, is a strong economic reason for assuming convexity.

4.5 Generalization to Many Commodities

Our discussion so far has been restricted to the case of two commodities only. Yet there is a simple and straightforward method of extending our analysis to the general case of many commodities. Instead of regarding X and Y as two physical commodities (or services), such as food and clothing, think of them as food (some physical commodity or service) and money (general purchasing power). Visualize the consumer as choosing between spending her income on food (X) or keeping it available for expenditure on other goods and services. As long as the prices of all goods and services besides X remain constant, we can draw up an indifference map summarizing the tastes of the consumer between X and money.

In the above formulation, "money" (or "commodity Y") represents "all other goods" and is referred to as a *composite good*. Further, the proposition that analytically we can treat the composite good as a single physical commodity is known as the *composite good theorem*.[8]

4.6 The Effects of Income Changes

The equilibrium of the consumer depends on two data: the indifference map (or tastes) and the budget line (or attainable set). When these two data change, the equilibrium of the consumer changes also.

Economists do not know exactly how tastes are formed and how they change. It is not possible to formulate empirically testable hypotheses with respect to tastes. For this reason, economists assume that tastes remain constant. This assumption, which reflects a fundamental aspect of economic methodology, is justified by the fact that tastes do not change continuously or erratically. Tastes tend to remain stable. The "stability" of tastes is inferred from the empirical observation that consumer behavior is "stable." Many empirical studies support this hypothesis.

Assuming that tastes remain constant, it is apparent that the equilibrium of the consumer can change only in response to changes in the budget line (or attainable set). Since the budget line depends on the consumer's income and the commodity prices, the consumer must be expected to adjust her equilibrium consumption basket in response to changes in her money income and the commodity prices. In this section we study the effects of income changes on the equilibrium consumption basket. As it turns out, familiarity with the effects of income changes facilitates the discussion of the effects of price changes. The latter are taken up in Sections 4.8 and 4.9.

Income Changes and Consumer Equilibrium

Consider a consumer who experiences a permanent increase in his money income per month, while the commodity prices remain unchanged. The lucky consumer could be a student whose thoughtful father pleasantly surprises him with an increase in his monthly allowance, or a worker whose employer has just granted him a raise, or an engineer who has just sold his latest invention to a big corporation. How will this income change affect the consumer's purchases of commodities, such as food, clothing, and entertainment?

Figure 4.8 illustrates the effects of income changes. Suppose that the consumer starts with an income of $0L_0$ in terms of commodity X, or $0B_0$ in terms of commodity Y. Initially, he is in equilibrium at point E_0, where his budget line B_0L_0 is tangent to indifference curve I_0. In this position, he purchases x_0 units of X and y_0 units of Y. As his income increases to $0L_1$ in terms of X, or $0B_1$ in terms of Y, the budget line shifts outward (the attainable set expands), as shown by line B_1L_1. The consumer moves to a new equilibrium point (E_1), where his new budget line B_1L_1 is tangent to indifference curve I_1. In this case, his purchases of X and Y *increase* to x_1 and y_1, respectively. Note that the consumer is better off at E_1 relative to E_0, because indifference curve I_1 is higher than I_0.

When the consumer's income increases further to $0L_2$ in terms of X, or $0B_2$ in terms of Y, he moves to equilibrium point E_2 on indifference curve I_2. At E_2, he is

[8]The composite good theorem is due to J. R. Hicks (1946, pp. 33–34, 312–313).

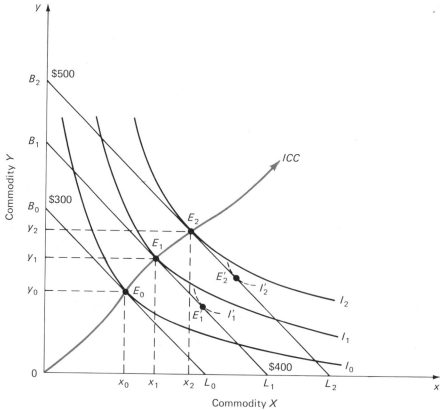

Figure 4.8 The income consumption curve. As the consumer's income increases from OB_0 to OB_1, and then to OB_2, while the commodity prices remain constant, the budget line shifts outward in a parallel fashion, from B_0L_0 to B_1L_1, and then to B_2L_2, respectively. The consumer equilibrium shifts from E_0 to E_1, and then to E_2. The locus of all equilibrium points is the income consumption curve, as shown by the curve labeled *ICC*.

better off (because indifference curve I_2 is higher than indifference curve I_1), and he purchases larger amounts of both X and Y.

When income increases but prices are held constant, the budget line shifts outward in a *parallel* fashion. (Recall that the absolute slope of the budget line is equal to the price ratio p_x/p_y, known as the relative price of X in terms of Y.) For instance, budget lines B_1L_1 and B_2L_2 are parallel to original budget line B_0L_0 and to each other.

The precise effect of an increase in income on the purchases of the consumer depends fundamentally on his tastes, that is, the nature of his indifference map. Had indifference curves I_1 and I_2 been drawn differently in Figure 4.8 (but without violating any of the general properties of indifference curves), as illustrated by dashed indifference curves I_1' and I_2', equilibrium would have occurred elsewhere on budget lines B_1L_1 and B_2L_2, as shown by points E_1' and E_2', respectively.

The Income Consumption Curve

By holding tastes and commodity prices constant, each level of income generates a distinct consumer equilibrium (equilibrium commodity basket). Points E_0, E_1, and E_2 in Figure 4.8 illustrate three such equilibria.

Now keep prices (and tastes) constant and allow income to vary from zero to any reasonable amount. At each level of income, draw the budget line and determine the corresponding equilibrium point. Finally, trace out a continuous line through all such equilibria, as shown in Figure 4.8 by the curve labeled *ICC*. The resultant curve is known as the *income consumption curve (ICC)*. It shows how the rational consumer's purchases respond to changes in income.

The precise shape and location of the income consumption curve depend on two elements: (1) the indifference map and (2) the level of the constant price ratio. For any given indifference map *and* constant price ratio, the income consumption curve is *uniquely* determined, as illustrated in Figure 4.8. But for any given indifference map, there is a whole *family* of income consumption curves, each corresponding to a different price ratio. In general, the family of income consumption curves differs from one indifference map, or consumer, to another.

The existence of a whole family of income consumption curves implies that the effect of an increase in income on the consumer's purchases depends crucially on the constant value of the price ratio p_x/p_y, because the price ratio restricts the consumer to a specific income consumption curve. With a different price ratio, the consumer shifts to a different income consumption curve, and there is no requirement that the consumer's behavior (or response to income changes) be the same along all income consumption curves.

Note also the following important characteristics of income consumption curves:

1. All income consumption curves start at the origin, because with zero income the consumer cannot purchase any positive amount of either X or Y.
2. An income consumption curve intersects each indifference curve only once.
3. Income consumption curves derived from the same indifference map (and thus corresponding to different price ratios) can never intersect one another.
4. An income consumption curve that corresponds to a lower relative price of X (i.e., p_x/p_y) lies closer to the x-axis than another income consumption curve that corresponds to a higher p_x/p_y.

Possible Shapes of the Income Consumption Curve

What shapes are possible for the income consumption curve? What is the economic significance of each particular shape? Some interesting shapes are illustrated in Figure 4.9. In interpreting this diagram, keep in mind that each income consumption curve is derived from a *different* indifference map; these five curves are brought together into a single diagram for comparison purposes only. Also note that each income consumption curve is drawn with an arrowhead pointing in the direction of rising income and ordinal utility. As shown below, the arrow is convenient in the interpretation of the diagram.

The most common income consumption curve slopes upward, as illustrated by ICC_1. In this case, as income increases, the consumer increases his consumption of both commodities. As we pointed out in Chapter 2, commodities that display this characteristic are known as *normal goods* (or *superior goods*).[9]

Curves ICC_2 and ICC_3 illustrate the case of *inferior goods*, that is, goods whose rate of consumption decreases as income increases. ICC_2 shows that beyond point A the consumer's purchases of Y fall as his income increases; thus beyond point A, commodity Y is inferior. Similarly, ICC_3 shows that commodity X is inferior beyond point B; that is, beyond B, the consumer's purchases of X fall as his income increases.

[9]Some authors draw a distinction between normal goods and superior goods according to whether the positive income elasticity of demand is less than unity or greater than unity, respectively. We do not follow this practice in this book.

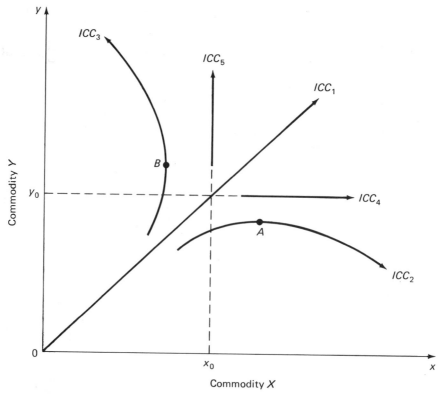

Figure 4.9 Shapes of the income consumption curve. ICC_1 illustrates the typical case in which both commodities are normal and the income consumption curve slopes upward (has a positive slope). ICC_2 shows that Y is inferior beyond A, while ICC_3 shows that X is inferior beyond B. ICC_4 and ICC_5 illustrate the limiting cases in which Y and X, respectively, are neutral.

Margarine is usually offered as an example of an inferior good. However, most of the poorer qualities of commodities (such as poor cuts of meat, poorly made clothes and shoes, low-grade gasoline, used cars, and bias-belted tires) tend to be inferior, as the consumer may be purchasing them only because he cannot afford better qualities.

Is it possible for all commodities purchased by the consumer to be inferior? No, this is not possible. The consumer's total expenditure on an inferior commodity (i.e., price times quantity) falls as income increases. If all commodities were inferior, the consumer's total expenditure on all commodities would fall as his income increased. This result contradicts the premise that the consumer's total expenditure remains constant and equal to his fixed income at all times. We, therefore, conclude that at least one commodity must be normal or superior. Accordingly, no income consumption curve will ever turn back toward the origin.

Note that neither inferiority nor superiority is an intrinsic property of any commodity. A commodity may be inferior (or superior) for some consumers but not for others. Similarly, a commodity may be inferior (or superior) over some income range only, or at some price ratio(s).

Curve ICC_4 illustrates the limiting case in which commodity Y is *neutral*. In this case, Y is neither superior nor inferior; rather, its rate of consumption (y_0) is independent of the income level. Similarly, ICC_5 illustrates the limiting case in which commodity X is neutral. The consumer purchases x_0 units of X at every income level.

The Engel Curve

We now turn briefly to the *Engel curve,* named after the nineteenth-century German statistician Ernst Engel (1821–1896), not to be confused with Karl Marx's friend and collaborator Friedrich Engels. Engel pioneered the study of family income and expenditure relationships. In particular, he asserted that if demographic factors are held constant, an increase in income will lower the proportion of income spent on food. This proposition, known as *Engel's law,* has been tested empirically and found valid throughout the world.

The Engel curve is a relationship between the quantity of a commodity purchased by the consumer and her money income. It is derived from the income consumption curve, as illustrated in Figure 4.10. Panel (a) reproduces the income consumption curve *(ICC)* of Figure 4.8; panel (b) shows the corresponding Engel curve for commodity X. At each point on the income consumption curve, we identify two numbers: (1) the level of income and (2) the amount of X purchased by the consumer. Given these two numbers, we plot the corresponding point on the Engel curve. For instance, at E_0 on *ICC,* the consumer's income is \$300 (or $0B_0$ in terms of Y) and she purchases x_0 units of X. This information is now sufficient to determine the corresponding point on the Engel curve, as shown by E_0' in panel (b). Points E_0', E_1', and E_2' in panel (b) correspond to points E_0, E_1, and E_2, respectively, in panel (a). For a normal (or superior) commodity, the Engel curve is upward sloping (as in Figure 4.10); for an inferior commodity, it is downward sloping; and for a neutral commodity, it is horizontal.

When the income consumption curve shifts (either because of a change in the price ratio or a shift of the indifference map resulting from a change in consumer preferences), the corresponding Engel curve shifts also. This should be obvious because the Engel curve is derived from the income consumption curve. But the Engel curve may shift even when the income consumption curve does not. To understand why, consider again point E_1 (on the *ICC*) and point E_1' (on the Engel curve). Suppose that money income and money prices increase by 25 percent. This change leaves both the budget line and the equilibrium at E_1 unchanged. Yet point E_1' on the Engel curve must shift to the right, as shown by E_1'', because now the consumer purchases x_0 units of X but her income is \$500 (i.e., 25 percent higher than \$400). As long as the Engel curve relates *money* income to quantity consumed, general inflation causes it to shift to the right (even though the income consumption curve remains the same).

There is also the *Engel expenditure curve* that relates expenditure (i.e., price times quantity) to income. For instance, while the Engel curve of Figure 4.10(b) relates x to I, the corresponding Engel expenditure curve relates $p_x \cdot x$ to I. Since p_x is constant by assumption, however, the expenditure on X is proportional to the units of X purchased. As a result, the Engel expenditure curve is very similar to the Engel curve, and further discussion of it appears unnecessary.

4.7 Cash Versus In-Kind Subsidy

In this section we show how the theory we have developed so far can be used to examine the effects of various types of subsidies provided by the government. Such subsidies can be made in cash or in kind. A *cash subsidy* involves the transfer of a certain amount of money which the recipient is free to use as he pleases. A *subsidy in kind* involves the transfer of a certain amount of a specific commodity, such as food, housing, and education.

In general, *a cash subsidy is more valuable to the consumer than an equivalent in-kind subsidy.* Yet the proponents of in-kind subsidies ignore this important principle. They argue that the purpose of an in-kind subsidy is to increase the con-

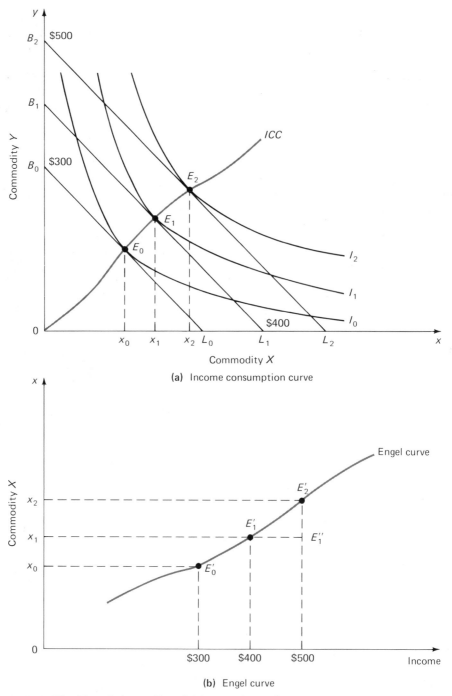

(a) Income consumption curve

(b) Engel curve

Figure 4.10 The Engel curve. Panel (a) reproduces the income consumption curve (*ICC*) of Figure 4.8. Panel (b) gives the coresponding Engel curve for commodity *X*. Each point on the Engel curve corresponds to a point on the income consumption curve. For example, points E_0', E_1', and E_2' in panel (b) correspond to points E_0, E_1, and E_2, respectively, in panel (a).

sumption of the subsidized commodity only, not to finance the consumption of other unnecessary commodities. Below we discuss these issues within the context of two examples of in-kind subsidies: the food stamp program and public education.

The Food Stamp Program of the United States

The food stamp program of the United States is designed to provide all poor American households with a nutritionally adequate diet. Until 1979 and under the provisions of the Food Stamp Act of 1964, as amended, eligible households could use a portion of their low income to purchase food stamps. In turn, they could use these food stamps as "money" to purchase food, and only food. The market value of the food so purchased was, of course, higher than the initial outlay for the purchase of the necessary food stamps, with the difference between market value and initial outlay being an income subsidy. As of January 1979, eligible low-income recipients are not required to pay for the food stamps they receive.

To ensure the success of the program, its originators saw fit to impose an important restriction: The recipients of the food stamps cannot legally trade food stamps, or food purchased with food stamps, on the market. Some of them do, of course, but it is illegal.

Figure 4.11 illustrates the effect of the food stamp program on a typical low-income consumer. Along the horizontal axis we measure food, and along the vertical

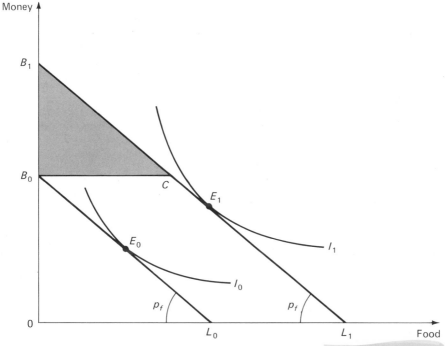

Figure 4.11 Effects of the food stamp program. Before the subsidy, the consumer purchases bundle E_0. A cash subsidy of B_0B_1 would shift the budget line from B_0L_0 to B_1L_1. With an equivalent food stamp subsidy, however, points in shaded triangular area B_0CB_1 are not attainable, because the consumer cannot spend on other commodities (composite good) more than her initial income of OB_0 dollars. In the present case, the cash subsidy and the food stamp subsidy have the same effect on the consumer: They both cause equilibrium to shift from E_0 to E_1. Note that at E_1 the consumer consumes more of all commodities, which means that the food stamp subsidy indirectly finances increased consumption of nonfood items.

axis "money" (i.e., a composite good representing "all other goods"). Initially, the consumer is at E_0, where her budget line B_0L_0 is tangent to indifference curve I_0. Since the price of the composite good, or money, is \$1, the slope of B_0L_0 gives the fixed price of food (p_f). The consumer's money income is shown by vertical distance $0B_0$.

Suppose now that this consumer receives food stamps worth B_0B_1 dollars. Had the consumer received a cash subsidy of B_0B_1 dollars instead, her budget line would shift to B_1L_1, which is parallel to B_0L_0. However, under the provisions of the food stamp program, the consumer must use the food stamps to buy food, and only food. Furthermore, she cannot legally sell the food stamps on the market. What do these restrictions mean for the consumer? What is the consumer's attainable set?

Since the consumer cannot use food stamps to purchase nonfood items, it follows that she cannot spend on other commodities (composite good) more than her initial income of $0B_0$ dollars. Thus points above horizontal line B_0C, indicated by shaded triangular area B_0CB_1, are not attainable. Area B_0CB_1 represents lost opportunities and constitutes the main difference between the food stamp subsidy and an equivalent cash subsidy. The attainable set (under the food stamp subsidy) coincides with area $0B_0CL_1$.

There is an alternative way of looking at the new budget line. Since the consumer cannot spend on nonfood items more than her initial income of $0B_0$ dollars, her budget line must start at point B_0. From B_0, the consumer can use her food stamp subsidy of B_0B_1 dollars to purchase up to B_0C units of food while continuing to spend her initial income ($0B_0$) on nonfood items, as illustrated by horizontal line segment B_0C. (Over the B_0C range, the opportunity cost of food is zero and the budget line is necessarily horizontal.) At point C, the consumer is completely out of food stamps. To purchase additional units of food, the consumer must pay the full market price of food (p_f), indicated by the absolute slope of straight-line segment CL_1. We therefore conclude that the consumer's budget line is given by kinked line B_0CL_1.

The food stamp subsidy can affect the recipient in one of two ways. One possibility is illustrated in Figure 4.11, where the food stamp subsidy causes equilibrium to shift from E_0 to E_1. In this case, the effect of the food stamp subsidy is exactly the same as the effect of an equivalent cash subsidy. Had the consumer received a cash subsidy of B_0B_1 dollars instead, she would still purchase commodity bundle E_1. The reason for this outcome is that with a cash subsidy, the consumer chooses to purchase more than B_0C units of food (i.e., the quantity of food provided by the food stamp subsidy).

The second possibility is illustrated in Figure 4.12. Budget lines B_0L_0 and B_1L_1 are the same as those of Figure 4.11. Before the subsidy, the consumer maximizes her utility at E_0 (as in Figure 4.11), where budget line B_0L_0 is tangent to indifference curve I_0. With a cash subsidy of B_0B_1 dollars, the consumer would purchase bundle G, indicated by the tangency between budget line B_1L_1 and indifference curve I_2. Because at G the consumer spends on nonfood items more than her initial money income of $0B_0$, point G is not attainable under the food stamp program. The consumer must now choose a point (commodity bundle) along kinked line B_0CL_1. The best option open to the consumer is bundle C, which lies on the highest attainable indifference curve (I_1).

In both cases (illustrated by Figures 4.11 and 4.12), the consumer increases her purchases of food. This result is necessary, because food is a normal commodity. But the consumer increases her purchases of all other goods (composite good) as well. This means that *the food stamp subsidy is indirectly used to finance increased consumption of nonfood items*. This conclusion should serve as a warning to those legislators who feel that they can pass a law restricting an in-kind subsidy to the consumption of the subsidized commodity only.

In Figure 4.12 the food stamp subsidy is clearly inferior to an equivalent cash

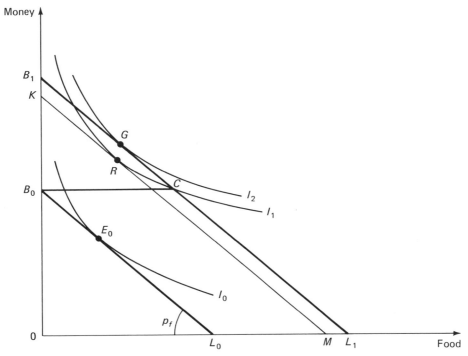

Figure 4.12 The deadweight loss of the food stamp subsidy. Budget lines B_0L_0 and B_1L_1 are the same as those of Figure 4.11. Before the subsidy, the consumer is at E_0. With a cash subsidy of B_0B_1 dollars, equilibrium shifts to G where new budget line B_1L_1 is tangent to indifference curve I_2. Under the food stamp program, point G is not available to the consumer because now her attainable set coincides with OB_0CL_1. With the food stamp subsidy, the consumer moves to C, which lies on I_1. The food stamp subsidy is now inferior to the equivalent cash subsidy because I_1 is lower than I_2. Actually, the food stamp subsidy of B_0B_1 is as valuable as a cash subsidy of only B_0K dollars (budget line KM is tangent to I_1 at R); that is, the food subsidy of B_0B_1 has a deadweight loss of KB_1 dollars.

subsidy: Indifference curve I_1 attained at C (food stamp subsidy) is lower than indifference curve I_2 attained at G (cash subsidy). Actually, the food stamp subsidy of B_0B_1 is just as valuable to the consumer as a cash subsidy of only B_0K dollars. Thus, with a cash subsidy of B_0K, the consumer's budget line shifts to thin line KM, which is tangent to indifference curve I_1 at point R. This means that the food stamp subsidy of B_0B_1 has a deadweight loss of KB_1 dollars. Clarkson (1976) estimated that in 1973 the deadweight loss of food stamp subsidies amounted to approximately 17 percent, a rather large amount.

We therefore conclude that, in general, in-kind subsidies are not as valuable to the recipient as equivalent cash subsidies. In some cases in-kind subsidies and cash subsidies give rise to identical results. However, a cash subsidy can never be inferior to an equivalent in-kind subsidy. Finally, an in-kind subsidy typically increases not only the consumption of the subsidized commodity, but also the consumption of other goods.

Public Education

It is not true that an in-kind subsidy always increases the consumption of the subsidized commodity. In some cases it may actually reduce it, despite the fact that the subsidized commodity is a normal good. This paradox can occur when the nature

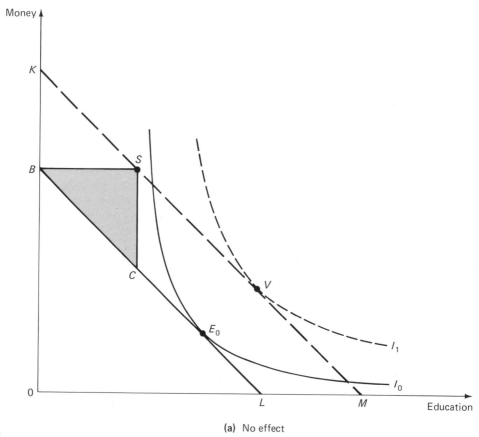

(a) No effect

Figure 4.13 The possible outcomes of the education subsidy. In all three panels, the presubsidy budget line is BL. With an education subsidy of BS units of free public education, the attainable set is enlarged by triangular area BSC, which is shaded in panel (a) only. In panel (a), the education subsidy has no effect: The person consumes at E_0 both before and after the subsidy. An equivalent cash subsidy, as indicated by dashed line KM, would have enabled the consumer to move to V. In panel (b), the education subsidy causes equilibrium to shift from E_1 to S. An equivalent cash subsidy would have enabled this person to move to T. Finally, panel (c) illustrates an important paradox: *The education subsidy reduces the consumption of education.* Before the subsidy, the consumer is at E_2; with the education subsidy, he moves to S. Had the education subsidy been given in the form of an equivalent cash subsidy, the consumer would have chosen point F, which implies more education relative to E_2.

of the subsidized commodity is such that the consumer cannot supplement the susidized quantity with additional purchases. Education is an important example of such a commodity. A person cannot be a full-time student both at a free public school (or college) and a private school (or college) at the same time. He can choose only one of the two. Moreover, if he chooses the private school, he must forgo the subsidy altogether and pay the entire cost of private education.

Figure 4.13 illustrates all possible outcomes of the education subsidy. In all three panels, the presubsidy budget line is BL. In the presence of the education subsidy (BS units of free public education), the budget line coincides with kinked line $BSCL$. The interpretation of this peculiar budget line is simple. The consumer can consume BS units of public education while spending his entire income ($0B$) on noneducation

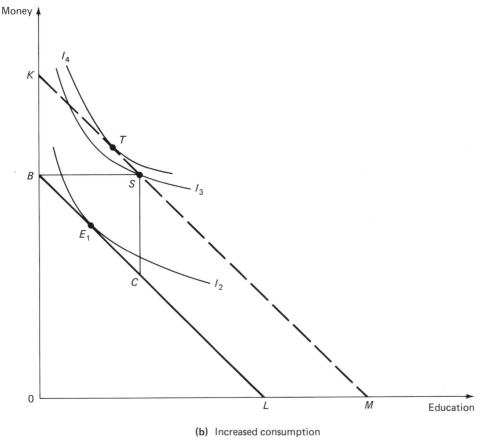

(b) Increased consumption

Figure 4.13 (Continued)

commodities, as indicated by point S. To consume more education than the subsidized quantity BS, the consumer must give up the education subsidy and bear the full cost of education, as shown by CL along presubsidy budget line BL. The effect of the education subsidy is to enlarge the attainable set by triangular area BSC, which is shaded in panel (a). Dashed line KM represents the budget line with an equivalent cash subsidy.

Panel (a) illustrates the case of a person who truly loves education. The availability of free public education has no effect on this person, who maximizes his utility at E_0. Note that with an equivalent cash subsidy (i.e., a subsidy of equal cost to the government as the education subsidy), this education-lover would consume at V, where he would purchase more education and more of all other goods (relative to E_0).

Panel (b) illustrates the case of someone who does not care much about education. Without the subsidy, this person would consume at E_1, where the quantity of education consumed is less than the quantity of free public education (BS). With the availability of free public education, this consumer moves to point S, where he increases his consumption of education as well as his consumption of all other goods (relative to E_1). With an equivalent cash subsidy, this consumer would maximize his utility at T.

Panel (c) illustrates the paradoxical outcome referred to above. In the absence of the education subsidy, the consumer maximizes his utility at E_2, where he purchases

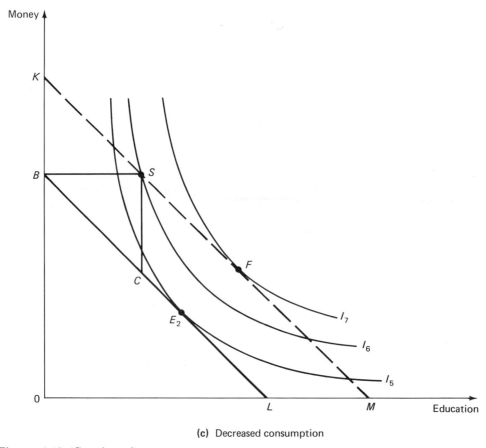

(c) Decreased consumption

Figure 4.13 (Continued)

a larger quantity of private education than the subsidized quantity *BS*. With the subsidy, he moves to point *S*, where he actually consumes *less* education relative to the presubsidy equilibrium at E_2. Note that this consumer prefers the private school and is willing to pay the difference in cost between public and private education in order to consume more education. (With an equivalent cash subsidy, this consumer would reach equilibrium at *F*.) But this option is not available to him. He can either go to the free public school or forgo the subsidy altogether and pay the entire cost of private education. Given his tastes, this consumer chooses the public school, even though this choice means less education consumed.

4.8 The Effects of Price Changes[10]

We now proceed to discuss the effects of price changes on the equilibrium consumption basket. This analysis is important because it lies at the very foundation of the theory of consumer demand. Indeed, our present analysis leads directly to the derivation of the consumer's demand curve. The following section probes even deeper into the underpinnings of the law of demand.

---

[10]This section can be read together with Sections A4.2 and A4.9 of the Appendix to Chapter 4.

Price Changes and Consumer Equilibrium

Throughout the following discussion we assume that the consumer's money income (I) and the price of Y (p_y) remain constant. Our objective is to investigate the effects of changes in the price of X (p_x) on the consumer's purchases of X and Y.

Consider Figure 4.14. The original equilibrium position is at E_0, where budget line BL_0 is tangent to indifference curve I_0. Starting with an income of $0B$ in terms of Y, the consumer purchases x_0 units of X and y_0 units of Y. How would the consumer react to a reduction in the price of X?

At the initial price of X, the consumer's fixed income would buy a maximum of $0L_0$ of X. When the price of X falls, the same money income will buy a larger amount of X, say, $0L_1$. However, because the price of Y remains constant, the consumer's income in terms of Y will remain fixed at $0B$. Accordingly, the reduction in the price of X will cause the consumer's budget line to swing outward (or counterclock-

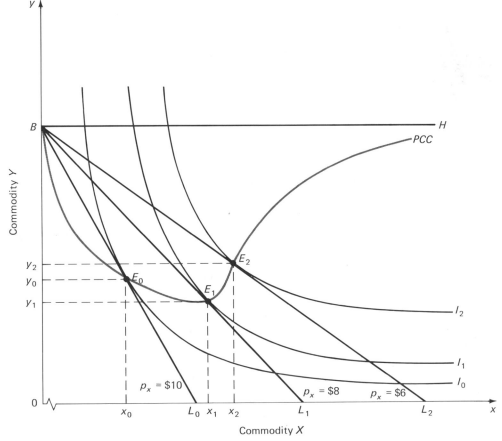

Figure 4.14 The price consumption curve. Equilibrium occurs initially at E_0, where budget line BL_0 is tangent to indifference curve I_0. As the price of X falls, the budget line rotates to BL_1 and equilibrium shifts to E_1. A further reduction in the price of X causes the budget line to rotate to BL_2, with equilibrium moving to E_2. The locus of all these successive equilibria, as shown by the curve labeled PCC, is the price consumption curve. In region BE_1, where the price consumption curve is downward sloping, the elasticity of demand for X is higher than unity; at E_1, where the tangent to PCC is horizontal, the elasticity of demand is unity; and beyond E_1 (in the direction of the arrow), the elasticity of demand for X is less than unity.

wise) from pivot point B, as illustrated by line BL_1. The new equilibrium position will be at E_1, where the consumer purchases x_1 units of X and y_1 units of Y. Note that the consumer is better off at E_1 relative to E_0, because indifference curve I_1 is higher than I_0.

When the price of X falls further, the budget line will swing further outward through pivot point B to, say, BL_2. Equilibrium will shift to E_2, where the consumer is better off relative to E_1. At E_2 she purchases x_2 units of X and y_2 units of Y.

The Price Consumption Curve

Holding money income and the price of Y constant, we find that each level of price of X results in a distinct consumer equilibrium point, as illustrated by points E_0, E_1, and E_2 in Figure 4.14. The locus of all these successive equilibrium points is known as the *price consumption curve (PCC)*. This is illustrated by the gray curve labeled *PCC*. In general, a price consumption curve shows how the rational consumer's purchases respond to changes in the price ratio, with money income remaining constant.

Figure 4.14 illustrates a typical price consumption curve. It starts at point B, the pivot point of the rotating budget line; it continues as a U-shaped curve; and finally, it becomes asymptotic to horizontal line BH. Note that the price consumption curve is drawn with an arrowhead pointing in the direction of lower prices of X and rising ordinal utility.

That the typical price consumption curve starts at the pivot point of the rotating budget line is not difficult to explain. Imagine that the price of X *increases* continuously, causing the budget line to move closer and closer to the vertical axis. When the price of X increases beyond a certain limit, the consumer will be forced to purchase only Y, that is, buy $0B$ units of Y.[11]

Further, the price consumption curve must lie below horizontal line BH, because the consumer cannot purchase more units of Y than the quantity ($0B$) that her income permits. Since it starts at pivot point B, it follows that, initially, it must have a negative slope. Eventually, however, as the price of X tends to zero, the price consumption curve will attain a positive slope, and eventually, it will tend to become asymptotic to horizontal line BH. This asymptotic behavior of the price consumption curve is not difficult to explain. As the price of X tends to zero and the budget line moves closer and closer to horizontal line BH, the consumer will be able to purchase unlimited amounts of X with a small and decreasing fraction of her income. Accordingly, the consumer will be able to increase her purchases of Y continuously, moving closer and closer to upper limit $0B$.

The price consumption curve intersects each indifference curve only once. Also, its precise location and shape depend on two elements: (1) the consumer's income in terms of the commodity whose price remains constant, that is, the location of pivot point B; and (2) the indifference map.

Finally, in Figure 4.14 we could derive another price consumption curve, showing the effect of a progressive reduction in the price of Y, with the price of X and income in terms of X remaining constant. We leave this as an exercise for the reader.

---

[11]The argument in the text implies that a "corner solution" exists at pivot point B. However, this is not always the case. For instance, the utility function $U = xy$ generates indifference curves that are asymptotic to both axes, and in this case, a corner solution is not possible. Under such circumstances, the price consumption curve cannot exist at pivot point B. Nevertheless, even in this case point B can be considered as a "limit point" of the price consumption curve, in the sense that the equilbrium point along the price consumption curve can be made to "get arbitrarily close" to pivot point B by allowing the price of X to increase beyond all bounds.

The Demand Curve of the Individual Consumer

We now proceed to derive the consumer's demand curve for a commodity from the price consumption curve. This step corresponds to the derivation of the Engel curve from an income consumption curve.

Consider Figure 4.15. For convenience, panel (a) reproduces the price consumption curve (*PCC*) of Figure 4.14. (Indifference curves I_0, I_1, and I_2 are now omitted.) Panel (b) shows the corresponding demand curve for commodity X. Each point on the price consumption curve of panel (*a*) gives rise to a point on demand curve DD' of panel (b). Thus at each point on the price consumption curve, we can identify two numbers: (1) the price of X and (2) the equilibrium quantity of X purchased by the consumer. Given these two numbers, we can plot a corresponding point on the consumer's demand curve for commodity X. For instance, at E_0 in panel (a) the price of X is \$10 and the consumer purchases x_0 units of X.[12] This information is sufficient to plot point E_0' on demand curve DD' in panel (b). Similarly, at E_1 the price of X is \$8 and the consumer purchases x_1 units of X. This price-quantity pair is sufficient to determine point E_1' on demand curve DD'. Finally, point E_2' on demand curve DD' corresponds to point E_2 on the price consumption curve. Connecting all points so determined (such as E_0', E_1', and E_2') with a continuous line, we obtain the consumer's demand curve for X, as shown in panel (b) by demand curve DD'.

Both the price consumption curve and the corresponding demand curve of Figure 4.15 are consistent with the law of demand: As the price of X falls, the quantity of X bought by the consumer increases. We return to this important principle in the following section.

Since the demand curve is derived from the price consumption curve, it follows that it is drawn on the same assumptions as the price consumption curve. Accordingly, the demand curve for a commodity is drawn on the assumption that the consumer's income, all prices other than the commodity's own price, and tastes remain constant. For instance, demand curve DD' in Figure 4.15 is drawn on the assumption that the indifference map, the price of Y, and money income are held constant. (Keep in mind, however, the homogeneity property explained in Section 4.1.)

Finally, as the price of X falls and the consumer moves down on her demand curve, say, from E_0' to E_1' (Figure 4.15), her ordinal utility increases. This proposition becomes obvious when we recall that points E_0' and E_1' correspond to points E_0 and E_1, respectively, on the price consumption curve, and that E_1 is preferred to E_0, because indifference curve I_1 is preferred to (higher than) indifference curve I_0.

The Price Consumption Curve and the Elasticity of Demand

It is interesting to note that the elasticity of demand can be inferred from the slope of the price consumption curve. Return to Figure 4.15, panel (a), and observe carefully that the vertical distances between the price consumption curve and the horizontal line BH indicate the consumer's total expenditure (in terms of Y) on commodity X. For instance, at point E_0 the consumer divides her fixed income $0B$

---

[12]For convenience, in Figure 4.15, panel (a), the price of X is registered along each budget line. In general, however, the slope of the budget line gives only the price ratio p_x/p_y. To determine the price of X from the diagram, we use the following simple formula:

$$\text{price of } Y \cdot \text{slope of budget line} = \text{price of } X$$

Bear in mind that the price of Y is already given and remains constant by assumption.

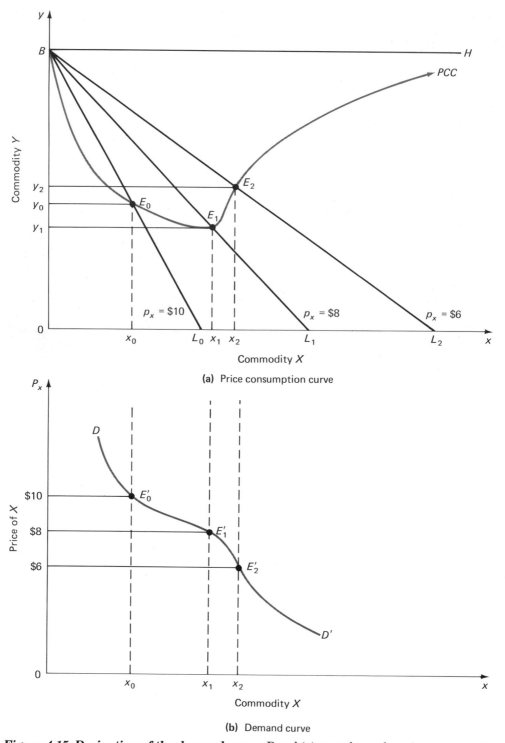

Figure 4.15 Derivation of the demand curve. Panel (a) reproduces the price consumption curve (PCC) of Figure 4.14. Panel (b) gives the corresponding demand curve for commodity X. Each point on demand curve DD' corresponds to a point on the price consumption curve. For instance, points E_0', E_1', and E_2' on DD' in panel (b) correspond to points E_0, E_1, and E_2, respectively, on PCC in panel (a).

into two parts: $0y_0$ and y_0B. She allocates $0y_0$ to Y and y_0B to X.[13] Similarly, at points E_1 and E_2, total expenditure on X is shown by vertical distances y_1B and y_2B, respectively.

A "small" reduction in the price of X causes the equilibrium point to move along the price consumption curve in the direction of the arrow. This movement causes the total expenditure on X to change. In particular, when the slope of the price consumption curve is negative, the reduction in the price of X causes the total expenditure on X to increase, revealing that the elasticity of demand for X is higher than unity. On the other hand, when the slope of the price consumption curve is positive, the reduction in the price of X causes the total expenditure on X to fall, disclosing that the elasticity of demand is less than unity. Finally, when the slope of the price consumption curve is zero (i.e., when its tangent is horizontal), the total expenditure on X is momentarily constant and the elasticity of demand is unity. For instance, at points E_0, E_1, and E_2 in Figure 4.15, the elasticity of demand is higher than unity, unity, and less than unity, respectively.

As the price of X falls progressively and the consumer moves along the price consumption curve in the direction of the arrow (Figure 4.15), the equilibrium quantities of both X *and* Y change. In general, the quantity of X increases. (A minor exception is discussed in the next section.) The quantity of Y, however, may increase, decrease, or remain the same, depending on the elasticity of demand for X. If the demand for X is *elastic*, the quantity of Y *decreases* (because the consumer increases her expenditure on X and necessarily reduces her expenditure on Y); if the demand for X is inelastic, the quantity of Y *increases* (as the consumer spends less on X and necessarily more on Y); and if the demand for X is unit elastic, the quantity of Y remains *constant* (as the consumer continues to allocate her income between X and Y in exactly the same way).

The Market Demand Curve

We finally show how the demand curves of individual consumers can be summed to form the market demand curve. As we saw in Chapter 2, the market demand curve registers the alternative quantities of a good, say, beef, that *all* consumers in the market are willing to purchase at various prices. Visualize each consumer as having a demand curve that depicts his or her willingness to purchase alternative amounts of beef at various prices. In general, each of these individual consumer demand curves slopes downward from left to right. To obtain the market demand curve graphically, we merely *add all individual consumer demand curves horizontally,* so that at each price the market demand curve does indeed give the total number of pounds of beef that all consumers as a group are willing to purchase.

Figure 4.16 illustrates the process of obtaining the total market demand curve from the individual consumer demand curves. For simplicity, we assume that there are only two consumers: A and B. Their individual demand curves, d_a and d_b, are given in panels (a) and (b), respectively. The market demand curve, D, is shown in panel (c). At each price, the market demand curve in panel (c) gives the combined demand of A and B. For instance, when the price is \$10, consumer A is willing to purchase 80 units [see point E_a in panel (a)], and consumer B, 60 units [see point E_b in panel (b)]. Accordingly, when the price is \$10, the total quantity demanded in the market is 140 [see point E in panel (c)]. Other points on the market demand curve are determined similarly.

---

[13]Keep in mind that $0B$, $0y_0$, and y_0B are all measured in terms of Y. However, this presents no problems, because the price of Y remains constant by assumption. Indeed, we may think of Y as "money" ("all other goods") whose price is always equal to \$1. Then all vertical distances would measure dollars.

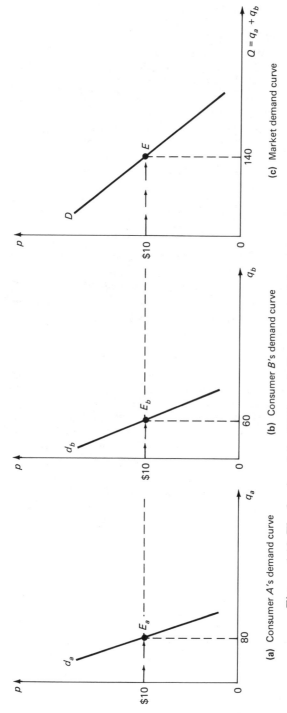

Figure 4.16 The horizontal addition of all consumers' demand curves. When the price is $10, consumer A is willing to purchase 80 units [see point E_a on A's demand curve d_a in panel (a)], and consumer B, 60 units [see point E_b on B's demand curve d_b in panel b]. Accordingly, when the price is $10, the total quantity demanded in the market is 140 (i.e., 80 + 60), as shown by point E on market demand curve D in panel (c).

(a) Consumer A's demand curve

(b) Consumer B's demand curve

(c) Market demand curve

114

We therefore conclude that the marekt demand curve is fundamentally the *horizontal summation* of the individual consumer demand curves.

4.9 Income and Substitution Effects[14]

We are finally ready to evaluate the law of demand. Does it follow from the axioms of consumer behavior that demand curves slope downward always? In other words, does a reduction in the price of a commodity cause the quantity demanded to increase? As it turns out, the law of demand does *not* follow from the pure logic of the model of consumer choice. It is rather an empirical proposition based on observation of the real world. This section clarifies these ideas by decomposing the total effect of a price change into a substitution effect and an income effect. Although this analysis is abstract, it allows us to probe more deeply into the foundations of the law of demand.

Nature of the Problem

A reduction in the price of a commodity has two different effects on the demand for it: an *income effect* and a *substitution effect*. On the one hand, a fall in the price of any commodity raises the "real income" of the consumer (i.e., it causes the budget line to "shift" outward and thus makes it possible for the consumer to attain a higher indifference curve), and the increase in "real income" influences the consumer's purchases (income effect). On the other hand, a fall in the price of a commodity induces the consumer to substitute that commodity for other commodities, because the commodity whose price has fallen has become a bargain relative to other goods whose prices have remained constant (substitution effect). The total effect of the price change is the sum of the income effect and the substitution effect.

Equivalent Variation, Compensating Variation, and Cost Difference

That the fall in the price of any commodity raises the consumer's "real income" seems clear enough. The price reduction makes the consumer better off; that is, the price reduction enlarges the consumer's attainable set (the budget line rotates outward), which in turn enables the consumer to move to a higher indifference curve. There is an ambiguity, however, in determining the precise income change that accompanies a *finite* price reduction. Because of this ambiguity, the decomposition of the total effect can be performed in many different ways (see Machlup, 1957). Presently, we discuss three such decompositions.

In all three panels of Figure 4.17, the initial equilibrium of the consumer is at E_0, where budget line BL_0 is tangent to indifference curve I_0. Thus initially, the consumer purchases x_0 units of X. As the price of X falls, the budget line rotates counterclockwise through pivot point B, as shown by BL_1 (in all three panels again), and equilibrium shifts to E_1, where budget line BL_1 is tangent to indifference curve I_1. At the new equilibrium, the consumer purchases x_1 units of X. Accordingly, the total price effect is $x_1 - x_0$. How do we split this total price effect into an income effect and a substitution effect? Each panel performs this decomposition in a different way. The trick is to isolate the income effect first.

Consider panel (a) first. It is apparent that the price reduction has increased the consumer's ordinal utility, because it has enabled the consumer to attain a higher indifference curve. But the same increase in ordinal utility could have been achieved,

---

[14]This section may be read together with Sections A4.4 to A4.9 of the Appendix to Chapter 4.

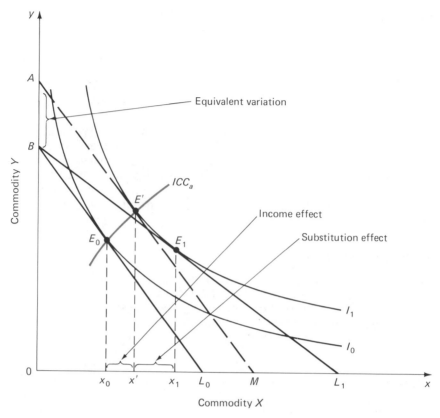

(a) Equivalent variation in income

Figure 4.17 Income and substitution effects. In all three panels, the initial equilibrium is at E_0 (where budget line BL_0 is tangent to indifference curve I_0). As the price of X falls, the budget line rotates counterclockwise through pivot point B, as shown by BL_1, and equilibrium shifts to E_1.

   Panel (a) decomposes the movement from E_0 to E_1 into a movement from E_0 to E' (through an equivalent variation in income equal to BA) plus a movement from E' to E_1. The movement from E_0 to E' corresponds to the income effect, and the movement from E' to E_1 to the substitution effect.

   In panel (b), the substitution effect is shown by the movement from E_0 to E' along I_0. The income effect (corresponding to a compensating variation in income equal to BF) is shown by the movement from E' to E_1.

   Panel (c) is similar to panel (b), except that auxiliary budget line CD is now made to pass through E_0. As a result, E' now lies on an indifference curve that is higher than I_0. The cost difference [BC in panel (c)] is always less than the compensating variation in income [BF in panel (b)]. Again, the movement from E_0 to E' corresponds to the substitution effect, and the movement from E' to E_1 to the income effect.

alternatively, by a hypothetical increase in income, without a price reduction. For instance, had the consumer's income increased by BA in terms of Y, budget line BL_0 would have shifted to dashed line AM, which is also tangent to indifference curve I_1. This hypothetical increase in income, BA, is known as the *equivalent variation*, because it represents the income variation that is equivalent to the price reduction insofar as concerns its effect on the welfare (ordinal utility) of the consumer.

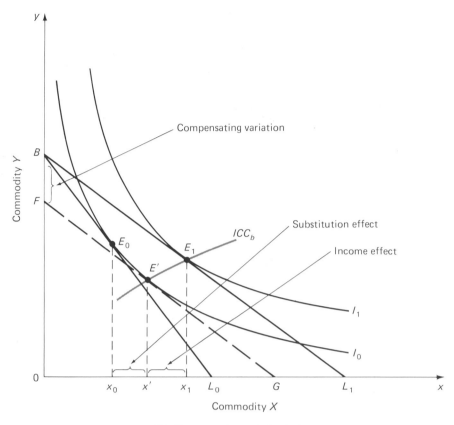

(b) Compensating variation in income

Figure 4.17 (Continued)

We can now identify in panel (a) the income and substitution effects. The equivalent variation in income causes the consumer to move from E_0 to E', increasing his purchases of X from x_0 to x'. This increase in demand, $x' - x_0$, is the income effect of the price reduction. Even though the equivalent variation in income has the same effect on ordinal utility as the price reduction, its effect on demand is different. The consumer cannot stay at E'. Because X has become cheaper relative to Y, the consumer must substitute X for Y until his marginal rate of substitution becomes equal to the new market price ratio. Accordingly, the residual movement from E' to E_1 along indifference curve I_1 corresponds to the substitution effect. That is, the increase in demand from x' to x_1 is the substitution effect of the price reduction.

Note that points E_0 and E' in panel (a) lie on an income consumption curve (ICC_a), while points E' and E_1 lie on an indifference curve. Accordingly, the income effect is associated with a movement along an income consumption curve, and the substitution effect with a movement along an indifference curve.

Turn now to panel (b). To isolate the increase in income due to the price reduction, we now think as follows. The price reduction causes the consumer's ordinal utility to increase. To offset this utility gain, we must take away from the consumer enough income to force him back to indifference curve I_0. What can we tax away from the consumer, after the price reduction, so that he is neither better off nor worse off than he was before the price reduction? Obviously, when the consumer's income is decreased by BF in terms of Y, budget line BL_1 will shift to dashed line FG, which

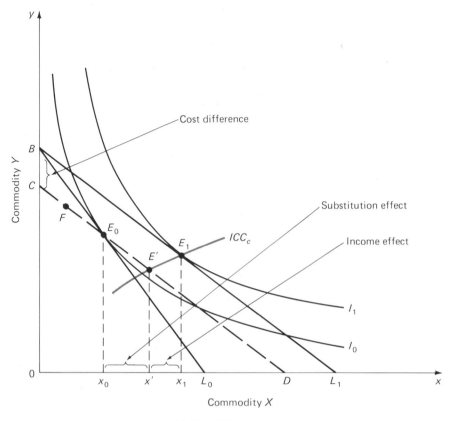

(c) Cost difference approach

Figure 4.17 (Continued)

is also tangent to indifference curve I_0, as is initial budget line BL_0. This hypothetical lump-sum tax, BF, is known as the *compensating* variation in income, because it compensates (in a negative way) for the welfare (ordinal utility) effects of the price reduction.

How is the total price effect, $x_1 - x_0$, decomposed into a substitution effect and an income effect in panel (b)? The movement from E_0 to E' along indifference curve I_0 is associated with the substitution effect, and the movement from E' to E_1 along income consumption curve ICC_b, with the compensating variation in income. Thus the increase in demand from x_0 to x' is the substitution effect, and the increase from x' to x_1 is the income effect.

In empirical investigations, neither the equivalent variation nor the compensating variation can be determined precisely, because the indifference curves are unknown. Panel (c) illustrates the *cost-difference* technique, which gives a conservative estimate of the compensating variation in income without full knowledge of the indifference map.

By means of direct observation of the market behavior of the consumer, we know that as the price of X falls he shifts from point (or commodity bundle) E_0 to E_1. Instead of removing the entire income gain as we did with the compensating variation in income, we now fix the lump-sum tax in such a way as to leave the consumer enough income to purchase the original commodity bundle, E_0, at the new prices. This is accomplished in panel (c) by reducing the consumer's income by BC in terms of Y (at the new prices), which causes budget line BL_1 to shift to dashed line CD. Thus the auxiliary budget line (CD) is now made to pass through point E_0, which, of course, is known to us. The hypothetical lump-sum tax, BC, is known as the *cost difference* because it represents the cost saving of the price reduction when the consumer purchases the original commodity bundle, E_0. In other words,

$$\text{cost difference} = \Delta p_x \cdot x_0 \tag{4.10}$$

where Δp_x is the reduction in the price of X. Equation (4.10) is very useful. It estimates a lower limit for the compensating variation in income, which in turn reveals the strength of the income effect.

We therefore conclude that in panel (c) the increase in demand from x_0 to x' (associated with the movement from E_0 to E') is the substitution effect, and the increase from x' to x_1 (associated with the movement from E' to E_1 along income consumption curve ICC_c) is the income effect.

Note that in panel (c), E' lies on a *higher* indifference curve than E_0. Since E_0 is the most preferred point when the budget line is BL_0, and E_0 is also available to the consumer (i.e., the consumer can purchase E_0) when the budget line is CD, it follows that with budget line CD the consumer can maintain his utility by choosing E_0. The fact that he chooses E' is an indication that E' is preferred to E_0.

Also, it must be obvious that E' must lie on line segment E_0D, which shows that the substitution effect must be negative. The income consumption curve ICC_c cannot possibly intersect line segment CE_0. If it did, the consumer would be contradicting himself. For instance, suppose that with budget line CD the consumer chooses point F, which in effect means that he prefers F to any point on CD, in particular point E_0. But we already know that with budget line BL_0 the consumer chose point E_0, which in effect means that E_0 is preferred to any point in the attainable set $0BL_0$, including F. Since the consumer cannot both prefer E_0 to F and F to E_0, we infer that E' must lie somewhere along segment E_0D.

In conclusion, the three methods we described above give rise to three alternative decompositions of the total price effect. The differences among these alternatives are due to the fact that we are dealing with finite price changes. In the limit, when the price changes become infinitesimal, all methods lead to exactly the same decomposition.

Implications of the Income and Substitution Effects

What are the implications of the decomposition of the total price effect into an income effect and a substitution effect? One important implication concerns the predictability of these individual effects. While the substitution effect is quite systematic and predictable, the income effect is unreliable in the sense that we cannot predict its sign. Therefore, to isolate the systematic behavior of the reliable substitution effect, we must first remove the unreliable income effect.

As we saw above, the substitution effect is basically associated with a movement along an indifference curve that is convex to the origin. Consequently, it is always *negative*: As p_x falls, the rate of consumption of X rises. This proposition is known as the *Slutsky theorem*.

That the income effect is unpredictable follows from the fact that it is always associated with a movement along an income consumption curve, as the reader can verify by inspecting again Figure 4.17. Since the slope of an income consumption curve is unpredictable (see Figure 4.9), it follows that the sign of the income effect cannot be predicted with certainty either. In particular, the income effect can be negative, positive, or zero, depending on whether the commodity whose price falls is normal, inferior, or neutral, respectively.[15]

What light can be shed on the law of demand? Simply this: The law of demand does not follow from the logic of the model of consumer choice. When the price of a *normal* commodity falls, the *negative income effect* reinforces the *negative substitution effect,* with the result that the demand curve has a *negative slope.* But when the price of an *inferior* commodity falls, the *positive income effect* works against the *negative substitution effect,* and as shown in the next subsection, it is possible for the adverse income effect to be strong enough to outweigh the favorable substitution effect. In that case the fall in price will cause the quantity demanded to *fall* (*not* to rise), a result that contradicts the law of demand. The circumstances of this truly paradoxical case are explained in the next subsection. It is rarely observed in practice.

We therefore conclude that the demand curve of a normal commodity has a negative slope. The same is true for a neutral commodity whose income effect is zero (because of the inherently negative substitution effect). However, the demand curve of an inferior commodity *may* have a positive slope in some region(s).

The Giffen Paradox

Sir Robert Giffen (1837–1910) was a British statistician and economist. He is quoted by Alfred Marshall [see Marshall (1961), p. 132] to have said that "a *rise* in the price of bread makes so large a drain on the resources of the poorer labouring families . . . that they are forced to curtail their consumption of meat and the more expensive farinaceous foods; and, bread being still the cheapest food which they can get and will take, *they consume more,* and *not less of it*" (italics added). Marshall was quick to point out that economic phenomena such as the Giffen case are extremely rare. They are almost never observed in empirical studies.

Figure 4.18 illustrates the Giffen paradox. The consumer is initially at E_0, where budget line BL_0 is tangent to indifference curve I_0. As the price of X falls, budget line BL_0 rotates outward to BL_1, and equilibrium shifts to E_1 on indifference curve I_1. Accordingly, as the price of X *falls,* the quantity demanded also *falls,* from x_0 to x_1.

What conditions are *necessary* for the emergence of the Giffen paradox? First, *commodity X must be inferior.* Second, *the consumer must spend a large share of his income on the inferior commodity.* The first condition guarantees that the income effect is positive and thus works against the substitution effect. The second condition ensures that the adverse income effect is large. Of course, the Giffen paradox occurs when the adverse income effect is strong enough to outweigh the favorable substitution effect.

Figure 4.18 shows clearly that commodity X is inferior and that the adverse income effect is stronger than the substitution effect. Thus BF is the compensating variation in income, as in Figure 4.17(b). The movement from E_0 to E' along indifference curve I_0 corresponds to the substitution effect, and the movement from E' to E_1 (along a backward-bending income consumption curve, such as ICC_3 in Figure 4.9) corresponds to the income effect. The favorable substitution effect is

[15]The income effect of a price reduction is *negative* for a *normal* commodity, and *positive* for an *inferior* commodity. As the price of a normal (inferior) commodity *falls,* the consumer's "real income" increases, causing the quantity demanded to *increase* (*decrease*). Some authors concentrate on the relationship between the *change in income* and the *change in the quantity demanded* and conclude that the income effect is positive for a normal commodity, and negative for an inferior commodity. Our approach is straightforward and avoids awkward statements such as this: "In the case of a *normal* commodity, the *positive* income effect *reinforces* the *negative* substitution effect; and in the case of an inferior commodity, the *negative* income effect *works against* the *negative* substitution effect."

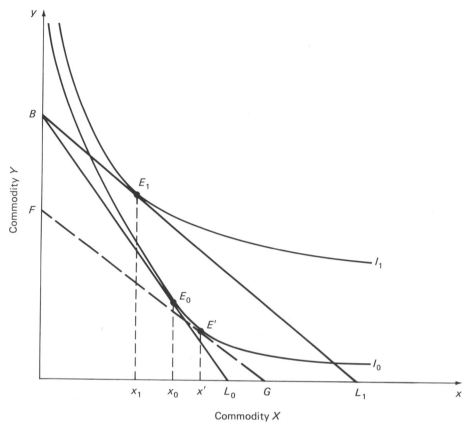

Figure 4.18 The Giffen paradox. Initially, equilibrium is at E_0, where budget line BL_0 is tangent to indifference curve I_0. As the price of X *falls*, BL_0 rotates to BL_1, and equilibrium shifts to E_1. Hence the quantity demanded *falls* from x_0 to x_1.

---

equal to the small *increase* in the quantity demanded from x_0 to x', while the adverse income effect is equal to the large *decrease* in the quantity demanded from x' to x_1. Accordingly, the income and substitution effects conspire to produce the Giffen paradox: A reduction in price leads to a reduction in quantity demanded.

When we shift our attention from the individual consumer demand curve to the market demand curve, we must add another condition for the occurrence of the Giffen paradox; that *commodity X must be a "Giffen good" for most consumers.* Otherwise, the "abnormal" behavior of some consumers can be offset by the "normal" behavior of others.

We therefore conclude that the Giffen paradox is a legitimate exception to the law of demand. Yet the conditions for its existence are so stringent that it is a most rare phenomenon. Accordingly, it seems safe to assume that market demand curves do slope downward.

4.10 The Return to the Gas-Guzzling V-8 Engine: Another Application

The behavior of American car buyers since the early 1970s provides an important application of the principle of commodity substitution in response to relative price changes. As the reader may recall, soaring gasoline prices in the 1970s persuaded consumers to substitute more-fuel-efficient four-cylinder and six-cylinder engines for the gas-guzzling V-8 engines. For a while it looked as if the V-8 engine were doomed and the auto industry sharply reduced its capacity to produce it. But the big V-8 engine is staging a comeback.

According to *The Wall Street Journal* (May 25, 1983, p. 33), during the first four months of the 1983 model year (i.e., September 1982–December 1982), 31 percent of all American-built cars were equipped with gas-fueled V-8 engines compared to only 21 percent in the same period one year earlier. It is evident from these figures (which represent an increase of about 50 percent in the share of such cars) that American consumers are returning to big cars equipped with big engines. What accounts for this phenomenon? Is it the legendary "love" of the American consumer for the full-size car? If that were the reason, why did the demand for big cars fall drastically in the 1970s? The primary reason for the return to the V-8 engine is the falling price of gasoline. The truth of the matter is that the cost of gasoline *per mile* is not higher now (1985) than it was before the energy crisis. A simple calculation should convince us of this fact.

Before the energy crisis, in the 1970s, the price of regular gasoline was about 30 cents a gallon. But the general price level increased from 100 before the energy crisis to about 250 in the early 1980s. (The numbers are rounded off for easy calculation.) Had the price of gasoline increased at the same rate as the general price level, it would be about 75 cents in 1985. Therefore, for a full-sized car equipped with a big V-8 engine with a rating of about 10 miles a gallon (which approximates the fuel efficiency conditions of the early 1970s), the fuel cost per mile at 1985 prices would be about 7.5 cents (i.e., 75 ÷ 10 = 7.5).

The price of regular unleaded gasoline is currently (April 1985) about $1.20 a gallon. However, V-8s are not as thirsty as they once were. Because of improvements in engine combustion technology, emission controls, carburation, transmission, and aerodynamics as well as reduction in car weight, V-8 engines achieve much better mileage now than they did a decade ago. For instance, a 1983 Thunderbird was rated at 17 miles a gallon in city driving; in the early 1970s a similarly equipped Thunderbird got barely 10 miles a gallon. For our purposes we may assume that the gas mileage of a full-sized car equipped with a big V-8 engine increased from about 10 miles per gallon in 1973 to about 16 miles per gallon in 1985. Accordingly, the fuel cost per mile in 1985 was 7.5 cents (i.e., 120 ÷ 16 = 7.5)—which is exactly *the same as it was in 1973!* Is it any wonder American car buyers are returning to big cars equipped with big V-8 engines?

SUMMARY

1. The consumer's budget line divides the commodity space into the attainable set and the unattainable set. Its absolute slope equals the ratio of commodity prices (or the opportunity cost of one commodity in terms of the other).

2. The objective of a rational consumer is to maximize her ordinal utility subject to her budget constraint. This objective is attained at the tangency of the budget line to the highest possible indifference curve, that is, when $MRS_{xy} = p_x/p_y$. Consumer equilibrium occurs on the budget line because of the axiom of nonsatiation.

3. Proportional changes in money income and all money prices leave the budget line unchanged; thus they have no influence on the equilibrium of the consumer (absence of money illusion). This means that the demand functions are homogeneous of degree zero with respect to money prices and income.

4. The marginal rate of substitution (MRS_{xy}) equals the ratio of marginal utilities (MU_x/MU_y). As a result, the condition $MRS_{xy} = p_x/p_y$ is equivalent to the equimarginal principle ($MU_x/p_x = MU_y/p_y$), but it is not based on cardinal utility.

5. Convex indifference curves are consistent with both interior solutions (diversification in consumption) and corner solutions (complete specialization in consumption). Concave indifference curves always lead to corner solutions. In general, nonconvexity of indifference curves may lead to many strange results (such as multiple equilibria, drastic changes in consumption patterns following small price changes, and exclusion of many commodity bundles as possible equilibria) that contradict observed behavior.

6. *Composite good theorem:* In drawing an indifference map, a group of commodities whose relative prices remain constant can be treated as a single composite good ("money" or "general purchasing power").

7. As the consumer's income increases while prices remain constant, the budget line shifts outward in a parallel fashion, causing the consumer equilibrium to change. The locus of all such equilibria is the income consumption curve; its precise shape and location depend on the indifference map and the price ratio.

8. Commodities are classified into normal, inferior, and neutral according to whether their consumption increases, decreases, or remains constant, respectively, as income increases. It is not possible for all commodities to be inferior (or neutral) at the same time.

9. *Engel's law:* When demographic factors are held constant, an increase in income lowers the proportion of income spent on food.

10. The Engel curve is a relationship between the quantity of a commodity purchased by a consumer and his money income. The Engel expenditure curve relates expenditure (price times quantity) to income. Both curves are derived from the income consumption curve.

11. In general, a cash subsidy is more valuable to the consumer than an equivalent in-kind subsidy. Typically, an in-kind subsidy increases the consumption of both the subsidized commodity and other goods. When the nature of the subsidized commodity (such as public education) is such that the consumer cannot supplement the subsidized quantity with additional purchases, an in-kind subsidy may actually *reduce* its consumption, even when the subsidized commodity is a normal good.

12. As the price of commodity X falls continuously, the budget line swings outward (counterclockwise) from its intercept with the Y-axis. The locus of the resultant equilibria is the price consumption curve (PCC), from which we derive the demand curve for X. At each point on PCC we identify the price and equilibrium quantity of X and thus determine a point on the demand curve for X.

13. The elasticity of demand for X is greater than, less than, or equal to unity according to whether the slope of the PCC is negative, positive, or zero, respectively (assuming that X is measured horizontally). The quantity of Y decreases, increases, or remains the same according to whether the elasticity of demand for X is greater than, less than, or equal to unity, respectively.

14. The total price effect is the sum of an income effect and a substitution effect. The substitution effect corresponds to a movement along a convex indifference curve; thus it is always negative (Slutsky theorem). The income effect is negative, positive, or zero according to whether the cheapened good is normal, inferior, or neutral, respectively.

15. The equivalent variation in income corresponds to a hypothetical increase in income which (in the absence of any price reduction) would put the consumer on the same indifference curve as the price reduction would. The compensating variation in income is equal to a hypothetical lump-sum tax, which (after the price reduction) would force the consumer back to the indifference curve attained before the price reduction. The cost difference provides a lower limit estimate for the compensating variation in income; it is equal to the amount of money that the consumer would save after the price reduction if he purchased the original commodity bundle.

16. The law of demand does not follow from the model of consumer choice. The law always holds for normal and neutral commodities. For an inferior commodity the positive income effect works against the negative substitution effect, and it is possible for the adverse income effect to outweigh the favorable substitution effect, giving rise to a positive slope of the demand curve (Giffen good).

QUESTIONS

1. Mr. Brown's indifference curves for food and clothing have two properties:
  1. They are asymptotic to each axis.
  2. They are *consistent* with the assumption that the marginal utility of each good is a decreasing function of its own quantity and independent of the quantity of the other good.

Explain briefly why you regard each of the following statements as true or false.

(a) Mr. Brown's indifference curves are necessarily strictly convex to the origin.

(b) Neither good is ever inferior for Mr. Brown.

(c) Neither good can ever be consumed to a point of satiation.

(d) Mr. Brown would never choose to consume only food or only clothing.

(e) Although consistent with the assumption of independent and decreasing marginal utilities, Mr. Brown's indifference map is consistent with *increasing* marginal utility for either or both of the two goods.

2. Is it true that a diminishing marginal rate of substitution of beef for vegetables necessarily implies diminishing marginal utilities of the two goods?

3. A consumer spends all her income on food and clothing. Given the current prices of the two commodities, she can purchase either a maximum of 20 units of food or a maximum of 100 units of clothing. She is maximizing her utility, however, by purchasing 10 units of food and 50 units of clothing.

(a) What is her marginal rate of substitution of food for clothing at the initial equilibrium point?

(b) Is the marginal rate of substitution at the initial equilibrium point diminishing, increasing, or constant?

(c) If the consumer assures us that at the initial equilibrium her marginal utility of food is 10 utils, can you determine her marginal utility of clothing?

(d) Suppose that the price of food falls so that the consumer can now buy a maximum of 30 units of food (or a maximum of 100 units of clothing, as before). Suppose further that the consumer now maximizes her utility by purchasing 9 units of food and 70 units of clothing. Is the consumer rational? Is food inferior or normal? Is clothing inferior or normal?

*4. A person's utility function is of the form $U = 5xy$. The prices of commodities X and Y are $p_x = \$4$ and $p_y = \$2$, respectively. The person's income is $1200.

(a) What quantities of X and Y should the consumer purchase to maximize his utility?

(b) Determine the person's income consumption curve. Explain whether each of the two commodities is normal or inferior.

(c) Suppose that the price of Y remains fixed at $p_y = \$2$ but the price of X is allowed to vary. Determine the person's price consumption curve and demand curve for X. At what price is the elasticity of demand for X equal to unity?

5. A consumer spends all his income on commodities X and Y. At the current price of Y, he could purchase a maximum of 100 units of Y. Suppose that the consumer's price consumption curve in the range $10 \le x \le 30$ is of the form $y = 10 + 2x$. Determine the consumer's demand curve in the range $10 \le x \le 30$.

6. Suppose that the local sales tax on food is abolished. How will this change affect a typical family's consumption of food?

7. Suppose that the deduction for home mortgage interest is abolished. At the same time, the federal government returns the tax revenue to the consumers by means of a reduction of the federal tax rates.

(a) Suppose that each citizen receives from the federal government the additional tax paid to the government because of the abolition of the interest deduction. How will the restructuring of the federal tax affect the average citizen's consumption of housing?

(b) Suppose that before the new law goes into effect, only 50 percent of all residents own their homes. How will the change affect the consumption of housing of an initial home owner? How about the consumption of housing of an initial renter (assuming that rents remain the same)?

8. The slope of a price consumption curve has definite implications about the price elasticity of demand. Suppose that quantities of commodity X are measured horizontally and quantities of money (or "all other goods") are measured vertically. State the implications about the price elasticity of demand for X if the price consumption curve runs:

(a) To the southeast.

(b) Straight to the east.

(c) To the northeast.

(d) Straight to the north.

(e) To the northwest.

9. A consumer's indifference map for commodity X and money (or "all other goods") is such that the marginal utility of income is constant. Which of the following statements are true and which are false? In each case, explain why.

(a) The income effect of any price change is zero.

(b) The marginal rate of substitution of X for money depends only on the quantity of X consumed.

(c) A line drawn perpendicular to the X-axis intersects all indifference curves at points of equal slope.

(d) The demand curve for commodity X is strictly negatively sloped.

(e) Commodity X is normal.

10. A consumer spends all her income on food and clothing. At the current prices of $p_f = \$10$ and $p_c = \$5$, the consumer maximizes her utility by purchasing 20 units of food and 50 units of clothing.

(a) What is the consumer's income?

(b) What is the consumer's marginal rate of substitution of food for clothing at the initial equilibrium?

(c) As the prices of food and clothing change to $p_f' = \$7.50$ and $p_c' = \$6$, respectively, the consumer purchases 18 units of food and 105 units of clothing. Is this choice consistent with the axioms of consumer choice? Is the consumer better off or worse off after the price change?

*11. A person's utility function is of the form $U = xy$. The person's income is $\$1500$, and the prices of commodities X and Y are $p_x = \$3$ and $p_y = \$1$, respectively.

(a) Determine the utility-maximizing quantities of X and Y.

(b) Suppose that the price of X falls to $p_x' = \$2$. Determine the new quantities of X and Y that maximize utility.

(c) Determine the cost difference, the equivalent variation, and the compensating variation of income of the price reduction.

(d) Decompose the total effect on the purchase of X into an income effect and a substitution effect in three alternative ways, using the results of your answer to part (c).

12. The income-consumption curve of the person in Question 11 is given by the equation $y = 3x$ (assuming that $p_x = \$3$ and $p_y = \$1$).

(a) Derive the Engel curve for X.

(b) Derive the Engel expenditure curve for X.

FURTHER READING

Baumol, W. J. (1977). *Economic Theory and Operations Analysis,* 4th ed. Prentice-Hall, Inc., Englewood Cliffs, N.J. Chapter 9.

Clarkson, K. W. (1976). "Welfare Benefits of the Food Stamp Program," *Southern Economic Journal,* Vol. 43 (July), pp. 864–878.

Ferguson, C. E. (1972). *Microeconomic Theory,* 3rd ed. Richard D. Irwin, Inc., Homewood, Ill. Chapters 2 and 3 (Sections 3.1–3.3).

Friedman, M. (1949). "The Marshallian Demand Curve," *Journal of Political Economy,* Vol. 57, pp. 463–495. Reprinted in M. Friedman, *Essays in Positive Economics.* The University of Chicago Press, Chicago, 1953.

Henderson, J. M., and R.E. Quandt (1980). *Microeconomic Theory,* 3rd ed. McGraw-Hill Book Company, New York. Chapter 2.

Hicks, J. R. (1946). *Value and Capital,* 2nd ed. Oxford University Press, New York. Chapters 1 and 2.

Machlup, F. (1957). "Professor Hicks' Revision of Demand Theory," *American Economic Review* (March), pp. 119–135. Reprinted in W. Breit and H. M. Hochman (eds.), *Readings in Microeconomics.* Holt, Rinehart and Winston, New York, 1968.

Marshall, A. (1961). *Principles of Economics,* 9th (variorum) ed., Macmillan & Company Ltd., London. Book III.

Samuelson, P. A. (1947). *Foundations of Economic Analysis.* Harvard University Press, Cambridge, Mass. Chapters 5–7.

Slutsky, E. E. (1915). "On the Theory of the Budget of the Consumer," *Giornale degli Economisti,* Vol. 51, pp. 1–26. Reprinted in G. J. Stigler and K. E. Boulding (eds.), *Readings in Price Theory,* Richard D. Irwin, Inc., Homewood, Ill. 1952.

CHAPTER 5

Applications and Extensions of Consumer Theory

In this chapter we discuss some important applications and extensions of the theory of consumer behavior. We begin in Section 5.1 with the important choice between leisure and income and the derivation of the supply of labor. In Section 5.2 we introduce the concept of an income-compensated demand curve, which is very useful in the study of the consumer's surplus, as explained in Section 5.3. Price and quantity index numbers form the subject matter of Section 5.4. Section 5.5 provides an application of the modern theory of demand to New York City's Mitchell-Lama middle-income housing program. The chapter concludes with Section 5.6, which extends the theory of consumer behavior to situations involving uncertainty.

5.1 The Choice Between Leisure and Income

So far, we have discussed the theory of consumer behavior on the assumption that the consumer's income is given. However, most people in our society *earn* their income by selling their personal services. Accordingly, the amount of income received by a typical consumer depends on the amount of *time* she allocates to work. How does the consumer-worker respond to an increase in the wage rate? Will President Reagan's income tax cut induce people to increase their work effort?

In this section we apply the tools of the theory of consumer behavior to explain how a worker chooses between work and leisure. We also generate the supply-of-labor schedule and study related issues.

The New Scenario

Consider a consumer who derives his income from the work he performs, that is, the amount of time he allocates to work. In particular, the consumer has at his disposal a fixed amount of time, such as 24 hours per day or 168 hours per week, which he divides between work and leisure. Obviously, leisure provides enjoyment (or utility) directly to the consumer. The time he allocates to work, on the other hand, provides him satisfaction (or utility) indirectly, through the commodities that his earned *income* commands.

On the basis of such a scenario, we must introduce leisure explicitly into the consumer's preference function. In order to be able to illustrate the argument graphically, we must also make use of the composite good theorem. In what follows we assume that the prices of the various commodities that the consumer purchases with his income remain *constant* throughout. Consequently, we treat income as a composite good (generalized purchasing power). The fundamental choice, therefore, is between income and leisure.

The consumer's preferences can be summarized by an indifference map in the income-leisure space. The consumer's problem is to choose the most preferred income-leisure combination, subject to the fixed number of hours available to him and the fixed hourly wage rate.

The Income-Leisure Equilibrium

Figure 5.1 measures the consumer's money income along the vertical axis and hours of leisure time along the horizontal axis. Straight line *BL* illustrates the budget line of a typical consumer-worker. The fixed amount of time at the disposal of the consumer (say, 24 hours per day) is shown by horizontal distance $0L$, which

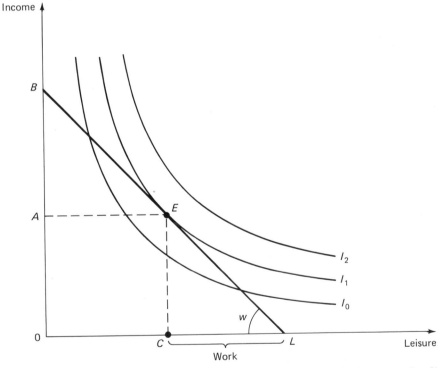

Figure 5.1 The consumer-worker equilibrium. The fixed amount of time at the disposal of the consumer (say, 24 hours per day) is shown by horizontal distance $0L$, which also corresponds to maximum leisure time. If the consumer worked 24 hours per day ($0L$), his maximum earned income would be $OB = w \cdot OL$. Accordingly, the consumer's budget line is given by line *BL*, whose (absolute) slope coincides with the fixed wage rate (w). Equilibrium occurs at *E*, where budget line *BL* is tangent to I_1. Thus the consumer-worker enjoys OC hours of leisure, earns an income of OA dollars per day, and works CL hours per day.

is the maximum amount of leisure time that the consumer can enjoy. On the other hand, if it were actually possible for the consumer to work 24 hours per day, his maximum earned income per day would be $0B$. Thus $0B = w \cdot 0L$, where w is the fixed hourly wage rate. Accordingly,

$$\text{slope of budget line } BL = \frac{0B}{0L} = w \qquad (5.1)$$

In other words, the (absolute) slope of budget line BL coincides with the fixed wage rate.

Note that *the wage rate is the opportunity cost of leisure.* To increase leisure time by 1 hour, the consumer must forgo the opportunity of working for that hour, which implies a reduction in income equal to the hourly wage rate. In other words, the hourly wage rate represents the sacrifice (opportunity cost) that the consumer must make for an extra hour of leisure.

The income-leisure indifference map is illustrated by indifference curves I_0, I_1, and I_2, which have all the usual properties of indifference curves (explained in Chapter 3). Equilibrium occurs at E, where budget line BL is tangent to indifference curve I_1. Accordingly, the consumer enjoys $0C$ hours of leisure and earns an income of $0A$ dollars per day. Because the total amount of time at the disposal of the consumer is fixed at $0L$ hours, it also follows that the consumer works $CL = 0L - 0C$ hours per day, as shown on the graph. Note also that

$$\text{income earned} = 0A = CE = w \cdot CL = \text{wage} \cdot \text{work} \qquad (5.2)$$

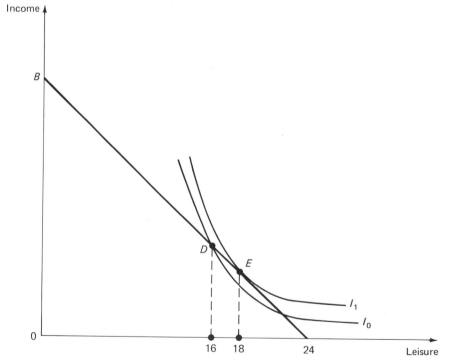

Figure 5.2 The effect of employment restrictions. Without any work restrictions, the consumer would be at E, where he would work only 6 hours per day (i.e., $24 - 18 = 6$). Because he must work 8 hours per day, however, he is forced to "disequilibrium" point D, which lies on lower indifference curve I_0.

Work Restrictions

In the above analysis, we implicitly assumed that the consumer may work as many hours as he wishes. However, the fact of the matter is that a worker must work a certain number of hours per day (say, 8 hours) or not work at all. What effect does this important restriction on employment have on the individual consumer?

Consider Figure 5.2, which is similar to Figure 5.1. Without any work restrictions, the consumer would be at E on indifference curve I_1, where he would work only 6 hours per day (i.e., $24 - 18 = 6$). Because he must work 8 hours per day, however, he is forced to "disequilibrium" point D, which lies on lower indifference curve I_0. We must therefore conclude that employment restrictions tend to prevent the individual worker from attaining the highest possible indifference curve (i.e., from maximizing his ordinal utility).

The Price Consumption Curve

How does the consumer-worker respond to changes in the wage rate? Consider Figure 5.3. As the wage rate rises, the budget line rotates in the clockwise direction through point T (which corresponds to the *fixed* amount of time available to the consumer), as shown by lines B_0T, B_1T, and B_2T which correspond to wage rates of \$8, \$12, and \$16, respectively. Each budget line gives rise to an equilibrium point. For instance, at $w = \$8$ equilibrium occurs at E_0, where B_0T is tangent to I_0; thus the consumer's income is L_0E_0, as he divides his time $0T$ into $0L_0$ (leisure) and TL_0

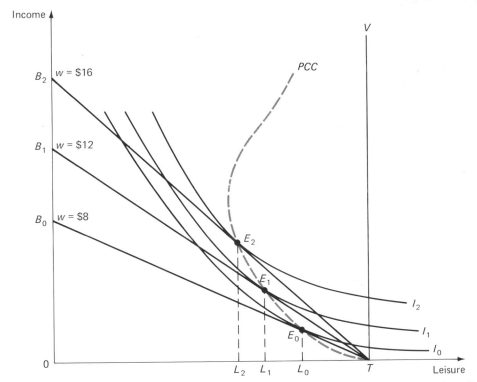

Figure 5.3 The price consumption curve. As the wage rate increases, the budget line rotates clockwise through pivot point T, as shown by lines B_0T, B_1T, and B_2T. Each budget line gives rise to an equilibrium point, as illustrated by E_0, E_1, and E_2. The locus of all such equilibria is the price consumption curve, as shown by dashed curve *PCC*.

(work). As the wage rate rises to $w = \$12$, equilibrium shifts to E_1, where $B_1 T$ is tangent to I_1, income $= L_1 E_1$, leisure $= 0 L_1$, and work $= T L_1$. Finally, when the wage rate rises to $w = \$16$, equilibrium moves to E_2, where $B_2 T$ is tangent to I_2, income $= L_2 E_2$, leisure $= 0 L_2$, and work $= T L_2$.

Allow the budget line to rotate clockwise through T from the horizontal position $T0$ (which corresponds to $w = 0$) to the vertical position VT (which corresponds to $w = \infty$). Connect the points of tangency between the various budget lines and indifference curves, as shown by dashed curve *PCC*, which is none other than our familiar *price consumption curve*. The only insignificant difference between this price consumption curve and the one we derived in Chapter 4 is that now the pivot point for the rotating budget line lies on the horizontal (not the vertical) axis. Accordingly, the price consumption curve in Figure 5.3 is backward bending, and as the wage rate increases beyond all bounds, it tends to become asymptotic to vertical line VT.

The Labor Supply Curve

We now derive the *labor supply curve* from the price consumption curve. At each point on the price consumption curve, we can identify (1) the wage rate and (2) the amount of time allocated to work (quantity of labor supplied). This information is sufficient to determine a point on the labor supply curve. This is shown in Figure 5.4, where labor supply curve *TS* corresponds to the price consumption curve of Figure 5.3. In particular, points T, E_0, E_1, and E_2 on the labor supply curve correspond to the synonymous points on the price consumption curve. Observe that

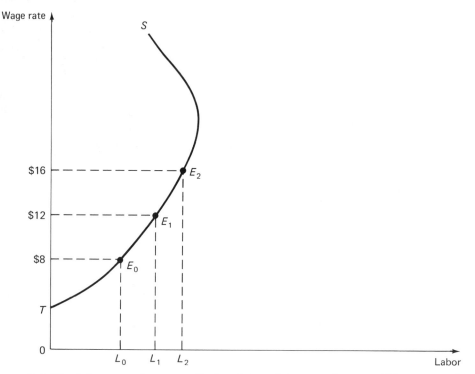

Figure 5.4 The labor supply curve. Each point on labor supply curve *TS* corresponds to a point on the price consumption curve of Figure 5.3. For instance, points T, E_0, E_1, and E_2 correspond to the synonymous points in Figure 5.3. Typically, the labor supply curve is backward bending, as shown.

the labor supply curve starts at point T on the vertical axis. The wage rate indicated by $0T$ (Figure 5.4) corresponds to the absolute slope of the indifference curve that passes through corresponding point T in Figure 5.3.

Typically, the labor supply curve is backward bending, as shown in Figure 5.4. This means that an increase in the wage rate may either increase or decrease the amount of labor supplied by the individual. The reason is simple. In the case of a supplier, the income and substitution effects of a *normal* commodity (such as leisure) pull in opposite directions and we cannot predict which effect will be stronger.

Consider Figure 5.5. The consumer is initially at E, where budget line BT is tangent to indifference curve I_0. As the wage rate increases, the budget line rotates to CT, and equilibrium shifts to F. Thus the quantity of labor supplied decreases from TL_0 to TL_1.

The total effect (L_0L_1) of the increase in the wage rate can be decomposed into an income effect and a substitution effect. Thus the consumer could have attained higher indifference curve I_1 by means of an *equivalent variation in income* equal to BA. This is shown by dashed line AG, which is parallel to BT and tangent to I_1 at G. (Note that points E and G lie on income consumption curve ICC.) The movement from E to G corresponds to the income effect. As his "real" income increases, the consumer increases his consumption of leisure and thus *reduces his supply of labor,* because leisure is a normal good. In particular, the consumer reduces his supply of labor by L_0L_2 (income effect). At the same time, the increase in the wage rate raises

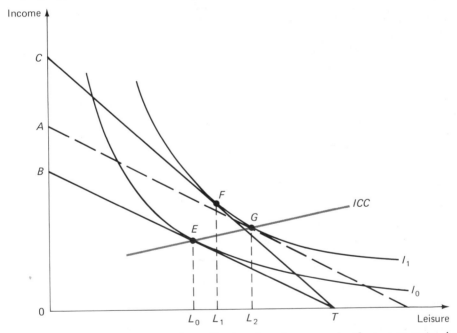

Figure 5.5 Income and substitution effects of an increase in the wage rate. As the wage rate increases, the budget line rotates from BT to CT and equilibrium shifts from E to F. The supply of labor decreases from TL_0 to TL_1. The total effect (L_0L_1) of the increase in the wage rate is decomposed into an income effect (L_0L_2) and a substitution effect (L_1L_2). The income effect (associated with the movement from E and G) tends to *decrease* the supply of labor because leisure is a normal good. The substitution effect (associated with the movement from G to F), however, tends to *increase* the supply of labor because the increase in the wage rate raises the price of leisure and causes the consumer to consume less of it. By construction, the income effect is larger than the substitution effect, and thus the supply of labor falls by $L_0L_1 = L_0L_2 - L_1L_2$.

the price of leisure, which causes the consumer to consume less leisure (and thus *supply more labor*) at any given level of satisfaction. This is shown by the movement from G to F along indifference curve I_1. The distance L_1L_2 is the subsitution effect.

In the example of Figure 5.5, the income effect (L_0L_2) is larger than the substitution effect (L_1L_2); and the increase in the wage rate causes the supply of labor to fall. But the reverse is also possible, as the reader should be able to demonstrate. We must therefore conclude that on theoretical grounds alone we cannot predict whether the slope of the labor supply curve is positive or negative at any particular wage rate.

The Workweek and Real Wage in U.S. Manufacturing Industries, 1909–1977

From colonial days to 1950, the average workweek declined gradually to a norm of 40 hours. At the same time the real wage rate has steadily increased. This empirical finding was taken by economists to mean that workers choose shorter working hours when their real income rises. However, things have changed since World War II.

During the postwar years the average workweek has remained at 40 hours even though the real wage rate has continued to rise. This somewhat surprising phenomenon is shown in Table 5.1, which focuses on the workweek and real wage of production workers in U.S. manufacturing industries, a group that has remained relatively homogeneous over time. Note that the workweek fell by about 20 percent from 1909 to 1950 but remained relatively flat from 1950 to 1977. The real wage, on the other hand, rose almost continuously from 1909 to 1977 at about 2 percent a year.

In terms of the theory of this section, we may say that the income effect dominated the substitution effect from 1909 to 1950; but that since 1950 the roles of the two effects have been switched. A possible explanation of such a switch in the roles of the income and substitution effects is that in 1950 the indifference curves of the average worker shifted permanently so that, for any given budget line, more income and less leisure was preferred. (This change in tastes can be illustrated by a counterclockwise tilt of the indifference curves of the individual worker.) Economists are not in agreement yet as to whether such a shift has taken place, or if it has occurred, what caused it. Brack and Cowling (1983) advance the hypothesis that such a shift in tastes did occur because of the increased intensity of advertising

Table 5.1 Average Workweek and Real Wage for Production Workers in U.S. Manufacturing Industries, 1909–1977

Period	Workweek	Real Wage[a]
1909–1919	48.9[b]	0.763[b]
1920–1929	44.7	1.017
1930–1939	38.1	1.278
1940–1949	41.5	1.818
1950–1959	40.2	2.250
1960–1969	40.6	2.733
1970–1977	40.1	3.012

Sources: Employment and Earnings, U.S. 1909–78, Bulletin 1312-11, pp. 52–53; *Handbook of Labor Statistics 1978,* Bulletin 2000, Table 116, U.S. Department of labor, Bureau of Labor Statistics, Washington, D.C., 1979.

[a]In 1967 dollars.

[b]Average for 1909, 1914, and 1919.

(due mainly to the evolution of television), which influences the desirability of goods in general.

5.2 Compensated Demand Curves[1]

The demand curve we derived from the price consumption curve (Chapter 4) is known as the *ordinary demand curve*. It rests on the assumption that *money* income remains constant and includes the total effect (i.e., the sum of the substitution effect and the income effect) of a price change.

For certain problems, such as the analysis of consumer surplus (Section 5.3), the ordinary demand curve is inappropriate, because we need a demand curve that is drawn on the assumption that *real* income (ordinal utility), as opposed to money income, is held constant. Such a demand curve is known as an *income-compensated demand curve* (or just "compensated demand curve"), because real income is held constant by making compensating variations in money income. The compensated demand curve includes the substitution effect only. Figure 5.6 illustrates how a compensated demand curve can be derived.

When the consumer's income is $0B$ and the price of X is p, the consumer is at E, where his budget line BL is tangent to indifference curve I_0 [panel (a)]. Accordingly, when the price of X is p, the consumer purchases x_0 units of X. Transferring this choice to panel (b), we determine point E' on the compensated demand curve that corresponds to indifference curve I_0.

Suppose now that the price of X falls to p' and at the same time we reduce the consumer's money income by AB so that his new budget line AM continues to be tangent to indifference curve I_0. The consumer moves from E to F (which is a pure substitution effect). Thus at p', the consumer purchases x_1 units of X, which fixes point F' on the compensated demand curve in panel (b). Other points can be derived in a similar way.

In general, the prices registered by the compensated demand curve show the consumer's marginal willingness to pay; that is, they correspond to the various marginal rates of substitution of X for "money" (all other goods) along the corresponding indifference curve.

Note that there is a different compensated demand curve for each indifference curve (level of ordinal utility). Since every point on an ordinary demand curve corresponds to a different level of ordinal utility, it follows that a different compensated demand curve must pass through each point of an ordinary demand curve. The precise relationship between an ordinary demand curve and a compensated demand curve is illustrated in Figure 5.7 (see p. 136).

In panel (a) we assume that commodity X is *normal*, which causes the compensated demand curve to be *steeper* than the ordinary demand curve. For instance, when the price of X falls from p_2 to p_1 but the consumer's money income is not adjusted, the quantity demanded increases from x_1 to x_3, as the consumer moves from A to B on the ordinary demand curve. With a reduction in money income that compensates for the fall in price, however, the quantity demanded does not increase as much. This is shown by the movement from A to C along the compensated demand curve through A. Thus, with compensation, the quantity demanded increases from x_1 to x_2 only.

Note that for a price increase, the compensated demand curve (for a normal good) must lie to the right of the ordinary demand curve, as actually shown in panel (a), because a price increase erodes the consumer's real income and thus the consumer

---

[1]This section may be read together with Section A5.1 of the Appendix to Chapter 5.

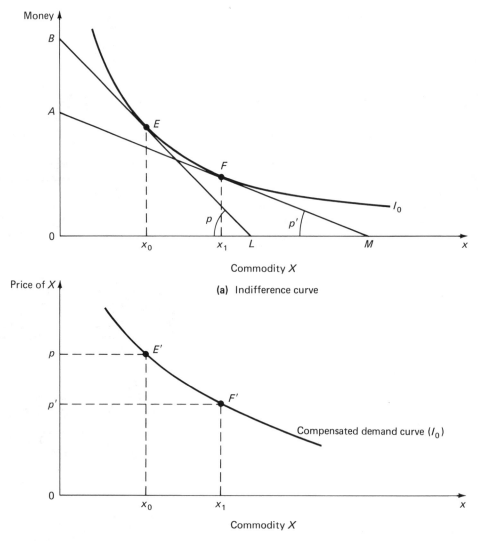

Figure 5.6 Derivation of a compensated demand curve. When the consumer's income is OB and the price of X is p, the consumer is at E [panel (a)] or E' [panel (b)]. When the price of X falls to p' and at the same time the consumer's income is reduced by AB (so that new budget line AM continues to be tangent to I_0), the consumer moves from E to F [panel (a)] and from E' to F' [panel (b)]. Points E' and F' lie on the compensated demand curve [panel (b)] that corresponds to indifference curve I_0 [panel (a)].

receives an infusion of money income that prevents his purchases from falling as much as without compensation.

In panel (b), commodity Z is *inferior*, which causes the compensated demand curve to be *flatter* than the ordinary demand curve. Thus, without compensation, a reduction in the price of Z from p_2 to p_1 causes the quantity demanded to rise from z_1 to z_2. With compensation (i.e., with an appropriate *reduction* in the consumer's money income), the quantity demanded increases to z_3, because the adverse income effect $z_2 z_3$ is removed. Surely, for a price increase the opposite is true: The consumer is compensated with extra money income, which induces him to reduce further his purchases of inferior good Z.

5.3 Consumer Surplus

In this section we deal with the concept of consumer surplus, which was first used by Dupuit in 1844 to measure the social benefit of such goods as bridges, canals, and highways. The concept was refined and popularized by Alfred Marshall. We begin our discussion with the Marshallian approach within the context of the cardinal utility model. Later we use the tools of the indifference curve approach to refine further the concept of consumer surplus.

The Nature of Consumer Surplus

Because of the fundamental law of diminishing marginal utility, the total utility obtained by a consumer from the consumption of a commodity exceeds the utility of its market value, that is, the utility of what could be obtained instead with its market value given the prices of other goods. For instance, the total utility obtained from air is boundless even though its market value is zero.

The difference between total utility (benefit to the consumer) and utility of market value (cost to the consumer) is a *surplus* that accrues to the consumer. Marshall sought to determine the *monetary* value of this surplus, that is, how many dollars it is worth to the consumer. It is the monetary measure of the surplus that Marshall called *consumer surplus*.

Marshall assumed explicitly that the marginal utility of money (or income) is constant. Accordingly, we can convert Marshall's monetary measure of the surplus into a *surplus of utility* by merely multiplying it by the constant marginal utility of money.

To determine the consumer surplus, it is necessary to determine two things: (1) the *monetary measure of total utility* (i.e., the maximum benefit to the consumer in monetary terms) and (2) the market value (i.e., price times quantity). The Marshallian concept of consumer surplus is given by the difference between these two quantities.

The market value is, of course, easily determined. But what is the monetary value of total utility enjoyed by the consumer? It is the *maximum amount of money that the consumer is willing to pay than go without the commodity*. We show below how to determine this amount.

Graphical Illustration

Figure 5.8 illustrates Marshall's approach to consumer surplus. We assume that the current price is $1.00 and the consumer buys 5 units per week, as shown by point F. What is the consumer's surplus equal to?

To discover the consumer surplus, forget for the moment that the current price is $1.00. Instead, suppose that the price is initially set at $1.80 and then falls gradually to $1.00. When the price is $1.80, the consumer is willing to purchase only 1 unit per week (point B). This shows that the satisfaction or utility that she obtains from *the first unit is at least worth $1.80 to her*. When the price falls to $1.60, the consumer is willing to purchase a second unit (point C). This again means that *the second unit is at least worth $1.60* to her; otherwise, she would not buy it. Similarly, *the third unit is worth at least $1.40 to the consumer* (point D); *the fourth*

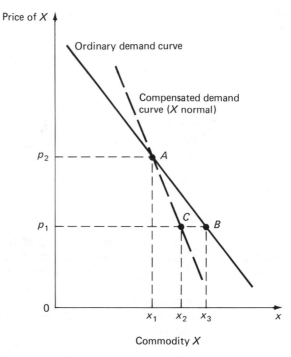

(a) Normal commodity

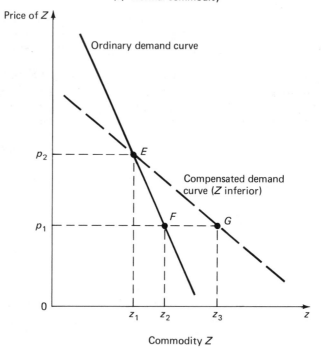

(b) Inferior commodity

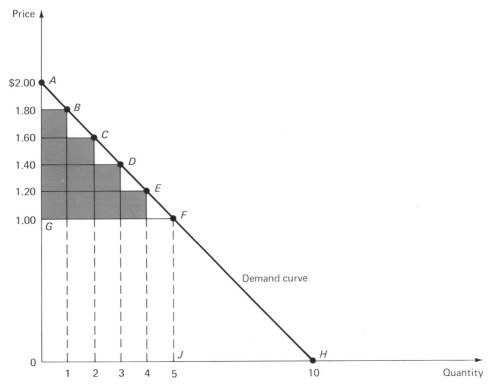

Figure 5.8 Consumer surplus. Each point on the demand curve shows the marginal valuation that the consumer places on the last unit he purchases. For instance, point B shows that the first unit is at least worth $1.80 to the consumer, point C shows that the second unit is at least worth $1.60, and so on. At the current price of $1, the consumer buys 5 units and derives a total benefit equal to the shaded area (i.e., $2.00), assuming that the commodity is indivisible. Given divisibility, however, the consumer surplus becomes equal to the entire triangular area AFG.

unit is worth at least $1.20 to her (point E); and finally, *the fifth unit is at least worth $1.00* to her (point F).

In general, we can interpret each point on the demand curve as showing the marginal valuation that the consumer places on the last unit demanded by her. Now recall that the current price is actually $1.00. Thus the consumer actually pays only $1.00 for each of the 5 units she purchases.

Table 5.2 summarizes the above information and shows the benefit (marginal valuation less price) derived by the consumer from each of the 5 units she purchases. Thus the consumer derives a benefit of at least $0.80 from the first unit, a benefit of at least $0.60 from the second unit, a benefit of at least $0.40 from the third unit,

---

Figure 5.7 Comparison between ordinary and compensated demand curves. Panel (a) illustrates the case of a normal commodity (X). The compensated demand curve (dashed line AC) is steeper than the ordinary demand curve (AB). Thus, as the price of X falls from p_2 to p_1, the quantity demanded (without compensation) increases from x_1 to x_3, and the consumer moves from A to B. With a reduction in money income that compensates for the price reduction, the quantity demanded increases to x_2 only (because X is normal), as the consumer moves from A to C. In panel (b), the compensated demand curve (EG) is flatter than the ordinary demand curve (EF) because commodity Z is inferior.

| Table 5.2 Consumer Surplus ||||
Units Consumed	Marginal Valuation	Price	Marginal Benefit
1	$1.80	$1.00	$0.80
2	1.60	1.00	0.60
3	1.40	1.00	0.40
4	1.20	1.00	0.20
5	1.00	1.00	0
		Total Consumer Surplus	$2.00

and a benefit of at least $0.20 from the fourth unit. The fifth unit is at least worth $1.00 to the consumer; by paying $1.00 for it, she does not become any worse off. The sum of these individual benefits (i.e., $0.80 + $0.60 + $0.40 + $0.20 = $2.00) is the consumer surplus, and it is shown in Figure 5.8 by the shaded area.

In other words, if the consumer had to pay a "fee" for the opportunity of entering a restricted market and buying as many units as she wished at the current price of $1.00 (such as a fee for joining a record club), she would be willing to pay a fee up to $2.00 (i.e., the consumer surplus).

The above example dealt with discrete units. We can generalize the analysis by assuming that the commodity is divisible. What is the total consumer surplus when the commodity is perfectly divisible? It is equal to the entire triangular area AFG. Thus the market value is given by the area of rectangle $0JFG$, and the maximum amount of money that the consumer is willing to pay for 5 units than go without the commodity altogether is given by the entire area $0JFA$. Accordingly, the consumer surplus is equal to the difference $0JFA - 0JFG = AFG$. Note that area AFG is equal to $2.50, which is larger than the $2.00 we obtained earlier.

Note that the consumer does not actually benefit at the expense of the seller(s). In a *voluntary* transaction, neither party loses! This important point must be stressed, because many people (including students of economics) often view trade as a process through which one party "exploits" another. To the extent that a transaction is voluntary, a person (buyer or seller) will not participate in it unless he or she expects to benefit from it. We return to this idea in Chapter 14.

An Application

To appreciate the significance of the concept of consumer surplus, consider a city of 1 million people who contemplate the construction of a bridge. To avoid the difficulty of interpersonal comparisons of utility, assume that all citizens have the same tastes and the same income. More specifically, assume that the demand curve depicted in Figure 5.8 shows each citizen's willingness to use the bridge. Along the horizontal (quantity) axis we now measure the number of times per week that a person would use the bridge, and along the vertical (price) axis, we measure the toll that the person will have to pay for each crossing. Suppose further that the costs of the bridge (i.e., depreciation, interest, and maintenance) are expected to be equal to the fixed amount of $8 per week per person, irrespective of the volume of traffic on the bridge.

Should the city build the bridge? On the face of it, it appears that the city should refuse to construct the bridge, because the maximum revenue that can be extracted from each citizen by means of tolls is only $5. (Total revenue is maximized at point F, where the elasticity of demand is unity, as the reader should be able to verify.) Thus if the city charged the revenue-maximizing toll of $1 per crossing, each person would cross the bridge five times per week, and the city would collect only $5 from each person. Accordingly, the city would have to provide a subsidy of $3 per person according to the formula: subsidy per person ($3) = cost per person ($8) − revenue per person ($5). However, even if the city taxed the entire consumer surplus of $2.50 away from each person, there would not be enough revenue for the financing of the subsidy. It therefore appears that the construction of the bridge is not in the best interests of the city. Or is it?

As it turns out, it would be foolish not to construct the bridge. Let the city finance the construction and maintenance of the bridge by raising $8.00 in taxes from each person. In return, the city can allow every citizen to use the bridge without any further charge (toll). Each citizen will then cross the bridge 10 times per week, since the toll per crossing is zero (point H). Each consumer's surplus is now given by the bigger triangular area $AH0$, which happens to be equal to $10. We therefore conclude that each citizen will enjoy a net benefit of $2; that is, consumer surplus ($10) − tax per person ($8) = net benefit per person ($2).

It is evident, then, that the concept of consumer surplus can be used to justify the development of a public project, such as a bridge or subway, where the price mechanism does not provide the correct signals.

Consumer Surplus and Compensating Variation in Income

We now turn to the indifference curve approach. Figure 5.9 illustrates how to measure the consumer surplus precisely. The consumer's money income is $0B$, and

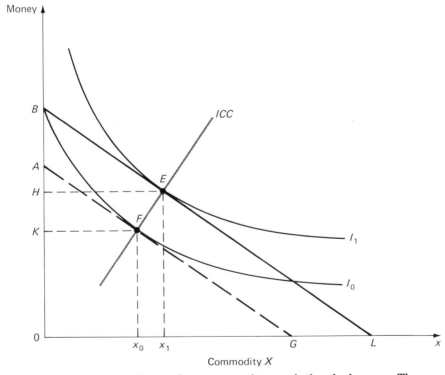

Figure 5.9 Consumer surplus and compensating variation in income. The consumer is at E, where budget line BL is tangent to I_1. He pays HB dollars for x_1 units of X. If he were unable to purchase X, he would be at B on lower indifference curve I_0. Accordingly, the consumer would be willing to pay a maximum amount of AB dollars (compensating variation in income) for the opportunity to purchase X at the current price. The amount AB is the consumer surplus.

the price of X is indicated by the slope of budget line BL. The consumer is at tangency E on indifference curve I_1, where he actually pays HB dollars for x_1 units of X. The opportunity to purchase X at the current price is beneficial to the consumer, because if he were unable to purchase X, he would be at B on lower indifference curve I_0. In fact, the consumer would be willing to pay something for this opportunity. How much? The compensating variation in income indicated by vertical distance AB. When AB dollars are taken away from the consumer, his budget line would shift from BL to parallel line AG, which touches indifference curve I_0 at F. We therefore conclude that vertical distance AB is the consumer surplus.

Observe that consumer surplus AB is equal to the difference between, KB and KA; that is, $AB = KB - KA$. Distance KA indicates the amount of money that the consumer actually pays for x_0 (not x_1) units of X; and distance KB corresponds to the maximum amount of money that the consumer would be willing to sacrifice for x_0 units of X (to move from B to F).

The Compensated Demand Curve and the Consumer Surplus

We mentioned above that we can measure the consumer surplus by the triangular area under the demand curve and above the commodity price. This procedure is accurate only when we use the compensated (*not* the ordinary) demand curve.

Return to Figure 5.9 and divide quantity x_0 that the consumer purchases at F into n equal parts, such as $\Delta x_1, \Delta x_2, \ldots, \Delta x_n$. Visualize the consumer at point B, and start offering him successively the various parts of x_0. For each successive part of x_0, the consumer is willing to give up a certain amount of money without becoming worse off, say ΔM_1 for Δx_1, ΔM_2 for $\Delta x_2, \ldots$, and ΔM_n for Δx_n. This is illustrated in Figure 5.10, which reproduces indifference curve I_0 from Figure 5.9. To avoid cluttering the diagram, the quantity x_0 is subdivided into four equal parts.

How much money is the consumer willing to pay for the entire quantity $x_0 = \Delta x_1 + \Delta x_2 + \Delta x_3 + \Delta x_4$ (and in general $x_0 = \Delta x_1 + \Delta x_2 + \cdots \Delta x_n$)? Obviously, the total amount must be $KB = \Delta M_1 + \Delta M_2 + \Delta M_3 + \Delta M_4$ (and in general $KB = \Delta M_1 + \Delta M_2 + \cdots + \Delta M_n$). How are the successive money quantities ΔM_1, $\Delta M_2, \ldots, \Delta M_n$ determined?

Recall that, in general, the marginal rate of substitution of x for money is equal to $MRS_{xM} = \Delta M/\Delta x$, where we assume that Δx is very, very small (and we also ignore the inherently negative sign); hence $\Delta M = MRS_{xM} \cdot \Delta x$. Accordingly, $\Delta M_1 = p_1 \cdot \Delta x_1$, where $p_1 = MRS_{xM}$ at point B. Similarly, $\Delta M_2 = p_2 \cdot \Delta x_2$, where $p_2 = MRS_{xM}$ at J; $\Delta M_3 = p_3 \cdot \Delta x_3$, where $p_3 = MRS_{xM}$ at H; and $\Delta M_4 = p_4 \cdot \Delta x_4$, where $p_4 = MRS_{xM}$ at N.

It should now be clear that the total amount of money that the consumer is willing to give up for x_0 without becoming worse off is equal to

$$KB = p_1 \Delta x_1 + p_2 \Delta x_2 + p_3 \Delta x_3 + p_4 \Delta x_4$$

and in general,

$$KB = p_1 \Delta x_1 + p_2 \Delta x_2 + \cdots + p_n \Delta x_n \qquad (5.3)$$

The accuracy of equation (5.3) depends, of course, on the assumption that the quantities Δx_i are very, very small.

Finally, recall that the marginal valuations $p_1, p_2, \ldots, p_n$ are the prices which are actually registered by the compensated demand curve that corresponds to indifference curve I_0, as illustrated in Figure 5.11. Accordingly, the sum ($p_1 \Delta x_1 + p_2 \Delta x_2 + \cdots + p_n \Delta x_n$) corresponds (in the limit) to area $0p_1F'x_0$. Since distance

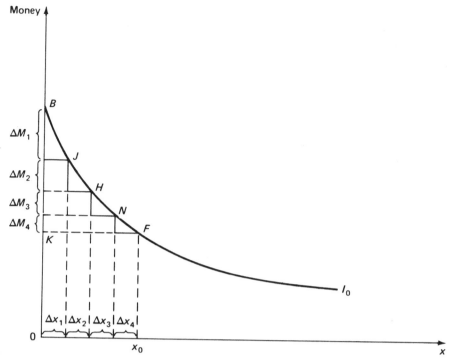

Figure 5.10 Determination of the amount of money that the consumer is willing to exchange for a given quantity of commodity X. Starting at B, the consumer is willing to give up ΔM_1 for Δx_1. Having arrived at J, the consumer is then willing to exchange ΔM_2 for Δx_2. At H, he is willing to give up ΔM_3 for Δx_3; and finally at N, he is willing to sacrifice ΔM_4 for Δx_4. Thus the consumer is willing to give up the total amount $KB = \Delta M_1 + \Delta M_2 + \Delta M_3 + \Delta M_4$ for $x_0 = \Delta x_1 + \Delta x_2 + \Delta x_3 + \Delta x_4$.

KA in Figure 5.9 (i.e., the amount of money that the consumer actually pays for x_0 units of X) corresponds to the area of rectangle $0p_nF'x_0$ (Figure 5.11), it follows that the consumer surplus is equal to shaded triangular area $p_1F'p_n$.

If we use the ordinary demand curve instead, our measurement will exceed the correct consumer surplus when X is normal (because then the ordinary demand curve originating at p_1 would lie to the right of the compensated demand curve); it will fall short of the exact consumer surplus when X is inferior (because then the ordinary demand curve would lie to the left of the compensated demand curve).

It is interesting to note that when commodity X is neutral, the income effect is zero and the ordinary and compensated demand curves coincide. In this limiting Marshallian case, it is immaterial which demand curve we use to measure the consumer surplus.

5.4 Index Numbers

In this section we deal with an important application of the theory of consumer behavior: the construction and interpretation of index numbers of price and quantity. Such index numbers are designed to mainly gauge the effect of inflation (deflation), that is, the overall rise (fall) in *money* prices of goods and services, on the standard of living (level of satisfaction, ordinal utility, or welfare) of consumers. For instance, during the last decade all countries of the world, without exception,

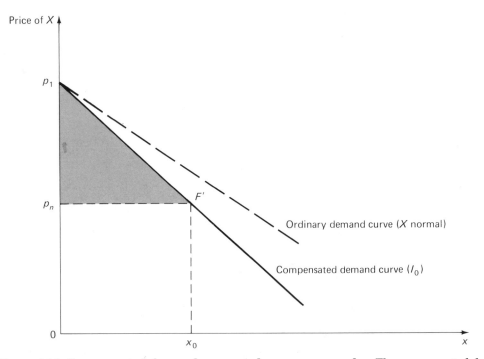

Figure 5.11 Compensated demand curve and consumer surplus. The compensated demand curve (p_1F') corresponds to indifference curve I_0 of Figure 5.9. Area $Op_1F'x_0$ (equivalent to vertical distance KB in Figure 5.9) shows the maximum amount of money that the consumer is willing to pay for x_0 units of X. On the other hand, the area of rectangle $Op_nF'x_0$ (equivalent to vertical distance KA in Figure 5.9) gives the amount of money that the consumer actually pays for x_0 units of X. Accordingly, shaded triangular area $p_1F'p_n$ (equivalent to vertical distance AB in Figure 5.9) corresponds to the consumer surplus.

experienced varying rates of inflation. Have wages kept up with the rising money prices? How did inflation affect the standard of living of a typical worker? Index numbers can shed some light on such questions.

In our society, index numbers are used for a variety of purposes: to adjust money wages and salaries, pensions, and welfare payments. They are even useful in adjusting the salaries of employees who are transferred to foreign countries. The most widely known index number in the United States is the Consumer Price Index, published each month by the Bureau of Labor Statistics.

The Ideal Price Index

We find it useful to begin our discussion with the construction of an *ideal price index* which, although not observable in empirical investigations, can serve as a standard of comparison for those index numbers that are actually constructed. Consider a consumer who in 1981 (base period) purchased 20 units of X and 50 units of Y at prices $p_x^1 = \$750$ and $p_y^1 = \$300$, respectively.[2] From this we immediately infer that the consumer's money income in 1981 was \$30,000 (i.e., money income = expenditure on commodities X and Y = $\$750 \times 20 + \$300 \times 50 =$

---

[2]Throughout our present discussion, we consistently use the numbers 1 and 2 either as superscripts or as subscripts to indicate the initial period (also known as the base period) and the current period, respectively.

$30,000). This information is summarized in Figure 5.12 by point Q_1, where budget line BL is tangent to indifference curve I_1.

Further suppose that in 1986 (current period) the prices of X and Y have risen to $p_x^2 = \$840$ and $p_y^2 = \$600$. By how much should the consumer's money income increase in 1986 so that she can maintain her 1981 standard of living (i.e., attain indifference curve I_1)? To answer this question, we must know the precise position and shape of indifference curve I_1, as in Figure 5.12. At the 1986 price ratio indicated by the slope of dashed line CD, the consumer must have enough money income (implied by CD) to be able to purchase commodity bundle G, which consists of 30 units of X and 30 units of Y. Accordingly, in 1986 the consumer will need a minimum income of \$43,200 (i.e., $\$840 \times 30 + \$600 \times 30 = \$43,200$). If the consumer's income actually rises above \$43,200, she will definitely be better off in 1986, but if it is less than \$43,200, she will definitely be worse off. Note that the movement from Q_1 to G represents a *pure substitution effect* because, by construction, the income effect of the change in prices is removed by a compensating variation in money income.

The ideal price index (ϕ) is defined as follows:

$$\phi \equiv \frac{\text{minimum income needed in current period}}{\text{income in base period}} = \frac{\$43,200}{\$30,000} = 1.44 \qquad (5.4)$$

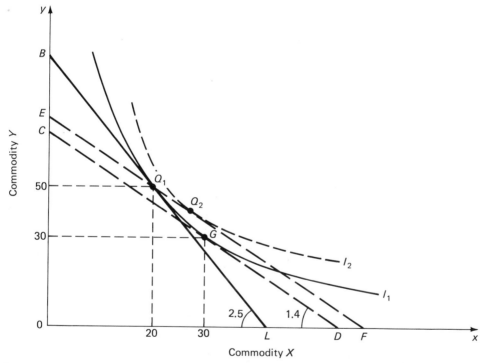

Figure 5.12 The ideal price index. In 1981 (base period), the consumer purchased 20 units of X and 50 units of Y at prices $p_x^1 = \$750$ and $p_y^1 = \$300$, respectively, as shown by point Q_1. From this information, we infer that in 1981 the consumer's income was \$30,000 (i.e., $\$750 \times 20 + \$300 \times 50$). In 1986 the two prices rise to $p_x^2 = \$840$ and $p_y^2 = \$600$, and the relative price of X falls, as shown by dashed line CD. To maintain her 1981 standard of living, her 1986 income must be at least as high as the cost of bundle G, where CD is tangent to I_1. Thus the consumer's income must rise to \$43,200 (i.e., $\$840 \times 30 + \$600 \times 30$). The ideal price index (ϕ) is given by the ratio \$43,200/\$30,000 = 1.44.

(or $\phi = 144$ percent, because price indexes are usually written as percentages). To determine whether the consumer is better off or worse off in 1986 relative to 1981, we simply compare the ideal price index, ϕ, to the *actual* income ratio (E), which is defined as follows:

$$E \equiv \frac{\text{actual income in current period}}{\text{actual income in base period}} \tag{5.5}$$

Obviously, the consumer is better off in the current period (1986) when $E > \phi$, and she is worse off when $E < \phi$. In the limiting case where $E = \phi$, the consumer's standard of living is exactly the same in the two periods. For instance, if in our illustration the consumer's income in 1986 is only \$42,000, we may conclude that she is worse off in 1986, because $E = \$42,000/\$30,000 = 1.4 < 1.44 = \phi$.

Several observations are now in order. First, the above analysis presupposes that the consumer's tastes (indifference curves) do not shift over the time period under consideration. This is a crucial assumption (and one that may not be valid in the real world, especially over long periods of time). We should always keep it in mind.

Second, the ideal price index is different from one person to another, because tastes differ between people (and income levels). We ignore this complication.

Finally, the ideal price index cannot be constructed until the precise shape of indifference curve I_1 is known. Since indifference curves are generally unknown, it follows that it is not possible empirically to construct an ideal price index (even for a single consumer). If this is so, can we actually construct any other indexes that may be reasonable approximations of the ideal price index? Indeed we can, as the remainder of this section shows.

The Laspeyres Price Index

Even though we do not know the exact shape and location of each indifference curve, we do know from direct observation what the consumer actually purchases in each period. As it turns out, this information is sufficient in most (but *not all*) cases to determine whether the consumer is better off in the current period relative to the base period, or vice versa.

Return to Figure 5.12. We do know that in 1981 the consumer is at Q_1. What we do not know is the precise shape of indifference curve I_1 and the exact location of point G. Suppose, however, that in 1986 the consumer has just enough income to purchase commodity bundle Q_1 (as illustrated by dashed budget line EF that passes through Q_1) but she actually buys bundle Q_2. Can we not then conclude that the consumer is better off in 1986? We certainly can, because in 1986 the consumer could choose Q_1 and be just as well off as in 1981. The sheer fact that she chooses Q_2 over Q_1 clearly indicates that she is actually better off.

It must be clear from Figure 5.12 that the cost of Q_1 at 1986 prices is *always* larger than the cost of G (also at 1986 prices), irrespective of how we actually draw indifference curve I_1. This becomes obvious when we notice that the marginal rate of substitution of X for Y at Q_1 (given by the slope of the 1981 budget line BL) must be larger than the relative price of X in 1986 (given by the slope of dashed line EF, which is parallel to CD). Accordingly, budget line EF *must intersect* convex indifference curve I_1 at Q_1 and lie above point G, as shown.

From the preceding comments it is clear that we can construct an index number, similar to the ideal price index, by merely replacing, in our earlier calculations, point G (which is unknown) by point Q_1 (which is known). That is, instead of determining the minimum income that will enable the consumer to attain indifference curve I_1 (whose precise shape is not known), we determine the minimum income that will permit the consumer to purchase bundle Q_1 at 1986 prices. With this substitution, we have the *Laspeyres price index* (L_p), named after Etienne Laspeyres (1834–1913), a nineteenth-century statistician. Thus we have

$$L_p = \frac{P_2 Q_1}{P_1 Q_1} > \phi \tag{5.6}$$

where $P_2 Q_1 = p_x^2 x_1 + p_y^2 y_1 = $ cost of $Q_1(x_1, y_1)$ at the current period's prices
          $P_1 Q_1 = p_x^1 x_1 + p_y^1 y_1 = $ income in base period

Because the cost of Q_1 is larger than the cost of G at current prices, it follows that $L_p > \phi$.

When the actual income ratio (E) equals or exceeds the Laspeyres price index (L_p), that is, when $E \geq L_p$, we can conclude that the consumer is unambiguously better off in the current period. But when the actual income ratio is less than the Laspeyres price index, we *cannot* conclude that the consumer is worse off in the current period. The main reason for this anomaly is that the Laspeyres price index is larger than the ideal price index ($L_p > \phi$), and we can conclude that the consumer is worse off in the current period only when the ideal price exceeds the actual income ratio ($\phi > E$). When $L_p > E$, we cannot exclude the possibility that $L_p > E > \phi$, in which case the consumer is actually better off in the current period. We therefore conclude that the inequality $E \geq L_p$ is a *sufficient* (but *not necessary*) condition for welfare improvement.

To illustrate this rule, suppose that in our original numerical example we learn that the consumer's money income in 1986 was actually $48,000. A quick calculation shows that $P_2 Q_1 = \$840 \times 20 + \$600 \times 50 = \$46,800$. Accordingly,

$$L_p = \frac{\$46,800}{\$30,000} = 1.56$$

$$E = \frac{\$48,000}{\$30,000} = 1.60$$

Since $E > L_p$, we must conclude that the consumer is better off in 1986.

The preceding analysis finds an important application in the cost-of-living adjustment to social security and welfare payments. These adjustments are tied to the Consumer Price Index, which is basically a Laspeyres price index. The objective of the adjustment, of course, is to permit the recipients to maintain their standard of living in the presence of inflation. Yet our analysis shows that such adjustments actually overcompensate the recipients, because the Consumer Price Index exceeds the ideal price index. Table 5.3 gives the Consumer Price Index from 1800 to 1982, using 1967 as the base year.

The economic implications of the Laspeyres price index are illustrated in Figure 5.13 (see p. 148). Assume that in 1981 the consumer purchases bundle Q_1 on budget line *BL*, and in 1986 she buys bundle Q_2 on budget line *EF*. The cost of Q_1 at 1986 prices is indicated by auxiliary line *CD*. Since *CD* lies closer to the origin than *EF*, it is evident that the consumer's income in 1986 is *larger* than the cost of Q_1 at 1986 prices. Accordingly, $E > L_p$, which means that the consumer is better off in 1986. Note that Q_1 lies inside budget line *EF*, which shows that Q_2 must be preferred to Q_1.

Alternatively, assume that the 1986 budget line is *GH* (instead of *EF*) and that the consumer actually purchases bundle Q_2' (instead of Q_2). Since *GH* lies inside *CD*, it follows that the 1986 income is less than the cost of Q_1 at 1986 prices. (Observe that Q_1 lies outside the 1986 attainable set, that is, area *0GH*.) Accordingly, $L_p >$

Table 5.3 Consumer Price Index, 1800–1982[a] (1967 = 100)					
Year	**CPI**	**Year**	**CPI**	**Year**	**CPI**
1800	51	1862	30	1924	51.2
1801	50	1863	37	1925	52.5
1802	43	1864	47	1926	53.0
1803	45	1865	46	1927	52.0
1804	45	1866	44	1928	51.3
1805	45	1867	42	1929	51.3
1806	47	1868	40	1930	50.0
1807	44	1869	40	1931	45.6
1808	48	1870	38	1932	40.9
1809	47	1871	36	1933	38.8
1810	47	1872	36	1934	40.1
1811	50	1873	36	1935	41.1
1812	51	1874	34	1936	41.5
1813	58	1875	33	1937	43.0
1814	63	1876	32	1938	42.2
1815	55	1877	32	1939	41.6
1816	51	1878	29	1940	42.0
1817	48	1879	28	1941	44.1
1818	46	1880	29	1942	48.8
1819	46	1881	29	1943	51.8
1820	42	1882	29	1944	52.7
1821	40	1883	28	1945	53.9
1822	40	1884	27	1946	58.5
1823	36	1885	27	1947	66.9
1824	33	1886	27	1948	72.1
1825	34	1887	27	1949	71.4
1826	34	1888	27	1950	72.1
1827	34	1889	27	1951	77.8
1828	33	1890	27	1952	79.5
1829	32	1891	27	1953	80.1
1830	32	1892	27	1954	80.5
1831	32	1893	27	1955	80.2
1832	30	1894	26	1956	81.4
1833	29	1895	25	1957	84.3
1834	30	1896	25	1958	86.6
1835	31	1897	25	1959	87.3
1836	33	1898	25	1960	88.7
1837	34	1899	25	1961	89.6
1838	32	1900	25	1962	90.6
1839	32	1901	25	1963	91.7
1840	30	1902	26	1964	92.9
1841	31	1903	27	1965	94.5
1842	29	1904	27	1966	97.2
1843	28	1905	27	1967	100.0
1844	28	1906	27	1968	104.2
1845	28	1907	28	1969	109.8
1846	27	1908	27	1970	116.3
1847	28	1909	27	1971	121.3

(*continued on the following page*)

Table 5.3 (Continued)					
Year	**CPI**	**Year**	**CPI**	**Year**	**CPI**
1848	26	1910	28	1972	125.3
1849	25	1911	28	1973	133.1
1850	25	1912	29	1974	147.7
1851	25	1913	29.7	1975	161.2
1852	25	1914	30.1	1976	170.5
1853	25	1915	30.4	1977	181.5
1854	27	1916	32.7	.	.
1855	28	1917	38.4	.	.
1856	27	1918	45.1	.	.
1857	28	1919	51.8	1978	195.4
1858	26	1920	60.0	1979	217.4
1859	27	1921	53.6	1980	246.8
1860	27	1922	50.2	1981	272.4
1861	27	1923	51.1	1982	289.1

Sources: Handbook of Labor Statistics 1978, Bulletin 2000, Table 116, U.S. Department of Labor, Bureau of Labor Statistics, Washington, D.C., 1979; *Handbook of Labor Statistics 1983,* Table 110, U.S. Department of Labor, Bureau of Labor Statistics, Washington, D.C. 1984.

[a]For the years 1978–1982 the numbers indicated refer to the CPI for all urban consumers.

E. Is the consumer worse off in 1986? We cannot tell. The indifference curve through Q_1 could pass above, below, or right through Q_2'.

Finally, note that the sufficient condition for welfare improvement ($E \geq L_p$) can be cast in the following equivalent forms:

$$\frac{P_2 Q_2}{L_p} \geq P_1 Q_1 \tag{5.7}$$

$$P_2 Q_2 \geq P_1 Q_1 \cdot L_p \tag{5.8}$$

Inequality (5.7) states that the consumer is unambiguously better off in the current period when her *current income (P_2Q_2), corrected (divided) by the Laspeyres price index, equals or exceeds her income in the base period (P_1Q_1).* Similarly, inequality (5.8) states that the consumer is unambiguously better off in the current period when her current income (P_2Q_2) equals or exceeds the base period income corrected (multiplied) by the Laspeyres price index ($P_1Q_1 \cdot L_p$).

The Paasche Price Index

The Laspeyres price index leads to a sufficient condition ($E \geq L_p$) for welfare improvement. But it cannot tell us when the consumer is actually worse off in the current period. Can we construct another price index that will give us this important information? We most certainly can.

Consider Figure 5.14, which is similar to Figure 5.13 except for the location of Q_1 and Q_2 (and the auxiliary budget line). The commodity bundle chosen in the current period (Q_2) lies totally inside the budget line of the base period (*BL*). Accordingly, the consumer could have chosen Q_2 in the base period, but she actually chose Q_1 instead. This choice reveals that Q_1 is preferred to Q_2. We therefore conclude that the consumer is unambiguously worse off in the current period.

The crucial element in the foregoing conclusion is the assumption that Q_2 is available to the consumer in the base period. In other words, the cost of Q_2 at base

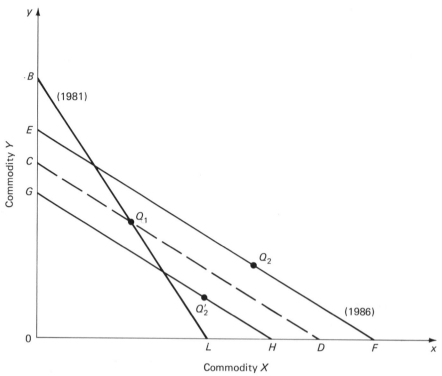

Figure 5.13 The Laspeyres price index. In 1981 the consumer purchases bundle Q_1 on budget line *BL,* and in 1986 she buys bundle Q_2 on budget line *EF.* The cost of Q_1 at 1986 prices is indicated by auxiliary line *CD,* which is parallel to *EF.* Because *CD* lies inside *EF,* the 1986 income is larger than the cost of Q_1 at 1986 prices. Thus the actual income ratio is higher than the Laspeyres price index, which means that the consumer is better off in 1986. That this is so follows also from the fact that Q_1 lies inside *EF.* Alternatively, if the 1986 budget line is *GH* and the consumer purchases bundle Q_2', we cannot tell whether she is better off in 1986.

period's prices did not exceed the consumer's income in the base period; that is,

$$P_1Q_2 \leq P_1Q_1 \tag{5.9}$$

(Strict equality holds when Q_2 coincides with *S*, that is, the point of intersection between the two budget lines.) This is illustrated in Figure 5.14 by the fact that dashed line *CD* (which corresponds to the cost of Q_2 at base period's prices) lies inside budget line *BL.*

We can now construct the *Paasche price index* (P_p), named after French statistician Hermann Paasche (1851–1925), as follows:

$$P_p \equiv \frac{P_2Q_2}{P_1Q_2} \tag{5.10}$$

The Paasche price index is similar to the Laspeyres price index, except that Paasche uses the current period's quantities (Q_2) as weights.

Note that inequality (5.9) is equivalent to

$$\frac{1}{P_1Q_2} \geq \frac{1}{P_1Q_1}$$

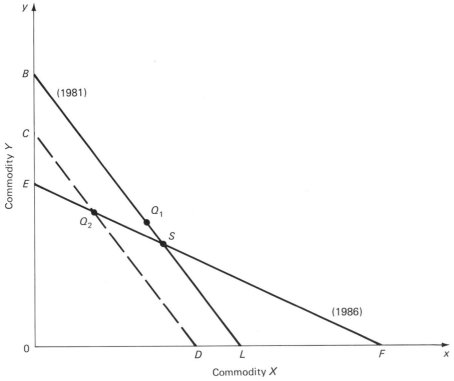

Figure 5.14 The Paasche price index. In 1981, the consumer chooses Q_1 on budget line *BL*, and in 1986 she chooses Q_2 on budget line *EF*. Since Q_2 lies in the 1981 attainable set (i.e., area *OBL*), the consumer is unambiguously worse off in 1986. Because the consumer could have chosen Q_2 in 1981 but chose Q_1 instead, it follows that Q_1 is preferred to Q_2.

or

$$\frac{P_2Q_2}{P_1Q_2} \geq \frac{P_2Q_2}{P_1Q_1} \tag{5.11}$$

or

$$\mathrm{P}_p \geq E$$

We therefore conclude that the consumer is unambiguously worse off in the current period when the Paasche price index equals or exceeds the actual income ratio (E). Inequality (5.11) can also be cast in the following equivalent forms:

$$P_1Q_1 \geq \frac{P_2Q_2}{\mathrm{P}_p} \tag{5.12}$$

$$P_1Q_1 \cdot \mathrm{P}_p \geq P_2Q_2 \tag{5.13}$$

Inequality (5.12) states that the consumer is unambiguously worse off in the current period when current income, corrected (divided) by the Paasche price index is less than, or equal to, the base period income. Similarly, inequality (5.13) declares that the consumer is unambiguously worse off in the current period when current income is less than, or equal to, base period income corrected (multiplied) by the Paasche price index.

Consider again the earlier numerical example. In the base period (1981), a consumer purchases 20 units of X and 50 units of Y at prices $p_x^1 = \$750$ and $p_y^1 = \$300$, respectively. Suppose that in the current period (1986) the same consumer purchases 23 units of X and 37 units of Y at prices $p_x^2 = \$840$ and $p_y^2 = \$600$, respectively. The consumer's income is \$30,000 in 1981 (i.e., $P_1Q_1 = \$750 \times 20 + \$300 \times 50$), and \$41,520 in 1986 (i.e., $P_2Q_2 = \$840 \times 23 + \$600 \times 37$). Similarly, the cost of Q_2 at 1981 prices is \$28,350 (i.e., $P_1Q_2 = \$750 \times 23 + \$300 \times 37$). Accordingly,

$$P_p = \frac{\$41,520}{\$28,350} = 1.465$$

$$E = \frac{\$41,520}{\$30,000} = 1.384$$

Since $P_p > E$, we must conclude that the consumer is worse off in 1986 than in 1981.

Again, the condition $P_p \geq E$ is *sufficient* (but not necessary) for a deterioration in the consumer's welfare. That is, E may be larger than $P_p(E > P_p)$, yet the consumer may still become worse off. This is illustrated in Figure 5.15, which is similar to

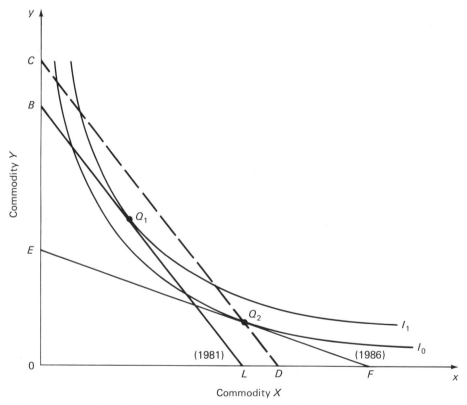

Figure 5.15 Ambiguity of the Paasche price index. Auxiliary budget line CD (through Q_2) lies beyond the 1981 budget line (BL). Thus the consumer's 1981 income is less than the cost of Q_2 at 1981 prices, which implies that the Paasche price index is less than the actual income ratio. Yet the consumer is worse off in 1986, as indicated by the fact that Q_2 lies on a lower indifference curve than Q_1.

Figure 5.14. Note that auxiliary budget line *CD* (through Q_2) lies beyond base period budget line *BL*. Thus the consumer's income in 1981 is less than the cost of Q_2 at 1981 prices, which implies that $P_p < E$. Yet Q_2 lies on a lower indifference curve than Q_1.

The Zone of Ignorance

Both the condition for welfare improvement ($E \geq L_p$) and the condition for welfare deterioration ($P_p \geq E$) are only *sufficient,* not necessary. Consequently, there is always a zone of ignorance (or ambiguity) defined by the following inequalities:

$$P_p < E < L_p \tag{5.14}$$

When the actual income ratio is less than the Laspeyres price index and higher than the Paasche price index, we are in the dark. We do not have enough information to determine whether the consumer is better off or worse off in the current period. This inherent ambiguity in the Laspeyres and Paasche indexes is illustrated in Figure 5.16.

Obviously, the consumer could not afford bundle Q_2 in 1981, because Q_2 lies outside the 1981 attainable set (0*BL*). Hence the 1981 money income is less than the cost of Q_2 at 1981 prices (i.e., $P_1Q_1 < P_1Q_2$), which leads to $P_p < E$. Similarly,

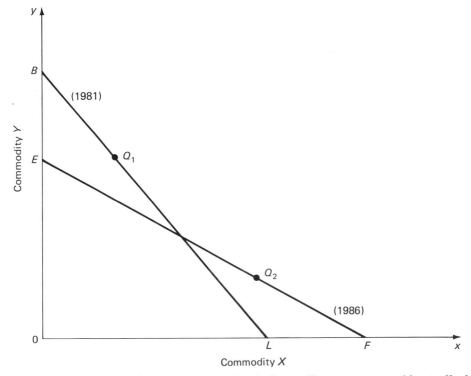

Figure 5.16 The inherent ambiguity of price indexes. The consumer could not afford Q_2 in 1981 because Q_2 lies beyond the 1981 budget line (*BL*). This implies that the Paasche price index is less than the actual income ratio, which is *not* sufficient to conclude that the consumer is worse off in 1986. Similarly, the consumer could not afford Q_1 in 1986, because Q_1 lies beyond the 1986 budget line (*EF*). This implies that the Laspeyres price index is higher than the actual income ratio, which is *not* sufficient to conclude that the consumer is better off in 1986. In this case, we are in the dark. The indifference curve through Q_1 could be drawn to pass above, below, or through point Q_2.

the consumer cannot afford Q_1 in 1986 because Q_1 lies beyond the 1986 budget line, *EF*. Consequently, the cost of Q_1 at 1986 prices exceeds the 1986 money income (i.e., $P_2Q_1 > P_2Q_2$), and this implies that $E < L_p$. We must therefore conclude that the consumer could be either better off or worse off in 1986 than in 1981. This ambiguity is actually confirmed by the fact that the indifference curve through Q_1 could be drawn to pass either above or below (or even coincide with) the indifference curve through Q_2 (without violating any fundamental properties), as the reader should be able to verify.

Index Numbers of Quantity

In addition to the price indexes that we considered above, there are also corresponding quantity indexes. There is no need to discuss the quantity indexes at any length, because they are related to the price indexes. For our purposes it is sufficient to show how they are defined, how they are related to the price indexes, and how the inequalities $E \geq L_p$ and $P_p \geq E$ can be cast in terms of them.

The *Laspeyres quantity index* (L_q) is defined as follows:

$$L_q = \frac{P_1Q_2}{P_1Q_1} \tag{5.15}$$

Similarly, the *Paasche quantity index* (P_q) is defined by

$$P_q = \frac{P_2Q_2}{P_2Q_1} \tag{5.16}$$

Both quantity indexes are attempts to find out whether the consumer actually purchases a larger "quantity" of commodities in the current period than in the base period. To convert a heterogeneous collection of commodities into a homogeneous entity, we use prices as weights. The Laspeyres quantity index uses the base period's prices as weights; the Paasche quantity index employs the prices of the current period as weights.

As it turns out, there exists the following fundamental identity among the price and quantity indexes and the actual income ratio:

$$L_p \cdot P_q = E = L_q \cdot P_p \tag{5.17}$$

The proof of this identity is straightforward. Substituting directly from the definitions of the various indexes, as given by equations (5.5), (5.6), (5.10), (5.15), and (5.16), we have

$$L_p \cdot P_q = \frac{P_2Q_1}{P_1Q_1}\frac{P_2Q_2}{P_2Q_1} = \frac{P_2Q_2}{P_1Q_1} = E$$

$$L_q \cdot P_p = \frac{P_1Q_2}{P_1Q_1}\frac{P_2Q_2}{P_1Q_2} = \frac{P_2Q_2}{P_1Q_1} = E$$

Obviously, the condition for welfare improvement $(E \geq L_p)$ is equivalent to

$$P_q \geq 1 \tag{5.18}$$

Similarly, the condition for welfare deterioration $(P_p \geq E)$ is equivalent to

$$L_q \leq 1 \tag{5.19}$$

Finally, the zone of ignorance is defined by the inequalities

$$P_q < 1 < L_q \tag{5.20}$$

5.5 The Mitchell–Lama Middle-Income Housing Program[3]

The Mitchell–Lama middle-income housing program was established by the New York State Limited Profit Companies Law (enacted in 1955). It involves the construction or rehabilitation of cooperative or rental housing by private developers (sponsors). The developers provide only 10 percent of the project cost (equity investment); New York City finances the rest of the project cost by means of low-interest, long-term mortgage loans. (When the project was planned, it was also eligible for exemption from real estate taxes.) Project construction and management are subject to public supervision. Tenant eligibility is determined by income and family size. In 1968 there were 123 projects providing subsidized housing to 57,000 households at a construction cost of slightly over $1 billion, which comes to approximately $17,500 per unit—a bargain in 1968.

How can we evaluate the success of the Mitchell–Lama program? Figure 5.17 illustrates the case of a typical household (consumer). We measure housing services h horizontally, and money M ("all other goods") vertically. Under free-market conditions, the consumer is at E_0, where budget line BL_0 is tangent to indifference curve I_0. Given his money income of $0B$, the consumer purchases h_0 units of housing at the market rental (slope of BL_0).

Suppose now that the government subsidizes housing. In particular, assume that the consumer is allowed to buy housing services at the lower rental indicated by the slope of line BL_1. As a result, he moves to E_1, where new budget line BL_1 is tangent to higher indifference curve I_1. What is the cost of the subsidy to the government? To purchase bundle E_1 at market prices, the consumer must have an income equal to $0C$, as indicated by solid budget line CD, which is parallel to BL_0 and passes through E_1. Accordingly, the cost of the subsidy to the government must be equal to BC, because the market value of E_1 (that is, $0C$) exceeds the consumer's income ($0B$) by BC.

What is the subsidy worth to the consumer in terms of money? In other words, how much money must the government give to the consumer, instead of granting him the subsidy, so that he can attain indifference curve I_1? This cash equivalent (or equivalent variation in income) is shown by BM; for when the consumer's income increases by BM, he can afford to pay the market rental and still attain indifference curve I_1, as shown by the tangency at W between line MS (which is parallel to BL_0) and indifference curve I_1. We must therefore conclude that the consumer's net benefit is equal to BM, which is less than the cost to the government (BC).

Nevertheless, the consumer does not ordinarily have the freedom to purchase as much subsidized housing as he wishes. The consumer may be restricted to a housing unit chosen by someone else. For instance, the consumer may be offered h' (instead of h_1) units of housing on a take-it-or-leave-it-basis. Since h' puts him at E' (on budget line BL_1), which lies on higher indifference curve I' (relative to I_0), we assume that the consumer accepts the offer. But now the consumer's benefit is reduced to BN, and the cost to the government is increased to BQ. (BN and BQ are determined in the same way as were BM and BC, respectively.)

The reduction in the consumer's benefit follows a general principle: *An in-kind income transfer (or subsidy) can never have a higher value to the recipient than an equivalent money transfer.* This important principle was discussed in Chapter 4.

In summary, at E' the consumer purchases h' units of housing whose market

[3]This section is based on DeSalvo (1975).

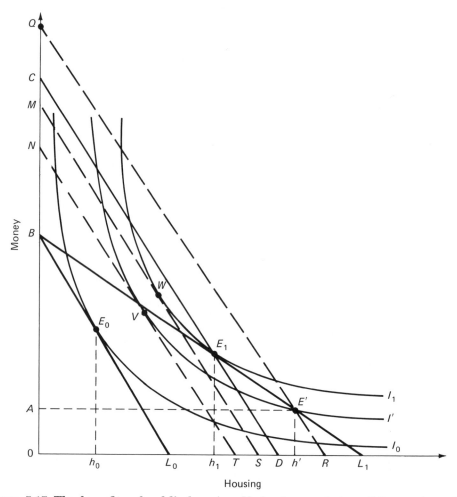

Figure 5.17 The benefits of public housing. Under free-market conditions, a household is at E_0, where budget line BL_0 is tangent to I_0. A government subsidy causes BL_0 to rotate to BL_1; and equilibrium moves to E_1. The cash equivalent to the subsidy is BM, but the cost to the government is BC. When the consumer is restricted to E' on BL_1, the consumer's net benefit falls to BN. At E' the consumer pays a rent of AB, while the market value of h' of housing is AQ. The difference $AQ - AB - BN = NQ$ is a deadweight loss that must be accounted for by other nontenant benefits.

value (and thus resource cost) is AQ. (By construction, QR is parallel to BL_0.) The rent that the consumer pays is only AB, while his net benefit is BN. Apparently, there is a deadweight loss equal to NQ, which must be accounted for by other nontenant benefits, such as the elimination of slums, the revival of downtown business areas, and the mitigation of poverty.

DeSalvo (1975) estimates that in 1968 the households that occupied the 57,000 subsidized dwellings of New York City paid total rents of $84 million, or $1476 per unit, and received net benefits of $25.6 million, or $450 per unit. The public subsidy amounted to $46.9 million, or $824 per unit.[4] This means that the total deadweight loss was $21.3 million (i.e., $46.9 − $25.6 million), or $374 per unit (i.e., $824 −

---

[4]For his estimates, DeSalvo (1975) uses the Cobb–Douglas utility function, $U = h^\beta x^{1-\beta}$, where h is the flow of housing services, x is all other goods, and $0 < \beta < 1$.

$450). DeSalvo (1975, p. 804) concludes that "rather substantial nontenant benefits ... would have had to be generated by the program for it to be considered an efficient use of resources in 1968." Unfortunately, DeSalvo could not make an estimate of nontenant benefits.

5.6 Behavior Under Uncertainty[5]

In our discussion so far, we have implicitly assumed that the individual consumer lives in a world of complete certainty and thus has perfect knowledge of the consequences of his or her decisions. Yet risk and uncertainty are fundamental characteristics of the real world. To bring our theory closer to reality, we discuss in this section the problem of decision making under uncertainty. This logical extension of the theory of consumer behavior to situations involving uncertainty has been largely accomplished during the last four decades.

Objective Versus Subjective Probability

We begin our discussion by considering the concept of probability. When we toss a coin, there are only two possible outcomes: heads or tails. What is the probability that heads will turn up? If the coin is unbiased (or ideal), the probability of heads must be $\frac{1}{2}$. What does this mean? Simply this: If the coin is tossed a large number of times, heads will appear in approximately one-half of the trials. Similarly, when we roll an unbiased die, the probability that a 4 will appear is $\frac{1}{6}$, because if we throw the die a large number of times a 4 will appear approximately one-sixth of the trials.

We therefore define the *probability* of an outcome to be *the limit of the relative frequency with which it occurs when the same experiment is repeated for an unlimited number of times.* Accordingly, the probability of an outcome is always given by a positive fraction (i.e., a number between 0 and 1). Two limiting cases are worth noting. First, the probability of an *impossible* outcome (i.e., an outcome that never occurs) is zero. For instance, the probability of immortality is zero. Second, the probability of a certain outcome is 1. For example, the probability of death is 1.

Consider now an experiment (such as rolling a die). Suppose that the outcome of this experiment can be one of several "simple" events: $E_1, E_2, \ldots, E_n$. These events are called *mutually exclusive* when the occurrence of any one of them precludes the occurrence of all others; they are called *collectively exhaustive* if the list of events exhausts all possible outcomes, that is, one of these events must occur on every trial. For instance, when we roll a die the outcome must be one of the following six: 1, 2, 3, 4, 5, or 6, and when, say, a 4 occurs, it is not possible for any other number to appear as well. Accordingly, the events (1, 2, 3, 4, 5, 6) are mutually exclusive and collectively exhaustive. As it turns out, the sum of the probabilities of a set of mutually exclusive and collectively exhaustive events must be 1 and reflects the fact that when the experiment is performed, one, and only one, of these events must always occur. For instance, in the case of an unbiased die, the sum of the probabilities of the set (1, 2, 3, 4, 5, 6) is equal to $\frac{1}{6} + \frac{1}{6} + \frac{1}{6} + \frac{1}{6} + \frac{1}{6} + \frac{1}{6} = 1$.

Economic phenomena are not quite as precise as the tossing of a coin or the rolling of a die. Typically, the decision maker cannot perform the experiment a large number of times before making a decision. Indeed, in many situations the decision maker may not be able to perform the experiment at all. As a result, economists use the concept of *subjective (or personal) probability,* which corresponds to the *beliefs* of the decision maker as to the likelihood of the different outcomes.

---

[5]This section may be read together with Section A5.3 of the Appendix to Chapter 5.

For instance, the subjective probability that a 4 will appear on a single roll of a die reflects the beliefs of the decision maker and could be very different from the corresponding objective probability. As it turns out, the behavior of a decision maker under uncertainty depends on what he or she actually regards as the probabilities of the various outcomes. Subjective probabilities have the same properties as objective probabilities.

Frank Knight (1885–1972) introduced the distinction between risk and uncertainty. Risk, according to Knight, refers to situations in which the probabilities of all possible outcomes are known in advance. For instance, the probability of winning the first prize of the New York state lottery can be calculated precisely. Uncertainty, on the other hand, refers to situations in which the probabilities of all possible outcomes are completely unknown or are not even meaningful. For instance, what is the probability that a cure for cancer can be found by 1990? Knight's distinction between risk and uncertainty has proved sterile. All decision makers must somehow assign probabilities to the possible outcomes of their actions, and it makes no difference whether these probabilities are *objective* (as in Knightian risk) or *subjective* (as in Knightian uncertainty). In this book we ignore Knight's distinction between risk and uncertainty.

The Neumann–Morgenstern Index

In the course of their work on game theory, John von Neumann and Oskar Morgenstern (1947) developed a utility index that can be used to predict the choices of an individual consumer in situations involving risk. Initially, the Neumann–Morgenstern index appeared to many economists to have "cardinal" properties. As it turned out, however, the Neumann–Morgenstern index has nothing in common with the neoclassical concept of cardinal utility. This subsection reviews briefly the Neumann–Morgenstern theory.

The essential idea of the Neumann–Morgenstern theory can be explained by means of a simple illustration. Return to the traveling salesman of Chapter 3. When we left him, he was in Atlanta trying to choose a restaurant. We know that he prefers restaurant a to restaurant b, restaurant b to restaurant c, and (by transivity) restaurant a to restaurant c. If the salesman were absolutely sure (as he was in Chapter 3) that each of the three restaurants would accommodate him, he would choose the most highly ranked restaurant, that is, a. Suppose, however, that the salesman is told that he can either have dinner at restaurant b for certain, or he can alternatively accept a gamble with dinner at restaurant a or dinner at restaurant c as the outcome. What will his choice be?

It is intuitively obvious that if the probability of winning dinner at restaurant a is sufficiently high, the salesman will probably accept the gamble. On the other hand, if the probability of winning dinner at restaurant c is very high, it is likely that the salesman will choose the certain option: dinner at restaurant b. Accordingly, as the probability of winning dinner at restaurant a is allowed to vary continuously from 1 to 0 (and thus the probability of winning dinner at restaurant c varies from 0 to 1, since the sum of these two probabilities must be equal to 1), the salesman's preference for the gamble must change into a preference for the certain option (dinner at restaurant b). It seems reasonable to assume that at a critical value of the probability of winning dinner at restaurant a, the salesman becomes indifferent between a certain dinner at restaurant b and the gamble whose outcome can be either dinner at restaurant a or dinner at restaurant c. For concreteness, assume that the gamble becomes equivalent to the certain option (dinner at restaurant b) when the probability of winning dinner at restaurant a assumes the critical value of $\Pi = \frac{3}{4}$ (and thus the corresponding probability of winning dinner at restaurant c is $1 - \Pi = \frac{1}{4}$).

We are now ready to construct the Neumann–Morgenstern index. We may recall from Chapter 3 that the salesman's ranking of restaurants a, b, or c can be represented by three *arbitrary* numbers that satisfy the inequalities: $U(a) > U(b) > U(c)$, where $U(a)$ = ordinal utility of a, $U(b)$ = ordinal utility of b, and $U(c)$ = ordinal utility of c. In the present context of uncertainty, however, once we arbitrarily choose two of the three numbers, the third is perfectly determined.

Suppose that we assign arbitrary utility numbers to a (the *most preferred* restaurant) and c (the *least preferred* restaurant). In particular, it is convenient to assume that

$$U(a) = 1$$
$$U(c) = 0 \tag{5.21}$$

even though any other pair of numbers is acceptable provided only that $U(a) > U(c)$. What utility number should we assign to b? The Neumann–Morgenstern convention is to assign the *expected utility* of the gamble, which is indifferent to the certain option (b). This expected utility is merely a *weighted average* of $U(a)$ and $U(c)$, where the weights are the probabilities of winning a and c, respectively, in the equivalent gamble. Accordingly,

$$
\begin{aligned}
U(b) &= \text{expected utility of equivalent gamble} \\
&= \Pi \cdot U(a) + (1 - \Pi) \cdot U(c) \\
&= \Pi \cdot 1 + (1 - \Pi) \cdot 0 \\
&= \Pi \\
&= \tfrac{3}{4}
\end{aligned}
\tag{5.22}
$$

Because of the judicious choice of the utility numbers we assigned to a and c, the utility number we attach to b is merely the probability of winning a in the equivalent gamble.

The above procedure can be easily generalized. Suppose that there are n bundles of commodities $(B_1, B_2, \ldots, B_n)$, and a consumer reveals to us that she prefers B_1 to B_2, B_2 to B_3, $\ldots$, and B_{n-1} to B_n. We want to assign utility numbers to these bundles. First, we arbitrarily assign a utility of 1 to B_1, and a utility of 0 to B_n; that is, we arbitrarily set $U(B_1) = 1$ and $U(B_n) = 0$. To all other commodity bundles, we assign the expected utility of equivalent gambles. For instance, to assign a utility number to B_i, we ask the consumer to tell us at what probability (say Π_i) he would be indifferent between B_i with certainty and a gamble whose outcome is either B_1 with probability Π_i or B_n with probability $(1 - \Pi_i)$. As before, the expected utility of the equivalent gamble coincides with Π_i, that is, the probability of winning B_1 in the equivalent gamble. In this way we can assign a utility number to every commodity bundle.

Note that the Neumann–Morgenstern utility index is unique only up to a "linear transformation," that is, up to a choice of origin and scale. Thus once we arbitrarily assign numbers to *two* commodity bundles (say, B_1 and B_n), the Neumann–Morgenstern method determines the remaining utility numbers uniquely. But for each arbitrary assignment of utility numbers to B_1 and B_n, we obtain, of course, a different *set* of utility numbers, and all such sets of utility numbers are linear transformations of each other. This problem is similar to the selection of temperature scales (Celsius, Fahrenheit, Kelvin).

Note also that the requirement that the Neumann–Morgenstern utility index be unique up to a *linear* transformation is much more stringent than the requirement (discussed in Chapter 3 and its appendix) that an ordinal utility function be unique up to a *monotonic* transformation.

In the Appendix to Chapter 5 we prove the basic Neumann–Morgenstern theorem according to which the Neumann–Morgenstern index can be used to rank gambles consistently and that rational persons seek to maximize their expected utility.

The Neumann–Morgenstern Index Versus Cardinal Utility

Turn now briefly to the question of whether the Neumann–Morgenstern utility index is equivalent to the neoclassical notion of cardinal utility. Return again to the example of the traveling salesman. We concluded above that on the basis of the Neumann–Morgenstern approach, the salesman attaches the utility numbers, 1, $\frac{3}{4}$, and 0 to restaurants a, b, and c, respectively. The numerical difference between the utility assigned to b and c (i.e., $\frac{3}{4} - 0 = \frac{3}{4}$) is *three times* that between a and b (i.e., $1 - \frac{3}{4} = \frac{1}{4}$). This is true for any initial choice of $U(a)$ and $U(c)$, as the reader should be able to show. [For instance, the numbers 200, 180, and 120 can also represent the ranking of a, b, and c, respectively, provided by the Neumann–Morgenstern approach because $180 - 120 = 3(200 - 180)$.] Accordingly, numerical differences between utility numbers assume now significance, and comparisons among them appear meaningful, as in the neoclassical model of cardinal utility.

Does the preceding conclusion mean that the Neumann–Morgenstern index rescues the concept of cardinal utility? Unfortunately, this is not the case. For one thing, the Neumann–Morgenstern index reveals nothing about the quantities of pleasure or satisfaction derived by the salesman (or consumer). We cannot assert that the salesman actually experiences 1 util of pleasure from having dinner at restaurant a. For another thing, the Neumann–Morgenstern index is constructed by asking the consumer to choose among risky alternatives, and thus *reflects the consumer's attitudes toward gambling*, not his evaluation of certain outcomes. For instance, if the salesman likes to take chances, he may be willing to accept a gamble in which the probability of having dinner at restaurant a is only $\frac{1}{5}$ instead of choosing the certain option (restaurant b). If the salesman dislikes gambling, he may choose restaurant b even when he is alternatively offered a gamble in which the probability of having dinner at restaurant a is $\frac{9}{10}$.

Luce and Raiffa (1957, p. 22) put the matter as follows: "The subject's preferences among alternatives and lotteries came prior to our numerical characterization of them. We do not want to slip into saying that he preferred A to B because A has the higher utility; rather, because A is preferred to B, we assign A the higher utility."

Fair Games and the St. Petersburg Paradox

In our discussion of the Neumann–Morgenstern theory, we used a rather general utility function. For the rest of this section we simplify our discussion by assuming that the consumer focuses her attention on one single variable—her money income (or wealth measured in monetary units). Accordingly, the utility index depends on the consumer's income and nothing else.

Suppose that the consumer is offered a gamble in which she has an even chance of winning or losing $100. The *expected value* of the gamble is simply the weighted average of the payoffs, where the weights are the respective probabilities. Thus the expected value of the present gamble is zero: $\frac{1}{2} \times 100 + \frac{1}{2} \times (-100) = 0$. A gamble whose expected value is zero (or, in general, one that costs its expected value for the right to play) is called a *fair game*.

Generally speaking, rational people tend to avoid fair games. This proposition is dramatized by the "St. Petersburg paradox," which was initially posed by Nicholas Bernoulli (who was interested in the operation of the gambling casinos of St. Petersburg). The major figure in the paradox is, however, Daniel Bernoulli (1700–1782), who actually solved it.

Table 5.4 The Bernoulli Game			
(1) Number of Trials	(2) Probability	(3) Payoff	(4) Expected Value
1	$\frac{1}{2}$	$ 2	$1
2	$\frac{1}{4}$	4	1
3	$\frac{1}{8}$	8	1
4	$\frac{1}{16}$	16	1
5	$\frac{1}{32}$	32	1
.	.	.	.
.	.	.	.
.	.	.	.
			$\overline{\$\infty}$

What is the St. Petersburg paradox? Consider a game in which an unbiased coin is tossed until heads first appears. The player is paid $\$2^n$ if heads appears on the nth trial. Evidently, this game has an infinite number of outcomes, which are summarized in Table 5.4. Column (2) gives the probability of obtaining heads on the nth trial, which is merely equal to $(\frac{1}{2})^n$. Column (3) gives the payoff ($\$2^n$) if heads appears on the nth trial. Finally, column (4) gives the products between payoffs and respective probabilities, and then shows the sum (i.e., the expected value of the game), which is *infinite*. If the game is to be fair, what fee must the player pay for the privilege to play? The expected value of the game, of course, which is infinite. Would any rational person be willing to pay an infinite amount of money in order to participate in Bernoulli's fair game? The answer is clearly "no." The paradox then is that the Bernoulli game is *not* worth its expected value.

Daniel Bernoulli resolved the paradox by arguing that rational people are concerned with *expected utility* rather than with expected payoffs. *When the marginal utility of income is diminishing,* a rational person will not participate in a fair game. For instance, I would not like to play a game in which I have an even chance of winning or losing $100, because the $100 I may win is not as worthwhile to me as the $100 I may lose. Bernoulli proved his point by adopting a logarithmic utility function [$U(I) = a \cdot \log I$, where I is income and a is some positive constant] and showing that the expected utility of the game of Table 5.4 is finite and perhaps reasonable.

Attitudes Toward Risk

We have just seen that a rational person whose marginal utility of income is diminishing will never accept a fair game. Such a person is usually referred to as *risk averse*. More formally, *a risk averter is a person who prefers the expected value of a gamble with certainty to the gamble itself.* This is illustrated in Figure 5.18.

For convenience, the Neumann–Morgenstern utility curve, $U = U(I)$, is drawn to pass through the origin (since the Neumann–Morgenstern utility index is arbitrary with respect to *origin* and scale). In addition, it has a strictly positive slope throughout (i.e., total utility always increases with income), because more income is always preferred to less. Finally, the utility curve of Figure 5.18 is strictly concave implying diminishing marginal utility of income.

Suppose now that the person's current income is $3000 and he is offered a gamble in which he has an even chance of winning or losing $1000. If he wins, his income will rise to $4000; and if he loses, his income will fall to $2000. Accordingly, if he accepts the gamble, the expected value of his income will be $3000 (i.e., $4000 ×

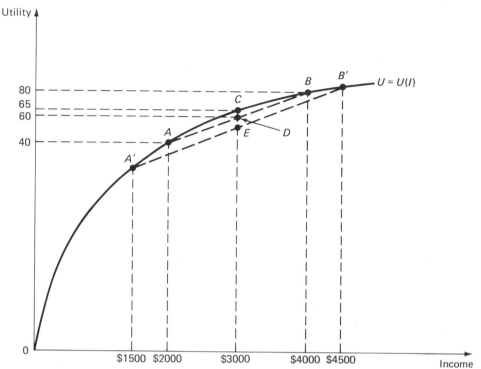

Figure 5.18 Risk aversion. The Neumann–Morgenstern utility curve starts at the origin (which is arbitrary) and has a positive slope throughout (because more income is preferred to less). The concavity of the utility curve reflects the assumption of diminishing marginal utility of income. The person's current income is $3000, and she is offered a gamble in which she has an even chance of winning or losing $1000. If she accepts the gamble, her expected income will be $3000, and her expected utility will be 60 (point *D* on straight-line segment *AB*), which is less than the utility of $3000 with certainty (point *C* on the utility curve). Thus the person prefers to have $3000 with certainty to the gamble. That is, the person is a risk averter.

$\frac{1}{2}$ + $2000 × $\frac{1}{2}$ = $3000). Of course, if he refuses the gamble, his income will remain at $3000 with certainty. Should he accept or refuse this fair gamble?

Because his marginal utility of income is diminishing, the person should refuse the gamble. To prove this proposition, we must show that the total utility of $3000 with certainty is higher than the expected utility of the gamble, whose expected value is also $3000. Thus the total utility of $3000 with certainty is 65 utils (as shown by point *C* on the utility curve). However, the expected utility of the gamble is only 60 utils, as illustrated by point *D* on straight line *AB*. Note that straight line *AB* is the locus of all points satisfying the equation

$$\text{expected utility} = \Pi \cdot U(\$4000) + (1 - \Pi) \cdot U(\$2000),$$

where Π is the probability of income being $4000. In the present case where $\Pi = \frac{1}{2}$, the expected utility of the gamble is equal to $\frac{1}{2} × 80 + \frac{1}{2} × 40 = 60$. Because of the assumed concavity of the total utility curve, straight line *AB* lies below the utility curve, and thus the expected utility of a gamble is always less than the utility of the expected value of the gamble.

We therefore conclude that if the consumer's marginal utility of income is diminishing, he will avoid fair games. But we can actually say more than this. Between two gambles that have the same expected value, a risk averter will always prefer the one that has the "smaller variability" of the outcomes. As we have seen, a risk averter prefers the expected value of a gamble with certainty (where variability is zero) to the gamble itself (where variability is certainly higher than zero). Figure 5.18 presents another example. Suppose that the person is now offered two fair gambles: (1) an even chance of winning or losing $1000, as before, and (2) an even chance of winning or losing $1500. It is evident from Figure 5.18 that the person prefers the first gamble (which has the lower variability of income). The expected utility of the first gamble is given by point D, while the expected utility of the second gamble is indicated by point E, which lies directly below D.

The opposite of a risk averter is a *risk lover*. In particular, a risk lover is a person who prefers a gamble to the gamble's expected value with certainty. The Neumann–Morgenstern utility curve of a risk lover is strictly convex, as illustrated in Figure 5.19. Strict convexity in this context reflects *increasing* marginal utility of income. Suppose again that a person whose current income is $3000 is offered a gamble in which he has an even chance of winning or losing $1000. If he accepts the gamble, his expected income will be $3000, and if he refuses the gamble, his income will be $3000 with certainty. Because of the assumed convexity of the utility curve, the expected utility of the gamble, as indicated by point D on straight line AB, is *higher* than the utility of the expected value of the gamble (point C on the utility curve).

Figure 5.19 also shows that between two gambles that have the same expected value, a risk lover always prefers the one that has the "larger variability" of the

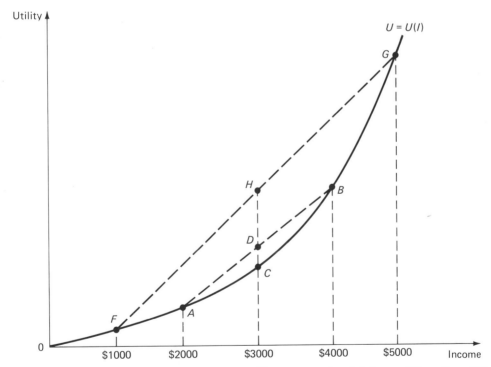

Figure 5.19 The Neumann–Morgenstern utility curve of a risk lover. When the utility curve is convex, the marginal utility of income is increasing, and the person is a risk lover. Thus, if the person's current income is $3000, she would gladly accept a gamble in which she has an even chance of winning or losing $1000 because the expected utility of the gamble (point D along straight-line segment AB) is higher than the utility of $3000 with certainty (point C on the utility curve).

outcomes. Suppose that the person (whose utility curve is shown in Figure 5.19) has an income of $3000. He is offered two fair gambles: (1) an even chance of winning or losing $1000, and (2) an even chance of winning or losing $2000. The expected value of both gambles is $3000, but the expected utility of the second gamble (indicated by point *H* along line segment *FG*) is higher than the expected utility of the first gamble (indicated by point *D*). Accordingly, the person will choose the second gamble, that is, the gamble with the larger variability.

The limiting case of a person who is neither a risk averter nor a risk lover is illustrated by a linear utility curve, as shown in Figure 5.20. Such a person, referred to as *risk neutral,* is *indifferent* between participating in a gamble and receiving the expected value of the gamble with certainty.

An Illustration

Consider a farmer who is debating whether or not to fertilize his land. He knows that the final outcome of either action depends on the weather. If he fertilizes, his income will be high (say, $4000 per month), but only if there is much rain; if it does not rain, his income will be low (say, $2000 per month), presumably because the fertilizer will burn a lot of the seed. If the farmer does not fertilize, his income will be moderate (say, $3000 per month) irrespective of whether it rains or not. This information is summarized in Table 5.5, which is often called the *payoff matrix.* In technical jargon, we say that the farmer chooses between two *actions* (fertilizing and no fertilizing), while nature "chooses" between two possible *states of the world* (rain and no rain).

Suppose, further, that the farmer believes that there is a 50–50 chance of rain, as shown in the last line of Table 5.5. It follows that the expected value of each of the two possible actions is equal to $3000: (0.5)4000 + (0.5)2000 = (0.5)3000 + (0.5)3000 = 3000. Which action will the farmer choose?

The answer depends on the farmer's attitude toward risk. The choice is between

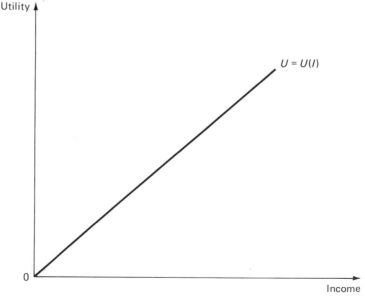

Figure 5.20 The Neumann–Morgenstern utility curve of a risk-neutral person. When the marginal utility of money is constant, the person is neither a risk averter nor a risk lover. He is rather risk neutral, and his utility curve is a straight line (through the origin), as shown.

Table 5.5 Farmer's Payoff Matrix		
	State of the World	
Action	Rain	No Rain
Fertilizing	$4000	$2000
No fertilizing	$3000	$3000
Probability	0.5	0.5

a *certain prospect* of $3000 and a *gamble* whose expected value is also $3000. If the farmer is a risk averter, as in Figure 5.18, he will not fertilize; that is, he will choose the certain prospect. If the farmer is a risk lover, as in Figure 5.19, he will fertilize; that is, he will choose the gamble. Finally, if the farmer is risk neutral, as in Figure 5.20, he will be indifferent between the two options.

Risk Aversion and Insurance

A risk averter is always willing to pay an insurance fee to avoid risk. In other words, a risk-averse person is willing to pay someone else (say, an insurance company) to replace an uncertain prospect (gamble) with an alternative that offers the expected value of the uncertain prospect with certainty.

Consider Figure 5.21, which shows the utility function of a risk averter. Suppose that this risk-averse person has an annual income of $50,000 but will lose, say, $30,000 if her house burns down. For concreteness, assume that the person believes that there is a 50–50 chance of losing her house through fire in a given year. In effect, this person faces a gamble that offers $50,000 with probability 0.50, and $20,000 again with probability 0.50. The expected value of the gamble is $35,000, which has an expected utility of 100 (as indicated by point C along straight-line segment AB).

Obviously, an income of $27,000 with certainty has the same utility as the gamble, as illustrated by point D on the utility curve. This means that this risk-averse person is willing to pay the insurance company up to $23,000 (i.e., $50,000 − $27,000 = $23,000) provided that the insurance company agrees to pay her $30,000 if the house burns down. This explains the *demand side* of insurance.

Typically, insurance companies are willing to accept the gambles that are offered to them at premiums that are much lower than those that risk-averse persons are willing to pay. But insurance companies are owned by stockholders, who are presumably risk averters also. What makes these companies willing to accept such gambles? In other words, what is the basis of the *supply* side of insurance?

The supply side of insurance is founded on the *law of large numbers*. Consider a large number (n) of people, all of whom face the same risky prospect. The ith person's income (I_i) is a *random variable*. Assume that each of these random variables has the same expected value $E(I)$ and the same *probability distribution*. Consider now the array of actual incomes of this group of n people in a certain year: $I_1, I_2, \ldots, I_n$. Let

$$\bar{I} = \frac{I_1 + I_2 + \cdots + I_n}{n}$$

be the average income of the group. The essence of the law of large numbers is this: As n tends to infinity, the probability that the absolute difference between $\bar{I}$ and $E(I)$ is less than *any* given positive number approaches 1. In other words, $\bar{I}$ will be very close to $E(I)$ provided that n is large. This means that even though we cannot

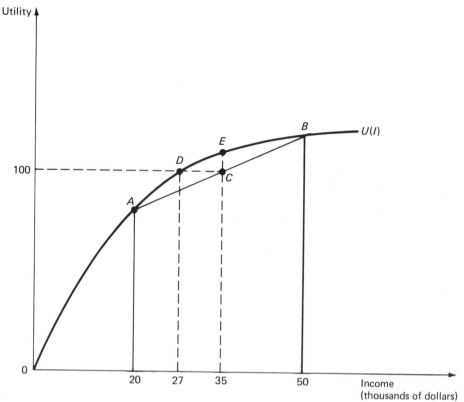

Figure 5.21 Risk aversion and insurance. This risk-averse person has an annual income of $50,000. However, he has a 50–50 chance of losing $30,000. The expected value of this uncertain income prospect is $35,000, which has an expected utility of 100, as indicated by point *C* on line segment *AB*. Since an income of $27,000 with certainty also has a total utility of 100 (point *D*), the person would be willing to trade his uncertain income prospect for an income of at least $27,000 with certainty. That is, the person would be willing to pay a maximum insurance premium of $23,000 in order to avoid the risk.

predict the actual income of any particular person, we can still predict the average income of the group with great accuracy.

Return now to the example of fire insurance (Figure 5.21). Suppose that n persons face the same risk. If n is very large, it will be almost certain that the average income of the group ($\bar{I}$) will be very close to $35,000 (assuming for the moment that the objective probability of losing a house through fire is 0.50). That is, if the n persons pooled their incomes and agreed that each would draw the average income ($\bar{I}$) out of the pool, each person would receive an income of about $35,000. The large variability of individual incomes would then be greatly reduced. Each person would be able to replace the uncertain prospect ($20,000 or $50,000 with equal probability) with the certain prospect of $35,000 (i.e., the expected value of the uncertain prospect). This is, of course, better than the minimum income of $27,000 with certainty that would be acceptable to each person. In effect, an insurance company indirectly accomplishes this kind of pooling of risks.

But there is another problem. Despite the fact that each person may feel that the probability of losing his house through fire is 0.50, the insurance company may objectively calculate that probability to be only 0.004. This means that the insurance company may calculate that out of every 1000 houses insured, only 4 burn down in any given year. If we assume that the insurance company writes a large number of policies, the annual total cost per house would then be 4 × $30,000/1000 = $120. If the insurance company also added, say, 25 percent for overhead costs and profit, the annual premium charged to each homeowner would be only $150—an insignificant amount compared to the maximum premium of $23,000 that each person would be willing to pay.

The Friedman–Savage Hypothesis

Finally, we may note that in real life there are many instances in which people behave both as risk averters (i.e., when they buy insurance) and as risk lovers (i.e., when they gamble at the casinos of Las Vegas, or purchase New York State lottery tickets, whose price is generally higher than their expected value). Such behavior could be irrational, of course. Or people who gamble may do so for the fun of it. Nevertheless, Friedman and Savage (1948) offer a rational explanation of this phenomenon in terms of a Neumann–Morgenstern utility curve that has both concave and convex sections, as shown in Figure 5.22.

The person's income is I^*. Suppose that this person feels that there is a 50–50 chance of losing $I^* - I_0$, say, through fire (as in Figure 5.21). The expected value of this uncertain income prospect is I_2. As explained in the preceding subsection,

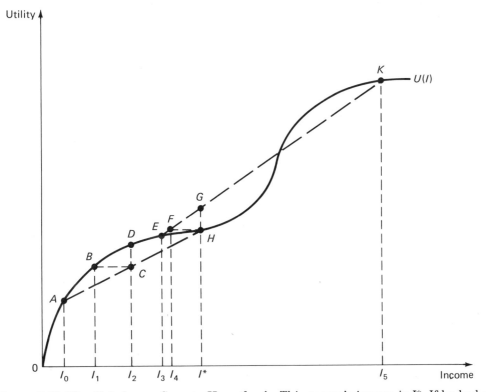

Figure 5.22 The Friedman–Savage Hypothesis. This person's income is I^*. If he had a 50–50 chance of losing $I^* - I_0$, the expected value of the uncertain income prospect would be I_2; and the person would be willing to buy insurance to eliminate the risk, provided that the insurance premium did not exceed $I^* - I_1$. Alternatively, suppose that at the small price of $I^* - I_3$ the same person could purchase a lottery ticket that offered him the chance of winning $I_5 - I^*$. If the expected value of the gamble were at least as high as I_4, the person would purchase the lottery ticket; that is, he would gamble.

the person would be willing to trade this uncertain prospect for an income of as little as I_1 with certainty. That is, the person would be willing to buy insurance. Note that if the person pays a premium that exceeds $I^* - I_2$, the insurance will be unfair; yet the person will buy it, provided that the premium is not higher than $I^* - I_1$.

Alternatively, suppose that at the small price of $I^* - I_3$ the same person can purchase a lottery ticket that offers him or her the chance of winning a large sum of money, say, $I_5 - I^*$. If the gamble were fair, its expected value would be I^*, and its expected utility (indicated by point G along straight-line segment EK) would exceed the utility of the sure prospect of I^* (indicated by point H). Thus the person would accept the fair gamble. Actually, this person would even accept an unfair gamble, provided that its expected value is at least as high as I_4, as the reader should verify.

SUMMARY

1. A consumer-worker attains equilibrium (i.e., allocates optimally his fixed time between work and leisure) at the tangency of his budget line to the highest possible indifference curve; that is, when the marginal rate of substitution of leisure for income equals the wage rate (opportunity cost of leisure). Work restrictions prevent the worker from maximizing his utility.

2. A wage increase gives rise to a substitution effect and an income effect. Because leisure becomes more expensive, the worker substitutes income for leisure; that is, she reduces leisure and increases her supply of labor (substitution effect). But her real income grows also, and she consumes more leisure (normal good), reducing her supply of labor (income effect). Thus the income and substitution effects work in opposite directions, and the slope of the labor supply curve may be positive or negative. Typically, the labor supply curve is backward bending.

3. The ordinary demand curve rests on the assumption that money income remains constant; it includes both the substitution effect and the income effect of a price change. The compensated demand curve is drawn on the assumption that real income (ordinal utility) is held constant; it includes the substitution effect only.

4. Because each point on the ordinary demand curve corresponds to a different level of ordinal utility, a different compensated demand curve passes through each point of the ordinary demand curve. The compensated demand curve is steeper than, flatter than, or coincides with the ordinary demand curve according to whether the commodity is normal, inferior, or neutral, respectively.

5. The consumer surplus is accurately measured by the triangular area under the compensated (not the ordinary) demand curve.

6. The consumer is better off or worse off in the current period relative to the base period according to whether $E > \phi$ or $E < \phi$, respectively, where E = actual income ratio and ϕ = ideal price index.

7. Because the Laspeyres price index (L_p) exceeds the ideal price index, the consumer is unambiguously better off in the current period when $E \geq L_p$.

8. The consumer is unambiguously worse off in the current period when $P_p \geq E$, where P_p is the Paasche price index.

9. The zone of ignorance of index numbers is defined by the inequalities: $P_p < E < L_p$.

10. Given n commodity bundles $(B_1, B_2, \ldots, B_n)$, where B_1 is preferred to B_2, B_2 to B_3, $\ldots$, and B_{n-1} to B_n, we arbitrarily set $U(B_1) = 1$ and $U(B_n) = 0$. To each other commodity bundle B_i the Neumann–Morgenstern index assigns the expected utility of an equivalent gamble (i.e., a gamble whose outcome is either B_1 or B_n and which is indifferent to B_i with certainty). Because $U(B_1) = 1$ and $U(B_n) = 0$, the expected utility of the equivalent gamble is Π_i where Π_i is the probability of winning B_1 in the equivalent gamble. The numerical differences between utility numbers are now important, but the N–M index does not rescue the concept of cardinal utility because (a) it does not measure quantities of satisfaction and

(b) it reflects attitudes toward gambling.

11. The marginal utility of money is increasing, decreasing, or constant according to whether the person is a risk lover, risk averter, or risk neutral, respectively. A risk averter prefers the expected value of a gamble with certainty to the gamble itself (i.e., he rejects fair gambles), a risk lover prefers the opposite, and a risk-neutral person is indifferent between the two alternatives.

QUESTIONS

1. "Backward-bending supply curves are more likely than backward-bending demand curves. This contrast is traceable to the different relationships between substitution and income effects on the supply side as compared with the demand side." Explain fully wherein you agree or disagree.

2. Suppose that my three goods (X_1, X_2, X_3) have independently additive utilities. In each case, marginal utility is diminishing.

(a) Explain how an increase of my income will affect my "marginal utility of income."

(b) How many inferior goods can I have? Explain why.

(c) Suppose that the price of X_1 rises. How will that affect my consumption of X_2 and X_3? Explain why. (*Hint:* First consider the case where X_1 has unitary own elasticity.)

(d) Is Giffen's paradox possible? Explain rigorously.

3. The proponents of "supply-side economics" argue that an income tax reduction raises wages, and the wage increase, in turn, induces people to work more. Does a wage increase cause people to work more? Explain why or why not.

4. In 1980 the income of Mr. Jones was $15,000 and the prices of commodities X and Y were $p_x^0 = \$100$ and $p_y^0 = \$150$, respectively. Mr. Jones maximized his utility by purchasing 90 units of X and 40 units of Y. In 1986 the income of Mr. Jones has risen to $24,000 as the prices of X and Y have increased to $p_x' = \$120$ and $p_y' = \$300$, respectively. As a result, Mr. Jones now maximizes his utility by consuming 160 units of X and 16 units of Y. Assuming that the tastes of Mr. Jones have not changed during the last 6 years, determine whether Mr. Jones is better off or worse off in 1986 than in 1980.

5. Mr. Roberts was transferred by his employer from New York to London, England. Mr. Roberts spends all his income on only three commodities: X (food), Y (clothing), and Z (shelter). The following table summarizes the prices of X, Y, and Z and the choices of Mr. Roberts in New York and London.

City	X	p_x	Y	p_y	Z	p_z
New York	80	$20	10	$40	50	$20
London	20	30	60	30	40	30

(a) What is Mr. Roberts' income in London? What was his income in New York? What was the raise Mr. Roberts received?

(b) Is Mr. Roberts better off in London than in New York?

(c) Find the *minimum* raise that would be necessary to ensure that Mr. Roberts is at least as well off in London as he was in New York. (*Reminder:* You do not know the exact shape of Mr. Roberts' indifference curves.)

(d) How would you answer part (c) if you actually knew Mr. Roberts' indifference map?

6. A person's utility function is of the form $U = zI$, where z is the leisure (hours per day, so that his maximum leisure is $z_0 = 24$) and I is the money income. The prices of all goods purchased by the person are constant so that I can be regarded as a composite good whose price is unity. His daily income from property that he owns is $I_0 = 12$.

(a) If he works $L = 24 - z$ hours per day at a fixed wage rate of w per hour, what is his income-leisure budget equation? What is the opportunity cost of leisure?

(b) What is his utility-maximizing equation? (*Hint:* Set the marginal rate of substitution of leisure for income equal to the opportunity cost of leisure.)

(c) What is the person's labor supply function? Determine L, z, and I assuming that $w = 2$.

(d) Suppose that $w = 2$ and a proportional tax of 25 percent is imposed on wage income only. What are the new values of L, z, and I?

(e) Alternatively, suppose that the government taxes the person's income from property in an amount that hurts him to the same extent as the above 25 percent tax on wage income. What are the new equilibrium values of L, z, and I?

7. A person's utility function is of the form $U = xyz$, where x and y are the consumption rates of commodities X (food) and Y (clothing), respectively, and z represents leisure (hours per day, so that his maximum leisure is $z_0 = 24$).

  (a) For any given wage rate (w) and prices of X and Y (p_x and p_y), show that the person works for 16 hours and divides his wage income equally between X and Y.

  (b) Suppose that it takes α hours (where $0 < \alpha < 1$) to consume 1 unit of X. How will this additional "cost" affect x, y, z, and the supply of labor? How will the new equilibrium quantities compare with the corresponding quantities when $\alpha = 0$?

8. A person's utility function is of the form $U = (x + 1)\, y$, where x and y are the quantities of commodities X and Y. The price of Y is $p_y = \$1$, so Y may be regarded as the composite of all goods (besides X) that he buys. His income is $\$100$.

  (a) Derive the ordinary demand curve for X.

  (b) At what price of X ($\bar{p}_x$) does the person purchase 12 units of X? Show that on the basis of the ordinary demand curve, the maximum amount of money that this person would be willing to pay for $x = 12$ is approximately $\$161$, which is much higher than his income! (*Hint:* Take the entire area under the ordinary demand curve $0 \le x \le 12$.) How is that possible?

  (c) Return now to the point on the ordinary demand curve where $x = 0$. Determine the person's utility (say, $\bar{U}$) at that point, and then derive his compensated demand curve for X (for $U = \bar{U}$).

  (d) Suppose that p_x is again equal to $\bar{p}_x$ [as in part (b)]. Show that $\bar{p}_x$ corresponds to exactly $x = 4$ on the compensated demand curve.

  (e) Using the compensated demand curve, calculate the correct consumer surplus when $p_x = \bar{p}_x$. Show also that the maximum amount of money that the person is willing

to pay for $x = 4$ is only $\$80$, which is certainly less than his income. Can you now resolve the puzzle of part (b)?

9. A farmer is debating whether or not to fertilize his land. He knows that the net return to fertilizer will depend on whether there is a favorable rainfall. He believes that the probability of rain is 0.50. The farmer's *net income* in each of the possible *states of the world* (rain or no rain) as a result of each possible *plan* (fertilizer or no fertilizer) is summarized by the following *payoff matrix*.

Plan		Rain	No Rain
A	Fertilizer	$50,000	$10,000
B	No fertilizer	$35,000	$25,000
Probability		0.50	0.50

What will the farmer do, if he is (a) a risk lover; (b) risk neutral; (c) risk averse? Illustrate the three possibilities graphically.

10. "Economics is nonsensical. If half of the wheat produced by the United States every year were destroyed, the price of wheat would more than double. Hence half the wheat would be worth more than all of it!" Can you resolve this puzzle?

11. (a) Define "fair" gambles.

  (b) Is it rational or irrational to accept fair gambles? Explain why.

12. A person has an expected utility function of the form $U = \log I$, where $I = $ income (or wealth). This person is spending a day at the races. His initial income is $I = \$5000$.

  (a) Show that the person is a risk averter. (*Note:* $d \log I/dI = 1/I$, and $d^2 \log I/dI^2 = -1/I^2$.)

  (b) The person considers how much to bet on a horse called Liberty in order to maximize his expected utility. If Liberty wins the race, he will receive $\$5$ (net) for each $\$1$ bet. If Liberty loses, he will just lose all the money he bets. If the person's subjective probability that Liberty will win is $\frac{2}{3}$, how much money should he bet in order to maximize his expected utility?

  (c) Alternatively, if the person bets $\$2000$ on Liberty, what is his subjective probability that Liberty will win?

13. Suppose that Mr. White believes that there is a 0.5 percent chance that his house will be totally destroyed by fire in any given year. The house is valued at $\$150,000$ and his annual

income is $200,000. Mr. White's expected utility function is of the form $U = \sqrt{I}$, where I is the income (or wealth).

(a) What is Mr. White's expected income?

(b) If an insurance company offers to insure Mr. White's house for an annual fire insur-

ance premium of $1000, will he be willing to purchase the insurance policy?

(c) What is the maximum fire insurance premium that Mr. White would be willing to pay?

FURTHER READING

Alchian, A. (1953). "The Meaning of Utility Measurement," *American Economic Review*, Vol. 43 (March), pp. 26–50.

Arrow, K. J. (1965). *Aspects of the Theory of Risk-Bearing*. Academic Bookstore, Helsinki.

Baumol, W. J. (1977). *Economic Theory and Operations Analysis*, 4th ed. Prentice-Hall, Inc., Englewood Cliffs, N.J. Chapter 17.

Bernoulli, D. (1954). "Exposition of a New Theory on the Measurement of Risk," *Econometrica*, Vol. 22 (January), pp. 23–36.

Brack, J., and K. Cowling (1983). "Advertising and Labour Supply: Workweek and Workyear in U.S. Manufacturing Industries, 1919–76," *Kyklos*, Vol. 36, pp. 285–303.

DeSalvo, J. S. (1971). "A Methodology for Evaluating Housing Programs," *Journal of Regional Science*, Vol. 11 (August), pp. 173–185.

DeSalvo, J. S. (1975). "Benefits and Costs of New York City's Middle-Income Housing Program," *Journal of Political Economy*, Vol. 83 (August), pp. 791–805.

Friedman, M., and L. J. Savage (1948). "The Utility Analysis of Choices Involving Risk," *Journal of Political Economy*, Vol. 56 (August), pp. 279–304.

Hicks, J. R. (1946). *Value and Capital*, 2nd ed. Oxford University Press, New York. Note to Chapter 2, and Chapter 3.

Hicks, J. R. (1956). *A Revision of Demand Theory*. Clarendon Press, Oxford.

Hirshleifer, J., and J. G. Riley (1979). "The Analytics of Uncertainty and Information—An Expository Survey," *Journal of Economic Literature*, Vol. 17 (December), pp. 1375–1421.

Knight, F. H. (1921). *Risk, Uncertainty, and Profit*. Houghton Mifflin Company, New York.

Luce, R. D., and H. Raiffa (1957). *Games and Decisions*. John Wiley & Sons, Inc., New York. Chapter 2.

Samuelson, P. A. (1947). *Foundations of Economic Analysis*. Harvard University Press, Cambridge, Mass. Chapters 5–7.

Samuelson, P. A. (1974). "Complementarity—An Essay on the 40th Anniversary of the Hicks-Allen Revolution in Demand Theory," *Journal of Economic Literature*, Vol. 12 (December), pp. 1255–1289.

Samuelson, P. A. (1977). "St. Petersburg Paradoxes: Defanged, Dissected, and Historically Described," *Journal of Economic Literature*, Vol. 15 (March), pp. 24–55.

von Neumann, J., and O. Morgenstern (1947). *Theory of Games and Economic Behavior*, 2nd ed. Princeton University Press, Princeton, N.J. Chapter 1 and Appendix.

Willig, R. D. (1976). "Consumer's Surplus Without Apology," *American Economic Review*, Vol. 66 (September), pp. 589–597.

PART THREE

Production
and
Cost

CHAPTER
6

Theory of Production

In a competitive market, equilibrium price is determined by supply and demand. In Part Two we examined those economic principles that lie behind the demand curve. We now wish to complete the picture by considering supply. What lies behind the supply curve?

As it turns out, two fundamental concepts lie at the very foundation of all supply decisions: the concept of *production* and the concept of *cost*. It is therefore natural to begin our discussion of supply by studying these concepts. This chapter deals exclusively with the general theory of production.

6.1 The General Model of Supply

Before embarking on a detailed discussion of the fundamental concepts of production and cost, we consider it useful to provide a bird's-eye view of the basic supply model.

The Concept of Production

The bare elements of the model of supply are not difficult to grasp. A casual look at the real world is enough to convince us that practically all economic goods and services consumed (demanded) by consumers come into existence through the process of production. The individual producing units of the economy—the *firms*—incessantly transform *inputs* of factors and goods into an *output* of goods and services. A good analogy is provided by the sausage machine: Several ingredients (inputs) are fed in at one end and a product (output) emerges at the other end.

We must emphasize at the outset that production is *not* restricted to manufacturing alone. Rather, *production includes all economic activity, other than ultimate consumption.* We must classify as production the rendering of legal services, the provision of medical services, the writing of books, and teaching. In addition, storage and transportation of commodities are part of the production process. Thus "storage" represents a transfer of commodities through *time* (i.e., storage gets the commodities to the consumers *when* they need them), while "transportation" represents a transfer of commodities through *space* (i.e., transportation gets the commodities to the consumers where they need them). Finally, production includes such activities as wholesaling, repackaging, and retailing.

Note also that production is not restricted to the activities of profit-seeking business enterprises alone. For instance, in the United States such business firms produce only 80 percent of all goods and services; federal, state, and local government agencies (such as the Department of Defense and the Georgia Department of Transportation) as well as nonprofit organizations (such as the Ford Foundation and the Red Cross) produce the rest.

Factors of Production

Typically, production processes utilize a wide variety of inputs (factors of production) which are conveniently grouped into the following four categories:

1. *Labor services,* such as the services provided by barbers, bricklayers, doctors, engineers, farmers, and teachers.
2. *Capital goods,* that is, all types of *producers' durables* (such as airplanes, buildings, boats, buses, computers, machinery, tools, tractors, and trucks) and *intermediate products* (such as bricks, coal, iron, oil, and wheat). Durable goods yield their services over an extended period of time; intermediate goods are used as inputs into a further stage of production, as illustrated by the use of wheat in the production of bread. All capital goods are *produced means of production;* that is, they are themselves the output of earlier production processes. We return to this point in Chapter 17.
3. *Land* of varying degrees of fertility, sunshine, and rainfall. Location is also important, as are oil and mineral deposits.
4. *Entrepreneurial* or *managerial skills* necessary for the provision of control, coordination, planning, supervision, risk taking, and leadership.

The Production Function

The theory of production deals primarily with the technical/engineering rules according to which firms convert inputs into output. Economists find it convenient to summarize all such engineering rules available to a firm by means of a *production function,* as explained in Section 6.2. In other words, the production function of a typical firm represents the "state of technology" and serves as a severe technical constraint in the process of converting inputs into output.

The Profit-Maximization Problem

We shall assume that the owner of a typical firm, the entrepreneur, seeks to maximize the firm's money profits. This is undoubtedly the most satisfactory assumption that could be made about the behavior of a rational entrepreneur.[1] It rests on the powerful argument that unless a firm maximizes profit, competition will sooner or later force it out of business.

Profit is the difference between revenue and cost. Thus, to produce output, the firm uses a variety of inputs purchasable in the marketplace. As the firm uses inputs, it incurs costs; and as it sells output, it receives sales revenue. The main

---

[1]See Section 8.3 for further discussion of the profit-maximization assumption and other alternatives.

objective of the firm is to maximize the difference between sales revenue and cost (i.e., profit).

The solution to the profit maximization problem yields (1) the optimal quantities of the various inputs used (demanded) by the firm at the current market prices, (2) the optimal output of the firm, (3) the lowest cost of producing that output, and (4) the maximum revenue secured by the sale of the optimal output.

Traditionally, the profit-maximization problem is solved in various steps. Our approach will be as follows. First, we study the production function and its general properties (Chapter 6). Second, we consider the problem of *cost minimization* (and its dual, output maximization), and derive the necessary cost curves (Chapter 7). Third, we determine the optimal (or profit-maximizing) output of the firm, given the cost curves (derived in the second step) and the demand schedule for the firm's product(s). Fourth, we examine the industry equilibrium under alternative market structures. (The third and fourth steps are taken up in Part Four.) Finally, in Part Five, we turn to the firm's (and the industry's) demand for factors of production (or inputs). Accordingly, the supply side forms the central theme of Parts Three to Five.

6.2 The Production Function

Even though production encompasses all economic activity other than ultimate consumption, we shall restrict our discussion to the cases of agriculture and manufacturing. This simplifying assumption makes the concept of production a lot clearer. In addition, we shall assume that the typical firm uses only two factors of production, homogeneous "labor" (L) and homogeneous "land" (T), and produces a single homogeneous product. As it turns out, this simplified model is sufficient for the discussion of most problems of production and cost and, in addition, facilitates the use of two-dimensional graphs, as shown below.

Consider a firm using two factors of production (inputs), labor L and land T, and producing a single output Q of a particular good. The firm's production function is merely a statement of the *maximal* quantity of output that it can produce with any specified quantities of labor and land.

It is important to remember that the production function is a purely *physical* concept; that is, it is a technical relationship between the *physical* quantities of inputs (so many workers and acres of land per unit of time) and the *physical* quantity of output (so many bushels of wheat per unit of time)—*not* their values. We shall introduce the prices of inputs and the price of final output in later chapters.

Further, the production function incorporates the concept of *engineering efficiency*. Thus the production function gives the *maximal* quantity of output for any specified amounts of labor and land. This implies that the production function summarizes only the *most efficient* methods of production, disregarding all inefficient ones. In other words, given any combination of inputs, the firm is assumed to choose only that method of production which *maximizes* output. Accordingly, the production function presupposes that the firm's engineers (or production managers) have already performed a sequence of optimality calculations and have selected the "best" (optimal) method in each case.

There is a very good reason for assuming engineering efficiency, of course. It is that those firms which, for some reason, refuse to adopt the best methods of production will incur higher production costs than other, more efficient competitors and that they will eventually go bankrupt. Because of this severe consequence, we may conclude that competition forces firms to adhere to the rules of engineering efficiency.

The production function (involving two inputs and one output) can be represented graphically by means of a *production surface* that is analogous to the consumer utility surface we discussed in Chapter 3. This is illustrated in Figure 6.1 with production surface 0*ABC*. A point in the labor–land plane represents a combination of given quantities of labor and land. For instance, point *E* represents 10 units of labor and 20 units of land. The perpendicular distance *DE* corresponds to the maximum quantity of output that the firm can produce with 10 units of labor and 20 units of land. (Point *D* necessarily lies on the production surface.) However, unlike utility, the quantity of output produced is cardinally measurable.

In the rest of this chapter, we consider some important properties of the production function by studying various cross sections of the production surface of Figure 6.1.

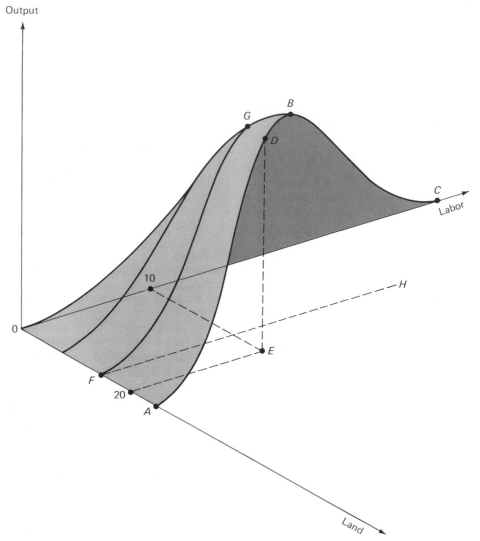

Figure 6.1 The production surface. A point in the labor–land plane (the "floor" of the diagram) represents a combination of labor and land. The perpendicular distance from production surface O*ABC* to the "floor" gives the quantity of output. Thus, with 10 units of labor and 20 units of land (point *E*), the firm produces *DE* units of output, where point *D* lies on the production surface directly above point *E*. When land remains fixed at O*F* while labor is variable, the firm can move along dashed line *FH*, which is parallel to the labor axis. To investigate the effect on total output, we must examine cross section *FG* of the production surface, which lies directly above line *FH*.

6.3 Production in the Short Run

Three-dimensional production surfaces are not convenient at all. As a result, economists have developed various ingenious ways of eliminating one dimension so that they can use two-dimensional graphs. In this section we examine some important properties of the production function when one input, say land T, is held *fixed,* while the other input, say labor L, is *variable.*

Short Run Versus Long Run

In discussing the theory of production as well as the related concept of costs of production, economists find it convenient to use an analytical device: the distinction between *fixed* and *variable* inputs, and the related distinction between *short run* and *long run.* A fixed input is an input whose quantity is fixed and cannot change during the period of time under consideration. On the other hand, a variable input is one whose quantity can be readily changed during the relevant period of time. Similarly, "short run" refers to a period of time during which at least one input is fixed, while "long run" corresponds to a situation in which all factors are variable.

The concepts of short run and long run do *not* correspond to definite periods of calendar time (so many months or years). Rather, the distinction between short run and long run is based on the degree of adjustability of inputs. "Short run" implies incomplete adjustability, while "long run" implies full (total or complete) adjustability. Indeed, it is convenient to think of the long run as the "planning stage," that is, the situation facing the firm before any plant and equipment are purchased or any other commitments are made. During the planning stage (long run), all options (concerning the size of the plant, the scale of operations, and so on) are open—the firm has the freedom to choose any combination of inputs it considers worthwhile. In the long run all inputs are necessarily variable.

As soon as the entrepreneur signs contracts and commits the firm to a given plant size and to other fixed capital equipment, however, the planning stage is over—the firm is in the short run. The firm's choices become limited, as the fixed inputs serve as constraints on the operations of the firm. Thus if the firm decides to either increase or decrease the size of its existing plant, it cannot do so at once; it must wait until a new plant can be implemented.

The definition of the long run is precise because it refers to the unique case in which all inputs are variable. The definition of the short run, however, cannot be formulated very precisely. This is because of the difference in time needed for the adjustment of the various inputs. Indeed, there is not a unique short run, but an infinite number of them. Thus at one extreme all inputs are fixed, as illustrated by the case of an already harvested crop. At the other extreme, all inputs are variable (long run). Between these two extremes, there is an infinite number of short runs, with progressively longer short runs shading gradually into the full long run.

When economists speak of "the" short run, they have in mind a typical situation in which the firm's plant and at least certain key pieces of fixed capital equipment are fixed and unadjustable. Finally, note that the duration of the typical short run may be different for an expansion of the fixed input than for a contraction.

The Total Product Curve

Return to the production surface of Figure 6.1 and assume that the input "land" remains *fixed* at $0F$ units while the input "labor" is variable. Accordingly, in this short run the firm can move along dashed line FH (which is parallel to the labor axis). We wish to investigate what happens to the rate of output as the firm moves from F toward H. For this purpose we must examine cross section FG of the production surface, which lies directly above line *FH*. For convenience, cross section *FG* is reproduced by itself in Figure 6.2 and is known as a *total product curve*.

The total product curve shows the total output of the firm for alternative quantities of the variable input (labor) on the assumption that the fixed factor (land) is held constant at $0F$ units. The total product curve starts at the origin (point F) because of the reasonable assumption that one input (land) alone cannot produce any output. When the firm employs L_1 units of labor (together with $0F$ units of land), total output is Q_1 units (as shown by point N). As the employment of labor increases to L_2 units, output increases to Q_2 units, as shown by point R, and so on. By assumption, total output continues to increase until L_3 units of labor are employed. At that point, output is actually maximized (as indicated by point M), and further increases in the employment of labor cause the total output to fall. The presumption is that increasing labor beyond L_3 has the effect of "overcrowding" the fixed factor, with workers getting into each other's way, so that total output begins to decline. It must be clear from the preceding discussion that a different total product curve can be drawn for each value of the fixed input.

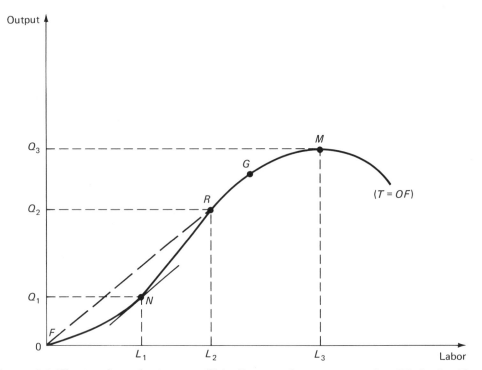

Figure 6.2 The total product curve. This diagram shows cross section *FG* (by itself) of Figure 6.1. It is known as the total product curve and shows the total output at alternative quantities of labor, on the assumption that land remains fixed at $0F$ units. It starts at the origin, because land alone cannot produce any output. As labor increases, output increases also until point M is reached. Increasing labor beyond L_3 causes output to decline, presumably because the numerous workers get into each other's way. When L_2 units of labor are employed, the firm produces Q_2 units of output, and the average product of labor is given by the slope of vector $0R$. The marginal product of labor is given by the slope of the total product curve. For instance, when L_1 units of labor are used, the marginal product of labor is given by the slope of the tangent at point N.

Average and Marginal Physical Products

We must now introduce two additional concepts: the concept of the *average physical product* and the concept of the *marginal physical product*. The average physical product of labor (APP_L) is simply total output (Q) divided by the amount of labor (L) used together with the fixed input to produce that output. In symbols,

$$APP_L = \frac{Q}{L} \tag{6.1}$$

For instance, if total output is 200 units when the firm employs 10 units of labor (along with the fixed input), the average physical product of labor is 20 units of output (i.e., $APP_L = 200 \div 10 = 20$).

At any level of employment of labor, the average physical product of labor can be easily read off the total product curve of Figure 6.2. For instance, when L_2 units of labor are employed, $Q_2 = L_2 R$ units of output are produced. Accordingly, the average physical product of labor is given by the ratio Q_2/L_2, which coincides with the slope of vector $0R$. The latter joins the origin with point R (corresponding to the current employment of L_2 units of labor).

On the other hand, the marginal physical product of labor (MPP_L) is the addition to total output that results from a unit increase in the employment of labor, assuming that the fixed input remains unchanged. For instance, if output increases from 200 units to 225 units as labor increases from 10 units to 11 units, the marginal physical product of labor (i.e., the contribution to total output made by the last unit of labor) is 25 units of output. In general, if output increases by ΔQ units when labor increases by ΔL units, the marginal physical product of labor is given by the ratio $\Delta Q/\Delta L$; that is,

$$MPP_L = \frac{\Delta Q}{\Delta L} \tag{6.2}$$

Graphically, the marginal physical product of labor is given by the slope of the total product curve at the current level of employment of labor. For instance, when L_1 units of labor are employed, the marginal physical product of labor is given by the slope of the tangent to the total product curve at point N.

There exists an important relationship between the average and the marginal physical product of labor. When the marginal product is higher than the average, the average product tends to increase as the employment of labor increases. On the other hand, when the marginal product is lower than the average, the average product tends to fall with further increases in labor. In the limiting case in which the marginal product is equal to the average product, the average remains constant for a small increase in labor.

The reason for this relationship between the average and the marginal physical products can best be explained by means of some examples. Suppose that the average weight in a class of 15 students is equal to 160 pounds and consider what happens to that average weight as another (marginal) student joins the class. If the new (marginal) student is very heavy, say 200 pounds, the average weight of the class will increase. On the other hand, if the new student is very light, say 130 pounds, the average weight of the class will decrease. In the limiting case in which the weight of the new student is exactly 160 pounds, the class average weight will remain constant at 160 pounds.

As another example, consider a baseball player's batting average, which is currently standing at .250. If at the next time at bat he has a hit, his batting average will rise (because marginal = 1.000 > .250 = average). On the other hand, if he strikes out, his average will fall (because marginal = .000 < .250 = average).

As a final example, you may consider the effect of the grade you will receive in microeconomics on your cumulative point average, which is currently standing at, say, 3.0. If you receive an A (which is equivalent to 4.0), your average will rise (because marginal = 4.0 > 3.0 = average). On the other hand, if you receive a C (which is equivalent to 2.0), your average will fall (because marginal = 2.0 < 3.0 = average). Your average will remain unchanged if, and only if, you receive a B (which is equivalent to 3.0).

Further Relationships Among Total Output, Average Physical Product, and Marginal Physical Product

In Figure 6.3, panel (a), we have reproduced the total product curve of Figure 6.2. As before, this curve rises initially (region $0M$); it reaches a maximum at point M; and it finally declines (region MS). But the total product curve has another feature which now must be made explicit: It has an *inflection point* (F). In the region $0F$ the curve is convex; at point F (inflection point), the curve ceases to be convex and begins to be concave. (In addition, at the inflection point F the total product curve crosses from one side of its tangent to the other.) The economic significance of the assumed inflection point is clarified below.

In panel (b), right below the total product curve, we have constructed the corresponding average and marginal (physical) product curves. Thus, at each level of employment of labor, we calculated the average and marginal physical products of labor from the total product curve in panel (a) and registered the results in panel (b). For instance, when the firm employs L_1 units of labor, the average product of labor is given by the slope of vector $0F$ in panel (a) or by vertical distance L_1F'' in panel (b), and the marginal product of labor is given by the slope of the tangent to the total product curve at point F in panel (a) or by vertical distance L_1F' in panel (b).

There are some important relationships among the three curves of Figure 6.3 that we now wish to summarize:

1. Both the average and the marginal product curves have the same positive intercept (point D) with the vertical axis. Surely, the marginal product of labor corresponds to the positive slope of the total product curve at the origin. But why should the average product of labor be equal to the marginal when both the employment of labor and total output are zero? To understand why, start at point F, panel (a), where the firm employs L_1 units of labor. Allow the employment of labor to decrease gradually from L_1 toward zero, causing point F to travel along the total product curve toward the origin. As that happens, the slope of vector $0F$ (which indicates the average product) falls continuously and tends to become equal to the slope of the tangent to the total product curve at the origin. In other words, the slope of the total product curve at the origin (which, by definition, gives the marginal product of labor when the employment of labor is zero) is the limiting value of the average product of labor, as the employment of labor tends to zero. Accordingly, positive intercept D of the average product curve in panel (b) merely signifies this limiting value.

2. The marginal product curve is upward sloping when the total product curve is *convex* (region $0F$); it is downward sloping when the total product curve is *concave* (region FS); it lies in the first quadrant (i.e., the marginal product of labor is positive) when the total product curve is upward sloping (region $0M$); it crosses the labor axis (i.e., the marginal product becomes zero) when the total product curve reaches a maximum (point M); and it lies in the fourth

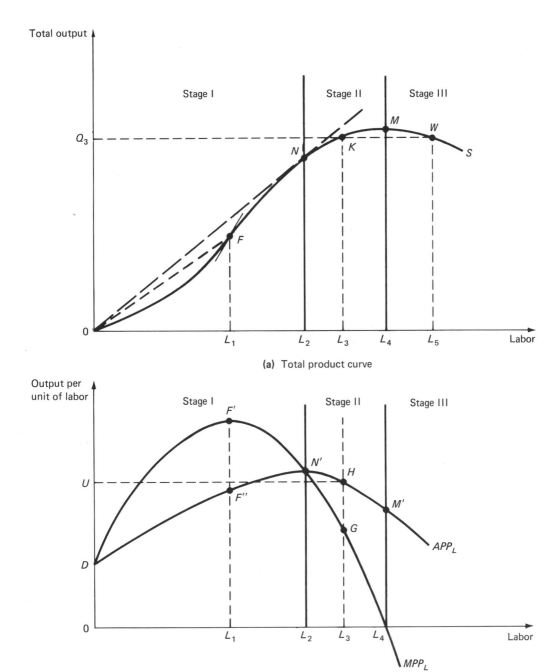

(a) Total product curve

(b) Average and marginal physical product curves

Figure 6.3 Total product, average product, and marginal product. Panel (a) reproduces the total product curve of Figure 6.2. Panel (b) exhibits the corresponding average and marginal product curves, labeled as APP_L and MPP_L, respectively. Both the APP_L and the MPP_L start at point D. [Distance OD coincides with the slope of the total product curve in panel (a) at the origin.] The MPP_L is upward (downward) sloping when the total product curve is convex (concave), as in region OF (FS); it crosses the horizontal axis (point L_4), when the total product curve reaches a maximum (point M); and it becomes negative when the total product curve is downward sloping (region MS). The MPP_L lies above (below) the APP_L, for levels of employment up to L_2 (beyond L_2), and it intersects the APP_L at N' where APP_L is at a maximum. The MPP_L reaches a maximum at F', which corresponds to the inflection point (F) of the total product curve. When L_3 units of labor are employed, total output is given by distance L_3K in panel (a), and also by area OL_3HU, or $OL_3GF'D$, in panel (b).

quadrant (i.e., the marginal product becomes *negative*) when the total product curve is downward sloping (region *MS*).

3. When the marginal product curve lies above the average product curve, as is the case for employment levels up to L_2, the average product curve is upward sloping (because marginal > average, causing the average product to rise). On the other hand, for employment levels beyond L_2, the marginal product curve lies below the average, causing the average product curve to be downward sloping.

4. The marginal product curve intersects the average product curve at point N', where the average product is *maximized*. This becomes evident when we notice that, in panel (a), vector $0N$ is actually tangent to the total product curve at N, which corresponds to N' of panel (b).

5. The marginal product curve reaches a maximum at a lower level of employment than does the average product curve. In particular, the marginal product curve reaches its maximum at point F', where the firm employs L_1 units of labor. Note than when L_1 units of labor are employed, the total product curve in panel (a) has an *inflection point* (F). That the marginal product curve reaches its maximum before the average does is implicit in properties 3 and 4. Thus when the average is rising, the marginal lies above it; and when the average is falling, the marginal must lie below it. Accordingly, at point N' where they become equal, the marginal must be *falling* in order to pass from above the average to below it. But this means that the marginal must have reached its maximum at a lower level of employment of labor.

6. For any level of employment of labor, we can determine total output from the average product curve. For instance, suppose that the firm employs L_3 units of labor. From panel (a) we know that the firm must be producing Q_3 units of output. Turning to panel (b), we observe that the average product of labor is equal to vertical distance L_3H. Accordingly, total output = $L_3 \cdot L_3H$ = area of rectangle $0L_3HU$. This is obvious from the definition of the average product. Thus equation (6.1) can be rearranged as follows:

$$Q = L \cdot APP_L \tag{6.1)'}$$

7. Similarly, for any level of employment of labor, we can determine total output as the area under the marginal product curve. For instance, when the firm employs L_3 units of labor, total output is given by area $0L_3GF'D$. This is similar to the relationship that exists between the marginal utility curve and total utility (discussed in Chapter 3) and follows from the fact that total output is the *sum* of marginal products.

The Three Stages of Production

The preceding relations among total output, average product, and marginal product are used to define three stages of production, as shown in Figure 6.3. Stage I corresponds to that range of employment of labor (from zero to L_2) over which the *average product of labor is increasing*. Stage II coincides with that range of employment of labor (from L_2 to L_4) over which the *average product of labor is declining and the marginal product of labor is positive*. Finally, stage III is defined as the range of *negative marginal product of labor* (or declining total output.)

It must be obvious from Figure 6.3 that a rational producer will never produce in stage III, where the marginal product of labor is negative. For he could always *reduce* the employment of labor (and the wage bill) and increase total output. For instance, consider a producer who is currently employing L_5 units of labor and produces Q_3 units of output, as shown in Figure 6.3, panel (a). Because he is in stage III, he can produce that same output with a smaller quantity of labor (L_3). Accordingly, to minimize his costs (which is necessary for profit maximization), the producer will never employ labor beyond L_4 units.

Although it may not be obvious from the diagram, a rational producer will never operate in stage I either. As explained in the Appendix to Chapter 6, in stage I where the average product of the variable input (labor) is rising, the marginal product of the fixed input (land) is necessarily negative, assuming that returns to scale are constant. (The commonsense explanation of this phenomenon is that in this stage, the fixed input is "too large" relative to the variable input.) Consequently, when market conditions are such that a small level of output must be produced (say, a level between zero and L_2N), it will be more efficient for the producer to use only a fraction of the fixed input (assuming that it is feasible) and thus produce on a different total product curve corresponding to that smaller quantity of the fixed input.

By elimination, therefore, we conclude that a rational producer will operate in stage II. We shall have more to say on this proposition in later chapters.

The Law of Diminishing Returns

The total product curve of Figure 6.3 (and that of Figure 6.2) embodies an important hypothesis: the *law of diminishing returns,* which states that as larger and larger quantities of the variable factor (labor) are applied to a constant quantity of the fixed factor (land), eventually a point is reached beyond which additional increases in the variable factor yield diminishing marginal contributions to total output.[2]

The law of diminishing returns is an important empirical proposition. If it were not for this law, the entire food supply of the world could be grown on a single acre of land (or even a single flowerpot) by employing only a sufficient quantity of labor.

Further, the law of diminishing returns lies at the heart of the theory of overpopulation of Thomas Malthus (1766–1834). In his *Essay on the Principle of Population* (1798), Malthus postulated that population (and thus labor), when unchecked, has a tendency to grow at a geometric progression. However, land is absolutely fixed in the long run, and given sufficient time all land will be brought into cultivation. Because of the law of diminishing returns, the production of food cannot continue to keep pace with the growth of population. Eventually, the output of food will fall below the minimum subsistence level necessary for sustaining life, and the growth of population will be kept in check by pestilence, famine, and war. Even though in later editions of his book, Malthus softened his initial, gloomy prediction by pointing out that the growth of population could also be checked by preventive measures that operate on the birth rate and advocating for moral restraint, the Malthusian doctrine was sufficient for Thomas Carlyle (1795–1881), an English historian, to characterize economics as the "dismal science."

Modern economists point out that while the law of diminishing returns is a valid empirical proposition, Malthus had not fully realized the potentiality of capital accumulation and especially technical progress. Thus the law of diminishing returns holds for a given state of technology. Rapid technical progress causes the total product curve to shift upward, pushing continuously the specter of Malthus into the distant future.

---

[2]The law of diminishing returns could also be cast in terms of the *average* product of the variable factor. Thus we could alternatively state that as the employment of labor increases while land is held constant, eventually a point is reached beyond which the average physical product of labor becomes diminishing.

6.4 Isoquants

We now turn to an examination of the long-run production function where all inputs are variable. Because the three-dimensional production surface of Figure 6.1 is not easy to handle, economists use the ingenious device of *isoquants* (or equal-product curves), which are analogous to the consumer indifference curves discussed in Part Two. This section shows how the isoquant map can be derived and what its properties are.

Derivation of Isoquants

What is an isoquant? It is a curve in input space that depicts all possible combinations of inputs that are physically capable of producing a given quantity of total output. In terms of the production surface of Figure 6.1, we can say that an isoquant is the locus of all points in the labor–land plane that correspond to the same height in the third dimension, that is, generate the same quantity of total output. This is illustrated in Figure 6.4.

Surface 0*DAFBE* illustrates a portion of the production surface of Figure 6.1. This surface is now viewed directly from behind. Imagine a horizontal plane (i.e., a plane parallel to the labor–land plane) intersecting the production surface at a certain height, say *A'A*, as shown by plane *ABC*. Project the cut of the surface (i.e., curve *AB*) onto the labor–land plane, as shown by dashed curve *A'B'*. This projection, *A'B'*, is an isoquant; it gives all combinations of labor and land that are capable of producing *A'A* units of output per period.

The concept of an isoquant emphasizes the fact that there are many ways of

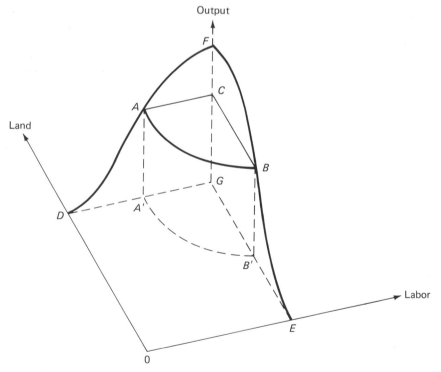

Figure 6.4 Derivation of isoquants. Horizontal plane *ABC* intersects production surface 0*DAFBE* at height *A'A*, as shown by curve *AB*. The projection of cut *AB* onto the labor–land plane, as shown by dashed curve *A'B'*, is an isoquant; it shows all combinations of labor and land that are capable of producing *A'A* units of output per period.

producing a given level of output. Indeed, a smoothly continuous isoquant, such as $A'B'$ in Figure 6.4, represents an infinite number of ways (or methods) of combining labor and land to produce, say, $A'A$ units of output. Each point on isoquant $A'B'$ corresponds to a method of production. As we move from one point of the isoquant to another, the actual (or observed) process of production may change drastically, as illustrated, for instance, by the replacement of workers by robots in the automotive industry.

Following the above procedure, we can derive as many isoquants as we wish. Thus, for each level of output, we use a horizontal plane to cut the production surface of Figure 6.4 at the appropriate height, and then project the cut of the surface onto the labor–land plane. The entire family of isoquants is known as the *isoquant map*.

An isoquant map represents the existing technology. Technical progress corresponds to a shift of the isoquant map. Unless explicitly stated otherwise, we assume that the isoquants do not shift; that is, we assume that technology remains constant throughout our analysis.

Isoquants Versus Indifference Curves

An isoquant map is very similar to an indifference map. Yet there are two important differences between them, because output is cardinally measurable whereas utility is not.

First, unlike indifference curves, we can accurately register on each isoquant the exact number of units of output it represents, as shown in Figure 6.5. Thus curves 1, 2, and 3 show all alternative combinations of labor and land that are capable of producing 10, 20, and 30 units of output, respectively.

Second, unlike indifference curves, we can precisely determine by how much the number of units of output registered on one isoquant is larger or smaller than that registered on another isoquant. For instance, isoquant 2 represents an output of 20 units, while isoquant 3 represents an output of 30 units. It follows, then, that isoquant 3 represents an output 10 units larger than that of isoquant 2.

General Properties of Isoquants

What are the general properties of isoquants? These are easily summarized as follows:

1. Isoquants *slope downward* (at least in the economically relevant middle region).
2. Isoquants *do not intersect* each other.
3. Isoquants lying *farther* from the origin correspond to *larger* amounts of output. (A movement from a "lower" to a "higher" isoquant implies an increase in output.)
4. Isoquants are *convex* to the origin.

The first property ("slope downward") follows from the justifiable assumption that additional units of any factor produce additional *positive* amounts of output; that is, each factor's (input's) marginal physical product is *positive*. Thus, as one input is increased, the second input must be decreased; otherwise, total output would rise and we would move to a "higher" isoquant.

How reasonable is the assumption that the marginal physical product of each factor is positive? As we saw in Section 6.3, there may exist situations where a sufficiently large quantity of labor may cause such an overcrowding of a fixed piece of land that the marginal physical product of labor may become negative—the employment of additional workers may actually reduce total output. This could

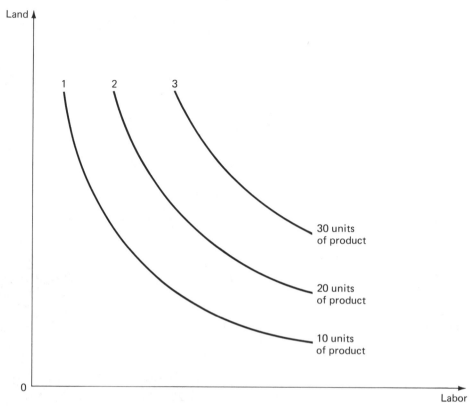

Figure 6.5 The isoquant map. Isoquants 1, 2, and 3 show all alternative combinations of labor and land that are capable of producing 10, 20, and 30 units of output, respectively. They all slope downward, are convex to the origin, and do not intersect; also, a movement from a "lower" isoquant to a "higher" one implies an increase in output. Unlike indifference curves, each isoquant is associated with a cardinal quantity of output.

happen, of course, but no rational producer would ever employ an input up to the point where its marginal physical product becomes negative (or even just zero). The reason should be obvious: Inputs have positive prices, and employing a factor (input) whose marginal product is negative would violate the principle of cost minimization (and that of profit maximization). Thus an upward-sloping isoquant indicates that a given output can be produced with less of both inputs and, therefore, at lower cost. We therefore conclude that no point on an upward-sloping region of an isoquant could ever represent an equilibrium position. Over the economically relevant range, isoquants slope downward.

There is another important reason why we should ignore an upward-sloping region of an isoquant. As we saw in Section 6.2, the firm's production function gives the *maximal* quantity of output for any specified combination of labor and land. To allow isoquants with positive slope, in effect, means that an input may become a positive nuisance without the firm being able to get rid of it costlessly. However, it may be difficult to accept the view that the mere availability of redundant labor or land would ever reduce output. The reason is simple: The entrepreneur has the option to let a redundant input (labor or land) to remain idle (free disposal). Not only is it not mandatory to "use" excess labor (or land) when it happens to be available, but also such output-reducing use of an excess input violates the very definition of the production function. Accordingly, we must not reject the possibility of "no use," because it may actually be the "best use." What we must reject is the compulsory use of redundant inputs.

The second property ("do not intersect") follows from the observation that a point of intersection between two isoquants would represent two *different* levels of *maximal* output, which is a logical contradiction.

The third property ("farther from the origin ... larger ... output") follows again from the reasonable assumption that in the economically relevant region, larger quantities of inputs produce more output.

The last property ("convex to the origin") is actually an additional assumption. Section 6.5 discusses its economic meaning and shows that convexity is a reasonable assumption.

6.5 The Convexity of Isoquants

This section deals with the economic interpretation of the shape of isoquants and, in particular, the assumption of convexity.

The Phenomenon of Factor Substitution

As we have seen, isoquants normally slope downward—at least within the relevant region. Within this range, factors are *substitutable*. For instance, Figure 6.6 shows that the firm can produce 50 units of output by any combination of inputs that coincides with a point on isoquant 1. In particular, the firm can use either combination A (i.e., L_1 units of labor and T_2 units of land) or combination B (i.e.,

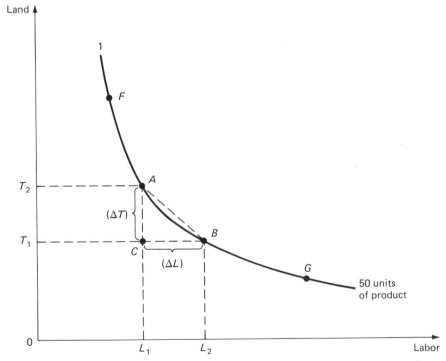

Figure 6.6 Factor substitution. To move from A to B, the firm substitutes ΔL (or $L_1 L_2$) units of labor for ΔT (or $T_1 T_2$) units of land. For this "large" movement, the marginal rate of technical substitution is given by the absolute slope of dashed line AB. As point B travels along isoquant 1 toward point A, the slope of AB approaches the slope of the tangent at A. For this reason, when the firm is at A, we define the absolute slope of the tangent at A to be the marginal rate of technical substitution of labor for land.

L_2 units of labor and T_1 units of land). In moving from point A to point B, the firm *substitutes* L_1L_2 (or ΔL) units of labor for T_1T_2 (or ΔT) units of land.

Input substitution is an important economic phenomenon. Examples are not difficult to find. Because of the energy crisis, some industries are now substituting labor for energy. For instance, to save fuel, airplanes fly more slowly, truckers drive more slowly, and during the summer months air-conditioning is turned down (reducing the efficiency of workers). Similarly, other corporations substitute coal for oil (or natural gas).

The Marginal Rate of Technical Substitution

Economists use the concept of the *marginal rate of technical substitution (MRS)* to measure the rate at which the entrepreneur can substitute "small" quantities of one input for "small" quantities of another input as he or she travels along an isoquant. More precisely, the marginal rate of technical substitution of labor for land (MRS_{LT}) gives the number of units of land (T) that can be replaced by one extra unit of labor, assuming that total output remains unchanged. In the example of Figure 6.6, the movement from point A to point B along isoquant 1 implies that *on the average*, $\Delta T/\Delta L$ units of land are replaced by each additional unit of labor employed.[3] Accordingly, the marginal rate of technical substitution of labor for land, designated by the symbol MRS_{LT}, is given by the absolute value of the ratio $\Delta T/\Delta L$. In other words,

$$MRS_{LT} = \left| \frac{\Delta T}{\Delta L} \right| \tag{6.3}$$

where ΔT and ΔL are "very small" quantities.

The marginal rate of technical substitution of labor for land coincides with the absolute slope of an isoquant at a specific point. This idea is very similar to the proposition that the marginal rate of substitution of commodity X for commodity Y is given by the absolute slope of an indifference curve, and the reader is referred to Section 3.6 for further discussion.

Marginal Product and Input Substitution

There is an important relationship between the marginal physical products of labor and land, on the one hand, and the marginal rate of technical substitution, on the other, just as there is a relationship between the marginal utilities of commodities X and Y and the marginal rate of substitution of X for Y.

Return to Figure 6.6 and assume again that we move from A to B. Divide this movement into two parts: (1) a movement from A to C and (2) a movement from C to B. In the first step, ΔT units of land are given up and output necessarily falls. By how much? By $\Delta T \cdot MPP_T$, where $MPP_T \equiv$ marginal physical product of land. In the second step, the employment of labor increases by ΔL units and output increases by $\Delta L \cdot MPP_L$, where $MPP_L \equiv$ marginal physical product of labor. What is the overall change in output? It must be zero, because in the final analysis we move along the same isoquant (from A to B). Accordingly, the sum of the two separate changes in output must be zero. In other words,

$$\Delta T \cdot MPP_T + \Delta L \cdot MPP_L = 0 \tag{6.4}$$

Finally, we can rearrange equation (6.4) as follows:

---

[3] All this is very simlar to the marginal rate of substitution in consumption, discussed in Section 3.6.

$$MRS_{LT} \equiv - \frac{\Delta T}{\Delta L} = \frac{MPP_L}{MPP_T} \qquad (6.5)$$

That is, the marginal rate of technical substitution of labor for land is equal to the ratio of the marginal physical product of labor to the marginal physical product of land.

The Law of Diminishing Marginal Rate of Technical Substitution

The assumption of convexity of isoquants implies that the marginal rate of technical substitution of labor for land diminishes as labor continues to replace land along an isoquant. For instance, as we travel from F to G along isoquant 1 of Figure 6.6, the marginal rate of technical substitution of labor for land (i.e., the absolute slope of the isoquant) tends to become smaller and smaller.

In general, convexity means that the substitution of one input for another tends to become progressively more difficult as it is pushed further and further. This phenomenon, known as the *law of diminishing marginal rate of technical substitution,* may be illustrated by an example. A tailor uses cloth and his labor to produce a suit. To save cloth, he must exercise great care in cutting; that is, he must work longer (use more labor). However, as this substitution of labor for cloth proceeds, the tailor is likely to find out that saving more cloth requires progressively more labor time, and that such substitution of labor for cloth cannot be pushed beyond a certain limit.

The main economic justification for the assumed convexity of isoquants is similar to the justification of convexity of indifference curves, discussed in Section 4.4. It is that equilibrium with both inputs used cannot occur at a point where the marginal rate of technical substitution is increasing. Concave isoquants would make it profitable to employ only one of the inputs by itself. In practice, however, we do not find firms that carry on production with only labor or only land. We rather observe production processes in which all four classes of factors enumerated in Section 6.1 cooperate with one another. This economic justification will be clarified in Chapter 7.

Ridge Lines

As we noted earlier, the substitution of one input for another does not only become progressively more difficult as it proceeds further and further; it also becomes impossible beyond a certain point. For instance, the tailor cannot substitute labor for cloth indefinitely; it is obvious that there is an upper limit to the quantity of cloth that he can save no matter how much labor he uses.

The boundaries to effective input substitution are known as *ridge lines*. In particular, the *labor ridge line* is the locus of points in input space where any further substitution of labor for land is impossible. In other words, the labor ridge line is the locus of points where the isoquants become parallel to the labor axis for the first time, that is, the points where $MRS_{LT} = 0$ (or $MPP_L = 0$).

Similarly, the *land ridge line* is the locus of points in input space where any further substitution of land for labor is impossible. In other words, the land ridge line is the locus of points where the isoquants become parallel to the land axis for the first time (or where $MPP_T = 0$).

The labor and land ridge lines are illustrated in Figure 6.7. Note that at points C and D, isoquants 1 and 2, respectively, become parallel to the labor axis. Similarly, at points A and B, isoquants 1 and 2 become parallel to the land axis. Also, the area bounded by the two ridge lines represents the economic region of production,

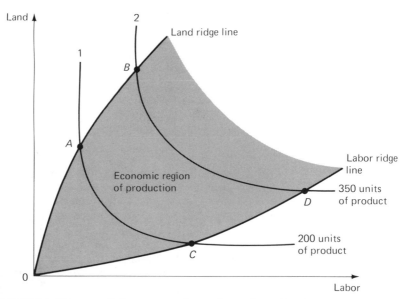

Figure 6.7 *Ridge lines and the economic region of production.* The labor ridge line is the locus of points, such as *C* and *D*, where the isoquants become parallel to the labor axis for the first time. Similarly, the land ridge line is the locus of points, such as *A* and *B*, where the isoquants become parallel to the land axis for the first time. The shaded area bounded by the two ridge lines represents the economic region of production.

that is, the second stage of production. A rational entrepreneur will never produce outside this region. Finally, isoquants 1 and 2 are drawn as straight lines and parallel to the axes beyond the ridge lines, because of our earlier decision to reject isoquants that have a positive slope (Section 6.4). Actually, it would make no difference if we drew the isoquants with a positive slope beyond the ridge lines, because no rational entrepreneur will ever operate there.

6.6 Returns to Scale

What happens to output when all inputs increase proportionately (i.e., by the same percentage)? For instance, what happens to output when all inputs are doubled? Or how does output respond to changes in the *scale* of the firm? The answer to this question may have serious consequences both for the survival of certain firm sizes and the very existence of perfect competition.

Definitions and Graphical Illustration

Economists use the term *returns to scale* to refer to the relationship between a proportionate change in the physical quantity of all inputs and the resultant change in the physical quantity of output. For instance, suppose that all inputs are variable (long run) and that the firm increases all of them by the same proportion. What happens to output? There are three possibilities:

1. *Constant returns to scale:* The physical quantity of output increases in the same proportion as all inputs. For instance, when all inputs are doubled, output doubles also.

2. *Increasing returns to scale:* The physical quantity of output increases by a greater percentage than all inputs. For instance, when all inputs are doubled, output more than doubles.
3. *Decreasing returns to scale:* The physical quantity of output increases by a smaller percentage than all inputs. For instance, when all inputs increase by 20 percent, output increases by only 15 percent.

A proportionate change in the physical quantity of all inputs leaves the proportion in which they are used constant. For instance, consider a firm that is currently employing 20 units of land and 10 units of labor; this means that the firm is using 2 units of land per unit of labor (i.e., land ÷ labor = 20 ÷ 10 = 2). Suppose now that the firm increases both inputs by 30 percent. Land increases to 26 units and labor to 13 units, but their ratio continues to be equal to 2 (land ÷ labor = 26 ÷ 13 = 2).

Graphically, we can represent a proportionate change in labor and land by a movement along a ray through the origin in the labor–land plane, as shown in Figure 6.8 (which is similar to Figure 6.4) by dashed line 0*B* on the "floor" of the three-dimensional diagram. Thus as the firm moves from point *A* to point *B*, the

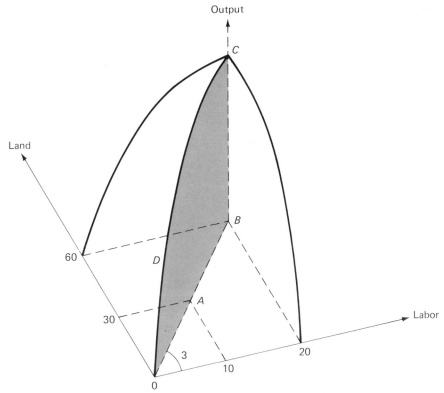

Figure 6.8 Proportional increases in inputs and the production surface. Along ray 0*B*, the firm uses land and labor in the fixed proportion 3:1, as shown by the slope of 0*B* with the labor axis. To find out what happens to output, we consider cross section 0*ABCD* of the production surface. This cross section is generated by a plane that is perpendicular to the "floor" of the diagram and passes through line 0*B*. This plane cuts the production surface along 0*DC*. Whether returns to scale are constant, increasing, or decreasing depends on the properties of curve 0*DC*.

employment of labor and land doubles, but the firm continues to use 3 units of land per unit of labor, as indicated by the slope of ray $0B$ with the labor axis.

To find out what happens to output as inputs change along ray $0B$, we take a cross section of the production surface, as indicated by shaded area $0ABCD$. Imagine a plane that is perpendicular to the labor–land plane and passes through line $0B$. This imaginary plane intersects the production surface, as shown by line $0DC$. Whether the returns to scale are increasing, constant, or decreasing depends on the properties of this cut of the production surface, that is, curve $0DC$.

Figure 6.9 presents three possible shapes of the cross section $0ABCD$ of Figure

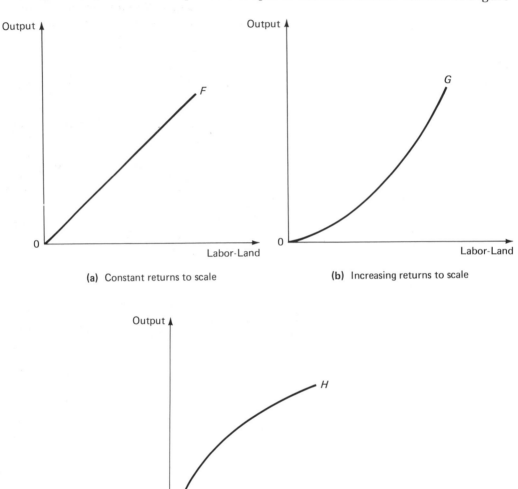

(a) Constant returns to scale

(b) Increasing returns to scale

(c) Decreasing returns to scale

Figure 6.9 Returns to scale. Panel (a) illustrates the case of constant returns to scale. Line $0F$ (corresponding to curve $0DC$ in Figure 6.8) is *straight*, indicating that output tends to increase at the same rate as all inputs. Panel (b) illustrates the case of increasing returns to scale—cross section $0G$ is *convex* with an *increasing* slope, indicating that output increases faster than all inputs. Finally, panel (c) illustrates the case of decreasing returns to scale— cross section $0H$ is *concave* with a *decreasing* slope.

6.8. Panel (a) illustrates the case of constant returns to scale. Here cross section line $0F$ (corresponding to curve $0DC$ in Figure 6.8) is *straight,* indicating that output tends to increase at the same rate as all inputs. Panel (b) illustrates the case of increasing returns to scale. Thus cross section $0G$ is convex with an *increasing slope,* indicating that output increases faster than all inputs. Finally, panel (c) illustrates the case of decreasing returns to scale. Cross section $0H$ is now concave with *decreasing slope,* indicating that output increases more slowly than all inputs.

Constant, increasing, and decreasing returns to scale can also be illustrated graphically by means of isoquants. This is shown in Figure 6.10. All three panels exhibit three illustrative isoquants for outputs of 10, 20, and 30 units, with a ray through the origin intersecting them at points A, B, and C, respectively. With constant returns to scale, it takes twice as much of both inputs to produce 20 units than to produce 10 units of output and three times as much of both inputs to pro-

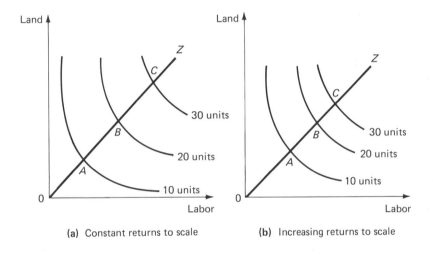

(a) Constant returns to scale   (b) Increasing returns to scale

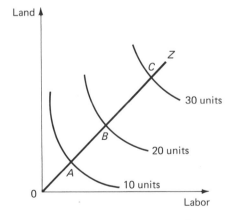

(c) Decreasing returns to scale

Figure 6.10 *Returns to scale and the isoquant map.* All three panels exhibit three illustrative isoquants for outputs of 10, 20, and 30 units, and ray $0Z$ intersects them at points A, B, and C, respectively. Panel (a) illustrates the case of constant returns to scale: The three isoquants intersect ray $0Z$ at equal distances (i.e., $OA = AB = BC$). Panel (b) illustrates the case of increasing returns ($OA > AB > BC$). Finally, panel (c) illustrates the case of decreasing returns ($OA < AB < BC$).

duce 30 units than to produce 10 units of output. This situation is illustrated in panel (a), where the three isoquants intersect ray $0Z$ at equal distances (i.e., $0A = AB = BC$). Panel (b) illustrates the case of increasing returns to scale. Now as we move from the origin along ray $0Z$, the distances between successive isoquants become smaller and smaller (i.e., $0A > AB > BC$). Equal increases in output can be produced with smaller and smaller increases of inputs. Finally, panel (c) illustrates the case of decreasing returns to scale. As we move from the origin along ray $0Z$, the distances between successive isoquants become progressively larger and larger (i.e., $0A < AB < BC$). In this case, equal increases in output require larger and larger increases of inputs.

Reasons for Increasing and Decreasing Returns to Scale

Whether returns to scale are constant, increasing, or decreasing is an empirical question. Nevertheless, there is a presumption that production functions should exhibit constant returns to scale. This presumption is based on the simple idea that a factory could always be duplicated, so that doubling all inputs (plant, workers, raw materials, etc.) must double the output. Unfortunately, this presumption is not correct, as there are important reasons for both increasing and decreasing returns to scale.

What are the most important reasons for the existence of increasing returns to scale? We can summarize them as follows:

1. *Indivisibilities:* Although it is true that it may be fairly easy to duplicate a plant or a process, it may not be possible to halve them. If a man operates a machine, or a computer, we could find a second man with roughly the same skills to operate a second machine, or a second computer. However, it may not be possible to devise a "half-machine" or a "half-computer" that can be operated by a "half-man." Accordingly, at a small scale of operations, a producer may be forced to employ less efficient inputs, because the more efficient inputs may be available only at a larger scale. Such indivisibilities give rise to increasing returns: As the scale of operations becomes larger, it becomes possible to use more efficient inputs and processes.

2. *Division of labor:* Adam Smith was the first economist to emphasize the importance of the economies generated by the division of labor. As the scale of operations increases, it becomes possible for workers to specialize on some of the many different tasks that are being performed. Such specialization leads to increased dexterity, and increased knowledge acquired through better familiarity with each task. Finally, such division of labor makes it possible for workers to avoid wasting time and effort in shifting from one task to another.

3. *Geometrical relations:* Doubling the walls of a warehouse *quadruples* warehouse space. For instance, consider a rectangular warehouse that is 100 by 150 feet and thus provides 15,000 square feet of space. A second rectangular warehouse that is 200 by 300 feet provides 60,000 square feet of space, four times as much space as the first warehouse. Accordingly, doubling the wall area (input) quadruples the warehouse space (output). Even though this simple calculation ignores other important aspects of the problem (such as the land, the roof, and the floor of the warehouse), it nevertheless makes a valid point.

   A similar problem arises in the case of a pipe that is used to transport, say, oil. Its capacity (output) is proportional to the square of its radius (r^2), whereas the quantity of the metal needed for its construction (input) is proportional to its diameter ($2r$). Accordingly, doubling its radius, say, from 2 feet to 4 feet, doubles the quantity of metal needed for its construction (because $2r$ doubles whenever r doubles) but quadruples its capacity (because r^2 quadruples whenever r doubles).

4. *Inventories:* Usually, the optimal level of inventories increases less than in proportion with the firm's output.

5. Finally, some inputs do not have to increase at all as the level of output increases. Some examples are the designing of a product such as an automobile, the proofreading of a book, and the collection of information.

Turn now to decreasing returns. What reasons can account for them? Basically two:

1. *Input limitations:* Even though output would double if *all* inputs were doubled, there are circumstances in which it might not be actually possible to double all inputs. This is especially true when some input is related to a state of nature. For instance, doubling the size of the fishing fleet may not double the catch of fish, because the natural availability of fish (one of the inputs) cannot be doubled. The same is true, of course, in other "extractive" industries, such as mining and hunting. Because economists are mostly concerned with those inputs that are actually under the control of the producer, they disregard inputs that are related to the state of nature. But then the relevant (or economic) production function, relating output to the truly economic inputs (say, the size of the fishing fleet but not the natural availability of fish), may exhibit decreasing returns to scale.

2. *Difficulties of supervision:* As the firm's scale of operations increases, it usually becomes necessary to establish a hierarchy of supervisors, with the first-line supervisors being supervised by a second line of supervisors, and so on. In addition, as the top supervisors are pushed farther and farther from the actual process of production, their efficiency tends to decline. These difficulties of supervision form by far the most important reason for decreasing returns to scale.

   Typically, the production function of a firm combines elements of constant, increasing, and decreasing returns to scale. Thus increasing returns at the beginning (due to "economies of large-scale production) are followed by constant and decreasing returns successively, presumably because of increasing difficulties of supervision.

6.7 Constant Returns to Scale

Constant returns to scale occupy an important place in economics. For this reason, we single them out for special scrutiny in this final section on the theory of production.[4]

The Industry Versus the Firm

Economists use the term "industry" to refer to a *group* of firms that produce a homogeneous product. This distinction between a "firm" and an "industry" will become very important in later parts of the book. For the moment, we wish to use it to justify the study of constant returns to scale.

As we pointed out in the preceding section, the typical production function of a firm is *not* characterized by constant returns to scale. Then why study constant

---

[4]This section may be read together with the Appendix to Chapter 6, which carries the discussion of constant returns to scale a little further.

returns to scale any further? Because constant returns to scale are not an unrealistic assumption for the entire *industry*.

For instance, suppose that each firm in an industry produces a single commodity using homogeneous labor and homogeneous land. Assume further that each individual firm's production function exhibits increasing returns to scale at the beginning, followed by constant and decreasing returns successively. In particular, at the current long-run equilibrium, each of the 1000 active firms uses 12 workers and 3 acres of land to produce 600 units of output. Thus the entire industry output is equal to 600,000 units. As a result of an increase in demand, the industry must increase its output by 10 percent (or 60,000 units). Broadly speaking, the assumption of constant returns to scale (at the industry level) means that *the number of active firms will increase* by 10 percent (or by 100 additional firms), with each new firm employing 12 workers and 3 acres of land and producing 600 units of output, just as each of the old firms did. Accordingly, from the point of view of the industry, both inputs (labor and land) and output will increase by exactly 10 percent, as is required by constant returns to scale.

The reader is urged to keep this scenario in mind in the subsequent discussion of constant returns to scale.[5]

Properties of Constant Returns to Scale

When returns to scale are constant, the production function has several important properties. We can summarize these properties as follows:

1. *The average physical product of each input depends only on the proportion in which labor and land are used.* For instance, in the above example each firm uses 12 workers on 3 acres of land (or 4 workers on each acre) and produces 600 units of output. Thus the average product of labor is 50 (i.e., $600 \div 12 = 50$) and the average product of land is 200 (i.e., $600 \div 3 = 200$). As long as each firm uses 4 workers on each acre of land, the average products of labor and land will remain constant at 50 and 200, respectively. These average products will change only when each firm uses labor and land in a different proportion.

2. *The marginal physical product of each input depends only on the proportion in which labor and land are used.* For instance, the marginal physical product of labor depends only on how many workers each firm uses on each acre of land and nothing else.

3. *The marginal rate of technical substitution depends on the proportion in which inputs are used.* This must be obvious from the fact that the marginal rate of technical substitution is given by the ratio of marginal physical products [as shown by equation (6.5)], and these depend on the proportion in which inputs are used. This property implies that any straight line through the origin (signifying a fixed labor/land ratio) will intersect all isoquants at points that have the same slope (i.e., the same marginal rate of technical substitution).

4. *The entire isoquant map is a blown-up version of the unit isoquant.* Thus when the unit isoquant (or any other isoquant, for that matter) is given, the whole isoquant map can be easily constructed.

5. *The total output, Q, is exactly exhausted by the distributive shares of all inputs when each input is paid its marginal physical product.* This is known as *Euler's theorem* or as the *adding-up theorem.*

   Here is a heuristic proof of Euler's theorem. Suppose that L_0 units of labor

---

[5]For a proof that the industry production function may be characterized by constant returns to scale, even though the production function of each individual firm is not, see Chacholiades (1978, pp. 96–101).

and T_0 units of land are currently employed in the production of Q_0 units of output. If labor increases by ΔL units, and land by ΔT units, output will increase by

$$\Delta Q = \Delta L \cdot MPP_L + \Delta T \cdot MPP_T \tag{6.6}$$

where MPP_L is the marginal physical product of labor and MPP_T the marginal physical product of land. Suppose now that the input increases, ΔL and ΔT, are actually proportional to the initial amounts L_0 and T_0, respectively; that is, $\Delta L = \mu L_0$ and $\Delta T = \mu T_0$, where μ is a constant number. Because of constant returns to scale, we must also have $\Delta Q = \mu Q_0$. Substituting the values μL_0, μT_0, and μQ_0 into equation (6.6), and dividing both sides by the common factor μ, we finally obtain

$$Q_0 = L_0 \cdot MPP_L + T_0 \cdot MPP_T \tag{6.7}$$

Equation (6.7) is Euler's theorem.

6. *When the isoquants are convex to the origin (i.e., when the law of diminishing marginal rate of technical substitution applies throughout), the marginal physical products of labor and land are diminishing (i.e., the law of diminishing returns also holds throughout).*

Property 6 is illustrated in Figure 6.11. Straight line $0Z$ intersects isoquants 1, 2, and 3 at points A, B, and C, respectively. The slopes at A, B, and C are identical (property 3), and thus the tangents to the three isoquants at A, B,

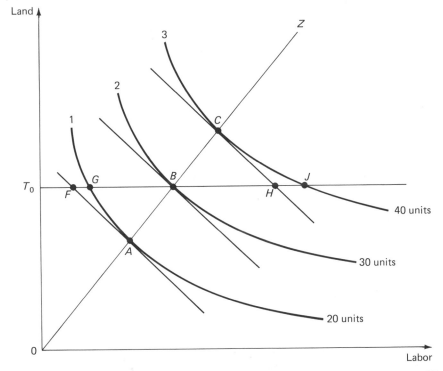

Figure 6.11 Constant returns to scale and the law of diminishing returns. Keeping land fixed at OT_0, we can increase output from 20 to 30 units by increasing labor by GB units. To increase output from 30 to 40 units, we must increase labor by BJ units. Since $GB < BJ$ (because $GB < FB = BH < BJ$), the marginal physical product of labor must be diminishing.

and C, respectively, are parallel to each other, as shown in Figure 6.11. Thus distance AB equals distance BC (because of the assumption of constant returns to scale). In addition, $FB = BH$. We now wish to show that keeping land fixed at $0T_0$, successive increases in labor by equal amounts cause output to increase by smaller and smaller amounts, or, which is the same thing, successive increases of output by equal amounts, say, 10 units, require larger and larger additions to labor.

Start at point G, where 20 units of output are produced. To increase output from 20 to 30 units (while we keep land fixed at $0T_0$), we must move from G to B, that is, we must increase labor by GB units; and to increase output from 30 to 40 units, we must move from B to J, that is, we must increase labor by BJ units. To prove that the marginal physical product of labor is diminishing, we must show that $BJ > GB$. However, this last inequality should be obvious from the construction of the diagram. Thus $FB = BH$ and $GB < FB = BH < BJ$. Q.E.D.

6.8 Selected Empirical Applications

We now turn briefly to a few empirical applications of the theory of production.

Substitution of Robots for Workers

Isoquants can clarify a wide range of issues. As oil prices rose sharply in the 1970s, American automobile manufacturers felt the intense competition by their Japanese counterparts, who were flooding the American market with small cars. To keep their costs low while producing the kind of automobile that the American public demanded, American producers, following the lead by the Japanese, introduced robots into their production lines. This automated approach was also followed by European producers.

Using robots means that fewer workers are needed for the production of the same number of automobiles. That is, robots can be substituted for labor. This relationship can be shown by an isoquant similar to that shown in Figure 6.6. The only difference is that now along the vertical axis we measure robot hours; along the horizontal axis we continue to measure labor hours.

Putting the matter thus, it becomes evident that there is a trade-off between robots and workers. The trade-off is measured, of course, by the marginal rate of technical substitution—a critical piece of information which can prove useful to producers, workers, and labor union leaders.

For the sake of argument, suppose that the marginal rate of technical substitution of robot hours for labor hours is unity. If a robot hour costs \$10, workers cannot insist on being paid \$20 an hour. If they do, rational producers will simply replace most of them with robots.

The Trade-off Between Insulation and Energy

Another case clarified by isoquants is the use of insulation to reduce heating and cooling bills. Today home builders can construct a house that is almost airtight. For instance, according to *The Wall Street Journal* (August 4, 1982, p. 23), a 2400-square foot home in Indianapolis had a heating bill of only \$148 during the 1981–1982 winter, a season that was slightly colder than normal.

We can think of insulation and energy as two inputs in the production of heat. Typically, more insulation enables a household to maintain a certain temperature in the house with less energy. This trade-off between insulation and energy can again be represented by an isoquant. The actual construction of such an isoquant is left as an exercise for the interested reader. (Along one axis measure units of insulation; along the other, measure units of energy. Draw a hypothetical isoquant corresponding to 75° Fahrenheit. Note that a different isoquant must be drawn for each home, depending on various characteristics, such as size and location.) Note again that the marginal rate of technical substitution of insulation for energy as well as the prices of these two inputs are very important in deciding how much insulation is optimal.

The Production Function for the Transportation of Crude Oil by Pipeline

An interesting application of the concept of production function is found in the transportation of crude oil by pipeline. The pipeline output, called "throughput," is the volume of liquid carried per unit of time, such as so many barrels of oil per day.

Table 6.1 The Production Function for the Transportation of Crude Oil by Pipeline

Inside Diameter of Pipeline (inches)	Hydraulic Horsepower			
	5,000	10,000	15,000	20,000
15.00		72,435		
15.65				100,000
16.62			100,000	
18.09		100,000		
20.00	92,570	118,807	137,479	152,480
20.92	100,000			
23.42				200,000
24.87			200,000	
25.00		174,392		
27.07		200,000		
29.64				300,000
30.00		238,627		
31.30	200,000			
31.48			300,000	
34.27		300,000		
39.62	300,000			

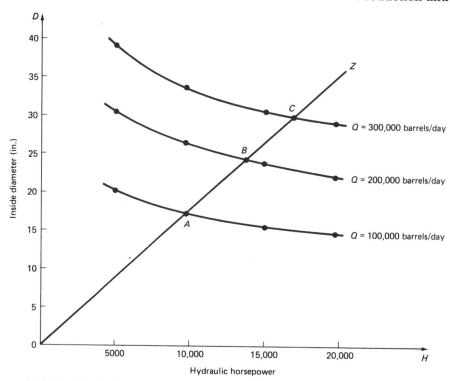

Figure 6.12 Trade-off between hydraulic horsepower and pipeline diameter in the transportation of crude oil. The three isoquants illustrated above correspond to throughputs of 100, 200, and 300 thousand barrels per day. Increasing returns to scale prevail throughout. Note that $OA > AB > BC$.

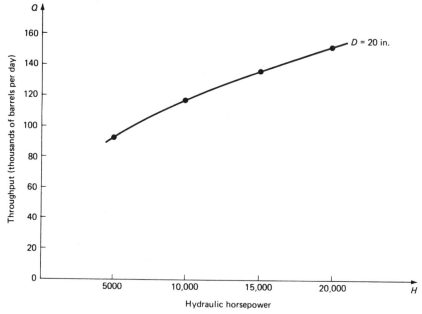

Figure 6.13 Throughput as a function of hydraulic horsepower. The pipeline diameter is held constant at 20 inches. As horsepower increases, throughput increases but at a diminishing rate.

We can also identify two inputs: the size of the inside diameter of the pipeline and the amount of hydraulic horsepower applied by the pumps to the oil carried. A given size of pipeline can be used to achieve several different throughputs by applying different amounts of hydraulic horsepower. Conversely, any given throughput can be attained with several combinations of pipeline sizes and horsepower. The relevant physical laws can be summarized by the following formula [production function; Pearl and Enos (1975, p.56)]:

$$Q = 24.95 \times H^{0.36} \times D^{1.72} \tag{6.8}$$

where Q = throughput of crude oil (barrels per day) of given density and viscosity (60 SUS/34°API)
H = hydraulic horsepower
D = inside diameter (inches) of the steel pipeline

Equation 6.8 was used to calculate the entries in Table 6.1. Each entry shows the throughput Q for the relevant combination of hydraulic horsepower H and inside diameter of the pipeline D. For instance, the throughput of 100,000 barrels per day can be produced with an inside diameter of 18.09 inches and 10,000 hydraulic horsepower. (As an exercise, the reader is encouraged to fill in the remaining blanks in Table 6.1.)

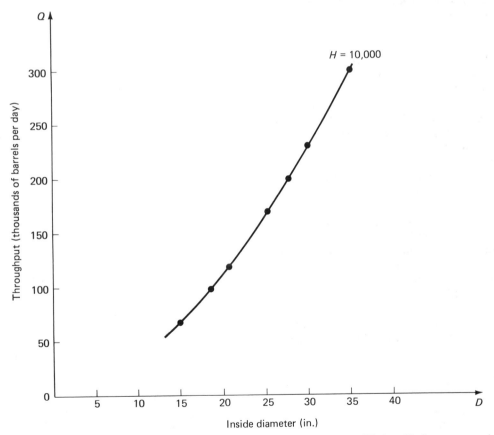

Figure 6.14 Throughput as a function of pipeline diameter. Hydraulic horsepower is held constant at 10,000. As the inside diameter of the pipeline increases, throughput increases at an increasing rate.

In turn, the entries in Table 6.1 were used to draw the three isoquants in Figure 6.12 and the total product curves in Figures 6.13 and 6.14. It is evident from Figure 6.12 [compare with Figure 6.10, panel (b)] that the transportation of crude oil by pipeline is subject to *increasing* returns to scale. The concavity of the total product curve in Figure 6.13 reveals that the average and marginal products of hydraulic horsepower are *diminishing*, as the reader can also verify directly from Table 6.1. Finally, the convexity of the total product curve in Figure 6.14 indicates that the average and marginal products of the inside diameter of the pipeline are *increasing*.

SUMMARY

1. Firms transform inputs (labor, capital, land, and entrepreneurship) into output. Their objective is to maximize profit (revenue less cost).

2. The firm's production function gives the *maximal* quantity of (physical) output that can be produced with any specified quantities of (physical) inputs.

3. A fixed input is an input whose quantity cannot change during the relevant period of time; a variable input is one whose quantity can be readily changed.

4. "Short run" refers to a situation in which at least one input is fixed. In the long run all inputs are variable.

5. The total product curve shows total output for alternative quantities of the variable input, on the assumption that the fixed input is held constant at some specified level.

6. The average physical product of labor (total output ÷ quantity of labor) is given by the slope of the vector that joins the origin with the relevant point on the total product curve.

7. The marginal physical product of labor (the addition to total output that results from a unit increase in the employment of labor while the fixed factor remains unchanged) is given by the slope of the total product curve.

8. The average physical product of labor increases, decreases, or remains the same according to whether it is lower than, higher than, or equal to the marginal physical product of labor.

9. The marginal product curve reaches its maximum before the average product curve does, and it intersects the latter at its maximum point. These two curves have the same vertical-axis intercept.

10. Total output is equal to the area under the marginal product curve; it also coincides with the area of the rectangle formed with reference to a specified point on the average product curve.

11. In labor's first stage of production, the average product of labor is increasing; in the second stage, the average product of labor is declining but the marginal product of labor is positive; in the third stage, the marginal product of labor is negative. A rational producer operates in the second stage.

12. *Law of diminishing returns:* As more of the variable factor is applied to the fixed factor, the marginal physical product of the variable factor eventually diminishes. This law lies at the heart of the Malthusian theory of overpopulation.

13. An isoquant is the locus of all (minimal) input combinations capable of producing a given total output. The entire family of isoquants (isoquant map) represents the existing technology.

14. Isoquants slope downward, do not intersect, and are convex to the origin. Because output is cardinally measurable, we can determine by how much the output registered on a higher isoquant exceeds the output registered on a lower one.

15. The marginal rate of technical substitution gives the number of units of one factor that can be replaced by one extra unit of the other, assuming that total output remains unchanged. Graphically, it coincides with the absolute slope of an isoquant; it is also equal to the ratio of the marginal physical products.

16. *Law of diminishing marginal rate of technical substitution:* The marginal rate of technical substitution of labor for land diminishes as labor continues to replace land along an isoquant. This law is implied by the assumed convexity of isoquants.

17. A factor's ridge line is the locus of points in input space where the marginal product of that factor becomes zero for the first time. The area bounded by the ridge lines corresponds to the economic region of production (second stage).
18. Returns to scale are constant, increasing, or decreasing according to whether the rate of change of output is equal to, greater than, or smaller than the proportionate change in all inputs.
19. Reasons for increasing returns to scale include indivisibilities, division of labor, geometrical relations, inventories, and once-and-for-all inputs (such as the designing of a product).

20. Decreasing returns to scale are due to difficulties of supervision and input limitations.
21. Under constant returns to scale the average and marginal physical products of each input as well as the marginal rate of technical substitution depend only on the proportion in which inputs are used; in addition, total output is exhausted by the distributive shares of all inputs when each is paid its marginal physical product (Euler's theorem or adding-up theorem); the isoquant map is a blown-up version of the unit isoquant; and when isoquants are convex, the law of diminishing returns holds throughout.

QUESTIONS

1. A commodity is produced with labor and land. The following table gives information about the production of the commodity when alternative quantities of labor (variable factor) are applied to a fixed piece of land (fixed factor).

Units of Labor	Total Output	Average Product of Labor	Marginal Product of Labor[a]
1	10	———	———
2	———	———	16
3	———	15	———
4	56	———	———
5	———	———	4
6	———	9	———

[a]In the present "discrete" case where labor and output do not change continuously, the marginal product of labor represents some *average* rate of change of total output per extra unit of labor between two "widely" separated outputs. Graphically, this discrete marginal product of labor is given by the slope of the straight line joining the two points on the total product curve.

(a) Fill in the blanks in the table.
(b) Use the information in the completed table to plot the relevant points on the curves of total product, average physical product. and marginal physical product of labor.
(c) Indicate on your diagram the ranges of employment of labor that correspond to labor's three stages of production.
2. Return to the completed table of Question 1 and assume constant returns to scale. Suppose also that the fixed piece of land is exactly

60 acres. Use the information in the completed table to plot six points on each of the three isoquants which correspond to 30, 45, and 60 units of output.
3. Empirical studies show that the yield-per acre on a French farm is typically much higher than the yield on an American farm devoted to the same crop. Does this mean that French farmers are more efficient than American farmers?
4. A firm uses 60 units of labor and 100 acres of land to produce 500 units of output. If the firm used only 50 units of labor, it would have to employ 120 acres of land in order to maintain total output at 500 units.
(a) What is the marginal rate of technical substitution of labor for land?
(b) What is the marginal physical product of land, assuming that the marginal physical product of labor is 8 units of output?
5. Show that under constant returns to scale, labor's first stage of production corresponds to land's third stage.
6. Suppose that a good is produced with two inputs, labor (L) and capital (K), according to the production function

$$Q = 10L + 20K$$

(a) Does this production function exhibit increasing, decreasing, or constant returns to scale?
(b) Is this production function consistent

with diminishing *marginal* returns to a variable factor? With diminishing *average* returns to a variable factor?

7. (a) Contrast the law of diminishing returns with the concept of decreasing returns to scale.

(b) Can the law of diminishing returns prevail even in the presence of increasing returns to scale?

(c) Is the law of diminishing returns applicable in the long run?

8. On the basis of the law of diminishing returns, Thomas Malthus reached a dismal conclusion about the future of the human race.

(a) Reconstruct the Malthusian thesis.

(b) Explain why the Malthusian prediction has not materialized so far.

9. A firm uses 10 workers and 20 acres of land and produces 500 units of output.

(a) Suppose that the marginal physical products of labor and land are 12 and 15, respectively. Does the firm's production function exhibit constant returns to scale?

(b) Alternatively, assume that the marginal physical product of labor is 12. What should the marginal physical product of land be for the production data to be consistent with constant returns to scale?

FURTHER READING

Baumol, W. J. (1977). *Economic Theory and Operations Analysis,* 4th ed. Prentice-Hall, Inc., Englewood Cliffs, N.J. Chapter 11.

Carlson, S. (1939). *A Study of the Pure Theory of Production.* P. S. King, London.

Cassels, J. M. (1936). "On the Law of Variable Proportions," in *Explorations in Economics,* McGraw-Hill Book Company, New York. Reprinted in W. Fellner and B. F. Haley (eds.), *Readings in the Theory of Income Distribution.* Richard D. Irwin, Inc., Homewood, Ill., 1946.

Chacholiades, M. (1978). *International Trade Theory and Policy.* McGraw-Hill Book Company, New York, Chapter 4.

Douglas, P. (1948). "Are There Laws of Production?" *American Economic Review,* Vol. 38 (March), pp. 1–41.

Hicks, J. R. (1946). *Value and Capital,* 2nd ed. Oxford University Press, New York. Chapters 6 and 7.

Machlup, F. (1936). "On the Meaning of the Marginal Product," in *Explorations in Economics,* McGraw-Hill Book Company, New York. Reprinted in W. Fellner and B. F. Haley (eds.), *Readings in the Theory of Income Distribution.* Richard D. Irwin, Inc., Homewood, Ill., 1946.

Pearl, D. J., and J. L. Enos (1975). "Engineering Production Functions and Technological Progress," *The Journal of Industrial Economics,* Vol. 24 (September), pp. 55–72.

Samuelson, P. A. (1947). *Foundations of Economic Analysis.* Harvard University Press, Cambridge, Mass. Chapter 4.

CHAPTER
7

Costs of Production

Having described the technology of the firm in Chapter 6, we now turn to the theory of cost. An understanding of the theory of cost is of paramount importance, primarily because cost is relevant to decision making. The rational firm must weigh the advantages or benefits against the disadvantages or costs of any potential action. A profitable action is one whose benefits exceed its costs. The firm is essentially interested in profitable actions.

We begin in Section 7.1 with a discussion of the nature of cost and explain several concepts of cost, such as explicit cost, implicit cost, accounting cost, and opportunity cost. We continue in Section 7.2 with the choice of optimal input combinations and study the dual problems of cost minimization and output maximization. In Section 7.3 we generalize the results of Section 7.2 by developing the firm's expansion path, which shows how the optimal input combination varies as output expands. Given the firm's expansion path, we proceed in Sections 7.4 and 7.5 with the derivation of the long-run total-cost curve and its properties, and then continue with the derivation and properties of the long-run average-cost and marginal-cost curves. In Section 7.6 we turn to the various short-run cost curves: total cost, total fixed cost, total variable cost, average cost, average variable cost, average fixed cost, and marginal cost. In Section 7.7 we examine the relationships that exist between the unique set of long-run cost curves and the whole family of sets of short-run cost curves. Finally, we conclude our discussion in Section 7.8 with several empirical applications.

7.1 The Nature of Cost

Within a static framework, the meaning of cost is rather simple. To produce a certain amount of output, a firm uses a variety of economic inputs (such as labor services, land services, and raw materials). These economic inputs are scarce and have prices. The total payments for the use of these inputs are the firm's *total cost* of the produced output. This sounds simple enough, but there are difficulties with regard to the identification of the economically relevant inputs and their prices. The purpose of this section is to clarify these issues.

Explicit Versus Implicit Costs

It is often thought that costs coincide with the *money outlays* that the firm makes in order to obtain the necessary inputs. This notion is not entirely correct. In some cases, a money outlay may not be a cost; conversely, a cost may not always appear as a money outlay.

In principle, the concept of cost includes both "explicit costs" and "implicit costs." Explicit costs are outlays made by a firm for purchased or hired factors of production. Examples of explicit costs are the payments for raw materials, utilities, wages, and rent for office space. Implicit costs, on the other hand, are the imputed costs of self-owned, self-employed factors of production. Examples of implicit costs are the salary of the entrepreneur, the return on the capital invested in a firm by the owner, the rent for self-supplied land and capital equipment, and the necessary compensation for risk bearing.

Consider a farmer who cultivates his own land with a hired laborer and a newly purchased tractor. What is the farmer's total cost of production? Obviously, the wage paid to the hired laborer (an explicit cost) is part of the farmer's total cost. However, it would be very misleading to regard the full price of the tractor as part of the total cost. It would be equally misleading to ignore the farmer's own labor service and the use of his own land just because there are no corresponding cash outlays. Rather, it would be more appropriate to include as cost an implicit rent for the services of the tractor, plus an implicit rent for the services of the self-supplied land, plus an implicit wage for the farmer's own labor service. How these "implicit costs," or "imputed costs," are actually determined is explained below.

Opportunity Cost

We have just concluded that the concept of cost includes both explicit costs and implicit costs. The explicit costs correspond to the actual payments for purchased and hired factors of production and are easily identifiable. However, the implicit costs are not so obvious, because no payments are made to anyone outside the firm. How are these implicit costs determined?

In evaluating the firm's implicit costs, economists are guided by an important principle called *opportunity cost*. According to this principle, *the cost of an input to a firm is the value forgone (or opportunity lost) by not employing it in its best alternative use.* For instance, in our earlier example, the farmer must include an implicit rent for the self-supplied land equal to the maximum rent that he might receive if he rented his land to someone else. Similarly, the farmer's implicit wage for his own labor service is equal to the maximum wage that he might receive if he worked for someone else.[1]

The concept of opportunity cost is fundamental in economics. In fact, when economists speak of cost they usually mean opportunity cost. In particular, the concept of opportunity cost is not restricted to the firm's implicit costs alone. The firm's explicit costs are also opportunity costs. For instance, when a firm purchases raw materials, it sacrifices the opportunity of acquiring something else that has the

---

[1]To the extent that one prefers to work for himself rather than for someone else, the relevant opportunity cost of a self-supplied factor of production is lower than the corresponding pecuniary returns in its best alternative use. In such cases, the opportunity cost of a self-supplied input is the *minimum* return that the person must receive if he is to continue using it in the role of entrepreneur.

same value; therefore, from the point of view of the firm, the purchase price of raw materials essentially reflects their opportunity cost. The same is true of the firm's payroll as well as other explicit costs.

The concept of opportunity cost has many other applications. For instance, suppose that a consumer purchases an automobile. The true cost to the consumer is best measured in terms of the alternative goods and services that he must forgo. Similarly, at the level of the entire economy, the true cost of producing an additional television set is best measured in terms of the other goods (such as refrigerators and washing machines) that the economy must sacrifice. Thus, to produce one additional television set, the economy needs additional resources which in the final analysis, must be diverted from the production of other goods. The opportunity cost of one additional television set is therefore the number of refrigerators (or washing machines) that the economy must sacrifice.

Depreciation

The principle of opportunity cost differs drastically from conventional accounting rules that place great emphasis on historical cost. This is especially true in the case of durable goods.

The purchase of durable goods, such as buildings, equipment, and machinery, represents an *investment*—not a current expense. Expense is incurred only as these durable goods are used by the firm. This expense, known as *depreciation*, is then charged off as a cost of output. In essence, depreciation reflects the loss in value due to *physical deterioration* (wear and tear) as well as the *obsolescence* of the durable good.

Accountants have developed an inexhaustible variety of alternative depreciation methods based on the price originally paid for the durable good. The simplest and most common method is *straight-line depreciation*, according to which the same fraction of the original price (historical cost) is charged to current costs each year of the expected useful life of the durable good. Unfortunately, the historical cost may be drastically different from the relevant opportunity cost.

Economists view the historical cost of a durable good as a "sunk cost," which is irrelevant to decision making on the principle that "bygones are bygones." The relevant issue concerns the opportunity lost, if any, by not employing the capital good in its best alternative use. Accordingly, economists invoke the opportunity-cost principle and set the implicit cost of the capital good equal to the highest rent that someone else would be willing to pay for its use. Indeed, if the capital good (say, a machine) happens to have no alternative uses whatsoever, its opportunity cost will be zero, despite the fact that the conventional accounting depreciation charge may be very high. Needless to say, the conventional accounting methods are very useful for other purposes, such as the determination of income tax liability.

7.2 The Optimal Combination of Inputs

How does a business firm decide on the proportions in which to use different inputs in the production of a commodity? For example, why is it that in producing a product like a road, an Indian construction firm uses an enormous number of workers who move earth and mix concrete with shovels, whereas an American construction corporation makes extensive use of bulldozers and other modern heavy equipment? The answer lies in the comparative costs of the different production methods.

In Chapter 6 we learned that there are many possible combinations of inputs that are physically capable of producing a given quantity of total output. All these input combinations are summarized by an isoquant. In general, each point on the isoquant corresponds to a different method of producing the specified output. Given these alternative technological methods, the firm must choose the *optimal* method (or input combination). This choice is an economic one, because it is not determined by entirely technical or engineering considerations. It depends, in addition, on the prices of the inputs and the behavioral assumption that firms try to minimize cost (which is part and parcel of the profit-maximization assumption). An *optimal input combination* (or method of production) is one that minimizes the total cost of producing the specified output. This section deals primarily with the cost-minimization problem and its dual, the output-maximization problem.

The Scenario

Consider a firm that uses two inputs, homogeneous labor and homogeneous land, and produces a single commodity. Assume that the firm is in the long run (planning horizon). Thus all inputs are variable (all options are open to the firm). Assume further that the firm purchases labor services and land services in perfectly competitive markets. In other words, the firm is a *price taker* in the factor markets; that is, the firm can purchase all the labor services and land services it wants at the prevailing rental rates.

The above situation is analogous to that of a consumer who is purchasing consumer goods in perfectly competitive markets at predetermined prices. An important difference, however, between the consumer and the firm lies in the fact that the consumer's expenditure on commodities is constrained by his fixed income, whereas the firm's total expenditure on inputs is variable.

The ultimate objective of the firm is to maximize its profit. For this purpose, the firm calculates (1) the minimum total cost and (2) the maximum total revenue at each level of output; and then selects that level of output at which total profit (i.e., total revenue minus total cost) is at a maximum. The first step in this process is therefore the minimization of total cost at each level of output, which the firm accomplishes by choosing the optimal input combination at each level of output, as explained below.

The Isocost Map

To solve the cost-minimization problem, it is necessary first to determine the various combinations of inputs that the firm can purchase with a fixed sum of money (expenditure). This is analogous to the budget line of a consumer. For instance, all alternative combinations of labor and land that the firm can obtain for a total outlay of C dollars must satisfy the following equation:

$$wL + rT = C \tag{7.1}$$

where L is the amount of labor service (worker-hours), T the amount of land service (acres of land per year), w the wage rate (per worker-hour), and r the rent (per acre per year). Equation (7.1) is called an *isocost equation* and is very similar to the consumer's budget equation (4.1). Figure 7.1 illustrates equation (7.1) graphically.

Isocost line AB shows all combinations of labor and land that the firm can purchase with the fixed amount of C dollars. In particular, the labor-axis intercept (B) is given by the ratio C/w and represents the maximum number of units of labor (worker-hours) that the firm can purchase with C dollars. Similarly, the land-axis intercept (A) is given by the ratio C/r and represents the maximum number of units

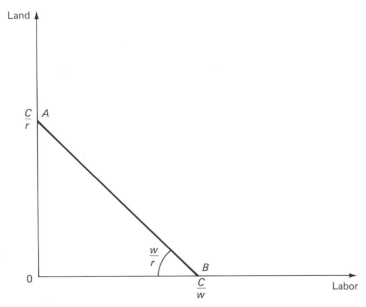

Figure 7.1 The isocost line. Given a total outlay of C dollars and assuming that the wage rate (w) and rent (r) are fixed, the firm can purchase any input combination on isocost line AB. Distance OB is given by the ratio C/w and represents the maximum number of units of labor that the firm can purchase with C dollars. Similarly, distance OA is given by the ratio C/r and represents the maximum number of units of land that the firm can purchase with C dollars. Finally, the absolute slope of line AB gives the wage/rent ratio (w/r).

of land that the firm can purchase with C dollars. Finally, the (absolute) slope of the isocost line gives the wage/rent ratio (w/r) and corresponds to the constant terms at which the firm can potentially exchange labor for land in the marketplace. All these properties of the isocost line must be obvious from our earlier discussion of the properties of the consumer's budget line in Section 4.1.

As mentioned above, a basic difference between a firm and a consumer lies in the fact that while the consumer's income is fixed, the firm's total outlay (cost) is a variable whose value must be determined. For this reason, a single isocost line is not sufficient to describe all purchasing possibilities by the firm, because the firm must know what combinations of labor and land it can purchase *for each alternative amount of total cost*. But this information is not difficult to obtain. For any given amount of total cost, we can draw an isocost line, as shown in Figure 7.2.

Isocost line T_1L_1 shows all alternative combinations of labor and land that cost exactly \$1000, isocost line T_2L_2 represents a total cost of \$2000, and finally, isocost line T_3L_3 corresponds to a total cost of \$3000. Note that as total cost increases, the firm shifts to an isocost line that lies farther from the origin.

In general, an isocost line passes through each point in the labor–land (or input) space. The totality of all isocost lines is called the *isocost map*. Note carefully that all isocost lines are parallel to each other. Their common (absolute) slope coincides, of course, with the wage/rent ratio.

Finally, observe that the isocost map is drawn on the assumption that the factor rentals (w and r) are given. When either factor rental changes, all isocost lines shift to a new position. For instance, when the wage rate rises, each isocost line rotates inward (clockwise) from its land-axis intercept, because the labor-axis intercept (C/w) decreases.

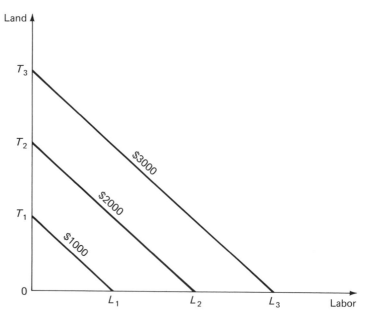

Figure 7.2 The isocost map. Given the factor rentals, the firm can draw an isocost line for each alternative amount of total cost. For instance, isocost lines T_1L_1, T_2L_2, and T_3L_3 give all alternative input combinations that the firm can purchase with $1000, $2000, and $3000, respectively. In general, an isocost line passes through each point in the input space. The totality of all isocost lines is called the *isocost map*. All isocost lines are parallel to each other, their common slope being given by the fixed wage/rent ratio.

Cost Minimization[2]

Suppose now that the firm wishes to produce a given output, say, 100 units. To do so, the firm must purchase a combination of labor and land that coincides with the coordinates of some point on the isoquant that corresponds to 100 units of output. But there are many such input combinations. Which labor–land combination will the firm actually choose? That combination which minimizes total cost. Graphically, this means that the firm will choose that point on the specified isoquant that puts it on the lowest possible isocost line. Figure 7.3 illustrates the cost-minimization procedure.

Isoquant 1 corresponds to 100 units, which is the stipulated output level. To produce 100 units of output, the firm must choose some input combination shown along this isoquant. By superimposing the isocost map, as illustrated by isocost curves, T_1L_1, T_2L_2, and T_3L_3, it becomes apparent that the firm must choose input combination E (i.e., L^* units of labor and T^* units of land) at a total cost of $2000. Input combinations that lie on the isocost lines that are lower than T_2L_2, such as N on T_1L_1, cost less than $2000 but are not capable of producing 100 units of output, because they lie below isoquant 1. On the other hand, all other input combinations along isoquant 1, such as V and U, that can produce the desired output imply a total cost that is higher than $2000, because they lie on isocost lines that are higher than T_2L_2.

Note carefully that at the optimum input combination (E) isocost line T_2L_2 is just *tangent* to isoquant 1. Indeed, under our assumptions, this tangency is the fundamental condition for cost minimization.

[2]This subsection can be read together with Section A7.1 of the Appendix to this chapter.

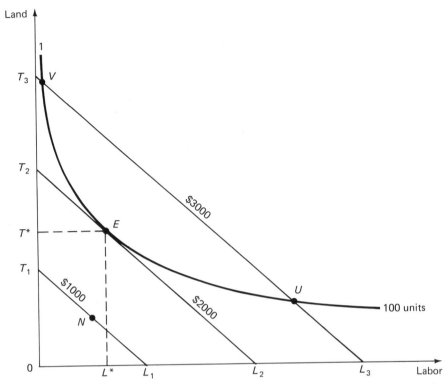

Figure 7.3 Cost minimization. Suppose that the firm wishes to produce 100 units of output. To accomplish this production level, the firm must choose an input combination (point) along isoquant 1. A rational firm will choose that input combination that minimizes total cost. By superimposing the isocost map, as illustrated by isocost curves T_1L_1, T_2L_2, and T_3L_3, it is evident that the firm must choose combination E, where isocost line T_2L_2 is just tangent to isoquant 1.

The tangency at point E implies that the absolute slope of isocost line T_2L_2 (i.e., w/r) is equal to the absolute slope of isoquant 1 (i.e., the marginal rate of technical substitution of labor for land) at E. Accordingly, the fundamental condition for cost minimization becomes

$$MRS_{LT} = \frac{MPP_L}{MPP_T} = \frac{w}{r} \tag{7.2}$$

[Recall that the marginal rate of technical substitution of labor for land (MRS_{LT}) is equal to the ratio of the marginal physical product of labor (MPP_L) to the marginal physical product of land (MPP_T).]

What is the commonsense meaning of the condition for cost minimization? We can discover the significance of equation (7.2) by considering situations in which it is not satisfied. In such situations, the firm can always reduce its total cost by a judicious substitution of one input for the other along the given isoquant. For instance, suppose that the firm arbitrarily chooses input combination V, where isoquant 1 is steeper than isocost line T_3L_3. For concreteness, suppose that the marginal rate of technical substitution of labor for land at V is equal to 4, while the common absolute slope of isocost lines is equal to only 2, because, say, $w = \$20$ and $r = \$10$. On the margin, therefore, the firm can replace 4 units of land by one extra unit of labor while maintaining output at 100 units, because $MRS_{LT} = 4$. On the other hand, the firm can obtain one extra unit of labor by giving up only 2 units of land, because the common absolute slope of isocost lines is 2. Thus the cost of one extra unit of labor in the marketplace (i.e., \$20) is equal to the cost of 2 units of land (i.e., $2 \times \$10$). Since technologically the firm can replace 4 units of land with one extra unit of labor, it follows that it can reduce its total costs by \$20 (the cost of 2 units of land) by merely substituting one extra unit of labor for 4 units of land. Such input substitution will continue to be beneficial along region VE, even though the cost reduction per extra unit of labor employed will progressively decline, because the marginal rate of technical substitution of labor for land is diminishing. We therefore conclude that moving from V toward E along isoquant 1 enables the firm to shift to progressively lower isocost lines.

If the firm starts at U instead of V, where the marginal rate of technical substitution of labor for land is lower than the wage/rent ratio, it will be able to reduce its total cost (while maintaining output at 100 units) by substituting land for labor. Thus, as the firm travels along isoquant 1 from U toward E, it moves to progressively lower isocost lines.

We must therefore conclude that total cost is minimized only when the marginal rate of technical substitution of labor for land is exactly equal to the wage/rent ratio.

An Alternative Interpretation of the Cost-Minimization Condition

There is an alternative interpretation of the cost-minimization condition which is also very illuminating. Rewrite equation (7.2) in the following equivalent form:

$$\frac{w}{MPP_L} = \frac{r}{MPP_T} \tag{7.3}$$

What is the economic meaning of equation (7.3)?

Consider first the economic interpretation of the ratio w/MPP_L. When the firm increases its employment of labor by 1 unit, two things happen: (1) the total cost increases by the wage rate w, and (2) the total output increases by the marginal physical product of labor MPP_L. Accordingly, the ratio w/MPP_L shows the cost per additional unit of output at the margin when the increase in output takes place through an increase in the employment of labor. For instance, if $w = \$20$ and $MPP_L = 2$, it follows that the cost of 1 extra unit of output (brought about by means of an appropriate adjustment in the employment of labor alone) is equal to \$10.

The additional cost that the firm may have to incur to increase output by 1 extra unit is usually called the *marginal cost* of output. Therefore, the ratio w/MPP_L gives the marginal cost of output, assuming that the firm actually increases the employment of labor only, while keeping land constant. Similarly, the ratio r/MPP_T gives the marginal cost of output when the firm actually increases the employment of land only, while keeping labor constant.

To minimize total cost, the firm must so adjust the employment of labor and land that the marginal cost of output is the same for both inputs; that is, equation (7.3) must hold. Otherwise, the firm can always reduce its total cost by transferring expenditure from the factor whose "marginal cost" is high to the other factor whose "marginal cost" is low.

For instance, return to Figure 7.3 and suppose that the firm is currently at point

V where

$$\frac{MPP_L}{MPP_T} > \frac{w}{r}$$

or

$$\frac{r}{MPP_T} > \frac{w}{MPP_L}$$

For concreteness, we may assume that $w = \$20$, $r = \$10$, $MPP_L = 4$, and $MPP_T = 1$. Thus $r/MPP_T = \$10$ and $w/MPP_L = \$5$. Evidently, the firm can reduce its total cost by transferring expenditure from land (where the marginal cost is $\$10$) to labor (where the marginal cost is only $\$5$), that is, by substituting labor for land and moving from V toward E along isoquant 1.

The common value of the ratios w/MPP_L and r/MPP_T at the cost-minimization point E is known as the firm's *long-run marginal cost*. We return to this important concept of cost in Section 7.5.

The Economic Reason for Convexity

We are now in a position to clarify the economic justification for assuming that isoquants are convex to the origin (law of diminishing marginal rate of technical substitution). A point of tangency between an isocost line and an isoquant represents a point of *minimum* total cost, only when the isoquant is convex to the origin. If the isoquant were *concave* to the origin, such a tangency would represent a point of *maximum* total cost, and the firm would never produce there.

Accordingly, with concave isoquants, the firm would never produce in the middle area of the input space; it would rather move to either axis (corner solution) depending on circumstances. This means that *the firm would employ one factor only.* Since such behavior contradicts the casual empirical observation that as a rule, firms use various combinations of all major classes of factors of production, we conclude that isoquants must be convex to the origin—at least in the economically relevant region.

The above argument does not, of course, rule out the possibility that isoquants may have concave parts. Nevertheless, we disregard such possibility because the firm will never choose an input combination along a concave region of an isoquant. (For further details, see the analogous discussion in Section 4.4 concerning the economic rationale for the convexity of indifference curves.)

Output Maximization[3]

The dual problem to cost minimization is merely *output maximization.* Suppose that the firm wishes to spend a fixed sum of money on labor and land. Obviously, it will be in the interests of the firm to choose that input combination along the relevant isocost line that *maximizes* total output.

Consider Figure 7.4. If the firm wishes to spend $\$10,000$ on labor and land, it can obtain one of the input combinations along isocost line $T_0 L_0$, such as R, E, or S. To maximize total output, the firm must choose combination $E = (L^*, T^*)$. Among

---

[3]This subsection may be read together with Section A7.2 of the Appendix to Chapter 7.

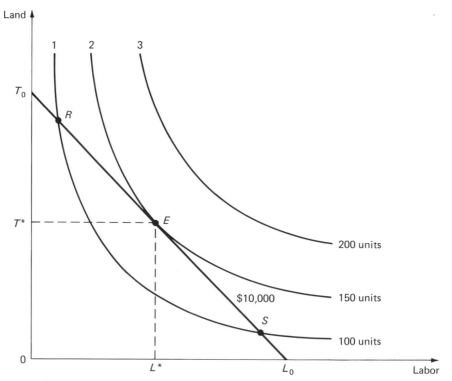

Figure 7.4 Output maximization. Suppose that the firm wishes to spend $10,000 on labor and land. It can obtain one of the input combinations along isocost line T_0L_0. A rational firm will choose that input combination that maximizes total output. By superimposing the isoquant map as illustrated by isoquants 1, 2, and 3, it is evident that the firm must choose combination E, where isocost line T_0L_0 is tangent to isoquant 2.

all the input combinations that lie along isocost line T_0L_0, only combination E enables the firm to attain isoquant 2 (i.e., produce 150 units). All other feasible input combinations along T_0L_0, such as R and S, put the firm on lower isoquants.

The problem of output maximization is analogous to the problem of utility maximization by the consumer. The condition for output maximization is identical to the condition for cost minimization. Thus the firm maximizes total output for the given expenditure on inputs at the point where the relevant isocost line is tangent to the highest attainable isoquant, that is, when the marginal rate of technical substitution of labor and land equals the wage/rent ratio. This should come as no surprise because as we already mentioned, output maximization is dual to cost minimization.

Because of the inherent relationship between cost minimization and output maximization, we can provide a third alternative interpretation of equation (7.2), which we rewrite as follows:

$$\frac{MPP_L}{w} = \frac{MPP_T}{r} \tag{7.4}$$

The ratio MPP_L/w shows the extra output that the firm produces by spending one additional dollar on labor. This we can see as follows. If the firm spends w extra dollars on labor, it will obtain 1 extra unit of labor, which will cause output to increase by the marginal physical product of labor (MPP_L). Accordingly, the firm's output increases by MPP_L/w per extra dollar spent on labor.

Similarly, the ratio MPP_T/r gives the extra output that can be made possible by spending one extra dollar on land. A rational firm maximizes its output by hiring factors until their marginal physical products per dollar are equalized.

The above proposition is analogous to the equimarginal principle for utility maximization. Readers may test their understanding of this proposition by showing that at R (Figure 7.4) the marginal physical product per dollar spent on labor is higher than the marginal physical product per dollar spent on land (i.e., $MPP_L/w > MPP_T/r$), and therefore the firm can increase output by transferring dollars from land to labor, thus moving from R toward E along isocost line T_0L_0.

7.3 The Expansion Path[4]

In Section 7.2 we discussed the problem of how a firm determines the optimal (or least-cost) input combination for producing a specified output. Indeed, we established an important condition for this purpose, namely, the tangency between the appropriate isoquant and the lowest possible isocost line. If the firm knew precisely how much output to produce, it is apparent that the preceding analysis would be sufficient.

In general, however, the optimal output is a variable whose value must be determined by the firm in its attempt to maximize profit. As a first step toward accomplishing its ultimate objective of profit maximization, the firm must repeat the analysis of cost minimization for each level of output. In other words, for each level of output the firm must determine the optimal input combination (i.e., that input combination that minimizes the total cost of producing the specified output). Once the firm solves the cost-minimization problem for each level of output, it can proceed with the determination of the optimal output.

Figure 7.5 illustrates the above procedure. The isocost map is superimposed on the isoquant map. Each tangency between an isocost line and an isoquant depicts an optimal input combination. For instance, a rational entrepreneur who wants to produce Q_1 units of output will employ input combination E_1, that is, the tangency between isocost line T_1L_1 and isoquant 1. Similarly, the optimal input combinations for Q_2 and Q_3 units of output are given by tangencies E_2 and E_3, respectively. The locus of all such cost-minimizing tangencies is known as the firm's *expansion path*. For the given wage/rent ratio (slope of isocost lines), the expansion path shows how the firm's optimal input combination varies as output expands.

The firm's expansion path is analogous to the consumer's income consumption curve. In the same way that we distinguish between normal and inferior goods on the basis of the "shape" of the income consumption curve, we could also distinguish between *normal* and *inferior inputs* on the basis of the shape of the firm's expansion path. (An inferior input is one whose quantity falls as output expands, whereas a normal input is one whose quantity increases with output.) While input inferiority cannot be ruled out as a theoretical possibility, it is highly unlikely that such comprehensive aggregates as "labor" and "land" (or "capital") could be inferior.[5] Unless explicitly stated otherwise, in the remainder of the book we assume that

---

[4]Sections 7.3 and 7.4 can be read together with Section A7.3 of the Appendix to Chapter 7.

[5]Inferiority becomes a real possibility in a disaggregated model with a detailed input classification. For instance, as output expands, the firm may use more *skilled* workers while reducing the employment of *unskilled* labor. Even though "labor" as an aggregate of skilled and unskilled workers may increase with output, unskilled labor may be an inferior input.

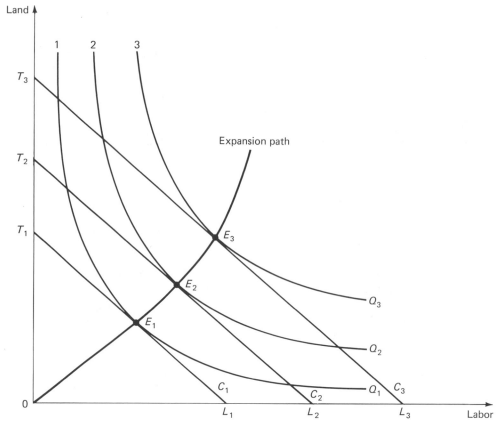

Figure 7.5 The expansion path. By superimposing the isocost map on the isoquant map, we can determine the optimal input combinations that a rational firm will choose at alternative levels of output (or total cost). These optimal input combinations occur at the tangencies between isoquants and isocost lines, as illustrated by points E_1, E_2, and E_3. The locus of all such tangencies is known as the firm's *expansion path*.

the expansion path has a positive slope (implying that the employment of both inputs increases as output expands).

In the case of constant returns to scale, the expansion path is necessarily a straight line through the origin. This follows from property 3 (see Section 6.7): The marginal rate of technical substitution depends on the proportion in which the inputs are used. Thus any straight line through the origin (signifying a fixed labor/land ratio) must intersect all isoquants at points that have the same slope. Given the wage/rent ratio, all cost-minimizing tangencies between isocost lines and isoquants must therefore occur along a straight line through the origin.

A constant-returns-to-scale production function is not the only one that has linear expansion paths. This becomes obvious when we notice that the shape of the expansion path depends on the geometric characteristics of isoquants (such as their curvature in relation to one another), not the units of output each isoquant represents. Starting with an isoquant map exhibiting constant returns to scale, we can alter at will the number of units of output that each isoquant represents (provided that a higher isoquant corresponds always to a larger output than a lower one). Such a change will obviously leave unchanged the geometric properties of isoquants, including the linearity of expansion paths. Such a general production function, whose expansion paths are straight lines through the origin while exhibiting a mixture of varying degrees of increasing, decreasing, and constant returns to scale, we call *homothetic*.

Finally, note that the expansion path is drawn for a given wage/rent ratio. When both the wage rate and the rent for land services change by the same percentage, their ratio (w/r) and the expansion path remain the same. However, the total cost (or expenditure) at each point on the expansion path changes by the exact percentage by which factor rentals change.

When only one factor rental changes, the expansion path shifts to a new position because the isocost lines shift. For instance, when the wage rate rises, each isocost line in Figure 7.5 rotates inward (clockwise) from its land-axis intercept, with the result that the expansion path rotates counterclockwise from the origin. Thus, as the wage rate rises, the firm substitutes land for labor at each level of output.

7.4 The Long-Run Cost Curves[6]

The least cost of producing a certain quantity of total output is known as the firm's *long-run total cost*. The relationship that exists between long-run total cost and alternative quantities of output is summarized by the firm's *long-run total cost curve* (or function), which shows how total cost varies as the level of output changes. The firm's long-run total-cost curve is the basic cost concept. However, we can obtain a deeper understanding of the firm's cost structure by introducing two additional concepts: the concept of the *long-run average cost* and the concept of the *long-run marginal cost*. This section deals with all three concepts of cost and studies their relationships. Section 7.5 provides further insights into the relationship between long-run average cost and the characteristics of the underlying technology.

Derivation of the Long-Run Total-Cost Curve

As it turns out, the expansion path gives all the information necessary for the derivation of the long-run total-cost curve. By construction, an isoquant and an isocost line pass through every point along the expansion path. The isoquant gives the amount of output produced; the isocost line gives the least cost of producing that output (i.e., the long-run total cost of production). This information is sufficient to determine a point on the long-run total-cost curve. By repeating the same experiment for each point on the expansion path, we can determine each corresponding point on the long-run total-cost curve.

Figure 7.6 illustrates the preceding procedure. The long-run total-cost curve C_L corresponds to (is derived from) the expansion path of Figure 7.5. For instance, point E_1' corresponds to point E_1 (Figure 7.5), where the firm produces Q_1 units of output at a long-run total cost of C_1 (because, by assumption, all points along isocost line T_1L_1 have a total cost of C_1 dollars). Similarly, points E_2' and E_3' on the long-run total-cost curve (Figure 7.6) correspond to points E_2 and E_3, respectively, on the expansion path (Figure 7.5).

The long-run total-cost curve has two important properties: (1) it starts at the origin and (2) it has a positive slope throughout. Property 1 follows from the observation that when the firm's output is zero, the long-run total cost is also zero, because all factors are variable (the firm is in the planning stage so to speak). Property 2 is attributed to the undeniable characteristic that the least cost of producing a larger output is higher than the least cost of producing a smaller output. That is, as the firm moves along the expansion path from a lower to a higher isoquant, it necessarily moves from a lower to a higher isocost line as well.

---

[6]This section can be read together with Section A7.3 of the Appendix to Chapter 7.

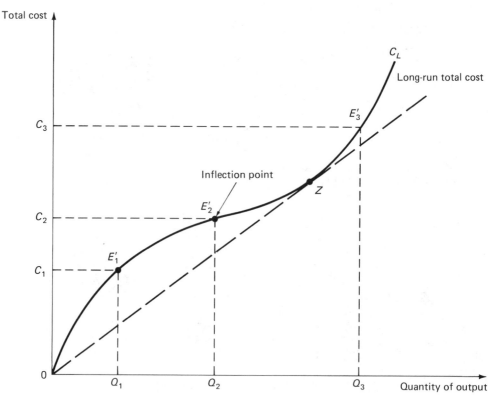

Figure 7.6 The long-run total-cost curve. Each point on long-run total-cost curve C_L corresponds to (is derived from) a point on the expansion path of Figure 7.5. For instance, points E_1', E_2', and E_3' on C_L correspond to points E_1, E_2, and E_3, respectively, on the expansion path (Figure 7.5). In general, the long-run total-cost curve starts at the origin and has a positive slope throughout.

The typical long-run total-cost curve is *concave* at low levels of output and eventually becomes *convex,* as illustrated by the long-run total-cost curve of Figure 7.6. The economic justification for this behavior is presented in Section 7.5.

The Long-Run Average-Cost Curve

The long-run average cost is, by definition, the long-run cost *per unit* of output. It is given by the *total cost/total output* ratio. For instance, if the long-run total cost of 100 units of output is $500, the long-run average cost is $5 (i.e., $500/100 = $5 per unit).

Given the long-run total-cost curve (C_L), we can easily determine the long-run average cost for any level of output, as shown in Figure 7.7 (see p. 220), which shows a typical long-run total-cost curve in panel (a). When the firm produces Q_1 units of output, the corresponding long-run total cost is C_1 (see point A). Accordingly, the long-run average cost is given by the ratio C_1/Q_1, which geometrically coincides with the slope of vector $0A$. The latter joins the origin with point A. We can follow a similar procedure and determine the long-run average cost at each level of output.

Based on the long-run total-cost curve of Figure 7.7(a), we constructed a long-run average-cost curve (AC_L), as shown in Figure 7.7(b). (For the moment, ignore the dashed curve labeled MC_L.) At each level of output, we calculated the slope of the vector from the origin to the corresponding point on the long-run total-cost curve and summarized the results in Figure 7.7(b).

Consider an imaginary trip along the long-run total-cost curve, starting at the origin. As we travel along the concave portion, say, from the origin to inflection point A, the long-run average cost continues to fall (the vector from the origin to the long-run total-cost curve becomes progressively flatter). However, the average cost does *not* stop falling at the inflection point. It continues to fall until we reach point B, where the vector from the origin actually becomes tangent to the total-cost curve. Beyond point B, the average cost increases (the vector from the origin becomes progressively steeper).

The long-run average-cost curve has a positive intercept (point G) with the vertical axis. This may be puzzling, because when output is zero, total cost is zero as well, and the ratio $0 \div 0$ is undefined. To understand the meaning of point G, start at point A, panel (a), where the firm produces Q_1 units of output at a total cost equal to C_1. Allow the level of output to decrease gradually from Q_1 toward zero, causing point A to travel along the long-run total-cost curve toward the origin. During this process, the slope of vector $0A$ rises continuously and tends to become equal to the slope of the tangent to the long-run total-cost curve at the origin. It is this limiting value of the long-run average cost as output tends to zero (i.e., the slope of the tangent to the long-run total-cost curve at the origin) that is actually being reflected by the intercept of the long-run average-cost curve with the vertical axis (point G).

For any level of output, we can determine the corresponding long-run total cost from the long-run average-cost curve. For instance, when the firm produces Q_1 units of output, the total cost of production is given by the area of rectangle $0Q_1A'H$. This follows from the fact that

long-run total cost $\equiv$ output $\times$ long-run average cost

The last identity is nothing more than a rearrangement of the definition of long-run average cost.

The Long-Run Marginal-Cost Curve

The long-run marginal cost is the addition to long-run total cost that results from a unit increase in total output. For instance, if long-run total cost increases from \$1000 to \$1050 as total output increases from 10 to 11 units, the long-run marginal cost (i.e., the extra cost incurred for producing the last unit of output) is \$50 (i.e., \$1050 − \$1000). In general, if long-run total cost increases by ΔC_L dollars when total output increases by ΔQ units, the long-run marginal cost (MC_L) is given by the ratio $\Delta C_L / \Delta Q$; that is,

$$MC_L = \frac{\Delta C_L}{\Delta Q} \tag{7.5}$$

Graphically, the long-run marginal cost is given by the slope of the long-run total cost curve at the current total output. This is illustrated in Figure 7.7. When the firm produces Q_0 units of output, the long-run marginal cost is given by the slope of the tangent to the long-run total-cost curve at point D, in panel (a). The same is true for any other level of output.

In panel (b), right below the long-run total-cost curve, we constructed the corresponding long-run marginal-cost curve (MC_L). At each level of output, we cal-

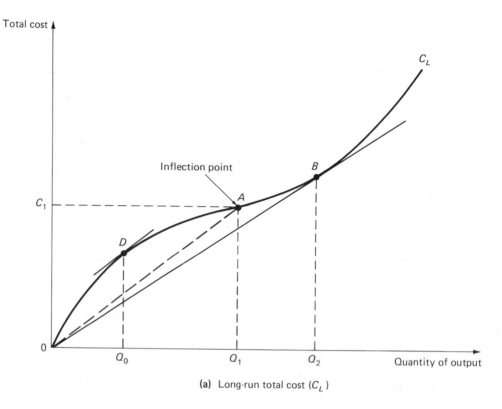

Total cost

C_L

Inflection point

C_1

A

B

D

0   Q_0 Q_1 Q_2 Quantity of output

(a) Long-run total cost (C_L)

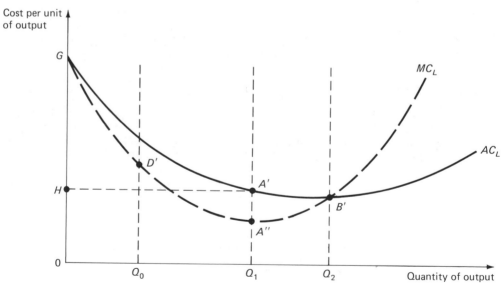

Cost per unit
of output

G

MC_L

AC_L

D'

H

A'

B'

A''

0   Q_0 Q_1 Q_2 Quantity of output

(b) Long-run average cost (AC_L) and marginal cost (MC_L)

culated the slope of the tangent to the long-run total-cost curve in panel (a) and registered the results in panel (b). This procedure is analogous to the derivation of the marginal utility curve from the total utility curve, and the marginal-physical-product-of-labor curve from the total product curve.

Consider again an imaginary trip along the long-run total-cost curve, starting at the origin. As we travel along the *concave* portion, that is, from the origin to inflection point A, the long-run marginal cost continues to fall (the tangent to the long-run total-cost curve becomes progressively flatter). At inflection point A, the long-run marginal cost reaches its minimum. As we continue to travel beyond point A along the *convex* portion, the long-run marginal cost begins to increase (the tangent to the long-run total-cost curve becomes progressively steeper). These observations explain the shape of the long-run marginal-cost curve in panel (b).

For any level of output, we can determine the corresponding long-run total cost of production as the area under the long-run marginal-cost curve. For instance, when the firm produces Q_0 units of output, the total cost of production is given by area $0GD'Q_0$. This is analogous to the relationship that exists between the marginal utility curve and total utility (discussed in Chapter 3) and between the marginal-physical-product curve and total output (discussed in Chapter 6). This property follows from the fact that the long-run total cost of production is the *sum* of long-run marginal costs.

The Relationships Between Long-Run Average and Marginal Cost

Turn now to the relationships that exist between the long-run average cost and marginal cost.

First, note that both the long-run average-cost and marginal-cost curves have the same positive intercept [point G in Figure 7.7(b)]. This should be obvious. Surely, the long-run marginal cost at zero output corresponds to the positive slope of the long-run total-cost curve at the origin [Figure 7.7(a)]; and as we explained earlier, the same slope of the long-run total-cost curve at the origin gives the limiting value of the long-run average cost as output tends to zero.

Second, when the long-run marginal cost is lower than the average, the long-run average cost tends to fall as output increases. When the long-run marginal cost is higher than the average, the long-run average cost tends to increase as output increases. In the limiting case in which the long-run marginal cost is equal to the average, the long-run average cost remains constant for a "small" change in output.

This important relationship is illustrated in Figure 7.7(b). For any output level less than Q_2, the long-run marginal-cost curve lies below the average, pulling the

---

Figure 7.7 Long-run total cost, average cost, and marginal cost. When the firm produces Q_1 units of output, the total cost of production is C_1, as illustrated by point A in panel (a). The corresponding long-run average cost is given by the ratio C_1/Q_1, which coincides with the slope of vector $0A$, and the corresponding long-run marginal cost is given by the slope of (the tangent to) the long-run total-cost curve at point A. By registering these results in panel (b), as illustrated by points A' and A'', and repeating the same experiment for all conceivable levels of output, we can trace out the long-run average-cost and marginal-cost curves, as shown. The long-run average-cost curve has the same positive intercept with the vertical axis (point G) as the marginal-cost curve, it is declining in the region where the marginal lies below it and rises in the region where the marginal lies above it, and finally, it reaches its minimum (point B') when the marginal intersects it (and vector OB is just tangent to C_L). The marginal-cost curve is declining when C_L is concave, it is rising when C_L is convex, and it reaches its minimum at inflection point A of C_L.

average down; for any output level higher than Q_2, the long-run marginal-cost curve lies above the average, pulling the average up; and when output is at Q_2, the marginal-cost curve intersects the average at its "minimum" point (see point B'), which is a "stationary" point.

The reason for this relationship is similar to that offered in Chapter 6 for the relationship between the average physical product and the marginal physical product of labor. A rigorous proof is given in the Appendix to this chapter.

That the long-run average-cost curve reaches its minimum at the point where it is intersected by the marginal-cost curve should be evident from Figure 7.7(a). As we mentioned above, the long-run average cost reaches its minimum at the point where the tangent to the long-run total-cost curve passes through the origin, as shown by point B. At that point, the slope of the tangent (i.e., the slope of vector $0B$) gives both the marginal cost and the average cost. Accordingly, when the average cost is at its minimum point, the marginal cost must be equal to it.

Finally, the long-run marginal-cost curve reaches its minimum at a lower output than the long-run average-cost curve. For instance, in Figure 7.7(a), the marginal-cost curve attains its minimum at inflection point A, whereas the average-cost curve reaches its minimum at a higher level of output, as illustrated by point B.

7.5 Returns to Scale and Long-Run Average Cost[7]

The precise shape of the long-run average-cost curve reflects the characteristics of the underlying technology (production function). In particular, it reflects the nature of returns to scale. When returns to scale are increasing, the long-run average-cost curve slopes downward; when they are decreasing, it slopes upward; and when they are constant, it is horizontal.[8] This section provides a heuristic proof of this proposition. A rigorous proof is provided in the Appendix to Chapter 7.

Constant Returns to Scale

We saw in the preceding section that in the special but important case of constant returns to scale, the expansion path is necessarily a straight line through the origin. In this case, the long-run total-cost curve is also a straight line through the origin, while the long-run average-cost curve is given by a horizontal line. To see why this is so, suppose that the firm increases its output along the linear expansion path. All inputs increase at the same rate as output (because of the very definition of constant returns to scale). Since by assumption factor rentals remain constant, it follows that the firm's total expenditure on inputs (i.e., long-run total cost) necessarily increases at the same rate as all inputs and output, and the firm's average cost remains constant. For instance, when output doubles, long-run total cost doubles also, while long-run average cost necessarily remains unchanged.

Increasing Returns to Scale

When returns to scale are *increasing* (when output increases faster than all inputs), the long-run total cost does not increase as fast as output. Consequently, the long-run average cost declines as output expands. This is shown in Figure 7.8, panel (a). For instance, as output increases from 100 to 200 units (i.e., doubles),

---

[7]This section may be read together with Section A7.4 of the Appendix to this chapter.

[8]Because of the strict relationship that exists between the long-run total-cost curve and the long-run average-cost curve, it must be evident that the shape of the long-run total-cost curve also reflects the underlying returns to scale.

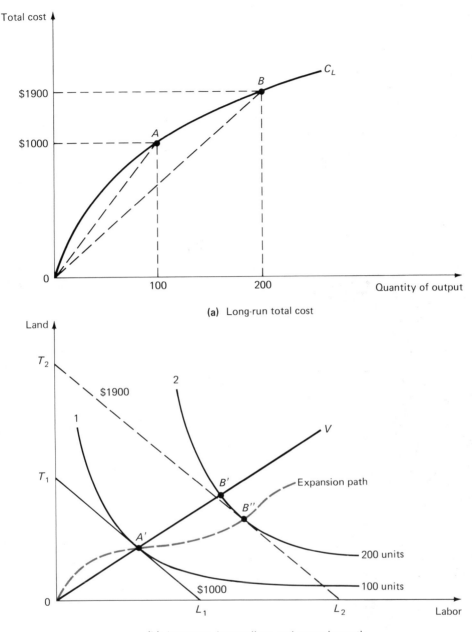

(a) Long-run total cost

(b) Isoquants, isocost lines, and expansion path

Figure 7.8 The shape of the long-run average-cost curve under increasing returns to scale. When returns to scale are increasing throughout, the long-run average-cost curve is downward sloping because total cost does not increase as fast as total output. For instance, if the firm wishes to double output from 100 to 200 units, total cost will rise from $1000 to only $1900, as shown in panel (a). As a result, average cost will fall from $10 to $9.50, as shown by the slopes of vectors OA and OB, respectively.

With a *homothetic* production function, the expansion path is linear, as illustrated by OV in panel (b). Because of increasing returns to scale, $A'B' < OA'$; therefore, the total cost at B' must be less than $2,000. Thus average cost at B' must be less than $10.

With a nonhomothetic production function, the expansion path may take the shape indicated by dashed line $OA'B''$. To produce 200 units, the firm must now choose input combination B'', which lies on a lower isocost line than B'. A fortiori, then, the total cost at B'' must be less than 2000, and the corresponding average cost must be less than $10.

long-run total cost increases from $1000 to $1900 only (as indicated by points A and B), causing the long-run average cost to decrease from $10 to $9.50.

Figure 7.8, panel (b), provides a heuristic proof of this proposition. Isoquants 1 and 2 represent 100 and 200 units of output, respectively. By assumption, the optimal input combination for producing 100 units of output occurs at A', where isocost line T_1L_1, corresponding to $1000, is tangent to isoquant 1. Point A' in panel (b) corresponds to point A in panel (a). The long-run average cost of 100 units of output is $10 (i.e., $1000/100). Suppose now that the firm increases its output from 100 to 200 units. The average cost at 200 units will be less than $10 if, and only if, total cost remains less than $2000. Is it possible for total cost to increase from $1000 to $2000 (or even higher)? No, in the presence of increasing returns to scale this is not possible.

If the production function were *homothetic*, the expansion path would be a straight line through the origin, as shown by vector $0V$. To increase output from 100 to 200 units, the firm would have to move from point A' to B'. Because of increasing returns to scale, distance $A'B'$ is necessarily less than distance $0A'$. (Recall Figure 6.10.) Accordingly, the isocost line passing through B' (not drawn) would correspond to a total cost of production that is less than twice the cost at A'. Suppose that, in fact, the total cost at B' is only $1950, giving rise to an average cost of $9.75 (which is less than $10). This is enough, of course, for the long-run average-cost curve to be downward sloping.

What if the production function is not homothetic? Well, the expansion path will pass through A' but will no longer be linear. This is actually shown by the dashed expansion path $0A'B''$. In this case, the optimal input combination for producing 200 units of output will be different from B'. In particular, in the example of Figure 7.8, the firm will produce at B''. Since the firm could have produced 200 units of output at B' but did not, we must infer that the total cost of production at optimal point B'' must necessarily be lower than the total cost at suboptimal point B'. A fortiori, the total cost of production at B'' must be less than $2000, since the cost at B' is already less than $2000. By implication, the long-run average cost at B'' must be less than $9.75 (i.e., the average cost at B'). In Figure 7.8 we assume that the total cost at B'' is only $1900 (see isocost line T_2L_2, which is tangent to isoquant 2 at B''), giving rise to an average cost of only $9.50. Point B'' in panel (b) corresponds to point B in panel (a).

We therefore conclude that in the presence of universal increasing returns to scale, and irrespective of whether the production function is homothetic or not, the long-run average cost of production decreases as output expands. As a result, the long-run average-cost curve is downward sloping.

Decreasing Returns to Scale

When returns to scale are *decreasing* (when output increases by a smaller percentage than all inputs), the long-run total cost increases faster than output, causing the long-run average cost to rise. This is shown in Figure 7.9, panel (a) on p. 226. For instance, as output increases from 100 to 160 units (by 60 percent), total cost increases from $500 to $1000 (by 100 percent), and average cost rises from $5.00 to $6.25; and when output increases further from 160 to 200 units (by 25 percent), total cost increases from $1000 to $1400 (by 40 percent), and average cost rises from $6.25 to $7.00.

Figure 7.9, panel (b), provides a heuristic proof of this proposition. Isoquants 1, 2, and 3 represent 100, 160, and 200 units of output, respectively. By assumption, the optimal input combination for producing 100 units of output occurs at A', where isocost line T_1L_1 (corresponding to $500) is tangent to isoquant 1. Accordingly, point A' in panel (b) corresponds to point A in panel (a). Suppose now that the firm wishes to double its output to 200 units. Under decreasing returns to scale, the firm's total cost will more than double and the average cost will rise.

If the production function were *homothetic,* the expansion path would be a straight line through the origin, as shown by vector $0V$. To increase output from 100 to 200 units, the firm would have to move from A' to C'. Because of decreasing returns to scale, distance $A'C'$ is necessarily larger than distance $0A'$. (Recall Figure 6.10.) Accordingly, the isocost line passing through C' (not drawn) would correspond to a total cost of production that is more than twice as large as the cost at A'. We may suppose that the cost at C' is actually \$1500, giving rise to an average cost of \$7.50 ($>$\$5.00). This is enough to cause the long-run average-cost curve to be upward sloping.

In the general case of a nonhomothetic production function, the expansion path will pass through A' but will no longer be linear. Accordingly, point C' will no longer represent the optimal input combination for producing 200 units of output. Rather, the firm will move to a different point on isoquant 3 by substituting one input for the other. By means of such input substitution, the total cost of production will definitely fall below \$1500 (total cost at C'), and the average cost will be less than \$7.50. Is it possible for the total cost of 200 units to fall below \$1000 (which is twice as large as the cost of 100 units), and for the average cost to fall below \$5.00? No, it is not possible. We can prove this by showing that the maximum output that the firm can achieve with a total cost of \$1000 is less than 200 units, which necessarily implies that the total cost of producing 200 units must be higher than \$1000. Thus the average cost at 200 units of output must be higher than \$5.00.

Consider isocost line T_2L_2, which corresponds to \$1000, and suppose that the firm maximizes output at point B'. (B' must be different from B'' because of the assumed nonhomotheticity of the production function). Draw vector $0B'$ and let it intersect isocost line T_1L_1 at point S. By construction, distance $0S$ must be exactly equal to distance SB'. At point S, the firm produces less than 100 units (say, 99), because point S lies below isoquant 1. Because of decreasing returns to scale, the output at B' must be less than twice the output at S. (As the firm moves from S to B', all inputs double but output does *not*.) For instance, the output at B' may be 160 units only, as shown by isoquant 2. Accordingly, the total cost of 200 units must be higher than \$1000—isoquant 3 must be tangent to an isocost line that is higher than T_2L_2. This necessarily implies that the average cost at 200 units of output must be higher than \$5.00 (i.e., \$1000/200).

We have, therefore, shown that when output doubles from 100 to 200 units, the total cost increases from \$500 to a figure that is definitely higher than \$1000. Thus the average cost increases as output expands. As a result, the long-run average-cost curve is upward sloping.

The Typical Long-Run Average-Cost Curve

As explained in Section 6.6, the production function of a typical firm combines elements of increasing, constant, and decreasing returns to scale. In particular, increasing returns to scale are usually observed at low levels of output (due to "economies" of large-scale production). As output expands, the initial increasing returns are followed successively by constant and then decreasing returns to scale, presumably because of increasing difficulties of supervision and, in general, inefficiencies in management.

We must, therefore, conclude that the typical long-run average-cost curve is U-shaped, as illustrated in Figure 7.7(b). In other words, average cost declines at low levels of output (because of the underlying increasing returns to scale). At the precise point (B') where the long-run average-cost curve attains a minimum, the firm experiences momentary constant returns to scale; thereafter, average cost increases

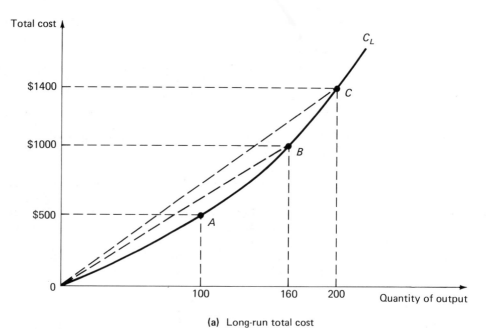

(a) Long-run total cost

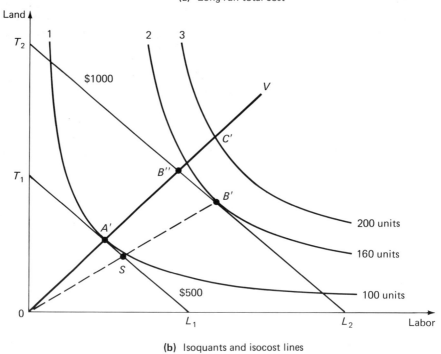

(b) Isoquants and isocost lines

226

because the firm encounters decreasing returns to scale. Evidently, a U-shaped long-run average-cost curve generates a long-run total-cost curve that is *concave* at low levels of output and becomes *convex* at high levels of output, as shown in Figures 7.6 and 7.7.

7.6 The Short-Run Cost Curves

The firm's long-run cost curves are drawn on the assumption that all factors are variable. As we explained in Section 6.3, in the long run the firm enjoys complete adjustability of all inputs. On the other hand, "short run" refers to a period of time during which some inputs are fixed and unadjustable. This lack of full adjustability of factor quantities is "the" distinguishing feature of the short run. This section develops the cost curves that are relevant for the short run, and studies their relationships.

Fixed Cost Versus Variable Cost

Because *factors* are classified into fixed and variable in the short run, the short-run total cost of production (C_s) consists of two components: (1) the total fixed cost (F), corresponding to the cost of fixed factors; and (2) the total variable cost (V), corresponding to the cost of variable factors. In other words,

$$C_s = F + V \qquad (7.6)$$

The distinction between fixed and variable cost is fundamental in economics. It is often thought that fixed cost is that part of total cost that remains constant at all levels of output. While this is also a feature of fixed cost, its crucial characteristic is simply that it is *unavoidable even at zero output*. A truly fixed cost is inherently a "sunk cost"; that is, it is a cost for an input that is irretrievably committed to the firm's own productive operations. This means, in effect, that fixed cost is not a true cost—the opportunity cost of a truly fixed (or "specific") factor is zero.

Examples of costs that have the appearance of being fixed but do not satisfy the crucial test (of being unavoidable at zero output) are not hard to find. For instance, the rent paid for a piece of land or a building may be held constant by a lease

---

Figure 7.9 The shape of the long-run average-cost curve under decreasing returns to scale. When returns to scale are universally decreasing, the long-run average-cost curve is upward sloping because total cost increases faster than output. For instance, in panel (a), as output increases from 100 to 160 and then to 200 units, total cost increases from $500 to $1000 and then to $1400, respectively. Accordingly, long-run average cost increases from $5.00 (at A) to $6.25 (at B) and then to $7.00 (at C), as shown by the slopes of vectors OA, OB, and OC, respectively. Panel (b) shows why this is so. With a linear expansion path (homothetic production function), doubling output from 100 to 200 units more than doubles cost because $A'C' > OA'$. With a nonlinear expansion path (nonhomothetic production function), it is evident that doubling cost from $500 to $1000 is not enough to double output. Thus, with $1000 total cost, the firm produces at B'. By construction, $SB' = OS$. But at S (which lies below isoquant 1) the firm produces less than 100 units. Because of decreasing returns to scale, the output at B' must be less than twice the output at S. In particular, we assume that total output is only 160 units at point B'. Accordingly, isoquant 3 (200 units of output) must be tangent to an isocost line that is higher than $T_2 L_2$ ($1000), and the long-run average cost at 200 units must be higher than $5.

agreement irrespective of the output of the firm. Yet such rent may not represent a sunk cost to the extent that the entrepreneur may actually sublease the land or the building to someone else. Of course, based on the fundamental principle of opportunity cost, the rent so retrieved must be considered as an element of the variable cost.

Similarly, the depreciation of a piece of capital equipment may not represent, in whole or in part, a truly fixed (or sunk) cost. To the extent that the equipment could be rented out to someone else, or to the extent that depreciation depended on the actual *use* of the equipment (not just the mere passage of time), and therefore its services could be transferred to a future period, current depreciation charges should not be viewed as a fixed (or sunk) cost.

The total variable cost, on the other hand, is that part of total cost that the firm can avoid completely by closing down. It corresponds precisely to the opportunity cost of the factors employed by the firm.

The significance of the distinction between fixed and variable cost springs from the fact that only the variable cost is relevant for making decisions. The fixed cost is a sunk cost that is totally irrelevant to decision making on the principle that bygones are bygones.

The Short-Run Total-Cost Curve

Figure 7.10 is similar to Figure 7.5. As before, in the long run the firm operates along the expansion path, which is the locus of tangencies between isocost lines (illustrated by T_1L_1, T_2L_2, and T_3L_3) and isoquants (illustrated by curves 1, 2, and 3). Suppose that the firm originally plans to produce a long-run-equilibrium output of Q_2 units. For this purpose it must purchase the input combination indicated by tangency E_2.

Assume further that while labor is a variable factor in the short run, land is not. Accordingly, having committed itself to the fixed amount, T_0, of land (fixed factor), the firm can change its output in the short run by adjusting labor (variable factor) only. Thus, in the short run, the firm can no longer move along the expansion path. Rather, it will move along horizontal line T_0Z.

Because along line T_0Z the isocost lines are not tangent to the isoquants (except at point E_2), the cost-minimization condition [equation (7.2)] is violated. Consequently, the short-run total cost of production is necessarily higher than the corresponding long-run total cost at all levels of output, except for the singular quantity Q_2 for which the size of the fixed factor (land) is optimal. For instance, if the firm wishes to produce Q_3 units of output, it would not be able to produce at E_3 simply because it lacks the capacity to adjust the fixed factor (land). It will rather produce at B, which lies on a higher isocost line (not drawn) than E_3. Thus incomplete adjustment means higher costs.

In Figure 7.11, panel (a), the gray curve C_L represents the long-run total-cost curve that corresponds to the expansion path of Figure 7.10. Points E_1', E_2', and E_3' on C_L correspond to points E_1, E_2, and E_3, respectively, on the expansion path. We assume that the total cost of the fixed factor is C_0. As we mentioned earlier, the total fixed cost is the same at every output, including zero; thus it is represented by horizontal line C_0F. The total variable cost is represented by curve V, which necessarily starts at the origin and has a positive slope throughout, reflecting the progressively higher wage bill for progressively larger outputs. The curve labeled C_s is the short-run total-cost curve; it gives the short-run total cost at alternative levels of output.

Since $C_s = F + V$ by definition, there is a strict relationship among the three short-run total-cost curves. In particular, the sum of the heights of the F and V curves at any output equals the height of the C_s curve. Alternatively, the verti-

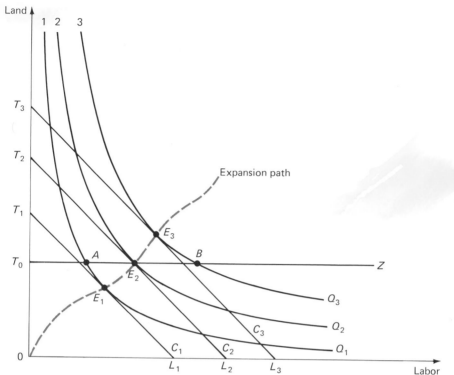

Figure 7.10 Production and cost in the short run. Originally, the firm plans to produce a long-run equilibrium output of Q_2 units and thus chooses input combination E_2. Having committed itself to T_0 units of land (fixed factor), the firm cannot move along the expansion path in the short run. If it wishes to change its output, it will have to move along horizontal line T_0Z by adjusting labor (variable factor) only. This incompete adjustment involves the penalty of a higher total cost. For instance, to increase output to Q_3, the firm must choose input combination B because the most efficient combination (E_3) is not available, but B lies on a higher isocost line than E_3. Similarly, to reduce output to Q_1 units, the firm must choose input combination A, which costs more than the least-cost combination E_1.

cal distance between the C_s and V curves is everywhere equal to the total fixed cost (F).

Note carefully that the short-run total-cost curve (C_s) is tangent to the long-run total-cost curve (C_L) at point E_2', corresponding to Q_2 units of output for which the size of the fixed factor is optimal. At any other level of output, the C_s curve is higher than the C_L curve, because of the higher costs involved in the short run due to incomplete adjustment.

Geometrically, points along the C_s curve correspond to points along horizontal line T_0Z in Figure 7.10. For instance, points A', E_2', and B' on C_s correspond to points A, E_2, and B, respectively, on horizontal line T_0Z. At point A, the firm produces Q_1 units of output but at a cost (C_1') that is higher than C_1. Similarly, at B the firm produces Q_3 units of output but at a cost (C_3') that is higher than C_3.

The Short-Run Average and Marginal-Cost Curves

Corresponding to the three species of short-run total cost (F, V, and C_s), there are also three species of short-run average cost: average fixed cost (AFC), average variable cost (AVC), and average cost (AC_s). These species of short-run per unit cost

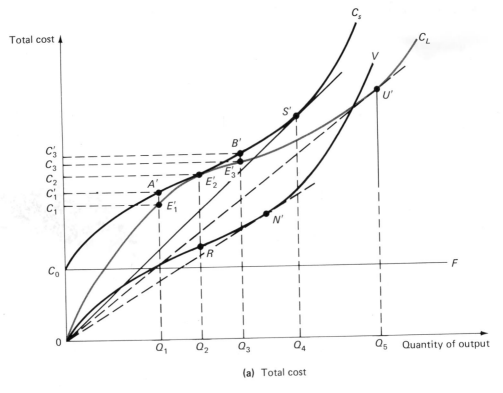

(a) Total cost

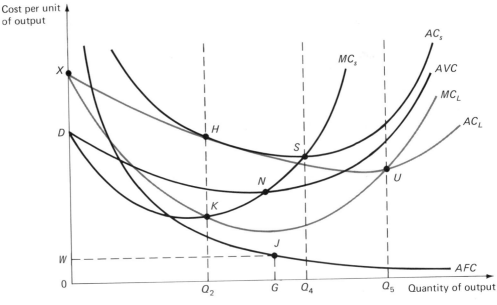

(b) Average and marginal cost

Figure 7.11 The short-run cost curves. In panel (a) we obtain the short-run total-cost curve (C_s) by displacing the total-variable-cost curve (V) vertically upward by the amount of the total fixed cost (F). C_s is tangent to the long-run total-cost curve (gray C_L curve) at Q_2 units of output, which is the output for which the fixed factor is optimal. C_s lies above C_L at all other outputs. Panel (b) shows the corresponding per unit curves for the long run (gray AC_L and MC_L) and the short run (AC_s, AVC, AFC, and MC_s). At the output level of Q_2 units, AC_s is tangent to AC_L and MC_s intersects MC_L from below. Also, MC_s intersects both AVC and AC_s at their respective minima (N and S, respectively). Curve AFC is a rectangular hyperbola.

are defined as follows:

$$AFC = \frac{F}{Q} \tag{7.7}$$

$$AVC = \frac{V}{Q} \tag{7.8}$$

$$AC_s = \frac{C_s}{Q} \tag{7.9}$$

In each case, the "average" is equal to the corresponding "total" divided by the firm's total output (Q).

The three species of per unit cost can be determined graphically from the corresponding species of short-run total cost. The rule is simple: *The "average" is equal to the slope of a line from the origin to any desired point on the corresponding "total" curve.* In Figure 7.11(b), we used this rule to construct the three "average" curves (AFC, AVC, and AC_s) from the corresponding "total" curves (F, V, and C_s) illustrated in Figure 7.11(a). The gray curves labeled AC_L and MC_L represent the long-run average-cost and marginal-cost curves, respectively, corresponding to the grey C_L curve in Figure 7.11(a). Note that the AC_s curve lies above the AC_L curve at all outputs except Q_2 where the curves are tangent to each other, reflecting the tangency at E_2' in Figure 7.11(a) between C_s and C_L.

Even though there are three different "total" (F, V, and C_s) and three different "average" curves (AFC, AVC, and AC_s), there is only one meaningful concept of short-run *marginal* cost (MC_s). This is analogous to the concept of long-run marginal cost and represents the extra total cost that the firm must incur in the short run in order to increase output by 1 unit. Because $C_s = F + V$ and F is constant, any change in C_s is necessarily equal to the change in V. Accordingly,

$$MC_s = \frac{\Delta C_s}{\Delta Q} = \frac{\Delta V}{\Delta Q} \tag{7.10}$$

Graphically, the short-run marginal cost is given either by the slope of the short-run total-cost curve (C_s), or by the slope of the total-variable-cost curve (V). These two slopes must be the same at any output because the C_s curve is merely a vertical displacement of the V curve.

The Relationships Among the Various Short-Run Cost Curves

We now proceed with a brief summary of some additional relationships among the various curves in Figure 7.11. There is no need for detailed proofs in most cases in view of our earlier discussion of the relationships among the long-run cost curves.

1. *The average-fixed cost curve (AFC) has the distinctive shape of a rectangular hyperbola.* The area of the rectangle formed with the axes from any point on it [such as $0GJW$ in Figure 7.11(b)] is always the same and equal to the total fixed cost. Thus, rearranging equation (7.7), we have $AFC \cdot Q = F$, where AFC and Q are the height and width, respectively, of the said rectangle. The AFC curve is asymptotic to both axes.

2. *The average-variable-cost curve (AVC) is typically U-shaped.* The economic reasons for this behavior are given in the next subsection.

3. *The height of AC_s at any output equals the sum of the heights of AFC and AVC.* This property follows from the fundamental identity $C_s = F + V$, which is equivalent to

$$AC_s = AFC + AVC \qquad (7.11)$$

Equation (7.11) is obtained from equation $C_s = F + V$ by dividing both sides of the latter equation by Q and then using the definitions of AC_s, AFC, and AVC as given by equations (7.7) to (7.9).

4. *The short-run average-cost curve (AC_s) is U-shaped and reaches its minimum at a higher level of output than does the average-variable-cost curve (AVC).* At low levels of output, AC_s declines because both AFC and AVC decline. Indeed, AC_s would be declining even if AVC were not, in view of the sharply falling AFC in its early stage (reflecting the spreading of the total fixed cost over a progressively larger number of units). Essentially for the same reason, AC_s continues to decline even after AVC turns upward, because the declining AFC outweighs the rising AVC. Eventually, however, AC_s turns upward also, reflecting the diminishing influence of AFC relative to the rising AVC. In Figure 7.11(b), AVC reaches its minimum at N while AC_s attains its minimum at a higher level of output, as illustrated by point S.

5. *The short-run average-cost curve (AC_s) reaches its minimum at that level of output for which the tangent to the short-run total-cost curve passes through the origin.*

6. *The average-variable-cost curve (AVC) reaches its minimum at that level of output for which the tangent to the total-variable-cost curve (V) passes through the origin (or when the tangent to C_s intersects the vertical axis at the level of total fixed cost).*

7. *The area of the rectangle formed at any desired point on AC_s gives the corresponding short-run total cost (C_s).*

8. *The area of the rectangle formed at any desired point on AVC gives the corresponding total variable cost (V).*

9. *The short-run marginal-cost curve (MC_s) is negatively sloped when C_s (or V) is concave, it is positively sloped when C_s (or V) is convex, and it reaches a minimum when C_s (or V) has an inflection point.*

10. *The short-run marginal-cost curve (MC_s) lies below AVC when AVC is declining, it lies above AVC when AVC is rising, and it intersects AVC at its minimum point,* as illustrated by point N in Figure 7.11(b).

11. *The short-run marginal-cost curve (MC_s) lies below AC_s when AC_s is declining, it lies above AC_s when AC_s is rising, and it intersects AC_s at its minimum point,* as illustrated by point S in Figure 7.11(b).

12. *The area under the short-run marginal-cost curve (MC_s) from the vertical axis to a vertical line drawn at any desired level of output gives the total variable cost (V).* MC_s is totally independent of the fixed cost.

13. *The average-variable-cost curve (AVC) and the short-run marginal-cost curve (MC_s) have the same positive intercept with the vertical axis,* as illustrated by point D in Figure 7.11(b).

14. *The short-run average-cost curve (AC_s) is asymptotic to the vertical axis, because the average-fixed-cost curve is asymptotic.*

15. *At the output for which the quantity of the fixed factor is optimal, C_s is tangent to C_L (and AC_s is tangent to AC_L). Accordingly, MC_s and MC_L are necessarily equal at that same output, but they are not tangent. In particular, MC_s intersects MC_L from left to right (or from below),* as illustrated by point K in Figure 7.11(b).

It is often thought that MC_L must be greater than MC_s, because MC_L depends on *full* cost (in the long run *all* costs are variable), while MC_s depends only on the total variable cost (not the fixed cost). This idea is wrong. Figure 7.11(a) shows clearly that C_s is steeper than C_L just to the right of tangency E_2', while C_L is steeper than C_s just to the left of E_2'. This is geometrically necessary if C_s is to be tangent to C_L at E_2' and at the same time lie above C_L everywhere else. What is the economic explanation for this apparently paradoxical phenomenon?

Return to Figure 7.10 and assume that the firm is currently producing at E_2. If the firm wishes to increase its output by 1 extra unit, it will have to move to a point, such as B, along horizontal line T_0Z where the cost-minimization condition is violated. Accordingly, the short-run marginal cost for *increasing* output by 1 unit must necessarily be higher than the long-run marginal cost. This reflects the fact that the firm pays a "penalty" for not being able to adjust optimally all factors of production.

Suppose, however, that starting at point E_2 the firm wishes to *reduce* output by one unit. Will the marginal cost be larger in the short run or in the long run? Be careful. For a reduction in output, we must *think in terms of the outlays that the firm can actually save*. As it turns out, the firm can save more in the long run (where it enjoys full adjustability) than in the short run (where the degree of adjustability is limited). Therefore, for a reduction in output, MC_L must be larger than MC_s. For instance, in Figure 7.10, the firm must move from E_2 to, say, A which is definitely inferior to E_1. Thus in the short run the total cost of production does not fall as rapidly as in the long run, which implies that MC_s (cost saving in the short run) is much lower than MC_L (cost saving in the long run).

The Relationship Between the Average Variable Cost and the Average Physical Product of Labor

We now wish to explain why the average-variable-cost curve is typically U-shaped. For this purpose we must unearth an important relationship that exists between the average variable cost (AVC) and the average physical product of labor (APP_L).

In the simple case of a single variable factor (labor), the total variable cost (V) is equal to the market rental of the factor (w) times the number of units of the variable factor employed. That is,

$$V = w \cdot L \tag{7.12}$$

where w is the wage rate and L the units of labor. Substituting equation (7.12) into equation (7.8), we obtain

$$AVC = \frac{V}{Q} = w \cdot \frac{L}{Q} = \frac{w}{Q/L} = \frac{w}{APP_L} \tag{7.13}$$

Accordingly, AVC is inversely related to APP_L. When APP_L is increasing (first stage of production), AVC is decreasing; when APP_L is declining (second and third stages of production), AVC is rising; and finally, when APP_L reaches a maximum, AVC is at its minimum.

Figure 7.12 illustrates the above relationship and shows how to derive the average-variable-cost curve from the average-physical-product-of-labor curve. In the fourth quadrant, we have the total-product curve, and in the third quadrant we show the corresponding average-physical-product-of-labor-curve. The shapes of these curves may seem a little unfamiliar, because labor (L) is measured vertically (moving downward from the origin). The curve in the second quadrant is a rectangular

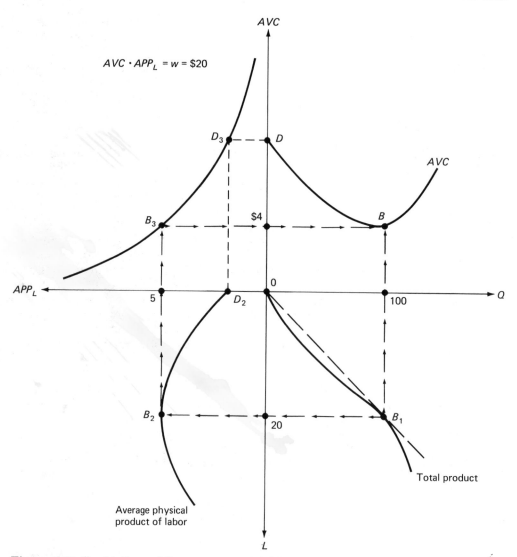

Figure 7.12 Derivation of the average-variable-cost curve. For any arbitrary point on the total product curve, such as B_1, we complete rectangle $B_1B_2B_3B$, whose corner (B) in the first quadrant gives a point on AVC. In this manner we can determine as many points as we please on the AVC curve.

hyperbola defined by the equation $AVC \cdot APP_L = w$, which is a simple rearrangement of equation (7.13). From the information given in quadrants 2, 3, and 4, we derive the average-variable-cost curve (AVC) in the first quadrant. For any arbitrary point on the total product curve, say, B_1, we complete rectangle $B_1B_2B_3B$, whose corner (B) in the first quadrant gives a point on AVC. In this manner we can determine as many points as we please on AVC. When we have enough points, we can trace out the entire curve (AVC) in the first quadrant.

The justification for this geometrical procedure is rather simple. At B_1 the firm employs 20 units of labor and produces 100 units of output. Moving vertically upward, we register the 100 units, which is the horizontal (or Q) coordinate of point B on AVC. To obtain the average variable cost at 100 units of output (i.e., the vertical coordinate of point B), we return to point B_1 and move horizontally to the left to point B_2 on the APP_L curve, which shows that at the current level of production, $APP_L = 5$. Moving vertically upward, we register 5 along the APP_L axis, and we continue until we reach point B_3 on the rectangular hyperbola in the second quadrant. The coordinates of B_3 show that when $APP_L = 5$, the corresponding average variable cost is \$4 (on the assumption that $w = \$20$). Moving horizontally to the right, we register \$4 along the AVC axis. We now have both coordinates of point B, which we determine perfectly by completing the rectangle.

Note carefully that the shape of the *long-run* average-cost curve depends on the behavior of *returns to scale*. On the other hand, the shape of AVC depends on the behavior of the *average physical product of the variable factor* (and the *law of diminishing returns*).

The Relationship Between the Short-Run Marginal Cost and the Marginal Physical Product of Labor

Before concluding this section it is interesting to note that in the simple case of a single variable factor (labor), the short-run marginal cost (MC_s) is inversely related to the marginal physical product of the variable factor (MPP_L). We can see this by rearranging equation (7.10) as follows:

$$MC_s = \frac{\Delta V}{\Delta Q} = \frac{\Delta V}{\Delta L} \cdot \frac{\Delta L}{\Delta Q} = \frac{\Delta V}{\Delta L} \div \frac{\Delta Q}{\Delta L} = \frac{w}{MPP_L} \qquad (7.14)$$

The ratio $\Delta V / \Delta L$ shows the change in total variable cost (wage bill) when labor (L) increases by 1 unit. Surely, this ratio must be equal to the wage rate (w). The ratio $\Delta Q / \Delta L$ is, by definition, the marginal physical product of labor (MPP_L).

Equation (7.14) shows clearly that MC_s is inversely related to the marginal physical product of labor. In particular, when MPP_L is rising, MC_s is falling; when MPP_L is falling, MC_s is rising; and when MPP_L is at a maximum, MC_s is at a minimum.

We leave as an exercise for the interested reader the derivation of the short-run marginal-cost curve (MC_s). For this purpose, Figure 7.12 should be amended as follows: *Replace the APP_L curve in the third quadrant by the MPP_L curve;* change the name of the variable measured along the horizontal axis (moving from right to left) from APP_L to MPP_L, and the name of the variable measured along the vertical axis (moving vertically upward) from AVC to MC_s. The rectangular hyperbola in the second quadrant is now the locus of points that satisfy the equation $MC_s \cdot MPP_L = w$. You can now start determining points on the MC_s curve (first quadrant) by completing rectangles, as before. ·

7.7 The Relationships of Long-Run Costs and Alternative Sets of Short-Run Costs

In the preceding section we discussed only one set of short-run cost curves—that set for which the fixed factor (T_0) was optimal for the production of Q_2 units of output. Assuming that the fixed factor (land) becomes continuously variable in the long run,[9] however, there must exist an infinite number of alternative sets of short-run cost curves—a different set for each alternative value of the fixed factor which

---

[9]This means that the fixed factor is perfectly divisible. The question of indivisibility, or "lumpiness," of the firm's fixed factor is considered below.

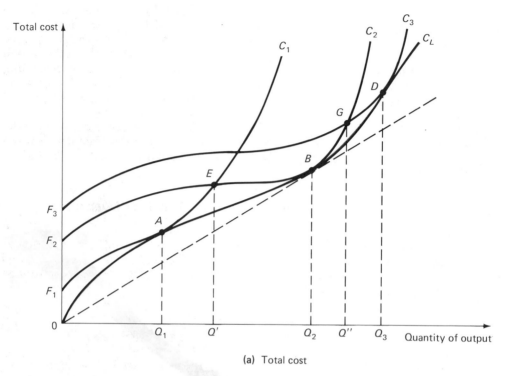

(a) Total cost

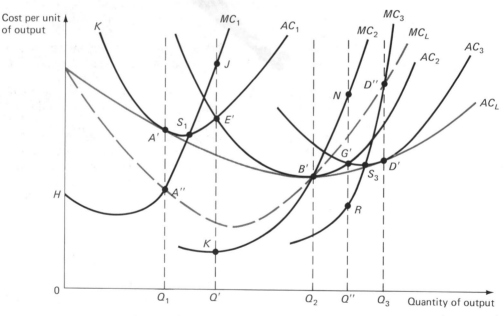

(b) Average and marginal cost

is optimal at a different long-run-equilibrium output. Each set of short-run cost curves must also bear the same relationships to the unique set of long-run cost curves as the relationships we studied earlier in Section 7.6 (particularly Figure 7.11). This is shown in Figure 7.13.

The long-run cost curves are shown by gray lines in both panels. The infinite family of sets of short-run cost curves is illustrated by only three sets identified with subscripts 1, 2, and 3. These three sets correspond to the long-run-equilibrium outputs of Q_1, Q_2, and Q_3 units, respectively. Accordingly, at Q_1, C_1 is tangent to C_L (point A) in panel (a), AC_1 is tangent to AC_L (point A') in panel (b), and MC_1 intersects MC_L (point A'') from below in panel (b).[10] The same relationships hold also between the other two sets of short-run cost curves (i.e., 2 and 3), on the one hand, and the unique set of long-run cost curves, on the other (at outputs Q_2 and Q_3, respectively).

Several observations are now in order. We summarize them briefly as follows:

1. The long-run total-cost curve (C_L) in panel (a) may be viewed as the *envelope* of the family of short-run total-cost curves. (As is well known, an envelope of a family of curves is a curve that is "touched" by all members of the family. At a point on the envelope, both the envelope and the particular member of the family touching it have the same slope.) To understand this, simply visualize the entire family of short-run total-cost curves and then consider their lower boundary line (envelope). This lower boundary line is none other than the long-run total-cost curve (C_L).
2. The long-run average-cost curve (AC_L) in panel (b) is also the envelope of the family of short-run average-cost curves; that is, AC_L is the lower boundary of the entire family of short-run average-cost curves.
3. Points A' and D' in panel (b) (i.e., the tangencies of AC_1 and AC_3, respectively, with AC_L) do *not* coincide with the minima of AC_1 and AC_3, respectively. In particular, AC_1 reaches its minimum at S_1 (where MC_1 intersects AC_1 from below), and AC_3 reaches its minimum at S_3 (where MC_3 intersects AC_3 from below).[11] The same is true, of course, at all other points along AC_L, except point B' (i.e., the point where the long-run average cost is at a minimum).
4. At output Q_1 (where $Q_1 < Q_2$), $AC_L = AC_s > MC_L = MC_1$. This is evident by comparing points A' and A'', and holds for all output levels that are lower than Q_2. Similarly, at output Q_3 (where $Q_3 > Q_2$), $AC_L = AC_s < MC_L = MC_3$.

Figure 7.13 The long-run cost curves as envelopes of alternative sets of short-run cost curves. The long-run cost curves are given by the grey lines in both panels. The infinite family of sets of short-run cost curves is illustrated by the three sets identified with subscripts 1, 2, and 3, which correspond to the long-run-equilibrium outputs of Q_1, Q_2, and Q_3, respectively. At output Q_1, C_1 is tangent to C_L (point A), AC_1 is tangent to AC_L (point A'), and MC_1 intersects MC_L (point A'') from below. The same relationships hold also between sets 2 and 3, on the one hand, and the long-run cost curves, on the other, at outputs Q_2 and Q_3, respectively. C_L in panel (a) is the *envelope* of the family of short-run total-cost curves. Similarly, AC_L is also the *envelope* of the family of short-run average-cost curves.

When the fixed factor is indivisible and sets 1, 2, and 3 are the only relevant sets of short-run cost curves, the long-run total-cost curve is given by $F_1AEBGDC_3$, the long-run average-cost curve by $KA'S_1E'B'G'S_3D'AC_3$, and the long-run marginal-cost curve by $HA''S_1JKB'NRS_3D''MC_3$.

[10]For simplicity, we omitted the separate curves of fixed and variable cost.

[11]At point A', both AC_1 and AC_L have the same slope. Since the slope of AC_L is negative at A', the same must be true of the slope of AC_1. But AC_1 attains a minimum when its slope is zero, and this occurs at a higher level of output, as illustrated by point S_1.

This becomes apparent when we compare points D' and D'', and holds for all output levels that are higher than Q_2. However, at output Q_2 (where AC_L is at a minimum), we have the important equation $AC_L = AC_2 = MC_L = MC_2$.

The above observations have important implications. If the firm wishes to produce a long-run equilibrium output, say, Q^*, that is different from Q_2 (where AC_L is at a minimum), it will *not* build a plant whose AC_s attains its minimum at Q^*. If Q^* is less than Q_2, as illustrated by Q_1 in Figure 7.13, the firm will choose that plant whose short-run average-cost curve is AC_1, and it will produce on the *downward-sloping* portion of AC_1. On the other hand, if Q^* is greater than Q_2, as illustrated in Figure 7.13 by Q_3, the firm will choose that plant whose short-run average-cost curve is AC_3, and it will produce on the *upward-sloping* portion of AC_3.[12]

5. When the fixed factor is indivisible, or "lumpy," only those short-run cost curves that correspond to the admissible values of the fixed factor become relevant; the rest are necessarily ruled out. For instance, suppose that there are only three sizes of plants, small, medium, and large, and that their short-run cost curves correspond to the sets labeled as 1, 2, and 3, respectively, in Figure 7.13. As a consequence, each plant (with its associated short-run cost curves) becomes optimal over some range of long-run-equilibrium outputs rather than just one such output as in the continuous case. In particular, the small plant is optimal for any output between zero and Q', the medium-size plant is optimal for any output between Q' and Q'', and the large-size plant is optimal for outputs higher than Q''. In this case the long-run total-cost curve is the "scalloped" locus of C_1, C_2, and C_3, that is, curve $F_1AEBGDC_3$. Similarly, the long-run average-cost curve is given by $KA'S_1E'B'G'S_3D'AC_3$ and the long-run marginal-cost curve by $HA''S_1JKB'NRS_3D''MC_3$. Note that the long-run marginal-cost curve has two discontinuities (one at Q' and the other at Q'') as a reflection of the discontinuities of slope of the long-run total-cost curve (at points E and G, respectively).

7.8 Selected Empirical Applications

In this section we present empirical evidence on the cost structure of two industries: the U.S. trucking industry and the cement industry.

The U.S. Trucking Industry

A number of studies confirm the hypothesis that there are significant economies of scale in the U.S. trucking industry. Typically, larger firms have distinctly lower costs. This hypothesis is illustrated in Table 7.1, which is based on a study by J. P. Rakowski (1978).

A sample of 371 firms (taken from a population of 479 carriers) is divided into 12 groups according to the size of their annual revenues. Column (2) gives the size of *average* revenue within each group. Group 1 consists of the smallest firms and group 12 of the largest.

As a proxy for output, we can use such physical measures as vehicle-miles (VM) or ton-miles (TM). Even though transportation economists never fail to remind us

[12]In a classic article, Jacob Viner (1931) asserted that AC_L is the locus of minima of the various short-run average-cost curves, such as points S_1 and S_3. He explained in a footnote (p. 36) that his "instructions to the draftsman were to draw" C_L as an *envelope* tangent to the various short-run average-cost curves *and* also passing through their minimum points. The draftsman, of course, promptly replied that this construction was impossible.

(1) Group	(2) Average Revenue (thousand dollars)	(3) *C/VM* (dollars)	(4) *C/TM* (dollars)
Table 7.1 Economies of Scale in U.S. Trucking			
1	862	2.361	0.337
2	1,482	2.117	0.321
3	2,084	2.142	0.251
4	2,812	2.070	0.294
5	3,870	1.969	0.293
6	5,646	2.081	0.296
7	8,164	1.911	0.202
8	11,182	1.925	0.206
9	15,111	1.793	0.174
10	21,492	1.844	0.168
11	43,098	1.987	0.158
12	135,406	1.443	0.109

Source: Adapted from Rakowski (1978, p. 167).

that 1 ton moved 100 miles is not the same thing as 100 tons moved 1 mile, we consider these imperfect physical measures as good enough for our purposes.

Column (3) gives the cost per vehicle-mile (*C/VM*); and column (4), the cost per ton-mile (*C/TM*). It is evident from columns (3) and (4) that the long-run average cost (*C/VM* or *C/TM*) in the U.S. trucking industry exhibits a definite downward trend as firm size increases. For instance, the cost per vehicle-mile is $2.361 for group 1, $2.081 for group 6, and only $1.443 for group 12. Similarly, the cost per ton-mile decreases from $0.337 (group 1) to $0.109 (group 12).

The Cement Industry

The production of cement takes place in three stages. The first stage involves assembling, preparing, grinding, and amalgamating the raw materials (limestone, cement rock, snail or oyster shell, and clay) in the appropriate proportions. In the

Costs/Barrel (1960 dollars)	Capacity (1000 barrels)						
	704	1230	1524	1990	2520	2990	5863
Table 7.2 Average Cost of Cement Manufacturing							
Direct labor	0.361	0.457	0.423	0.397	0.341	0.300	0.153
Raw materials	0.114	0.114	0.114	0.114	0.114	0.114	0.114
Power	0.358	0.358	0.358	0.358	0.358	0.358	0.358
Fuel	0.404	0.404	0.404	0.404	0.404	0.404	0.404
Indirect labor and overhead costs	0.575	0.534	0.507	0.481	0.426	0.392	0.275
Depreciation on fixed capital	0.841	0.767	0.744	0.691	0.631	0.592	0.431
Interest on fixed capital	0.663	0.605	0.587	0.546	0.498	0.467	0.341
Average total costs	3.586	3.239	3.137	2.991	2.772	2.627	2.076

Source: McBride (1981, p.109).

second stage, the mixture produced by the first process is roasted at high temperatures (approximately 2700°F) in rotary kilns (fired by coal, gas, or oil) to form cement clinker. In the final stage, the clinker is mixed with small amounts of gypsum (retarding agent) and ground into the fine powder known as cement.

The cement production process employs several large units of capital equipment and exhibits significant economies of scale. This is shown in Table 7.2. As capacity increases from 704 thousand barrels to 5863 thousand barrels, the average cost of cement (last line) decreases from $3.586 to $2.076. Note that the largest element of cost is depreciation on fixed capital followed by interest on fixed capital. Raw materials constitute a negligible part of cost.

Table 7.2 shows clearly that the cost of raw materials, fuel, and power usage per unit of output are invariant with respect to scale. The primary sources of economies of scale are capital costs (depreciation and interest) along with direct and indirect labor. As capacity increases from 704 to 5863 thousand barrels, depreciation and interest fall by 49 percent, while direct and indirect labor fall by 58 and 52 percent, respectively.

SUMMARY

1. The concept of cost includes both explicit costs and implicit costs (or imputed costs).

2. The opportunity cost of an input is the value forgone (or opportunity lost) by not employing the input in its best alternative use.

3. Depreciation is based on historical cost (sunk cost), which need not coincide with the opportunity cost of the durable good.

4. An isocost line is the locus of all alternative combinations of inputs (labor and land) that the firm can purchase with a given amount of dollars. Its absolute slope shows the ratio of input prices (w/r).

5. The whole family of isocost lines (each drawn for a different amount of dollars) is called the isocost map. All isocost lines have the same slope (w/r).

6. An optimal input combination is indicated by the tangency between an isocost line (corresponding to, say, C^* dollars) and an isoquant (corresponding to, say, Q^* units of output). This tangency (which takes three alternative forms: $MRS_{LT} = MPP_L/MPP_T = w/r$, $w/MPP_L = r/MPP_T$, or $MPP_L/w = MPP_T/r$) is the fundamental condition (a) for cost minimization (the problem of selecting that input combination which minimizes the total cost of Q^*) and (b) output maximization (the problem of choosing that input combination which maximizes output subject to the total cost C^*).

7. The assumption that isoquants are convex rests on the argument that nonconvexity is un-

acceptable because it leads to results which are inconsistent with observed behavior. Concave isoquants lead to corner solutions—use of one factor only.

8. The expansion path is the locus of all optimal input combinations. Under constant returns to scale, the expansion path is a straight line through the origin. (In general, all homothetic production functions have linear expansion paths.)

9. A different expansion path is drawn for a different wage/rent ratio. As w/r falls, the firm substitutes labor for land at all levels of output and the expansion path tilts toward the labor axis.

10. The long-run total-cost curve is derived from the expansion path and shows how (minimized) total cost varies as output changes. It has two general properties: (a) it starts at the origin (zero output is associated with zero cost) and (b) it has a positive slope (larger output involves higher total cost).

11. The average cost (total cost/total output) coincides with the slope of the vector joining the origin with the relevant point on the total-cost curve. Total cost (average cost × total output) coincides with the area of the rectangle formed with respect to the relevant point on the average-cost curve. The average-cost curve reaches a minimum at that output for which the tangent to the total-cost curve passes through the origin. (These relationships hold between C_L and AC_L, C_s and AC_s, and V and AVC.)[13]

12. Marginal cost is the addition to total cost (C_s, V, or C_L) that results from a unit increase in output. It is given by the slope of the total-cost curve (C_s, V, or C_L). As output expands, the marginal cost falls or rises according to whether the total-cost curve (C_s, V, or C_L) is concave or convex, respectively; it reaches a minimum at the inflection point of the total-cost curve (C_s, V, or C_L). The total variable cost (V or C_L) coincides with the area under the marginal-cost curve.

13. The average-variable cost curve (AVC or AC_L) and the marginal-cost curve have the same vertical-axis intercept. The average-cost curve (AC_s, AVC, or AC_L) falls or rises according to whether the marginal-cost curve lies below it or above it, respectively; it reaches a minimum at the point where the marginal-cost curve intersects it. The marginal-cost curve reaches its minimum at a lower output than does the average-cost curve (AC_s, AVC, or AC_L).

14. The slope of the *long-run* average-cost curve is negative, positive, or zero according to whether *returns to scale* are increasing, decreasing, or constant.

15. The short-run total cost is the sum of (a) the total fixed cost (which is unavoidable even at zero output) and (b) the total variable cost. Because of the existence of fixed factors, the firm does not operate on the long-run expansion path and thus violates the cost-minimization condition; hence $C_s > C_L$. When the size of the fixed factor happens to be optimal, C_s is tangent to C_L (and AC_s is tangent to AC_L), and MC_s intersects MC_L from below.

16. The average-fixed-cost curve is a rectangular hyperbola. The U-shaped short-run average-cost curve is asymptotic to the vertical axis and reaches its minimum at a higher output than does the average-variable-cost curve.

17. The short-run average variable cost and marginal cost are inversely related to the average and marginal physical product of labor (variable input), respectively.

18. The long-run total-cost curve may be viewed as the envelope of all short-run cost curves; and the long-run average-cost curve, the envelope of all short-run average cost curves.

19. If the firm wishes to produce a long-run equilibrium output Q_0, it will not always build a plant whose AC_s attains its minimum at Q_0. The rule is to build that plant whose AC_s at Q_0 is lower than that of any other conceivable plant.

QUESTIONS

1. A firm uses labor (L) and capital (K) to produce output Q). Capital is a fixed factor; labor is variable. Suppose that the wage rate is $10. The following table gives information about the production function.

(a) Fill in the blanks in the table.

(b) Use the information in the completed table to plot the relevant points on the curves of average physical product of labor (APP_L) and marginal physical product of labor (MPP_L).

(c) On a separate diagram, plot the relevant points on the curves of average fixed cost (AFC), average variable cost (AVC), short-run average cost (AC_s), and short-run marginal cost (MC_s).

L	Q	APP_L	MPP_L	AFC	AVC	AC_S	MC_S
1	___	5	___	$100	___	___	___
2	___	___	7	___	___	___	___
3	___	7	___	___	___	___	___
4	32	___	___	___	___	___	___
5	___	___	3	___	___	___	___
6	___	6	___	___	___	___	___
7	35	___	___	___	___	___	___

[13]To avoid repetition, statements 11, 12, and 13 are cast in general terms. They are valid both in the long run and the short run.

(d) Compare the curves of APP_L and AVC. Do you detect any pattern?

(e) Compare the curves of MPP_L and MC_s. Do you detect any pattern?

2. (a) Prove that constant returns to scale lead to a horizontal average-cost curve.

(b) Prove that increasing returns to scale lead to a negatively sloped average-cost curve.

(c) Prove that decreasing returns to scale lead to a positively sloped average-cost curve.

3. Suppose that your firm uses labor and land in the production of a certain commodity. You are currently employing 10 workers and 20 acres of land. The total wage bill is $800 per day; the total rent is $1200 per day.

(a) Suppose that the marginal physical products of labor and land are 16 and 14, respectively. Is your firm minimizing long-run costs?

(b) Alternatively, assume that your firm is indeed minimizing long-run costs. What is the long-run marginal cost of output if you are certain that the marginal physical product of land is 10?

4. In a famous article, Jacob Viner (1931) asserted that the typical U-shaped long-run average cost curve is the locus of the minimum points of the family of short-run average cost curves associated with all conceivable scales of plant. His draftsman protested that such a drawing was impossible to construct. In criticizing the draftsman, Viner said: "My instructions to the draftsman were to draw the $[AC_L]$ curve so as never to be above any portion of any $[AC_s]$ curve. He is a mathematician, however, not an economist, and he saw some mathematical objection to this procedure which I could not succeed in understanding."

(a) Who was correct in this debate, Viner or his draftsman?

(b) Are there any conceivable circumstances in which the draftsman would not have raised any objections to Viner's procedure?

(c) What is the economic implication of the draftsman's objection?

5. Explain how the curves of AC_L, MC_L, AC_s, AFC, AVC, and MC_s as well as the expansion path will shift in each of the following cases:

(a) The government imposes a $1 tax per unit of output.

(b) The firm is required to pay a licence fee of $1000 per year for the privilege of doing business irrespective of how much output it produces.

(c) The wage rate rises by $1.

6. A corporation is exploring the construction of one of three alternative plants for manufacturing a new product. The average costs at alternative levels of output for each of the three plants are indicated below.

Output	Plant A	Plant B	Plant C
30	$10		
40	6		
50	4	$15	
60	7	7	
70	20	2	
80		8	$ 8
90		30	5
100			9
110			18

(a) Determine the long-run average-cost curve.

(b) Indicate the range of output over which each plant is optimal.

(c) Approximately what is the long-run marginal cost at $Q = 50$, or $Q = 70$, or $Q = 90$?

*7. A firm uses labor L and land T to produce total output Q according to the production function

$$Q = 10L^{3/4}T^{1/4}$$

Suppose that the wage rate and rent are $w = 10 and $r = 5, respectively.

(a) Calculate the firm's expansion path and the curves of AC_L and MC_L.

(b) Suppose that land is held fixed at $T = 625$. Calculate the curves of AVC, AFC, AC_s, and MC_s. What is the marginal cost of the fiftieth unit?

(c) Suppose the firm wishes to spend $1000 on labor and land. What input combination should it purchase in order to maximize output?

8. Regulatory commissions in the United States allow public utilities to raise their prices sufficiently so as to earn a "fair rate of return" on their capital. Does a guaranteed rate of return interfere with the goal of cost minimization? Why or why not?

9. A firm has three plants whose total costs for various outputs are indicated below.

Output	Total Cost		
	Plant *A*	Plant *B*	Plant *C*
0	$200	$1000	$500
1	210	1002	505
2	222	1008	513
3	236	1019	528
4	252	1036	554
5	270	1061	594

(a) Determine how the firm should allocate among the three plants the following alternative total outputs: 1, 2, 3, 5, 9, 11, and 14.

(b) Sketch the firm's curves of short-run average cost and marginal cost.

10. In the fall of 1983 President Reagan signed the social security bill, which contained a new method of financing health costs for the elderly. In the past, the government paid whatever it cost to treat Medicare patients (within certain limits). On the basis of the new method, the government will decide in advance how much it will pay for treating each of 467 types of medical problems. Explain how, in your opinion, the new method of financing will affect the cost of health care.

FURTHER READING

Baumol, W. J. (1977). *Economic Theory and Operations Analysis,* 4th ed. Prentice-Hall, Inc., Englewood Cliffs, N.J. Chapter 11.

Marshall, A. (1920). *Principles of Economics,* 8th ed. Macmillan & Company Ltd., London. Book 5, Chapters 8–11.

McBride, M. E. (1981). "The Nature and Source of Economies of Scale in Cement Production," *Southern Economic Journal,* Vol. 48 (July), pp. 105–115.

Rakowski, J. P. (1978). "Economies of Scale in U.S. Trucking," *Journal of Economics and Business,* Vol. 30 (Spring/Summer), pp. 166–176.

Samuelson, P. A. (1947). *Foundations of Economic Analysis.* Harvard University Press, Cambridge, Mass. Chapter 4.

Shepard, R. W. (1953). *Cost and Production Functions.* Princeton University Press, Princeton, N.J.

Viner, J. (1931). "Cost Curves and Supply Curves," *Zeitschrift für Nationalökonomie,* Vol. 3, pp. 23–46. Reprinted in K. E. Boulding and G. J. Stigler (eds.), *Readings in Price Theory.* Richard D. Irwin, Inc., Homewood, Ill., 1952.

PART FOUR

The Firm and the Industry

CHAPTER
8

The Firm:
Its Environment
and Goals

This part of the book examines the problem of determining price and output levels in alternative market structures: perfect competition, monopoly, oligopoly, and monopolistic competition. In each case the analysis proceeds from the equilibrium of the firm to the equilibrium of the industry. Of course, in the case of monopoly the equilibrium of the firm coincides with the equilibrium of the industry, because in monopoly the firm happens to be the industry. In essence, the present discussion is an elaboration of the Marshallian partial-equilibrium supply–demand analysis of Chapter 2. In this fashion we finally begin to see how the decisions and actions of millions of diverse individual consumers and producers lead, through a system of prices and markets, to the allocation of resources—a problem that we investigate further in Parts Five and Six.

This chapter serves as an introduction to Part Four. In Section 8.1 we begin with a preliminary classification of "selling markets" and then discuss the most important features of each market structure. In Section 8.2 we examine the various aspects of the firm's revenue. Finally, in Section 8.3 we discuss first various alternatives to profit maximization and then present the reasons why we assume that firms maximize profits.

8.1 Market Structures

Because the determination of equilibrium prices and output levels depends crucially on the particular market forms (or structures) in which firms sell their products, we provide in this section a preliminary taxonomy of "selling markets." Although oversimplified, this taxonomy is very useful as a first approximation, especially when the implied groups of the firms constitute well-defined industries. In addition, it serves both as an introduction and a guide to the discussion in this part of the book.

A Classification of Market Structures

To classify industries (or groups of firms) into various meaningful categories, we initially concentrate on two criteria: (1) the number of firms in the industry and (2) the nature of the product produced by the firms that constitute the industry. On the basis of the first criterion ("number of firms in the industry"), we classify industries according to whether they have *many, few,* or *one* firm. On the other hand, on the basis of the second criterion ("nature of product"), we divide industries into two categories according to whether the products of the rival firms are *homogeneous* (i.e., identical) or *differentiated.* Table 8.1 summarizes the resultant two-way classification.

Note that there are only five meaningful market types: *perfect competition, monopolistic competition, pure oligopoly, differentiated oligopoly,* and *monopoly.* The situation where a single firm produces differentiated products is not relevant— especially since we are assuming that each firm produces only one product.

In the terminology of Table 8.1, the terms "competition," "oligopoly," and "monopoly" refer to the number of firms in the industry. In particular, "competition" denotes that the rival sellers are "many." Similarly, the term "oligopoly" suggests that there are only a "few" rival firms in the industry, and "monopoly" refers to the situation where a single firm is the sole producer in the industry.[1]

On the other hand, the adjectives "perfect" and "pure" connote "homogeneous" or perfectly substitutable products, in contrast to the adjectives "monopolistic" and "differentiated," which suggest "differentiated" products (i.e., products that are relatively close but not perfect substitutes, as explained below).

It is important to note that in the present context the term "competition" does not have the same meaning as in its usage in everyday speech. In particular, competition does *not* mean *rivalry* (i.e., the ability and willingness of producers to encroach upon each other's market). As stated earlier, competition means a situation in which an industry consists of *many* firms. Indeed, because of the large number of producers in a competitive industry, direct confrontation, or rivalry, between firms is totally absent. Accordingly, a competitive industry functions in an "impersonal" fashion in response to market stimuli.

All market structures other than the polar case of perfect competition are often grouped together under the general heading of *imperfect competition.* Monopoly, then, may be viewed as the "most imperfect" market structure, while monopolistic competition may be considered to be the "least imperfect" market structure. Oligopoly necessarily occupies a middle position between monopoly and monopolistic competition.

The classification of market structures summarized in Table 8.1 focuses on the sellers' side of the market. On the basis of the buyers' side we may distinguish among three types of markets: perfectly competitive (many small buyers each of

Table 8.1 Classification of Market Structures

Nature of Product	Number of Firms		
	Many	Few	One
Homogeneous	Perfect competition	Pure oligopoly	Monopoly
Differentiated	Monopolistic competition	Differentiated oligopoly	

[1]The term "oligopoly" is derived from the Greek words "ὀλίγος" (meaning "some" or "few") and "πωλῶ" (meaning "sell"). Similarly, the term "monopoly" is derived from the Greek words "μόνος" (meaning "single") and "πωλῶ" (meaning "sell").

whom is a price taker), *oligopsonistic* (few buyers), and *monopsonistic* (single buyer). When economists refer to the model of the perfectly competitive market, they mean a market structure that is competitive both on the sellers' side and the buyers' side, as in Chapter 2. *Bilateral monopoly* refers to the situation where a single seller (monopoly) faces a single buyer (monopsony).

Homogeneous Versus Differentiated Products

Before proceeding with a preliminary examination of the basic features of each of the five market structures summarized in Table 8.1, we must discuss briefly the meaning of the terms "homogeneous" and "differentiated" products.

As we pointed out in Chapter 2, a product is called homogeneous when all units of the product offered for sale are of the same quality, at least in the eyes of the buyers. Accordingly, when we say that an industry produces a homogeneous product, we must understand a situation in which each firm produces a product that is identical to the product produced by every other firm in the industry. In essence, this means that the products produced by the various firms in the industry are *perfect substitutes*. As a result, buyers are indifferent about the particular firm they may purchase the product form, as long as all firms charge the same price.

On the other hand, by "differentiated products" we must understand products that are not identical. Typically, such products are different from one another in some respects, although their differences may be more apparent than real. In technical terms, we may say that differentiated products are not perfect substitutes; rather, they are imperfect substitutes. Economists usually require differentiated products to be *close* substitutes for the simple reason that generally there is some substitutability between any two commodities. After all, as our discussion in Part Two made clear, all commodities compete for the consumer's fixed income.

However, there is not a generally acceptable definition of what constitutes "close" substitutability. Because of this, the definition of "product" is necessarily arbitrary, because it depends on an arbitrarily specified degree of substitutability. Consequently, an industry that produces a differentiated product cannot be defined in a strict and precise way. For instance, suppose that we wish to study the market for "automobiles." What products should we include in the study? Should we include station wagons? How about Jeeps, pickup trucks, trucks, and buses? To go even further, should we also include motorcycles? If so, how about bicycles? Or skate boards and roller skates? Where exactly do we draw the line? It must be obvious that whatever definition we adopt, it will be arbitrary.

In the rest of the book, we assume that it is possible to define precisely the product and its market. This simplification is necessary and should not frighten the reader. The purpose of all theory is to simplify. A model should not be expected to capture all aspects of the real world. Rather, it should concentrate on what the theorist believes to be the most crucial elements of reality and ignore all unnecessary details. Indeed, most of our discussion will revolve around the concept of a homogeneous product, even though we shall occasionally refer to the complications raised by differentiated products.

Perfect Competition

As implied by Table 8.1, a perfectly competitive industry is characterized by many producers of a homogeneous product. Yet, as will become evident in Chapter 9, perfect competition can exist only when some additional conditions prevail. What are these additional conditions?

In the first place, each of the many firms in the industry must be *small* in the sense of producing a very small and insignificant percentage of the total industry output. Indeed, the output of a perfectly competitive firm must be so small relative to the industry output that in the entrepreneur's perception no increase or decrease in the firm's production, however large, can have any appreciable effect on the market price. Essentially, this means that each individual firm accepts the prevailing market price as a datum; that is, each perfectly competitive firm is a *price taker*.

On the demand side, there must be many individual buyers, with each individual buyer purchasing only a small percentage of the total volume of the commodity traded in the market. This means that buyers are price takers also.

Further, a perfectly competitive industry requires *perfect factor mobility;* that is, all factors of production must be able to move freely not only among the firms that constitute the industry, but also between the perfectly competitive industry and the rest of the economy.

Perfect factor mobility necessarily implies *perfect labor mobility*. Labor should be able to move freely from one region to another as well as from one occupation to another without being restrained either by any natural barriers, such as the need to acquire new skills, or by any artificial devices, such as apprenticeship programs and union membership.

Furthermore, perfect factor mobility implies *perfect capital mobility* also. Such devices as copyrights and patents that restrict the flow of capital from one industry to another should not exist. Capital should be free to move into that industry that provides the highest return.

The most important implication of perfect factor mobility is that *firms can enter or exit the industry at will*. In the long run, new firms should be able to enter the industry and existing firms should be able to suspend production depending on market conditions—and they should be able to do so *freely and costlessly*.

Finally, perfect competition requires that consumers, producers, and owners of factors of production have *perfect knowledge* of all aspects of the market and the economy. For instance, they must know the prices of all commodities and factors of production that prevail throughout the economy. No consumer should ever pay for a commodity a price that is not equal to the lowest price existing in the economy. Similarly, no owner of a factor of production should ever accept a price for the services of his or her factor that is not equal to the highest available price. Finally, no producer should ever pay more for any factor services than the lower possible prices.

Moreover, in the purest forms of perfect competition perfect knowledge is not restricted to the present alone. On the contrary, market participants should also possess perfect knowledge of the future; that is, they must also have *perfect foresight*—uncertainty should be completely absent, a condition that has never been satisfied in the real world and never will.

The preceding conditions are so severe that only a few markets in the real world can claim that they are perfectly competitive, even approximately. The closest examples of perfectly competitive markets are the market for agricultural crops (grains) and the stock market, even though these markets do not meet all requirements of perfect competition in its purest form. Does this sad conclusion mean that the study of perfectly competitive markets is without merit? Not at all. As we already pointed out, a model may be useful even though its assumptions may violate reality. Indeed, the model of perfect competition is most useful and widely used by economists, mainly because it performs remarkably well in the sense of explaining and predicting behavior in the real world. In addition, as we shall see in Part Six, the model of perfect competition possesses important properties concerning economic efficiency and the optimal allocation of resources. Policymakers and economists must be aware of these properties irrespective of whether perfect competition exists in the real world or not and also irrespective of whether they live in a democratic nation, such as the United States, or under a communist regime. The reason is simple: When a real economic system does not have the properties of prefect competition, it must be wasting valuable resources. To avoid inefficiency and waste, a real economic system, whether that of the United States or that of the Soviet Union, must organize its production according to the fundamental properties of perfect competition. Consequently, in addition to its ability to explain and predict behavior, the model of perfect competition is useful both for identifying areas of inefficiencies in a real economy and also for prescribing the right policies for the elimination of those inefficiencies.

Monopoly

According to Table 8.1, a monopoly exists when there is one, and only one, seller of a product. This is, of course, the most important characteristic of monopoly. Nevertheless, the existence of monopoly requires that at least two additional conditions be satisfied as well: (1) the monopolist's product must have no *close substitutes*, and (2) there must exist natural or artificial barriers preventing other firms from entering the industry. We discuss both of these conditions below.

The first condition ("no close substitutes") implies that not only should there be no rival firms producing the same product as the product of the monopolist, but also there should be no other firms producing similar products. Accordingly, the demand for the monopolist's product must be reasonably independent of the price of other products. (Technically, this condition means that the cross-elasticity of demand between the monopolist's product and any other product is approximately zero.)

It is apparent, then, that the monopolist faces no direct competition from rival firms and does not anticipate any retaliation for his policies and actions. In other words, the monopolist has significant market power. Nevertheless, the monopolist's market power is not unlimited, simply because he also faces constraints. For instance, one such constraint is provided by the demand for the monopolist's product. Because he is the sole producer in the industry, the demand curve for the product of the monopolist coincides with the entire market demand curve. In turn, this demand curve serves as a severe constraint on the monopolist's price–output policies. In particular, the existence of such a demand curve prevents the monopolist from fixing his price and output independently of each other. If he fixes his price, he must allow the market to determine his output, because he just cannot force the consumers to purchase the quantity he wants to sell at the price he specifies. Similarly, if he fixes his output, he must allow the market to determine the price. In short, the monopolist always operates within the constraint imposed by the market demand curve; he can arbitrarily fix either his price or his output, but not both.

Implicit in the above argument is the undeniable proposition that even though he has no direct rivals by assumption, the monopolist faces *indirect* competition from other producers in the economy. This indirect competition is, of course, based on the fact that *all* commodities are rivals for the consumer's limited income. Ultimately, all commodities compete against one another because each one seeks a place in the consumer's budget.

Furthermore, the market power of the monopolist can be eroded even further by the existence of substitutes. Of course, as we already pointed out, the monopolist's product must be unique and should have no close substitutes. Nevertheless, some imperfect substitutes may exist. For instance, telephone service, a classic example of a monopolized commodity, may have to compete with the telegram, teletype, mail, radio communication, and ordinary messenger service.

Because of the existence of indirect competition, it is not unusual for a monopolist to pursue actively a sales promotion campaign in an attempt to increase his sales volume without lowering his price. The main objective of such sales activities (e.g., advertising) is to *shift* the demand curve to the right. To be successful in this endeavor, the monopolist must be able to convince consumers to spend more of their income on the monopolist's product by diverting it away from other commodities.

Whenever a monopoly is lucrative, the monopolist must remain vigilant against *potential* competition. Naturally, the existence of a huge monopoly profit is a strong inducement for other firms to enter the monopolized industry. Undoubtedly, many potential competitors will be eager to enter such an industry in an attempt to capture part of the profit. A profitable monopoly can persist in the long run only when such entry is somehow blocked. But how can a profitable monopolized market be shielded from potential competition? By the existence of *barriers to entry,* which is the second condition mentioned above. These barriers may take a variety of forms.

Perhaps the most prominent barrier to entry is the presence of pronounced *economies of scale.* This simply means that the minimum average cost of production occurs at a rate of output that is very high relative to the market. Accordingly, at any price that is at least equal to the minimum average cost of production, the monopolist has the capability of satisfying the entire market, leaving no room for other competitors. If a second producer were to enter the industry, neither firm would be able to cover the full cost of production, as explained in detail in Chapters 9 and 10. Certainly, this is not a very enticing prospect for a potential competitor.

A monopoly that is founded on the existence of pronounced economies of scale is usually called a *natural monopoly.* Examples of natural monopolies are provided by virtually all public utilities, such as electrical power companies, municipal waterworks, sewage disposal systems, and telephone companies. As a rule, the behavior of natural monopolies is regulated by the government, as explained in Chapter 10.

Sometimes the monopolist may be able to bar entry into the industry by controlling the entire supply of a key raw material that is absolutely necessary for the manufacture of the product. The most frequently cited example of this type of barrier to entry was provided by the Aluminum Company of America (Alcoa). Before World War II, Alcoa owned almost all sources of bauxite (a key input in the production of aluminum) in the United States. As a result, Alcoa reigned as the sole producer of aluminum in the United States until the courts broke its monopoly in the 1940s.

Other barriers to entry include franchises and patents. A franchise is awarded to the firm by the government. It entitles the recipient firm to be the sole producer-seller of a certain commodity in a specified geographical area. In return for this exclusive privilege, the government reserves the right to regulate certain aspects of the recipient firm's market behavior in order to minimize (or eliminate) the risk of abuse of the government-created monopoly power.

On the other hand, a firm may obtain a patent either for the manufacture of a certain *product* or for a low-cost *process* for manufacturing a product. In the United States, such patents give the inventor-innovator exclusive rights to the patented product or process for 17 years. Of course, after the initial 17-year period elapses, patents may be renewed. Nevertheless, patents are at best temporary barriers to entry, because they cannot guarantee the existence of monopoly on a permanent basis. As the Japanese have convincingly demonstrated, competitors often exhibit remarkable ingenuity in imitating a patented product or process. In addition, in an era of rapid technical progress, better products and more efficient processes become continuously available.

Whenever potential competition is a real possibility, it behooves the monopolist to take note of it and formulate his price–output polices accordingly. As we have seen, whenever profit prospects are bright, it is natural to expect that many potential competitors will be attracted into the market. To preserve his monopoly power, the monopolist may have to avoid being too "greedy." More specifically, in such situations the monopolist may have to pursue a moderate pricing policy, even though such policy may prevent him from maximizing his short-run profit. But surely, whenever the monopolist follows this course, he does so because he wants to maintain his monopoly power and maximize his profit *in the long run,* not because he is a good-hearted humanitarian. In other words, the monopolist may often decide *not* to maximize his short-run profit in order to keep potential competitors out of the market.

Finally, note that whether monopoly exists in its pure form or not, the principles of monopoly are indispensable for two reasons. First, these principles are applicable to all those industries that approach the model of monopoly. Second, these same principles are invaluable in the study of oligopoly and monopolistic competition. It is for these reasons that Chapter 10 is devoted exclusively to the study of monopoly.

Monopolistic Competition

Until the 1920s, economists were completely satisfied with the polar cases of perfect competition and monopoly. Until that time, it is fair to say that the models of perfect competition and monopoly constituted the bulk of microeconomics. However, in the 1920s economists became aware of a serious inconsistency in the Marshallian theory of the firm. In particular, Marshall (1961, p. 318) stated that "an increase in the aggregate volume of production of anything will generally increase the size, and therefore the *internal economies* possessed by such a representative firm; that it will always increase the external economies to which the firm has access; and thus will enable it to manufacture *at a less proportionate cost* of labour and sacrifice than before" (italics added). In effect, Marshall maintained that a perfectly competitive firm could be in equilibrium with *unexhausted internal economies,* a proposition that is shown in Chapter 9 to be false. Because of this inconsistency and the resultant controversy in the economic journals, economists followed the suggestion of Piero Sraffa (1926) to turn their attention to the "middle ground" between monopoly and perfect competition. Within a few years, the economics profession witnessed the simultaneous publication of two seminal works dealing with the middle ground, one by Joan Robinson (1933) of Cambridge University and one by Edward H. Chamberlin (1933) of Harvard University. The model of monopolistic competition was developed exclusively by Chamberlin.

Chamberlin based his theory of monopolistic competition on the empirical observation that a large number of industries are composed of many small firms that produce *differentiated products* (i.e., products that have many close, but not perfect, substitutes). As Chamberlin (1933, p. 56) pointed out, product differentiation may be "real or fancied"; furthermore, it "may be based on certain characteristics of the product itself, such as exclusive patented features; trade marks; trade names; peculiarities of the package or container, if any; or singularity in quality, design, or style. It may also exist with respect to the conditions surrounding its sale."

It is interesting to note that for purposes of product differentiation the meaning of "product" must be a broad one. It must include not only the *physical* characteristics of the tangible product but also many other elements, such as credit terms, packaging, delivery, installation, subsequent maintenance or repair, warranties, and even such intangible and subjective elements as the personality of the salesperson and the environment in which the sale is transacted. Product differentiation may be based on either the physical characteristics of the product itself or any other element(s) included in the broad definition of "product."

Product differentiation is the main distinguishing feature of monopolistic competition. In all other respects, monopolistic competition is similar to perfect competition. In particular, in monopolistic competition, as in perfect competition, there are *many* firms in the industry, with each firm being very *small* in relation to the market. This means that each individual seller's actions (or policies) do not have any appreciable effect on any other firm in the industry, simply because such effects are spread over many rivals and consequently are greatly diluted. Because of this, each firm can pursue its own policies without any fear of retaliation from any other rival firm(s).

Further, entry into a monopolistically competitive industry is relatively easy, but not as easy as in perfect competition. The main reason for this is the inherent product differentiation that prevails under monopolistic competition. Because of product differentiation, a new firm that wishes to enter a monopolistically competitive industry must meet two requirements: (1) it must produce its own version of the product and (2) it must persuade enough customers to switch to the new brand. The first requirement involves investment in research and development; the second requirement involves investment in a vigorous sales promotion campaign to win consumers away from already established firms. Accordingly, a newcomer to a monopolistically competitive industry faces greater obstacles (in the form of greater capital requirements) than a newcomer to a perfectly competitive industry.

To increase its volume of sales, a firm in a monopolistically competitive industry can follow three different courses of action: (1) it may reduce its price, (2) it may vary the nature of its product, and/or (3) it may intensify its advertising (or sales promotion) campaign. The first course of action ("price reduction") represents a *movement* along the demand curve for the product of the firm. The last two courses of action ("product variation" and "sales promotion") represent attempts to *shift* that demand curve to the right, but they also involve an upward shift in the firm's average cost curve.

Unlike a perfectly competitive firm, a monopolistically competitive firm is *not* a price taker. Because of the prevailing product differentiation, the monopolistically competitive firm has limited monopoly power: The demand curve for its product is downward sloping—not horizontal (infinitely elastic) as in perfect competition. Because consumers become attached to particular brand names, a monopolistically competitive firm may increase its price without losing all its customers to its competitors—it loses only some "marginal" customers. Similarly, when a monopolistically competitive firm reduces its price, it may attract some marginal customers only. Nevertheless, the demand curve for the product of a monopolistically competitive firm must be very elastic, because of the assumed close substitutability among the products of rival firms. Strong "brand loyalties" and "company loyalties" cannot persist in the presence of wide differences in the prices charged by the rival firms.

Some examples of monopolistically competitive industries are the construction industry, gas stations, drugstores, and the textile industry, to name only a few. Part A of Chapter 11 deals with the main features of the theory of monopolistic competition as developed by Chamberlin.

Oligopoly

Oligopoly is a market structure that is characterized by the existence of a relatively *small number of firms*. On the average, oligopolistic firms are *large relative to the size of the market* they serve—a feature that has important implications for their market behavior, as explained below.

Typically, oligopoly prevails in the corporate sector, where each oligopolistic firm is not only large relative to the size of the market it serves, but also it is large in absolute terms. Nevertheless, the absolute size of oligopolistic firms is only an incidental characteristic of many actual oligopolies. Oligopoly is by no means limited to the corporate sector, and there are many examples of oligopolistic industries with only a few "small" firms. For instance, consider the case of a few drugstores, or grocery stores, in a small town; or the case of two (or a few) ice cream sellers, or chestnut sellers, stationed at a busy street corner in Manhattan.

In terms of the number of firms in the industry, oligopoly occupies the middle ground. Monopoly requires a *single* seller; perfect and monopolistic competition require *many* small sellers. Oligopoly, on the other hand, has a *few* sellers. This fewness of firms in oligopoly has an important consequence: *Oligopolistic firms are closely interdependent.* Indeed, the strong interdependence among oligopolistic firms is *the* main distinguishing feature of oligopoly—a feature that actually sets oligopoly apart from all other market structures.

Both in monopoly and in perfect (and monopolistic) competition a producer formulates its price-output policies independently of all other producers in the economy. In other words, neither a monopolist nor a perfect competitor needs to worry about the reactions of his competitors. As we saw above, a monopolist has no direct rivals at all. At the other extreme, the rivals of a perfect competitor are so numerous that the effects of his policies on any one of them are negligible. Therefore, a perfect competitor has no reason to expect any reaction to his policies, because none of his many competitors notices his policies.

On the other hand, each oligopolist's policies (with regard to price and output, but also product variation and sales promotion in the case of differentiated products) necessarily have an *appreciable* effect on each of his rivals, especially when all firms in the industry are of comparable size. Because of this, any policy change by one of the oligopolists is likely to provoke some *reaction* on the part of the other rival firms. For instance, when General Motors announces a rebate program in order to boost sales, both the Ford Motor Company and the Chrysler Corporation counter with a plan of their own; otherwise, they will lose many customers to General Motors. It is this type of interdependence that constitutes the distinguishing characteristic of oligopoly and the central complication in its systematic analysis.

In formulating his policies, the oligopolist must take into consideration what he believes to be the likely reactions of his rivals. Because an oligopolist cannot know in advance and with complete certainty what the reactions of his rivals will be, he cannot predict with certainty the final effects of his policies on the volume of sales and profitability of his firm. As a consequence of the strong interdependence among all oligopolistic firms and the basic inability of the individual oligopolist to predict the reactions of his rivals, we cannot even determine a demand curve for the product of an oligopolistic firm. However, the oligopolist knows that such a demand curve, whenever it exists, must have a negative slope—given the nature of his product and the intensity of his sales promotion, the oligopolist recognizes that he cannot substantially increase his sales volume without a significant price reduction.

The relatively few firms in an oligopolistic industry may produce either a homogeneous product (pure oligopoly) or a differentiated product (differentiated oligopoly). Examples of pure oligopoly are provided by the markets for aluminum, cement, chemicals, copper, explosives, and steel, to name only a few. On the other hand, typical examples of differentiated oligopoly are the markets for air conditioners, automobiles, automobile tires, cigarettes, computers, electric razors, refrigerators, soft drinks, television sets, and toothpaste. Obviously, the degree of interdependence among oligopolists depends, in addition to how few the rival firms happen to be, on the degree of product differentiation. Further, in pure oligopoly the prices charged by the various rival firms must be virtually identical, whereas in differentiated oligopoly different firms can, and do, charge different prices.

Finally, note that an oligopoly can persist in the long run only if barriers to entry, natural or artificial, prevent new firms from entering the market. As with monopoly, the most important barrier is provided by economies of scale, which make it inefficient and unprofitable for more than a few firms to operate in the market. Other possible barriers to entry are control over key resources (such as mineral deposits and land locations), patents to a certain product or process, exclusive franchises, and large financial requirements related to plant construction, distribution network costs, and initial advertising expenditure. In addition, the existence of unused capacity and a moderate pricing policy by existing oligopolists may also deter potential competitors from entering the industry.

8.2 The Revenue Curves of the Firm[2]

Before we can even analyze the market behavior of a typical firm, we must introduce three important revenue curves: the *average-revenue curve,* the *total-revenue curve,* and the *marginal-revenue curve.* Combined with the firm's cost curves (studied in Chapter 7), these revenue curves can be used to determine the profit-maximizing output of the firm, as shown later in this part of the book. The purpose of this section is to discuss the three revenue curves of the firm.

Average and Total Revenue

The firm's "average revenue" (or revenue per unit of output sold) is merely another name for the "price" at which the firm sells all its output. Similarly, the "average-revenue curve" coincides with the demand curve for the firm's output, which shows the various prices at which the firm can sell various alternative outputs. For our present purposes, it is convenient to assume that the firm faces some definite demand curve. Initially, we also assume that this demand curve is downward sloping, as shown in Figure 8.1, panel (a), by the curve labeled AR (for "average revenue").

The firm's "total revenue" is equal to average revenue times quantity sold. Geometrically, total revenue is given by the area of a rectangle constructed with respect to a desired point on the average-revenue curve. For instance, when the firm sells 20 units of output at $3 per unit (point N), total revenue is $60. This is illustrated by the shaded rectangle, which is, of course, drawn with respect to point N. In Figure 8.1, panel (a), we followed this procedure to calculate the firm's total revenue implied by each point that lies on the average-revenue curve. In turn, we used this information to draw the firm's total-revenue curve, as shown by curve $0N'T'S'$ in panel (b). The latter curve gives directly the firm's total revenue for various alternative outputs (volumes of sales). (The reader must be familiar with the notion of a total-revenue curve from our discussion in Section 2.6, in particular Figure 2.9.)

What are the properties of the total revenue curve? First, it necessarily starts at the origin (provided that the average-revenue curve has a finite vertical-axis intercept). The reason is simple: As output approaches zero, total revenue must also approach zero, irrespective of how high the price happens to rise (provided that it remains finite). Second, total revenue is again zero (and thus the total-revenue curve intersects the horizontal axis) when average revenue is zero, irrespective of how large output happens to be. Thus point S' in panel (b) corresponds to point S in panel (a). Third, for any given output, the slope of a line from the origin to the relevant point on the total-revenue curve gives the corresponding average revenue, as illustrated in panel (b) by the slope of vector $0N'$. In addition, we shall always assume that the total-revenue curve has a unique maximum point, as illustrated by point T'.

Marginal Revenue

As will become clear in the following chapters, the firm is interested not only in the prices at which it may sell various alternative outputs, but also in the change of total revenue as it adjusts its output. This is particularly true when the demand curve facing the individual firm is downward sloping. In that case, the extra revenue

---

[2]This section may be read together with the Appendix to Chapter 8.

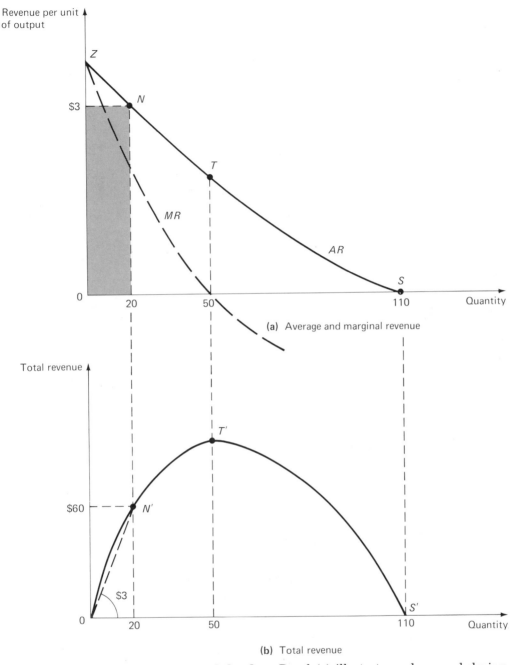

(a) Average and marginal revenue

(b) Total revenue

Figure 8.1 The revenue curves of the firm. Panel (a) illustrates a downward-sloping average-revenue curve (labeled AR) and the corresponding marginal-revenue curve (labeled MR). Panel (b) gives the corresponding total-revenue curve. When the firm sells 20 units at $3 each, as indicated by point N on the average-revenue curve, total revenue is equal to $60, as shown by the area of the shaded rectangle in panel (a). Point N' in panel (b) corresponds to point N in panel (a), and the slope of vector ON' gives the firm's average revenue (which is $3). The marginal-revenue curve lies everywhere below the average-revenue curve except at the vertical-axis intercept (point Z). In addition, the marginal revenue is positive, zero, or negative according to whether the slope of the total-revenue curve is positive (region OT'), zero (point T'), or negative (region $T'S'$), respectively. Finally, the total-revenue curve has a single maximum (point T') and intersects the horizontal axis at two points: (a) at the origin (where output is zero), and (b) at point S' (where average revenue is zero).

obtained from the sale of one additional unit of output is necessarily less than the price—in fact, it may even be negative!

For instance, suppose that a firm is currently selling 100 units of output at $10 per unit, obtaining a total revenue of $1000 (i.e., $10 × 100 = $1000). Suppose further that to increase its sales to 101 units, the firm must lower its price to, say, $9. The firm's total revenue will *not* increase by $9 (i.e., by the price of the additional unit sold). Thus the *new* total revenue will be $909 (i.e., $9 × 101 = $909) only. In other words, by increasing its sales by 1 unit, the firm will actually experience a *reduction* in its total revenue equal to $91 (i.e., $1000 − $909 = $91), instead of gaining an additional amount of $9. The reason for this anomaly is that in cutting the price on *all* units that it sells, the firm must take into consideration not only the price received for the extra unit (i.e., $9) but also the revenue that it "loses" by selling the "original" units at a *reduced price*. In our example, this loss of revenue is equal to $100, because the "original" 100 units could have been sold at $10 each but are actually sold at only $9 each. Accordingly, total revenue falls by $91, which is the difference between the "loss" of $100 (on the original units) and the "gain" of $9 (from sale of the extra unit).

The change in total revenue that results from a unit increase in the quantity sold is known as *marginal revenue*. More precisely, *marginal revenue is the rate of change of total revenue per extra unit of quantity sold*. Geometrically, marginal revenue is given by the *slope* of the (tangent to the) total-revenue curve at any specified point. Accordingly, when the total-revenue curve is positively sloped [as in region $0T'$, Figure 8.1, panel (b)], marginal revenue is positive; when it is negatively sloped (as in region $T'S'$), marginal revenue is negative; and when it reaches a maximum (as at point T'), marginal revenue is zero.

In Figure 8.1, panel (a), we also constructed a marginal revenue curve and labeled it *MR* for "marginal revenue." This new curve gives directly the firm's marginal revenue (or slope of total revenue curve) at various alternative levels of output. Note that the marginal-revenue curve necessarily has the same vertical-axis intercept as the average-revenue curve (for the same reason that, say, the average-physical-product curve has the same vertical-axis intercept as the marginal-physical-product curve). Everywhere else, the marginal-revenue curve lies below the average-revenue curve because the latter slopes downward (just as the marginal-cost curve lies below the average-cost curve when the latter slopes downward).

Furthermore, the area under the marginal-revenue curve, between the origin and any specified positive output, gives the firm's total revenue (for that output). This follows from the simple idea that total revenue is merely the *sum* of the marginal revenues of all units sold. This is again very similar to the proposition that total (variable) cost is given by the area under the marginal-cost curve. Even though the calculation of total revenue as the area under the marginal-revenue curve is not always easy (especially when the marginal-revenue curve is curvilinear), we must emphasize that this property is of the utmost importance in theoretical work. This will become clear in Chapters 9 to 11.

Average and Marginal Revenue and the Elasticity of Demand

The reader may recall from Chapter 2 that there is an important relationship between the shape of the total revenue curve and the elasticity of demand. In particular, the elasticity of demand is greater than unity, less than unity, or unity according to whether the slope of the total-revenue curve is positive, negative, or zero, respectively.

We can easily restate the above proposition in terms of the concept of marginal revenue. Thus we may say that the elasticity of demand is greater than unity, less than unity, or unity according to whether marginal revenue is positive, negative, or zero, respectively. Actually, there exists a precise formula relating the coefficient of elasticity (e) to average and marginal revenue:

$$|e| = \frac{AR}{AR - MR} \tag{8.1}$$

(This formula gives the value of the coefficient of elasticity in absolute terms, without the negative sign.) Since this formula is often very useful, we explain below how it is derived. (For a rigorous development of the formula, see the Appendix to Chapter 8.)

Initially, we assume that the demand curve happens to be a straight line, as shown in Figure 8.2 by line AB. Then the corresponding marginal-revenue curve

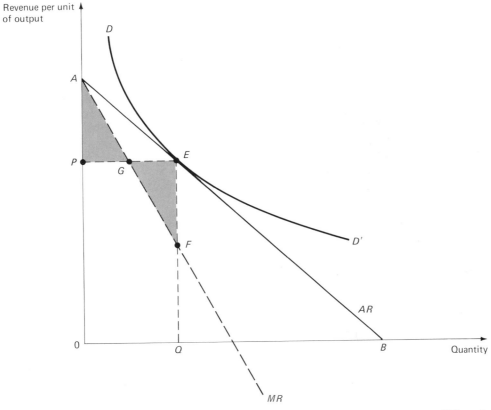

Figure 8.2 The relationship of elasticity to average and marginal revenue. When the average-revenue curve is a straight line, as shown by the line labeled AR, the corresponding marginal-revenue curve is also a straight line, as illustrated by the dashed line labeled MR. At OQ units of output, total revenue is given both by the area of rectangle $OQEP$ and the area of trapezoid $OQFA$, both of which have area $OQFGP$ in common. Accordingly, similar triangles GEF and GPA have the same area, which means that they are identical. Thus $PG = GE$ and $AP = EF$. The equality $PG = GE$ shows that the linear marginal-revenue curve bisects the horizontal distance between any point on the linear average-revenue curve and the vertical axis, while the equality $AP = EF$ shows that average revenue at OQ units of output (i.e., QE) exceeds marginal revenue (i.e., QF) by the amount indicated by vertical distance AP. The elasticity of demand at E is given by the ratio $QE/(QE - QF)$. This continues to be true even when the true demand curve is curvilinear, as shown by the curve labeled DD', provided that straight line AB is tangent to DD' at E.

is necessarily a straight line also. We already know that the marginal-revenue curve has the same vertical-axis intercept as the demand curve. But how can we identify the marginal-revenue curve completely?

Consider some arbitrary output level, say $0Q$. Obviously, the total revenue for that output level is given by the area of rectangle $0QEP$ (which is the equivalent to price times quantity). But the total revenue at $0Q$ units of output must also be equal to the area under the unknown marginal-revenue curve from 0 to Q. For instance, if dashed line AF were the marginal-revenue curve, the total revenue at $0Q$ units of output would also be equal to the area of trapezoid $0QFA$. Therefore, for dashed line AF to be the true marginal-revenue curve, it is required that the area of trapezoid $0QFA$ be equal to the area of rectangle, $0QEP$. Since area $0QFGP$ is common to both the rectangle and the trapezoid, it follows that the two shaded triangles (GEF and GPA) must have the same area. Nevertheless, these triangles are also similar, as the reader should verify. Accordingly, the two shaded triangles must be congruent (identical), so that $PG = GE$ and $AP = EF$.

These last equalities give two alternative rules for drawing the marginal-revenue curve. In particular, the equality $PG = GE$ means that the *marginal-revenue curve necessarily bisects the horizontal distance between any point on the linear demand curve (such as point E) and the vertical axis.* Alternatively, the equality $AP = EF$ gives the amount by which average revenue (QE) exceeds marginal revenue (QF) at any specified output level. (Note that distance AP is determined from the demand curve alone.) The reader may recognize distance EF (or AP) to be the "correction factor" that the entrepreneur must subtract from the average revenue in order to obtain the marginal revenue—that is, the revenue "lost" in relation to the "original" units when the entrepreneur increases his output by 1 unit.

We are now ready to prove formula (8.1). Recall from Chapter 2 the following definition of (point) elasticity (in absolute terms):

$$|e| = -\frac{dq}{dp}\frac{p}{q} \tag{8.2}$$

The derivative dq/dp corresponds to the reciprocal of the slope of the demand curve at some specified point, and the terms p and q correspond to the price (or average revenue) and quantity, respectively, at that same point. For instance, at point E on linear demand curve AB of Figure 8.2, we have $dq/dp = -PE/AP$, $p = QE$, and $q = 0Q$. Substituting these values into equation (8.2), we obtain

$$|e| = \frac{PE}{AP}\frac{QE}{0Q}$$

$$= \frac{QE}{AP} \qquad \text{(because } PE = 0Q\text{)}$$

$$= \frac{QE}{EF} \qquad \text{(because } AP = EF\text{)}$$

$$= \frac{QE}{QE - QF} \qquad \text{(because } EF = QE - QF\text{)}$$

$$= \frac{AR}{AR - MR} \qquad \text{(because } QE = AR \text{ and } QF = MR\text{)}$$

This establishes formula (8.1), because the above relationships hold for each point on the linear demand curve.

Formula (8.1) is not valid for linear demand curves only. It is also valid when the demand curve is not linear. To determine the elasticity (and marginal revenue) at a specified point on a nonlinear demand curve, we first construct a straight line that is tangent to the demand curve at the given point; then we proceed as if the straight line (tangent) itself were the true demand curve. For instance, suppose that DD' is the true demand curve in Figure 8.2. Then the elasticity at point E and the corresponding marginal revenue will continue to be given by $QE/(QE - QF)$ and QF, respectively, because straight line AB is tangent to curve DD' at point E.

Finally, we may summarize the following conclusions, which follow easily from formula (8.1):

1. When $AR > MR > 0$, $|e| > 1$ (demand is elastic).
2. When $AR > MR = 0$, $|e| = 1$ (demand is unit elastic).
3. When $AR > 0 > MR$, $|e| < 1$ (demand is inelastic).
4. When $AR = MR > 0$, $|e| = \infty$ (demand is perfectly elastic).

The last case is important for the analysis of a perfectly competitive firm to which we now turn.

The Revenue Curves of a Perfectly Competitive Firm

As we already know, a perfectly competitive firm is a price taker; it can sell any output that it chooses at the prevailing price, because it is too small relative to the market and cannot appreciably affect the market price by any conceivable change in its output. Accordingly, the average-revenue curve of a perfectly competitive firm is necessarily horizontal, as shown in Figure 8.3, panel (a).

The total revenue of a perfectly competitive firm is necessarily proportional to the given market price. Therefore, the total-revenue curve is a straight line from the origin. This is shown in Figure 8.3, panel (b), by vector $0R$, whose slope indicates, of course, the firm's average revenue (AR), that is, the given market price.

Because the perfectly competitive firm can always sell additional units of output without affecting the price, it follows that its marginal revenue (i.e., the extra revenue per extra unit of output sold) is necessarily equal to the average revenue (price). This is also illustrated in Figure 8.3, panel (a), where the marginal-revenue curve coincides with the average-revenue curve. To emphasize this fact, we used the equality $AR = MR$ to label the horizontal line. As we already know, the elasticity of a horizontal demand curve, such as the one shown in Figure 8.3, panel (a), is infinite.

8.3 The Assumption of Profit Maximization

What is the objective of firms? What do firms maximize? Before we consider their market behavior, we must know what it is that firms are trying to achieve. As we pointed out in Section 6.1, in the classical tradition firms are said to *maximize profit*, which is the difference between revenue and (opportunity) cost. In this section we first review briefly some of the alternatives to profit maximization, and then we proceed to discuss the basic rationale for the assumption of profit maximization.

Challenges to Profit Maximization

The assumption of profit maximization has been challenged by several economists. For instance, Tibor Scitovsky (1943) suggested that in the case of small, unincorporated businesses the entrepreneur (who happens to be the owner and manager of the firm) aims at maximum utility (satisfaction); in the final analysis,

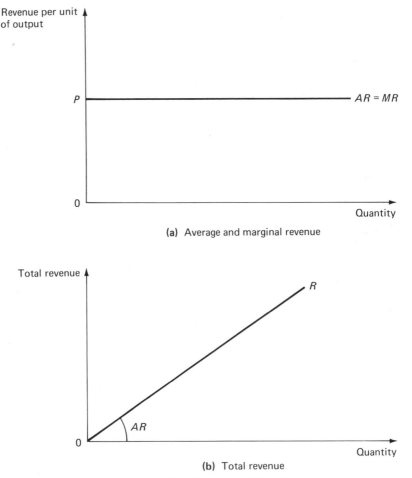

Figure 8.3 The revenue curves a perfectly competitive firm. Both the average-revenue curve and the marginal-revenue curve of a perfectly competitive firm are given by the same horizontal line, as illustrated in panel (a) by the line labeled $AR = MR$. In panel (b) the corresponding total-revenue curve is a straight line from the origin (OR) whose slope gives the firm's constant average revenue.

utility is a function of the firm's profit and the amount of leisure enjoyed by the entrepreneur. The implication of this hypothesis, of course, is that the entrepreneur may sacrifice some profit for some extra leisure.

On the other hand, some observers of the modern corporation reject the assumption of profit maximization, basically because of the separation of management from ownership. William Baumol (1967) claims, for example, that management is more preoccupied with the maximization of *sales revenue* (at least after profits reach acceptable levels), presumably because executive salaries (and other benefits, such as luxurious offices) are more closely correlated with the firm's scale of operations than with its profitability. Similar claims have been advanced by John K. Galbraith (1967), who argues that the main goals of the "technostructure" (a fancy word for the complex decision-making mechanism of the modern corporation) are *growth of sales* and *stability*. Finally, Herbert A. Simon (1959) suggests that firms attempt to achieve a "satisfactory" rate of profit, not a "maximum" rate.

In addition to the more serious alternatives to profit maximization mentioned above, there is often reference to less important goals, such as having a "good image," being "socially responsible," increasing or maintaining the market share, and being the leader in a certain field.

Undoubtedly, there is some grain of truth in each of the preceding alternatives to profit maximization. Yet so far at least, none of these alternative goals has emerged as a possible candidate for replacing the behavioral assumption of profit maximization in a general formulation of the microeconomic theory of the firm.

The Case for Profit Maximization

What supporting arguments can we offer for the classical behavioral assumption of profit maximization? The following two arguments are overwhelming and they seem to clinch the case for profit maximization.

First, there is the *survivorship principle:* Unless a firm that happens to exist in a very competitive environment maximizes profit, there is danger that it may not be able to survive in the long run. Accordingly, profit maximization is the most satisfactory assumption in all those cases where competition is keen. Under these circumstances, any successful firms that we may observe in the economy are likely to be profit maximizers.

The survivorship principle is also consistent with our earlier observation in Section 8.2, namely, that monopolies and oligopolies may avoid profit maximization in the short run in order to repel potential competition. Evidently, the main objective in such situations is to *maximize profits in the long run.* The same is true for most other alternatives to profit maximization enumerated above. To the extent that these other goals are means to achieve maximum profits in the long run, any inconsistency between them and the goal of profit maximization is only apparent.

Second, microeconomic theory is concerned with the construction of a general model that is capable of explaining and predicting the behavior of *industries* and *markets,* as opposed to the behavior of *particular firms.* We study the theory of the firm not for its own sake but as an important theoretical link in the analysis of the entire economic process. In other words, the main object of analysis in microeconomics is the whole economy, not the firm. By necessity, then, the microeconomic theory of the firm must be abstract. At such a level of generality and abstraction, profit maximization is the most satisfactory assumption that we can make.

In this connection we may observe that neither a model nor its assumptions can be totally "realistic" in the sense of describing reality accurately. Every model or assumption is unrealistic, or false, to a certain extent. This is necessary, however, because a theory must be able to cut through the massive and confusing details of the real world in order to explain certain aspects of reality. After all, a model that is as extensively descriptive as reality must necessarily be totally useless, because such a model is actually provided by the real world itself. This complication is very much like the problem experienced by a person who happens to be driving from, say, Atlanta to New York. For such a driver, a road map that shows every little street along the way is necessarily confusing and useless. What the driver actually needs is a road map that shows only the major highways.

If an assumption is inherently unrealistic, how can we tell whether it is a good or a bad assumption? Friedman (1953, pp. 21–23) argues that the ultimate test for an assumption is its predictive capability. As an example, he considers the problem of predicting the shots made by an expert billiard player who nevertheless has no knowledge of the rules of physics that determine the movements of the balls on the table. To predict the player's shots accurately, *we may assume that he knows and applies instantly the complicated mathematical formulas that govern the movements of the balls, despite the fact that he is totally unfamiliar with such laws.*

The above resolution has important implications for the profit-maximization hypothesis. Business and corporate managers may be telling the truth when they declare that they do not consistently and faithfully pursue the goal of profit maximization, either because they lack the necessary information about their cost curves and the demand curves for their products, or because they think that they are simultaneously pursuing other goals as well. Yet profit maximization may still be a valid assumption to the extent that it enables us to predict the behavior of firms accurately. This brings us back to the survivorship principle. As Friedman (1953, p. 22) puts it, "unless the behavior of businessmen in some way or other approximated behavior consistent with the maximization of returns, it seems unlikely that they would remain in business for long." In other words, we can make accurate predictions with a model in which firms behave *as if* they were seeking to maximize their profits, just as we can predict the shots of the expert billiard player when we assume that he behaves as if he were familiar with the relevant laws of physics.

SUMMARY

1. From the sellers' side, markets are classified into five types (structures): (a) perfect competition (many small sellers of a homogeneous product), (b) monopolistic competition (many small sellers of differentiated products), (c) pure oligopoly (few sellers of a homogeneous product), (d) differentiated oligopoly (few sellers of differentiated products), and (e) monopoly (one seller).

2. The technical term "competition" means "many sellers;" it does not mean rivalry (ability and willingness of producers to encroach on each other's market).

3. A product is called homogeneous when all its units are of the same quality (perfect substitutes), at least in the eyes of the buyers. Products which are close substitutes and have "small" differences (real or apparent) are called differentiated.

4. In addition to many small sellers and a homogeneous product, perfect competition requires also perfect factor mobility (costless entry or exit), perfect knowledge, and perfect foresight.

5. For the existence of monopoly, two conditions must be met: (a) the monopolist's product must have no close substitutes, and (b) there must exist natural or artificial barriers to entry.

6. Natural monopolies are created by the existence of pronounced economies of scale.

7. Entry into a monopolistically competitive industry is not as easy as in perfect competition, because of product differentiation.

8. A monopolistically competitive firm is *not* a price taker (the demand curve for its product

is downward sloping but very elastic). To increase its volume of sales such a firm may reduce its price, vary the nature of its product, or intensify its advertising campaign.

9. Each oligopolist's policies have an appreciable effect on his rivals, who often retaliate. This interdependence constitutes the distinguishing feature of oligopoly.

10. From the buyers' side markets are classified into three types: perfect competition (many small buyers), oligopsony (few buyers), and monopsony (single buyer). Bilateral monopsony refers to the market structure where a single seller faces a single buyer.

11. Average revenue is another name for price ($AR = pq/q = p$). The average-revenue curve coincides with the demand curve for the firm's output.

12. Total revenue (pq) is given by the area of the rectangle constructed with respect to a point on the AR curve; it is zero either when $p = 0$ or $q = 0$.

13. The slope of a line joining the origin and a point on the total-revenue curve gives the corresponding average revenue.

14. The marginal revenue (the rate of change of total revenue per extra unit of output sold) coincides with the slope of the total-revenue curve; it is positive, negative, or zero according to whether the elasticity of demand is greater than, less than, or equal to unity, respectively.

15. The area under the marginal-revenue curve gives the firm's total revenue.

16. The elasticity of demand (e) is related to the average and marginal revenue by the formula $e = AR/(AR - MR)$.

17. The *MR* curve bisects the horizontal distance between any point on a linear demand curve and the price axis.

18. A perfectly competitive firm is a price taker (the demand curve for its product is horizontal). Hence market price = *AR* = *MR*, and the *MR* curve coincides with the *AR* curve. The total revenue curve is a straight line through the origin; its slope gives the market price.

19. Despite the fact that it has been challenged by many economists, profit maximization still remains the most satisfactory assumption concerning the behavior of firms.

QUESTIONS

1. Complete the following table.

Price (dollars)	Quantity (bushels)	Total Revenue (dollars)	Marginal Revenue (dollars)	Elasticity $\|e\| = \dfrac{AR}{AR - MR}$
10.00	1	———	n.a.	n.a.
9.90	2	———	———	———
9.50	3	———	———	———
———	4	———	7.50	———
8.00	5	———	———	2.0
———	6	42.00	———	1.4
———	7	———	0.00	———
5.00	8	———	———	———

*2. A monopolist faces the following linear demand curve: $p = 250 - 0.3q$.

  (a) Determine the functions of total revenue $(R = pq)$ and marginal revenue $(MR = dR/dq)$.

  (b) Use the functions of average revenue, marginal revenue, and total revenue to calculate the unknown quantities in the various cells of the following table.

p	q	$R = pq$	$AR = \dfrac{R}{q}$	$MR = \dfrac{dR}{dq}$	$\|e\| = \dfrac{AR}{AR - MR}$
10					
50					
100					
125					
200					
250					

  (c) Plot carefully on graph paper the curves of average and marginal revenue, and on a separate diagram directly below the first (with the same *q*-scale) plot the total revenue curve. Identify on both diagrams the points involved in the table above.

3. The assumption of profit maximization as the goal of firm behavior has been criticized by several economists.

  (a) Discuss some of the arguments that can be made both for and against the assumption of profit maximization.

  (b) Suggest one or two alternatives to profit maximization.

  (c) If the assumption of profit maximization is not valid (as suggested by Herbert Simon and others), why is so much emphasis given to it in the formal teaching of microeconomic theory?

FURTHER READING

Baumol, W. J. (1967). *Business Behavior, Value and Growth,* rev. ed. Harcourt Brace Jovanovich, Inc., New York.

Chamberlin, E. H. (1933). *The Theory of Monopolistic Competition.* Harvard University Press, Cambridge, Mass.

Friedman, M. (1953). "The Methodology of Positive Economics," in *Essays in Positive Economics.* The University of Chicago Press, Chicago.

Galbraith, J. K. (1967). *The New Industrial State.* Houghton Mifflin Company, Boston.

Knight, F. H. (1971). *Risk, Uncertainty and Profit.* The University of Chicago Press, Chicago. (Originally published in 1921 by Houghton Mifflin Company.)

Marshall, A. (1961). *Principles of Economics,* 9th (variorum) ed., Macmillan & Company Ltd., London.

Robinson, J. (1933). *The Economics of Imperfect Competition.* Macmillan & Company Ltd., London.

Scitovsky, T. (1943). "A Note on Profit Maximization and Its Implications," *The Review of Economic Studies,* Vol. 11 (Winter), pp. 57–60.

Simon, H. A. (1959). "Theories of Decision Making in Economics and Behavioral Science," *American Economic Review,* Vol. 49 (June), pp. 253–283.

Sraffa, P. (1926). "The Laws of Returns Under Competitive Conditions," *The Economic Journal,* Vol. 36, pp. 535–550.

CHAPTER
9

Perfect Competition

Having completed our investigation of the fundamental principles that underlie demand and supply behavior in Parts Two and Three, respectively, we are now ready to reconsider the workings of the law of supply and demand. In a sense, the present discussion is an elaboration of the preliminary analysis of the law of supply and demand presented in Chapter 2.

Our discussion in this chapter is divided into three parts. Part A deals with the static equilibrium of the perfectly competitive firm in both the long run and the short run. Part B continues with the static equilibrium of the perfectly competitive industry and explains the circumstances for the various shapes of the long-run industry supply curve. Finally, Part C concludes with several applications of the tools developed in Parts A and B.

PART A. STATIC EQUILIBRIUM OF THE PERFECTLY COMPETITIVE FIRM

Our present discussion is based on two important assumptions: (1) The firm faces some definite set of revenue and cost curves, and (2) the firm's only motive is to maximize its total profit. Indeed, a firm is said to be in *static equilibrium* when it produces that output, known as the *equilibrium output,* that yields the maximum total profit. The main objectives of this part of the chapter are (1) to identify the necessary and sufficient conditions for profit maximization both in the long run and the short run, and (2) to study the implications of the profit-maximizing decision.

9.1 Long-Run Equilibrium of the Perfectly Competitive Firm

A perfectly competitive firm is in (static) long-run equilibrium when it maximizes its (total) profit with respect to its long-run cost curves. This implies, of course, that the firm is able to adjust all its factors of production in order to achieve the lowest possible total cost for its long-run equilibrium output.

The Total Revenue-Total Cost Approach

It is convenient to begin our analysis of the equilibrium of the perfectly competitive firm with reference to its total revenue and total cost, as illustrated in Figure 9.1. The firm's total-revenue curve is given by straight line OR (whose slope coincides with the constant price for the firm's product), and its long-run total-cost curve is shown by the curve labeled C_L. Both of these curves necessarily start at the origin (why?).

At any output, the vertical distance between the total-revenue and total-cost curves represents total profit. Evidently, profit is negative over the range of outputs less than q_1 units, it is positive over the middle range of outputs between q_1 and

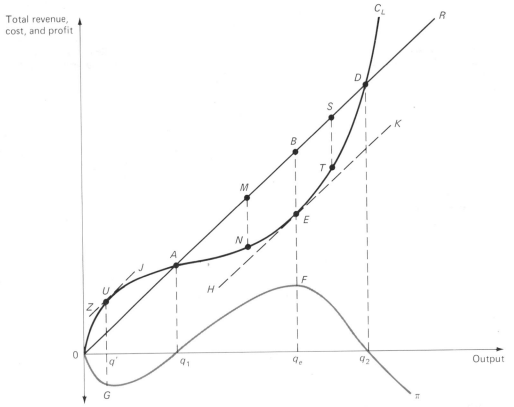

Figure 9.1 Long-run equilibrium of the perfectly competitive firm in terms of total revenue and cost. To determine the equilibrium output, displace vertically downward the linear total-revenue curve (OR) until it is just tangent to the total-cost curve (C_L), as shown by line HK. When the firm produces q_e, it enjoys a maximum total profit indicated by vertical distance EB. This is confirmed by the fact that the total-profit curve (π) attains a maximum (point F) at q_e. Note that in the neighborhood of E (where profit is maximized) the long-run total-cost curve (C_L) is *convex* and lies above its tangent (HK). On the other hand, in the neighborhood of U (where profit is minimized), C_L is *concave* and lies totally below its tangent (ZJ).

q_2 units, and it becomes negative again over the range of outputs greater than q_2 units. (Note also that total profit is exactly zero at only three levels of output: zero, q_1, and q_2.) Accordingly, total profit must be maximized at some output between q_1 and q_2 units. How can we determine the equilibrium output precisely?

To ascertain the equilibrium output, we displace vector $0R$ vertically downward until it is just tangent to the total-cost curve, as shown by dashed line HK, which is tangent to the C_L curve at E. Because line HK is by construction parallel to vector $0R$, it must be evident that the firm can achieve a maximum total profit indicated by vertical distance EB when it produces q_e units of output. At any other rate of output, the vertical distance between the total-revenue and total-cost curves, such as NM and TS, is necessarily smaller than distance EB.

This conclusion is also confirmed by the shape of the *total-profit curve,* as illustrated by the curve labeled π. At each level of output, the height of the π curve registers the positive or negative vertical distance between vector $0R$ and the C_L curve. It is apparent that the π curve attains a maximum (point F) at the equilibrium output of q_e units.

Because dashed line HK is by construction parallel to vector $0R$, it follows that *at the profit-maximizing output the slopes of the total-revenue and total-cost curves are necessarily equal.* In turn, this implies that profit maximization occurs at the precise output where *marginal revenue* (slope of the total-revenue curve) *equals marginal cost* (slope of the total-cost curve).

Although necessary, the equality of marginal revenue and marginal cost is not sufficient for profit maximization. For instance, at q' units of output the slope of the total-cost curve is again equal to the slope of the total-revenue curve, as evidenced by the fact that the tangent to the C_L curve at U is parallel to vector $0R$. However, at q' units of output the firm is *minimizing* its total profit, or rather it is *maximizing its total loss.* This conclusion is confirmed by the fact that at q' units of output the π curve has a trough (point G) in the *negative* quadrant.

How can we analytically distinguish between points of profit *maximization* (such as point E or F) and points of profit *minimization* (such as point U or G)? In addition to the first-order condition (i.e., the equality of marginal cost with marginal revenue), we must also apply a second-order condition. Note that at point E, the total-cost curve is *convex* and lies totally *above* and to the left of its tangent (line HK), but at point U, it is *concave* and lies totally *below* and to the right of its tangent (line ZJ). Accordingly, *in the vicinity of the equilibrium output (q_e) the total-cost curve must be convex.*

What is the economic meaning of the required convexity of the total-cost curve? It is that the *marginal cost must be increasing* in the neighborhood of equilibrium. For instance, as we travel along the total-cost curve from, say, N to T, we observe that the slope of (the tangent to) the C_L curve (i.e., marginal cost) continuously increases. We return to the implications of increasing marginal cost in the next subsection.

In summary, we may say that a perfectly competitive firm maximizes its long-run total profit at its current output if, and only if, the following two conditions are satisfied:

1. *First-order condition:* The long-run marginal cost must be equal to the marginal revenue (= average revenue = price).
2. *Second-order condition:* The marginal cost must be rising.

These two conditions guarantee that the total-profit curve (π) is at a *peak,* although that peak may lie in the negative quadrant (i.e., it may correspond to a *loss*), as explained below.

The Marginal Approach

We can gain additional insights into the profit-maximization problem by employing the marginal approach. The essence of this approach is that the firm (or entrepreneur) gropes toward the equilibrium point by making marginal adjustments to output. When marginal revenue exceeds marginal cost, an output expansion adds more to total revenue than to total cost, and total profit rises. On the other hand, when marginal cost exceeds marginal revenue, the firm can increase its total profit by *reducing* its output, because then the *cost saved* (MC_L) is larger than the *revenue lost* (MR) per unit decrease in output. Evidently, the firm maximizes its total profit when it cannot increase it by either expanding or contracting its output, a state of affairs that prevails only when marginal cost equals marginal revenue ($MC_L = MR$).

The marginal approach is illustrated in Figure 9.2. The long-run average-cost and marginal cost curves (AC_L and MC_L, respectively) correspond to the long-run total-cost curve (C_L) of Figure 9.1. In addition, Figure 9.2 shows the average-revenue curve ($AR = MR$) corresponding to the total-revenue curve (vector $0R$) of Figure 9.1. As explained in Section 8.2, in the present case the average-revenue curve is also the firm's marginal-revenue curve, and for this reason we label that horizontal line $AR = MR$.

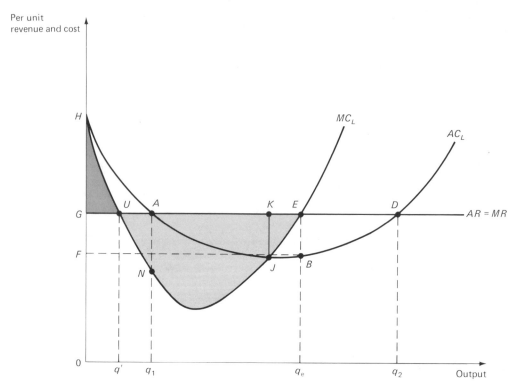

Figure 9.2 The marginal approach to profit maximization. The firm maximizes its total profit at point E, where the MC_L curve intersects the $AR = MR$ line from below. Total profit is given by the area of rectangle $GFBE$. Alternatively, total profit coincides with the difference between the positive profit area $UNJE$, and the negative profit area, HGU. Since area HGU equals area UNA—at q_1, total profit is zero—total profit is indicated by area $ANJE$. Note that at U, where the MC_L curve intersects the $AR = MR$ line from above, total profit is at a minimum. Finally, the firm does *not* maximize its profit per unit (point J). If it did, it would fail to capture the additional profit indicated by triangular area KJE.

The firm's long-run equilibrium output (q_e) is now indicated by the *intersection* (point E) of the marginal-cost and marginal-revenue curves (MC_L and MR, respectively). Surely, it is much easier to detect an intersection between the MC_L and MR curves than it is to identify the point on the total-cost curve where the tangent happens to be parallel to the linear total-revenue curve (as we actually did in Figure 9.1).

The intersection of the MC_L and MR curves is only the first-order condition for a profit *maximum*. To ensure that it is a profit maximum (and not a profit minimum), however, we also need a second-order condition: *The marginal-cost curve must intersect the marginal-revenue curve from below.* This secondary condition is also satisfied at point E.

For outputs immediately larger than q_e, marginal cost exceeds marginal revenue. Consequently, an output increase will cause total profit to fall, because the additional cost will exceed the additional revenue. Similarly, for outputs immediately smaller than q_e, marginal revenue exceeds marginal cost. Accordingly, an output reduction will also cause total profit to decline, since the revenue lost will exceed the cost saved. We must, therefore, conclude that total profit is at its peak (or maximum) when the firm produces q_e units.

To appreciate the importance of the second-order condition ("MC_L must intersect MR from below"), consider point U, which is the other intersection of the MC_L and MR curves. At U, the marginal-cost curve intersects the marginal-revenue curve from *above*. As a result, the firm can augment its profit by either increasing or decreasing its output. For instance, an output expansion will add more to total revenue than to total cost, because for outputs immediately larger than q', $MR > MC_L$; and similarly, an output contraction will result in a larger reduction in cost than in revenue, because for outputs immediately smaller than q', $MC_L > MR$.

Measurement of Profit

Before we go any further, it is important to show how to graphically measure the firm's maximum profit. The simplest way is to take profit per unit (BE) times number of units sold (FB), which coincides with the area of rectangle $GFBE$ in Figure 9.2. The rationale for this approach follows from the identity

$$
\begin{aligned}
\text{total profit} &= \frac{\text{total profit}}{\text{output}} \cdot \text{output} \\
&= \text{average profit} \cdot \text{output} \\
&= (AR - AC_L) \cdot \text{output}
\end{aligned}
$$

There is an alternative approach, however, which is in the spirit of marginalism. As we saw in Chapter 7, the area under the MC_L curve (from the vertical axis to some specified level of output) coincides with the long-run total cost. Thus, when the firm produces q_e units of output, its total cost is given by area $H0q_eE$. On the other hand, total revenue is given by the area of rectangle $G0q_eE$. Since these two areas have in common area $G0q_eEJNU$, it follows that total profit is given by shaded area $UNJE$ *minus* shaded triangular area HGU.

The actual measurement of irregular areas, such as $UNJE$ and HGU, is not an easy matter. Yet the above approach is very useful in many analytical problems, as will become evident in the rest of this book. For the moment, we may use it to sharpen our understanding of the marginal approach to profit maximization.

Imagine that the firm allows its output to gradually increase from zero to, say, q_2 units. Let the firm register the positive or negative contribution to total profit made by each additional unit (marginal profit). At any level of output, total profit must be equal to the *sum* of marginal profits generated by all units sold.

Since marginal profit necessarily coincides with the difference between marginal revenue and marginal cost, it is graphically indicated by the vertical distance between the MR and MC_L curves at each level of output. From zero to q' units, marginal profit is negative; between q' and q_e units, marginal profit is positive; and for outputs higher than q_2, it again becomes negative.

Accordingly, at all outputs less than q' units, the firm experiences losses. In this range of outputs, the firm's total loss increases with output. Indeed, when the firm produces q' units exactly, its total loss is at a (local) maximum. This maximum total loss coincides with shaded triangular *area HGU*, which corresponds to the *sum* of marginal profits of all units up to q'.

As the firm expands its output beyond q' units, its total loss begins to decline, because marginal profit is now positive ($MR - MC_L > 0$). In particular, when it increases its output to q_1 units exactly, the firm just breaks even—its total profit becomes zero. Dashed area UNA, corresponding to the positive contribution to total profit made by all units from q' to q_1, just matches the area of negative profit (HGU). This becomes evident when we notice that at q_1 units of output $AC_L = AR$ or $AR - AC_L = 0$ (i.e., per unit profit is zero).

As output increases beyond q_1 units, the firm begins to enjoy a positive profit which continues to grow until output rises to q_e units. At that point, as we saw above, total profit is maximized. In fact, that maximum profit is given by area $ANJE$ (i.e, the area between the MR and MC_L curves from q_1 to q_e). Obviously, total profit begins to fall when the firm expands its output beyond q_e units, because over that range of outputs marginal profit is negative (i.e., $MR - MC_L < 0$).

As a consequence of the preceding discussion, it must be absolutely clear that a profit-maximizing firm does *not* maximize its profit per unit. For instance, in Figure 9.2, the per unit profit is maximized at point J, where AC_L is at its minimum. If the firm were to produce at J, it would fail to capture the additional profit indicated by shaded triangular area KJE.

The Condition for Nonnegative Profit

We saw that when the marginal-cost curve intersects the marginal-revenue curve from below, profit is at a maximum (or loss is at a minimum). However, this condition does not automatically guarantee that that maximum profit will actually be positive—it could very well be negative! Because in the long run the firm always has the option of not existing at all (a situation that implies zero revenue, zero cost, and therefore zero profit), we must explicitly rule out the possibility of negative profit. This last condition may be expressed in any one of the following three alternative ways:

$$\text{total profit} \geq 0 \qquad (9.1)$$

or

$$\text{total revenue } (R) \geq \text{total cost } (C_L) \qquad (9.2)$$

or

$$\text{average revenue } (AR) \geq \text{average cost } (AC_L) \qquad (9.3)$$

The implications of the above condition are illustrated in Figure 9.3, which is similar to Figure 9.2 except for the fact that the $AR_0 = MR_0$ line now lies below the AC_L curve. (For the moment, ignore the $AR_1 = MR_1$ line.) The marginal-revenue curve intersects the marginal-cost curve at points U and E. We can rule out point

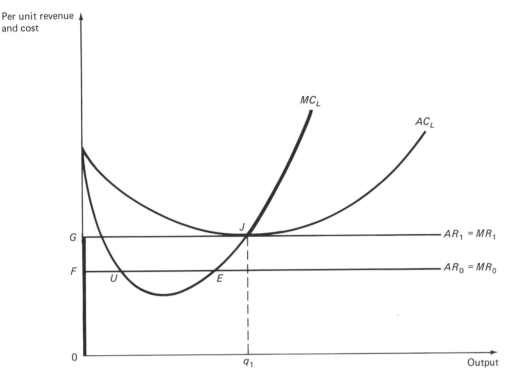

Figure 9.3 The condition of nonnegative profit and the long-run supply curve. At point E, where the MC_L curve intersects the $AR_0 = MR_0$ line from below, the maximum total profit is *negative* (i.e., a loss), and the firm will choose to leave the industry and make zero profit. The firm's long-run supply curve consists of the two disconnected and heavily drawn line segments: (a) segment OG along the vertical axis, and (b) the rising segment of the MC_L curve above point J. The long-run supply curve does not exist over the range of outputs where the AC_L curve is negatively sloped—it skips discontinuously from G to J.

U because at that point the slope of the MC_L curve is negative. However, at E, the MC_L curve intersects the MR curve from below; and according to our earlier analysis, total profit attains a maximum at E. Yet total profit at E is necessarily *negative* (i.e., it is a *loss*) because the average revenue (or price) falls short of the long-run average cost (AC_L). Accordingly, E is not an eligible point of long-run equilibrium either—the firm can achieve zero profit at zero output (i.e., by closing down).

In general, the firm will refuse to remain in business if the price (average revenue) is lower than the *minimum* long-run average cost of production, for it will not be able to cover its costs at any positive output.

The important special case where the price happens to be exactly equal to the minimum long-run average cost is illustrated by the horizontal $AR_1 = MR_1$ line, which is just tangent to AC_L at its minimum point (J). In this special case, the firm has two equally attractive options: it may produce q_1 units of output, or it may cease to exist. In either case, total profit is zero.

The Long-Run Supply Curve of the Perfectly Competitive Firm

The long-run supply curve of a perfectly competitive firm shows the alternative quantities of output that the firm is willing to produce and sell at various prices. As we explained above, for all prices up to the one corresponding to the minimum long-run average cost, the firm's best option is to close down—all positive outputs necessarily imply losses. Accordingly, for this range of prices, the firm's long-run supply curve coincides with the vertical axis, as illustrated by the heavy line segment $0G$ in Figure 9.3.

When the price is exactly equal to the minimum long-run average cost (i.e., $0G$), the firm has two possible offers: it can either close down (as shown by point G), or it can produce q_1 units (as shown by point J). Accordingly, at this special price, the supply curve is discontinuous—it jumps from point G on the vertical axis to point J (the point of minimum AC_L).

For any price above the minimum long-run average cost, the firm maximizes its profit at the intersection of the horizontal price line ($AR = MR$) with the rising segment of the long-run marginal-cost curve. Consequently, for this range of prices the supply curve coincides with the rising segment of the firm's long-run marginal cost curve, as illustrated in Figure 9.3 by the heavy line starting at point J.

The Incompatibility of Perfect Competition with Decreasing Cost (or Increasing Returns to Scale)

As we saw above, the perfectly competitive firm is in equilibrium at the point where the long-run marginal-cost curve intersects the horizontal average-revenue curve *from below.* This obviously means that *the perfectly competitive firm cannot be in equilibrium over the range of outputs where its long-run marginal cost is decreasing.* But this is not all. Implicit in our preceding analysis is also the proposition that *the perfectly competitive firm cannot be in equilibrium over the range of outputs where its long-run average cost is decreasing.* (Recall that the firm's long-run supply curve does not exist over that range of outputs—it skips discontinuously from the vertical axis to the point where the long-run average-cost curve attains its minimum.)

We therefore conclude that the perfectly competitive firm cannot be in long-run equilibrium either with decreasing marginal cost or decreasing average cost. If this is so, what happens when the long run average cost continuously declines as output expands?

There are two possibilities. If the downward-sloping average-cost curve happens to remain *above* the average-revenue curve, as shown in panel (a) of Figure 9.4, the firm will close down, because it will be unable to cover its costs at any output. On the other hand, if the average-cost curve dips below the average-revenue curve and continues to decline as output expands, as shown in panel (b) of Figure 9.4, the firm will wish to expand output beyond all bounds because in this case total profit tends to increase indefinitely with output. (This follows from the fact that total profit = ($AR - AC_L$) × output, and beyond point B, $AR > AC_L$ and AC_L continues to decline as output expands.) Nevertheless, the tendency and ability of the firm to expand output indefinitely is incompatible with the assumptions of perfect competition because the firm will no longer be able to sell all it wants at a fixed price. On the contrary, the firm will soon discover that to increase its volume of sales, it must lower its price. In other words, the firm will cease being a price taker (or a perfect competitor).

Now recall from our discussion in Section 7.5 that the phenomenon of decreasing long-run average cost is due to *increasing returns to scale.* We must therefore conclude that perfect competition is incompatible with increasing returns to scale.

As we anticipated in Chapter 8, perfect competition may not exist even when the long-run average-cost curve of a typical firm is U-shaped. This is the case when the average cost attains its minimum at a rate of output that is very large relative to the market demand. Under these circumstances, the market demand may be satisfied by a single firm (natural monopoly) or, at best, by only a few firms (oligopoly).

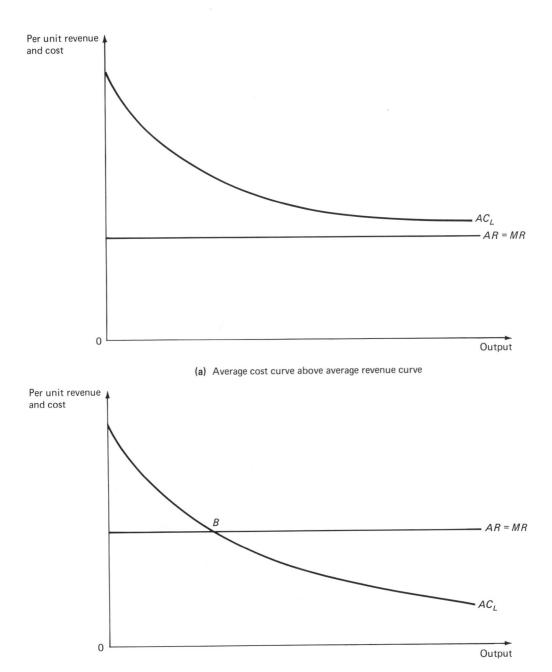

(a) Average cost curve above average revenue curve

(b) Average cost curve dips below average revenue curve

Figure 9.4 The incompatibility of perfect competition with decreasing cost. In panel (a) the downward-sloping AC_L curve remains above the $AR = MR$ line. The firm cannot remain in business because it cannot cover its costs at any output. In panel (b) the AC_L curve dips below the $AR = MR$ line and continues to decline as output expands. Since the firm now has a tendency to expand output indefinitely, it cannot remain a perfect competitor— its output decisions will eventually affect price.

This is an important reason why perfect competition cannot exist in many actual cases.

9.2 Short-Run Equilibrium of the Perfectly Competitive Firm

We now turn to the concept of static short-run equilibrium of the perfectly competitive firm. This is analytically similar to the concept of static long-run equilibrium, except for the fact that short-run equilibrium is compatible with negative profit (loss). Indeed, the possibility of loss is the main distinguishing feature of short-run equilibrium, and it is a reflection of the inability of the firm to adjust its *fixed inputs* whose cost (total fixed cost) therefore becomes *unavoidable even at zero output* (sunk cost).

The Conditions of Short-Run Equilibrium

In the short run, the perfectly competitive firm maximizes its profit with respect to its short-run cost curves. In this process the firm is constrained by its fixed factors, which are irretrievably committed to its productive operations. Except for this complication, the short-run profit-maximization conditions are analogous to the conditions developed in Section 9.1 for maximizing profit in the long run.

The firm's short-run equilibrium output is again indicated by the intersection of the marginal-cost curve (MC_S) with the horizontal average-revenue curve. Moreover, for a profit maximum the MC_S curve must intersect the $AR = MR$ line *from below*. The justification for these two conditions is exactly the same as before, except for the insignificant difference that the *short-run* marginal-cost curve now replaces the long-run marginal-cost curve.

Nevertheless, the third condition—summarized by inequalities (9.1) to (9.3)—needs to be reformulated. As the reader may recall, inequalities (9.1) to (9.3) require the total profit to be nonnegative, because in the long run the firm has the option of not existing at all—a situation that implies zero revenue, zero cost, and *zero profit*. On the other hand, if the firm suspends production in the short run, it will have to bear the full burden of the total fixed cost (F). For this reason it may be to the advantage of the firm to remain active in the short run even though it may suffer a loss, provided only that the short-run loss does not exceed the total fixed cost. Of course, if the minimum short-run loss with positive production happens to be larger than the total fixed cost, the firm will choose to close down even in the short run.

We therefore conclude that *the total fixed cost (F) represents the maximum loss that the firm may have to suffer.* Accordingly, the third condition for short-run equilibrium at some *positive* output takes the form

$$\text{total profit} \geq -\text{total fixed cost } (F) \tag{9.4}$$

Inequality (9.4) replaces inequality (9.1).

Inequality (9.4) can be rearranged into two alternative forms which are analogous to inequalities (9.2) and (9.3). Recall that the short-run total cost (C_S) is equal to the total-variable cost (V) plus the total-fixed cost (F); that is, $C_S = V + F$. Furthermore total profit is equal to total revenue (R) minus total cost (C_S); that is, total profit = $R - C_S$. Accordingly, inequality (9.4) may be written as follows:

$$R - C_S \geq -F \tag{9.4'}$$

or

$$R - (V + F) \geq -F$$

or

$$R \geq V \tag{9.5}$$

Inequality (9.5) corresponds to inequality (9.2). It states that in the short run *a firm will choose to produce a positive output if, and only if, it can at least cover its total variable cost.*

Further, dividing both sides of (9.5) by output (q), we get

$$\frac{R}{q} \geq \frac{V}{q}$$

or

$$AR \geq AVC \tag{9.6}$$

where AR is the average revenue (or price) and AVC the average variable cost. Inequality (9.6) corresponds to inequality (9.3). It states that in the short run *a firm will choose to produce a positive output if, and only if, the price is at least as high as the average variable cost.* The usefulness of inequality (9.6) will be recognized below in relation to the graphical representation of the firm's short-run equilibrium.

It is interesting to note that contrary to appearances, the third condition for short-run equilibrium is not really different from the third condition for long-run equilibrium. After all, long run is that special situation where all costs are variable and total fixed cost is zero. Inequality (9.1) is nothing else but a special case of inequality (9.4), where F is set equal to zero. Similarly, inequality (9.2) is a special case of inequality (9.5), where C_L corresponds to V; and inequality (9.3) is a special case of (9.6), because in the long run $AC_L = AVC$. To emphasize the strict correspondence between short-run and long-run equilibrium, we summarize the preceding discussion in the form of the following two general propositions:

Proposition 1. *The firm can remain in business (i.e., produce a positive output) only if it can at least cover its variable cost.*

Proposition 2. *The total fixed cost represents the maximum loss that the firm may suffer.*

The above propositions are valid both in the long run and the short run.

The Irrelevance of Total Fixed Cost

The firm's short-run equilibrium is totally independent of the total fixed cost. In other words, the firm can determine its short-run equilibrium output without knowing the magnitude of its total fixed cost. This important proposition confirms our statement in Chapter 7 that fixed cost is not a true cost; it is inherently a sunk cost.

Recall that profit $= R - C_S = (R - V) - F$. Since F is by definition constant, maximization of profit is equivalent to maximization of $R - V$, that is, the difference between total revenue (R) and total variable cost (V). Accordingly, the short-run equilibrium is wholly independent of F. In other words, the firm can determine its short-run equilibrium output from its knowledge of its total-revenue and total-variable-cost curves only.

The above proposition is also implicit in the three conditions of short-run equilibrium discussed above. We already know that the short-run marginal cost is independent of the total-fixed cost. Hence the first two conditions ("$MC_S = AR$" and "MC_S intersects $AR = MR$ from below") are also independent of F. Similarly, the third condition does not involve the magnitude of the total-fixed cost, despite the misleading impression given by inequality (9.4). This becomes evident from inequalities (9.5) and (9.6), which require $R \geq V$ and $AR \geq AVC$, respectively.

The total-fixed cost (F) is needed only for the calculation of the precise magnitude of the firm's short-run profit ($R - V - F$). If F were to change, total profit would also change, but the firm's equilibrium output would remain the same.

A Comparison Between Long-Run and Short-Run Equilibrium

When a firm is in long-run equilibrium, it must necessarily be in short-run equilibrium also. On the other hand, when a firm is in short-run equilibrium, it need not (although it may) be in long-run equilibrium. The commonsense explanation of this proposition should be obvious.

Long-run equilibrium is a situation in which the firm cannot increase its profit by adjusting any one input (or combination of inputs). Naturally, whatever adjustment(s) the firm may wish to perform in the short run, it could also perform in the long run. If the firm cannot increase its profit in the long run, *a fortiori* it must not be able to do so in the short run, where its degree of adjustability is rather limited. We therefore conclude that if the firm is in long-run equilibrium, it must automatically be in short-run equilibrium as well.

The converse is not true, however. That is, when a firm is in short-run equilibrium, it need *not* be in long-run equilibrium (although it may). This is also attributable to the firm's greater adjustability in the long run relative to the short run. Suppose that an initial long-run equilibrium is disturbed by an increase in price, presumably because of an increase of the market demand. In the short run, the firm will be able to increase its profit by adjusting its variable factors only. In the long run, however, the firm will increase its profit even further by adjusting those factors which were fixed in the short run.

Graphical Illustration

Figure 9.5 gives the per unit short-run cost curves of a perfectly competitive firm along with three alternative horizontal demand lines labeled $AR_0 = MR_0$, $AR_1 = MR_1$, and $AR_2 = MR_2$, corresponding respectively to prices p_0, p_1, and p_2. For simplicity, we omit the average-fixed-cost curve for two reasons: (1) it is not needed, and (2) we can always identify the average-fixed cost at any output by the vertical distance between the AC_S and AVC curves, since $AC_S = AVC + AFC$. Recall that the short-run marginal-cost curve (MC_S) passes through the respective minimum points (E_0 and M) of the AVC and AC_S curves.

If the firm is to make a positive profit in the short run, its average-revenue curve must lie above the AC_S curve for a certain range of outputs, as illustrated by the horizontal line labeled $AR_2 = MR_2$. In this case the firm would maximize its short-run profit at point E_2, where the MC_S curve intersects the $AR_2 = MR_2$ line from below. The per unit profit would be given by vertical distance E_2K_2, the firm's equilibrium output would be equal to q_2 units, and total profit would be equal to a rectangular area (not shown) whose height is E_2K_2 and its width coincides with horizontal distance p_2E_2 (corresponding to the firm's equilibrium output).

The horizontal demand line $AR_1 = MR_1$ lies totally below the average-cost curve (AC_S). In this case the firm cannot cover its full cost at any output and therefore

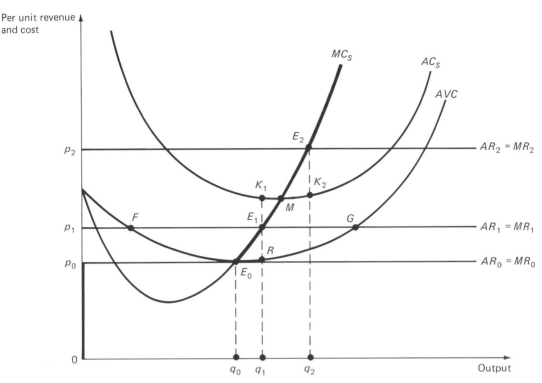

Figure 9.5 *Short-run equilibrium of the perfectly competitive firm and the short-run supply curve.* At price p_2 the firm maximizes its short-run total profit at point E_2, where the MC_S curve intersects the $AR_2 = MR_2$ line from below. When the price falls to p_1, the firm produces at E_1, where it suffers a short-run loss. The firm chooses to produce at E_1 rather than close down because the average revenue (p_1) exceeds the average variable cost: $p_1 = q_1E_1 > q_1R = AVC$. The least favorable demand situation is shown by the $AR_0 = MR_0$ line, which is just tangent to the AVC curve at its minimum point (E_0). In this case it is a matter of indifference to the firm whether it produced at E_0 or shut down production altogether. In either case, the firm will suffer the maximum loss $(=$ total-fixed cost$)$. The firm's short-run supply curve is illustrated by the two disconnected and heavily drawn line segments: segment Op_0 and the rising segment of the MC_S curve above point E_0. The supply curve does not exist over the range of outputs where the AVC curve is negatively sloped—it skips from the vertical axis to point E_0.

loss is unavoidable. Nevertheless, the firm will not shut down altogether because the $AR_1 = MR_1$ line does lie above the average-variable-cost curve (AVC) between points F and G. It is evident, then, that in this range of outputs (FG), the firm can more than cover its variable cost, with the difference $R - V$, or $(AR - AVC)q$, serving as a partial recovery of the total fixed cost. Naturally, the firm will produce at E_1, where the MC_S curve intersects the $AR_1 = MR_1$ line from below, and the price (p_1) is higher than the average-variable cost (q_1R), as required by inequality (9.6). The firm's total loss would be equal to the rectangular area (not drawn) whose height is E_1K_1 and its width coincides with horizontal distance p_1E_1. This loss is, of course, smaller than the total-fixed cost, which coincides with a rectangular area whose height is given by RK_1 and its width is the same as that of the minimum-loss area.

The horizontal demand line $AR_0 = MR_0$ is just tangent to the AVC curve at its minimum point (E_0) and represents the least favorable demand situation. By producing at the tangency (E_0), the firm will just cover its total-variable cost and suffer a loss equal to its total fixed cost. At any other positive output, the firm cannot cover even its variable cost. We therefore conclude that in this case it is a matter of indifference to the firm whether it produced at E_0 (i.e., q_0 units of output) or shut down production altogether, because in each case its total loss would be equal to its total fixed cost.

It should be obvious from the preceding comments that if the price were to fall below p_0, the firm would unambiguously go out of business (in the short run). Figure 9.5 illustrates the firm's short-run supply curve as well. Thus for prices between zero and p_0, the firm prefers to remain inactive; thus its supply curve coincides with the vertical axis, as shown by heavy line segment $0p_0$. When the price is exactly equal to p_0, there is a two-point indeterminacy: The firm may choose to remain inactive (produce zero output), or it may produce q_0. Accordingly, at p_0 the supply curve "jumps" from the vertical axis to point E_0. For prices above p_0, the supply curve coincides with the rising segment of the MC_S curve, as illustrated by the heavy line starting at E_0.

Finally, note that the perfectly competitive firm cannot be in short-run equilibrium with decreasing marginal or average-variable cost. That marginal cost must be rising in the neighborhood of equilibrium follows from the fact that the MC_S curve must intersect the $AR = MR$ line *from below*. Furthermore, over the range of outputs where the average-variable cost is declining, the firm's supply curve does not exist at all—it skips from the vertical axis to the minimum point of the AVC curve (i.e., point E_0 in Figure 9.5). Incidentally, note that the law of diminishing returns guarantees that beyond some finite level of output, both the short-run marginal-cost curve and the average-variable-cost curve must "turn up," as explained in Section 7.6.

Nevertheless, the perfectly competitive firm could be in short-run equilibrium with decreasing full average cost (AC_S), as illustrated by region E_0M along the supply curve of Figure 9.5. But note that along region E_0M the firm necessarily incurs losses. This is, of course, in contrast with the situation in the long run, where the firm could not be in equilibrium with declining average cost (AC_L).

PART B. STATIC EQUILIBRIUM OF THE PERFECTLY COMPETITIVE INDUSTRY

We now turn to the static equilibrium of a perfectly competitive industry in which a large number of small firms supply a homogeneous commodity. As we anticipated in Chapter 2, perfect competition is the only market structure where prices are determined by the law of supply and demand. Throughout the present discussion, we assume that the demand curve for the industry's commodity is given, simply because we have already explained in Part Two how a demand curve is derived. For convenience, we also assume that this demand curve is largely independent of the prices of other commodities in the economy. In this part of the chapter we focus our attention on one central concept: The *industry supply curve,* which, in general, represents a horizontal summation of the supply curves of the member firms.

9.3 The Notion of Industry Equilibrium

As we have already explained, in the long run firms enjoy complete adjustability in their supply decisions. This means that each firm is free to adjust *all* its inputs, because in the long run all inputs are variable. Naturally, this notion of full adjustability includes both the freedom of existing (or active) firms to leave the industry, if they wish to do so, without paying a penalty, and the freedom of potential (new) firms to enter the industry and organize production.

A perfectly competitive industry is said to be in long-run equilibrium when the following two conditions are met:

1. Each of the *active* firms must be maximizing its long-run profit. That is, no active firm should have any incentive to alter its output or leave the industry.

2. No *potential* firm should have any incentive to enter the industry. That is, no potential firm should think that it could do better by entering the industry and organizing production.

Taken together, the above conditions mean that a perfectly competitive industry is in long-run equilibrium when all its member firms, both actual and potential, happen to be in static long-run equilibrium.

In the short run, on the other hand, each active producer is committed to certain fixed factors, such as the firm's plant and major pieces of capital equipment and machinery. This means that in the short run, no existing firm is free to leave the industry without suffering a loss equal to its total fixed cost. Moreover, potential producers cannot enter the industry even when they have a positive inducement to do so, because they just do not have the time to acquire the necessary fixed inputs. In other words, in the short run all potential producers remain dormant irrespective of how bright market conditions happen to be. As a consequence, the number of actual producers cannot exceed the number of firms that already possess the relevant fixed inputs.

In contrast with the situation in the long run, therefore, a perfectly competitive industry is said to be in static short-run equilibrium when none of the existing firms has any positive incentive to alter its output. This means that each firm that happens to be committed to the relevant set of fixed factors must be maximizing its total profit with reference to its short-run cost curves. This situation need not always involve positive profits; it may very well mean *negative* profits (losses) for some or all such firms. However, such losses, if any, may not exceed the corresponding total fixed costs. Naturally, those firms that cannot cover their variable costs must suspend production even in the short run.

9.4 Constant-Cost Industries

For pedagogical reasons, we begin our discussion of industry equilibrium with the special but most important case of a constant-cost industry. As we show below, in this case the long-run industry supply curve is horizontal (infinitely elastic). The class of constant-cost industries is the borderline between the class of increasing cost industries (studied in Section 9.5) and the class of decreasing-cost industries (considered in Section 9.6).

Prerequisites for the Existence of a Constant-Cost Industry

A constant-cost industry can exist only when the following two conditions are satisfied: (1) all firms that are actual or potential members of the industry have the same long-run average-cost curve, and (2) as the industry output expands (or contracts) these identical average-cost curves do not shift.[1]

---

[1]Strictly speaking, a constant-cost industry requires that all member firms have the same *minimum* long-run average cost only, *not* the same long-run average-cost *curve*.

The first condition ("identical long-run average-cost curves") is obviously met when all factors of production, including the entrepreneurial factor, are homogeneous. The homogeneity of the entrepreneurial factor means that each firm will be able to combine the same factors in the same way; that is, all firms will have the same production function. Furthermore, perfect competition in the factor markets will guarantee that all firms pay the same factor prices for the same factors. But identical factor prices and identical production functions necessarily generate identical cost curves.

The second condition ("the identical long-run average-cost curves *do not shift* as output changes") is a little more complicated. It means that both the factor prices paid by each firm and the technical efficiency of all factors used by each firm remain constant as the industry output changes.

Consider first the requirement that factor prices remain constant as the industry output expands. Evidently, this condition means that the industry is a price taker in the factor markets. In other words, the factor-supply curves facing this industry must be perfectly elastic (horizontal). In turn, this implies that the industry's factor demands represent only a small fraction of the corresponding supplies traded in the factor markets. Consequently, a constant-cost industry cannot use any factors that are specific (or peculiar) to it even in the long run. Rather, the industry should employ only general (nonspecific) factors that are used by many other industries in the economy.

Finally, the requirement that the technical efficiency of all factors used by each firm remains constant as the industry output expands rules out the possibilty of *technological external economies and diseconomies*. These phenomena are briefly discussed in Sections 9.5 and 9.6.

Long-Run Equilibrium

When the foregoing conditions are fulfilled, *the long-run equilibrium price must be equal to the common minimum long-run average cost of production, irrespective of how large the quantity demanded at that price happens to be*. Obviously, when the price is lower than the common minimum long-run average cost, no firm can remain in business because that would involve negative profits. On the other hand, when the price is higher than the common minimum long-run average cost, every potential producer will be attracted into the industry (by the prevailing positive profits) and an indefinitely large quantity of output will be forthcoming. Naturally, neither of these two alternatives is consistent with the requirements of static long-run equilibrium. (For convenience, we ignore the uninteresting case in which the equilibrium industry output is zero.)

However, when the price is just equal to the common minimum long-run average cost, it is a matter of indifference to any one firm whether it produces or not. Under these circumstances, active producers just cover their costs and make zero profits. Similarly, potential producers can continue to remain outside the industry (where they enjoy zero profits), because they know they cannot do better by becoming active producers. Accordingly, all firms in the industry can simultaneously be in long-run equilibrium.

Furthermore, the price mechanism ensures that just the right number of firms become active. If more firms than necessary were in the industry, price would fall below the common minimum long-run average cost, causing a gradual exit of firms until the correct number was reached. On the other hand, if the existing firms were fewer than necessary (relative to demand), price would rise above the common minimum long-run average cost until a sufficient number of new firms entered the industry.

The above proposition, namely, that the long-run equilibrium price is necessarily

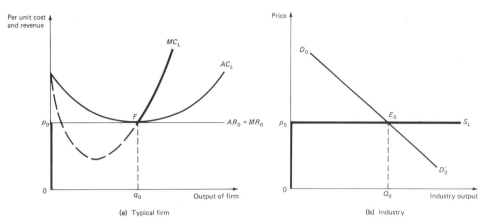

Figure 9.6 A constant-cost industry in static long-run equilibrium. All potential firms have the same set of long-run cost curves, as shown in panel (a). The long-run supply curve of the typical firm consists of the two disconnected and heavily drawn line segments: Op_0 and the rising segment of the MC_L curve above point F. Panel (b) shows the long-run industry supply curve (S_L). The latter coincides with the vertical axis for all prices lower than p_0, and at p_0, it becomes a horizontal line—the industry can produce any output (including zero) by adjusting the number of active firms. Long-run equilibrium occurs at E_0, where the industry demand curve (D_0D_0') intersects the industry supply curve. At that equilibrium the demand curve facing the typical firm of panel (a) is given by the $AR_0 = MR_0$ line. Accordingly, each active firm produces q_0. Since the total industry output is Q_0, we may also infer that the number of active firms is $n_0 = Q_0/q_0$.

equal to the common long-run minimum average cost *irrespective of the precise position of the demand curve,* necessarily implies that the industry supply curve is horizontal at that price. This is illustrated in Figure 9.6.

Panel (a) shows the long-run average-cost and marginal-cost curves of a typical firm. The common minimum long-run average cost ($=$ price p_0) occurs at q_0 units of output, as shown by point F. The long-run supply curve of the typical firm consists of the two disconnected and heavily drawn line segments: (1) segment $0p_0$ along the vertical axis and (2) the rising segment of the long-run marginal-cost curve (MC_L) above point F.

Panel (b) illustrates the corresponding long-run industry supply curve (S_L), which is also heavily drawn. For prices lower than p_0, S_L coincides with the vertical axis, because no firm is willing to enter the industry and produce. At price p_0, S_L becomes a horizontal line—the industry can produce any quantity of output (including zero) *by properly adjusting the number of active firms.* For this reason, the typical firm's long-run supply curve for prices higher than p_0 (above point F) becomes totally irrelevant in the determination of the long-run industry supply curve.

The industry's long-run equilibrium output (Q_0) is determined by the intersection of the long-run industry-supply curve (S_L) and the industry-demand curve (D_0D_0'), as shown by point E_0 in panel (b). The demand curve facing the typical firm of panel (a) is given by horizontal line $AR_0 = MR_0$. Assuming that all firms have the same long-run cost curves (not just the same minimum average cost), it is evident that each active firm produces q_0 units of output. Since the industry's long-run equilibrium output is Q_0 units, we can also infer that the equilibrium number of active firms (n_0) is given by

$$n_0 = \frac{Q_0}{q_0} \tag{9.7}$$

It is an important characteristic of the long-run equilibrium of a constant-cost industry that each firm makes a zero total profit. This characteristic is not a goal of the typical firm, because evidently all firms prefer to earn positive profits. The zero-profit state is brought about by the long-run operation of the market: When profits are positive, new firms are willing to enter the industry; and when profits are negative, hitherto active firms gradually leave the industry.

The Short-Run Industry Supply Curve

In the short run, only the finite number of existing firms can produce output. Potential producers cannot enter the industry. The short-run industry supply curve then represents a horizontal summation of the short-run supply curves of the existing firms.

In any particular short run, each of the existing firms may be committed to a different set of fixed factors and short-run cost curves, particularly because of the incessant dynamic changes that take place in any economic system. Presently, however, we shall make the simplifying assumption that all existing firms are committed to the same set of short-run cost curves, because we are mainly interested in the process of moving from one long-run equilibrium to another.

In the long-run equilibrium portrayed in Figure 9.6, each of the n_0 active firms necessarily commits itself to a short-run average-cost curve that is tangent to the long-run average-cost curve (AC_L) at point F (minimum point). This short-run average-cost curve (AC_S) is shown explicitly in Figure 9.7, panel (a), together with the average-variable-cost curve (AVC) and the short-run marginal-cost curve. The two disconnected parts of the typical firm's short-run supply curve are indicated by the two heavy line segments.

The corresponding short-run industry supply curve (S_S) is illustrated by the heavy line in Figure 9.7, panel (b). Because the short-run supply curves of the n_0 firms are identical, the quantity supplied in the short run by the entire industry is just equal to n_0 times the quantity supplied by the typical firm at any specified price. For instance, at p_0 the typical firm is willing to supply q_0 units (point F) while the industry is willing to supply Q_0 units (point E_0), where $Q_0 = n_0 q_0$. Actually, the short-run industry supply curve in panel (b) looks identical to the typical firm's short-run supply curve in panel (a). This is due to our judicious choice of scales along the respective horizontal axes: The same horizontal distance represents in panel (b) n_0 times the quantity it represents in panel (a).

Nevertheless, the short-run supply curves of firm and industry shown in Figure 9.7 differ in one important respect: At p_1 (= minimum average-variable cost), the firm's supply curve has a horizontal gap that stretches from the vertical axis to

---

Figure 9.7 The relationships of short-run and long-run equilibrium. Panel (a) gives the short-run per unit cost curves (AC_S, AVC, and MC_S) of each of the n_0 firms which are in long-run equilibrium in Figure 9.6. [The initial long-run industry equilibrium is also reproduced in panel (b) for convenience.] The two disconnected parts of the typical firm's short-run supply curve are indicated by the two heavy line segments. The corresponding short-run industry supply curve is shown by the heavy line labeled S_S in panel (b). The S_S curve necessarily passes through the initial long-run equilibrium point (E_0). When the industry demand curve shifts to the right from $D_0 D_0'$ to $D_2 D_2'$, equilibrium moves quickly to M_2 (market-period equilibrium) and then travels downward along the $D_2 D_2'$ curve to point S_2 (short-run equilibrium) and finally to E_2 (new long-run equilibrium). Alternatively, when the demand curve shifts to the left from $D_0 D_0'$ to $D_1 D_1'$, equilibrium moves to M_1 (market period), then to N' (short run), and finally settles at E_1 (long run).

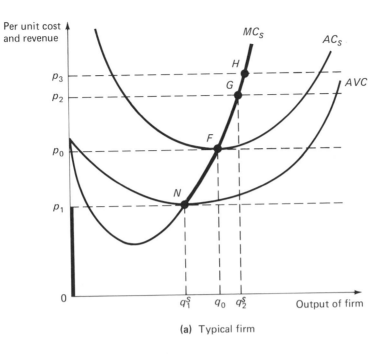

(a) Typical firm

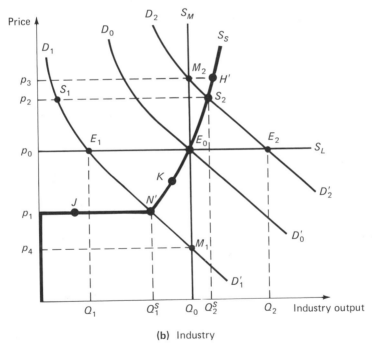

(b) Industry

285

point N, while the industry's supply curve is essentially a solid horizontal line segment (p_1N'). The reason for this difference is simple. At p_1, the typical firm is willing to either close down or produce exactly q_1^S units of output. The industry, on the other hand, is willing to supply all intermediate quantities between zero and Q_1^S units, because it can adjust the number of active firms.

Finally, note that the short-run industry supply curve (S_S) necessarily intersects the long-run industry supply curve (S_L) at point E_0, that is, the point of the initial long-run equilibrium.

Short-Run Equilibrium and the Process Toward Long-Run Equilibrium

Return again to Figure 9.7 and consider the initial long-run equilibrium at E_0 where each of the n_0 active firms supplies q_0 units of output at the price p_0. Naturally, the industry is also in short-run equilibrium, as is evident by the fact that the short-run industry supply curve passes through E_0. We now wish to study the sequence of adjustments that the industry will go through following a shift of the market demand curve.

Suppose that the industry demand curve shifts to the right, as shown by D_2D_2'. In the Marshallian market period where the output to be sold (Q_0) is already produced and absolutely fixed, equilibrium will shift to the intersection of D_2D_2' with the vertical market-period supply curve S_M (i.e., point M_2), and price will rise quickly to p_3. With the passage of time, however, all active firms will tend to increase their output by employing additional units of the variable inputs. For instance, at the price p_3 the typical firm in panel (a) attains short-run equilibrium at point H, and the entire industry will be willing to supply the quantity indicated by point H' in panel (b). Since at p_3 short-run supply (p_3H') exceeds demand (p_3M_2), price will continue to fall until short-run equilibrium is reestablished at point S_2 (i.e., the intersection of D_2D_2' and S_S).

Nevertheless, the short-run equilibrium at point S_2 cannot last for long either. Because the price p_2 is higher than the minimum long-run average cost, new firms will begin to enter the industry. This process will continue until a new long-run equilibrium is reached at point E_2 (i.e., the intersection of D_2D_2' and the horizontal long-run industry-supply curve S_L).

At the new long-run equilibrium (point E_2) the price is again equal to p_0. This means that at E_2 the typical active firm is producing the same long-run equilibrium output as at E_0 (initial long-run equilibrium point), that is, q_0. Because the industry output is higher at E_2 than at E_0, however, we can infer that the total number of active firms must have increased to $n_2 = Q_2/q_0$. This is the only significant difference between the initial equilibrium at E_0 and the final equilibrium at E_2.

Alternatively, suppose that the industry demand curve shifts to the left, as shown by D_1D_1'. In the Marshallian market period, equilibrium will shift to M_1 (the intersection of D_1D_1' and S_M). Price will fall to p_4, which happens to be lower than the minimum average-variable cost (p_1). In the short run, each active firm will reduce its output (by adjusting its variable factors) and equilibrium will shift to the intersection of D_1D_1' and S_S (i.e., point N'), where the price (p_1) is just equal to the minimum average-variable cost. At N' all the initial n_0 firms will necessarily remain active in the short run, but each firm will suffer its maximum loss (= total fixed cost). In the long run, firms will be leaving the industry until a new long-run equilibrium is attained at E_1 (i.e., the intersection of D_1D_1' and S_L), where the price is again equal to p_0 (= minimum long-run average cost). Accordingly, everything is the same at E_1 as it was originally at E_0, except that the number of active firms is now smaller: $n_1 = Q_1/q_0 < Q_0/q_0 = n_0$.

If D_1D_1' intersected S_S to the left of point N' (say, at point J), some firms would drop out even in the short run. On the other hand, if $D_1 D_1'$ intersected S_S between points N' and E_0 (say, at K), all the n_0 firms would again remain active in the short run, because their losses would be less than their respective total-fixed costs.

9.5 Increasing-Cost Industries NO

When the conditions underlying a constant-cost industry do not prevail, the long-run industry supply curve may become either positively sloped (increasing-cost industry) or negatively sloped (decreasing-cost industry). This section deals exclusively with the important case of increasing-cost industries. The analysis is focused on the *long-run* industry-supply curve, but similar considerations also influence the shape of the *short-run* industry supply curve in much the same way.

External Diseconomies

External diseconomies occur where an expansion of the industry output leads to higher costs for each individual firm in the industry. They are divided into *pecuniary external diseconomies* and *technological external diseconomies*. The former ("pecuniary") reflect an increase in factor *prices;* the latter ("technological") reflect reduced *efficiency* of each individual firm, which is a peculiarity of the production function itself.

A perfectly competitive firm, such as a single farmer, can double his output and substantially increase his employment of inputs, such as land, seed, fertilizer, labor, and tractors, without putting any upward pressure on the prices of these inputs. However, when the *industry as a whole* expands its output, the prices of those factors that are heavily employed by that industry will tend to increase, causing the average-cost curve of each firm to shift upward. This factor-price effect is known as a "pecuniary external diseconomy." It is "pecuniary" because it involves an increase in factor *prices*. It is "external" (to the firm) because it is not caused by the output decision and factor demands of any single firm. Finally, it is a "diseconomy" because it involves an increase in costs.

A similar phenomenon occurs when some factors are not homogeneous, and as the industry expands, it becomes necessary to attract less efficient units away from other industries. Typically, the prices of these additional units are not low enough to compensate for their inefficiency. The reason is simple. Such factors may be attracted away from other industries where they happen to be highly efficient, and their prices necessarily reflect their forgone incomes in their best alternative uses. For instance, land that may be good for growing grapes may have to be used for producing wheat, or workers that are highly skilled in the production of clothing may have to be employed in the production of food, where they lack the necessary skills. We therefore conclude that as less and less efficient inputs are employed by the industry, the costs of each individual firm tend to rise.

Typically, technological external diseconomies reflect the unrestrained exploitation of some scarce resource that is not owned by anybody. For example, consider the case of neighboring farmers who irrigate their farms by pumping up water from underground wells. When one farmer intensifies his effort to irrigate his farm, he necessarily drains water away from his neighbors' wells, thus causing their costs to increase. Similarly, when people are free to hunt in a forest or fish in a lake, an increase of such productive endeavor results in a higher cost per animal or fish caught, because of the law of diminishing returns. This external diseconomy is "technological" because it reflects a dependence of the output of one firm on the factor quantities employed and/or the output produced by other firms—an expansion of the industry has an adverse effect on the technology of each firm.

It is interesting to note that both the technological and the pecuniary external diseconomy depend on the greater scarcity of some factor. When the scarce factor is appropriated and subject to the pricing process, the external diseconomy is pecuniary; and when the scarce factor is unappropriated and unpriced, the external diseconomy is technological.

The Positively Sloped Long-Run Industry Supply Curve

External diseconomies, both pecuniary and technological, cause the cost curves of the individual firm to shift upward as the industry output expands. As a result, the supply price of the product rises with the industry output, causing the long-run industry supply curve (S_L) to become positively sloped, as shown in Figure 9.8.

We assume that the industry is in long-run equilibrium at point E_0. The initial equilibrium price is p_0, and the industry output is Q_0. At this equilibrium, the relevant long-run cost curves of the typical firm are shown in panel (a) by the curves labeled AC_0 and MC_0. Accordingly, the typical firm produces q_0, and the number of active firms is $n_0 = Q_0/q_0$.

Suppose now that the demand curve for the industry's product shifts to the right from D_0D_0' to D_1D_1', causing the industry output to expand from Q_0 to Q_1. Because of the underlying external diseconomies, the typical firm's cost curves shift to AC_1 and MC_1, and the equilibrium price rises to p_1, which is exactly equal to the new, higher minimum long-run average cost. By allowing the industry demand curve to shift continuously to the right, we can determine as many points on the long-run industry supply curve as we wish, as illustrated by points E_0 and E_1. As long as the external diseconomy persists, the typical firm's average cost curve will continue to shift upward with every expansion of the industry output, causing the long-run industry supply curve (S_L) to have a positive slope, as in Figure 9.8.

Several observations are now appropriate. First, the optimal output of the typical firm may rise, fall, or remain the same as its long-run average-cost curve shifts upward. This is immaterial. The crucial implication of the external diseconomy is that the minimum long-run average cost rises as industry output expands.

Second, the increase in the equilibrium price from, say, p_0 to p_1, as industry output expands from Q_0 to Q_1 does not imply any positive profits for any of the active firms. The higher price reflects either higher incomes to those factors whose prices have increased (when the external diseconomy is pecuniary) and/or a reduced efficiency in producing the greater industry output (when the external diseconomy is technological).

Finally, external diseconomies may have similar effects on the industry's short-run supply curve. Indeed, pecuniary external diseconomies are usually more pronounced in the short run because factor mobility among industries is lower in the short run than in the long run.

Differences in the Cost Curves of Individual Firms

So far we have been assuming that the entrepreneurial factor is a homogeneous one. Now we wish to drop this assumption. In particlar, we assume that all entrepreneurs are different from one another with respect to their efficiencies both in the perfectly competitive industry under consideration and especially in other industries.

When the entrepreneurial factor is not a homogeneous one, each firm has a different minimum long-run average cost for two reasons. First, each firm has a

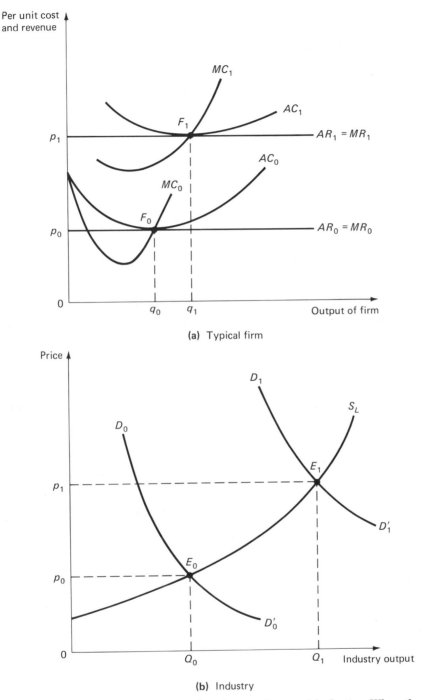

(a) Typical firm

(b) Industry

Figure 9.8 The long-run supply curve of an increasing-cost industry. When the initial long-run equilibrium at E_0, panel (b), is disturbed by a rightward shift of the industry demand curve from D_0D_0' to D_1D_1', the industry output expands from Q_0 to Q_1. Because of the underlying *external diseconomy*, the typical firm's cost curves shift *upward* from AC_0 and MC_0 to AC_1 and MC_1, as shown in panel (a). The new higher equilibrium price (p_1) coincides with the new higher minimum long-run average cost indicated by point F_1.

different production function because by assumption all entrepreneurs differ from one another with respect to their efficiencies in the industry under consideration. Second, each firm includes a different entrepreneurial income (implicit cost) in its long-run total cost. [Recall that on the basis of the principle of opportunity cost (discussed in Chapter 7), each firm must include in its long-run total cost the maximum entrepreneurial income that its organizer and manager could earn in his best possible alternative employment.]

Note that a low-cost producer need not be more efficient than a high-cost producer. The reason is simple. An entrepreneur who happens to be very efficient in the industry under consideration is likely to be highly efficient in other industries as well. Hence, her opportunity cost of organizing production in this industry (i.e., the highest income that she could earn in some other industry) will be relatively high, with the result that her minimum long-run average cost may be higher than the corresponding cost of some other less efficient entrepreneur.

When each firm has a different minimum long-run average cost, the long-run industry supply curve is positively sloped, even in the absence of any external diseconomies. The reason is simple. In the absence of any externalities (economies or diseconomies), the industry supply curve is obtained by a straightforward horizontal summation of the supply curves of all potential producers. At any given price, the total quantity supplied is necessarily finite, because only those firms whose minimum long-run average cost does not exceed the given price are willing to produce any positive output. As the price rises, the total quantity supplied increases for two reasons: (1) Each hitherto active firm increases its output (by moving along its long-run marginal-cost curve), and (2) new firms enter the industry. Therefore, the long-run industry-supply curve has a positive slope.

Figure 9.9 illustrates the long-run equilibrium of such an industry. Imagine the various firms in order, starting with the lowest-cost producer at the extreme left of the diagram and continuing to the right with successively higher-cost producers. For obvious reasons, we show the cost curves of only two such firms in this chain—firm 300 in panel (a) and firm 900 in panel (b). By assumption, the cost curves of the various firms are independent of the industry output. The positively sloped long-run industry supply curve (S_L) is shown in panel (c).

When the industry demand is at D_0D_0', equilibrium occurs at E_0 with p_0 as the equilibrium price and Q_0 as the industry output. The corresponding average-revenue curve of each firm (actual or potential) is at the level of $AR_0 = MR_0$, as shown in panels (a) and (b). Evidently, firm 300 is on the margin of profitability—it just covers its long-run costs by producing exactly q_0 units of output. Any fall in price would, in the long run, send firm 300 out of the industry. For this reason we call firm 300 a "marginal" firm.

Surely, all other 299 firms to the left of firm 300 (i.e., firm 1, firm 2, . . . , firm 299) earn positive profits even in the long run because by assumption their respective minimum long-run average costs are less than p_0. All such firms are described as "intramarginal" firms. On the other hand, all firms to the right of firm 300, such as firm 900 shown in panel (b), remain outside the industry because they cannot cover their costs.

When the industry demand increases to D_1D_1', equilibrium shifts to E_1. The equilibrium price rises to p_1 as output expands to Q_1. The average-revenue curve of each firm now shifts to the level of $AR_1 = MR_1$, as shown in panels (a) and (b). Six hundred new firms (i.e., firm 301 through firm 900) enter the industry. Firm 300 is no longer the marginal firm. That role is now assumed by firm 900. The profits of the 300 initially active firms (i.e., firm 1 through firm 300) are increased as are their outputs. For instance, firm 300 now produces q_1 units of output and enjoys a total profit indicated by the area of shaded rectangle p_1KHF_1.

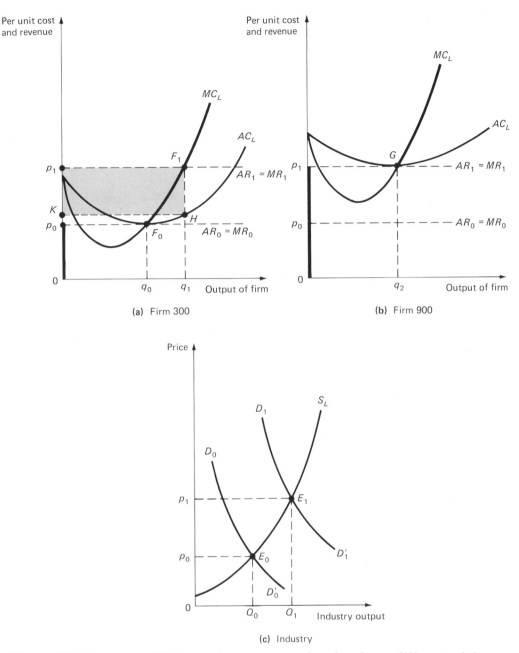

(a) Firm 300

(b) Firm 900

(c) Industry

Figure 9.9 Industry equilibrium when every member firm has a different minimum long-run average cost. Each firm has a different minimum long-run average cost. All firms are arranged in order from left to right, beginning with the lowest-cost producer (firm 1) and proceeding with successively higher-cost producers. Only two such firms are shown: firm 300 in panel (a) and firm 900 in panel (b). The positively sloped industry supply curve (S_L) in panel (c) represents a horizontal summation of the supply curves of all potential producers. When the industry demand is at D_0D_0', equilibrium occurs at E_0 and the corresponding average-revenue curve of each firm is at the level of $AR_0 = MR_0$, as shown in panels (a) and (b). Firm 300 is the "marginal firm" because it just breaks even. When the industry demand curve shifts to D_1D_1', equilibrium moves to E_1, the average-revenue curve of each firm shifts to the level of $AR_1 = MR_1$, and 600 new firms enter the industry (firm 301 through firm 900). Firm 900 is now the new marginal firm.

9.6 **Decreasing-Cost Industries**

We now turn briefly to the less important case of decreasing-cost industries. In this case, external economies (the opposite of external diseconomies) cause the cost curves of the individual firms to shift downward as the industry output expands. As a result, the long-run industry supply curve becomes negatively sloped (or forward falling).

External Economies

External economies are cost reductions that occur when the industry output expands. They are divided into *pecuniary external economies* (when the cost reductions are attributed to lower factor prices) and *technological external economies* (reflecting increased efficiency of each firm).

Pecuniary external economies cannot be observed in the case of primary factors, such as labor and land. They can only be observed in the case of intermediate goods provided that the supplying industry is either noncompetitive (such as monopoly or oligopoly) or a decreasing-cost perfectly competitive industry subject to technological external economies. In the former case, perfect competition is ruled out; in the latter, the pecuniary economies arise because of the existence of the second species of external economies, that is, those of the technological variety.

Examples of technological external economies are scanty. Recall the previous example of neighboring farmers and suppose now that the farms are too wet (or swampy) rather than too dry. If one farmer drains his field, he may thereby increase his neighbors' output as well as his own. A similar phenomenon occurs when a farmer undertakes a program of weed control. Another important example is to be found where the efficient development of an industry may require a large pool of trained labor, or large-scale information services for the exchange of technical information, or finally efficient transportation and communications networks—all of which are made possible as the industry becomes larger and larger.

Unlike external diseconomies, external economies are not important in the short run. If they exist at all, they exert their influence only in the long run.

The Forward-Falling Long-Run Industry Supply Curve

Return to the earlier scenario where all firms, both active and potential, have the same cost curves. In contrast with the foregoing example of external diseconomies, however, assume that the industry is now subject to external economies. As the industry output expands, the long-run average-cost curve of each firm shifts downward, causing the long-run industry supply curve (S_L) to exhibit a *negative* slope, as shown in Figure 9.10, panel (b).

Assume that the industry is initially in long-run equilibrium at point E_0, where the industry demand curve ($D_0 D_0'$) intersects the industry supply curve. The corresponding long-run cost curves of the typical firm are shown by AC_0 and MC_0 in panel (a). At the initial equilibrium price p_0, the typical firm produces q_0 units of output and makes zero profit.

As the industry demand curve shifts to the right from $D_0 D_0'$ to $D_1 D_1'$, the industry output increases (from Q_0 to Q_1). Because of the underlying external economies, the industry expansion causes the cost curves of each of the identical firms to shift downward from AC_0 and MC_0 to AC_1 and MC_1. Each firm's minimum long-run average cost decreases from p_0 to p_1, which is consistent with the new industry equilibrium at point E_1.

We, therefore, conclude that in the presence of extrenal economies (both pecuniary and technological) the long-run industry supply curve is negatively sloped—as the

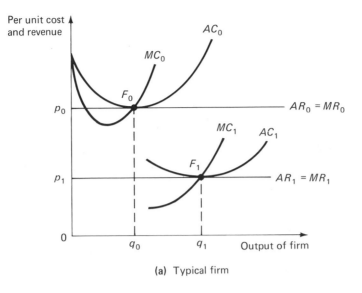

(a) Typical firm

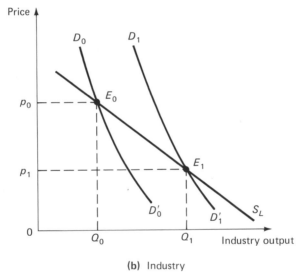

(b) Industry

Figure 9.10 *The long-run supply curve of a decreasing-cost industry.* When the initial equilibrium at E_0, panel (b), is disturbed by a rightward shift of the demand curve from D_0D_0' to D_1D_1', the industry output expands to Q_1. Because of the underlying *external economy,* the typical firm's cost curves shift *downward* from AC_0 and MC_0 to AC_1 and MC_1, as shown in panel (a). The new lower equilibrium price (p_1) coincides with the new lower minimum long-run average cost indicated by point F_1.

industry output expands, the minimum long-run average cost of the typical firm, and thus the supply price, tends to fall.

PART C. APPLICATIONS

Having examined the short-run and long-run equilibrium of the perfectly competitive firm and industry, we now turn to some important applications: the introduction of superior equipment and the problem of obsolescence, the effects of taxes, the degree of competition in the U.S. economy, and the recent adjustment in the U.S. copper industry.

9.7 The Introduction of Superior Equipment

Technical progress is often *embodied* in newer and more productive capital goods (superior machines). Such embodied technical progress becomes effective after the installation of the new machines—a process that is likely to be more or less gradual not because the new machines cannot be installed quickly but because hitherto active firms may choose to continue using the older machines until they wear out or they become totally obsolete, as explained below.

Consider a constant-cost industry that is in long-run equilibrium before a new machine is introduced, as shown in Figure 9.11. The typical firm's AC_L curve is shown in panel (a) together with the more important short-run cost curves: AC_S, AVC, and MC_S. Panel (b) displays the initial long-run industry supply curve (S_L), the corresponding short-run industry supply curve (S_S), and the market demand curve (DD'). (For the moment ignore the S'_L and S''_L curves.) Equilibrium occurs at E, where the industry output is Q_0 and the equilibrium price is p_0.

Now suppose that the superior new machines become available. For convenience, assume that the new machines are installed by new firms only. If the minimum long-run average cost of a typical new firm happens to be lower than the minimum average-variable cost of a typical old firm (i.e., p_2), as shown by the AC''_L curve in panel (c), the old machines will become totally obsolete as fast as the new machines can be installed. The new long-run industry supply curve will be S''_L, equilibrium will shift to K, and each new firm will produce q_2, while each old firm will leave the industry.

However, the minimum long-run average cost of a new firm may be higher than the minimum AVC (but lower than p_0), as shown by the AC'_L and MC'_L curves in panel (c). In this case the new long-run industry supply curve will be S'_L, and long-run equilibrium will occur at J. Nevertheless, even in the short run price and industry output will move to their new long-run equilibrium magnitudes (p_1 and Q_2) as soon as a sufficient number of new firms entered the industry. In particular, when new firms are able to produce HJ (or $Q_2 - Q_1$), price will fall to p_1 and industry output will rise to Q_2. But such a state of affairs is not a true long-run equilibrium, because each of the old firms will be incurring short-run losses. (The typical old firm will be producing at G.) Gradually, either because the old machines physically wear out or because their minimum AVC rises above p_1, old firms will be leaving the industry making room for more new firms.[2] Long-run equilibrium will be restored after all old firms are replaced by new firms.

[2]Typically, as machines grow older their variable costs tend to rise, as any driver of an older car may verify.

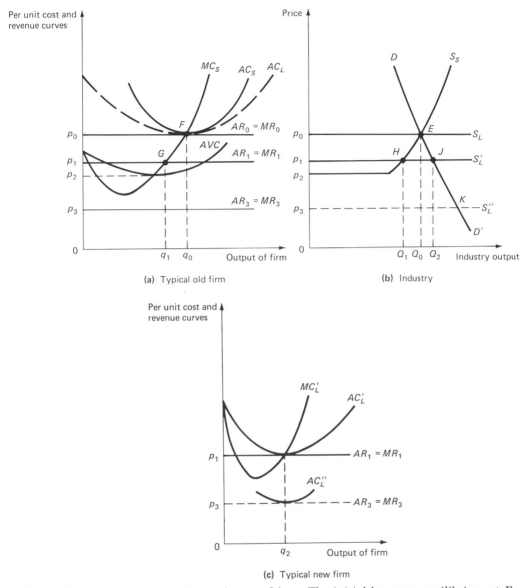

(a) Typical old firm

(b) Industry

(c) Typical new firm

Figure 9.11 Introduction of superior machines. The initial long-run equilibrium at E, panel (b), is disturbed by the availability of superior new machines. If the minimum long-run average cost of the typical new firm was p_3, as indicated by the AC_L'' curve in panel (c), the old machines would become totally obsolete as fast as the new machines were installed, and equilibrium would move to K. However, suppose that the cost curves of the typical new firm are those labeled AC_L' and MC_L'. As soon as new firms enter the industry and produce HJ (or $Q_2 - Q_1$), price will fall to p_1 and industry output will rise to Q_2. Each old firm will operate at G, panel (a). Full long-run equilibrium at J, however, will be restored after all old firms are replaced by new firms.

9.8 The Effects of Commodity Taxes

Because we have already discussed the effects of commodity taxes in the context of our preliminary investigation of the law of supply and demand (Chapter 2), our present comments will be very brief. As we pointed out in Chapter 2, a commodity tax may be legally fixed either as a certain sum of money per physical unit sold (specific tax) or as a percentage of the value of the commodity (*ad valorem* tax). The effects of an ad valorem tax are more or less the same as the effects of an equivalent specific tax. For this reason we study the effects of a specific tax only.

To determine the effects of a specific tax on the equilibrium price and the industry output, we shift the market demand curve vertically downward, as explained in Chapter 2. (For our present purposes, this procedure is superior to the alternative upward shift of the industry supply curve.) The new "after-tax demand curve" gives directly the net prices received by producers at alternative industry outputs, after the tax is subtracted from the corresponding prices paid by consumers.

Because the market demand curve is generally downward sloping, a downward shift causes it to also move to the left. Therefore, the imposition of a specific tax is equivalent to a leftward shift of the market demand curve. Since we examined the effects of such leftward demand shifts in part B of this chapter, there is no need to repeat that discussion in detail. We rather summarize the effects of a specific tax for the case of a constant-cost industry. The interested reader may extend the present analysis to the cases of decreasing-cost and increasing-cost industries, including industries with backward-bending supply curves.

Drawing on the analysis of Section 9.4 (particularly Figure 9.7), it is evident that in the short run the imposition of a commodity tax causes the industry output to fall as equilibrium moves downward along the short-run industry supply curve. The price received by producers also falls (generally by less than the full amount of the tax), although it cannot fall below the minimum AVC of the typical firm. All active firms will suffer short-run losses. Each firm will reduce its output and some firms may even leave the industry. The price paid by consumers will rise but not by the full amount of the tax.

In the long run some firms will have to leave the industry and the full burden of the tax will be shifted to consumers. The industry output will fall even further. However, the price received by producers will be restored to its pretax level (equal to the minimum long-run average cost of the typical firm). The typical active firm will return to the same position as in the pretax long-run equilibrium.

9.9 The Effects of Lump-Sum Taxes

Turn now to the effects of a lump-sum tax, which involves the payment of a fixed amount of money to the government. For instance, each firm in an industry may be required to pay a lump-sum tax per year (known as a "franchise tax") for the privilege of doing business.

It is important to note from the start that the lump-sum tax is not a true fixed cost, even though its amount does not change with the firm's output. The reason is simple: A firm can avoid the lump-sum tax by closing down altogether. In principle, therefore, a lump-sum tax is a variable cost. However, because its amount is by definition constant, we may refer to it as a quasi-fixed cost.

Consider again a constant-cost industry in long-run equilibrium (before the imposition of the tax), as shown in Figure 9.12. The pretax long-run cost curves of the typical firm are shown in panel (a) by the curves labeled AC_L and MC_L, and the corresponding long-run industry supply curve is given by the horizontal line labeled S_L in panel (b). The initial long-run equilibrium is at E_0. The equilibrium price is p_0 (= minimum long-run average cost), and the industry output is Q_0. The typical firm produces q_0 (point F_0).

Suppose now that the government imposes a lump-sum tax on each active firm. In the short run, this tax will have no effect on either the price or the industry

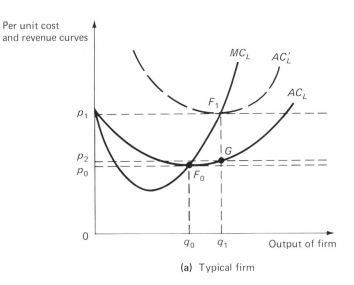

(a) Typical firm

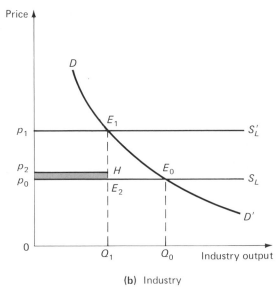

(b) Industry

Figure 9.12 Effects of a lump-sum tax. Before the imposition of the lump-sum tax, the industry is in long-run equilibrium at E_0, panel (b), and the typical firm produces q_0 (point F_0). The lump-sum tax causes the AC_L curve to shift upward, as shown by the dashed curve labeled AC_L'. The MC_L curve does *not* shift. Consequently, the typical firm's long-run supply curve starts at F_1, and the long-run industry supply curve shifts to S_L'. Equilibrium moves from E_0 to E_1, and each active firm increases its output to q_1, where the average cost of production (point G) is higher than p_0. As a result, there is a harmful increase in the total cost of Q_1 indicated by the area of shaded rectangle $p_0E_2Hp_2$. The government's tax revenue is given by the area of $p_2HE_1p_1$. With an equivalent commodity tax instead, the total cost of Q_1 remains equal to the area of $OQ_1E_2p_0$, and shaded area $p_0E_2Hp_2$ becomes part of the revenue collected by the government.

output, assuming that the tax is not larger than the typical firm's total-fixed cost.[3] However, the typical firm will suffer a short-run loss equal to the lump-sum tax.[4]

Now turn to the long-run. Evidently, the lump-sum tax does not affect the typical firm's long-run marginal-cost curve because it is a quasi-fixed cost. Nevertheless, it causes the long-run average-cost curve to shift upward, as shown in Figure 9.12, panel (a), by the dashed AC'_L curve. [Note that the AC'_L curve is also intersected at its minimum (point F_1) by the stable MC_L curve.] Consequently, the typical firm's long-run supply curve now starts at F_1, and the after-tax long-run industry supply curve is shown by the horizontal line labeled S'_L in panel (b). Equilibrium moves from E_0 to E_1, industry output falls from Q_0 to Q_1, and the price rises to p_1. The typical firm increases its output from q_0 to q_1. The number of active firms falls both because the industry output declines and the output of each firm increases.

Figure 9.12 shows clearly that the lump-sum tax has deleterious effects on economic efficiency. Because each firm is induced to increase its output beyond q_0, the long-run average cost of production rises to p_2. In other words, the typical firm operates at G instead of F_0. As a result, the industry produces the new equilibrium output (Q_1) at a higher total cost (excluding the tax) than it should. This harmful increase in cost is indicated in panel (b) by the area of shaded rectangle $p_0 E_2 H p_2$.

An alternative way of looking at the inefficiency of the lump-sum tax is to compare it with a specific tax. Suppose that the government imposes instead a specific tax equal to $p_1 - p_0$ (equal to distance $E_2 E_1$). The after-tax demand curve will then pass through E_2, where the new long-run equilibrium will actually occur. The industry output will fall to Q_1, but *the price received by producers will remain at p_0*. Hence each firm will produce q_0 (point F_0) compared with q_1 (point G) under the lump-sum tax. The total cost of production of Q_1 will now be equal to the area of rectangle $0 Q_1 E_2 p_0$ (compared with $0 Q_1 H p_2$ under the lump-sum tax). The tax revenue collected by the government will be equal to the area of rectangle $p_0 E_2 E_1 p_1$ (compared with $p_2 H E_1 p_1$ under the lump-sum tax). It is therefore evident that under a commodity tax, shaded rectangular area $p_0 E_2 H p_2$ will be part of the revenue collected by the government rather than part of the production cost. Thus the commodity tax is more efficient than the lump-sum tax.

The commodity tax involves a deadweight loss that is also shared by the lump-sum tax. For instance, in Figure 9.12, panel (b), as the price paid by consumers rises from p_0 to p_1 (after the imposition of the tax), the consumers' surplus falls by the area of $p_0 E_0 E_1 p_1$. As we mentioned above, the area of rectangle $p_0 E_2 E_1 p_1$ corresponds to revenue collected by the government. It follows, then, that triangular area $E_2 E_0 E_1$ represents a deadweight loss that is caused by the tax. In the case of a specific tax, this is the only economic loss, but in the case of a lump-sum tax, there is the additional loss indicated by the area of shaded rectangle $p_0 E_2 H p_2$.

9.10 The Degree of Competition in the U.S. Economy

As noted in Chapter 8, the theoretical requirements of the model of perfect competition are so severe that only a few markets in the real world can come close to meeting them. How useful, then, is the model of perfect competition? This is an

---

[3]When the lump-sum tax is larger than the typical firm's total-fixed cost, some firms will leave the industry even in the short-run, causing the price to rise and the industry output to fall. In particular, the price will have to rise sufficiently to cover each active firm's minimum average-variable cost *including the lump-sum tax*.

[4]By assuming that the lump-sum tax is not larger than the firm's total-fixed cost, the firm can maximize its after-tax profit by maximizing its pretax profit (because the tax is fixed). When each firm is in long-run equilibrium before the imposition of the tax, the tax will have no effect (in the short run) on the firm's output, but the firm will incur a loss equal to the tax.

important question. As it turns out, over three-fourths of the U.S. national income is now produced under conditions that are effectively competitive. This is the astonishing conclusion reached in a recent study by W. G. Shepherd (1982). His findings for the years 1939, 1958, and 1980 are summarized in Table 9.1. These findings show how indeed very relevant is the model of perfect competition.

On the basis of (1) structural evidence (mainly market shares, concentration ratios, and barriers to entry) and (2) behavioral evidence (mainly pricing behavior), all markets in the U.S. economy are classified into four types: (1) *pure monopoly* (market share at or near 100 percent, effective barriers to entry, and effective monopoly control over the level and structure of prices); (2) *dominant firms* (market share of 50 to over 90 percent, no close rival, strong barriers to entry, ability to control prices, and rates of return above the competitive level); (3) *tight oligopoly* (four-firm concentration above 60 percent, stable market shares, medium or high entry barriers, and rigid prices); and (4) *effective competition* (four-firm concentration below 40 percent, unstable market shares, flexible pricing, low entry barriers, little collusion, and low profit rates). The fourth category, effective competition, lumps together such market types as "loose" oligopoly, monopolistic competition, and pure competition.

It is evident from Table 9.1 (top part) that since 1939 effective competition has been the predominant market structure in agriculture, mining, wholesale and retail trade, and financial markets. In all sectors except the transportation and utility sectors, the majority of activity was effectively competitive.

Table 9.1 Trends of Competition in the U.S. Economy, 1939–1980

Sectors of the Economy	National Income in Each Sector, 1978[a] (billion dollars)	Percent of Each Sector That Was Effectively Competitive		
		1939	1958	1980[a]
Agriculture, forestry, and fisheries	54.7	91.6	85.0	86.4
Mining	24.5	87.1	92.2	95.8
Construction	87.6	27.9	55.9	80.2
Manufacturing	459.5	51.5	55.9	69.0
Transportation and public utilities	162.3	8.7	26.1	39.1
Wholesale and retail trade	261.8	57.8	60.5	93.4
Finance, insurance, and real estate	210.7	61.5	63.8	94.1
Services	245.3	53.9	54.3	77.9
Total	1512.4	52.4	56.4	76.7

		Percent of Each Category in Total National Income		
		1939	1958	1980
1. Pure monopoly	38.2	6.2	3.1	2.5
2. Dominant firm	42.2	5.0	5.0	2.8
3. Tight oligopoly	272.1	36.4	35.6	18.0
4. Others: effectively competitive	1157.9	52.4	56.3	76.7
Total	1512.4	100.0	100.0	100.0

Source: Shepherd (1982, p. 618). Permission granted by the North-Holland Publishing Company, Amsterdam.

[a]1980 figures reflect competitive conditions as of 1980. The industry weights are based on 1978 data for national income, the latest year available.

The main trends are also interesting. All sectors except agriculture have experienced an increase in competition throughout the 1939–1980 period. This rise in competition was rather slow from 1939 to 1958 (mainly in construction and transportation) but accelerated tremendously from 1958 to 1980 and became more widespread throughout the U.S. economy.

The lower part of Table 9.1 gives the overall percentage shares of U.S. national income produced by each of the four market categories. Note that the percentage of U.S. national income produced under effective competition experienced a modest rise of about four points from 1939 to 1958, increasing from 52.4 percent to 56.3 percent, but jumped to 76.7 percent in 1980, a fantastic surge of competition. The combined share of pure monopolies and dominant firms shrank from about 11 percent in 1939 to 8 percent in 1958, and to only 5 percent in 1980. The share of tight oligopoly was halved, from about 36 percent in 1939 and 1958 to 18 percent in 1980. Market power is still high in many markets, such as computers, drugs, locomotives, newspapers, photographic film, soups, and in various utilities and city services.

Shepherd (1982, p. 618) points out that the evidence about this remarkable surge in competition is not very sensitive to a few large industries, such as automobiles, steel, and telephone equipment, which have been classified as becoming more competitive in 1980. Even if these three industries (automobiles, steel, and telephone equipment) were left in their 1958 market categories, the revised share of effective competition would drop to only 74.3 percent, which is still very high.

Shepherd attributes the rise in effective competition to three main causes: increased import competition, antitrust actions, and deregulation.

9.11 Adjustment in the U.S. Copper Industry

The industry adjustment that follows a reduction in demand is always very painful, although such concomitant agony, distress, pessimism, and suffering are not captured by supply-and-demand diagrams. The recent history of the U.S. copper industry, as reported through the columns of *The Wall Street Journal,* illustrates these adjustment difficulties well.

The U.S. copper industry faces three fundamental, intractable problems: (1) It is by far the world's highest-cost major producer, (2) it must compete with foreign mines that are heavily subsidized, and (3) it has been experiencing a secular decline in demand. We discuss each of these problems below.

The operating costs of the U.S. mines are much higher than those of foreign mines for two reasons. First, the deposits in American copper mines contain only 13 pounds of copper per ton of rock, compared with 20 to 25 pounds overseas. The lower grade of ore increases U.S. costs, because much more rock has to be moved per pound of copper in the United States than in foreign countries. Second, U.S. costs for labor and antipollution equipment have surged since the mid-1970s to many times the levels at mines in developing nations.

Further, foreign mines are largely owned and subsidized by governments in such countries as Chile, Peru, Zaire, and Zambia. About 50 percent of world copper capacity is controlled by foreign governments, which tend to keep their mines open, despite operating losses, not only to provide employment for their people, but also to secure foreign exchange earnings to finance their imports.

However, the root of the plight of the U.S. copper industry can be traced to the secular decline in demand for copper. This secular decline is probably due to a fundamental structural change in the American economy—a shift away from traditional heavy industries and toward the service and high-technology sectors. As a result, the U.S. share of the world copper market has dropped from 35 percent in 1950 to about 19 percent in 1981. Indeed observers of the world copper market predict that Chile may soon surpass the United States as the world's largest copper producer.

The problems of the U.S. copper industry were compounded by the worldwide recession in the early 1980s. Many copper-using industries, such as automobiles, construction, and electrical equipment, reduced their operations sharply, causing the demand for copper to fall even further. Copper prices dropped precipitously. In 1982, U.S. copper producers were getting about 70 cents a pound, a price that is far below the average cost of production of copper in the United States (estimated to be in the range of 90 cents to $1.50). In Arizona, which produces two-thirds of this nation's copper, mine after mine was closed, and 12,500 miners (or 60 percent of the state's copper work force of 21,000) found themselves unemployed. Mining towns were devastated. As it turns out, the adjustment is especially painful in an industry such as mining because many workers live in remote little towns where there is nothing but the mine. When the mine closes down, these places turn quickly into ghost towns.

In a recent report *The Wall Street Journal* (September 16, 1982, p. 56) tells the moving story of a quiet little town, Silver Bell, which was unfortunate enough to fall victim to the cruelty of industry adjustment under adverse market conditions. Silver Bell is located in the middle of the cactus-dotted desert northwest of Tucson, Arizona, and a stone's throw from the mine. In December 1981, Asarco Inc. indefinitely closed the mine, laid off 240 of the 305 workers, and evicted many of them from company-owned houses that they had rented for as little as $100 a month. Anguish, despair, distress, grief and melancholy spread throughout the little town. The wooden ranch houses remained curtainless, dark, and silent. The Little League baseball team, whose uniforms and equipment were provided by the company, was disbanded. The beauty salon and the grocery store folded. Even the Catholic church was closed. The honest workers in this hard-hit region were permanently scarred. Each one will surely have his own stories to tell. Such are the chilling, demoralizing effects of a downward industry adjustment.

To ease the blow, Arizona officials allocated $140,000 in federal and state money to the Displaced Copper Workers Project, the first comprehensive aid program for unemployed miners. Housed in a vocational center in Tucson, the project trains laid-off miners for other jobs, helps them with job-interview techniques, and teaches them how to adjust to long-term unemployment.

SUMMARY

1. A perfectly competitive firm maximizes its long-run total profit when (a) $MC_L = MR$, (b) MC_L is rising, and (c) $AR \geq AC_L$ (or $R \geq C_L$). It does not maximize its per-unit profit.

2. Long-run total profit $= R - C_L = (AR - AC_L) \cdot$ output. It is also given by the algebraic sum of the areas between the curves of MR and MC_L.

3. The long-run supply curve of a perfectly competitive firm coincides with the rising segment of MC_L, starting at the point of minimum AC_L.

4. The perfectly competitive firm cannot be in long-run equilibrium with decreasing MC_L or AC_L. Hence perfect competition is incompatible with increasing returns to scale. (Perfect competition may also fail when the U-shaped AC_L curve of a typical firm reaches its minimum at a high rate of output, restricting entry to only a few producers.)

5. A perfectly competitive firm maximizes its short-run total profit at the point where the MC_S curve intersects from below the horizontal $AR = MR$ curve, provided that $R \geq V$ (or $AR \geq AVC$). The total fixed cost F represents the maximum loss that the firm may suffer, but the short-run equilibrium is totally independent of F.

6. The perfectly competitive firm cannot be in short-run equilibrium with decreasing MC_S, but it can do so with decreasing AC_S.

7. When a firm is in long-run equilibrium, it is in short-run equilibrium also. The converse need not be true.

8. The short-run supply curve of a perfectly competitive firm coincides with the rising segment of its MC_S curve, starting at the point of minimum AVC.

9. Short-run total profit $= R - C_S = (AR - AC_S) \cdot$ output. The algebraic sum of the areas between the curves of MR and MC_S equals total profit plus total fixed cost.

10. A perfectly competitive industry is in long-run equilibrium when (a) each active firm is maximizing its long-run profit and (b) no potential firm has any incentive to enter the industry.

11. A perfectly competitive industry is in short-run equilibrium when each active firm is maximizing its short-run profit. In the short run all potential producers remain dormant.

12. A constant-cost industry (horizontal industry supply curve) can exist when (a) all firms (actual and potential) have the same AC_L curve (or, more accurately, the same minimum AC_L) and (b) external economies and diseconomies are absent. Equilibrium price is equal to the common minimum AC_L, and each firm makes zero profit.

13. External diseconomies (cost increases) are divided into pecuniary (reflecting increases in factor prices) and technological (reflecting reduced efficiency). As the industry output expands, they cause the cost curves of firms to shift upward.

14. External economies (cost reductions), both pecuniary (due to lower factor prices) and technological (due to increased efficiency), cause the cost curves of firms to shift downward as industry output expands.

15. The long-run industry supply curve is positively or negatively sloped according to whether the industry is subject to external diseconomies or external economies, respectively.

16. When each firm has a different minimum AC_L, the long-run industry supply curve is positively sloped even in the absence of extrenal diseconomies.

QUESTIONS

1. The following table shows how a perfectly competitive firm's long-run average cost changes as output increases.

Output	Average Cost
1	$40
2	35
3	29
4	25
5	24
6	24
7	26
8	30
9	36
10	46

How much should the firm produce to maximize its long-run profit at the following alternative prices: (a) $30; (b) $17; (c) $40; (d) $57?

2. Explain why a perfectly competitive firm can be in equilibrium with decreasing average cost in the short run but not in the long run.

3. Define and give an example of an external economy. Explain why the industry supply curve may be downward sloping because of external economies but not internal economies.

4. The production functions of all individual firms in a perfectly competitive industry are the same in all respects. In addition, they are characterized by constant returns to scale.

(a) Will this peculiarity of production functions lead to any kind of indeterminacy as far as the equilibrium of the individual firm is concerned? Explain.

(b) If there exists some type of indeterminacy, does it destroy the perfectly competitive character of the industry?

5. Show graphically the short-run and long-run effects of a $1 per unit tax on a competitive industry. Consider three possibilities: constant-cost industry, increasing-cost industry, and decreasing-cost industry. In each case, begin with the impact of the tax on the cost curves of the individual firms, then indicate the effect on the long-run and short-run industry supply curves, and finally, compare the post-tax long-run equilibrium with the pretax equilibrium, also discussing the transition.

6. In a certain community, there are two lakes where fish may be caught. In lake A the cost per bushel of fish per week is $24. In lake B, which is more generously endowed, the cost per bushel of fish per week is $15, provided that no more than 600 bushels of fish are taken per week; above 600 bushels, the average cost per bushel rises by a nickel for each extra bushel taken. In this community, there are many potential fishermen who have free access to either lake. They are willing to turn to fishing from other pursuits provided that the price of fish is at least as great as their current average cost.

(a) Describe the supply curve of the fishing industry. Draw it on graph paper.

(b) Suppose that demand conditions are such that 1000 bushels of fish are sold each week. Determine the equilibrium price of fish and the number of bushels fished out of lake A. Calculate also the total cost of 1000 bushels.

(c) Show that the society can get the same total quantity of fish (1000 bushels) at a lower total cost. Calculate the lower total cost and explain why market forces lead to a higher cost.

(d) Suppose that the community allocates its fishing resources efficiently between the two available lakes. Describe and then draw on graph paper the fishing industry's supply curve.

7. How can you reconcile the assumption that the perfectly competitive firm faces a horizontal demand curve with the fact that the market demand curve is downward sloping?

8. In a perfectly competitive industry, there are many potential producers. Each producer can produce 80 units of output at a minimum long-run average cost of $90 per unit. (Other outputs involve a somewhat higher average cost.) The industry demand curve is $Q_d = 5800 - 20p$.

(a) Draw the industry's long-run supply schedule.

(b) Determine the long-run equilibrium price, industry output, output of each active firm, number of active firms, and total profit of each firm.

(c) When each active firm is in long-run equilibrium, its short-run total cost is given by the function

$$C_S = 1600 + 50q + 0.25q^2$$

and therefore, its short-run marginal cost, by the equation

$$MC_S = 50 + 0.50q$$

Calculate the average-variable cost function, the short-run supply schedule of the individual firm, and the short-run industry supply curve.

(d) Suppose now that the industry demand suddenly shifts. Consumers wish to buy 2400 units more now than before at any given price. Calculate the effects on the equilibrium price, industry output, output of each firm, number of active firms, and total profit of each firm (1) in the market period (when firms cannot increase their outputs at all), (2) in the short run, and (3) in the long run. Illustrate your results graphically.

9. The long-run equilibrium of a constant-cost industry, using labor and land, is disturbed by an increase of the wage rate. Explain all adjustments (by each consumer and firm) as the industry moves to the new long-run equilibrium.

10. There are just 1000 acres of land suitable only for the production of wheat. This land has no other use. Technology is such that each acre of land must be combined with 10 units of labor, with no deviation from this fixed proportion being possible. Each acre of land produces exactly 100 bushels of wheat. The wage rate is fixed at $20. The demand for wheat is given by the function $Q_d = 5,000,000/p$, where Q_d is the bushels of wheat and p the price per bushel.

(a) Calculate the equilibrium price of wheat.

(b) Determine the equilibrium rent per acre.

(c) Suppose that an ad valorem sales tax of 20 percent is imposed on wheat. Calculate the effects of the sales tax on the price paid by consumers, the price received by producers, the quantity of wheat, and the rent for each acre of land.

11. According to *The Wall Street Journal* (August 10, 1982, p. 56), Canadian fishermen are catching most of Lake Erie's fish (perch, walleye, smelt, and white bass). These fishermen earn an average of $21,000 a year, about three times the income of East Coast Canadian fishermen. But the government, worried that some Lake Erie species are being overfished, has imposed quotas on walleye fishing and is considering additional quotas on perch fishing.

(a) Is the government justified in its interference with market forces by means of quotas?

(b) Can you think of any economic reasons why Lake Erie may be overfished?

FURTHER READING

Ellis, H. S., and W. Fellner (1943). "External Economies and Diseconomies," *American Economic Review,* Vol. 33 (September), pp. 493–511.

Henderson, J. M., and R. E. Quandt (1980). *Microeconomic Theory: A Mathematical Approach,* 3rd ed. McGraw-Hill Book Company, New York. Chapter 6.

Marshall, A. (1959). *Principles of Economics,* 8th ed. Macmillan & Company Ltd., London. Book 5.

Robinson, J. (1933). *The Economics of Imperfect Competition.* Macmillan & Company Ltd., London. Chapters 6–9.

Scitovsky, T. (1954). "Two Concepts of External Economies," *Journal of Political Economy.* Vol. 17 (April) pp. 143–151.

Shepherd, W. G. (1982). "Causes of Increased Competition in the U.S. Economy, 1939–1980," *The Review of Economics and Statistics,* Vol. 64 (November), pp. 613–626.

Stigler, G. J. (1966). *The Theory of Price,* 3rd ed. The Macmillan Company, New York. Chapter 10.

Viner, J. (1931). "Cost Curves and Supply Curves," *Zeitschrift für Nationalökonomie,* Vol. 3, pp. 23–46. Reprinted in G. J. Stigler and K. E. Boulding (eds.), *Readings in Price Theory.* Richard D. Irwin, Inc., Homewood, Ill., 1952.

CHAPTER
10

Monopoly

This chapter is divided into three parts. In Part A we examine the basic theory of monopoly and expose the many fallacies that still surround this market structure. In Part B we continue with various extensions and applications of the basic theory of monopoly, such as shifts in the demand for the monopolist's product, price discrimination, and dumping. In Part C we conclude with the issues raised by the desire to regulate monopolies by means of taxation and price controls.

PART A. THE BASIC THEORY OF MONOPOLY

As we explained in Chapter 8, a monopoly exists when the industry consists of a single producer. The product of the monopolist has no close substitutes, and barriers to entry prevent potential rivals from entering the industry. In practice, this includes many utilities and patented goods. The monopolist faces the industry demand curve, and his equilibrium coincides with the equilibrium of the industry.

In this part of the chapter we deal with the static equilibrium of the monopolist. In particular, we develop the conditions for profit maximization (both in the long run and the short run) and dispel several misconceptions surrounding the behavior of monopoly. We also compare the monopoly equilibrium with the equilibrium of a perfectly competitive industry.

10.1 Monopoly Equilibrium in the Long Run[1]

A monopolist is said to be in static long-run equilibrium when he chooses that price–output combination that maximizes his total profit with reference to his long-run cost curves. The monopolist's equilibrium conditions are analogous to those we

[1]This section may be read together with the Appendix to this chapter.

developed in Chapter 9 for the case of the perfectly competitive firm. These conditions are

1. *The long-run marginal cost must be equal to the marginal revenue ($MC_L = MR$).*
2. *The long-run marginal-cost curve must intersect the marginal-revenue curve from below.* In other words, marginal revenue must exceed marginal cost at all outputs that are immediately lower than the equilibrium output, and marginal cost must exceed marginal revenue at all outputs that are immediately higher than the equilibrium output.
3. *The maximized profit should not be negative.* If it is, the monopolist will simply close down.

As the reader may recall, condition (3) can also be expressed in either one of the following two alternative forms:

3.′ Total revenue (R) should not be less than the long-run total cost (C_L); that is, $R \geq C_L$.
3.″ The monopolist's price (or average revenue) should not be less than his long-run average cost; that is, $AR \geq AC_L$.

These conditions are illustrated in Figure 10.1. Panel (a) gives the solution in terms of the total-revenue and total-cost curves. The monopolist's total profit is maximized at output Q^*, where the total-revenue and total-cost curves are farthest apart. By necessity, the slopes of these two curves at the equilibrium output, as indicated by the dashed tangent lines at points T and S, are equal. The maximized profit is shown by the heavily drawn vertical distance ST. Note that at Q^* total revenue (given by vertical distance Q^*T) exceeds total cost (given by vertical distance Q^*S), and any deviation from the equilibrium output necessarily results in a lower total profit.

Panel (b) presents the same solution in terms of the monopolist's per unit revenue and cost curves, that is, AR, MR, AC_L, and MC_L. Equilibrium is now indicated by point E, where the MC_L curve intersects the MR curve from below. Projecting point E onto the horizontal axis, as suggested by the arrows, we obtain the equilibrium output (Q^*). To determine the equilibrium price, we return to point E and move vertically upward to the demand curve (AR), as indicated by point H. Then we project point H onto the vertical axis, as shown by the arrows, to get the equilibrium price (P^*), that is, the price at which the market is willing to absorb (purchase) the monopolist's equilibrium output (Q^*). The monopolist's total profit now corresponds to the area of rectangle $DJHP^*$.[2]

It must be evident from the above analysis that the monopolist's equilibrium cannot be specified with reference to either the revenue or cost concepts alone. In particular, the notion that a profit-maximizing monopolist always produces at the point of minimum long-run average cost is fallacious. Similarly, there is no basis for the often-quoted aphorism that the monopolist charges "what the traffic will bear," a phrase that signifies preoccupation with the concept of revenue (especially price). Because the demand curve facing the monopolist is inherently downward sloping, there is no doubt that he can raise the price by reducing output. Past point H in Figure 10.1 (b), however, the higher price does not compensate the monopolist for the reduced output, and his total profit begins to fall.

---

[2]Alternatively, the monopolist's total profit can be calculated as the area between the MR and MC_L curves, extending from the vertical axis to vertical line Q^*H.

Similarly, the monopolist does not maximize his total revenue. [In Figure 10.1(a) total revenue attains its maximum at point F, which corresponds to zero marginal revenue.] This is actually dramatized by the conflict that exists between publisher and author. Typically, the author of a book is paid a royalty, which is a fixed percentage of the publisher's total revenue. Accordingly, the author would prefer that price-quantity combination that maximizes the publisher's total revenue (and by implication, the author's royalty), without regard to cost. The publisher, on the other hand, would maximize his net profit only if he chose a smaller output (number of books) and a higher price than the combination preferred by the author. The reason for this conflict is simple. The publisher's marginal cost is necessarily positive, and his profit attains a maximum when marginal revenue is still positive (i.e., when his total revenue is still rising).

Finally, the monopolist does not maximize his per unit profit (or average profit). As we know, total profit = average profit · output. Suppose that the monopolist's output is such that the *average profit* is at a maximum. If he reduced his output, the average profit would also fall, causing total profit to decline. If he increased his output, the average profit would again fall, but now the monopolist can balance the unfavorable effect of a declining average profit against the favorable effect of a larger output. Usually, the point of maximum total profit occurs in the region of declining average profit.[3] The only exception to this proposition is the case of profitless monopoly (discussed in more detail in Section 10.4), where average profit is zero at a single positive output and negative everywhere else. In the latter case, should the monopolist choose to remain in business, he must produce at that point where the average profit is at a maximum (zero)—at any other positive output both the average and total profit are negative.

10.2 Monopoly Equilibrium in the Short Run

In the short run, the monopolist maximizes his total profit with reference to his short-run cost curves. His equilibrium output is indicated by the point where the short-run marginal-cost curve (MC_S) intersects the marginal-revenue curve (MR) from below. His equilibrium price is again determined with reference to the demand curve (AR), as in Figure 10.1(b). To remain in business in the short run, the monopolist must at least cover his variable costs.

There is no need to discuss in more detail the short-run equilibrium of the monopolist. In the remainder of this chapter we restrict our comments to the case of long-run monopoly equilibrium, but the reader should have no trouble adapting that analysis to the circumstances that are peculiar to the short run.

10.3 Fundamental Properties of Monopoly Equilibrium

The monopoly equilibrium has several important properties not shared by the equilibrium of a perfectly competitive industry. The purpose of this section is to study these properties. Additional differences between monopoly and perfect competition will be noted in other parts of this chapter.

---

[3]Total profit is at a maximum when the "elasticity" of the downward-sloping average-profit curve is *unity*. In the case of smoothly continuous curves, the elasticity at the point of maximum average profit is infinite (because at that point the tangent is horizontal). Hence total profit attains its maximum at a higher output, that is, in the region of declining average profit.

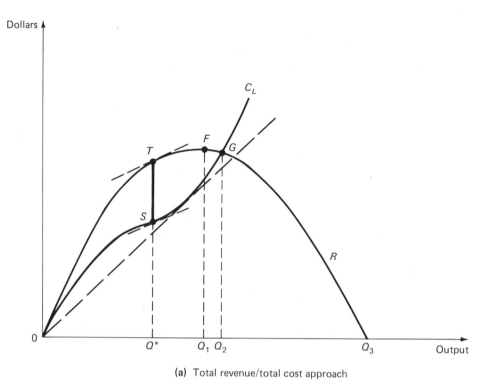

(a) Total revenue/total cost approach

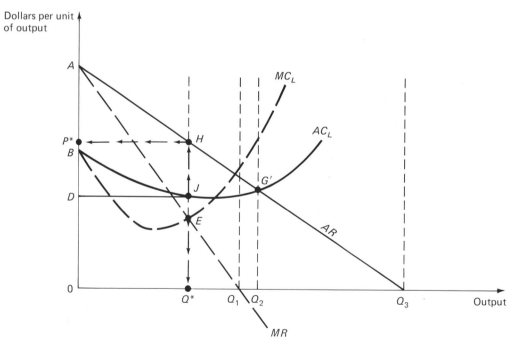

(b) Marginal approach

The Relationship Between Marginal Cost and Price

Because the demand curve facing the monopolist is inherently downward sloping, his marginal revenue is consistently lower than his average revenue; that is, $MR < AR$. (The reader may wish to refer to the argument presented in Section 8.2.) Further, the monopolist's equilibrium is dictated by the equality of marginal cost and marginal revenue; that is, $MC = MR$. It follows, therefore, that the monopolist's equilibrium price (AR) necessarily exceeds his marginal cost:

$$MC = MR < AR \qquad\qquad (10.1)$$

This is a significant deviation from perfect competition, where $MC = MR = AR$. As explained in Chapter 9, the demand curve facing each perfectly competitive firm is horizontal and thus $MR = AR$.

The inequality between marginal cost and price represents the basic evil of monopoly. As we know, the price (or average revenue) corresponds to the marginal valuation that consumers place on the last unit purchased. On the other hand, the monopolist's marginal cost reflects the social costs of producing that last unit. To maximize social welfare, production must proceed up to the point where $AR = MC$, a condition that is satisfied under perfect competition but violated under monopoly.

Figure 10.2 illustrates the harmful effect of monopoly on the allocation of resources. For simplicity, we assume that average and marginal costs are constant, as shown by the horizontal line labeled $AC = MC$. If the monopolist behaved like a perfectly competitive industry, he would operate at point G, where $MC = AR$. In the interests of profit maximization, however, he restricts his output to Q_m (indicated by the intersection of the MR and MC curves, that is, point E) and raises his price to P_m. The result is a loss of consumer surplus equal to the area of shaded triangle EFG. This is a deadweight loss due to monopoly.

It is often thought that the evil of monopoly lies with the huge monopoly profit. This is absolutely fallacious. It is true, of course, that a huge monopoly profit represents an "income transfer" from the consumers to the monopolist. Whether such a transfer is good or bad, however, must be judged on ethical grounds, as explained in Part Six of the book. Worse yet, the basic misallocation of resources would persist even if we taxed all profit away from the monopolist by means of a lump-sum tax (as explained in Section 10.9) and redistributed the proceeds to more deserving individuals.

Harberger (1954) provided a rough estimate of the aggregate magnitude of the deadweight loss of monopoly in the United States for the period 1924–1928. His estimate was surprisingly low—just a little less than one-tenth of 1 percent of national income. He concluded (p. 87): "We can neglect monopoly elements and still gain a very good understanding of how our economic process works and how our resources are allocated." Harberger was criticized for assuming unitary demand elasticities and constant marginal cost in all industries. Whether Harberger's estimates are correct and why is still a controversial issue.

Figure 10.1 Monopoly equilibrium. Panel (a) shows that the monopolist's total profit is maximized at output Q^*, where the curves of total revenue (R) and total cost (C_L) are farthest apart. The tangents at T and S are parallel, and the maximized profit is equal to vertical distance ST. In panel (b), equilibrium is indicated by point E, where the MC_L curve intersects the MR curve from below. The projection of E onto the horizontal axis, as suggested by the arrows, denotes the equilibrium output (Q^*). To determine the equilibrium price (P^*), we move vertically upward from E to H on the AR curve, and then we project H onto the vertical axis, as shown by the arrows. The monopolist's total profit is given by the area of rectangle $DJHP^*$.

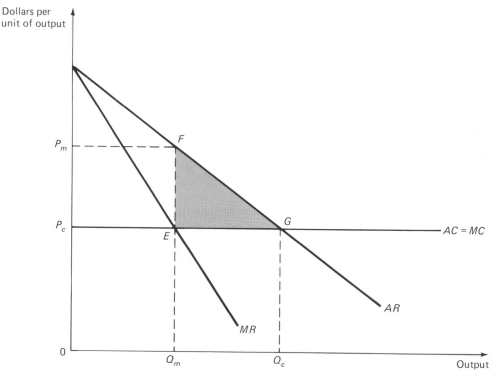

Figure 10.2 The effect of monopoly on economic efficiency. If the monopolist behaved like a perfectly competitive industry, he would operate at G where $MC = AR$. Actually, the monopolist restricts his output to Q_m and raises his price to P_m. The result is a loss of consumer surplus equal to the area of shaded triangle *EFG*, which is the deadweight loss of monopoly.

Monopoly Equilibrium and Decreasing Cost

As we explained in Chapter 9, a perfect competitor cannot be in equilibrium under conditions of decreasing average or marginal cost. This is not true in the case of monopoly. In particular, a monopolist may produce under decreasing, constant, or increasing costs. Figures 10.1 and 10.2 actually illustrate monopoly equilibrium under decreasing and constant average cost, respectively.

The Relationship Between Supply and Demand

Under perfect competition, the equilibrium price is such that the quantity supplied equals the quantity demanded. Each buyer purchases all he wants at the equilibrium price, and similarly each seller sells all he wants.

Under monopoly, however, supply exceeds demand because price is higher than marginal cost. For instance, in terms of Figure 10.1(b), the monopolist would be happy to sell a larger output than Q^* at P^*, because $P^* > MC_L$ ($= Q^*E$). Why, then, does he refrain from increasing his output? Because if he were to do so, he would have to lower his price on *all* units sold, with the result that his total revenue would not increase by as much as his total cost. But if he were able to sell more units *without reducing the price,* he would be delighted to do so. On the other hand, a perfect competitor sells all he pleases at the equilibrium price, and he would not be willing to sell more even at the same price.

The excess supply over demand has at least two important implications. First, it prevents us from analyzing the equilibrium of a monopolistic market in terms of supply and demand curves. That is, the law of supply and demand is applicable only to the case of perfectly competitive markets. Second, the excess of supply over demand provides the rationale for advertising—an attempt to shift the monopolist's demand curve to the right. The use of advertising as an important business strategy is actually a convincing proof of the existence of excess supply: Not only is the monopolist willing to sell more at the current price, but he is even willing to incur extra cost (advertising expenditure) to achieve his goal.

10.4 Some Misconceptions About Monopoly

The theory of monopoly is full of misconceptions. The most troublesome misconceptions are two: (1) The monopolist faces an *inelastic* demand curve, and (2) the monopolist makes huge profits.[4] We are now in a position to explain why these assertions are false.

Monopoly Equilibrium and the Elasticity of Demand

As we explained in Section 10.1, the first-order condition for profit maximization requires marginal revenue to be equal to marginal cost; that is, $MR = MC$. Since marginal cost is generally positive—the least cost of producing a larger output is always higher than the least cost of producing a smaller output—it follows that the marginal revenue of a profit-maximizing monopolist must be greater than zero ($MR = MC > 0$). But we know from our discussion in Section 8.2 that when $MR > 0$ the demand curve must be elastic—increasing the volume of sales by 1 unit by means of a judicious price reduction causes total revenue to increase by $MR > 0$. [Recall that $|e| = AR/(AR - MR)$.]

Conversely, when the demand curve is inelastic, the monopolist's marginal revenue is necessarily negative ($MR < 0$), and a negative MR cannot possibly be equal to a positive MC. We therefore conclude that a profit-maximizing monopolist will never fix his output at a level where the elasticity of his average-revenue curve is less than unity. A monopolist's equilibrium will always occur at a point where the elasticity of demand for his product is greater than unity.

Do Monopolists Make Huge Profits?

Another common misconception is that monopolists necessarily make huge (or "excess") profits. There is no analytical foundation for this assertion. Contrary to what many people believe, a monopolist is not free to set both his price and output at the levels he wants, because of the constraint imposed on him by the average-revenue curve. He can fix either his price, or his output, but not both. Of course, if it were true that the monopolist could simultaneously fix his price and output at the levels he desired, he would be able to make all the profit he wished. As it is, however, *the monopolist can make a positive profit only to the extent that his average-revenue curve lies above his average-cost curve over some range of outputs.* If this condition is not satisfied, the monopolist may have to suspend production altogether, as investors in many American railroads found out the hard way.

Figure 10.3 illustrates the case of profitless monopoly—the least favorable circumstances under which a monopolist may produce a positive output. The average-

---

[4]Recall that in Section 10.1 we showed that the following propositions are also false: (1) The monopolist produces at the point of minimum long-run average cost; (2) the monopolist charges the highest possible price; (3) the monopolist maximizes his total revenue; and (4) the monopolist maximizes his per unit profit.

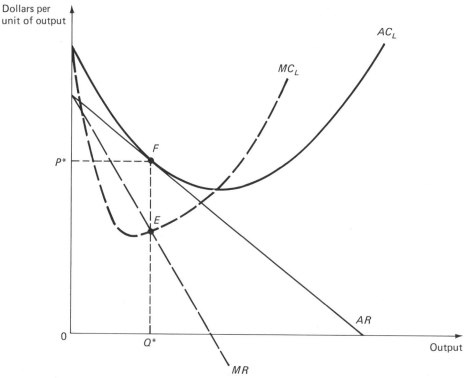

Figure 10.3 The case of profitless monopoly. The AR curve is just tangent to the AC_L curve at F. Everywhere else, the AR curve lies below the AC_L curve. The only positive output where the monopolist can cover his costs is Q^*, corresponding to the intersection (E) of the MR and MC_L curves. It is a matter of indifference to the monopolist whether he produces Q^* or closes down. In either case his total profit is zero.

revenue curve (AR) happens to be tangent to the long-run average-cost curve (AC_L) at point F. Everywhere else, the AR curve lies below the AC_L curve. It is therefore evident that the monopolist can just cover his costs only if he produces Q^*—the output indicated by the intersection (E) of the MR and MC_L curves.[5] At all other outputs, his total profit is negative. It is thus a matter of indifference to the monopolist whether he produces Q^* or closes down. In either case, his total profit is exactly zero.

The case of profitless monopoly represents the borderline between profitable and unprofitable monopolies, and it is a strong reminder that not all monopolists are capable of reaping huge profits.

10.5 Degrees of Monopoly

As we explained in Section 10.3, the monopolist's equilibrium price (AR) exceeds his marginal cost (MC). This fundamental property of monopoly equilibrium represents a significant deviation from perfect competition, where $MC = MR = AR$. Further, this important difference between monopoly ($AR > MC$) and perfect com-

---

[5]The tangency between the AR and AC_L curves at point F corresponds to another tangency between the curves of total revenue and total cost (not shown). It is the latter tangency that explains the intersection of the MR and MC_L curves at point E.

petition ($AR = MC$) reflects the fact that the monopolist faces a *downward-sloping* demand curve (which necessarily implies that $AR > MR$), whereas a perfectly competitive firm faces a *horizontal* demand curve (which means that $AR = MR$).

This basic difference between monopoly and perfect competition suggests that the relative gap between marginal cost and price can serve as an appropriate measure of the "degree of monopoly power" exercised by a firm. Indeed, this is the logic behind the index of monopoly power proposed by Lerner (1933).

Lerner's Index of Monopoly Power

Lerner defines the degree of monopoly power, designated as L (for Lerner), as follows:

$$L = \frac{AR - MC}{AR} \tag{10.2}$$

Lerner's index has several properties. First, it is a *dimensionless* number. Both the numerator ($AR - MC$) and the denominator (AR) have the same dimensionality: monetary units (dollars) per unit of output.

Second, within the context of static equilibrium, Lerner's index always lies between zero and unity; that is,

$$0 \leq L \leq 1 \tag{10.3}$$

In particular, when the firm is perfectly competitive ($AR = MR = MC$), Lerner's index becomes zero because $AR - MC = 0$. In other words, a perfectly competitive firm has no monopoly power at all.

A monopolistic firm has a positive degree of monopoly because $AR - MC > 0$. In addition, for any given value of marginal cost, the higher the price, the greater becomes the degree of monopoly power. Indeed, if price were to tend to infinity, Lerner's index would approach its upper limit of unity.

Lerner's index actually becomes unity in the special case of zero marginal cost ($MC = 0$). In this case, a positive price, however small, is "infinitely large" relative to the zero marginal cost.

Finally, Lerner's index would exceed unity if marginal cost were negative. But it is reasonable to exclude negative marginal cost as a practical possibility.

Lerner's Index and the Elasticity of Demand

Within the context of static equilibrium, Lerner's index (L) is equal to the reciprocal of the absolute value of the elasticity of demand ($|e|$) at the profit-maximizing output. In other words,

$$L = \frac{1}{|e|} \tag{10.4}$$

The derivation of equation (10.4) is simple. Recall from our discussion in Section 8.2 the important relationship that exists between the elasticity of demand, on the one hand, and the average and marginal revenue, on the other hand; that is, $|e| = AR/(AR - MR)$. When the firm is in static equilibrium, marginal revenue equals marginal cost ($MR = MC$). Substituting MC for MR in the elasticity formula, we have $|e| = AR/(AR - MC) = 1/L$, from which we obtain equation (10.4) by merely solving for L.

As equation (10.4) clearly shows, the degree of monopoly power is inversely related to the elasticity of demand at the profit-maximizing output. The lower the elasticity of demand is, the greater the degree of monopoly.

Finally, recall from Section 10.4 that monopoly equilibrium always occurs at a point where the elasticity of demand is greater than unity, because $AR > MR = MC \geq 0$. In the special case of zero marginal cost, the monopolist maximizes his profits at the point where $MR = 0$, $|e| = 1$, and the degree of his monopoly power is unity (or 100 percent). In all other cases, the degree of monopoly power is positive but less than unity, because $+1 < |e| < +\infty$.

Note also that the zero degree of monopoly power under perfect competition reflects the infinite elasticity of demand facing the perfectly competitive firm. As the elasticity of demand tends to infinity, the degree of monopoly power approaches zero.

PART B. EXTENSIONS OF THE BASIC THEORY OF MONOPOLY

In this part of the chapter we study various extensions and applications of the basic theory of monopoly. We begin in Section 10.6 with the effects of a shift in the demand for the monopolist's product, we continue in Section 10.7 with the special issues of price discrimination, and we conclude in Section 10.8 with a brief discussion of dumping.

10.6 The Effects of Shifts in Demand

The analysis of the effects of shifts in demand on an initial equilibrium position is much more complex under monopoly than it is under perfect competition, even though under monopoly the "firm" coincides with the "industry." The basic reason for this difference lies in the fact that the equilibrium of a perfectly competitive industry depends *only* on the *position* of the market demand curve, whereas the equilibrium of the monopolist depends both on the *position and shape* of his average-revenue curve.

Monopoly Equilibrium and the Shape of the Demand Curve

Before considering an unambiguous increase (or decrease) of demand, it is useful to explore a rather special and artificial change: a *rotation* of the average-revenue curve through the initial price–quantity combination. Surely, a rotation of the market demand curve through a competitive-equilibrium point would not influence the industry equilibrium at all—the industry supply and demand curves would continue to intersect at the initial equilibrium point. Yet under monopoly such demand rotation most certainly will affect the monopolist's price, output, and profits, as illustrated in Figure 10.4.

The solid revenue curves, AR and MR, correspond to the initial situation. The monopolist's initial equilibrium output (Q_0) is indicated by point E_0, where the marginal-cost curve (MC) intersects the MR curve from below. (To keep the diagram as clear as possible, we omitted the average-cost curve, which is not necessary for our present purposes.) Accordingly, the monopolist's initial price–quantity combination is denoted by point F on the AR curve.

Suppose now the average-revenue curve rotates through point F becoming flatter (i.e., more elastic at F), as shown by the dashed AR' curve. We wish to show that

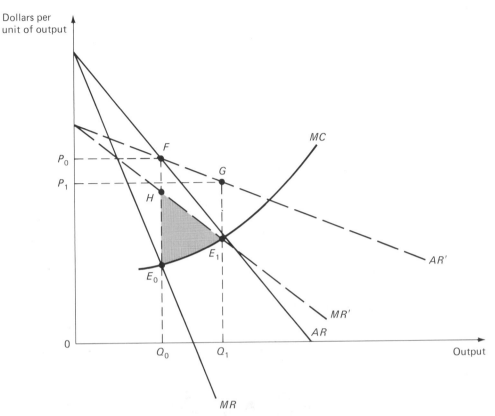

Figure 10.4 Monopoly equilibrium and the shape of the demand curve. The solid AR and MR lines correspond to the initial situation, where the monopolist produces and sells Q_0 at the equilibrium price P_0. Suppose now that the AR curve rotates through F becoming flatter (more elastic), as shown by the AR' curve. The MR curve shifts to the position shown by the MR' curve. The new equilibrium output (Q_1) is now indicated by E_1, where the MC curve intersects the MR' curve from below. The price falls to P_1. The monopolist's profit increases by shaded "triangular" area HE_0E_1. Because at F the AR' curve is *more elastic* than the AR curve, the MR' curve must lie *above* the MR curve at Q_0 (compare H with E_0).

the monopolist's *output will increase* (from Q_0 to Q_1), his *price will fall* (from P_0 to P_1), and his *profits will increase* (by shaded area HE_0E_1).

Graphically, the solution seems clear. When the average-revenue curve rotates to AR', the marginal-revenue curve shifts to MR'. The new equilibrium output is now indicated by point E_1, where the MC curve intersects the MR' curve from below. Accordingly, the monopolist's output increases from Q_0 to Q_1. If we tentatively accept this conclusion, we can also infer that the monopolist price must necessarily fall and his profits must increase.

The price must fall (from P_0 to P_1) because the monopolist's output increases— by assumption, the new demand curve (AR') passes through F and is negatively sloped. The monopolist's profit should increase because the monopolist could make the same profit as before without changing his output or price. The fact that he changes his price–quantity combination is evidence that his profit increases. In particular, the increase in total profit is necessarily equal to the shaded area between the MR' and MC curves extending from output Q_0 to Q_1.

To prove rigorously that the monopolist increases his output, we must show that at the initial output (Q_0) the new marginal revenue (indicated by point H) necessarily exceeds marginal cost (indicated by point E_0). But this must be so because the new AR' curve is more elastic at F than the original AR curve. We can see this clearly by rearranging the earlier elasticity formula as follows:

$$MR = AR\left(\left(1 - \frac{1}{|e|}\right)\right) \tag{10.5}$$

The factor AR is the same for both demand curves at point F (i.e., $AR = P_0$). The expression $(1 - 1/|e|)$, however, is larger for the AR' curve, which is more elastic than the AR curve. Accordingly, the MR' curve must lie *above* the old MR curve (and thus above the MC curve) at the initial equilibrium output (Q_0).

The Effects of an Increase of Demand

Suppose now that the average-revenue curve shifts unambiguously to the right (and upward). We wish to determine the effects on the monopolist's output, price, and profits.

The effect on output depends again on the relationship between the old and new marginal-revenue curves in the vicinity of the initial equilibrium output. Normally, the marginal-revenue curve will also shift upward and to the right, and in that case output will increase. But this is by no means the only result. As we know, marginal revenue is given by the slope of the *total* revenue curve; and it is conceivable that as the total revenue curve shifts upward at all outputs, its slope *in the neighborhood of the initial equilibrium output* may decrease, causing the new marginal-revenue curve to lie below the old one over the relevant range. In this exceptional case, *the monopolist's output will fall,* and thus the price will rise. His profits will increase though, as explained below.

Return now to the normal case in which the marginal-revenue curve shifts unambiguously upward and to the right. Although this is sufficient to cause the monopolist's output to rise, the effect on the equilibrium price is uncertain. This is illustrated in Figure 10.5, which summarizes those special circumstances which guarantee that the monopolist's price remains constant. The marginal-cost curve (MC) is horizontal, at least in the relevant range. (The average-cost curve is again omitted for simplicity.) The curves of average and marginal revenue are shown by the solid lines labeled AR and MR, respectively. The monopolist's initial equilibrium output (Q_0) is indicated by the intersection of MC and MR at E_0. The initial equilibrium price is, of course, P_0.

Suppose now that the original AR line rotates counterclockwise through its vertical-axis intercept (V), as suggested by the dashed AR' line. As we know from Section 2.6, the elasticity of AR' at G is necessarily equal to the elasticity of AR at F, because they are both given by the ratio $0P_0/P_0V$. It follows, then, from the fundamental formula $|e| = AR/(AR - MR)$ that MR at output Q_0 (point E_0) must be equal to MR' at output Q_1 (point E_1) because the elasticities of AR and AR' at the price P_0 and the respective outputs Q_0 and Q_1 are by construction equal. In conjunction with the assumed constancy of marginal cost, the intersection of the MC and MR' curves at point E_1 establishes Q_1 and P_0 as the new equilibrium magnitudes of output and price, respectively.

The monopolist's profit increases by the sum of the two shaded areas: (1) rectangle P_0FHP_1 and (2) triangle E_0E_1J. The justification for this proposition is fairly simple. The monopolist could keep his output constant at Q_0 by raising his price to P_1. In that case, his profit would increase by the area of shaded rectangle P_0FHP_1. But

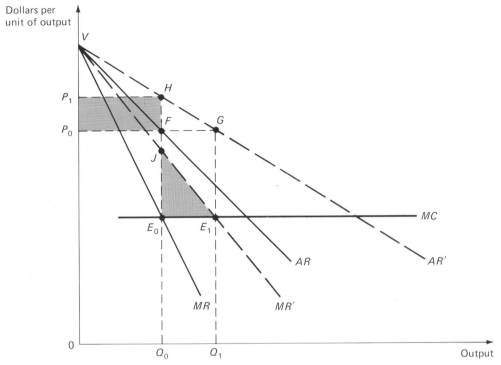

Figure 10.5 The effects of an increase of demand. With reference to the solid AR and MR lines, the monopolist initially produces and sells Q_0 at the price P_0. When the AR curve rotates counterclockwise through V, as suggested by the AR' line, the monopolist increases his output to Q_1 but keeps his price constant at P_0. This result is guaranteed by two circumstances: (a) the constancy of marginal cost and (b) the fact that the elasticity of AR at F is equal to the elasticity of AR' at G, implying that $QE_0 = Q_1E_1$. The monopolist's total profit increases by the sum of the two shaded areas: (1) rectangle P_0FHP_1, plus (2) triangle E_0E_1J.

the monopolist can actually increase his profit even more by expanding his output to Q_1. The additional increase in profit coincides with the area bounded by the *new* marginal-revenue curve (MR') and the unchanged marginal-cost curve (MC) between Q_0 and Q_1, that is, shaded triangular area E_0E_1J.

With reference to the limiting case described above, we can now identify the conditions under which an increase of demand will cause the monopolist's price to either increase or decrease. In particular, the monopolist's price will increase above P_0 if, and only if, the profit-maximizing output is less than Q_1. This will be the case (1) if the marginal-cost curve is upward sloping in the vicinity of the initial equilibrium output (Q_0), and/or (2) if the AR' curve is less elastic than the AR curve at the initial price (P_0). On the other hand, the monopolist's price will fall below P_0 if, and only if, the profit-maximizing output increases beyond Q_1. This will be the case (1) if the marginal-cost curve is downward sloping in the neighborhood of Q_0, and/or (2) if the AR' curve is more elastic than the AR curve at P_0.

If the marginal-cost curve is upward sloping in the vicinity of Q_0 and at the same time the AR' curve is more elastic than the AR curve at P_0, the effect on the monopolist's price will depend on which of these two opposing forces is stronger. The same is true when the marginal-cost curve is downward sloping and the AR' curve is less elastic than the AR curve at P_0.

In all cases in which the demand for the monopolist's product unambiguously increases, the maximized total profit necessarily increases. This must be so because the monopolist can always sell the same output as before at a higher price. To the extent that he also adjusts his output, his profit must increase even more.

The Degree of Monopoly Power and Total Profit

It is often thought that there exists a systematic relationship between the degree of monopoly power and the total profit of the monopolist. Unfortunately, this is not so, and the reader should resist the feeling that a higher total profit necessarily implies a greater degree of monopoly power. This is illustrated in Figure 10.5.

Following the increase of demand, the monopolist increases his output from Q_0 to Q_1. As we explained above, total profit also increases (by the sum of the two shaded areas). However, the degree of monopoly power remains constant because the monopolist's price and marginal cost remain unchanged.

In fact, if the AR' curve were more elastic than the AR curve at P_0, the monopolist's output would be higher than Q_1, the price would be lower than P_0, and total profit would be even higher. Yet the degree of monopoly power would become lower.[6]

10.7 Price Discrimination

Up to now we have assumed that the monopolist charges a uniform price to all customers. In this section we wish to study the problem of price discrimination, that is, the practice of selling the same commodity at different prices.

Nature of the Problem

Price discrimination occurs when a monopolist sells different units of the same homogeneous commodity at different prices. For instance, movie houses usually charge higher prices for adults than for children; a surgeon may charge different fees for an appendectomy depending on the wealth of the patient; and a Japanese steel producer may charge a higher price to domestic (Japanese) customers than to American or other foreign buyers. In such cases the observed price differentials cannot reflect differences in quality because all units sold are assumed to be identical in their physical characteristics. Nor should they reflect any systematic differences in cost due to, say, transportation.

Price discrimination becomes possible only when the different parts of the monopolist's market are separated (or insulated) from one another. Consumers (or traders) should not be able to purchase the commodity in the low-price sector of the market and resell it in the high-price sector. Whenever such *commodity arbitrage* is possible, the monopolist's price-discrimination scheme cannot survive. Similarly, customers in the dearer sector should not be able to transfer themselves into the cheaper sector in order to benefit from the lower price.

This condition is satisfied whenever consumers are not fully informed about any existing price differentials. For instance, when a commodity is sold on special orders, an individual buyer may have no way of knowing what prices are being charged to other customers. The condition is also satisfied whenever consumers happen to have the irrational feeling that a higher price reflects better quality.

---

[6]Rearrange equation (10.2) as follows: $L = (AR - MC)/AR = 1 - (MC/AR)$. When AR falls while MC remains constant, the value of the ratio MC/AR increases, causing the index of monopoly power (L) to decrease.

Price discrimination often occurs in the sale of direct personal services, the resale of which is impossible. It also occurs in international trade because the various national markets are separated from one another geographically and by tariff walls or other barriers to trade. In the latter case, the cost of transferring goods from the cheaper market to the dearer market is usually prohibitive.

The Principle of Equal Marginal Revenue

Suppose now that the monopolist's market can be broken up into two sectors that are fairly insulated from each other. Under what circumstances will he find it profitable to practice price discrimination? In other words, what additional *economic condition* must be satisfied (in addition to the requirement that the two segments of the market can be separated) for price discrimination to result in higher total profit? Further, if price discrimination is indeed possible and profitable, how much output will the monopolist sell in each sector of the market and at what prices?

To simplify the problem, we initially assume that the monopolist has a fixed amount of output to sell. Since the output is already produced, all costs are fixed. Accordingly, profit maximization in this case coincides with total-revenue maximization.

How should the discriminating monopolist allocate the fixed output between the two sectors of the market in order to maximize total revenue? He must do so in such a way that *the marginal revenue of the last unit sold in the first sector is equal to the marginal revenue of the last unit sold in the second sector.* Otherwise, the total revenue can always be increased by transferring sales from the sector in which the marginal revenue is low to the sector in which the marginal revenue is high.

Figure 10.6 shows how to solve the revenue-maximization problem for all "fixed" outputs once and for all. Panels (a) and (b) give the average and marginal-revenue curves of sectors 1 and 2, respectively. In panel (c), the curve labeled ΣAR represents the horizontal summation of the AR_1 and AR_2 curves given in panels (a) and (b), respectively. The ΣAR curve should be recognized as the initial market demand curve, that is, the market demand curve which exists before the discriminating monopolist segregates the market into the two sectors. Finally, the curve labeled ΣMR in panel (c) represents the horizontal summation of the MR_1 and MR_2 curves given in panels (a) and (b), respectively. The monopolist's fixed output is Q_0, as shown in panel (c) by vertical line $Q_0 S$. For the moment, ignore the MC curve in panel (c).

If the monopolist did not wish to practice price discrimination, he would charge the uniform price P_0, as shown by point C_0, that is, the intersection of the market demand curve ΣAR and vertical line $Q_0 S$. By projecting price P_0 back to panels (a) and (b), it becomes obvious that the monopolist would sell Q_1 in sector 1 and Q_2 in sector 2, where $Q_1 + Q_2 = Q_0$.

Can the monopolist increase his total profit (or revenue) by means of price discrimination? He most certainly can, because at P_0 the marginal revenue in sector 1 ($Q_1 H_1$) is lower than the marginal revenue in sector 2 ($Q_2 H_2$). Accordingly, the monopolist can increase his total revenue (and profit) by transferring sales from sector 1 to sector 2. To determine the optimal allocation of Q_0 between the two sectors, we begin in panel (c) at the intersection of vertical line $Q_0 S$ and the ΣMR curve (i.e., point E_0), which determines the common marginal revenue ($Q_0 E_0$). Then we project point E_0 into panels (a) and (b), as shown by the arrows, to determine the optimal allocation: Q_1' (sales in sector 1) and Q_2' (sales in sector 2). Thus, in the final analysis, the discriminating monopolist must transfer $Q_1 Q_1'$ (or $Q_2 Q_2'$) from sector 1 to sector 2. The price in sector 1 must *rise* from P_0 to P_1, while the price in sector 2 must *fall* from P_0 to P_2, as suggested by the arrows.

What is the economic reason why price discrimination is profitable in the example

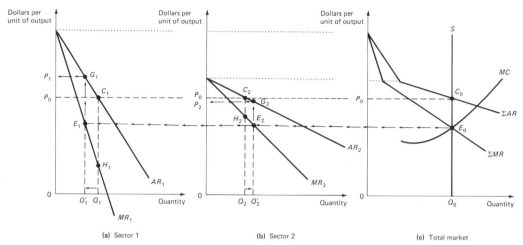

Figure 10.6 Price discrimination. The curve labeled $\Sigma\, AR$ in panel (c) represents the horizontal summation of the AR_1 and AR_2 curves of sectors 1 and 2, respectively, as shown in panels (a) and (b). Similarly, the $\Sigma\, MR$ curve in panel (c) represents the horizontal summation of MR_1 and MR_2 curves given in panels (a) and (b), respectively. The monopolist's equilibrium output (Q_0) is indicated by intersection E_0 of the MC and $\Sigma\, MR$ curves in panel (c). Projecting point E_0 into panels (a) and (b), as shown by the arrows, we also determine the monopolist's sales in the two sectors, namely, Q_1' in sector 1 and Q_2' in sector 2. The price is higher in sector 1, where the elasticity of demand is lower; that is, $P_1 > P_2$.

---

of Figure 10.6? As we pointed out above, the reason is that at P_0 the marginal revenue in sector 1 is lower than the marginal revenue in sector 2. In turn, this difference in marginal revenues reflects the fact that at P_0 the elasticity of demand in sector 1 is lower than the elasticity of demand in sector 2. If the elasticities of AR_1 and AR_2 at points C_1 and C_2, respectively, were the same, the marginal revenues would also be the same [because of the fundamental formula $|e| = AR/(AR - MR)$], and the monopolist would have no incentive to charge different prices.

We therefore conclude that *price discrimination is profitable only if the elasticity of demand in one sector is different from the elasticity of demand in the other.* Furthermore, *the price is necessarily higher in the sector with the lower elasticity of demand.* This again follows from the formula $|e| = AR/(AR - MR)$ when we remember that at the optimal allocation, the marginal revenue must be the same in both sectors. This type of price discrimination (charging different prices in different sectors) is known as third-degree price discrimination.

Variable Output

We can now generalize the above analysis to the case where production is also variable. We already know how the discriminating monopolist should allocate a fixed quantity. The question now is: How much should the monopolist produce in the first place?

When production is variable, not only should marginal revenue be the same in each sector of the market, but also the common marginal revenue should be equal to the marginal cost of the last unit of output produced. In other words, the equilibrium condition for a discriminating monopolist is $MR_1 = MR_2 = MC$. As should be evident, this condition is merely a refinement of the principle that "in equilibrium marginal revenue equals marginal cost."

The above solution is illustrated in Figure 10.6 also. The discriminating monopolist's optimal output (Q_0) is indicated in panel (c) by intersection E_0 of the marginal cost curve (MC) and the ΣMR curve. Once the monopolist knows how much to produce, he can treat that amount as a "fixed" output and proceed, as above, to determine its optimal allocation between the two sectors of the market. As we have seen, the monopolist must sell Q_1' in sector 1 at the price P_1, and Q_2' in sector 2 at the price P_2. Note again that the price is necessarily higher in sector 1, where the elasticity of demand is lower.

Perfect Price Discrimination

Perfect price discrimination (also known as *first-degree* price discrimination) occurs when the monopolist charges a different price for each unit sold, extracting the entire consumer surplus from each and every consumer. Although perfect price discrimination is not a practical possibility, its implications are very interesting and instructive.

Figure 10.7, panel (a), exhibits the ordinary demand curve D_c of a typical consumer. For simplicity, we assume that the income effect is zero (the commodity is neutral), so that the ordinary demand curve coincides with the income-compensated demand curve. This assumption ensures that the higher prices paid by the consumer for the initial units do not affect the later quantities purchased at lower prices. In panel (b), the market demand curve D_m represents the horizontal summation of all individual consumers' demand curves. If the monopolist did not practice price discrimination, his output would be indicated by intersection F of the marginal-cost curve (MC) and the marginal-revenue curve (MR). Thus he would sell Q_1 units of output at the price P_1. The typical consumer would purchase q_1 at P_1 and enjoy a total consumer surplus indicated by shaded triangle AJP_1.

Suppose now that the monopolist is able to practice perfect price discrimination. This means that the monopolist is able to charge different prices for different units, and it is to the advantage of the monopolist to set each unit's price equal to the buyer's marginal valuation. Assuming that each unit is sufficiently small, the monopolist can extract the entire consumer surplus from each consumer. For instance, the monopolist would be able to extract from the typical consumer of panel (a) the additional amount indicated by shaded triangle AJP_1. By repeating this process with every individual consumer, the monopolist would be able to increase his total revenue (and thus total profit) by the area of shaded triangle GHP_1, before he even adjusted his output.

What is the optimal output of the monopolist under perfect price discrimination? To answer this question, we must first identify the true marginal-revenue curve for the perfect price discriminator. Because now the discriminating monopolist does not lower the prices on previous units as he expands his sales, the usual marginal-revenue curve (of the simple monopolist) is no longer relevant. *For the perfect price discriminator, the marginal revenue coincides with the price.* Accordingly, the true marginal-revenue curve for the perfect price discriminator is identical with the market demand curve! This means that the perfect price discriminator will actually expand his output all the way to Q_0, as shown in panel (b) by intersection E_0 of marginal-cost curve MC and market demand curve D_m. This output expansion will actually cause his profits to increase further by shaded triangular area FE_0H.

In other words, the total profit of a perfect price discriminator exceeds the total profit of a simple monopolist by the sum of the two shaded triangular areas in panel (b): area GHP_1 plus area FE_0H. The entire consumer surplus of the typical consumer, that is, shaded triangular area ABP_0 in panel (a) is transferred to the monopolist.

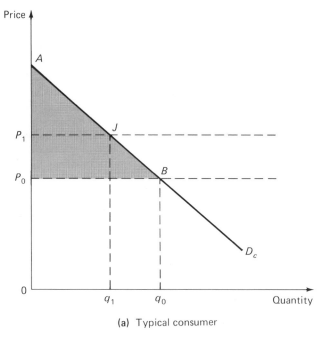

(a) Typical consumer

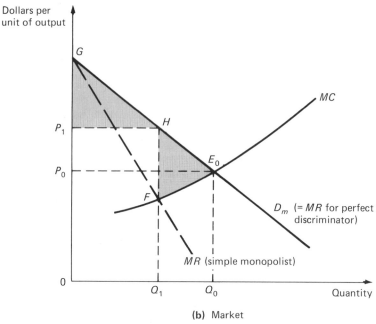

(b) Market

Figure 10.7 Perfect price discrimination. For simplicity assume that the income effect is zero. If the monopolist did not practice discrimination, he would produce and sell Q_1 at the price P_1, as shown in panel (b). The typical consumer would purchase q_1 at P_1 and enjoy a total consumer surplus equal to shaded triangle AJP_1, as shown in panel (a). A perfect price discriminator, on the other hand, would expand his output to Q_0, as indicated in panel (b) by intersection E_0 of the MC and D_m curves. The total profit of a perfect price discriminator would exceed the total profit of a simple monopolist by the sum of the two shaded triangular areas in panel (b): area GHP_1 plus area FE_0H. The entire consumer surplus of the typical consumer, that is, shaded triangular area ABP_0 in panel (a), is transferred to the monopolist.

It is somewhat paradoxical that when the monopolist exploits his market power to the maximum extent possible through perfect price discrimination, his degree of monopoly drops to zero (because price = marginal cost, as illustrated by point E_0) and the evil of monopoly disappears! In other words, the perfect discriminator does not produce too little output as the simple monopolist does; rather, he produces the same output that a perfectly competitive industry would produce. This conclusion dramatically shows that there exists no systematic relationship either between profit and the degree of monopoly power, or between total profit and the magnitude of economic inefficiency due to monopoly.

Multipart Pricing

Perfect price discrimination (or *first-degree* price discrimination) is a limiting case. Often in practice, a discriminating monopolist may be able to extract only part, but not all, of the consumer surplus. This is accomplished by means of a multipart pricing scheme (also known as *second-degree* price discrimination), illustrated in Figure 10.8.

Assume again for simplicity that the typical consumer's ordinary demand curve D_c coincides with the income-compensated demand curve, because the income effect is zero. Suppose further that a simple monopolist (charging the same price for all

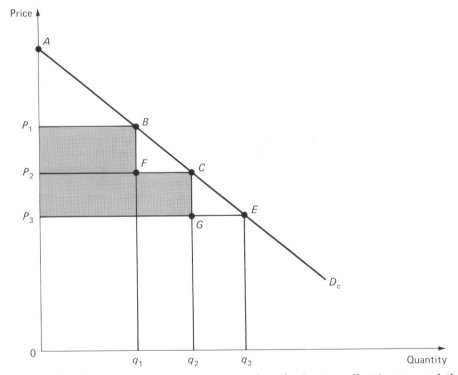

Figure 10.8 Multipart pricing. Assume again that the income effect is zero, and that a simple monopolist (charging the same price for all units sold) would fix his price at P_3. The typical consumer would purchase q_3 (point E) and enjoy a consumer surplus equal to the area of triangle AEP_3. With a three-part pricing scheme, the typical consumer must pay the high price P_1 for any quantity up to q_1, the middle price P_2 for any quantity from q_1 to q_2, and the lower price P_3 thereafter. This pricing scheme enables the monopolist to expropriate a certain portion of the consumer's surplus, as indicated by shaded area P_1BFCGP_3.

units sold) would fix his price at P_3. At that price, the typical consumer would purchase q_3 (point E).

With a multipart pricing scheme, however, the monopolist can extract more revenue from the consumer. For instance, Figure 10.8 illustrates a three-part pricing scheme where the typical consumer must pay the high price P_1 for any quantity up to q_1, the middle price P_2 for any quantity from q_1 to q_2, and the lower price P_3 thereafter. Since the income effect is by assumption zero, the typical consumer will purchase a total amount of q_3, but he will pay the price P_1 for the first q_1 units, the price P_2 for the next $q_2 - q_1$ units, and finally the price P_3 for the last $q_3 - q_2$ units. The revenue of the discriminating monopolist will thus be greater than the revenue of the simple monopolist by shaded area P_1BFCGP_3. Consequently, multipart pricing enables the monopolist to expropriate part, but not all, of the consumer's surplus.

Multipart pricing is often practiced by electric and water utilities. In addition, "quantity discounts," whether at the supermarket or the department store, are also indicative of this type of price discrimination.

10.8 Dumping: An Application

Dumping is international price discrimination. It takes place when a commodity is sold to foreign buyers at a price that is lower (net of transportation costs, tariffs, etc.) than the price charged domestic customers for the same (or a comparable) commodity. Dumping is made possible by the fact that domestic and foreign markets are separated from each other geographically as well as by tariff walls, quotas, and other barriers to trade.

Economists usually distinguish among three different types of dumping: *persistent, predatory,* and *sporadic.* Persistent dumping arises from the pursuit of maximum profits by a monopolist who realizes that the domestic and foreign markets are disconnected. Because the elasticity of demand for a commodity is usually higher in the world market than in the domestic market (mainly because of the greater competition among nations, and the greater availability of substitutes in the world market relative to the domestic market), the monopolist maximizes profits by charging a higher price to domestic customers (where the demand elasticity is low) than to foreign buyers (where the elasticity of demand is high).

Predatory dumping is usually classified as an "unfair method of competition." It occurs when a producer deliberately sells abroad at a reduced price for a short period of time in an effort to eliminate competitors and gain control of the foreign market. After this policy succeeds, the producer exploits the newly acquired monopoly power by raising the price substantially. Even though predatory dumping may involve short-run losses, the main objective of the producer is to maximize his long-run profit by driving competitors out of business.

Sporadic dumping is occasional price discrimination by a producer who happens to have an occasional surplus (presumably because of excess capacity, or unanticipated changes in market conditions, or just poor production planning). To avoid spoiling the domestic market, the producer sells the surplus to foreign buyers at reduced prices—a phenomenon that is reminiscent of "going out of business" sales by domestic department stores.

It is interesting to note that because of the special status of agriculture, governments frequently practice dumping to dispose of accumulated surpluses of agricultural products. Thus, in an effort to support domestic farmers, a government may institute a price floor well above the equilibrium price and purchase from the farmers, at the stipulated price floor, any quantity they cannot sell. The government later sells the accumulated surplus to foreign buyers at reduced prices.

Dumping benefits the consumers of the importing country, although predatory dumping may eventually become very harmful. If successful, predatory dumping would drive domestic producers out of business and penalize consumers (in the long run) with much higher prices. Importing countries typically retaliate against dumping either by imposing antidumping, or countervailing, duties to offset the price differential (or by threatening to do so). The main justification for this policy, of course, is the immense pressure put on the governments of the importing countries by their producers, who seek protection against the "unfair" foreign competition.

In the United States, antidumping legislation dates back to the Anti-Dumping Act of 1921. The 1974 Trade Act provides that the U.S. government may impose countervailing duties or other restrictions under two conditions: (1) the U.S. Treasury Department must first determine that an imported commodity is sold in the United States at a price which is lower than the price prevailing in the exporting country, and (2) the International Trade Commission must testify that American industry "is being or is likely to be injured or is prevented from being established" by reason of such imports.

In recent years, we have experienced many cases of dumping. Japan has repeatedly been accused of dumping steel and television sets, and European producers have been accused of dumping cars and steel. Most of these dumpers eventually raised their prices to avoid countervailing duties.

PART C. REGULATION OF MONOPOLIES

The objectives of public regulation of monopoly are two: (1) to prevent the monopolist from making abnormal profits, and (2) to induce the monopolist to expand his output (ideally to the level that would prevail under perfect competition). The former goal concerns the distribution of income; the latter, the efficient allocation of resources. In this last part of the chapter we examine the two prevalent methods of regulating a monopoly: taxation (Section 10.9) and price controls (Section 10.10).

10.9 The Effects of Taxes

In this section we study the effects of taxation on the monopolist's output, price, and profits. In the context of the present analysis, we distinguish among four types of taxes: a profit tax, a lump-sum tax, a specific tax, and an ad valorem tax.

Net Profit Versus Gross Profit

It is useful to state explicitly the simple relationship that exists between net profit (i.e., profit after taxes) and gross profit (i.e., profit before taxes). In all cases, the relationship takes the form

$$\text{net profit} = \text{gross profit} - \text{tax revenue} \tag{10.6}$$

The magnitude of gross profit in this formula does *not* correspond to the monopolist's profit *before* the tax is imposed. Rather, it corresponds to the monopolist's gross profit at the equilibrium he attains *after* the imposition of the tax. The distinction is important. These two magnitudes of gross profit are not always equal. As shown below, they are equal only when either a profit tax or a lump-sum tax is imposed, but when a commodity tax is levied (whether a specific tax or an ad valorem tax), the "gross profit after the tax" is necessarily lower than the "profit before the tax."

It must be evident from the discussion above that a tax does not always cause the monopolist's profit to fall just by the amount of the tax revenue collected by the government. To the extent that it causes the "gross profit after the tax" to fall below the "profit before the tax," the monopolist's profit will decrease by more than the tax revenue.

Note that the "gross profit after the tax" can never exceed the "profit before the tax." The reason is simple. By assumption, the monopolist is *maximizing* his "gross" profit before the tax is imposed. Therefore, a tax cannot cause the "gross" profit to increase, although it may cause it to decrease.

Perhaps an example may clarify these distinctions. Assume that in the absence of any tax the maximum monopoly profit is $10,000. Suppose further that the government imposes a tax (never mind what type) and eventually collects $2000 from the monopolist. If after the imposition of the tax the monopolist could maintain his gross profit at $10,000, his net profit (after taxes) would be $8000 (i.e., $10,000 − $2000 = $8000). But as shown below, the imposition of the tax may actually prevent the monopolist from maintaining his gross profit at $10,000. For concreteness assume that after the imposition of the tax, the monopolist can attain a gross profit of only $9000. [The monopolist cannot achieve a gross profit of more than $10,000, because he was initially maximizing his (gross) profit.] His net profit is then $7000 (i.e., $9000 − $2000 = $7000). Compared with the pretax situation, the tax causes the monopolist's net profit to fall by $3000 (which exceeds the tax revenue of $2000), from $10,000 (when tax revenue was zero) to $7000.

The Effects of a Profit Tax

As the name implies, a profit tax is a tax on profit. It is usually specified as a certain percentage of gross profit. Assuming that the profit-tax rate is less than 100 percent, a profit tax will reduce the monopolist's net profit, but it will not affect his profit-maximizing output-price combination.

Since the profit tax is a certain percentage (t_p) of the gross profit, it follows that net profit is proportional to gross profit. In particular

$$\text{net profit} = (1 - t_p)(\text{gross profit}) \qquad (10.7)$$

where t_p is the profit-tax rate. Equation (10.7) shows clearly that to maximize his net profit, the monopolist must first maximize his gross profit—an objective that he presumably attains even before the tax is imposed.

We therefore conclude that a profit tax cannot affect the optimal price–quantity combination of a profit-maximizing monopolist. In turn, this means that a profit tax cannot rectify the misallocation of resources introduced by the monopoly. Nevertheless, by reducing the monopolist's profit, the profit tax may improve the distribution of income.

The Effects of a Lump-Sum Tax

The effects of a lump-sum tax (such as a license fee) are very similar to the effects of a profit tax. This becomes obvious when we realize that in identity (10.6) the amount of tax revenue is "fixed," and thus maximization of net profit coincides with maximization of gross profit. Since the monopolist is maximizing his profit before the tax is levied, a lump-sum tax cannot have any effect on the monopolist's optimal price–output combination (assuming that the lump-sum tax does not exceed the gross profit). Accordingly, the lump-sum tax does nothing to cure the basic inefficiency of monopoly; its only effect is a distributional one—the entire tax revenue comes out of the monopolist's gross profit.

It is interesting to note that, under monopoly, the lump-sum tax does not introduce any inefficiency of its own as it does under perfect competition. From this point of view, the lump-sum tax is an "efficient" tax. Obviously, the same is true of the profit tax.

The Effects of a Specific Tax

A commodity tax always reduces monopoly profit and, in addition, leads to a lower output and a higher price. This is true irrespective of whether the commodity tax is legally specified as a fixed sum of money per physical unit sold (specific tax) or as a fixed percentage of the value of the commodity (ad valorem tax).

The effects of a specific tax are illustrated in Figure 10.9. For simplicity, we assume that the average-revenue curve (AR) is linear and the marginal-cost curve (MC) is horizontal (at least in the relevant range). Before the tax, the monopolist's price and output are P_0 and Q_0, respectively. When a specific tax equal to vertical distance AB is imposed, the average-revenue curve shifts vertically downward by

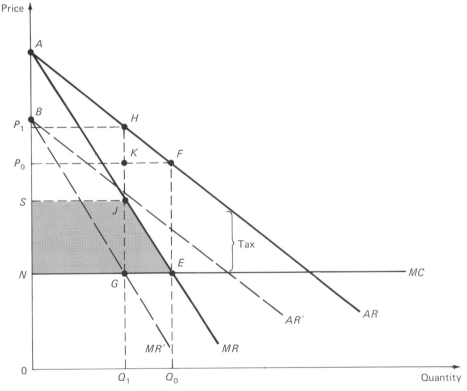

Figure 10.9 The effects of a specific tax. Before the tax, the monopolist's price and output are P_0 and Q_0, respectively. A specific tax equal to vertical distance AB causes the AR curve to shift vertically downward, as shown by the AR' line. The MR curve also shifts downward as shown by the MR' line. The monopolist reduces his output to Q_1 (as indicated by G) and raises his price to P_1. In this special case, the price increase $(P_1 - P_0)$ is just half the amount of the tax, mainly because the slope of AR is just half the slope of MR and marginal cost is constant. However, the monopolist's total profit falls by the area of shaded trapezoid *NEJS*, which is larger than the total tax revenue (*NGJS*) by the area of shaded triangle *GEJ*.

the precise amount of the tax, as shown by the dashed AR' curve. Consequently, the marginal-revenue curve also shifts vertically downward by the amount of the tax which is reasonable—as output increases by 1 unit after the tax, total revenue increases by the pretax marginal revenue minus the tax. As a result, the monopolist reduces his output to Q_1 (as indicated by intersection G of the unchanged MC curve and the new MR' curve) and raises his price to P_1. Note that even after the tax the original AR schedule continues to reflect the *gross demand price*.

In this special case of linear demand and horizontal marginal cost, the price increase $(P_1 - P_0)$ is just half the amount of the tax. This follows from the fact (implicit in the discussion of Section 8.2) that the slope of the AR line is just half the slope of the corresponding MR line. (Recall that the MR line necessarily *bisects* the horizontal distance between any point on the AR line and the vertical axis.) Since $GE = KF = Q_0 - Q_1$, it follows that GJ is twice as large as KH. But $KH = P_1 - P_0$ and $GJ =$ tax per unit—as mentioned above, the vertical shift of the MR curve (GJ) must be equal to the specific tax.

The above conclusion may actually give the impression that the burden of the tax is shared equally by the monopolist and the consumers. Such inference, however, is quite misleading, *because the monopolist's profit actually falls by more than the total tax revenue*. If we refer back to the basic identity (10.6), it is obvious that the monopolist's profit always falls by at least the amount of the tax revenue. (Graphically, the total tax revenue is shown by the area of shaded rectangle $NGJS$.) Because the specific tax induces the monopolist to reduce output and raise his price, however, his gross profit also falls. In particular, referring to the MC curve and the original MR line, we see that the monopolist's gross profit falls by the area of shaded triangle GEJ. We therefore conclude that the monopolist's profit falls by the area of shaded trapezoid $NEJS$.

It is obvious from the above discussion that a specific tax on the monopolist's product creates more problems than it solves. The monopolist suffers because his profit falls (by more than the total tax revenue), the consumers also suffer because they pay a higher price, and the misallocation of resources is made worse because the monopolist *reduces* his output. A specific tax is a very poor way of regulating the monopolist's behavior.

Finally, note that a specific tax may actually result in an increase of price that is higher than the tax. This is illustrated by the case of a demand curve that is constant elastic, that is, one that exhibits the same elasticity throughout its length, as explained in Section 2.6. For instance, suppose that the constant elasticity of demand (in absolute terms) is 2, and the marginal cost remains constant at \$4. Before the tax, the monopolist maximizes his profits at the point where $MR = MC = \$4$. Thus the pretax price must be equal to \$8.[7] When a specific tax equal to \$3 is imposed, the price will rise to \$14, that is, the price paid by consumers will rise by \$6, which is more than the tax.[8]

10.10 Price Controls

A price ceiling is an effective means of regulating monopolies. In contrast with perfect competition, where a price ceiling below the equilibrium price typically reduces output and creates a shortage of the controlled commodity, a "moderate"

[7]The equilibrium price is obtained by solving the fundamental equation $|e| = AR/(AR - MR)$ for AR, and setting $|e| = 2$, and $MR = MC = \$4$. Thus $AR = [|e|/(|e| - 1)]MR = (2/1)4 = 8$.

[8]To determine the after-tax price, we merely treat the specific tax as a variable cost that raises the marginal cost by the amount of the tax. Hence the relevant marginal-cost figure after tax becomes \$7 (i.e., \$4 + \$3). Solving the equation $2 = AR/(AR - 7)$ for AR, we obtain $AR = \$14$.

price ceiling imposed on a monopolist typically causes output to increase and enables the consumers to purchase all they want.

A Price Ceiling and the Curves of Average and Marginal Revenue

Before examining the effects of a price ceiling on the behavior of a monopolist, we must consider how this type of price control distorts the curves of average and marginal revenue. This is shown in Figure 10.10.

Before any price ceiling is imposed, the monopolist's curves of average and marginal revenue are given by the two straight lines labeled AR and MR, respectively. After a price ceiling is imposed at the level of P_c, dashed segment BD of the original AR curve becomes irrelevant and obsolete. Because the monopolist can sell any quantity from zero to Q_c at P_c, dashed segment BD is replaced by the heavily drawn horizontal line segment P_cD. For all prices lower than P_c, the original AR curve remains in effect. Accordingly, after the imposition of the price ceiling, the monop-

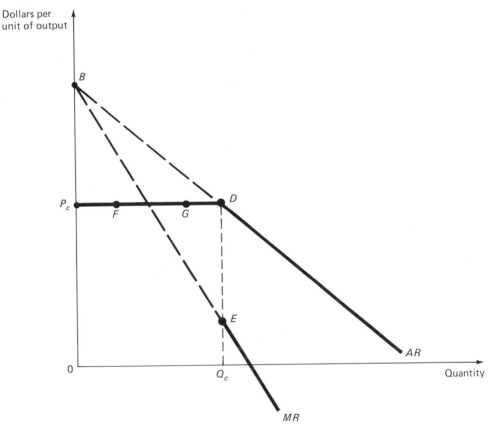

Figure 10.10 The effects of a price ceiling on the curves of average and marginal revenue. Before any price ceiling is imposed, the curves of average and marginal revenue are given by the AR and MR lines, respectively. After the imposition of the ceiling at the level of P_c, dashed segment BD of the original AR is replaced by the heavily drawn horizontal line segment P_cD, and the monopolist's average-revenue curve is distorted to the heavily drawn kinked line P_cDAR. Segment BE of the original MR curve is also replaced by horizontal line segment P_cD, so that the monopolist's marginal-revenue curve (after the imposition of the price ceiling) consists of two disconnected segments: P_cD and EMR.

olist's average-revenue curve is given by the heavily drawn kinked line P_cDAR, which necessarily has a discontinuity of *slope* at point D.

Turn now to the marginal-revenue curve. Over the range of outputs where the original AR curve is deleted, that is, from zero to Q_c, the original MR curve becomes irrelevant also. In this range of outputs, the marginal-revenue curve (after the imposition of the price ceiling) coincides with horizontal line segment P_cD, because the monopolist can increase his volume of sales (say, from F to G) without having to reduce his price.

For outputs higher than Q_c, however, the original MR curve, as indicated by the heavily drawn line segment EMR, continues to be relevant. In this range of outputs, the original total-revenue curve (not shown) necessarily remains unchanged because the original AR curve (segment DAR) is intact. Since marginal revenue corresponds to the slope of the total-revenue curve, it follows that the original MR curve (segment EMR) must remain in effect also.

We therefore conclude that after the imposition of the price ceiling, the monopolist's marginal-revenue curve consists of two disconnected segments: horizontal segment P_cD and original segment EMR. The vertical discontinuity of the marginal-revenue curve at Q_c reflects the discontinuity of *slope* of the AR schedule at point D (and, by implication, the discontinuity of slope of the corresponding total-revenue schedule at Q_c).

The Effects of a Price Ceiling

Consider Figure 10.11. Without any regulation, the monopolist would maximize his profit by selling the output Q_0 at the price P_0. Obviously, a price ceiling cannot be effective (or binding) unless it is lower than P_0, although it cannot be lower than the monopolist's minimum average cost, that is, P_1. (Evidently, at prices below P_1, the monopolist would not remain in business, because he would not be able to cover his costs.) Suppose, therefore, that the price ceiling is set at P_c, where $P_1 < P_c < P_0$. How would this price ceiling affect the monopolist's behavior?

The price ceiling at P_c has the effect of replacing segment KD of the original AR curve and segment KJ of the original MR curve by horizontal line segment P_cD. Because the marginal-revenue curve now becomes P_cDJMR, the monopolist increases his output to Q_c, which, of course, he sells at the price P_c.

Since marginal revenue is indeterminate at Q_c (the MR curve jumps discontinuously from D to J), the above equilibrium does *not* correspond to an *equality* of marginal cost and marginal revenue. (Note that at the output Q_c, the MC_L curve passes between the two disconnected segments of the MR curve.) Yet the monopolist's profit is at a maximum, because a change in output in either direction reduces profit. For outputs lower than Q_c, marginal revenue (P_c) exceeds marginal cost, and any output reduction (below Q_c) would reduce total profit. On the other hand, for outputs greater than Q_c, marginal cost exceeds marginal revenue, and any output expansion (above Q_c) would reduce total profit also.

How does the price ceiling affect the monopolist's total profit? It reduces it by the area of shaded triangle EJH, which is the area between the MC_L curve and the original MR curve over the range of outputs from Q_0 to Q_c. The consumers benefit, of course, because they pay a lower price (P_c instead of P_0). In particular, the consumers' surplus increases by the area of trapezoid P_0FDP_c. Note also that the price ceiling at P_c does not give rise to any shortage of supply—the consumers buy all they want at P_c.

Finally, the increase in output from Q_0 to Q_c is a step in the direction of correcting the basic inefficiency implied by an unregulated monopoly. Think of marginal cost as a measure of the value of resources used up in producing an additional unit of the product. Similarly, think of the price as a measure of the value of the product

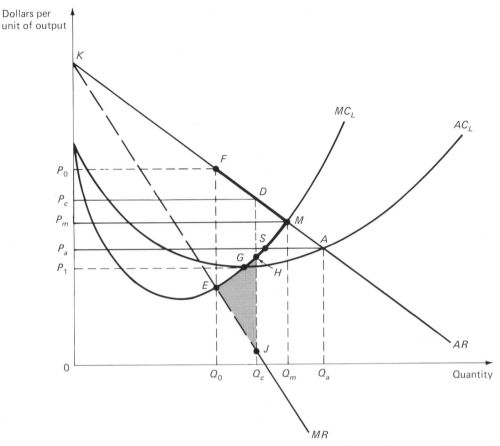

Figure 10.11 *The effects of a price ceiling.* Without any regulation, the monopolist would maximize his profit by selling Q_0 at P_0. When a price ceiling is imposed at the level of P_c, the monopolist would increase his output to Q_c, and total profit would fall by shaded area *EJH*. The consumers' surplus would increase by area P_0FDP_c. If we visualize the price ceiling falling gradually from P_0 to P_1, we can see that the monopolist's equilibrium point will travel from F to M, and then from M to G. The ideal price ceiling (P_m) is given by the intersection M of the MC_L and AR curves and is often referred to as *marginal-cost pricing*. At this ideal ceiling, the net gain to society is indicated by area *FEM*. *Average-cost pricing* is illustrated by P_a, which is determined by intersection A of the AC_L and AR curves.

to the consumers. It follows, then, that the expansion of output from Q_0 to Q_c is socially desirable, because in this range of outputs price exceeds marginal cost. The social cost of the additional output ($Q_c - Q_0$) is given by area Q_0EHQ_c, while the social value created by it coincides with area Q_0FDQ_c. Accordingly, the net benefit to society is given by area *EFDH*.

The Ideal Price Ceiling

As we saw above, a modest price ceiling has beneficial effects to society. Would these social benefits become larger with a still lower price ceiling? How low should the ceiling be? What is the ideal price ceiling?

Visualize the price ceiling falling gradually from P_0 to P_1. Initially, the monopolist's output will be rising, and it will continue to do so until the price ceiling falls to P_m. At P_m the monopolist's equilibrium would be indicated by point M, which is the intersection of the MC_L curve and the original AR curve. As the price ceiling falls below P_m, the monopolist's output will begin to fall, as the equilibrium production point will be traveling downward along the MC_L curve from M to G.

We therefore conclude that as the price ceiling is gradually reduced from P_0 to P_1, the monopolist's equilibrium point first travels along the heavily drawn segment FM of the original AR curve, and then continues downward along the heavily drawn segment MG of the MC_L curve. Accordingly, the monopolist's output is maximized when the price ceiling is at P_m, which induces the monopolist to produce Q_m.

Evidently, the ideal price ceiling must be P_m, because it forces the monopolist to expand his output until marginal cost becomes equal to the price (as indicated by point M). Compared with the unregulated, static equilibrium at P_0 and Q_0, the ideal equilibrium at P_m and Q_m implies maximum social benefits. The net gain to society is indicated by area FEM. Incidentally, at this ideal equilibrium the degree of monopoly power is reduced to zero, because MC_L = price, but the monopolist's profit is still positive, because price $> AC_L$.

Setting the ceiling equal to the price indicated by the intersection of curve MC_L and the original average-revenue curve (i.e., P_m) is often referred to as *marginal-cost pricing*. This regulated monopolistic equilibrium reproduces the basic attributes of a perfectly competitive equilibrium: Price is equal to marginal cost (which implies that the degree of monopoly is zero); supply is equal to demand.

Finally, note that a price ceiling lower than P_m necessarily generates a shortage of supply. For instance, when the price ceiling is set at P_a, the monopolist would produce at S and a shortage equal to horizontal line segment SA would appear.

Incidentally, setting the ceiling equal to the price indicated by the intersection of the AC_L curve and the original average-revenue curve (i.e., P_a) is usually referred to as *average-cost pricing*. From the point of view of economic efficiency, average-cost pricing is inferior to marginal-cost pricing, even if the monopolist were forced to produce the total quantity demanded at P_a (i.e., Q_a). Despite the fact that the monopolist's profit would be zero, resources would be misallocated—the monopolist's output (Q_a) would be higher than what is socially optimal (Q_m).

Regulation of Natural Monopolies

In the United States permanent regulation is universal for public utilities supplying electricity, gas, telephone service, water, and so forth, in any particular locality. These public utilities are generally considered to be natural monopolies, because in each case the industry output is more cheaply produced by a single firm.

Ordinarily, a natural monopolist operates under conditions of steadily decreasing average cost, as shown in Figure 10.12. Because of this, the marginal-cost curve (MC_L) consistently lies below the average-cost curve (AC_L). Under these circumstances, marginal-cost pricing is not feasible, unless the regulatory authority is prepared to subsidize the regulated firm. For instance, if the price ceiling is set at P_m (indicated by intersection M of the MC_L and AR curves), the monopolist will go out of business, because he would not be able to cover his costs ($AC_L = Q_mG > Q_mM$ = price). The monopolist can remain in business only if the regulatory authority grants him a total (lump-sum) subsidy which is at least as large as the area of shaded rectangle P_mMGH per period of time.

Because of the political problems associated with subsidizing natural monopolies[9] plus the practical difficulties surrounding the determination of true long-run marginal costs, regulatory commissions have turned to average-cost pricing. Thus the

[9]The reluctance to provide public subsidies is probably due to the naive belief held by most laypersons that the price of any commodity *ought* to be high enough to cover its long-run average cost.

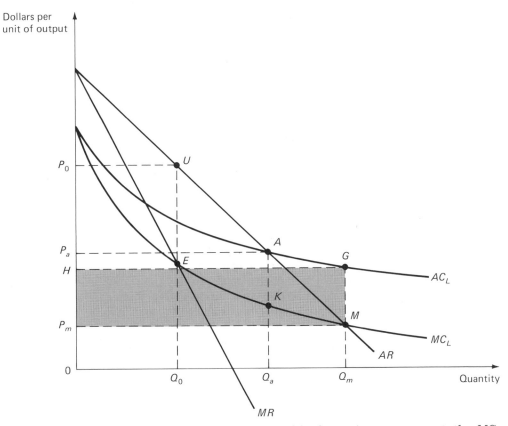

Figure 10.12 Natural monopoly. Because of steadily decreasing average cost, the MC_L curve lies consistently below the AC_L curve. Setting the ceiling at P_m (marginal cost pricing) would drive the monopolist out of business unless the regulatory authority grants the monopolist a lump-sum subsidy at least as large as shaded area $P_m MGH$. To avoid the subsidy, the regulatory authority usually aims at a price ceiling at the level P_a (average cost pricing). The monopolist would then produce Q_a. Average cost pricing is superior to unregulated monopoly equilibrium (point U), but it is inferior to marginal cost pricing (point M) because it perpetuates at least part of the original deadweight loss.

usual regulatory goal is that prices should be such as to enable the regulated firm to earn a "fair return" on its investment. In principle, the fair return corresponds to the opportunity cost of the owner's capital, with due allowances for risk, and as the reader may recall, all opportunity costs are already included in what we have defined as long-run average cost.

In terms of Figure 10.12, the regulators aim at a price such as P_a. At that price the monopolist will produce Q_a and make zero *economic* profit. The fair return on the monopolist's capital is, of course, part of the long-run average cost ($Q_a A$), which is just covered by revenue. Note that even though the monopolist's profit is reduced to zero, the degree of monopoly power remains strictly positive, because price exceeds marginal cost.

There are many problems associated with average-cost pricing. On the theoretical level, average-cost pricing is inferior to marginal-cost pricing because it perpetuates at least part of the deadweight loss (economic inefficiency) that the unregulated monopolistic equilibrium usually implies. In comparison with the unregulated equilibrium at U in Figure 10.12, the equilibrium at A (under average-cost pricing) implies additional net social benefits equal to area *UEKA*. Yet marginal-cost pricing could result in even more net social benefits (indicated by area *AKM*), by pushing equilibrium to point *M*.

Furthermore, there are cases where the demand curve lies totally below the long-run average-cost curve. In such cases, average-cost pricing cannot be implemented because there does not exist enough revenue to cover all costs at any positive output. Yet our analysis of the concept of consumer surplus in Section 5.3 warns that such projects as bridges and monorails for urban commuters may be highly desirable.

On the practical side, there are many problems in setting prices that will give the company "a fair return on its capital." Aside from the difficulty of defining what a "fair return" is, there is the problem of identifying the exact value of the capital to which the fair return is to be applied. Should the regulatory commission adopt the concept of "original cost" or the concept of "reproduction cost"? It usually makes a substantial difference which of these two alternative valuations is used. For instance, during the inflationary situation of the last two decades, *reproduction* cost is consistently greater than historical or *original* cost, and allowing public utilities to earn a fair return on the reproduction cost of their plant and equipment leads to higher permitted profits and higher prices to the consumers.

Finally, to the extent that a fair return is guaranteed, a public utility may not have any incentive to be efficient in the sense (discussed in Chapter 7) of producing each level of output at the lowest possible cost. This is, of course, in complete contrast with the case of a perfectly competitive firm which cannot remain in business unless it is efficient. Therefore, in the interests of economic efficiency, the regulators must not only define the fair return and agree on the proper valuation of the utility's fixed capital, but also must be prepared to monitor and scrutinize almost all aspects of the utility's behavior. Regulatory commissions must always remain vigilant against the possible use of inefficient equipment or processes and misleading accounting techniques. Cost supervision is at least as important as any other activity of public regulatory commissions.

10.11 Selected Empirical Applications

The discussion of this section is divided into two parts. The first part deals with the problem of third-degree price discrimination in the municipal water industry and the relative effectiveness of state versus local regulation. The second part gives a summary of various estimates of monopoly welfare losses in three countries: the United States, the United Kingdom, and France.

Price Discrimination in the Municipal Water Industry

Public utilities have always practiced third-degree price discrimination because of the convenient separation of their customers into three classes: residential, commercial, and industrial. Typically, public utilities charge the highest rates to the residential customer class and the lowest rates to the industrial class. The rates that they charge to the commercial users lie between the residential rates and the industrial rates.

Municipally owned utilities are divided into two sectors: the unregulated sector and the regulated sector. In most states municipally owned utilities establish their rates subject to the approval of the municipal government (mayor, city council, or public works commission). This group is known as the unregulated (or locally regulated) sector. However, in Maine, Indiana, Montana, West Virginia, and Wisconsin municipally owned utilities are regulated at the state level. The latter group is referred to as the regulated sector.

In a recent study, T. H. Bruggink (1982) provides some evidence concerning the practice of third-degree price discrimination by municipally owned water utilities, which account for about 85 percent of all water utilities. Bruggink is also interested in the problem of whether there exist significant differences between the regulated sector and the unregulated (or locally regulated) sector of water utilities.

To test his hypotheses, Bruggink calculated the mean ratios of price to long-run marginal cost (AR/MC) among the three traditional customer classes (residential, commercial, and industrial) for both regulated and unregulated municipally owned water utilities. His results are summarized in columns (1) and (4) of Table 10.1.

On the basis of the estimates provided in columns (1) and (4) plus the assumption of profit maximization, we also calculated in columns (2) and (5) the corresponding demand elasticities implied for each of the three customer classes; and in columns (3) and (6), the corresponding degrees of monopoly using Lerner's index (L). Recall that

$$|e| = \frac{AR}{AR - MR} = \frac{AR}{AR - MC} = \frac{1}{1 - MC/AR} \quad \text{and} \quad L = \frac{1}{|e|}$$

What conclusions can we derive from the information given in Table 10.1? First, the data confirm the practice of third-degree price discrimination by both the regulated and the unregulated water utilities. The price-marginal cost ratios (AR/MC) for residential, commercial, and industrial classes are, respectively, 3.12, 1.81, and 1.04 in the regulated sector, and 3.45, 2.32, and 1.52 in the unregulated sector. In both sectors, the AR/MC ratio of the industrial class is substantially lower than the corresponding ratio of the commercial class, and the AR/MC ratio of the commercial class is substantially lower than the corresponding ratio of the residential class. It is evident that the industrial class is the main beneficiary of this price discrimination. Thus, in the regulated sector, the AR/MC ratio of the industrial class is 67 percent below that of the residential class and 43 percent below that of the commercial class. In the unregulated sector, the corresponding numbers are 56 and 34 percent, respectively.

The second conclusion that can be derived from Table 10.1 is that the AR/MC ratios are much lower for all customer classes in the regulated sector than in the unregulated sector. For instance, the AR/MC ratio of the residential class is 10 percent lower in the regulated sector than in the unregulated sector. For the commercial class, the corresponding reduction is 22 percent, and for the industrial class, 32 percent. Although it is true that these reductions are uneven among classes, with the industrial and commercial customer classes receiving larger absolute and percentage reductions than the residential class, the fact remains that regulation seems to reduce substantially the scope of price discrimination and monopoly pricing.

Table 10.1 Price Discrimination in the Municipal Water Industry					
	(1) (2) (3) Regulated Utilities			(4) (5) (6) Unregulated Utilities		
Customer Class	*AR/MC*	|e|	L	*AR/MC*	|e|	L
Residential	3.12	1.47	0.68	3.45	1.41	0.71
Commercial	1.81	2.23	0.45	2.32	1.76	0.57
Industrial	1.04	26.00	0.04	1.52	2.92	0.34

Source: Adapted from Bruggink (1982). Permission granted by The University of Wisconsin Press.

Table 10.2 Summary of Estimates of Monopoly Welfare Loss			
	Loss (percent of national income)		
Author(s)	**United States**	**United Kingdom**	**France**
Cowling and Mueller (1978)	3.96	3.86	
Harberger (1954)	0.08		
Jenny and Weber (1983)			0.85–7.39
Kamerschen (1966)	5.4–6.2[a]		
Sawyer (1980)		4.5–11.5	
Schwartzman (1961)	0.13		
Siegfried and Tiemann (1974)	0.073		
Worcester (1973)	0.203–0.440[a]		

[a]This range is only one of a number of them given by the author.

Estimates of Monopoly Welfare Loss

We have already mentioned in Section 10.3 the low estimate of monopoly welfare loss in the United States reported by Harberger (1954) for the period 1924–1928. In Table 10.2 we summarize several other findings, mostly for the United States, but also for the United Kingdom and France. It is evident from Table 10.2 that these estimates range from an insignificant level to a very large percentage of national income. Thus, for the United States, the monopoly welfare loss ranges from a little less than one-tenth of 1 percent to over 6 percent of U.S. national income. For the United Kingdom the estimates range from a little less than 4 percent to over 11 percent, and for France, the spread is 0.85 to 7.39.

The large spread between the lowest and highest estimates of monopoly welfare loss is disturbing. If monopoly welfare loss is in the neighborhood of one-tenth of 1 percent of national income, monopoly power is not as detrimental to national welfare, but if it is in the vicinity of, say, 10 percent of national income, monopoly is quite harmful.

All we can say at the present time is that the issue of monopoly welfare loss has not been settled yet. We do know that monopoly gives rise to a welfare loss, but we still do not know how important quantitatively that loss is.

SUMMARY

1. The monopolist's long-run equilibrium conditions (analogous to those of the perfectly competitive firm) are (a) $MC_L = MR$, (b) the MC_L curve must intersect the MR curve from below, and (c) maximized profit ≥ 0 ($AR \geq AC_L$ or $R \geq C_L$).

2. A profit-maximizing monopolist does not maximize his total revenue or the per unit profit, does not charge the highest possible price, and does not produce at the point of minimum AC_L.

3. The monopoly equilibrium has three important properties: (a) $MC < AR$ (evil of monopoly, (b) supply > demand, and (c) a monopolist may produce not only under increasing cost, but also under constant or decreasing (average or marginal) cost.

4. It is often erroneously believed that the monopolist faces an inelastic demand and makes huge profits.

5. Lerner's index of monopoly power [$L = (AC - MC)/AR = 1/|e|$] has two properties: (a) it is a dimensionless number, and (b) $0 \leq L \leq 1$. For a perfectly competitive firm ($|e| = \infty$), $L = 0$ because $AR = MC$. There is no systematic relationship between the degree of monopoly power and total profit.

6. The equilibrium of the monopolist depends both on the position and shape of the demand curve.

7. A rotation of the demand curve through an initial p–q combination increases or decreases the monopoly output (and decreases or increases the monopoly price) according to whether the demand curve becomes more or less elastic, respectively. The monopoly profit increases always.

8. An increase in demand that causes the MR curve to shift unambiguously upward and to the right increases both the monopolist's output and his profit. The effect on the monopoly price is uncertain, depending on (a) the slope of the MC curve and (b) the elasticity of the new demand curve relative to the old demand curve at the initial monopoly price.

9. Price discrimination is possible when the different parts of the monopolist's market are insulated from one another, and profitable when the elasticity of demand differs from one sector to another. The monopolist charges a higher price in the segment with the lower demand elasticity. For two sectors, the equilibrium condition is $MR_1 = MR_2 = MC$.

10. Perfect (or first-degree) price discrimination occurs when the monopolist charges a different price for each unit sold, extracting the entire consumer surplus from each consumer. In this case, MR = price, and the demand curve becomes the MR curve also; thus the degree of monopoly drops to zero, and the inefficiency of monopoly disappears. The perfect discriminator produces the same output as a perfectly competitive industry would produce.

11. With multipart pricing (second-degree price discrimination) the monopolist takes only part (but not all) of the consumer surpluses.

12. Dumping (international price discrimination) is divided into persistent, predatory, and sporadic.

13. The objectives of public regulation of mo-nopoly are (a) to prevent the monopolist from making abnormal profits and (b) to induce the monopolist to expand his output (ideally to the competitive level).

14. Neither a profit tax nor a lump-sum tax can affect the optimal p–q combination of a profit-maximizing monopolist; they merely reduce his profit. (*Note:* If the lump-sum tax is set above the level of the pretax monopoly profit, the monopolist will close down.)

15. A commodity tax (specific or ad valorem) decreases the monopoly output and raises the price paid by consumers (in some cases, by more than the tax); it also reduces the monopolist's net profit by more than the tax revenue. Such a tax is a poor way of regulating the monopolist's behavior.

16. A moderate price ceiling reduces monopoly profit and raises monopoly output. The ideal price ceiling (marginal cost pricing) coincides with the price indicated by the intersection of the curves of MC and AR. The resultant monopoly equilibrium has the basic attributes of a perfectly competitive equilibrium: price = MC and supply = demand.

17. Average-cost pricing (a price ceiling set equal to the price indicated by the intersection of the curves of AC and AR) is inferior to marginal-cost pricing as it perpetuates at least part of the inefficiency of unregulated monopolies.

18. In the case of natural monopolies (steadily decreasing AC) marginal-cost pricing is not feasible (unless combined with politically undesirable subsidies); thus regulatory commissions have turned to average-cost pricing. Aside from its inferiority to marginal-cost pricing, average-cost pricing faces also practical problems: how to define a fair return, how to identify the proper value of the monopolist's capital (original cost versus reproduction cost), and how to guard against the inefficiency bred by a guaranteed fair return.

QUESTIONS

1. A profit-maximizing monopolist has the following data on average cost and demand:

Quantity	Price	Average Cost
1	$15	$ 5
2	14	6
3	13	7
4	12	8
5	11	9
6	10	10
7	9	11

Determine the profit-maximizing monopoly output and price. Also determine the maximum profit.

2. The production function of a monopolist is characterized by constant returns to scale. At the current factor rentals, $w = \$3$ and $r = \$1$, the monopolist's optimal input combination at the unit level of output (i.e., for $Q = 1$) is 1 unit of labor and 1 unit of land.

(a) Determine the monopolist's total-cost, average-cost, and marginal-cost curves.

(b) At the current equilibrium, the monopolist is selling 50,000 units. The elasticity of demand for the monopolist's product is -2. Determine the monopolist's price and total profits. How would the monopolist alter his behavior if the government imposed on him a lump-sum tax of $200,000 per period?

(c) Return to the equilibrium of part (b) and assume that the demand curve becomes more elastic at that point. In particular, assume that the new elasticity is -6. How would this increased elasticity affect the monopolist's price, output, and total profit?

(*Note:* If you cannot determine the precise equilibrium value of any variable, show whether it will increase or decrease and explain why.)

3. Two firms A and B face the same downward-sloping straight-line demand curve. Firm A maximizes its profits when it produces 100 units of its product and sells them at a price of $10 a piece. The marginal cost of this firm if $5 when it produces 100 units. On the other hand, firm B maximizes its profits when it produces 120 units and sells them at a price of $9 a piece. Answer the following questions to the extent that this information is sufficient. If the information is insufficient, state what additional information would be needed.

(a) What is the point elasticity of demand at the point where firm A maximizes its profits?

(b) What is the point elasticity of demand at the point where firm B maximizes its profits? What is the marginal cost of this firm at that point?

(c) Which firm is making the larger profits?

4. The production function of a monopolist is characterized by constant returns to scale. The monopolist purchases inputs (labor services and land services) in perfectly competitive factor markets. Currently, the monopolist maximizes his long-run profits by selling 1000 units of

commodity X at a price $p_x = \$10$. The point elasticity of demand at $p_x = \$10$ is 2.5 (in absolute terms).

Answer the following questions to the extent that the information given is sufficient. If the information is not sufficient, state what additional information is needed and why.

(a) What is the marginal revenue of the monopolist at the current profit-maximizing output (i.e., $X = 1000$)?

(b) What are the monopolist's total profits?

(c) What would the monopolist change his price (p_x) and output (X) to if the government imposed either a specific tax on X at the rate of $2 per unit or a lump-sum tax of $2000?

5. A firm is currently selling 12,000 units of its product per month at a price of $20 per unit. Its marginal cost is constant at the level of $15 per unit within the output range 10,000 to 30,000 units. Its fixed costs are $12,000 per month.

Answer the following questions to the extent that the information given is sufficient. If the information is insufficient for any of the questions, indicate what additional information would be needed.

(a) What is the firm's current profit per month?

(b) If the firm is maximizing its profit, what is the elasticity of demand at the current equilibrium point?

(c) What is the firm's degree of monopoly at the current equilibrium point?

(d) If the firm were to cut its price to $18, how much would it have to sell to keep its total profit unchanged?

6. A profit-maximizing firm marks up its price 50 percent above its constant average variable cost. What is the (point) elasticity of its demand curve at the quantity it actually sells?

7. A woman inherits a certain number of acres of standing timber that can be sold either for Christmas trees or for firewood. In either case she has no costs whatsoever.

(a) If she knows the demand curves of each type of possible purchaser, how should she determine her sale and price of acres of trees for each purpose? Show graphically.

(b) Could she ever sell less than all her acres? Show on a diagram.

8. (a) With reference to both pure competition and monopoly, specify the circumstances, if any, under which a specific commodity tax may (i)

...ause the gross price paid by consumers to rise ...y more than the amount of tax, or (ii) cause ...hat price to fall.

(b) Again with reference to both pure competition and monopoly, explain whether a specific tax and an ad valorem tax can have identical effects.

...9. A discriminating monopolist is selling a ...product in two isolated markets whose corre...sponding demand functions are

$$P_a = 12 - Q_a$$
$$P_b = 20 - Q_b$$

The monopolist's total-cost function is

$$C = 3 + 2Q$$

(a) Determine the discriminating monopolist's prices, sales volume, and marginal revenues in the two markets as well as his total profit.

(b) Alternatively, suppose that the monopolist cannot discriminate. What will be his price, output, and profit?

10. The marginal cost of a monopolist is constant at $10. Assuming that price discrimination is possible in markets A and B and also that the elasticities of demand in the two markets are respectively -2 and -3 (at all points of the individual demand curves), can you find out what prices this monopolist will charge at the two markets in order to maximize his profits? Could you say that this monopolist must be making more than normal profits? Justify your answer.

11. "The apparatus of 'supply and demand' is properly applied only to purely competitive industries, never to monopolistic ones. This becomes perfectly clear when we undertake to analyze the comparative effects, under pure competition and monopoly, of demand changes, cost changes, and taxes of various kinds." Discuss.

12. A product can be produced at decreasing average cost and constant marginal cost. At no price is demand great enough so that the price will cover average cost.

(a) With reference to the indifference maps of potential consumers, explain under what circumstances they can benefit from a subsidized production of the good, without hurt to anyone else.

(b) Under what further special circumstances can the analysis be made simply with reference to cost and demand curves? Explain.

13. Regulatory commissions frequently require public utilities to set a price that yields the going rate of return, that is, equate price to long-run average cost. Economists prefer a price equal to marginal cost on the grounds of economic efficiency. What problems arise with the selection of either of these two price schemes?

FURTHER READING

Averch, H., and L. L. Johnson (1962). "Behavior of the Firm Under Regulatory Constraint," *American Economic Review,* Vol. 52 (December), pp. 1052–1069.

Bruggink, T. H. (1982). "Third-Degree Price Discrimination and Regulation in the Municipal Water Industry," *Land Economics,* Vol. 58 (February), pp. 86–95.

Cowling, K., and D. C. Mueller (1978). "The Social Costs of Monopoly Power," *Economic Journal,* Vol. 88 (December), pp. 727–748.

Harberger, A. C. (1954). "Monopoly and Resource Allocation," *American Economic Review,* Vol. 44 (May), pp. 77–87.

Hicks, J. R. (1935). "Annual Survey of Economic Theory: The Theory of Monopoly," *Econometrica,* Vol. 3 (January), pp. 1–20.

Jenny, F. and A. P. Weber (1983). "Aggregate Welfare Loss due to Monopoly Power in the French Economy: Some Tentative Estimates," *The Journal of Industrial Economics,* Vol. 32 (December), pp. 113–130.

Kamerschen, D. R. (1966). "An Estimation of the Welfare Losses from Monopoly in the American Economy," *Western Economic Journal,* Vol. 14 (Summer), pp. 221–236.

Lerner, A. P. (1933). "The Concept of Monopoly and the Measurement of Monopoly Power," *Review of Economic Studies,* Vol. 1 (June), pp. 157–175.

Robinson, J. (1933). *The Economics of Imperfect Competition.* Macmillan & Company, Ltd., London. Chapters 3–5 and 11–16.

Sawyer, M. C. (1980). "Monopoly Welfare Loss

in the United Kingdom," *The Manchester School of Economic and Social Studies,* Vol. 48 (December), pp. 331–354.

Schwartzman, D. (1961). "The Effects of Monopoly: A Correction," *Journal of Political Economy,* Vol. 69, p. 494.

Siegfried, J. J., and T. K. Tiemann (1974). "The Welfare Cost of Monopoly: An Inter-industry Analysis," *Economic Inquiry,* Vol. 12, pp. 190–202.

Worcester, D. (1973). "New Estimates of the Welfare Loss to Monopoly: U.S. 1956–69," *Southern Economic Journal,* Vol. 40 (October), pp. 234–245.

CHAPTER
11

Monopolistic Competition and Oligopoly

Having discussed the theory of price under the polar cases of perfect competition (Chapter 9) and pure monopoly (Chapter 10), we now turn to the "middle ground," that is, monopolistic competition and oligopoly. The discussion is divided into two parts. In Part A we develop Chamberlin's model of monopolistic competition. In Part B we review some of the most widely known models of oligopoly.

PART A. MONOPOLISTIC COMPETITION

As explained in Chapter 8, the model of monopolistic competition (developed in the 1930s by Edward H. Chamberlin) revolves around the empirical observation that a large number of industries are composed of many small firms that produce *differentiated* products. Even though it is not an easy matter to define an "industry" in the presence of product differentiation, Chamberlin believes that it is still useful and meaningful to lump together firms producing similar products and call them a *product group*. In all other respects besides the idea of product differentiation, monopolistic competition is similar to perfect competition.

11.1 The Scenario of Monopolistic Competition

The model of monopolistic competition is based on the following assumptions:

1. There is a well-defined group ("industry") of many small suppliers of physically similar but economically differentiated products.
2. The number of firms in the group is sufficiently large so that each firm can pursue its own policies without any fear of retaliation from any other rival firm(s).

3. All of the actual and potential members of the group have the same cost curves and face the same demand curves. This is obviously a restrictive assumption; with differentiated products, one would expect the demand and cost curves of the member firms to be dissimilar. The main justification for the miraculous identicalness of cost and demand curves among member firms is analytical convenience. Because of this assumption, the entire analysis of group equilibrium can be performed in terms of a "representative" firm.

4. The cost curves of the member firms do not shift with changes of the group's size and aggregate output. This simplifying assumption excludes the possibility of external economies or diseconomies, whether pecuniary or technological.

5. The group (or "industry") is small relative to the rest of the economy, so that partial equilibrium techniques are applicable.

To keep our discussion of monopolistic competition within manageable proportions, we also assume in this chapter that both product quality and selling costs happen to be at their optimal levels.

11.2 Proportional Versus Perceived Demand

The graphical analysis of the model of monopolistic competition makes use of two different demand curves: the *proportional* demand curve (*D*) and the *perceived* demand curve (*d*). It is important to clarify the distinction between these two curves before proceeding with the analysis of a monopolistically competitive industry (group).

The Proportional Demand Curve

Because the analysis of a monopolistically competitive industry is usually carried out in terms of a "representative firm," it is necessary to scale down the "industry demand curve" in proportion to the individual firm. This "scaled-down" industry demand curve is known as the "proportional demand curve." *At any specified price, the proportional demand curve gives the representative firm's share of the total market quantity demanded, on the assumption that all firms charge the same price.*

The proportional demand curve is illustrated in Figure 11.1. The industry demand curve is given in panel (b), and the corresponding proportional demand curve is shown in panel (a) by line *D*. For concreteness, we assume that there are just 1000 active firms in the industry (group), and when all firms charge the same price, the consumer purchases are always distributed evenly among these firms. This means that at each price the sales volume of the representative firm is equal to 0.001 of the total market quantity demanded. For instance, when the price is $10, the total market quantity demanded is 15,000 units, as indicated by point A on the industry demand curve in panel (b); therefore, the representative firm must be able to sell 15 units (i.e., 0.001 of 15,000), as shown by point A' on the proportional demand curve *D* in panel (a).

Because of a judicious choice of scales, the same distance along the respective quantity axes represents in panel (b) 1000 times the quantity it represents in panel (a). As a result, the proportional demand curve in panel (a) and the industry demand curve in panel (b) are pictorially the same.

The role of the proportional demand curve in the analysis of monopolistic competition is the same as the role of the industry demand curve in the analysis of perfect competition: to identify whether the excess demand in the market is positive, negative, or zero. This is explained in Sections 11.3 and 11.4.

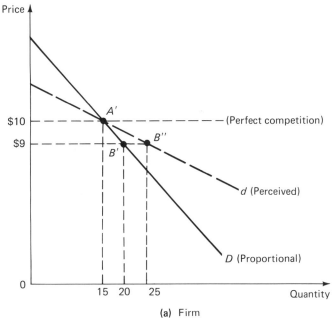

(a) Firm

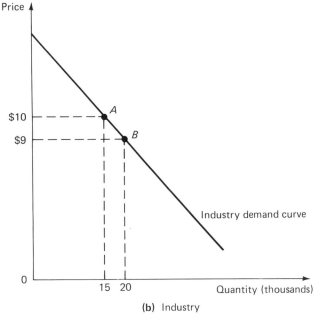

(b) Industry

Figure 11.1 Proportional versus perceived demand. The "industry demand curve" is given in panel (b). Assume that there are 1000 active firms in the group. At each price, the sales volume of the representative firm is 0.001 of the total market quantity demanded, as shown by the proportional demand curve (*D*) in panel (a). For instance, when the price is $10, the total market quantity demanded is 15,000 (point *A*), and the representative firm is able to sell 15 units (point *A'*). When the representative firm reduces its price to $9, it is under the illusion that other firms will keep their prices at $10, so it expects its sales volume to increase to 25, as shown by point *B''* on the perceived demand curve (*d*), as opposed to point *B'* on the proportional demand curve.

The Perceived Demand Curve

Suppose that all firms in the group are currently charging the same price, say, $10. We already know that at this price the representative firm can sell a maximum of 15 units, as shown by point A' in panel (a). This would be true even if the industry were perfectly competitive. Yet a perfectly competitive firm would have the illusion that it could sell any quantity it wished at the market price, as indicated by the dashed horizontal line through point A'. In other words, the demand curve *perceived* by the individual *competitive* firm would be horizontal (infinitely elastic) at the level of the current market price. All this is very familiar to us from the discussion in Chapter 9.

Under monopolistic competition, however, the demand curve perceived by the representative firm is not horizontal, although it is very elastic. Return again to point A' in panel (a). At the current market price of $10, the representative firm can sell a maximum of 15 units only. Suppose that to increase its sales volume, the representative firm reduces its price to $9. If all other firms reduced their prices to $9 also, the representative firm would be able to increase its sales to 20 units only, as shown by point B' on the proportional demand curve. But because the representative firm is very small relative to the market, it is under the illusion that other firms will maintain their prices at $10—the representative firm's price reduction is not expected to have any appreciable effect on any other firm in the group. Under these circumstances, the representative firm would expect to attract some marginal customers away from the other rival firms, with the result that its sales volume would exceed 20 units. In Figure 11.1(a) we assume that the representative firm expects to sell 25 units, as shown by point B'' on the perceived demand curve (d).

Note that when the representative firm increases its price while all other firms in the group keep their prices constant, the representative firm loses some marginal customers to other firms. Accordingly, its sales volume falls more rapidly than indicated by the proportional demand curve, as shown by the perceived demand curve.

We therefore conclude that the *perceived demand curve shows the alternative quantities that the representative firm expects to sell at various prices on the assumption that the prices of all the other firms in the group remain constant.* The perceived demand curve is necessarily more elastic than the proportional demand curve at point A'.

11.3 Short-Run Group Equilibrium

We are now ready to discuss the attainment of short-run equilibrium in a monopolistically competitive industry (group). As with perfect competition, we assume that only a finite number of firms are active producers. These are the firms that happen to possess the necessary plant and equipment (fixed factors) for the production of output. In the short run, new firms cannot enter the group.

The short-run group equilibrium is illustrated in Figure 11.2. The proportional and perceived demand curves of Figure 11.1(a) are now reproduced in panel (a), as shown by the curves labeled D and d, respectively. We assume that the initial market price is $10 and the representative firm sells 15 units.

As we explained in Section 11.2, the perceived demand curve d is the relevant demand curve for the representative firm's price and output decisions, because the firm believes that any change in its price will not be matched by all the other firms in the group. On the basis of the perceived demand curve d, we have also constructed the firm's marginal revenue curve (*MR*). Evidently, the representative firm will attempt to increase its output to 25 units and lower its price to $9, as implied by

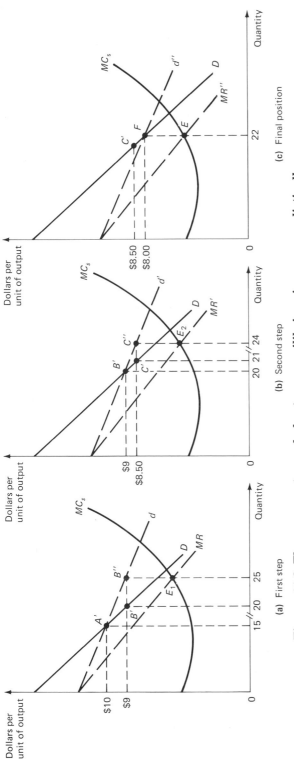

Dollars per unit of output

$10
$9

0   15 20 25   Quantity

A'
B''
B'
E₁
MC_s
d
D
MR

(a) First step

Dollars per unit of output

$9
$8.50

0   20 21 24   Quantity

B'
C''
C'
E₂
MC_s
d'
D
MR'

(b) Second step

Dollars per unit of output

$8.50
$8.00

0   22   Quantity

C'
F
E
MC_s
d''
MR''
D

(c) Final position

**Figure 11.2 The process toward short-run equilibrium is a monopolistically com-
petitive industry.** The proportional and perceived demand curves of Figure 11.1(a) are now
reproduced in panel (a), as shown by D and d, respectively. The initial market price is $10
and the representative firm sells 15 units (point A'). To maximize its short-run profit, the
representative firm must increase its output to 25, as indicated in panel (a) by intersection
E_1 of the curves of marginal cost (MC_s) and marginal revenue (MR). (The MR curve is
marginal to the d curve.) But every other firm will have the same incentive as the representative firm: to reduce its price to $9 and increase its output to 25. As a result, each firm
will be able to sell only 20 units (point B' on D), and the perceived demand curve will slide
downward along the D curve, as shown by d' in panel (b). But now, as shown in panel (b),
combination B' no longer represents equilibrium. The representative firm will again have
an incentive to reduce its price to $8.50 in order to sell 24 units (point C''), and so on. The
final equilibrium is shown in panel (c). The presentative firm produces 22 units, as indicated
by intersection E of MC_s and MR''. Note that the new d'' curve intersects the D curve at the
equilibrium price–output combination (point F).

345

intersection E_1 of the curves of marginal revenue (MR) and short-run marginal cost (MC_s). This is the "monopolistic" aspect of monopolistic competition.

The foregoing equilibrium position of the representative firm can actually be achieved and maintained only if the other firms in the group do indeed keep their prices constant, as the representative firm initially assumed. But each of the other firms will actually be confronted with exactly the same situation as that depicted in panel (a), because *each* firm will make the assumption that any change in its *own* price will not be matched by the other firms. Accordingly, *each firm will attempt to increase its output to 25 units and reduce its price to $9*. When they all reduce their prices in unison, however, each firm will be able to sell only 20 units, as shown by point B' on the proportional demand curve D. Thus the plans of all firms will be frustrated, and what is more important to us, the perceived demand curve will slide downward along the proportional demand curve, as shown by d' in panel (b). In other words, the *new* perceived demand curve will intersect the proportional demand curve at point B', which corresponds to the newly established market price.

Having arrived at the position shown in panel (b), the representative firm will continue to assume naively that any change in its price will not be matched by the other firms. Therefore, it will again attempt to maximize its short-run profit on the basis of the d' curve. In particular, it will lower its price to $8.50 under the illusion that it will be able to sell 24 units, as implied by the intersection E_2 of the new MR' curve and the original MC_s curve. But again each firm in the group will actually attempt to do the same thing. The result, of course, is that at the new market price of $8.50, each firm will be able to sell only 21 units (instead of 24 units), as shown by point C' on the unchanged proportional demand curve D in panel (b).

The process described above will continue until the representative firm has no incentive to alter its price–output combination, as shown in panel (c). Note that the representative firm produces 22 units of output, as indicated by intersection E of the MC_s curve and the relevant MR'' curve. In addition, at the equilibrium price of $8, the new d'' curve intersects the proportional demand curve D, as shown by point F. Accordingly, at the equilibrium price of $8, each firm is actually able to sell exactly the output that it initially expected to sell, that is, 22 units.

We therefore conclude that the representative firm formulates its price–output policies with respect to the perceived demand curve. Yet group equilibrium can prevail if, and only if, the representative firm's optimal price–output combination coincides with a point on the proportional demand curve.

11.4 Long-Run Group Equilibrium

In the long run, the monopolistically competitive firms, like the perfectly competitive firms, are able to adjust the size of their plant (fixed inputs) and to enter or leave the group (industry). Entry and exit are costless, as in perfect competition.

The long-run market adjustment mechanism rests on a most sensible assumption (borrowed from the model of perfect competition): The existence of economic profits in the group attracts new firms, while the presence of economic losses forces hitherto active firms to leave the group. Long-run equilibrium is established when all firms earn zero economic profits.

Figure 11.3 illustrates the long-run group equilibrium. To begin with, suppose that the short-run proportional and perceived demand curves are D_s and d_s, respectively, with MR_s being the marginal revenue curve that corresponds to d_s. In the short run, therefore, the representative firm sells q_s at p_s (point S). This initial position is determined by intersection E_s of the curves of short-run marginal revenue (MR_s) and long-run marginal cost (MC_L). Since price (p_s) exceeds the long-run av-

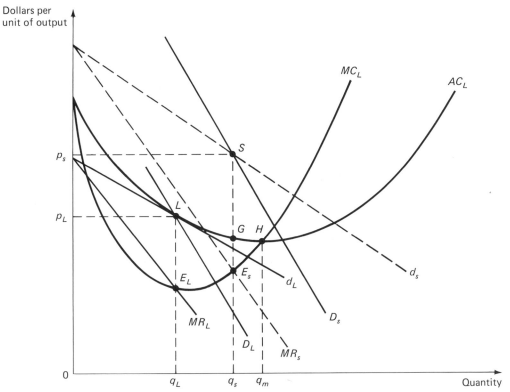

Figure 11.3 Long-run group equilibrium. Intersection E_s of short-run marginal-revenue curve (MR_s) and long-run marginal-cost curve (MC_L) determines the initial position where the representative firm sells q_s at p_s (point S). The existence of positive economic profits ($p_s > AC_L$) attracts more firms into the group, causing a gradual shift to the left of the proportional demand curve (D_s), as shown by D_L. The long-run equilibrium output (q_L) is again determined by intersection E_L or MR_L and MC_L, but now we have the added feature that the perceived demand curve (d_L) is tangent to AC_L at the equilibrium price–output combination (point L). Note that the long-run proportional demand curve (D_L) continues to pass through the equilibrium price–output combination (point L).

erage cost (q_sG), the representative firm earns positive economic profits, which attract new firms into the group.

The entry of new firms causes both the proportional and the perceived demand curves to gradually shift to the left—with more firms in the group, the representative firm's market share shrinks. Eventually, the two demand curves (D_s and d_s) shift to the position indicated by D_L and d_L, respectively, with MR_L being the marginal revenue curve that corresponds to d_L. The representative firm is finally in long-run equilibrium where it sells q_L at p_L (point L). At this long-run equilibrium, the representative firm is earning zero economic profit, as the perceived demand curve (d_L) is tangent to the long-run average-cost curve (AC_L) at L.

In summary, the long-run group equilibrium is characterized by two conditions: (1) the perceived demand curve (d_L) is tangent to the long-run average-cost curve (AC_L) at the equilibrium output (q_L), and (2) the proportional demand curve (D_L) intersects both the perceived demand curve (d_L) and the long-run average-cost curve (AC_L) at the point of tangency (L). Note that the tangency of d_L to AC_L at L implies that the marginal revenue curve (MR_L) intersects the long-run marginal-cost curve (MC_L) at the equilibrium output (q_L), as shown by point E_L.

11.5 Characteristics of Monopolistic Competition

The group equilibrium described in the preceding section has two important characteristics. These characteristics are

1. *Price exceeds marginal cost.* As in monopoly, the demand curve facing a monopolistically competitive firm is inherently downward sloping. In equilibrium, then, price necessarily exceeds marginal cost, which indicates that monopolistic competition leads to the same inefficiency as monopoly: Output is low and price is high. Unlike perfect competition, monopolistic competition does not produce enough output to maximize social welfare. But the more elastic is the perceived demand curve, the smaller becomes the divergence between the output of monopolistic competition and the efficient output.

2. *Excess capacity.* In a monopolistically competitive industry, there appear to exist too many active producers, each with excess capacity. Go back to Figure 11.3 and note that the representative firm's equilibrium output (q_L) is less than the output (q_m) where the long-run average cost is at a minimum. The difference between q_L and q_m (i.e., $q_m - q_L$) is called excess capacity, and it is a direct consequence of the fact that the demand curve facing the monopolistic competitor slopes downward.

Is excess capacity bad? Some critics of the model of monopolistic competition think it is. These critics point out that in comparison with perfect competition, monopolistic competition wastes scarce resources. The same total output could be produced with fewer firms at a lower per unit cost to society. Suppose that in Figure 11.3 $q_m = 100$, $q_L = 60$, and that there are 1000 active firms producing 60,000 units of output per unit of time (i.e., $60 \times 1000 = 60{,}000$) at an average cost of $p_L = \$20$. The same output could be produced by only 600 firms, with each firm producing 100 units at an average cost of, say, $\$17 = q_m H < p_L$.

This criticism is not convincing. The comparison with perfect competition is misleading, because perfect competitors deal in a *homogeneous* product. The reduction in the number of monopolistic competitors necessarily results in a diminished variety of products available to consumers. To the extent that product variety is desirable, the benefit to society resulting from lower per unit costs must be weighed against the loss of product variety. We must therefore conclude that the excess capacity that prevails under monopolistic competition is not necessarily a sign of waste of valuable resources; it may be viewed as the cost of achieving a socially desirable degree of product variety.

11.6 Concluding Remarks

Since its formulation in the early 1930s, the model of monopolistic competition has been severely criticized on both theoretical and empirical grounds.[1] Today, it is fair to say, Chamberlin's contribution is still controversial and there is no unanimity among economists as to its significance. But even though the model of monopolistic competition has never played a central role in economic theory, it brings out quite sharply several important aspects of economic reality and economists are not yet ready to discard it. It is apparent that much more research is needed in this area. The numbers are not all in yet for a final appraisal.

---

[1]For a critical view of monopolistic competition, see Stigler (1949) and Cohen and Cyert (1975). For a sympathetic view, see Bishop (1964).

PART B. OLIGOPOLY

As we explained in Section 8.1, oligopoly is a market structure that is characterized by a small number of sellers. Its main distinguishing feature is the strong interdependence that exists among the sellers. Because of the fewness of firms, each oligopolist's policies (with respect to price and output, but also product variation and sales promotion in the case of differentiated products) necessarily have an appreciable effect on each of his rivals. For this reason, a change of price or output by one of the oligopolists is likely to provoke some reaction on the part of the other rival firms. In formulating his policies, a rational oligopolist must take into consideration the likely reactions of his rivals. Of course, an oligopolist can never be absolutely sure what the reactions of his rivals will be. A variety of reaction patterns are possible, and as a result economists have developed a large number of theories of oligopoly. In this chapter we survey only the principal models of oligopoly.

The problem raised by oligopolistic interdependence can be conveniently studied within the framework of *duopoly,* a special case of oligopoly where there are just *two sellers.* For this reason, most (but not all) of our discussion in this chapter will be devoted to duopoly.

11.7 The Cournot Duopoly Model[2]

The first serious model of duopoly was published in 1838 by a French mathematician, Augustin Cournot (1801–1877). Cournot imagines two mineral springs, each producing at zero cost an abundant supply of an identical (homogeneous) but otherwise unique type of mineral water. One spring is owned by firm A, the other by firm B. Each firm is interested in maximizing its own profit (or total revenue, since costs are zero).

To obtain a unique static equilibrium, Cournot introduces two additional assumptions. First, as an institutional assumption, each firm determines its profit-maximizing *output* (not price), and the sum of the outputs of the two firms fixes the equilibrium price on the basis of the market demand curve for mineral water. Second, as a behavioral assumption, each firm acts independently of the other in the sense that in determining its most profitable output, *each firm takes the rival's output as constant.*

For convenience, we suppose that the market demand curve for mineral water is linear, as shown in Figure 11.4 by line DD'. By assumption, a zero price would require an output of 480. For any arbitrary output q_b of firm B, the relevant demand curve for firm A coincides with that portion of the market demand curve that corresponds to outputs greater than q_b (i.e., FD') because firm A assumes that B's output will remain constant at q_b. Graphically, this means that firm A visualizes the vertical (price) axis at the level of B's current output, as shown by dashed line L. On the basis of this "reconstituted demand curve," the profit-maximizing output of firm A (q_a) is given by the simple formula

$$q_a = \frac{480 - q_b}{2} \tag{11.1}$$

The logic behind equation (11.1) must be clear from our discussion in Chapters 8 and 10. When the average-revenue curve is linear, as shown by FD', the marginal-revenue curve is also linear and just twice as steep, as shown by dashed line FH, which intersects the quantity axis at a point (H) just halfway between q_b and D'.

---

[2]This section could be read together with Sections A11.1 and A11.2 of the Appendix to Chapter 11.

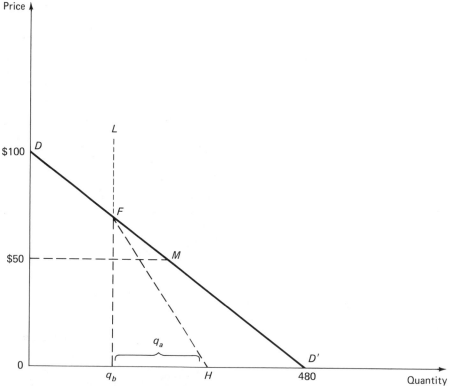

Figure 11.4 The "reconstituted demand curve" in the Cournot model. The market demand schedule is shown by DD'. For any arbitrary output q_b of firm B, the relevant demand curve for firm A coincides with the portion of the market demand curve that corresponds to outputs greater than q_b, that is, FD'; and the profit-maximizing output of firm A is equal to q_bH, or $(480 - q_b)/2$ because it is at that output where A's marginal revenue equals its marginal cost (zero).

Total revenue (and with zero cost, total profit as well) is maximized at H. Hence q_a is given by distance q_bH, or $(480 - q_b)/2$. This proves equation (11.1).

To determine the profit-maximizing output of firm B for any given output q_a of firm A, we simply reverse the roles of the two firms in the above reasoning. We conclude that for any arbitrary output q_a of firm A, the profit-maximizing output q_b of firm B is given by the formula

$$q_b = \frac{480 - q_a}{2} \tag{11.2}$$

Equation (11.2) is easily obtained from equation (11.1) by simply switching the subscripts a and b, a procedure that is equivalent to the reversal of roles of firms A and B.

Equations (11.1) and (11.2) are known as the *reaction functions* of firms A and B. Their simultaneous solution gives the equilibrium outputs of the two firms:

$$q_a = q_b = \frac{480}{3} = 160 \tag{11.3}$$

Note that at the equilibrium point the expectations of both firms are fulfilled: Each firm produces 160 units on the assumption that the other firm will continue producing 160 units also.

The Cournot model implies a dynamic process—an infinite series of adjustments and counteradjustments. Besides being interesting in itself, this process exposes the basic flaw in Cournot's analysis. Consider Figure 11.5, where we used equations (11.1) and (11.2) to obtain the *reaction curves* of firms A and B, respectively. A's reaction curve, corresponding to equation (11.1), shows firm A's profit-maximizing quantity (q_a) given B's current output (q_b) and the crucial assumption that firm A regards q_b as determined independently of its own q_a. For instance, when firm B produces nothing ($q_b = 0$), firm A produces the monopoly output $q_a = 240$, as shown by point G, and when $q_b = 120$, then $q_a = 180$, as shown by point E. Similarly, B's reaction curve, corresponding to equation (11.2), shows firm B's profit-maximizing output (q_b) given A's current output (q_a). For example, when $q_a = 0$, firm B produces the monopoly output $q_b = 240$, as shown by point H, and when $q_a = 240$, then $q_b = 120$ (point D).

The static Cournot equilibrium occurs at the intersection (C) of the two reaction curves. Note that the Cournot equilibrium implies an aggregate output ($q_a + q_b = 160 + 160 = 320$) that is larger than the monopoly output (240). To confirm this proposition graphically, draw dashed line GH connecting the monopoly outputs.

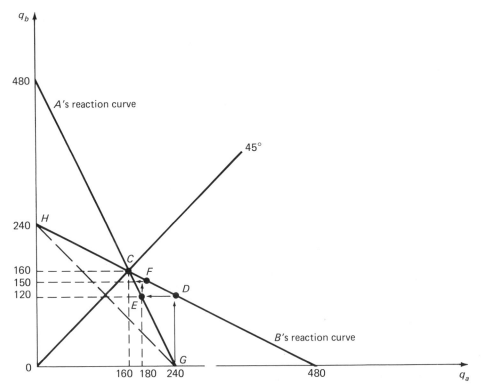

Figure 11.5 The Cournot solution. *A*'s reaction curve gives *A*'s profit-maximizing output (q_a) given *B*'s output (q_b); and *B*'s reaction curve shows *B*'s profit-maximizing output given q_a. Static equilibrium occurs at intersection C of the two reaction curves. Note that C lies on the 45° line (which implies $q_a = q_b$) and above and to the right of line GH which is the locus of points where $q_a + q_b = 240 =$ monopoly output. Firm A enters the market first and produces 240 units (point G). Firm B follows with an output of 120 (point D); and the system follows the adjustment path (GDEF . . . C) until equilibrium is eventually attained at C.

Points on line *GH* give all alternative combinations of q_a and q_b whose sum equals the monopoly output. That is, all points along line *GH* satisfy the equation $q_a + q_b = 240$. Since the Cournot equilibrium point (*C*) lies above and to the right of line *GH*, the combined output of firms *A* and *B* is necessarily larger than the monopoly output. This conclusion also implies that compared with monopoly, the Cournot equilibrium leads to a lower price and a smaller combined profit. Note also that in the symmetrical case of Cournot where both firms have identical (zero) costs, the final equilibrium occurs on a 45° line, as shown in Figure 11.5, implying equal market shares for the two firms (i.e., $q_a = q_b$).

Turn now to the adjustment process itself. Suppose that initially firm *A* happens to be alone in the market (i.e., $q_b = 0$). On the assumption that firm *B* will continue to produce nothing, firm *A* maximizes its profit by selling the monopoly output, 240 units, as shown by point *G*. Now let firm *B* enter the market. In the naive view that Cournot imposes on each duopolist, firm *B* expects q_a to remain constant at 240 and therefore sells 120 units, as shown by point *D*. Contrary to *B*'s expectation, however, firm *A* reconsiders its initially selected quantity. Being also a victim of the shortsightedness specified by Cournot, firm *A* takes q_b as fixed at 120. Accordingly, firm *A* reduces its output to 180, as indicated by point *E*. In turn, this curtailment of output by firm *A* changes the market position of firm *B*, which, in the same naive manner as before, increases its output to 150, as shown by point *F*. The increase in *B*'s output causes firm *A* to adjust its quantity, and so on. Clearly, this adjustment process continues until equilibrium is eventually established at *C*. The "adjustment path" implied by the foregoing sequence of output adjustments is shown by the arrows. It is evident from the diagram that the outputs of *A* and *B* converge rapidly to their respective equilibrium levels indicated by point *C*. This conclusion remains valid for any arbitrarily selected initial values for q_a and q_b.

We can now see the inherent flaw in Cournot's analysis. In adjusting its output, each firm assumes that the other firm's quantity is a constant, independent of its own. Yet as the adjustment process reveals, this is not the case, except at the singular Cournot-equilibrium point. Despite this fact, neither duopolist seems to learn from experience, and each continues to foolishly make the same naive assumption. One would expect the duopolists to quickly recognize their mutual interdependence and act accordingly.

11.8 The Bertrand Duopoly Model

In 1883, 45 years after the publication of the Cournot model, another French mathematician, Joseph Bertrand (1822–1900), reviewed Cournot's work and offered what he believed to be a correction of Cournot's analysis. Actually, Bertrand's criticism and alleged correction of Cournot turned out to be an alternative theory of duopoly.

Bertrand follows Cournot in assuming that each mineral-spring owner has an unlimited supply of homogeneous mineral water, available at zero cost. But where Cournot assumes that each entrepreneur's decision variable is the *quantity* to be sold, Bertrand assumes that each duopolist quotes a certain *price* (not quantity) and stands ready to supply as much as may then be demanded at that price—an assumption that Bertrand erroneously attributes to Cournot. Bertrand completes his model by adopting a naive behavioristic assumption analogous to that of Cournot, namely, that each duopolist regards the other's *price* as constant.

Under these assumptions, Bertrand concludes that a price war between the two rival firms will drive the price to zero (competitive level). For instance, return to Figure 11.4 and assume that initially firm *A* is alone in the market, presumably because the price quoted by firm *B* is higher than $100. On the assumption that firm *B* will keep its price above $100, firm *A* maximizes its profit by charging the monopoly price of $50. When firm B enters the market, it takes firm A's price as constant and sets its own price just below $50, say at $49.99, foolishly expecting to capture the entire market. Firm A, however, reacts by setting its own price just a bit lower than B's price, in the naive expectation that firm B would keep its own price fixed. This effectively transfers all the business back to firm A, at least until firm B adjusts its own price; and so on. This successive undercutting of one another's price comes to an end only when the price drops to zero, that is, the competitive level.

As in the Cournot model, neither duopolist is capable of learning from experience. Their expectations are never fulfilled, except at the final equilibrium. Actually, Bertrand makes his duopolists appear even more stupid than those of Cournot. Each time a duopolist cuts his price, he foolishly believes that his rival will quietly accept his *total exclusion* from the market.

11.9 The Edgeworth Duopoly Model

Francis Y. Edgeworth (1845–1926), an English mathematical economist, concurred with Bertrand's criticism of Cournot and developed a duopoly model that differs from the Bertrand model in only one respect. Where Bertrand assumes that each mineral-spring proprietor has an unlimited supply of an identical product, Edgeworth assumes that each duopolist has a capacity constraint, and as a result neither duopolist is able to supply the entire market demand at a perfectly equilibrium price. On the basis of this assumption, Edgeworth concludes that there exists no unique solution, but instead, a "perpetual motion" of price and quantity.

To illustrate Edgeworth's argument, assume that the market demand curve is linear, as shown in Figure 11.6 by DD'. Each firm has a capacity of 350 units, so that their aggregate supply is 700 units, as shown by vertical supply curve S. To sell their entire supply, as in a perfectly competitive equilibrium, the duopolists must set their price equal to $30, as indicated by intersection E of S and DD'. On the other hand, if the firms were to collude, they would charge the monopoly price of $50 and sell only 500 units, as implied by intersection F of the marginal revenue curve (MR) and the horizontal axis. (Because costs are zero, their combined profit is maximized when marginal revenue is zero.) Edgeworth first demonstrates that neither of these two positions is consistent with a stable equilibrium.

The monopoly equilibrium ($p = \$50$) is unstable for Bertrand's reason. Since the monopoly output is only 500, at least one (and perhaps both) of the sellers will be unable to sell his entire supply. On the naive assumption that the other seller will keep his price at $50, the frustrated duopolist will have an incentive to reduce his price below the monopoly price of $50 in an attempt to sell his entire output of 350 units. The ensuing price war will then cause the price to fall further.

For the moment, suppose that the price falls all the way to the perfectly competitive level of $30, where each duopolist is able to sell his entire supply. As Edgeworth explains, this price is not stable either. Certainly, neither duopolist has any incentive to lower the price below $30, but each has an incentive to raise it all the way to the monopoly level of $50, because the other seller is unable to satisfy all consumers at the low price of $30.

To gain further insight into Edgeworth's argument, assume that there are just 100 individual consumers, each with the same linear demand curve given by the equation $q = 10 - 0.1p$ (where p is price and q is quantity). The total market demand Q is 100 (consumers) times the individual demand; that is, $Q = 100q = 100(10 - 0.1p) = 1000 - 10p$, which is actually the equation for the linear demand curve of Figure 11.6. When the price is $30, each consumer purchases 7 units ($q = 10 - 0.1 \times 30 = 7$). With the fixed supply of 350 units, each duopolist is then able

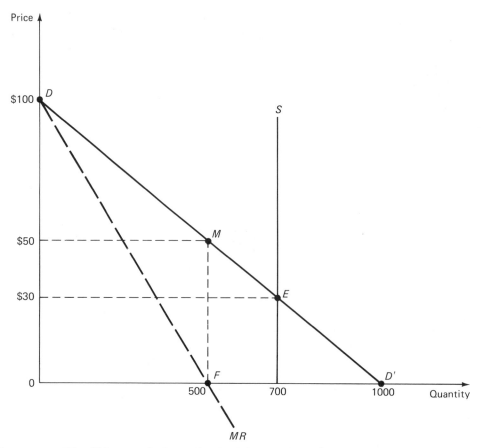

Figure 11.6 The Edgeworth duopoly model. Each firm has a capacity of 350 units. Aggregate supply is shown by vertical line S. The monopoly price is $50 (where $MR = 0$, as shown by F) and the competitive price is $30, as shown by E. Neither price is consistent with a stable equilibrium. Starting with the monopoly price, Bertrand-like monopoly war drives the price toward the competitive level; but then each duopolist has a strong incentive to raise it to the monopoly level again, and a new cycle begins.

to serve 50 customers only, obtaining a total revenue (and profit) of $10,500 (i.e., $30 \times 350 = $10,500$).

We now can see why each duopolist has a strong incentive to raise his price to the monopoly level of $50. Consider the argument of firm A. At the competitive price of $30, firm B is serving 50 customers only, which is the most it can do with its entire supply of 350 units ($350 \div 7 = 50$). The other 50 are glad to be served by firm A at any price that is less than $100. What price is most advantageous to firm A? That price that maximizes the total revenue (profit) extracted from each individual buyer. This price happens to be the monopoly price of $50. (The monopoly price is the same for the market demand curve as it is for the demand curve of each individual consumer.) Accordingly, by raising its price from $30 to $50, firm A can increase its profit from $10,500 to $12,500. (*Note:* At $p = 50, each consumer purchases $q = 10 - 0.1 \times 50 = 5$ units, spending a total of $pq = $50 \times 5 = 250.)

As Edgeworth himself was aware, the Bertrand price cutting will not continue until the perfectly competitive price of $30 is reached. The truth of the matter is that there exists a critical price (p^*), above $30, at which it becomes advantageous to either duopolist to raise his price to the monopoly level. What does this mean?

As we noted earlier, before the price drops to the competitive level of $30, it is not possible for both firms to sell their entire supplies simultaneously. To be sure, the low-price firm is always able to sell its entire supply, but the high-price firm is always left with a surplus (and a smaller profit). It follows that the high-price firm can always increase its profit by setting its price just below the price of the rival firm. (Thus, with an imperceptible price reduction, the hitherto high-price firm can switch roles with the hitherto low-price firm.) When the price falls below the critical level (p^*), however, it is more advantageous to raise the price to the monopoly level rather than reduce it further. What is this critical price?

To determine the critical price (p^*), we use an obvious relationship: The total profit of the firm, say B, that sells its entire output at p^* is exactly equal to the total profit of the other firm, say A, that sells only a fraction of its supply at the monopoly price. In our illustration, firm B must be selling $q^* = 10 - 0.1p^*$ to each of its customers, earning a total profit of $\$350p^*$. How many customers does firm B serve? Only $n_b = 350/q^* = 350/(10 - 0.1p^*)$ customers. How many customers remain to be served by firm A? Obviously, $n_a = 100 - n_b = 100 - 350/(10 - 0.1p^*)$. We already know that when firm A charges the monopoly price of $50, each customer's total expenditure is $250. Hence firm A's total profit is $\$250 \times n_a = \$250[100 - 350/(10 - 0.1p^*)]$. Accordingly, the critical price is the solution to the equation $350p^* = 250[100 - 350/(10 - 0.1p^*)]$, or $p^* = \$33.71$ (approximately).

It must be emphasized that Edgeworth's conclusion concerning the perpetual motion of price and quantity is valid only when the aggregate supply of the sellers exceeds the monopoly output of 500 units. To illustrate this point, suppose that each duopolist has a capacity of 200 units only. To sell their entire supply, as in perfectly competitive equilibrium, the duopolists must set their price equal to $60, enjoying a total profit of $12,000 each. Each duopolist serves just 50 consumers. Since each consumer happens to be at the elastic portion of his demand curve, however, it is no longer attractive to either duopolist to raise his price, because any increase in price would *reduce* the total revenue (and profit) obtained from each consumer. In this case the result is the competitive price, as in the Bertrand model.

Since Edgeworth adopted the same naive behavioristic assumption as Bertrand, his conclusions are subject to the same criticism as those of Bertrand.

11.10 The Chamberlin Duopoly Model

Edward H. Chamberlin (1933, pp. 46–51) criticized the naive behavioral assumptions of Cournot, Bertrand, and Edgeworth. He pointed out that, in general, oligopolists do recognize their interdependence and act accordingly. Chamberlin's main conclusion is that once the oligopolists recognize that their fortunes are interdependent, they will be driven to the monopoly equilibrium; that is, they will sell the monopoly output at the monopoly price and share the monopoly profits. Chamberlin reaches this conclusion irrespective of whether the oligopolists adjust their outputs (as in the Cournot model) or their prices (as in the models of Bertrand and Edgeworth).

For his analysis, Chamberlin adopts the Cournot duopoly model, except for the novel assumption that firms now recognize their market interdependence. For convenience, we reproduce in Figure 11.7 the same market demand curve DD' that we used in Figure 11.4 to study the Cournot model. Again let firm A start first by producing the monopoly output, 240 units, as shown by point M. Firm B then enters the market, and the best it can do is to supply 120 units, which reduces the price from $50 to $25, as shown by point C, exactly as Cournot suggested. How does firm A respond? Where Cournot postulates that firm A will adjust its output on the naive assumption that firm B will maintain its quantity at 120 units, Chamberlin suggests

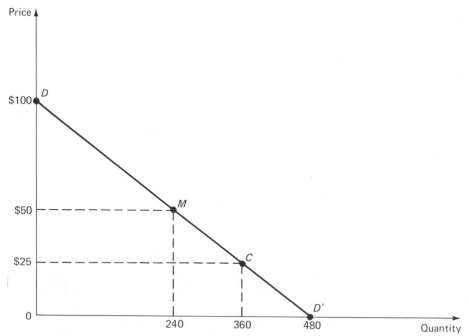

Figure 11.7 The Chamberlin duopoly model. As in the Cournot model, firm *A* begins by producing 240 units (monopoly output). Firm *B* enters and the best it can do is to supply 120 units, exactly as Cournot suggests. But now Chamberlin argues that firm *A* will recognize its interdependence with firm *B*, and firm *A* will reduce its output to 120 in order to share the monopoly profit equally with its rival.

that firm *A* will reduce its output to 120 units, and the total supply of 240 units (*A*'s output plus *B*'s output) will bring the monopoly price of $50. Why will firm *A* behave this way? Because it will recognize that firm *B* will react to *A*'s output adjustments, and that the *ultimate* consequences of any other chain of adjustments will be less attractive than sharing the monopoly profit equally with its rival. Because firm *B* will also reach this conclusion, the Chamberlin solution will prevail.

The foregoing conclusion remains valid even when the duopolists adjust their prices instead of their quantities. Each firm will realize that any reduction in its own price will have a considerable effect on its rival, and that the rival firm will retaliate by cutting its price also. But starting with the monopoly price, any cut will inevitably reduce the profits of all sellers, including the one who initiates the price reduction. For this reason, no rational seller will cut the price below the monopoly level. As Chamberlin (1933, p. 47) puts it, the monopoly price "is perfectly stable . . . for either seller would, by departing from it, bring disaster upon *himself* as well as upon his rival."

11.11 The Kinked Demand Curve Model

Despite moderate changes in cost and demand conditions, prices in oligopolistic markets tend to be rigid in the absence of collusion. The kinked demand curve model of differentiated oligopoly developed by Paul Sweezy (1939) offers an explanation of this observed price rigidity. The central idea of the Sweezy model is that the demand curve facing a typical oligopolistic firm has a "kink" at the prevailing equilibrium price.

To determine the relevant demand curve for its product, an oligopolistic firm must take into consideration the probable reactions of its rivals. In this connection, Sweezy argues, the rivals react differently according to whether the oligopolist raises or lowers the price. When an oligopolist lowers the price, he expects the rival firms to match that reduction, because they want to avoid losing customers; but when the oligopolist raises the price, he expects the rival firms to keep their prices constant, because they will welcome the gain in business. It is this asymmetry in the expected reactions of the rival firms that gives rise to the kink of the demand curve.

Figure 11.8 illustrates the kinked demand curve. (For the moment, ignore the marginal cost curve *MC*.) Drawing on Chamberlin's theory of monopolistic competition, we begin with two demand curves, *KET* and *FEG*, passing through the current equilibrium point *E*. The steeper demand curve (*KET*) is analogous to Chamberlin's proportional demand curve; it shows the relevant price and output combinations on the assumption that rival firms *match* this oligopolist's prices. The flatter demand curve (*FEG*) corresponds to Chamberlin's perceived demand curve; it reflects the relevant price and output combinations on the assumption that *the prices of rivals remain constant*. Because of Sweezy's basic assumption that rivals ignore

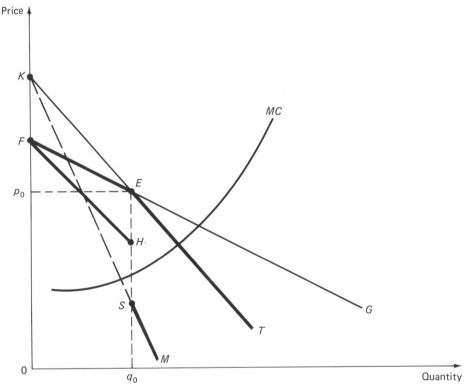

Figure 11.8 The kinked demand curve. Demand curve *KET* is analogous to Chamberlin's proportional demand curve; *FEG* corresponds to the perceived demand curve. These two curves intersect at the current equilibrium point *E*. If the oligopolist raises his price above p_0, rival firms will not follow—they will welcome the gain in business; and the relevant demand curve would be *FE*. If the oligopolist lowers his price below p_0, his rivals will lower their prices also (to avoid losing customers), and the relevant demand curve would be *ET*. The oligopolist's full demand curve *FET* has a kink at *E*, giving rise to a vertical discontinuity (*HS*) of the marginal-revenue curve (*FHSM*). Note that the marginal-cost curve (*MC*) passes through the discontinuity of the marginal-revenue curve.

price increases but match price reductions, the relevant demand curve for the oligopolist's product is the heavily drawn kinked line *FET*.

What is the oligopolist's marginal revenue curve, given kinked demand curve *FET*? First, note that *KSM* is marginal to *KET*, and *FH* is marginal to *FEG*. For outputs higher than q_0 where demand curve *KET* is applicable, marginal revenue curve *KSM* is relevant; and for outputs lower than q_0 where demand curve *FEG* is pertinent, marginal revenue curve *FH* becomes relevant. Accordingly, the oligopolist's marginal revenue curve consists of two disconnected segments: *FH* and *SM*. The kink in demand curve *FET* becomes a vertical discontinuity (*HS*) of the marginal revenue curve.

We can now confirm that equilibrium occurs at the initial price–output combination indicated by the kink (*E*). At the current output, q_0, the marginal-cost curve (*MC*) passes through the vertical discontinuity of the marginal-revenue curve (*FHSM*). Even though there is no equality of marginal cost and marginal revenue—the marginal-revenue curve does not exist from *H* to *S*—total profit is at a maximum, because a change in output in either direction reduces profit.

Note that a small upward or downward shift of the marginal cost curve has no effect on the profit-maximizing price and output—for small changes in cost, the marginal-cost curve continues to pass through the vertical discontinuity of the marginal-revenue curve. The same is true for small shifts of the demand curve, provided only that the kink remains at the initial price (p_0). Accordingly, oligopoly price tends to be rigid (or sticky).

Sweezy's contribution was at first hailed by many economists as a general theory of oligopoly. It soon became apparent, however, that the kinked demand curve model is deficient and incomplete. Although it explains how a *kink* may occur, it does not explain how the *initial price* is determined. In the absence of such explanation, the kinked demand curve model becomes an *ex post* rationalization of price rigidity rather than an *ex ante* theory of oligopoly pricing.

The Sweezy model has also been criticized on empirical grounds. The empirical evidence does not provide much support for the existence of a kink. For example, George Stigler (1947) found no asymmetry in the reactions of rival firms. In seven oligopolistic industries (anthracite, automobiles, cigarettes, dynamite, gasoline, potash, and steel) Stigler found that price *increases* by one firm were often matched by rivals, whereas in one industry (potash) price reductions were not followed. Subsequent studies supported Stigler's findings.

11.12 Price Leadership

In some oligopolistic industries, one of the firms may play the role of a *price leader*. The price leader initiates all price changes; the rest of the firms just follow the leader. Price leadership removes the uncertainty that surrounds the reactions of rivals to price adjustments. In effect, price leadership rules out the possibility of a kink (at the equilibrium price) in the demand curve facing an oligopolist, because all firms in the industry always match *all* price changes initiated by the leader. Although price leadership requires no formal agreement between the leader and the followers, the oligopolists must at least tacitly accept the arrangement. In some industries, price leadership may constantly rest with the same firm; in other industries, the price leader may change over time. Some examples of price leadership are provided by such industries as virgin aluminum, cigarette, cement, tin cans, and agricultural implements.

Economists have developed several models of price leadership. In this section we restrict our comments to only one of these models, known as the *dominant-firm model*. This model highlights the most typical form of price leadership; it applies to industries that are composed of a single large firm (the dominant firm) and a number of small ones. The dominant firm controls a substantial percentage of the total industry output. Each small firm produces only a negligible quantity relative to the industry output. The dominant firm serves as the price leader; the small firms act as price takers, selling all they wish to sell at the price set by the dominant firm.

How does the dominant firm determine the price that maximizes its profit while allowing the small firms to sell all they wish at that price? To answer this question, we must first determine the curves of average and marginal revenue of the dominant firm; then we can proceed as if the dominant firm were a monopolist. This solution is clarified in Figure 11.9.

The curve labeled DD' is the market demand schedule for the industry's output, while P_1S is the aggregate supply curve of the small firms. Because each small firm is a price taker, curve P_1S represents the horizontal summation of the marginal-cost curves of the small firms, as in a perfectly competitive industry. To derive the average-revenue curve of the dominant firm, at each price we subtract the quantity supplied by the small firms from the total market demand. For instance, at price P_2 the quantity supplied by the small firms equals the total quantity demanded, as indicated by the intersection (H) of DD' and P_1S; thus the dominant firm sells

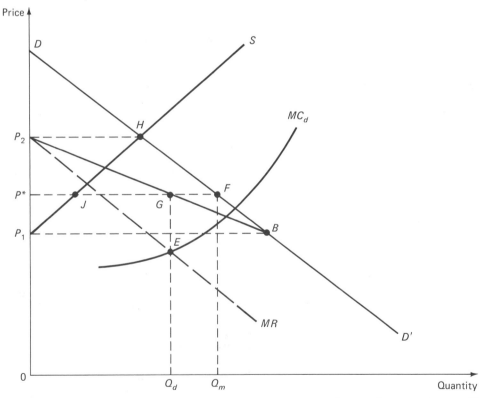

Figure 11.9 The dominant-firm model. At each price we subtract the quantity supplied by the small firms (read off P_1S) from the total market demand (read off DD') to determine the sales volume of the dominant firm. Thus the average-revenue curve of the dominant firm is given by P_2BD'. The associated marginal revenue curve over the relevant range of outputs is given by the dashed line labeled MR. To maximize its profit, the dominant firm must sell Q_d (determined by intersection E of MR and MC_d) at P^* (determined by point G). The small firms as a group sell $P^*J = GF$.

nothing and point P_2 lies on its average-revenue curve. Over the range of prices (P_1 or below) where the supply of small firms is zero, the dominant firm's average-revenue curve coincides with the market demand curve (region BD'). At any price between P_1 and P_2, the dominant firm's average-revenue curve is given by line P_2B, which represents the horizontal distances between lines DD' and P_1S. For example, at P^*, we have $P^*G = P^*F - P^*J$, which also implies that $P^*G = JF$ and $P^*J = GF$. We therefore conclude that the dominant firm's average-revenue curve is given by kinked line P_2BD'. The associated marginal-revenue curve over the relevant range of outputs is given by the dashed line labeled MR.

To maximize its profit, the dominant firm must produce Q_d units of output, as indicated by intersection E of the dominant firm's marginal-cost curve (MC_d) and the marginal-revenue curve (MR). Accordingly, the dominant firm sets its price equal to P^*, as shown by point G on average-revenue curve P_2BD' (*not* the market demand curve). At the equilibrium price, the small firms sell $P^*J = GF$ units of output.

11.13 Cartels

In an effort to exploit their joint monopoly power, oligopolists may form a *cartel*; that is, they may enter into a formal agreement to coordinate their pricing and output decisions. The advantages of forming a cartel are obvious: decreased competition and uncertainty in the market, and increased profit.

To prosper, a cartel must resolve several difficult problems: What should the price be? How should the industry's total output (sales volume) be divided among the cartel members? These are important questions, and the conflicting interests of the oligopolists may even prevent the cartel from getting off the ground.

If the main objective of the cartel is to maximize the total cartel profit, it must behave like a *multiplant monopolist*. As we know, profit maximization presupposes cost minimization. To minimize the cost of its aggregate output, the cartel must always allocate the total volume of sales among the member firms in such a way that all firms have the same marginal cost. But how much should the cartel produce in the first place? That output where the common marginal cost equals marginal revenue, as in monopoly. This solution is illustrated in Figure 11.10 for the case of two firms, A and B.

The marginal cost curves of firms A and B are given by MC_a and MC_b in panels (a) and (b), respectively. On the simplifying assumption that pecuniary and technological external economies and diseconomies are absent, we determine the horizontal summation of MC_a and MC_b, as shown in panel (c) by MC_c. The latter curve (MC_c) is the cartel's marginal-cost curve. The demand curve facing the cartel is also given in panel (c) by the AR curve, with MR being the associated marginal-revenue curve. To maximize total profit, the cartel must produce Q_c and sell it at the monopoly price p_c. Transferring the cartel's equilibrium *marginal cost* (Q_cE) from panel (c) to panels (a) and (b), as shown by the arrows, we determine the optimal allocation of the cartel's sales volume (Q_c) between the cartel members. Accordingly, firm A must produce q_a, as shown by point F in panel (a), and firm B must produce q_b, as shown by point G in panel (b).

In an ideal cartel, all firms have identical costs. Under these circumstances, a profit-maximization solution, analogous to Figure 11.10, may be quite acceptable to all cartel members because the total sales and profits are then shared equally by the cartel members. However, the ideal solution is not likely to occur in practice.

Typically, member firms have different costs and productive capacities. In this case, the maximization of total cartel profit leads to unequal shares of sales and profit among the cartel members. This is evident from Figure 11.10, where the low-

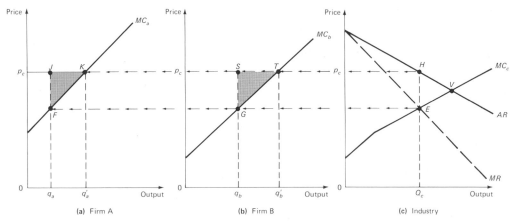

Figure 11.10 Maximization of cartel profit. The marginal-cost curves of firms A and B are given by MC_a and MC_b in panels (a) and (b), respectively. Their horizontal summation, MC_c in panel (c), represents the cartel's marginal-cost curve. To maximize total profit, the cartel must sell Q_c (determined by intersection E of MR and MC_c) at the monopoly price p_c. Projecting point E horizontally into panels (a) and (b), as shown by the arrows, we see that firm A must produce q_a (point F) and firm B must produce q_b (point G). However, firm A has an incentive to cheat: Firm A is under the illusion that it can increase its own profit by shaded area FJK by expanding its output to q_a'. Similarly, firm B has an incentive to increase its output to q_b'. The incentive to cheat is the most important reason for the eventual collapse of the cartel.

cost firm (B) comes out ahead. In such cases the cartel-profit-maximization solution may not be acceptable to the high-cost producer(s), unless it is supplemented by a satisfactory profit-sharing scheme. Alternatively, with different costs, cartel members are not likely to agree on what price to charge.

It is evident, then, that the pricing and output decisions of the cartel may be the result of intense negotiations among the cartel members. Normally, the distribution of the total volume of sales among the cartel members takes the form of quotas. In general, the quotas may reflect either the relative sales of each member firm in some precartel year, or its relative productive capacity. Another possibility is to divide the market geographically, with each member firm serving only one region.

11.4 The Instability of Cartels

In the United States, the formation of cartels is prohibited by the Sherman Antitrust Act, passed in 1890. In many European countries, though, cartels are legal. Yet even when they are legally acceptable, cartels usually suffer from internal pressures that tend to tear them apart. Their mortality rate is very high, mainly because each cartel member has a strong incentive to cheat on the cartel agreement.

The incentive to cheat is evident from Figure 11.10, even though a model with more cartel members than just firms A and B would be more appropriate. Panel (c) shows that to maximize its total profit, the cartel must restrict its output to Q_c and charge the monopoly price (p_c). This goal can be achieved only if firms A and B are persuaded to restrict their outputs to q_a and q_b, as shown in panels (a) and (b), respectively. Yet each firm has a strong incentive to produce much more than its quota. For instance, on the assumption that firm B will continue to adhere to the official cartel policy, firm A has the illusion that it can increase its *own* profit by expanding its own output to q_a', where A's marginal cost equals the official cartel price (point K). The expected gain in profit is indicated by (approximately) shaded triangular area FJK.[3]

Note that firm B has the same incentive as firm A. On the naive assumption that firm A will continue to abide by the cartel agreement, firm B also has the illusion that it can increase its own profit by raising its own output to q'_b, where B's marginal cost equals the official cartel price (point T). B's expected gain in profit is shown by (approximately) shaded triangular area GST.

Note also that when one cartel member cheats while all other members remain faithful to the cartel agreement, the cheater (or "chiseler," as he is more commonly called) does better for himself but the profit of the other members necessarily decreases. This should be evident from our earlier discussion in this chapter.

When greedy cartel members selfishly attempt to capture more profits for themselves, it becomes obvious that the cartel cannot effectively restrict output. Hence the cartel cannot preserve the monopoly price. Experience shows that this is the most important reason for the eventual collapse of a cartel.

The behavior of greedy cartel members reminds one of a fable of Aesop. A dog had stolen a piece of meat and was crossing a river on his way home when he saw his own shadow reflected in the stream below. Thinking that it was another dog with a larger piece of meat, he snapped at the supposed treasure. In the process, he dropped the bit he was carrying, and so lost all.

11.15 The Prisoners' Dilemma

The internal pressures of a cartel are highlighted by the so-called *prisoners' dilemma,* which is based on the following story. The police have just apprehended two criminals, A and B, but have no hard evidence against them. Without a confession, both criminals will be given light sentences, say, 50 days' imprisonment. To encourage a confession, the police first place the two criminals in separate cells in order to prevent direct communication between them. Then the police make this offer to each criminal: "If you confess while the other keeps silent, we will set you free but punish the other with 2000 days' imprisonment. If, however, the other also confesses, then each of you will spend 1000 days in prison." The choices facing each prisoner (criminal) are summarized in Table 11.1, which is known as a *payoff matrix.*

A quick inspection of Table 11.1 reveals the following important truth: *It is in the self-interest of each prisoner to confess.* Consider A's case first. There are two possibilities for B's behavior: B will either confess or keep silent. Suppose that B confesses. Then A will suffer only 1000 days' imprisonment if he (A) confesses, compared with 2000 days' imprisonment if he (A) does not confess. Hence it is in A's interest to confess. Or suppose that B does not confess. Then A will be free if he (A) confesses, compared with 50 days' imprisonment if he (A) does not confess. So again it is in A's interest to confess.

Following the same logic, we also conclude that it is in B's interest to confess.

Table 11.1 The Prisoners' Dilemma

		A's choices	
		Confess	**Don't confess**
B's choices	**Confess**	A: 1000 days B: 1000 days	A: 2000 days B: Free
	Don't confess	A: Free B: 2000 days	A: 50 days B: 50 days

---

[3]The expected gain is only *approximated* by shaded triangular area FJK because any expansion of output will cause the price to fall.

Accordingly, both prisoners confess, and each suffers 1000 days' imprisonment. Self-interest prevents the two prisoners from attaining the best solution for themselves (50 days' imprisonment), which can be achieved only if neither prisoner confesses.

Turn now to Table 11.2, which summarizes the profitability of two firms, *A* and *B*, the only members of a cartel. If both firms cooperate with the cartel agreement, each firm makes $30,000. If both firms cheat, each firm's profit falls to $10,000. If firm *A* cheats while firm *B* cooperates, *A* makes $50,000 but *B*'s profit drops to only $2000. Finally, if firm *B* cheats while firm *A* cooperates, *B*'s profit rises to $50,000 but *A*'s profit shrinks to $2000. Under these circumstances, each cartel member has a strong incentive to cheat. For instance, if firm *B* remains faithful to the cartel agreement, firm *A*'s best option is to cheat ($50,000) instead of cooperating ($30,000), and if *B* cheats, *A*'s best strategy is again to cheat ($10,000) rather than to cooperate ($2000). The same conclusion is true for firm *B* as well. Accordingly, both firms will cheat. Self-interest will bring about the breakdown of the cartel.

1.16 OPEC: An Empirical Application

In the late 1950s, competition among the major oil companies led to a fall in the price of crude oil. To stabilize the price of oil and prevent further erosion of their royalty revenues, the major oil exporters formed in 1960 the Organization of Petroleum Exporting Countries (OPEC). Initially, cartel membership was limited to five countries: Iran, Iraq, Kuwait, Saudi Arabia, and Venezuela. However, by 1973 eight additional countries (Algeria, Ecuador, Gabon, Indonesia, Libya, Nigeria, and the United Arab Emirates) had joined the cartel, with the result that OPEC accounted for about two-thirds of world oil reserves and over 85 percent of total world crude oil exports—a remarkable concentration of power.

During the first dozen years of its existence, OPEC functioned quietly and succeeded only in its initial objective of preventing further erosion in the royalties of the oil exporters. But the serenity of the world oil markets was shattered in 1973 with the Arab–Israeli "Yom Kippur War." In an effort to pressure the West to restrain Israel, the Arab members of OPEC temporarily embargoed oil exports to the United States and other pro-Israeli countries. Even though the Arab oil embargo was lifted in 1974, OPEC took advantage of the temporary supply shortage to quadruple the price of crude oil within three months, from $2.59 to $11.65 a barrel. OPEC had finally learned how to exploit its enormous market power.

The price of oil (in real terms) remained fairly stable at its new higher level until 1978, when as a result of the Iranian revolution, Iranian oil exports (which accounted for about 20 percent of all OPEC exports) almost disappeared completely. Naturally, the price of oil took another upward bound. The upward trend in the price of oil was further precipitated by the Iran–Iraq War, which resulted in further reductions in oil exports. By 1981 the price of Saudi Arabian light crude oil had climbed to $32 a barrel.

Which model best describes the post-1973 world oil market? Perhaps the domi-

		Firm *A*	
		Cheat	Cooperate
Firm *B*	Cheat	A: $10,000 B: $10,000	A: $2000 B: $50,000
	Cooperate	A: $50,000 B: $2000	A: $30,000 B: $30,000

Table 11.2 **Payoff Matrix for Cartel Members**

nant-firm model, but with the qualification that the dominant firm is actually a cartel. Thus we may assert that the low oil price (in real terms) which had prevailed up to 1973 corresponded to the *competitive price,* while the substantially higher price (in real terms) since 1973 is more or less the *monopoly price* charged by the dominant firm (OPEC).

Since 1973 OPEC has maintained the most lucrative monopoly in the history of the world. Many billions of dollars have been transferred from the oil-importing countries to the oil exporters. What accounts for the success of OPEC? The most important economic reason is the low price elasticity of demand for imports of oil by the rest of the world, which actually reflects the influence of three factors: (1) The price elasticity of demand for oil is very low, especially in the short run because there are no good substitutes for oil; (2) the elasticity of supply of oil by nonmembers of OPEC is also very low, because oil exploration and production is a very time consuming process; and (3) OPEC controls most of the proven oil reserves and exports of the world.

Because OPEC is a cartel (and not just a single dominant firm), it is also subject to all those internal pressures (discussed in Sections 11.14 and 11.15) that account for the observed instability of all cartels. An important necessary condition for the success of a cartel is that all members should adhere to the official set of policies (with respect to price and output) of the cartel. But as we saw in Section 11.14, cartel members have an incentive to cheat, with the result that the cartel cannot effectively restrict output and preserve the monopoly price. It is for this reason that many economists, most notably Milton Friedman, were predicting that after the lifting of the 1973–1974 oil embargo OPEC would break up and the price of oil would fall back to the competitive level. This prediction, of course, has not been borne out by the facts. The OPEC members have so far avoided the prisoner's dilemma and instead, have behaved more or less like the Chamberlin oligopolists.

The coherence of OPEC was tested in 1982. Because of declining world demand for oil (due to many energy conservation measures and the world recession) and increased oil output by non-OPEC countries (mainly due to oil discoveries in the North Sea and Mexico and the completion of the Alaskan pipeline), OPEC provided in 1982 only 34 percent of the world's oil output, down from 51 percent in 1977. At the same time, most OPEC members had developed enormous domestic needs and desperately required additional funds. For the first time OPEC appeared weak and many economists thought that this was the beginning of the end. But OPEC was able to weather the storm. In March 1983, the OPEC members agreed on a daily production ceiling of 17.5 million barrels (which incidentally was much higher than the approximately 12 million barrels that OPEC was able to sell daily at that time) and to *cut* its base price from $34 to $29 a barrel. Most OPEC members have so far stuck to the agreed prices and production quotas. It remains to be seen whether this kind of unity among such strange bedfellows will be maintained in the future.

11.17 Pricing Strategies in the Australian Newspaper Industry: Another Empirical Application[4]

The prisoners' dilemma emphasizes the inherent conflict that exists between oligopolists—a conflict that can only be resolved artificially and temporarily by collusive price leadership or similar practices. Even in what appear to be very "stable" oligopolies, there is always a latent power struggle between major firms. A case in point is a key sector of the Australian newspaper industry—the Sydney evening market—where on July 7, 1975, a price war broke out between News Limited, publisher of the *Daily Mirror,* and John Fairfax and Sons, publisher of the *Sun.*

[4]This episode is based on a recent study by Merrilees (1983).

The overt rivalry, which lasted for 42 months, shattered a long period of harmonious and peaceful coexistence.

Table 11.3 summarizes the behavior of cover prices in the Sydney evening newspaper industry from 1930 to 1981. Between 1941 and 1973, the prices of the *Sun* and the *Mirror* were identical to the day. Indeed, both papers gave simultaneous notices of two, five, and four days for the 1964, 1970,and 1974 price increases, respectively. This behavior may be taken as an indication of prior mutual agreement and tacit cooperation.

On July 7, 1975, price coordination collapsed. The *Sun* raised its price from 10 to 12 cents, but the *Mirror* did not go along. In retrospect, the chief reason for the *Mirror*'s refusal to match the *Sun*'s price increases seems to have been the intense desire of News Limited to seize the price leadership role from Fairfax. At the same time, Fairfax was determined to retain its role as a price leader in the evening newspaper market and was prepared to sacrifice profits in the process. The result was inevitably a prolonged conflict. The battle continued until January 1979, when the *Sun* finally decided to swallow its pride and drop its price back to 10 cents. The *Mirror*'s price of 10 cents lasted for five years, from November 1974 to November 1979.

In view of the fact that during the 1970s inflation was running at an average rate of 10 percent per annum, the constancy of nominal prices during the 1975–1979 period meant that the *real* cover prices of the Sydney evening newspapers fell continuously (at about 10 percent per annum). However, the *Mirror* remained cheaper than the *Sun* throughout this period.

News Limited's resolve not to follow the price increase posted by Fairfax was probably encouraged by two facts: (1) the passage of the 1974 Trade Practices Act, whose purpose was to discourage collusion; and (2) a temporary windfall in the cost of newsprint enjoyed by News Limited, but not Fairfax. In Australia, A.N.M. (Aus-

Table 11.3 Cover Prices in the Sydney Evening Newspaper Industry, 1930–1981

Date of Change	Price of the *Sun* (cents)	Price of the *Mirror* (cents)
1930, Aug. 4	1.3	—
1940, Feb. 5	1.7	—
1941, May 12		1.7 (entry)
1949, Sept. 12	2.5	2.5
1951, Mar. 12	3.3	3.3
1956, Oct. 8	4.2	4.2
1964, Sept. 14	5.0	5.0
1970, Mar. 31	7.0	7.0
1974, Jan. 21	8.0	8.0
1974, Sept. 30	9.0	—
1974, Oct. 1	—	9.0
1974, Nov. 25	10.0	—
1974, Dec. 10	—	10.0
1975, July 7	12.0	
1979, Jan. 15	10.0	
1979, Nov. 1	15.0	15.0[a]
1980, July 7	20.0[a]	20.0
1981, Sept. 21	25.0	25.0[a]

Source: Merrilees (1983, p. 295). Permission granted by Basil Blackwell, Oxford, England.

[a]Denotes price leader in terms of the first firm to announce a price rise, effective on the same date for both firms.

tralian Newsprint Mills) has a monopoly in the production of newsprint, which is a major cost element of newspapers. In 1966, A.N.M. introduced 10-year contracts with its customers, most of whom had a holding interest in A.N.M. The annual price increases provided by these contracts were very small, and with the acceleration of inflation in the early 1970s, A.N.M. found itself in a desperate financial situation. To ensure the survival of A.N.M. and hence the continuity of future supplies, A.N.M.'s customers voluntarily agreed to pay more for their newsprint. But unlike Fairfax, News Limited did not have a holding interest in A.N.M. and refused to cooperate. As a result the costs of newsprint for the *Mirror* did not rise as fast as those of the *Sun*. It is probably this cost differential (about $6 million) which provided the leverage for the pricing strategy of News Limited.

Table 11.4 gives the market shares of the *Mirror* and the *Sun* during the 1973–1981 period. Prior to the July 1975 (nominal) price change, the sales volumes of the two evening papers were about the same, and their market shares remained virtually constant. With the emergence of the price differential in July 1975, however, the *Mirror*'s market share increased from 50.1 percent (March 1975) to 54.1 percent (March 1977), a rise of about 8 percent.

The profits of the two newspapers also changed drastically during the 1975–1979 period. This is illustrated in Table 11.5, which gives the change and composition of profits for the 1975–1976 year compared to the preceding year. (The profit picture for later years was very similar to 1975–1976.) Excluding the special effects of higher newsprint prices ($0.3 million) and additional promotional expenses ($0.1 million), the *Sun*'s annual profit *fell* by $1.3 million while the profit of the *Mirror* *rose* by $1.6 million.

Fairfax clearly outperformed News Limited in terms of circulation revenue. With a constant price and increased circulation, the *Mirror* increased its circulation rev-

Table 11.4 Sales and Market Shares in the Sydney Evening Newspaper Industry, 1973–1981

Six-Month Period Ending:	Average Sales of *Mirror*	Average Sales of *Sun*	*Mirror*'s Market Share (percent)
March 1973	349,522	347,437	50.2
Sept. 1973	361,549	352,709	50.6
March 1974	304,317	301,017	50.3
Sept. 1974	369,153	364,288	50.3
March 1975	358,836	356,994	50.1
Sept. 1975	379,081	340,434	52.7[a]
March 1976	371,944	326,990	53.2
Sept. 1976	389,078	341,754	53.2
March 1977	375,107	318,370	54.1
Sept. 1977	377,508	328,731	53.5
March 1978	361,615	318,558	53.2
Sept. 1978	391,393	331,530	54.1
March 1979	387,173	338,511	53.4[b]
Sept. 1979	399,450	374,726	51.6
March 1980	361,520	342,284	51.4
Sept. 1980	358,907	348,715	50.7
March 1981	345,917	342,244	50.3
Sept. 1981	387,868	358,825	51.9

Source: Merrilees (1983, p. 301). Permission granted by Basil Blackwell, Oxford, England.

[a]Half of this six-month period involved a newly established price differential. [b]The last two months of this six-month period involved the elimination of the price differential.

Table 11.5 Increments in Company Profits, 1974–1975 to 1975–1976 (million dollars)		
	Mirror	*Sun*
Increment to Revenue		
Circulation revenue	+0.4	+0.8
Advertising revenue	+4.4	+0.3
Total	+4.8	+1.1
Increment to costs		
Mirror's Cost	+3.2	+3.2
Higher Newsprint Prices for Sun		+0.3
Higher Promotional Costs for Sun		+0.1
Lower Production Costs for Sun		−0.8
Total	+3.2	+2.8
Increment to gross profit	+1.6	−1.7

Source: Merrilees (1983, p. 304). Permission granted by Basil Blackwell, Oxford, England.

enue by $0.4 million. But with a higher price and reduced circulation, the *Sun* increased its circulation revenue by twice as much ($0.8 million). The fact that the *Sun*'s circulation revenue increased when its price rose leads to the surprising conclusion that the demand for the *Sun* was *inelastic* (with *negative* marginal revenue). But how can a profit-maximizing duopolist set his price at an inelastic part of his demand curve?

Circulation revenue (cover price times circulation) is only about one-third of total revenue. Advertising revenue (advertising rate times volume of advertising) makes up the other two-thirds. Other things being equal, a newspaper's advertising effectiveness and rate are increasing functions of its circulation. For instance, about half of the *Mirror*'s increased advertising revenue shown in Table 11.5 is attributable to its increased circulation. (Greater advertising volume explains the remainder.) Accordingly, the true marginal revenue of a unit increase in circulation far exceeds the marginal change in circulation revenue. The correct marginal revenue (to be compared with marginal cost) must also include the indirect effect on advertising revenue. This explains why a duopolist like Fairfax may rationally choose a cover price for which the demand may appear to be inelastic.

Prior to mid-1975, the *Mirror*'s advertising rate was slightly above the *Sun*'s, reflecting an historical advantage in advertising effectiveness. During 1975–1976 the *Mirror*'s relative circulation rose by 7 percent, and its advertising rate rose by 15 percent compared with 8 percent for the *Sun*.

On January 1979, a temporary truce went into effect. Backed by a $500,000 advertising campaign, the *Sun* retreated to 10 cents. This move signaled a tactical victory to News Limited, which demonstrated their newly won price leadership by initiating the November 1979 price increase. But on June 30, 1980, Fairfax once more seized the initiative and raised the price of the *Sun* to 20 cents. Because of ground lost to inflation since 1974, the *Mirror* followed suit. How long will the lull last? Nobody knows for sure.

SUMMARY

1. The model of monopolistic competition rests on five assumptions: (a) There is a well-defined group of small producers of differentiated prod- ucts; (b) the number of firms is large, and each pursues its own policies without fear of retaliation; (c) all firms have the same cost curves and face the same demand curves; (d) there exist no externalities; and (e) the "industry" is small relative to the rest of the economy.

2. At any specified price charged by all firms in the group, the proportional demand curve gives the representative firm's share of the total market quantity demanded.

3. The perceived demand curve, which is more elastic than the proportional one, shows the alternative quantities that the representative firm expects to sell at various prices on the assumption that the prices of all the firms in the group remain constant. The representative firm formulates its price-output policies with respect to the perceived demand curve.

4. Short-run group equilibrium (fixed number of active producers) prevails when the representative firm's optimal price-ouput combination coincides with a point on the proportional demand curve.

5. As in perfect competition, long-run group equilibrium is characterized by zero profit. The perceived demand curve is tangent to the AC_L curve at the equilibrium output, and the proportional demand curve intersects both the perceived demand and the AC_L curve at their point of tangency.

6. Group equilibrium has two important properties: (a) price > marginal cost, and (b) each producer has excess capacity.

7. Each oligopolist's policies (with respect to price, output, product variation, and sales promotion) have an appreciable effect on his rivals, who can react in many different ways. As a result, there are many theories of oligopoly.

8. In Cournot duopoly each firm determines its profit-maximizing output (not price) by naively taking the rival's output as constant. Each duopolist's behavior is captured by a reaction curve. Equilibrium occurs at the intersection of the two reaction curves.

9. In Bertrand duopoly each firm determines its price (not output) by naively regarding its rival's price as constant. The ensuing price war between the duopolists drives the price down to the competitive level. As in the Cournot model, neither duopolist is capable of learning from experience.

10. Unlike Bertrand, who assumes that each duopolist has an unlimited supply of an identical product, Edgeworth assumes that each duopolist has a capacity constraint and that neither firm can supply the entire market at the competitive price. His model leads to a "perpetual motion" of price and quantity.

11. Chamberlin argued that oligopolists do recognize their interdependence; whether they adjust price or output, they attain the monopoly equilibrium.

12. The kinked demand curve model is an attempt to explain the observed price rigidity in oligopolistic markets. The "kink" of the demand curve gives rise to a vertical discontinuity of the MR curve, and small shifts of the MC curve (or the demand curve) have no effect on the profit-maximizing price and output.

13. In some oligopolistic markets, a price leader initiates all price changes; all other firms follow the leader. Price leadership removes the uncertainty of rival reactions; it also rules out the possibility of a "kink."

14. The dominant-firm model highlights the most typical form of price leadership; it applies to industries composed of a single large firm (dominant firm) and many small ones. Each small firm sells all it wishes to sell at the price set by the dominant firm (price leader).

15. To exploit their joint monopoly power, oligopolists may form a cartel (formal agreement coordinating their pricing and output decisions). To prosper, a cartel must agree (by negotiation) on the price and how to divide the total sales volume among its members. Typically, cartels disintegrate fast because each member has a strong incentive to cheat on the agreement. The internal pressures of a cartel are highlighted by the prisoner's dilemma.

QUESTIONS

1. According to *The Wall Street Journal* (December 13, 1983, p. 16), the Chevrolet Division of the General Motors Corporation sold to the General Services Administration 12,571 cars and trucks for $68.3 million, or $5433 a unit. Compared with retail sticker prices, the federal government saved $22 million on this transaction, which amounts to a 24 percent discount. The general manager of the Chevrolet division was very pleased, an indication that the transaction was profitable for the company also. If this is so, why is it that General Motors Corporation does not reduce its prices to the American public by, say, 20 percent? Such a move would certainly motivate many American buyers to shift from, say, Toyotas to General Motors cars.

2. Demand and cost curves are the "same" for a group of producers of differentiated products. The number of such producers is limited by government licencing, as compared with the number that would otherwise operate.

    (a) Explain the nature of the group equilibrium when the firms are sufficiently numerous to rule out any oligopolistic element.

    (b) Under stationary conditions, would there be any value to a perpetually valid license? If yes, on what would it depend?

    (c) Suppose that a specific tax equal to the preexisting per unit profit is now imposed on the outputs of the group. What will be the effects of such a tax? How does the analysis differ, if at all, from that of a pure monopoly?

3. An industry is made up of just two firms, A and B. These two firms produce a homogeneous product under constant returns to scale. The common average cost of production is $2. The market demand curve for the industry's product is given by the equation

$$p = 400 - 4Q$$

where p is the price of the product and Q the industry output.

    (a) On a diagram, draw each firm's marginal cost curve.

    (b) Suppose that firm A enters the industry first. What quantity should A produce to maximize its own profit? What would the equilibrium price be? Firm A's total profit?

    (c) At the solution reached in (b), suppose that firm B enters the industry and behaves like a Cournot duopolist. Determine the output and profit of each firm and the equilibrium price. [Assume that firm A maintains its output at the level attained in part (b).]

    (d) Suppose that each firm behaves like a Cournot duopolist. Determine their reaction curves.

    (e) Finally, determine the Cournot equilibrium. (Calculate each firm's output and total profit as well as the equilibrium price.)

4. Return to the initial scenario of Question 3 and consider the following alternative situations:

    (a) Suppose that firms A and B collude and act as a monopoly. Determine the industry's output, price, and total profit.

    (b) Suppose, alternatively, that the two firms behave as perfect competitors. Again calculate the industry output, price, and profit.

    (c) What would the equilibrium solution (outputs, profits, and price) be if firms A and B behaved in accordance with the Bertrand assumptions?

    *(d) Finally, suppose that firm A were to act as a leader and firm B as a follower, in accordance with the Stackelberg model. What would be each firm's output and profit and the product's price?

5. (a) Discuss the meaning of monopolistic competition, the conditions that accompany it, and the major elements that distinguish it from perfect competition.

    (b) Compare monopolistic competition and perfect competition from the point of view of productive efficiency.

6. Firms A and B are contemplating two different advertising strategies. Their payoff matrix is shown at the bottom of the page.

    The entries in each cell show profits of the two firms for each combination of strategies.

    (a) Under what circumstances are both firms likely to spend more on advertising than their long-run best interests would require?

| | | **Firm B's Advertising Expenditure** | |
		$4 million	**$6 million**
Firm A's Advertising Expenditure	**$4 million**	A: $10 million B: $10 million	A: $6 million B: $12 million
	$6 million	A: $12 million B: $6 million	A: $8 million B: $8 million

(b) Under what circumstances are the two firms likely to adopt that strategy which maximizes their combined profit?

7. Assume that you are an antitrust economist and you observe the following phenomena in a particular industry:

(a) The number of buyers of the industry's product is large, and each buyer is fairly small in terms of sales.

(b) The *relative* market position of the major firms has been relatively stable over the past five years, but each firm's share of industry sales has decreased somewhat.

(c) Firms in the industry appear to be offering much more elaborate services and advertising much more than they had previously.

(d) The profit rates of the smaller firms have been increasing relatively more rapidly than the profit rates of the larger firms.

(e) The product is relatively homogeneous.

(f) Recent empirical studies have found that the price elasticity of demand at the industry output and average price is -1.8.

(g) Average costs of the larger firms do not seem to be at a minimum.

(h) Entry of new firms has been increasing slightly compared to past years.

In light of this evidence, would you argue in favor of initiating a price fixing investigation? Would *all* these phenomena point in that direction? (Discuss briefly the significance of *each* bit of evidence.)

8. An industry is composed of a dominant firm that controls a significant percentage of the total industry output and a large number of very small firms, each producing only a negligible quantity relative to the industry output. The combined supply curve of all small firms is given by the equation

$$P = 2 + Q_s$$

where P is the price and Q_s the combined output of small firms. The industry demand curve is given by

$$P = 20 - 0.10Q_d$$

where Q_d is the total quantity demanded.

(a) Derive the curves of average revenue and marginal revenue for the dominant firm. Show your results graphically.

(b) Suppose that the marginal cost curve of the dominant firm is given by the equation

$$MC = 3 + 1.5Q$$

where Q is the output of dominant firm. Determine the price that maximizes the dominant firm's profit. Also determine the output and profit of the dominant firm and the combined output of the smaller firms.

9. An industry is made up of just two firms, A and B, whose average costs of production are given in columns (2) and (3), respectively, of the table below. Data on the demand for the (homogeneous) product of these two firms are given in columns (4) and (5).

(a) Suppose that firms A and B form a cartel. Determine the equilibrium price, industry output, and each firm's individual output and profit, assuming that the objective of the cartel is to maximize total cartel profit.

(b) Explain why firm A (and alternatively firm B) would have an incentive to cheat on the cartel agreement.

| Output (Firm) (1) | Average Cost | | Industry Demand | |
	Firm A (2)	Firm B (3)	Output (Industry) (4)	Price (5)
1	$ 3	$ 5	4	$20
2	4	6	5	19
3	5	7	6	18
4	6	8	7	17
5	7	9	8	16
6	8	10	9	15
7	9	11	10	14
8	10	12	11	13

FURTHER READING

Bertrand, J. (1883). "Théorie mathématique de la richesse sociale," *Journal des Savants,* pp. 499–508.

Bishop, R. L. (1964). "The Theory of Monopolistic Competition After Thirty Years: The Impact on General Theory," *American Economic Review,* Vol. 54 (May), pp. 33–43.

Chamberlin, E. H. (1933). *The Theory of Monopolistic Competition,* Harvard University Press, Cambridge, Mass.

Cohen, K. J., and R. M. Cyert (1975). *Theory of the Firm: Resource Allocation in a Market Economy,* 2nd ed. Prentice-Hall, Inc., Englewood Cliffs, N.J. Chapters 11 and 12.

Cournot, A. (1897). *Researches into the Mathematical Principles of the Theory of Wealth,* trans. Nathaniel T. Bacon. The Macmillan Company, New York. Chapter 7.

Edgeworth, F. Y. (1925). "The Pure Theory of Monopoly," in *Papers Relating to Political Economy,* Vol. 1, Macmillan & Company, Ltd., London, pp. 111–142, especially pp. 116–126.

Merrilees, W. J. (1983). "Anatomy of a Price Leadership Challenge: An Evaluation of Pricing Strategies in the Australian Newspaper Industry," *The Journal of Industrial Economics,* Vol. 31 (March), pp. 291–311.

Stigler, G. J. (1947). "The Kinky Oligopoly Demand Curve and Rigid Prices," *The Journal of Political Economy,* Vol. 55, pp. 432–449.

Stigler, G. J. (1949). *Five Lectures on Economic Problems.* Longmans, Green & Company, London.

Sweezy, P. M. (1939). "Demand Under Conditions of Oligopoly," *The Journal of Political Economy,* Vol. 47, pp. 568–573.

Von Stackelberg, H. (1952). *The Theory of the Market Economy,* trans. A. T. Peacock. Oxford University Press, New York.

PART FIVE

Factor
Markets

CHAPTER 12

The Theory of Distribution

So far we have investigated the question of how the prices of commodities are determined in perfectly and imperfectly competitive markets. We now shift our attention to the problem of how the prices of factors of production are determined. Traditionally, the theory of factor pricing has been known as the *theory of distribution*.

In this chapter we present the neoclassical theory of distribution under perfectly competitive conditions. The basis of this theory is the *marginal productivity theory*. In Chapter 13 we analyze the implications of various imperfections of competition in both factor and product markets. Both chapters deal with general principles only. A complete understanding of factor markets requires, in addition, familiarity with the institutional framework within which factor supply and factor demand interact; but this type of knowledge lies beyond the scope of this book.

12.1 Introduction

In this introductory section we clarify several concepts that are of paramount importance to the study of the theory of distribution.

Factors of Production

Factors of production are the *services* of resources (or productive agents), not the resources themselves. Even though there are many factors of production, it is convenient to group them into a small number of categories, such as the services of *land, labor,* and *capital.* We are already familiar with these broad categories of factors of production from our discussion in Chapter 6. In the real world, each of these categories consists, of course, of many heterogeneous elements. (Where there is no possibility of confusion, we use the terms "labor" and "labor services" interchangeably. We follow this practice for all factors.)

The prices that form the subject matter of this chapter are then the prices of the services of land, labor, and capital, not the prices of the resources themselves. For instance, we are interested in the *wage rate,* which is the price of labor services per unit of time, not the price of bodies. Indeed, in a nonslave society there is no market in bodies. Similarly, we are interested in the rent of land services, not the price of a piece of land.

Supply and Demand

Like all prices, the prices of factors of production are determined by the forces of supply and demand (at least under perfectly competitive conditions). Thus the first step in our investigation is to discuss the general principles that govern both the supply of, and the demand for, factors of production as well as their interaction in the factor markets. As it turns out, we shall have much more to say on the demand for factors of production than on the supply.

Note that in comparison with the commodity markets, the roles of the leading actors are reversed in the factor markets. Business firms are now buyers, while individuals (or households) are sellers (at least of labor services).

The Principle of Derived Demand

It is a fundamental proposition in economics that the demand for a factor of production is usually a *derived demand.* That is, a business firm demands (or purchases) a factor *not* because of any *direct* satisfaction it anticipates to get from it, but because of the extra production and revenue it hopes to secure *indirectly* from it. For instance, the demand for shoemakers is derived from the demand for shoes, and the demand for weavers is derived from the demand for cloth. Personal services are an exception to this rule.

As explained below, the key to factor pricing lies in *marginal productivity.* In the final analysis, the remuneration of a factor is based on what it produces. But it must be clear from our discussion in Chapter 6 that marginal productivity is not a given number; rather, it is a function of many variables. For instance, the marginal productivity of labor depends not only on the skills of the work force, but also on the quantities of other factors (such as capital), the state of technology, and even the institutional structure of the market in which the final product is sold.

The Need for General Equilibrium Analysis

Even though factor prices are determined by supply and demand, we shall soon find out that the Marshallian partial equilibrium approach (which has proved so useful in the analysis of commodity markets) is not adequate for the analysis of factor markets. As will become increasingly evident in this chapter, the proper development of the theory of distribution requires a general-equilibrium approach for three reasons. First, there exists a strong interdependence between factor and commodity markets, as underscored by the very notion of derived demand. Second, there exist strong interrelationships among factors, as emphasized in Chapter 6. Finally, each general factor of production (such as labor, land, and capital) is likely to be employed by all (or at least many) industries. Thus the analysis of a single factor market will sooner or later require us to consider the entire economy. These general equilibrium aspects of the theory of distribution cannot be easily ignored.

Because general equilibrium analysis is inherently difficult, economists have constructed several simplified *macro*economic models of distribution. Such models are quite manageable because they hypothesize theoretical relationships among a small number of aggregate economic variables. Even though the process of aggregating diverse economic variables into a homogeneous economic entity does violate reality, such macroeconomic models often offer fruitful insights into the problem at hand. One such macroeconomic model of distribution is presented below in Section 12.9. A more disaggregated model of distribution must wait until Part Six.

Personal Versus Functional Distribution

Economists usually distinguish between two aspects of distribution theory: (1) the *personal* distribution and (2) the *functional* distribution. The personal distribution refers to the breakdown of national income (i.e., the aggregate income of society) among individuals (or households). Why are some people poor and some people rich? Are the poor getting poorer and the rich richer? Or are the poor becoming relatively richer and the rich relatively poorer? Why does a famous thoracic surgeon earn over $1 million a year while an elementary school teacher gets under $20,000 a year? Such questions illustrate the subject matter of the theory of personal distribution.

The functional distribution concerns the allocation of national income among the major factors of production: *rents* to land, *wages* to labor, and *profits* to capital.

Because factor prices are determined by supply and demand, the problem of functional distribution is merely part of the general theory of prices. The personal distribution, on the other hand, depends, in addition to the factor prices, on the *ownership* of the factors of production. This becomes evident when we realize that the income of any person depends on two elements: (1) the quantity of resources she owns, and (2) the price received for the services of each type of resource. The distribution of resources among individuals, however, does not belong to the study of economics, because it is the result of historical processes that are greatly influenced by the institutions of society with regard to inheritance, marriage, and so on. It is for this reason that traditionally economists have been concerned with the theory of functional distribution.

It is interesting to note that in the classical world of Adam Smith (1723–1790), David Ricardo (1772–1823), and John Stuart Mill (1806–1873) there was equivalence between personal and functional distribution theory, because the factors land, labor, and capital corresponded to three broad social groups. Land was owned by the landlords (aristocracy), labor was the province of the wage earners (working class, or proletariat), and capital was the property of the capitalists (rising middle class, or bourgeoisie). Incidentally, entrepreneurship was added as a fourth factor toward the end of the nineteenth century. Then profits were viewed as the price of entrepreneurship, and interest as the price of capital services.

Income Distribution and Justice

The great American economist John Bates Clark (1847–1938) regarded the theory of marginal productivity as a normative principle of *distributive justice*. Clark was convinced that distributing income according to each factor's marginal productivity leads to a *fair* division of products among economic agents, because each agent of production receives the amount of wealth which that agent creates.

Modern economists reject Clark's idea of distributive justice. To say that the distribution of income (whether it is based on the principle of marginal productivity or any other principle) is just is to make a judgment of a purely ethical nature. Ethical judgments have nothing to do with economics. (We return to this topic in Chapter 16.) The purpose of the marginal productivity theory is a more modest one, namely, to explain (rather than justify) the distribution of income observed in our society.

12.2 Profit Maximization and Input Employment

Consider a firm that uses two factors of production, homogeneous labor (L) and homogeneous land (T), and produces a single homogeneous product. Assume that both factor markets as well as the product market are perfectly competitive, so that the firm is a price taker in all markets. How much labor and how much land should the firm employ to maximize its profit? Are there any rules that the firm can follow in its search for the profit-maximizing levels of labor and land? The reader will be delighted to learn that the correct answers to these questions are implicit in our analysis of Chapters 7 and 9.

Recall that Sections 9.1 and 9.2 discussed how the firm determines its profit-maximizing *output*. Naturally, when the firm produces its optimal output, it must *ipso facto* employ certain equilibrium quantities of the relevant factors. This aspect of the firm's equilibrium was concealed in our earlier discussion, because our analysis was carried out in terms of the firm's cost curves. But as we showed in Chapter 7, the firm's cost curves are derived from the production function, which relates the output of the firm to the employment of factors of production. We must now untangle the key relationships between the firm's decision to produce a particular output and its decisions to hire certain quantities of factors.

The Cost-Minimization Condition

As we learned in Section 7.2, if the firm is to produce any output at least total cost, it must choose its factor quantities, L and T, so that the marginal rate of substitution of labor for land (MRS_{LT}) is equal to the wage/rent ratio (w/r)—a condition that is equivalent to the *tangency* between an isocost line and the relevant isoquant. Because the marginal rate of substitution of labor for land is equal to the ratio of the marginal physical product of labor (MPP_L) to the marginal physical product of land (MPP_T), the fundamental cost-minimization condition can be put in the following equivalent form:

$$\frac{w}{MPP_L} = \frac{r}{MPP_T} \tag{12.1}$$

where both ratios, w/MPP_L and r/MPP_T, are equal to the long-run marginal cost of the firm's output (MC). Equation (12.1) holds for each and every output along the firm's long-run cost curves; thus it must also hold when the firm produces its profit-maximizing output.

The Marginal Conditions for Profit Maximization

As we know from Section 9.1, if a firm is to maximize its total profit, it must operate at a point where marginal cost equals marginal revenue (MR). Combining this information with equation (12.1), we finally obtain the key factor-employment equilibrium conditions:

$$\frac{w}{MPP_L} = \frac{r}{MPP_T} = MR \tag{12.2}$$

In addition to introducing revenue data into our analysis of the factor-employment equilibrium of the firm, this last step yields two equations—one for each factor—that are valid only when marginal cost equals marginal revenue. To gain further insight into the significance of equations (12.2), we rearrange them as follows:

$$MR \cdot MPP_L = w \qquad (12.3)$$

$$MR \cdot MPP_T = r \qquad (12.4)$$

What is the economic meaning of these equations?

First, consider equation (12.3), which is the fundamental equilibrium condition for the employment of labor. Obviously, the right-hand side gives the wage rate (w), which represents the extra total cost per unit of extra labor, or the marginal cost of labor. The left-hand side ($MR \cdot MPP_L$) represents what is called the *marginal-revenue product* of labor (MRP_L), which is equal to the extra total revenue per extra unit of labor employed. When the firm increases its employment of labor by 1 unit, its total output increases by the marginal physical product of labor (MPP_L), and total revenue increases by the extra revenue per extra unit of output (i.e., MR) times the number of extra units of output (i.e., MPP_L).[1] For instance, if $MPP_L = 3$ and $MR = \$2$, $MRP_L = \$6$.

We therefore conclude that equation (12.3) requires the firm to increase its employment of labor until the extra revenue per extra unit of labor (i.e., MRP_L) equals the extra cost per extra unit of labor (i.e., the marginal cost of labor, or w). Surely, when $MRP_L > w$ the firm can increase its profit by hiring more labor, because some additional labor will add more to the firm's total revenue than it will add to its total cost. Conversely, when $MRP_L < w$ the firm can increase its profit by curtailing the employment of labor.

In the present case of perfect competition, $MR = AR = $ product's price. Hence $MRP_L = MR \cdot MPP_L = AR \cdot MPP_L$. Now the expression $AR \cdot MPP_L$ represents what is known as the *value of marginal product* of labor (VMP_L). In general, the latter concept (i.e., VMP_L) plays no role whatever in the analysis of the firm's equilibrium, but as will become clear in Chapter 13, its relationship to MRP_L is significant as a reflection of the competitive conditions in the firm's product market. Even though $VMP_L = MRP_L$ when the product market is perfectly competitive, we will continue to use the more significant concept of MRP_L.

Equation (12.4) is the fundamental equilibrium condition for the employment of land. Its interpretation is similar to that of equation (12.3). Thus equation (12.4) says that the firm must increase its employment of land until the *marginal-revenue product* of land ($MRP_T = MR \cdot MPP_T$) equals the marginal cost of land (r).

These conditions generalize easily to any number of factors of production. In general, the firm must increase the employment of each factor up to the point where its marginal-revenue product equals its marginal cost.

The Average-Revenue Product and the Decision to Produce a Positive Output

Finally, note that even when the foregoing marginal conditions are satisfied, the firm's maximum profit need not be positive—it may be negative. As we know, in the long run the firm will choose to close down rather than accept a negative profit. In the short run the firm will choose to produce a positive output (and thus employ positive amounts of labor and land) if, and only if, its total revenue is at least as high as its total variable cost. The latter condition can be conveniently specified in terms of the variable factor's *average-revenue product* (ARP).

The average revenue product of a factor, say labor, is defined as the firm's total revenue per unit of labor employed. That is,

---

[1]Analytically, we define $MRP_L = \Delta R/\Delta L$, where $R = pq = $ total revenue. But $\Delta R/\Delta L = (\Delta R/\Delta q)(\Delta q/\Delta L)$, where $\Delta R/\Delta q = MR$ and $\Delta q/\Delta L = MPP_L$. Accordingly, $MRP_L = MR \cdot MPP_L$.

$$ARP_L = \frac{R}{L} \tag{12.5}$$

where R is the total revenue. But total revenue is simply equal to average revenue (AR) times the quantity of output produced (q); that is, $R = AR \cdot q$. Accordingly, equation (12.5) can be rearranged as follows:

$$ARP_L = \frac{R}{L} = AR \cdot \frac{q}{L} = AR \cdot APP_L \tag{12.6}$$

where $APP_L = q/L$. In other words, the average-revenue product of labor is equal to the price of the product (AR) times the average physical product of labor (APP_L).

When labor is the only variable factor, the firm's total variable cost (V) is equal to the total wage bill; that is, $V = wL$. For the firm to be willing to remain in business, it is necessary that $R \geq V$, or $L \cdot ARP_L \geq wL$, or (dividing both sides of the last inequality by L)

$$ARP_L \geq w \tag{12.7}$$

Inequality (12.7) states that in the short run the firm will choose to produce a positive output (and thus employ a positive amount of labor) if, and only if, the average-revenue product of labor is at least as high as the wage rate.

Note that in the long run, the average-revenue product of labor must be much higher than the wage rate, because total revenue must be high enough to cover the total cost of all factors, not just the cost of labor.

12.3 The Firm's Short-Run Demand for Labor

We are now ready to derive the firm's demand curve for a factor of production, say, labor. To simplify the exposition, we begin in this section with a short-run setting where all other factors, besides labor, are fixed. We relax this assumption in Section 12.4.

The Curves of Marginal- and Average-Revenue Product

Figure 12.1 illustrates the curves of the average- and marginal-*revenue* product of labor. These curves are pictorially the same as the corresponding curves of the average and marginal *physical* product of labor (Figure 6.3), except for an appropriate change of vertical scale which reflects our current interest in values. For convenience, the hypothetical vertical scale of the physical product curves is retained on the right-hand side of the diagram. The construction of the left scale presupposes a product price of \$10. For instance, 6 units of output per unit of labor (right scale) translate into \$60 (i.e., \$10 $\times$ 6) per unit of labor (left scale).

The Firm's Demand for Labor

The firm's short-run demand curve for labor shows the quantity of labor which the firm is willing to purchase at each possible wage rate. It is easily obtained with the aid of Figure 12.1.

Suppose that the wage rate is \$60 per worker, as shown by the horizontal labor supply schedule labeled w_0. Following the analysis of the preceding section, it must be clear that the firm will employ 145 workers, as shown by point E where

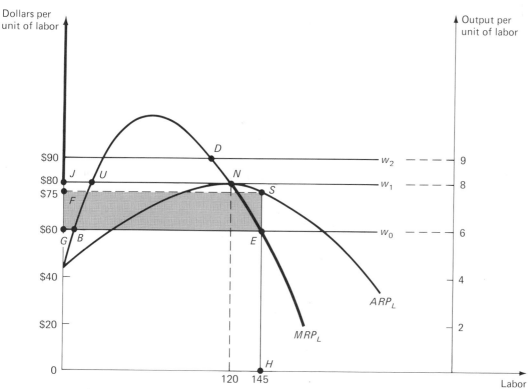

Figure 12.1 The firm's short-run demand curve for labor. When the wage rate is $60 per worker, as shown by horizontal labor supply schedule w_0, the firm maximizes its total profit by employing 145 workers, as shown by point E. The firm's total profit is equal to shaded area $GESF$ minus the total fixed cost. For wage rates lower than the maximum ARP_L (i.e., $80), the firm's demand for labor coincides with the MRP_L curve, as illustrated by the heavy line starting at N. For wage rates higher than $80, the demand for labor coincides with the vertical axis.

$MRP_L = \$60$. The firm's total wage bill will be $\$60 \times 145 = \$8700$, as indicated by the area of rectangle $OHEG$. The firm's total revenue, on the other hand, will be $\$75 \times 145 = \$10,875$, as shown by area $OHSF$. Shaded area $GESF$ (or $10,875 - \$8700 = \$2175$) shows the excess of total revenue over total variable cost. The firm's total profit is equal to shaded area $GESF$ (or $2175) minus the total fixed cost.

Note that all profit-maximization conditions are satisfied at point E. First, $MRP_L = w = \$60$. Second, the MRP_L curve is declining in the neighborhood of E. Thus, increasing the employment of labor above 145 workers causes the marginal-revenue product of labor to fall below the wage rate ($MRP_L < w$), and total profit declines. Conversely, if the firm employed less than 145 workers, it could increase its total profit by hiring more workers (because $MRP_L > w$). Finally, $ARP_L = \$75 > \$60 = w$, which implies that the firm's total revenue exceeds its total variable cost.

To appreciate the importance of the foregoing conditions, consider point B, where $MRP_L = \$60$ also. Because in the neighborhood of B the MRP_L curve is rising, the firm can augment its profit by either increasing or decreasing its employment of labor. In addition, at B the MRP_L curve lies above the ARP_L curve, which implies that $w = MRP_L > ARP_L$. Hence at B, total variable cost exceeds total revenue.

Next, suppose that the wage rate rises to $80. This case is illustrated by the horizontal labor supply curve w_1, which intersects the MRP_L curve at N (and U). Note that point N also happens to be the maximum point of the ARP_L curve. If the firm produces at all, it must hire 120 workers exactly, because at all other employment levels the average-revenue product of labor is lower than the wage rate ($ARP_L < w$). But at N the average-revenue product of labor is just equal to the wage rate ($ARP_L = w = \$80$). Hence the firm's total revenue ($ARP_L \times 120$) just equals its total variable cost ($\$80 \times 120$), and the firm suffers its maximum loss (total fixed cost). Accordingly, it is a matter of indifference to the firm whether it operates at N; it may alternatively shut down production altogether and incur exactly the same loss.

Should the wage rate rise above $80, the firm would immediately suspend production. This is illustrated in Figure 12.1 by the horizontal labor supply curve w_2, which corresponds to $w = \$90$. At D, $MRP_L = \$90$ and the MRP_L curve is negatively sloped. Yet the firm will shut down because, at D, $ARP_L < w = \$90$, which implies that $V > R$.

From the preceding discussion, we conclude that the firm's short-run demand curve for labor coincides with the vertical axis for all wage rates greater than the maximum average revenue product of labor, as shown by the heavy ray starting at point J. For all wage rates that are less than the maximum ARP_L, the firm's demand curve for labor coincides with the downward-sloping portion of its MRP_L curve, as illustrated by the heavy line starting at N. In the borderline case of a wage rate just equal to maximum ARP_L, there is a two-point indeterminacy: The firm may refuse to hire any labor (as indicated by point J), or it may employ the labor quantity indicated by point N (i.e., the maximum point of the ARP_L curve).

Observe that the firm's short-run demand curve for labor necessarily slopes downward. There are no exceptions here as with consumer demand.

12.4 The Firm's Long-Run Demand for Labor

In the long run, all factors are variable and the derivation of the firm's demand curve for labor is inherently more complex. The main reason lies in the fact that the marginal productivities of the various factors are interdependent. For instance, the marginal physical product of labor depends not only on the quantity of labor, but also on the associated employment of other factors, such as capital and land. Because of this, a change of the wage rate now leads to a variation in the quantities of other factors, which in turn shifts the marginal-physical-product curve of labor. Therefore, the demand curve for labor can no longer be identified with a unique MRP_L curve.

Factor Complementarity and Rivalry

Two factors are said to be *complementary* if an increase in the quantity of one of them *raises* the marginal physical product of the other. Complementarity signifies a mutually advantageous cooperation of factors, as illustrated by the following examples: computers and computer programmers, airplanes and pilots, bricklayers and bricks, and executives and secretaries.

Factor rivalry is the opposite of complementarity. It is often called "anticomplementarity," "inverted complementarity," "substitutability," or "competitiveness." Two factors are said to be *rival* if increased employment of one actually *reduces* the marginal physical product of the other. Rival factors are usually close substitutes of each other, as illustrated by the following examples: jumbo jets and small jets;

two similar, but slightly different, grades of labor (such as male and female workers); and electronic typewriters and word processors.

In the borderline case where a change in the employment of one factor has no effect whatsoever on the marginal physical product of the other, the two factors are called *independent* (or *neutral*). Factor independence means complete absence of any interaction between the two factors.

Note that factor complementarity and rivalry are *symmetrical* relationships. For instance, if labor is complementary to land (because MPP_L changes in the same direction as the quantity of land), land is automatically complementary to labor (i.e., MPP_T must necessarily change in the same direction as the quantity of labor). Similarly, if labor is rival to land, it is automatically true that land is rival to labor. The only proviso for this symmetry is that the production function is smoothly continuous.[2]

Derivation of the Long-Run Demand Curve for Labor

Suppose that the firm now uses two variable factors, labor (L) and land (T). The rent (r) for land services and the price of the firm's product are given. Also the firm's production function is assumed to remain unchanged throughout our discussion.

Initially, we suppose that the wage rate is at the level of w_1 and that the firm maximizes its total profit by employing the appropriate quantities of labor and land, say, L_1 and T_1, respectively. This initial equilibrium is illustrated by point A in Figure 12.2, where the schedule of the marginal-revenue product of labor, $MRP_L(T_1)$, is drawn on the assumption that the quantity of land is fixed at T_1.

Now let the wage rate fall to w_2. If the quantity of land remained unchanged, as in Figure 12.1, the firm would increase its employment of labor to L_2, as shown by point B on $MRP_L(T_1)$, and that would be the end of the matter. But in the present case, the increased employment of labor will cause the marginal-revenue product of land to rise or fall according to whether labor and land are complementary or rival factors, respectively, and it will be in the interests of the firm to adjust its employment of land also, which in turn will cause the entire MRP_L curve to shift. Therefore, the firm will adjust its employment of labor again; and so on. In principle, there will be an infinite number of such cycles, but the successive changes in the quantity of each factor will become smaller and smaller. As it turns out, the cumulative change of each factor will approach some finite limit, at which point equations (12.3) and (12.4) will be restored and the firm will again be in long-run equilibrium.

It is an important proposition that *whether labor and land are complementary or rival factors, the firm's adjustment of the employment of land in response to a wage-rate reduction, as described in the preceding paragraph, will always shift the entire MRP_L schedule to the right.* This is illustrated in Figure 12.2 by the $MRP_L(T_2)$ schedule, which is drawn on the assumption that the quantity of land has been completely adjusted from its initial magnitude of T_1 to its new equilibrium level at T_2. For the moment accept this proposition as true. When the wage rate drops to w_2, the firm's long-run equilibrium quantity of labor will increase to L_3, as indicated

---

[2]Mathematically, the rate of change of MPP_L (or $\partial q/\partial L$) with respect to T is given by the second-order cross-derivative $\partial(\partial q/\partial L)/\partial T = \partial^2 q/\partial L\,\partial T$. Similarly, the rate of change of MPP_T (or $\partial q/\partial T$) with respect to L corresponds to $\partial(\partial q/\partial T)/\partial L = \partial^2 q/\partial T\,\partial L$. As is well known, if $\partial q/\partial L$, $\partial q/\partial T$, and $\partial^2 q/\partial T\,\partial L$ are continuous, then $\partial^2 q/\partial T\,\partial L = \partial^2 q/\partial L\,\partial T$. The two factors are complementary, rival, or independent according to whether the common second-order cross-derivative is positive, negative, or zero, respectively. Because the second-order cross-derivatives are equal, it also follows that the quantitative measures of complementarity (or rivalry) are exactly the same.

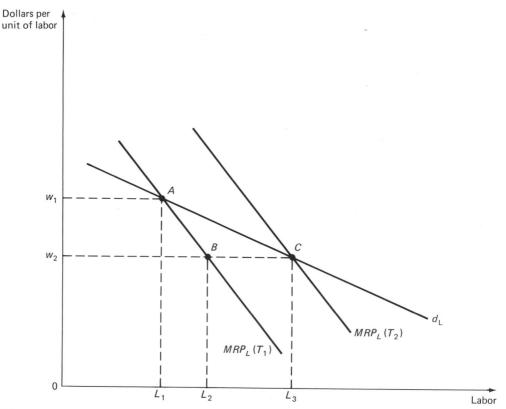

Figure 12.2 The firm's long-run demand curve for labor. When the wage rate is w_1, the firm employs L_1 and T_1 units of labor and land, respectively, as shown by point A on the $MRP_L(T_1)$ curve. As the wage rate falls to w_2, the firm adjusts its employment of land to T_2, causing the marginal revenue-product-of-labor curve to shift to $MRP_L(T_2)$; thus the firm increases its employment of labor to L_3 (not L_2), as shown by point C. The locus of all alternative points of long-run equilibrium, such as A and C, is the firm's long-run demand curve for labor, as indicated by the schedule labeled d_L.

by point C on the $MRP_L(T_2)$ schedule. The locus of all these alternative points of long-run equilibrium, such as points A and C, represents the firm's *long-run demand curve for labor* (d_L), as shown in Figure 12.2.

The most significant feature of the long-run demand curve for labor (d_L) is that it is flatter, or *more elastic*, than any of the MRP_L schedules at their respective points of intersection. For instance, d_L is more elastic than $MRP_L(T_1)$ at A; similarly, d_L is more elastic than $MRP_L(T_2)$ at C. Therefore, *the demand for labor (or any other variable factor) is more elastic in the long run* (where the quantities of all other "fixed" factors can also be optimally adjusted) than in the short run.

We now return to the proof of the main proposition concerning the rightward shift of the MRP_L schedule. Suppose first that labor and land are complementary factors. Following a wage-rate reduction, the firm initially increases its employment of labor, as shown in Figure 12.2 by the movement from A to B along the $MRP_L(T_1)$ schedule. Because labor and land are complementary factors by assumption, the initial increase of labor causes the schedule of the marginal physical product of land, and thus the MRP_T schedule, to shift upward and to the right, inducing the firm to *increase* its employment of land. As land increases, the MRP_L schedule shifts upward and to the right, prompting a further increase in the employment of labor; and so on. We therefore conclude that in the final equilibrium the firm hires more labor and more land. In terms of Figure 12.2, $L_3 > L_2 > L_1$ and $T_2 > T_1$.

What about rivalry? Do not fall into the trap of believing that because rivalry is the opposite of complementarity, the MRP_L schedule will shift downward and to the left (i.e., in a direction that is *opposite* to the one implied by complementarity). Let us see why such a conclusion is unwarranted. As w falls, the initial increase of labor now causes the schedule of the marginal physical product of land, and thus the MRP_T schedule, to shift downward and to the left, so that the quantity of land is *reduced*. Because rivalry is a symmetrical relationship, the reduction of land causes the marginal physical product of labor to *increase*, and the MRP_L schedule to shift upward and to the right, just as in the case of complementarity. The only difference now is that the successively relevant quantities of land are progressively smaller than the initial quantity of T_1. Thus, in the presence of rivalry, it must be true that $T_2 < T_1$.

In the borderline case where labor and land are independent factors, the interaction effect disappears completely, and the initial MRP_L schedule continues to represent the firm's long-run demand curve for labor, just as in the short-run case.

The analysis of this section and the preceding one shows conclusively that the demanded quantity of labor (or any other input for that matter) is inversely related to the wage rate (the input's price). A Giffen paradox (in which a reduction in the price of a commodity leads to a reduction in the quantity purchased by an individual consumer) cannot occur in the theory of the firm either in the short run or in the long run.

A Digression on Regressive Factors

Before concluding this section, we wish to comment briefly on a paradoxical phenomenon, which Sir John R. Hicks calls *regression*. Typically, one would expect a reduction in the price of an input to lead to an expansion of output, because of the concomitant cost reduction. This is no doubt the normal effect. But on some rare occasions, the cheapening of an input may actually lead to a *reduction* in output, in which case the cheapened input is called "regressive."

It is true, of course, that a reduction of an input price results in a cost reduction. But it is the *total* cost which is reduced, not necessarily the *marginal* cost. When the marginal cost falls *pari passu* with the total cost, output naturally expands. But marginal cost, being given by the *slope* of the total-cost curve, might increase while the total-cost curve shifts downward. When that happens, output contracts, and the cheapened input is said to be regressive.

The paradoxical phenomenon of regression is illustrated in Figure 12.3 in terms of the curves of total revenue (R) and total cost (C). Initially, the firm produces q_0 units of output and enjoys a maximum profit equal to vertical distance AB. As the price of a "regressive" input falls, the total-cost curve shifts downward, as shown by gray curve C'. Because the cheapened input is regressive, C' is actually steeper than C in the neighborhood of the initial output of q_0, implying an upward shift of the marginal-cost curve. As a result, the firm *reduces* its output to q_1 and enjoys a maximum profit equal to vertical distance DE.

Note that the phenomenon of regression can occur only in the long run. For instance, in the short run when only labor is a variable factor, a wage-rate reduction always reduces the short-run marginal cost (MC_s) in the vicinity of the initial output. This conclusion follows from the equality $MC_s = w/MPP_L$. As w falls, the ratio w/MPP_L also falls at each level of employment of labor; thus MC_s falls at each level of output including the initial output.

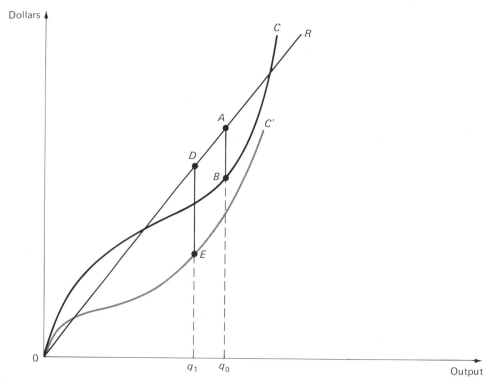

Figure 12.3 Regression. Initially, the firm produces q_0 and enjoys a maximum profit equal to vertical distance AB. As a "regressive" input becomes cheaper, the total-cost curve shifts downward, as shown by gray curve C'. Eventually, the firm reduces its output to q_1 and increases its profit to DE.

12.5 Industry Demand for Labor

The quantity of labor employed by an industry is the sum of the labor quantities employed by the industry's active firms. For this reason, it may appear that the industry demand curve for labor corresponds to the horizontal summation of the individual demand curves for labor of all active firms, just as the market demand curve for a commodity corresponds to the horizontal summation of the individual demand curves of all consumers. As shown in this section, such an inference is incorrect for several reasons, such as the product–price effect and the entry–exit effect.

The Product–Price Effect

Consider a perfectly competitive industry in *short-run* equilibrium. Assume that there are exactly n active firms in the industry. At the initial equilibrium product price (P_0), the typical firm's demand curve for labor is given in Figure 12.4, panel (a), by the curve labeled $d_L(P_0)$, which incidentally coincides with the firm's MRP_L curve (as in Figure 12.1). The curve labeled $\Sigma\, d_L(P_0)$ in panel (b) represents the horizontal summation of the individual demand curves for labor of the n active firms. For instance, at the current wage rate of w_0, the typical firm in panel (a) employs L_0 units of labor (point A), and the industry in panel (b) employs nL_0 (point A'). Evidently, point A' is a point on the industry demand curve for labor.

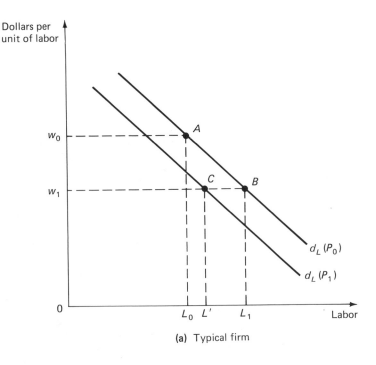

(a) Typical firm

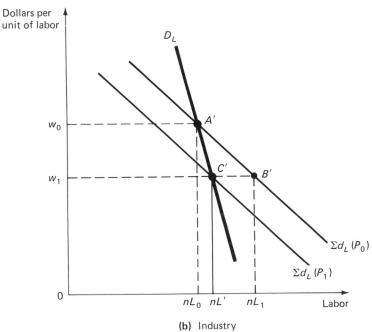

(b) Industry

Figure 12.4 The industry demand curve for labor. At the current product price P_0, $d_L(P_0)$ in panel (a) represents the typical firm's demand curve for labor; and $\Sigma\ d_L(P_0)$ in panel (b) represents the horizontal summation of the demand curves of n active firms. At the current wage rate w_0, the typical firm employs L_0 units of labor (point A), and the industry nL_0(point A'). As the wage rate falls to w_1, the industry's supply of the product increases, causing the product's price to fall to P_1. As a result, $d_L(P_0)$ shifts down to $d_L(P_1)$, and $\Sigma\ d_L(P_0)$ to $\Sigma\ d_L(P_1)$. At w_1, the typical firm employs L' units of labor (point C), and the industry nL'(point C'). The industry demand curve D_L is the locus of points such as A' and C', as shown in panel (b).

387

Let now the wage rate fall to w_1. Other things being equal, the typical firm would move along the initial demand curve, $d_L(P_0)$, to point B, increasing its employment of labor to L_1 units; and the entire industry would move along $\Sigma \, d_L(P_0)$ to point B', increasing aggregate employment to nL_1. But other things cannot remain equal. The increased employment of labor causes the output of the typical firm to increase; hence at the current product price of P_0, the aggregate output of the industry necessarily expands. This means that the wage-rate reduction causes the market supply curve of the commodity produced by the industry to shift to the right, generating a fall in the price of the product, as explained in Chapter 2. As the product price falls, the typical firm's demand curve for labor shifts downward and to the left.

Suppose that at the new equilibrium, the product price falls to P_1, and the typical firm's demand curve for labor shifts to the curve labeled $d_L(P_1)$. The corresponding horizontal summation of the $d_L(P_1)$ curves is now shown in panel (b) by the curve labeled $\Sigma \, d_L(P_1)$. Therefore, at the lower wage rate of w_1, the typical firm in panel (a) employs only L' units of labor (point C), and the industry in panel (b) employs nL' (point C'). Point C' is another point on the industry demand curve for labor.

By varying the wage rate and working as above, we can generate any number of points like A' and C'. The locus of all these points is, of course, the industry demand curve for labor (D_L), as shown in panel (b) by the heavy line passing through points A' and C'. The most significant feature of the industry demand curve for labor is the fact that it is steeper, or *less elastic,* than any of the horizontal-summation curves at their respective points of intersection.

The Entry–Exit Effect

In deriving the industry *long-run* demand curve for labor from the long-run demand curves for labor of the individual firms, we must again take into account the product–price effect, as illustrated in Figure 12.4. But this is not all, because now we must also take into consideration the entry of new firms (or the exit of old firms).

Return to Figure 12.4 and assume now that all curves are of the long-run variety. As the wage rate falls from w_0 to w_1, the long-run curves of the typical firm's average and marginal cost shift downward and thus production becomes more profitable. As the industry moves to its new long-run equilibrium, industry output expands while the product's price falls. Provided that the typical firm's optimal output does not overexpand (or, more precisely, it does not expand by the same or higher percentage than the growth rate of industry output), the new industry equilibrium will necessarily imply a larger number of active producers than the initial equilibrium (say, $n' > n$). The increase in the number of active producers will have the effect of mitigating the leftward shift of the summation curve $(\Sigma \, d_L)$, with the result that the industry demand curve for labor will be flatter (more elastic) than otherwise.

Other Effects

The product–price effect and the entry–exit effect do not exhaust all possibilities. For instance, the wage-rate reduction will also reduce the costs of other producers of both related and unrelated commodities. As the prices of these other commodities adjust to their new equilibrium levels, the market demand curve for this industry's product will almost surely shift (to the left or to the right depending on circumstances) with obvious consequences on both the product–price effect and the entry–exit effect. Furthermore, as the industry output expands, the industry employment of other factors (such as land and capital) will tend to rise, driving their prices up. Such factor-price changes will eventually affect all commodity and factor markets. We can now see more clearly why factor pricing can be satisfactorily analyzed only by general-equilibrium methods.

12.6 Determinants of the Elasticity of Derived Demand[3]

To measure the degree of responsiveness in the demand for labor to a change in the wage rate, we use the concept of (price) elasticity of demand for labor. The latter is defined and measured the same way as the (price) elasticity of demand for a consumer good. Accordingly,

$$\text{elasticity of labor demand} = \frac{\% \text{ change in quantity of labor}}{\% \text{ change in wage rate}}$$

and with obvious modifications, all the discussion in Section 2.6 becomes again relevant.

The elasticity of derived demand varies enormously from one input to another. What determines whether the elasticity of demand for some input (or factor) is high or low? We can conveniently summarize the determinants of the elasticity of derived demand in four propositions.

Proposition 1. *The demand for an input is more elastic, the larger is the elasticity of demand for the final product.*

The logic of this proposition is implicit in our earlier discussion in Section 12.5 in relation to the product–price effect and the construction of Figure 12.4. As the wage rate falls from w_0 to w_1, the product price falls from P_0 to P_1, causing the typical firm's demand curve to shift downward and to the left, as shown by $d_L(P_1)$ in panel (a). The industry as a whole moves from A' to C' in panel (b), as explained before. Had the final product's demand been a little more (less) elastic, the product price would have fallen by a little less (more); and the industry output as well as the employment of labor would have increased by a little more (less). Hence the industry demand for labor would have been a little more (less) elastic.

Proposition 2. *The demand for an input is more elastic, the more easily other inputs can be substituted for it.*

The relevant degree of substitutability between inputs in the present context concerns the curvature of isoquants, and it is properly measured by the *elasticity of substitution*, a concept that we discuss in Section 12.9. For the moment, we may note this: When the degree of substitutability between inputs is very low, a large change in the price of an input will result in a small change in its use (i.e., the elasticity of derived demand will be low). For instance, the 1973–1974 quadrupling in the price of oil did not immediately result in a substantial reduction in the use of oil, precisely because the degree of substitutability between oil and other energy sources (such as solar energy, nuclear energy, and coal) was very low.

Proposition 3. *The demand for an input is more elastic, the larger is the (price) supply elasticity of other factors.*

As we saw in Section 12.4, a wage-rate reduction increases in the long run not only the employment of labor, but also the employment of complementary factors, such

---

[3]This section can be read together with Section A12.2 of the Appendix to Chapter 12.

as land. However, in Section 12.4 we assumed that the rent for land services was fixed, or equivalently the supply of land was infinitely elastic. What difference does it make to the elasticity of demand for labor if the supply of land is less than infinitely elastic and the rent rises? We can consider the increase of the rent as a separate change and ask how it affects the employment of labor. Because complementarity is a symmetrical relationship, we can easily conclude that an increase in the rent leads to a *reduction* in the employment of labor at the current wage rate, just as a wage-rate reduction leads to an increase in the employment of land. We therefore conclude that when the (price) supply elasticity of land is less than infinite, a given wage-rate reduction will lead to a smaller increase in the employment of labor; that is, the demand for labor will be less elastic.

Proposition 4. *The demand for an input is more elastic in the long run than in the short run.*

This proposition is related to Proposition 2. The degree of substitutability between inputs is greater in the long run than in the short run because it takes time to adjust fully to an input-price change. When this observation is combined with Proposition 2, Proposition 4 follows easily. As we explained in Section 12.4, the firm's demand for labor is likely to be more elastic in the long run. The recent painful adjustment of industry around the world to the skyrocketing price of oil serves as a strong reminder of Proposition 4.

12.7 The Supply of Factors of Production

Having completed our discussion of factor demand, we now turn briefly to factor supply. For most purposes, economists adopt the convenient assumption that the supply curves of factors of production are perfectly inelastic (or vertical); that is, the total factor quantities, such as the total amounts of land, labor, and capital offered for sale, are fixed. This simplifying assumption is useful because it enables us to establish nearly all important propositions in the theory of distribution without having to introduce unnecessary complications. Because we shall use this assumption repeatedly in the rest of this book, we think it is appropriate in this section to make some general observations concerning the true shape of factor supply curves.

Our present discussion is limited to the supply of labor. The supply of intermediate goods (i.e., goods produced by the economic system itself and used as inputs in the production of other commodities, such as coal used in the production of steel) is governed by the general principles of supply of commodities, discussed in Chapter 9, and needs no further discussion. The supply of land is discussed in Section 12.8.

To avoid confusion, it is important to distinguish among three different types of factor supply curves: (1) the aggregate factor supply to the *economy* as a whole, (2) the factor supply facing a particular *industry,* and (3) the factor supply facing a particular firm. We illustrate these concepts below in relation to the supply of labor.

In Section 5.1 we explained how the labor supply curve of the individual worker is derived. Basically, the individual worker divides her available time between work and leisure in such a way as to maximize her utility, given her preferences and the wage rate (which is the opportunity cost of leisure). Typically, the individual labor supply curve is backward-bending (Figure 5.4).

To obtain the aggregate supply of labor *to the economy as a whole,* we merely add horizontally all individual labor supply curves. Because each individual labor supply curve is backward bending, the aggregate labor supply is also likely to be backward bending.

Incidentally, in the early nineteenth century economists believed that the long-run aggregate labor supply curve was horizontal (infinitely elastic) at the minimum subsistence wage rate. The basis for this "iron law of wages" was the belief that any rise in wages above the subsistence level would always bring about such an increase in population as to force wages down to the level of subsistence.[4] As is well known, the iron law has been contradicted by the facts and has long ceased to be the accepted view. At least in the more advanced countries of the world, wages have increased substantially during the twentieth century. Yet in Europe and North America birth rates dipped below 20 per thousand and were the lowest on the planet.

The supply of labor facing a particular industry (or type of employment) does not necessarily have the same characteristics (or shape) as the aggregate labor supply curve. Typically, the supply of labor confronting a particular industry is *much more elastic* than the aggregate supply of labor. For instance, suppose that an increase in wages actually *reduces* the aggregate supply of labor, because the economy is currently operating on the backward-bending portion of the aggregate supply curve. This does not mean that the supply of, say, weavers to the clothing industry is also backward bending. An increase in the wage rate paid to weavers would certainly attract to weaving workers from many other sectors of the economy, causing the supply curve of weavers to be upward sloping. Indeed, if the number of weavers is only a negligible fraction of the total labor force, the supply of weavers may be horizontal (infinitely elastic).

Finally, the labor supply curve facing a perfectly competitive firm is infinitely elastic (i.e., horizontal at the current wage rate). We used this supply curve repeatedly in this book in all those cases where we assumed that the wage rate paid by the individual competitive firm was fixed.

The reader should be able to distinguish among the various labor supply curves discussed in this chapter: the labor supply curve of an individual worker, the aggregate labor supply curve (economywide), the labor supply curve facing a particular industry, and the labor supply curve facing a firm.

12.8 The Theory of Rent

During the Napoleonic Wars food prices rose considerably, causing a sharp increase in rents. At that time, most people (trapped by the misleading impression that there is just a one-way cause-and-effect relationship from cost to price) attributed the high food prices to the high rents and felt that landlords were profiting from the misfortunes of the rest of society. David Ricardo (1772–1823) disagreed and argued convincingly that "corn is not high because a rent is paid, but a rent is paid because corn is high." The marginal productivity theory was largely an outgrowth of the Ricardian theory of rent.

In this section we begin with the Ricardian theory of rent, which treats rent as the return to the factor "land" whose supply is perfectly inelastic (or fixed). Then we generalize the analysis to any other factor, besides land, whose supply happens to be inelastic or imperfectly elastic.

The Supply of Land

Ricardo claimed that rent is a payment for the "original and indestructible powers of the soil," such as fertility, location, and mineral content. But the powers of the soil are neither original nor indestructible. The present landscape of most countries combines not only what nature has given, but also the human effort and capital investment that has been expended throughout the ages to reshape and improve

---

[4]The term "iron law of wages" was coined by Ferdinand Lassalle (1825–1864), a German socialist writer.

the original gift of nature. Furthermore, the supply of fertile land is not inexhaustible, and its productive power can be maintained only by continuing human effort and sacrifice.

What Ricardo really meant by his nebulous phrase is that land has the special property that in its fundamental sense as location and area, its supply to the economy is fixed. Additional land cannot be produced by the economic system in response to a greater demand for it. Reclamation of land from the sea is not quantitatively important and could be safely ignored. For all practical purposes, the supply of land is vertical (perfectly inelastic).

The Ricardo–Viner Model

We can illustrate the Ricardian theory of rent by means of a simplified model developed by the late Jacob Viner (1892–1970) and known as the Ricardo–Viner model. Consider a perfectly competitive industry producing a particular species of grape which requires a special type of vineyard land. Assume that this land is homogeneous, absolutely fixed in supply (say, 1000 acres), totally valueless in any other use, and widely owned (so that each landowner is a price taker). All other factors used by this industry, such as labor, capital equipment, and fertilizer, are available in perfectly elastic supply (i.e., at fixed prices). It is also convenient (but not necessary) to assume that each firm in the industry always chooses to cultivate a unique quantity of land (say, 1 acre) under all circumstances. Accordingly, there can never be more than 1000 active firms in the industry at any one time. Finally, assume that all firms have the same set of long-run cost curves.

In Figure 12.5, panel (a), the long-run average cost curve (AC) of the typical firm is drawn on the assumption that the vineyard land is available at zero rent. At the specific price of \$100 per wagonload of grapes (which coincides with the minimum AC), the output of the typical firm is exactly 5 wagonloads (point N); thus the *maximum* output of the industry is 5000 wagonloads, as shown by point N' in panel (b). Note that point N' is the terminal point of the horizontal stretch of the long-run industry supply curve S. Initially, suppose that at the price of \$100, the quantity of grapes demanded is exactly 5000 wagonloads, as indicated by industry demand curve $D_0 D_0'$. Thus initially, all potential producers are active and all the available vineyard land is used to produce grapes, even though the rent is zero.

For the moment, continue to assume that the vineyard land is available at zero rent and draw in panel (b) the long-run industry supply curve (S) by summing horizontally the long-run supply curves of all active firms, as explained in Chapter 9. (Recall that the typical firm's long-run supply curve coincides with the MC curve above point N, that is, the minimum point of AC.) Now let the industry demand curve shift to the right, as shown by $D_1 D_1'$, causing equilibrium to shift to F'. Evidently, the price of grapes will rise to \$150 and the industry output will expand to 6000 wagonloads. At the higher price of \$150, the typical firm will increase its output to 6 wagonloads, as indicated by point F in panel (a).

It should be obvious from panel (a) that if the rent of vineyard land were to continue to be zero, each firm would be able to make a positive profit equal to \$240, that is, $6 \times (\$150 - \$110)$. Can these profits be maintained? Certainly not, because the existence of positive profits would attract into the industry any number of potential producers who would be willing to pay *higher* rents for the scarce parcels of vineyard land. Competition among grape growers will continue to push rents higher and higher until all profits are completely eliminated. Because each firm's long-run equilibrium quantity of vineyard land remains constant by assumption, the extra rent paid by each firm is similar to an increase of just *fixed* cost in the short run; thus each firm's MC curve stays the same while its AC curve shifts upward, as shown by dashed curve AC^1 in panel (a). The new minimum AC occurs now at point F on the original MC curve.

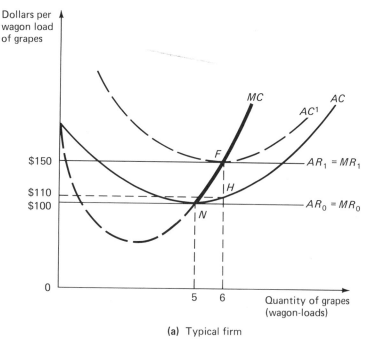

(a) Typical firm

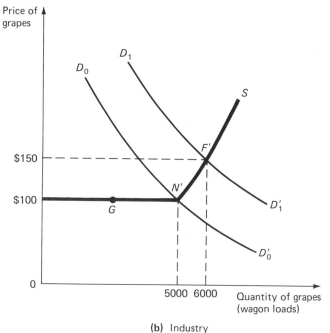

(b) Industry

Figure 12.5 The Ricardo–Viner Model. *AC* in panel (a) is drawn on the assumption that the rent for land is zero. The heavily drawn industry supply *S* in panel (b) is the horizontal summation of the long-run supply curves of 1000 active producers. As the industry demand increases from $D_0 D_0'$ to $D_1 D_1'$, the price of grapes rises from \$100 to \$150 per wagonload. The typical firm increases its output to 6 wagonloads, as shown by point *F*. If the rent were to continue to be zero, the typical firm would enjoy a profit of \$240, that is, $6 \times (\$150 - \$110)$. However, competition among grape growers raises the rent to exactly \$240 and eliminates all profits. As the rent rises, *AC* shifts upward, as shown by dashed AC^1.

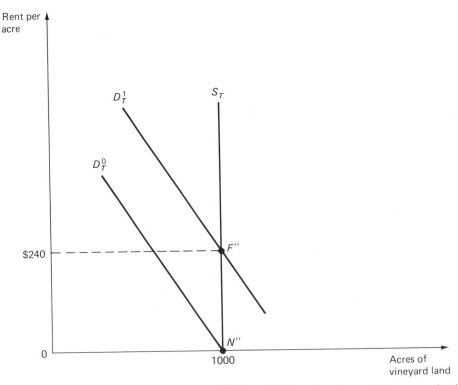

Figure 12.6 The market for vineyard land. When the industry demand for grapes is given by D_0D_0' in Figure 12.5, the industry demand for land coincides with D_T^0, implying a zero rent. As the demand for grapes increases to D_1D_1', the demand for land shifts to D_T^1, causing rent to rise to $240, as shown by point F'''.

Figure 12.6 gives the corresponding supply and demand situations in the rental market for vineyard land. The vertical supply schedule S_T reflects the fact that there are just 1000 acres of homogeneous vineyard land. When the demand for grapes is given by D_0D_0' in Figure 12.5, panel (b), the industry demand for land coincides with D_T^0 in Figure 12.6; thus equilibrium in the market for vineyard land occurs at N'', which implies a zero rent. As the demand for grapes increases to D_1D_1', the industry demand for land shifts upward to D_T^1, and equilibrium shifts to F'', where the rent per acre of land is $240. Note that the figure of $240 corresponds to the rent paid by the typical firm in Figure 12.5, panel (a).

Differential Rents

Ricardo himself did not assume that all land is homogeneous. Rather, he assumed that different parcels of land differ in fertility. This type of situation is said to cause *differential rents*. Rent is different on each grade of land, with more fertile land commanding a higher rent than less fertile land.

Ricardo's model of differential rents is technically similar to the case, studied in Section 9.5, where the entrepreneurial factor instead is not homogeneous. The only insignificant difference is that the intramarginal firms (or parcels of land) now earn differential rent instead of profit. (As explained below, the differential profit of Section 9.5 is actually economic rent accruing to the imperfectly supplied entrepreneurial talent.) The market price of the particular crop produced is again equal to the costs of the marginal parcel of land (i.e., the most infertile parcel of land farmed). Surely, the marginal land pays no rent.

We must be careful not to attribute rent to the existence of inferior land. On the contrary, rent is due to the scarcity of existing land. What the availability of inferior (less fertile) land does is merely to set a limit to the rent that can be earned on the most fertile land.

Transfer Earnings and Economic Rent

So far we have been assuming that land is "specific" to one crop (grape). Because such land is valueless for any other use, it has no place else to go, and it will always work for whatever it can earn in the grape industry. There is no need for grape growers to make any payments to keep land in the grape industry. This situation is not realistic, however.

Typically, land can produce more than one crop, such as grape, corn, wheat, and rye. To remain in the grape industry, land must be paid at least as much as it can earn in its best possible alternative employment. For instance, if 1 acre of land could earn $500 per year in the wheat industry, it would not remain in the grape industry unless it was paid at least $500. This minimum income ($500) is known as the land's *transfer earnings* (or *transfer price*).

More generally, by transfer earnings of a factor of production we mean the price at which the factor is indifferent between transferring into or out of some type of employment. From another angle, transfer earnings of a factor is the income forgone by not being employed in its best alternative use; that is, *transfer earnings is the opportunity cost of the factor.* Any payment to a factor of production in excess of its transfer earnings is a surplus called *economic rent.* Because economic rent is not a payment that is necessary for keeping the factor in its present employment, *it can be taxed away without affecting the allocation of resources.*

Pure economic rent is not a true, price-determining cost; but whether a factor's income (or some part of it) is economic rent depends on the viewpoint. For instance, suppose that land is perfectly inelastic (vertical) from the point of view of the economy as a whole. This means that for the economy as a whole, land has no alternative use and its transfer earnings are zero; thus all its income, if any, is economic rent.

Now look at the problem from the point of view of a small industry that faces a *perfectly elastic* (horizontal) supply of land. To keep land from transferring to its next best use, the small industry must pay the market price (rental). Accordingly, from the point of view of the small industry the entire income of land is transfer earnings, a true element of cost; thus land earns no economic rent at all. Similarly, from the point of view of an individual farmer who is a price taker, the entire payment for land services is a cost—the cost of keeping the land from transferring to someone else.

The Modern Theory of Rent

Ricardo limited his theory of rent to land, presumably the only factor fixed in available supply to society. But as we observed above, the supply of land is *not* fixed (perfectly inelastic). Furthermore, the supplies of other factors, such as skilled labor of a particular grade (physicists, surgeons, or computer programmers), may be fixed at least in the short run. The theory of rent is applicable to all such cases. More generally, the theory of rent is applicable to any factor whose supply is not perfectly elastic in the relevant economic context.

It was in this connection that Marshall extended the doctrine of Ricardian rent to embrace what he called "quasi-rent." Marshall observed that machines and other capital goods are highly specific factors whose supply is temporarily fixed. In the short run, such factors (inputs) cannot transfer to any other employment; that is, their transfer earnings are zero. Accordingly, in the short run the returns to such fixed factors are similar to Ricardian rent, or as Marshall put it, the earnings of fixed factors are quasi-rents. The Ricardian principles are applicable to such cases as well.

12.9 The One-Sector Model of Income Distribution

In this section we present a simplified macroeconomic model of income distribution. The foundation of this model is an aggregate production function for the economy as a whole, relating total output to the quantities of the factors employed. The *elasticity of substitution,* a new concept defined below, also plays a crucial role in this model.

The Aggregate Production Function

We now shift our attention from the individual firm (or industry) to the entire economy. To avoid unnecessary detail, we throw away our microscope and instead concentrate on the economy's three important aggregates: total labor, total capital, and total output. Generalizing from the theory of the firm, we postulate an aggregate production function

$$Q = F(L, K) \qquad (12.8)$$

relating total output (Q) to the total quantities of labor (L) and capital (K). This procedure is wrought with difficulties; yet it is useful in giving a broad picture of the entire economy. As the saying goes, we sacrifice the individual trees for the view of the entire forest.

We assume that both labor and capital are homogeneous factors, but labor is a primary factor (produced outside the economic system), while capital represents means of production produced by the economic system itself. Accordingly, we view capital as made of the same stuff as output. For simplicity, we assume that the quantities of labor and capital are fixed; that is, their supply schedules are perfectly inelastic (vertical).

As noted earlier in this chapter, it is necessary to distinguish between the *services* of factors sold in the market and the quantities of the factors themselves. The former (factor services) are *flows* (having the dimensions of quantity per unit of time), whereas the latter are *stocks.* We assume that the flow of services deriving from a factor is strictly proportional to the size of its stock. Surely, the arguments in the aggregate production function, L and K, represent the flows of labor services and capital services, respectively. (The terms "capital" and "capital services" as well as "labor" and "labor services" are used interchangeably where there is no possibility of confusion.)

Finally, we assume that the aggregate production function exhibits constant returns to scale: Total output increases in the same proportion as the total quantities of labor and capital employed. For instance, when L and K double, Q also doubles. As explained in Section 6.7, the assumption of constant returns to scale implies that the marginal physical product of each factor as well as the ratio of marginal products (i.e., the marginal rate of technical substitution) depend only on the proportion in which the two factors are employed. Graphically, the isoquants of the aggregate production function have the same slope along rays drawn from the origin. The entire isoquant map is a blown-up version of the unit isoquant.

In our formulation, land and natural resources are implicitly held constant; thus they are left out of the aggregate production. Because of this, a nineteenth-century follower of Malthus and Ricardo would expect our aggregate production function to exhibit diminishing (not constant) returns to scale. Yet most economists today ignore this possibility, because land's significance has declined sharply. For instance, in the United States land's contribution has declined to about 50 percent of its magnitude at the turn of the century. Land's present contribution is estimated around 5 percent for the entire economy, and much less for manufacturing alone.

The Geometry of Income Distribution[5]

Suppose that the economy uses L_0 units of homogeneous labor and K_0 units of homogeneous capital and produces Q_0 units of output per unit of time (year). This situation is depicted in Figure 12.7, where point E (whose coordinates indicate the given quantities of labor and capital) lies on the isoquant labeled Q_0.

We assume that competition ensures that the two factors are paid their marginal products. Thus

$$w = p \cdot MPP_L \tag{12.9}$$

$$r = p \cdot MPP_K \tag{12.10}$$

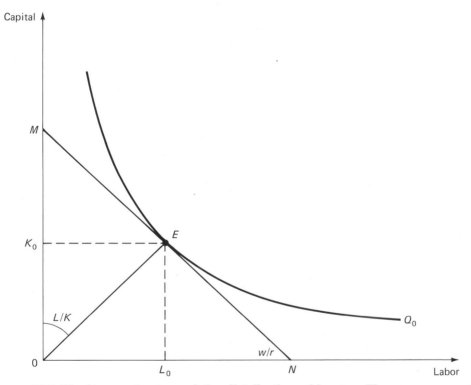

Figure 12.7 The isoquant map and the distribution of income. The economy uses L_0 units of labor and K_0 units of capital and produces Q_0 units of output. The absolute slope of (isocost) line MN, which is tangent to isoquant Q_0 at E, gives the equilibrium wage-rent ratio. Labor's absolute share is given by $0L_0$ in labor terms, and K_0M in capital terms. Similarly, capital's absolute share is given by OK_0 in capital terms, and L_0N in labor terms. The relative share of labor is $0L_0/0N$, or $K_0M/0M$. Finally, the relative share of capital is $L_0N/0N$, or $0K_0/0M$.

---

[5]This subsection could be read together with Section A12.3 of the Appendix to Chapter 12.

where w is the money wage rate, r the rental rate for capital services, and p the nominal (money) price of output. Equations (12.9) and (12.10) correspond to equations (12.3) and (12.4), because under perfect competition price equals marginal revenue ($p = MR$). Accordingly, the factor/price ratio w/r equals the ratio of marginal products MPP_L/MPP_K, which corresponds to the slope of isoquant Q_0 at point E.

It is an important proposition that the sum of the total income of labor (wL_0) plus the total income of capital (rK_0) equals the value of total output (pQ_0); that is,

$$pQ_0 = wL_0 + rK_0 \qquad (12.11)$$

The proof of equation (12.11) is simple. Thus, by a simple substitution from equations (12.9) and (12.10), $wL_0 + rK_0 = p \cdot MPP_L \cdot L_0 + p \cdot MPP_K \cdot K_0 = p(MPP_L \cdot L_0 + MPP_K \cdot K_0)$. Now equation (12.11) follows at once because $MPP_L \cdot L_0 + MPP_K \cdot K_0 = Q_0$, as implied by Euler's theorem discussed in Section 6.7 [see equation (6.7)].

It is important to distinguish between the *absolute shares* and the *relative shares* of the factors in the total output. The absolute share of a factor is its total income; its relative share is its absolute share divided by the total output. Expressing all shares in real terms, we have

$$\text{labor's absolute share} = \frac{wL_0}{p} = MPP_L \cdot L_0$$

$$\text{labor's relative share} = \frac{wL_0}{pQ_0} = \frac{MPP_L \cdot L_0}{Q_0} = \frac{MPP_L}{APP_L}$$

$$\text{capital's absolute share} = \frac{rK_0}{p} = MPP_K \cdot K_0 \qquad (12.12)$$

$$\text{capital's relative share} = \frac{rK_0}{pQ_0} = \frac{MPP_K \cdot K_0}{Q_0} = \frac{MPP_K}{APP_K}$$

Dividing both sides of equation (12.11) by pQ_0, we also obtain

$$1 = \frac{wL_0}{pQ_0} + \frac{rK_0}{pQ_0} \qquad .$$

or

$$\text{labor's relative share + capital's relative share} = 1 \qquad (12.13)$$

That is, the sum of the relative shares equals unity.

Now return to Figure 12.7 and observe that the line MN, which has all the properties of an isocost line, is tangent to isoquant Q_0 at employment point E. The absolute slope of MN gives the equilibrium factor-price ratio w/r, as shown. Because the total cost of output is identically equal to total income ($wL_0 + rK_0$), horizontal distance $0N$ corresponds to total income expressed in terms of labor; that is,

$$\text{total income in terms of labor} = \frac{wL_0 + rK_0}{w} = L_0 + \left(\frac{r}{w}\right)K_0 = 0L_0 + L_0N$$

But $0L_0$ is the value of labor's income in terms of labor (i.e., $wL_0/w = L_0$), and L_0N is the value of capital's income in terms of labor (i.e., rK_0/w). Accordingly, the relative share of labor in total income is $0L_0/0N$, and the relative share of capital in total income is $L_0N/0N$.[6]

Alternatively, expressing total income and income shares in terms of capital, we have $0M$ = total income, $0K_0$ = capital's total income (or absolute share), and K_0M = labor's total income (or absolute share). Furthermore, capital's relative share = $0K_0/0M = L_0N/0N$ and labor's relative share = $K_0M/0M = 0L_0/0N$.

An alternative presentation of the functional distribution of income is in terms of the curves of the marginal physical product of each factor, as shown in Figure 12.8. Panel (a) gives the curve of the marginal physical product of labor derived from the aggregate production function on the assumption that the capital stock remains constant at the level K_0. Because of constant returns to scale and the implicit assumption that isoquants are convex to the origin, the $MPP_L(K_0)$ curve exhibits diminishing returns (negative slope) right from the start. When L_0 units of labor are employed (together with K_0 units of capital, of course), the marginal physical product of labor is given by distance $0A$ (or L_0C), as indicated by point C. Hence labor's absolute share in real terms ($wL_0/p = MPP_L \cdot L_0$) coincides with the area of rectangle $0ACL_0$. As explained in Section 6.3, total output is given by the area under the $MPP_L(K_0)$ curve; that is, total output = area $0BCL_0$. Accordingly, capital's absolute share is necessarily equal to the residual triangular area ABC.

Panel (b) reverses the roles of the two factors. Labor is now kept fixed at L_0, and increasing amounts of capital generate a diminishing marginal physical product of capital, as shown by the $MPP_K(L_0)$ curve. When K_0 units of capital are employed, capital's absolute share in real terms ($rK_0/p = MPP_K \cdot K_0$) is given by the area of rectangle $0DFK_0$ while labor's absolute share (in real terms) coincides with the residual triangular area DEF.

Figure 12.8 establishes the complete symmetry of the factors. When this diagram is properly drawn, it is always true that area $0ACL_0$ in panel (a) equals residual area DEF in panel (b), and area $0DFK_0$ in panel (b) equals residual area ABC in panel (a). It is therefore evident that all factors have their distributive income shares determined simultaneously by their respective interdependent marginal physical products.

The Effects of Factor Growth

How does an increase of labor (or capital) affect the absolute and relative shares of the factors in the total product? Can labor growth actually reduce the absolute share of labor ($L \cdot MPP_L$)? Its relative share ($L \cdot MPP_L/Q$)?

It should be evident from Figure 12.8 that increasing the quantity of one factor must increase the absolute share of the other factor. For instance, when labor increases from L_0 to L_1, capital's absolute share expands from residual triangular

---

[6]Labor's relative share (wL_0/pQ_0) is equal to its marginal physical product divided by its average physical product. Thus labor's relative share = $wL_0/pQ_0 = MPP_L \cdot L_0/Q_0 = MPP_L/APP_L$. Furthermore, labor's relative share is equal to the elasticity of output with respect to labor (ϵ_L):

$$\text{labor's relative share} = \frac{MPP_L}{APP_L} = \frac{\partial Q}{\partial L}\frac{L_0}{Q_0} = \epsilon_L$$

Similar relationships hold for capital as well. Thus capital's relative share (rK_0/pQ_0) is equal to its marginal physical product divided by its average product; it is also equal to the elasticity of output with respect to capital.

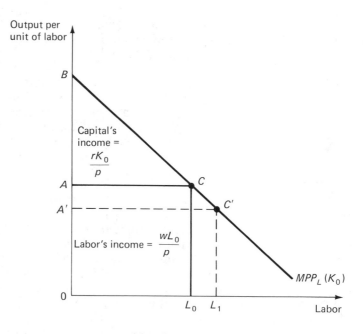

(a) Capital's income as a residual

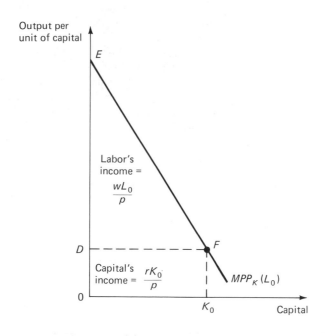

(b) Labor's income as a residual

Figure 12.8 The income distribution in terms of the marginal product curves. The $MPP_L(K_0)$ curve in panel (a) is derived from the aggregate production function on the assumption that capital is fixed at K_0. Labor's absolute share is given by area $0L_0CA$, and capital's absolute share by area ABC. In panel (b), the $MPP_K(L_0)$ curve is derived on the assumption that labor is fixed at L_0. The absolute shares of capital and labor are given by areas $0DFK_0$ and DEF, respectively.

400

area ABC to $A'BC'$, as shown in panel (a). However, the effects of labor growth on the absolute and relative shares of labor as well as the relative share of capital depend crucially on the characteristics of the aggregate production function. No possibility can be ruled out a priori except one: If the absolute share of labor (the augmented factor) does not rise, its relative share must fall. That is, if $L \cdot MPP_L$ falls or remains the same while Q rises, labor's relative share $L \cdot MPP_L/Q$ must fall.

We can easily infer from Figure 12.8, panel (a), what happens to the absolute share of labor (the augmented factor) if we know the elasticity of the $MPP_L(K_0)$ curve at the initial point (C), which is actually the *elasticity of demand for labor*. This relationship is the same as that between the elasticity of demand for a commodity and total revenue, studied in Section 2.6. Consequently, the absolute share of labor (the augmented factor) increases, remains unchanged, or decreases according to whether the elasticity of demand for labor is greater than, equal to, or smaller than unity.

When the interest lies in the effects of factor growth on the *relative* shares of the factors, the relevant parameter is the *elasticity of substitution*.

The Elasticity of Substitution[7]

Recall that under constant returns to scale the marginal rate of substitution of labor for capital (MRS_{LK}) depends only on the proportion (L/K) in which the factors are used, *not* their absolute quantities (L and K). Because of the law of diminishing marginal rate of substitution, MRS_{LK} is a *decreasing* function of L/K, as the reader can verify by inspecting Figure 12.7. But $MRS_{LK} = w/r$ (for cost minimization). Therefore, in the final analysis, the factor/price ratio $w/r = \phi$ is a decreasing function of the labor/capital ratio $L/K = \rho$, as shown in Figure 12.9.

Given the economy's labor/capital ratio, $L_0/K_0 = \rho_0$, we can determine directly from Figure 12.9 the equilibrium wage/rent ratio, $w_0/r_0 = \phi_0$, as shown by point E. Evidently, the product $(w_0/r_0)(L_0/K_0) = \phi_0\rho_0$, which corresponds to the shaded rectangular area under the functional relationship, equals the share of labor divided by the share of capital. Just as with an ordinary demand curve, that shaded area will increase, remain the same, or decrease as the labor/capital ratio (ρ) increases according to whether the elasticity of the functional relationship is greater than, equal to, or less than unity. The elasticity of substitution is none other than the elasticity of the functional relationship between ϕ and ρ depicted in Figure 12.9.

More formally, the elasticity of substitution (σ) is defined as follows:

$$\sigma = -\frac{\phi}{\rho}\frac{d\rho}{d\phi} \tag{12.14}$$

By definition, the elasticity of substitution is nonnegative, and its value may vary from zero to infinity.

The elasticity of substitution is zero in the case of *fixed coefficients of production*. In this case the isoquants are L-shaped and the two factors are always used in the same proportion (ρ) irrespective of the wage/rent ratio (ϕ). Hence the functional relationship between ϕ and ρ becomes vertical (perfectly inelastic).

At the other extreme, the elasticity of substitution becomes infinite when the isoquants are straight lines, so that MRS_{LK} (and thus ϕ) does not change as ρ varies. In this case, the functional relationship between ϕ and ρ becomes horizontal (perfectly elastic).

The elasticity of substitution is very useful in the study of the effect of changes

---

[7]This section could be read together with Section A12.1 of the Appendix to Chapter 12.

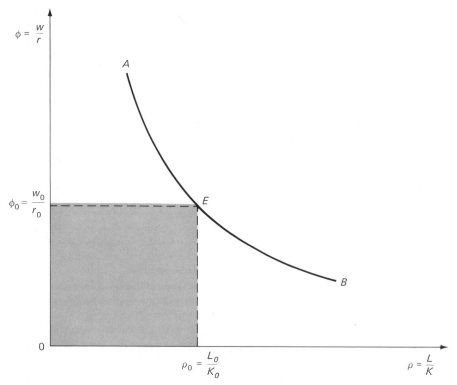

Figure 12.9 The elasticity of substitution. Because of constant returns to scale, the factor/price ratio $\phi = w/r$ is a decreasing function of the labor/capital ratio $\rho = L/K$, as shown by curve AB. The elasticity of curve AB at a point, such as E, is known as the elasticity of substitution. The shaded rectangular area gives the ratio of labor's relative share to capital's relative share. As ρ increases, that shaded area (ratio of relative shares) increases, remains the same, or decreases according to whether the elasticity of substitution is greater than, equal to, or less than unity.

in the labor/capital ratio on relative income shares. There exists a substantial amount of empirical evidence, suggesting that the relative income share of labor has remained relatively constant over a long period of time (at approximately 75 percent). For this reason many economists believe that the elasticity of substitution is unity, but there is no unanimity of opinion. Whether the elasticity of substitution is or is not equal to unity is an empirical matter. There is no a priori justification for making the assumption that $\sigma = 1$.

12.10 Selected Empirical Applications

We conclude this chapter with two empirical applications. The first application deals with the functional distribution of income of the United States for two recent years. The second application discusses the emergence of economic rents in the production of Wyoming coal in the 1970s.

The Functional Distribution of Income in the U.S. Economy

Table 12.1 presents both the absolute and relative income shares of the various factors of production in the U.S. economy for 1982 and 1983. Compensation of employees includes not only wages, but also benefits, such as health insurance and

Table 12.1 Income Distribution in the U.S. Economy				
	1982		1983	
Categories of Income	Billions of Dollars	Percent[a]	Billions of Dollars	Percent[a]
Compensation of employees	1865.7	76.14	1990.2	75.10
Proprietors' income	109.0	4.45	128.5	4.84
Rental income	49.9	2.04	54.8	2.07
Corporate profits	164.8	6.73	229.1	8.64
Net interest	261.1	10.66	247.5	9.34
National income	2450.4	100.00	2650.1	100.00

Source: Survey of Current Business, March 1984.

[a]Sums of percentages are not equal to 100.00 because of rounding.

contributions to pension funds and social security. This is by far the largest category of income. In both 1982 and 1983 compensation of employees accounted for over 75 percent of U.S. national income.

Proprietors' income refers to the income of unincorporated enterprises, such as small businesses, farms, partnerships, and professions. About one-fifth of the total proprietors' income was farm income. Typically, proprietors' income, which in 1982 and 1983 accounted for less than 5 percent of U.S. national income, includes (1) the wages for the labor put into the businesses by their owners, and (2) the return on the owners' investment in those businesses. Empirically, it is difficult to separate these two components of proprietors' income.

Rental income includes rents paid to persons, the imputed rent for owner-occupied housing, and income from patents and royalties. It is not a significant category of income. For 1982 and 1983, rental income accounted for a little over 2 percent of U.S. national income.

Corporate profit is the return on capital (machines, buildings, patents) in the corporate sector. It includes both dividends (i.e., actual payments to owners for the use of their capital and the risk they take) and undistributed profits (i.e., retained earnings). For 1982 and 1983, corporate profits amounted to approximately 7 to 8 percent of U.S. national income.

Finally, net interest represents the interest payments by U.S. businesses and the rest of the world to American firms and households that have lent to them money. This income category, which in 1982 and 1983 was about one-tenth of U.S. national income, does not include interest payments by U.S. households or the U.S. government, because according to current thinking the latter payments are not based on any production of goods and services.

Economic Rents in the Production of Wyoming Coal[8]

As a result of the policies of the Organization of Petroleum Exporting Countries (OPEC), the price of oil rose rapidly throughout the 1970s. Producers and consumers around the world switched gradually to other alternative energy sources, such as coal and natural gas, driving their prices higher and higher. As predicted by the Ricardo–Viner model, the widespread rise of energy prices generated economic rents. We illustrate this phenomenon with the case of Wyoming coal, where the opportunity to earn economic rents arose at various stages of the production–distribution process.

Producers of Wyoming coal, workers, owners of coal mineral rights, state and local governments, and even railroads—they all benefited from the increased de-

[8]This subsection is based on Mutti and Morgan (1983).

mand for coal. The precise overall rents as well as their distribution among these beneficiaries are difficult to ascertain. Yet there is no doubt that each of these groups reaped significant revenues at least in the short run.

During the early 1970s most Wyoming coal was sold via long-term fixed supply contracts to thermal plants designed to handle coal of a particular Btu, ash, and sulfur content. Initially, prices ranged from $1.57 to $2.50 per ton for northern Wyoming coal. (Perhaps the prices at the lower end were disequilibrium prices, arising from the desire of new firms to establish markets for their output.) With the onset of the energy crisis, Wyoming coal prices rose quickly, reflecting the general trend in U.S. bituminous coal prices. For instance, between June 1973 and March 1975 Wyoming coal prices doubled while average prices for crude materials increased by a meager 3 percent. Since 1975, however, the rate of increase of Wyoming coal prices has slowed down. Thus, from March 1975 to August 1977, Wyoming coal prices rose by about 30 percent; from August 1977 to June 1981, they increased by a little more than 3 percent; and from June 1981 to February 1982 (a time of declining oil prices), they remained stable.

This evidence suggests that during the 1973–1977 period the increased demand for coal resulted in economic rents to the Wyoming coal producers. Such economic rents, however, must be temporary (quasi-rents), reflecting the inability of coal producers to install additional mining equipment in the short run. Since Wyoming's known coal reserves are so vast that they could sustain the current rate of production for over 550 years, the increased demand for coal cannot be expected to lead to a permanent increase in the real price of coal.

Wyoming coal workers also benefited from the increased demand for coal. Typically, new workers cannot be attracted to the mines on short notice, because of relocation costs and other considerations. Hence those who had the good fortune of being at the right place at the right time collected temporary economic rents. Thus during the 1973–1978 period, the real wages of the Wyoming coal workers rose steadily while the real wages of private nonfarm workers declined. Indeed, during the 1973–1978 period the gap between the real wages of these two groups of workers rose by over 24 percent, but declined after 1978.

Nearly all coal is presently moved by railroad. At the national level, the increased volume of coal transported did not result in abnormally high U.S. coal transportation rates. (The wholesale price index for coal transportation rose only 5 percent faster than the comparable index for railroad freight for the entire 1973–1981 period.) However, coal rates from Powder River Basin, Wyoming, to Elmendorf, Texas, nearly tripled between December 1976 (the date coal shipments to Texas commenced) and January 1981. (For the same period, the national price index for coal transportation rose by only 62 percent.) It is, therefore, evident that Burlington Northern, which operates the Wyoming Texas rail line, was the recipient of substantial economic rents.

The state and local governments of Wyoming also benefited from the increased demand for coal. This is evident from the fact that during the 1973–1979 period Wyoming's coal severance tax rates increased steadily from 1 percent to 10.5 percent while production levels rose by over 600 percent and prices more than tripled. Surely not all of the additional tax revenues were net gain to the state because of the social costs associated with the expanded production of coal, such as increased air and water pollution, increased crime, congestion, and the need to provide extra public facilities for a growing population. Yet coal-importing states felt that they were being penalized by the heavy taxes imposed by the coal-producing states, and their representatives in Congress introduced severance tax limitations bills in an attempt to confine the sum of all such taxes to 12.5 percent.

Finally, the owners of coal mineral rights also benefited from the increased demand for coal. This is evident from the fact that the federal government was able to raise the federal royalty rates from a maximum of 20 cents per ton to nearly $1 per ton (or 12.5 percent royalty rate applied to the coal price of $7.50 per ton).

SUMMARY

1. Factors of production (labor, land, and capital) are the services of resources, not the resources themselves. Factor prices (the rates of wages, rent, and profit) are the prices of factor services, not the prices of bodies, acres of land, and machines.

2. Under perfect competition, factor prices are determined by supply and demand. But partial equilibrium analysis is no longer adequate; a general equilibrium framework is more appropriate.

3. The demand for a factor is a derived demand; it is derived from the demand for the final product it helps to produce.

4. Functional distribution is the breakdown of national income into wages, rents, interest, and profits. Personal distribution is the allocation of national income among individuals. The latter depends on both factor prices and factor ownership.

5. The purpose of the marginal productivity theory is to explain, not justify, the observed income distribution.

6. For long-run profit maximization, each factor's employment is increased until its *MRP* becomes equal to its price.

7. The short-run profit maximization conditions take the form (a) $w = MRP_L$, (b) MRP_L must be declining, and (c) $ARP_L \geqslant w$.

8. The firm's short-run demand curve for labor consists of two disconnected parts: (a) It coincides with the vertical axis for $w >$ maximum ARP_L, and (b) it follows the downward-sloping MRP_L curve for $w <$ maximum ARP_L. When $w =$ maximum ARP_L, a two-point indeterminacy arises.

9. Two factors are said to be complementary, rival, or neutral according to whether an increase in the quantity of one raises, lowers, or leaves unchanged the marginal physical product of the other, respectively. These relationships are symmetrical.

10. The firm's demand for a variable factor is more elastic in the long run than in the short run except when the two factors are independent, in which case the two demand curves

coincide. In all cases, the demand curve for a variable factor slopes downward.

11. When the price of a "regressive" factor falls, the product's *MC* curve shifts upward and output falls. Regression is possible only in the long run.

12. The industry demand curve for labor is *not* given by the horizontal summation of the individual demand curves for labor of all active firms, because of the product–price effect, the entry–exit effect, and other effects.

13. The elasticity of demand for an input is high (a) when the elasticity of demand for the final product is high, (b) other inputs are easily substituted for it, and (c) the supply elasticity of co-operant factors is high. It is also higher in the long run than in the short run.

14. We distinguish among (a) the labor supply curve of a worker, (b) the aggregate labor supply to the economy, (c) the labor supply curve facing an industry, and (d) the labor supply curve facing a firm.

15. In the Ricardo–Viner model, rent depends on the demand for grapes (final product). An increase in the demand for grapes raises their price and profits emerge, but competition among grape growers pushes rents higher until all profits are eliminated.

16. Differential rents are based on fertility differences, with more fertile land commanding a higher rent than less fertile land. Marginal land pays no rent.

17. A factor's transfer earnings (or opportunity cost) is the price at which the factor is indifferent between transferring into or out of some type of employment. Any payment in excess of transfer earnings is a surplus (economic rent) that can be taxed away without any effect on resource allocation.

18. Marshall extended the doctrine of Ricardian rent to capital goods (machines) whose supply is fixed in the short run. Such fixed factors earn quasi-rent.

19. The aggregate production function relates total output to the total quantities of homogeneous labor and homogeneous capital. In the presence of constant returns to scale, competition ensures that each factor is paid its marginal product. The sum of (real) absolute shares equals aggregate output. The sum of relative shares is unity.

20. Increasing the quantity of one factor raises the absolute share of the other factor. The absolute share of the augmented factor increases, remains unchanged, or decreases according to whether the elasticity of demand for the augmented factor is greater than, equal to, or less than unity. If the absolute share of the aug-

mented factor does not rise, its relative share must fall.

21. The elasticity of substitution (σ) is the elasticity of the functional relationship between w/r and L/K. In the case of fixed coefficients, $\sigma = 0$, and when isoquants are straight lines, $\sigma = \infty$.

22. As the L/K ratio increases, the relative share of labor rises, remains the same, or falls according to whether the elasticity of substitution is greater than, equal to, or less than unity.

QUESTIONS

1. A perfectly competitive firm uses labor (L) and a *fixed* factor to produce output (Q). The following table gives the average-revenue product of labor (ARP_L) at alternative employment levels of labor under the assumption that the market price for the firm's output is $10.

Labor, L (worker-hours)	Average-Revenue Product of Labor, ARP_L
1	$80
2	70
3	60
4	50
5	40

(a) Determine the marginal physical product of labor (MPP_L) and the marginal-revenue product of labor (MRP_L) for the employment levels given in the table.

(b) Suppose that the firm maximizes its profit by employing 3 units of labor. Determine the limits of the wage rate currently paid by the firm.

(c) Suppose, alternatively, that the wage rate is $20. Determine the profit-maximizing labor employment by the firm and the quasi-rent for the fixed factor.

2. Two perfectly competitive firms, A and B, use the same type of labor (available at the same wage rate to both firms) to produce their respective products which happen to be totally unrelated. At the current profit-maximizing outputs of these two firms, we know that:

A's marginal product of labor $= 8$
B's marginal product of labor $= 12$
price of A's product $= \$6$

Determine the wage rate and the price of B's product.

*3. Consider a firm using land (T) and labor (L) in the production of output according to a homogeneous production function: $Q = f(L, T)$. Assume that the firm pays all factors of production the value of their marginal products.

Demonstrate that if the production function is subject to constant returns to scale, profits will be zero, if it is subject to increasing returns to scale, profits will be negative, and if it is subject to decreasing returns, profits will be positive.

[*Note:* If you cannot work with the general production function $Q = f(L, T)$, you may use the function $Q = T^a L^b$.]

4. An industry consists of a large number of small producers, each of whom has the same production function and cost curves. Each firm employs two factors, labor (variable factor) and land (fixed factor). An initial long-run industry equilibrium is disturbed by an increase in the wage rate from $10 to $15 an hour. Discuss the short-run and long-run effects of the wage increase on the following:

(a) The equilibrium quantities of labor and land employed by each firm.

(b) The equilibrium quantities of labor and land employed by the entire industry.

(c) The quantity of output produced by each firm and the industry.

(d) The price of output.

(*Note:* If the above information is not sufficient to answer any part of the question, state what additional piece of information is needed and why.)

5. There happen to be just 1000 acres of homogeneous vineyard land, uniquely suitable for growing a particular species of grape. For simplicity, it is assumed that this land is completely valueless in any other use. Depending on the demand for the grapes, however, the land may command a positive rent in its one distinctive use. Both the grape market and the rental market for the vineyard land are perfectly competitive.

The nonrent costs of growing the grapes on a single acre are given by the following functions:

$$C = 42q - 0.6q^2 + 0.01q^3$$
$$MC = 42 - 1.2q + 0.03q^2$$

where C is the total cost, MC the marginal cost, and q the quantity of grapes (wagonloads). It may be assumed throughout that 1 acre is the suitable unit for grape growing, irrespective of the price of grapes and the rent of the vineyard land.

(a) Suppose that the rent per acre is zero. What is the minimum price per wagonload of grapes (p_0) at which each farmer could afford to operate? What quantity of grapes (q_0) would he choose to produce?

(b) What is the maximum industry output (Q_0) that could be satisfied at the price p_0? What does this imply about the industry supply schedule up to the quantity Q_0?

(c) What is the supply–price schedule of a representative farmer in the range of outputs greater than q_0?

(d) What is the supply–price schedule of the industry in the range of outputs greater than Q_0?

(e) Suppose that the industry demand for grapes is given by the function

$$p = 46.2 - 0.00055Q$$

Calculate the long-run equilibrium magnitudes of (i) price p_1, (ii) the industry quantity Q_1, (iii) each active farmer's output q_1, (iv) the number n_1 of active farmers, and (v) the annual rent r_1 per acre of the vineyard land.

(f) Suppose that the demand for grapes increases to

$$p = 64 - 0.00055Q$$

Calculate the long-run equilibrium magnitudes of the variables listed in part (e).

6. As in the Ricardo–Viner case, a fixed quantity of homogeneous vineyard land is available for the production of a distinctive species of grape. The land would be valueless for any other purpose, but it happens to command a high rent in the grape-growing use. All other relevant factors are in perfectly elastic supply. Product and factor markets are all purely competitive.

(a) Analyze the long-run effects of a specific tax (of some moderate magnitude) levied on the grapes.

(b) What difference, if any, would there be if the government instead raised the same total revenue by means of a tax on the vineyard land? Explain.

7. Suppose that compared with 1984, the capital/labor ratio increased by 0.2 percent, the nominal price of capital increased by 3 percent, and the nominal price of labor rose by 4 percent.

(a) What is the value of the elasticity of substitution?

(b) Is the relative share of labor higher or lower in 1986 compared with its level in 1984?

8. According to a recent article in the *Atlanta Constitution* (March 18, 1984, p. 55J), America is on the verge of a second industrial revolution made possible by the computer. For instance, General Electric has built a factory in which one enormous locomotive engine frame is produced daily in a process that involves no production workers at all. The plant replaces one that used to employ 68 workers, who produced only one such frame in 16 days.

(a) Does automation destroy jobs? Is automation the enemy of labor?

(b) Will the robotics revolution reduce the standard of living of workers?

9. "If we can obtain the market demand curve for wheat by horizontally summing the demand curves of all individual buyers of wheat, we can certainly follow the same procedure when we want to determine the long-run demand curve for bricks. I see no difference between the demand curve of one commodity and that of another. After all, the aggregate quantity of bricks purchased during any particular month is made up of the purchases of all individual buyers of bricks." Do you agree with this statement? Why or why not?

10. The demand for bricklayers is given by the function

$$L_d = 1000 - 20w$$

and the supply of bricklayers is given by the function

$$L_s = 5w + 910$$

where L_d is the number of bricklayers demanded, L_s the number of bricklayers seeking jobs, and w the wage rate.

(a) Determine the equilibrium wage rate and the number of bricklayers employed.

(b) Suppose that 10 bricklayers immigrate from a foreign country and are willing to work at almost any wage rate they may find. What will this influx of workers do to the equilibrium wage rate and the number of initially employed workers? Finally, how will the *total* wage income of all domestic workers change and why?

(c) Illustrate your results graphically.

FURTHER READING

Bronfenbrenner, M. (1971). *Income Distribution Theory.* Aldine-Atherton, Inc., Chicago.

Chacholiades, M. (1980). "Complementarity, Rivalry, and Regression: A Geometrical Note," *Greek Economic Review,* Vol. 2 (April), pp. 65–70.

Clark, J. B. (1899). *The Distribution of Wealth.* Macmillan & Co., New York.

Douglas, P. H. (1934). *The Theory of Wages.* The Macmillan Company, New York.

Hicks, J. R. (1932). *The Theory of Wages.* Macmillan & Company Ltd., London.

Hicks, J. R. (1946). *Value and Capital,* 2nd ed. Oxford University Press, New York. Chapters 6–8.

Johnson, H. G. (1973). *The Theory of Income Distribution.* Gray-Mills Publishing Ltd., London.

Marshall, A. (1920). *Principles of Economics,* 8th ed. Macmillan & Company Ltd., London. Books V and VI.

Mutti, J. H., and W. E. Morgan (1983). "Changing Energy Prices and Economic Rents: The Case of Western Coal," *Land Economics,* Vol. 59 (May), pp. 163–176.

Samuelson, P. A. (1947). *Foundations of Economic Analysis.* Harvard University Press, Cambridge, Mass. Chapter 4.

Stigler, G. J. (1941). *Production and Distribution Theories.* The Macmillan Company, New York.

Viner, J. (1931). "Cost Curves and Supply Curves," *Zeitschrift für Nationalökonomie,* Vol. 3, pp. 23–46. Reprinted in K. E. Boulding and G. J. Stigler (eds.), *Readings in Price Theory,* Richard D. Irwin, Inc., Homewood, Ill., 1952.

CHAPTER
13

Factor Market Imperfections

In Chapter 12 we analyzed the problem of factor pricing and employment on the assumption that perfect competition prevailed both in the final product market and the factor market. But imperfections may exist in either market (or both). For instance, in the product market the firm could be monopolistic or oligopolistic, and in the factor market, the firm could be *monopsonistic* (single buyer) or *oligopsonistic* (few buyers). The purpose of this chapter is to show how the behavior of firms is modified by such market imperfections.

13.1 Monopoly in the Product Market[1]

As in Chapter 12, consider a firm that uses two factors of production, homogeneous labor (L) and homogeneous land (T), and produces a single homogeneous product. Assume that the firm is a perfect competitor in both factor markets (i.e., it can purchase unlimited amounts of labor and land at fixed factor prices, w and r, respectively). In the product market, however, the firm possesses some *monopoly power*; that is, it faces a downward-sloping demand curve for its product. For simplicity, we assume that the firm is a monopolist in the product market (even though the same principles apply to oligopolists and monopolistic competitors).

The Primary Condition for Profit Maximization

How much labor and how much land should the monopolist employ to maximize her profit? By what rule will the monopolist be guided in her pursuit of maximum profits?

The primary marginal requirement for the monopolist's long-run equilibrium is

[1]This section could be read together with the Appendix to Chapter 13.

that each factor's marginal revenue product must be equated to that factor's price (or rental):

$$MRP_L = MR \cdot MPP_L = w \tag{13.1}$$

(12.3) repeated

$$MRP_T = MR \cdot MPP_T = r \tag{13.2}$$

(12.4) repeated

The monopolist will continue to expand employment of factors as long as hiring one more unit adds more to revenues than to costs.

Note that equations (13.1) and (13.2) coincide with equations (12.3) and (12.4), respectively. Does this mean that there is no difference between a firm that is a perfect competitor in the product market and a firm that is a monopoly? Not at all. When the firm sells its product in a perfectly competitive market, it faces a horizontal product demand, with average revenue (AR) equal to marginal revenue (MR); *hence the value of the marginal physical product of a factor* ($VMP = AR \cdot MPP$) *is equal to the marginal revenue product of that factor* ($MRP = MR \cdot MPP$). However, when the firm has some positive degree of monopoly power, the demand for its product is downward sloping, with $AR > MR$; hence the *value of the marginal physical product of a factor exceeds its marginal revenue product* ($VMP > MRP$). Combining this information with equations (13.1) and (13.2), we conclude that *under monopoly the equilibrium value of the marginal physical product of a factor exceeds the price (or rental) of that factor.* That is, $VMP_L > w$ and $VMP_T > r$.

The Curves of MRP_L, ARP_L, and VMP_L

Suppose that the quantity of land is fixed at its long-run equilibrium magnitude. Then given the curves of average and marginal *physical* product of labor (APP_L and MPP_L) as well as the curves of average and marginal revenue (AR and MR), we can derive the schedules of average and marginal *revenue* product of labor (ARP_L and MRP_L) and the schedule of the value of the marginal physical product of labor (VMP_L), as shown in Figure 13.1.

Panel (a) reproduces the familiar curves of average and marginal physical product of labor (APP_L and MPP_L), and directly below it, panel (b) gives the *value*-product curves: ARP_L, MRP_L, and VMP_L. Because AR is decreasing and $AR > MR$, these value-product schedules *cannot* be obtained from the relevant *physical*-product schedules (APP_L and MPP_L) by an appropriate change of vertical scale as in Figure 12.1. Rather, the three value-product schedules represent only distorted reflections of the corresponding physical-product schedules.

It is useful to summarize the main features of the various schedules illustrated in Figure 13.1 as follows.

1. All three value-product schedules (ARP_L, MRP_L, and VMP_L) have the same vertical-axis intercept (V). This follows from two facts: (a) the schedules of APP_L and MPP_L have a common vertical-axis intercept (D), and (b) the schedules of AR and MR (not shown) also have a common vertical-axis intercept.

2. The maximum $ARP_L = AR \cdot APP_L$ (point E_1) necessarily occurs at a lower labor quantity (L_1) than that (L_0) where APP_L reaches its maximum (point E_0'). The reason for this is because AR is *declining* (by assumption). Note that between L_1 and L_0, ARP_L is declining while APP_L is increasing.

3. For all positive values of labor, the schedule of VMP_L lies above the sched-

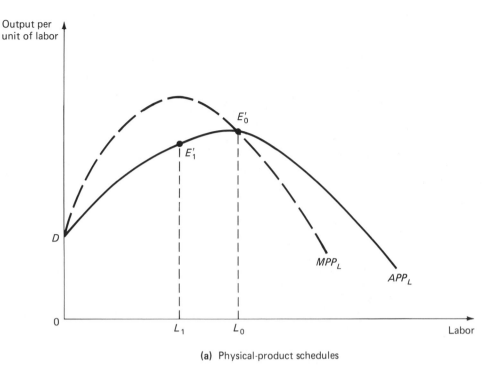

(a) Physical-product schedules

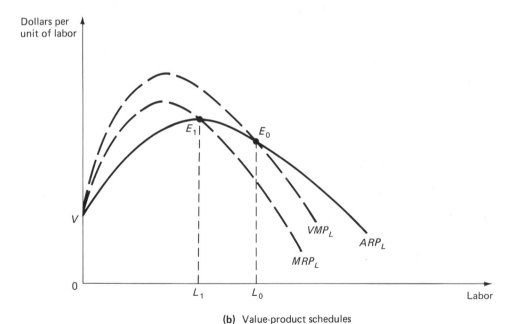

(b) Value-product schedules

Figure 13.1 Derivation of the monopolist's value product schedules. Panel (a) shows the familiar *physical* product curves: APP_L and MPP_L. Directly below it, panel (b) gives the three *value*-product curves: ARP_L, MRP_L, and VMP_L. The MRP_L curve lies above (below) ARP_L when ARP_L is rising (falling), and MRP_L intersects ARP_L at the latter's maximum point (E_1). The curve of VMP_L lies always above MRP_L because $AR > MR$. The maximum ARP_L (point E_1) occurs at a lower labor quantity (L_1) than that (L_0) at which APP_L reaches its maximum (point E'_0).

ule of MRP_L. This property must be obvious, because $VMP_L = AR \cdot MPP_L$, $MRP_L = MR \cdot MPP_L$, and $AR > MR$; hence $VMP_L > MRP_L$.

4. The schedule of VMP_L lies above (below) the schedule of ARP_L when the schedule of MPP_L lies above (below) the schedule of APP_L. Furthermore, the schedules of VMP_L and ARP_L intersect (point E_0) at the precise labor quantity (L_0) where MPP_L intersects APP_L (point E_0', or maximum APP_L). Since $VMP_L = AR \cdot MPP_L$ and $ARP_L = AR \cdot APP_L$, it follows that $VMP_L \gtrless ARP_L$ when $AR \cdot MPP_L \gtrless AR \cdot APP_L$, or $MPP_L \gtrless APP_L$.

5. The schedule of MRP_L lies above (below) the schedule of ARP_L when ARP_L is rising (declining), and MRP_L intersects ARP_L at the latter's maximum point (E_1). This is the same relationship that exists between all pairs of marginal-average concepts. [Recall from Chapter 12 that $MRP_L = MR \cdot MPP_L = (\Delta R/\Delta q)(\Delta q/\Delta L) = \Delta R/\Delta L$; and $ARP_L = AR \cdot APP_L = (R/q)(q/L) = R/L.$]

The Monopolist's Demand for Labor

Given the curves of marginal and average revenue product, we can derive the monopolist's short-run demand curve for labor by following, step by step, the procedure of Section 12.3. This is a necessary consequence of our assumption that the monopolist purchases labor (variable input) in a perfectly competitive labor market.

Consider Figure 13.2, which reproduces the value-product schedules (ARP_L, MRP_L, and VMP_L) of Figure 13.1. At the current wage rate $\overline{w}$, the monopolist maximizes her profit by employing $\overline{L}$ units of labor, as illustrated by the intersection (F) of horizontal labor supply schedule L_s and the downward-sloping MRP_L schedule. Point F lies on the monopolist's demand for labor. By allowing the wage rate to vary, as

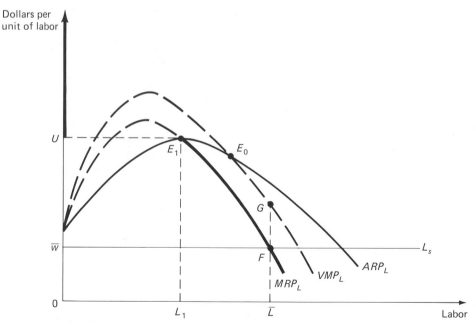

Figure 13.2 The monopolist's short-run demand for labor. At the current wage rate $\overline{w}$, the monopolist maximizes her profit by employing $\overline{L}$ units of labor, as shown by the intersection (F) of horizontal labor supply schedule L_s and the downward-sloping MRP_L schedule. The monopolist's demand for labor coincides with the vertical axis for all wage rates above $0U$ (or maximum ARP_L); and for all wage rates below $0U$, it follows the MRP_L schedule. The two disconnected segments of the labor demand are heavily drawn for easy identification.

in Chapter 12, we can determine as many points as we like on the monopolist's demand for labor. The end result is the same as in Chapter 12: For all wage rates lower than the maximum ARP_L (i.e., $0U$), the monopolist's short-run demand for labor coincides with the MRP_L schedule; for all wage rates higher than $0U$, the demand for labor coincides with the vertical axis; and for the specific wage rate $0U$ (maximum ARP_L), the demand for labor is either zero (point U) or equal to L_1 (point E_1). Accordingly, the demand for labor is indicated by the two disconnected and heavily drawn line segments.

The derivation of the monopolist's long-run demand for labor is left as an exercise for the interested reader. The procedure is the same as that employed in Section 12.4.

Some Properties of Monopolistic Equilibrium

Figure 13.2 teaches us an important lesson. At the monopolist's equilibrium point, it is always true that $MRP_L < VMP_L$. For instance, when the firm employs $\bar{L}$ units of labor, $MRP_L = \bar{L}F < \bar{L}G = VMP_L$. This property of the monopolist's equilibrium is traced back to the basic inequality between average and marginal revenue ($AR > MR$). It is therefore obvious that *in the presence of monopoly power in the product market, the value of the marginal physical product of labor* ($VMP_L = AR \times MPP_L$) *is always lower than the wage rate (which is equal to MRP_L)*.

Joan Robinson (1933, Chap. 25) calls the gap between VMP_L and MRP_L (shown by vertical distance FG in Figure 13.2) *monopolistic exploitation*. We return to Robinson's idea of monopolistic "exploitation" in Section 13.4.

Note that the inequality $VMP_L > MRP_L = w$ is essentially due to the inequality $AR > MR$ (i.e., the existence of a positive degree of monopoly in the product market) and nothing else. Consequently, the inequality $VMP_L > w$ will persist in the long run as well.

The precise magnitude of the gap between VMP_L and MRP_L (or w) depends on the elasticity of demand for the monopolist's product. Recall from Chapter 8 that the elasticity of demand in absolute terms is given by the formula

$$|e| = \frac{AR}{AR - MR}$$

(13.3)
(8.1) repeated

Solving equation (13.3) for MR, we have

$$MR = AR \left(1 - \frac{1}{|e|}\right)$$

(13.4)
(A8.4) repeated

Accordingly,

$$w = MRP_L = MR \cdot MPP_L$$

$$= AR \left(1 - \frac{1}{|e|}\right) MPP_L$$

or

$$w = \left(1 - \frac{1}{|e|}\right) VMP_L$$

(13.5)

When the elasticity of demand is infinite, $w = MRP_L = VMP_L$ because $AR = MR$ and $1/|e| = 0$. When the elasticity of demand is less than infinite, $w < VMP_L$. In fact, the lower is $|e|$, the larger becomes the gap between w and VMP_L.

13.2 Monopsony in the Factor Market[2]

So far our analysis has rested on the assumption that the firm is a perfect competitor in the factor market; that is, the factor supply curve facing the firm is horizontal (infinitely elastic) at the prevailing factor price. But there are many situations in which the firm faces an upward-sloping factor-supply curve. In such cases the firm can expand its factor employment but only if it is prepared to pay higher factor prices. To illustrate the consequences of this factor-market imperfection, we examine the polar case of *monopsony* (single buyer)[3]. The typical example of monopsony is the "company town" in which a single firm is the primary source of factor employment.

Marginal Factor Cost and Monopsony Power

Once again we use labor as an example of an input purchased by a single buyer (monopsonist). The labor supply curve confronting the monopsonist is upward sloping, which indicates that the monopsonist exercises some market power (*monopsony power*) on the wage rate she pays. For instance, starting from any initial position, the monopsonist may cause a fall in the wage rate by reducing the quantity of labor. (Monopsony power is similar to monopoly power whereby the monopolist may raise her price by reducing her output.)

Because changes in the monopsonist's employment of labor affect the wage rate, the marginal expense of hiring an extra worker is *not* equal to the wage rate.[4] For instance, suppose that the monopsonist is currently employing 50 workers at a wage rate of \$40, but to increase her employment by one extra worker, she must pay a wage rate of \$41 to all 51 workers. What is the marginal expense of hiring the fifty-first worker? Obviously, the marginal expense of the fifty-first worker is higher than the wage rate of \$41, because the monopsonist must also raise the wage rate of the other 50 workers from \$40 to \$41. Thus the marginal expense of the fifty-first worker is equal to \$91; that is, $\$41 + (\$41 - \$40) \cdot 50 = \$91$.

We can also discover the marginal expense of hiring the fifty-first worker by alternatively calculating the change of the total wage bill of the monopsonist. As total employment increases from 50 to 51 workers, the monopsonist's total labor cost changes from \$2000 (i.e., \$40 × 50) to \$2091 (i.e., \$41 × 51); hence it changes by exactly \$91, which confirms the earlier calculation.

The wage rate corresponds to the *average expense of labor* (AE_L). Because the wage rate (or average expense of labor) rises as the monopsonist hires more workers, the additional cost of hiring an extra worker, or the *marginal expense of labor* (ME_L), is necessarily higher than the wage rate (i.e., $ME_L > AE_L$). This result is just another instance of the fundamental average-marginal relationship.

Factor Employment Equilibrium

Suppose now that labor is the only variable factor of production. How much labor should the monopsonist employ in order to maximize her profit? Will the monopsonist continue to expand her employment of labor until the marginal revenue product of labor becomes equal to the wage rate?

---

[2]This section could be read together with the Appendix to Chapter 13.

[3]The analytical principles developed in the text in relation to monopsony are also applicable to *oligopsony* (few buyers) and *monopsonistic competition* (many small buyers of a differentiated input). We leave this extension of the theory as an exercise for the interested reader.

[4]To avoid confusion with the concept of marginal *cost* of output (MC), we adopt the term "marginal *expense* of labor."

The cardinal rule that *every* profit-maximizing producer must follow is to continue *to expand the employment of a variable input as long as the extra revenue derived from the employment of an extra unit (i.e., the marginal revenue product of the input) is at least as large as the extra cost of the extra unit of the input (i.e., the marginal expense of the input)*. Accordingly, the primary marginal condition for profit maximization is

$$MRP_L = ME_L \qquad\qquad (13.6)$$

where ME_L is the marginal expense of labor. Evidently, when the firm does not possess any monopsony power, the marginal expense of labor coincides with the wage rate ($ME_L = w$), and equation (13.6) reduces to equation (12.3) or (13.1). But equation (13.6) is more general and fundamental than equation (12.3), because it applies to *all* market structures.

The monopsonist's factor-employment equilibrium is illustrated in Figure 13.3. In panel (a), the monopsonist is assumed to be a perfect competitor in the product market with exactly the same types of value–product schedules, ARP_L and $MRP_L = VMP_L$, as in Figure 12.1. In panel (b), the monopsonist is assumed to be a monopolist in the product market, facing a downward-sloping demand for her product; hence $VMP_L > MRP_L$ (because $AR > MR$), as in Figure 13.2. In both panels, the labor supply schedule (AE_L) is positively sloped, implying that increasing quantities of labor can be purchased only at a steadily increasing, rather than a constant, wage rate (or average expense, AE_L). Because the AE_L schedule is positively sloped, the marginal expense of labor exceeds the wage rate (i.e., $ME_L > AE_L$) at every positive labor quantity, as shown by the fact that the ME_L schedule lies above the AE_L schedule. The monopsonist's equilibrium quantity of labor (L_0) is indicated, in both panels, by point E where the ME_L schedule intersects the MRP_L schedule from below; and the equilibrium wage rate (w_0) is determined (in both panels) by point H on the AE_L schedule, because exactly L_0 units of labor are offered only when the wage rate is w_0.

Note that in any short-run equilibrium, as in Figure 13.3, the monopsonist will choose to remain in business as long as the average-revenue product of labor is at least as high as the equilibrium wage rate (i.e., $ARP_L \geq w$). When $ARP_L < w$, the monopsonist will not be able to cover her total variable cost and she will suspend production altogether.

Some Implications of Monopsonistic Equilibrium

Return to Figure 13.3 and observe that in both panels *the marginal-revenue product of labor exceeds the wage rate ($MRP_L > w$)* at the monopsonistic equilibrium. The gap between MRP_L and w can be traced back to the monopsony power possessed by the firm. Because the firm adjusts the employment of labor until $MRP_L = ME_L$, the inequality $MRP_L > w$ can exist if, and only if, the marginal expense of labor exceeds the wage rate ($ME_L > w$), that is, if the firm possesses some positive degree of monopsony power.

The inequality $MRP_L > w$ is the central implication of monopsony power. Joan Robinson (1933, Chap. 26) labels the divergence between the marginal revenue product of labor and the wage rate (shown by vertical distance HE in both panels of Figure 13.3) *monopsonistic exploitation*. Total monopsonistic exploitation coincides with rectangular area w_0HEG (in both panels).

Note also that in Figure 13.3, panel (a), where the firm is a perfect competitor in the product market but a monopsonist in the labor market, the total gap between VMP_L and w (i.e., HE) is due to monopsonistic exploitation, because $VMP_L = MRP_L$. However, in panel (b) where the firm is both a monopolist in its product market

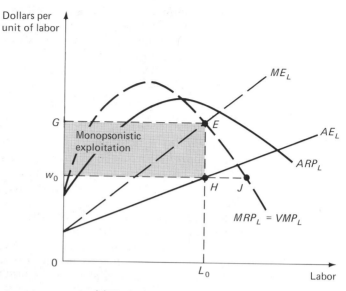

(a) Perfect competition in the product market

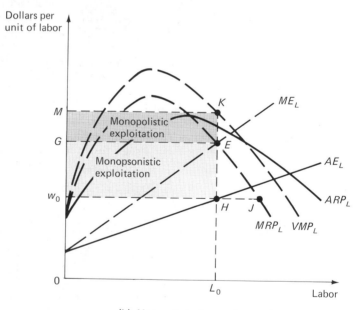

(b) Monopoly in the product market

Figure 13.3 *The monopolist's factor-employment equilibrium.* The monopolist's equilibrium quantity of labor (L_0) is indicated in both panels by the intersection (E) of the schedules of ME_L and MRP_L, and the equilibrium wage rate (w_0) is shown by point H on the AE_L schedule. In both panels total monopsonistic exploitation is shown by area w_0HEG. In panel (a) the firm is a perfect competitor in the product market (with $MRP_L = VMP_L$); hence the total gap between VMP_L and w (i.e., HE) is due to monopsonistic exploitation. In panel (b) the firm is a monopolist in its product market (with $AR > MR$ and $VMP_L > MRP_L$); hence the total gap between VMP_L and w (i.e., HK) is the sum of monopsonistic exploitation (HE) plus monopolistic exploitation (EK). Total monopolistic exploitation is shown in panel (b) by area $GEKM$.

416

and a monopsonist in the labor market, the total gap between VMP_L and w (i.e., HK) can be decomposed into two parts, HE plus EK. Distance HE represents again monopsonistic exploitation, because it reflects the divergence between ME_L and w, and distance EK indicates monopolistic exploitation (as FG in Figure 13.2) because it reflects the gap between MRP_L and VMP_L (which in turn is a consequence of $AR > MR$). Total monopsonistic exploitation coincides again with rectangular area w_0HEG, while total monopolistic exploitation is given by area $GEKM$.

Another important implication of monopsony power is that the firm's demand for labor exceeds the supply of labor in the actual monopsonistic equilibrium, as illustrated in Figure 13.3. Thus, in both panels, the quantity of labor (L_0) purchased by the monopsonist is less than the quantity (indicated by point J) that she would buy *if* the supply of labor were horizontal (infinitely elastic) at the equilibrium wage rate (w_0). Accordingly, monopsonistic equilibrium signifies a "sellers' market," in which the factor suppliers can sell all the labor (or some other input) they wish to sell, while the monopsonist is unable to buy as much as she would like to buy—at the wage rate that she herself sets.

This property of monopsonistic equilibrium is analogous to a similar property of monopolistic equilibrium. As we noted in Section 10.3, under monopoly supply exceeds demand, because price exceeds marginal cost. Just as monopsonistic equilibrium gives rise to a sellers' market, monopolistic equilibrium signifies a "buyers' market," in which it is easy to buy but hard to sell; and in the same way that the excess of supply over demand provides the monopolist with an incentive to advertise her willingness to sell additional output, the excess of factor demand over factor supply gives the monopsonist an incentive to advertise her willingness to hire additional help.

The Cost-Minimization Condition Again: Digression

Consider now a monopsonist who uses more than one variable input. To maximize total profit, the monopsonist must adjust the quantities of inputs until the marginal revenue product of each input becomes equal to that input's marginal expense. For instance, suppose that there are only two variable inputs, labor (L) and land (T). Profit maximization requires the monopsonist to hire labor and land so that

$$MRP_L = ME_L \qquad\qquad (13.7)$$
$$(13.6)\,\text{repeated}$$

$$MRP_T = ME_T \qquad\qquad (13.8)$$

where ME_T is the marginal expense of land.

Implicit in equations (13.7) and (13.8) is an important proposition concerning cost minimization. As we explained in Section 7.2, the fundamental condition for minimizing the total cost of *a firm that takes factor prices as given* (has no monopsony power) is

$$MRS_{LT} = \frac{MPP_L}{MPP_T} = \frac{w}{r} \qquad\qquad (13.9)$$
$$(7.2)\,\text{repeated}$$

where MRS_{LT} is the marginal rate of technical substitution of labor for land. Equation (13.9) is no longer valid when the firm has monopsony power. Let us see why.

Divide the left-hand side (right-hand side) of equation (13.7) by the left-hand side (right-hand side) of equation (13.8) to obtain

$$\frac{MRP_L}{MRP_T} = \frac{ME_L}{ME_T}$$

or
$$MRS_{LT} = \frac{ME_L}{ME_T} \tag{13.10}$$

because $MRP_L = MR \cdot MPP_L$, $MRP_T = MR \cdot MPP_T$, and thus $MRP_L/MRP_T = MPP_L/MPP_T = MRS_{LT}$. Accordingly, a monopsonist should set the marginal rate of technical substitution equal to the ratio of marginal expense of inputs (ME_L/ME_T), not the ratio of the input prices (w/r).

The main reason for the peculiarity of monopsony described above is due to the fact that changes in the volume of employment of an input cause changes in that input's price, with the result that the isocost "lines" of the firm are no longer linear. As shown below, in the presence of monopsony, the absolute slope of an isocost curve at a certain point coincides with the ratio of marginal expense of inputs, not the ratio of input prices. Hence the tangency of an isocost curve to an isoquant is equivalent to equation (13.10).

Write the equation of an isocost curve as follows:

$$C = E_L + E_T \tag{13.11}$$

where E_T is the total expense on labor, E_T the total expense on land, and C the given total cost. From an initial input combination whose total cost is C, allow the monopsonist to increase the employment of labor by ΔL and decrease the employment of land by ΔT so that total cost continues to remain equal to C. As L increases by ΔL, total cost increases by $\Delta L \cdot ME_L$ (*not* $\Delta L \cdot w$); and as T decreases by ΔT, total cost decreases by $\Delta T \cdot ME_T$ (*not* $\Delta T \cdot r$). Because total cost remains constant, by assumption, the total change of total cost must be zero; that is,

$$\Delta L \cdot ME_L + \Delta T \cdot ME_T = 0$$

from which we obtain

$$\text{slope of isocost curve} = -\frac{\Delta T}{\Delta L} = \frac{ME_L}{ME_T} \tag{13.12}$$

Equation (13.10) is a general rule valid in all cases. Note that equation (13.9) is a special case of equation (13.10). When the input markets are perfectly competitive, the marginal expense of an input is equal to the input's price; that is, $ME_L = w$ and $ME_L = r$, so that equations (13.9) and (13.10) are equivalent. In the presence of monopsony power, however, equation (13.9) no longer holds, and the general rule summarized by equation (13.10) must be applied.

13.3 Summary of Factor-Employment Equilibria

Table 13.1 summarizes the profit-maximizing conditions and the implications of the four alternative factor-employment situations that we have studied so far. Labor is used as an example. In all alternative market structures, profit maximization requires the equality of $MRP_L = ME_L$, as shown in all four boxes of the table.

When the firm is a perfect competitor in the product market (first row of table), equilibrium implies $VMP_L = ME_L$, because $AR = MR$ (no monopoly power) and

	Factor Market	
Product Market	**Perfect Competition** $(w = ME_L)$	**Monopsony** $(w < ME_L)$
Perfect competition $(AR = MR)$	$VMP_L = MRP_L = ME_L = w$ (no exploitation)	$VMP_L = MRP_L = ME_L > w$ (monopsonistic exploitation = $MRP_L - w$)
Monopoly $(AR > MR)$	$VMP_L > MRP_L = ME_L = w$ (monopolistic exploitation = $VMP_L - w$)	$VMP_L > MRP_L = ME_L > w$ (monopolistic exploitation = $VMP_L - MRP_L$; monopsonistic exploitation = $MRP_L - w$)

Table 13.1 Alternative Factor-Employment Equilibrium

thus $VMP_L = MRP_L$ (no monopolistic exploitation). When the firm has monopoly power in its product market (second row), it follows that $VMP_L > ME_L$, because the inequality $AR > MR$ implies $VMP_L > MRP_L$ (monopolistic exploitation).

When the firm is a perfect competitor in the factor market (first column), equilibrium implies that $MRP_L = w$ (no monopsonistic exploitation), because $ME_L = w$ (no monopsony power). In the presence of monopsony power (second column), however, $MRP_L > w$ (monopsonistic exploitation), because $ME_L > w$ (monopsony power).

13.4 Exploitation Versus Distributive Justice

A factor of production, most notably labor, is said to be "exploited" when it receives not what it "deserves," but much less. The deviation between the actual and the "just" factor price is a measure of "exploitation." It is obvious, then, that the concept of exploitation rests on the assumption that the economist knows how to determine the "fair" or "just" factor price, but this assumption is wrong. Economic analysis alone can never identify a "proper" or "just" factor price and thus cannot provide any measure of exploitation.

Whether the distribution of income is "fair" or "just" depends on one's ethical judgment. Usually, different ethical observers have divergent views as to what constitutes distributive justice. We must therefore recognize that the term "exploitation" primarily signifies an ethical judgment as to the justice of income distribution. To avoid confusion, ethical judgments must always be stated explicitly, because they have nothing to do with economic analysis. It is unfortunate that in the past many a great economist did not explicitly state their ethical judgments, but rather attempted to stretch the results of their positive economic analysis to legitimize what they believed to be a "just" income distribution. This practice must be avoided.

The idea of exploitation goes back to Karl Marx (1818–1883). In Marx's view, labor produces the whole product and therefore should receive it all. Labor is exploited, according to Marx, to the extent that any part of the product accrues to other factors; that is, labor is exploited when the wage rate is less than the average revenue product of labor ($w < ARP_L$).

Joan Robinson's concept of exploitation is not as radical as the Marxian concept. As noted in Sections 13.1 and 13.2, Joan Robinson (1933) affixed the label of exploitation to any situation in which the price of a factor falls short of the value of its marginal product. In doing so, she was actually adopting the definition of exploitation that was originally formulated by Arthur C. Pigou (1877–1959).[5] But Robinson sharpened and extended Pigou's definition. Whereas Pigou always associated the concept of exploitation with monopsony in the factor market, Robinson demonstrated for the first time that exploitation in Pigou's sense may also be the result of monopoly in the product market.

The origins of the Pigou–Robinson concept of exploitation are to be found in the early developments of the marginal productivity theory of income distribution. As noted in Section 12.1, J. B. Clark believed that the exact contribution of a factor to the total product corresponds to its marginal physical product; hence each factor is justly remunerated when it receives its marginal product. In addition, Clark claimed that perfect competition (the only market structure he studied) leads to a just distribution of income because, as he had demonstrated, under perfect competition each factor actually receives its marginal product. Unlike Marx who had regarded labor as the sole productive factor, Clark took the more even-handed view that all scarce factors are productive.

The Pigou–Robinson concept of exploitation is a logical implication of Clark's ethical scheme. If a factor's just price (in real terms) is its marginal physical product, the factor is "exploited" whenever it receives less than its marginal product. Clark himself did not explicitly state the exploitation corollary, because he never carried his analysis beyond the confines of perfect competition. But Pigou and Robinson did take this extra step.

The Pigou–Robinson concept of exploitation is objectionable because of its strong ethical overtones and implications. In the first place, it condones Clark's view of distributive justice (that each factor should receive its marginal product), irrespective of how uneven the resultant income distribution may be. Furthermore, the Pigou–Robinson definition is arbitrary in its implied disapproval of situations involving exploitation because there is no correlation between exploitation and low factor prices. Exploitation is not necessarily absent when factor prices are high, nor is it necessarily present when factor prices are low. Should we, as ethical observers, follow Pigou and Robinson and consider as fair the pitifully low wage (perhaps a subsistence wage) received by an "unexploited" worker, but regard as unfair the income of an "exploited" landlord, even though the landlord's income is very high?

13.5 Labor Unions

A labor union is an association of individual workers that represents them in negotiations with their employers. Workers join unions in order to obtain a voice in the determination of their wages and fringe benefits, the improvement of their hours and working conditions, and the security of their jobs. About one-fourth of all American nonfarm workers are now members of labor unions. As a result, labor unions have a profound effect on the economy of the United States. A comprehensive study of labor unions lies beyond the scope of this book. In this section we discuss briefly the economic effects of labor unions within the partial equilibrium framework.

Perfect Competition in the Labor Market

Consider a perfectly competitive labor market in which a large number of small firms (demanders) interact with a large number of unorganized workers (suppliers) to determine the equilibrium wage rate. This is shown in Figure 13.4. Equilibrium occurs at the intersection (E) of the market supply and demand curves for labor, S_L and D_L, respectively.

---

[5]See Pigou (1932, pp. 551, 556–557, and 813–814).

Next, suppose that the workers organize themselves into a union and press for a higher wage, and by the threat of a strike, the labor union succeeds in enforcing a higher wage rate. What are the effects of the higher wage rate? Do the workers become better off after the formation of the labor union?

Return to Figure 13.4 and suppose that the labor union raises the wage rate from w_0 to w_1. Graphically, this means that the dashed portion of the labor supply curve (*FB*) is now replaced by horizontal line w_1B, which intersects the market demand curve at point *A*. *The unavoidable outcome of the rise in wages is a decline in employment (from L_0 to L_1) and the emergence of an excess supply of labor (AB).* Note that the excess supply of labor (*AB*) is larger than the reduction of employment because more labor is supplied at the higher wage rate. Surely those workers who are lucky enough to remain employed are clearly better off, because their incomes are higher. But their fellow workers who lose their jobs are worse off.

To be sure, our partial equilibrium analysis cannot tell us exactly what happens to those workers who lose their jobs, because it fails to consider repercussions in other sectors of the economy. The usual assumption is that those workers who leave the industry find employment elsewhere in the economy. If these workers receive the same wage that they earned before the union was formed, the only damage they suffer (in addition to the ephemeral difficulties of having to change jobs) is as consumers of the product now produced at a higher price in the unionized industry.

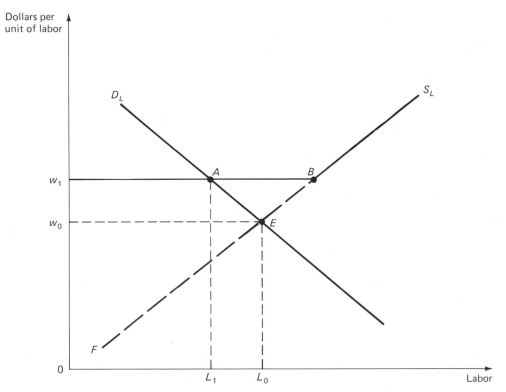

Figure 13.4 The effects of a union in a competitive labor market. Initially, equilibrium occurs at *E*. After a labor union raises the wage rate from w_0 to w_1, the dashed portion of the labor supply curve (*FB*) is replaced by horizontal line w_1B, and equilibrium shifts to point *A*. Employment declines from L_0 to L_1; but the excess supply of labor (*AB*) at w_1 is larger than the reduction of employment (L_1L_0) because more labor is supplied at w_1 than at w_0. However, total wage income is higher at the higher wage rate (i.e., $w_1L_1 > w_0L_0$) only when the demand for labor is inelastic.

The other side of the coin, of course, is that these workers may remain unemployed for some time, and when they do finally find a job, the wages they receive may be lower than what they initially earned.

Nevertheless, it is conceivable that a labor union may benefit all workers, not just some of them. For instance, if the market demand for labor is *inelastic*, the rise in the wage rate (from w_0 to w_1) will result in an increase in total wage income earned by the unionized workers. (That is, $w_1L_1 > w_0L_0$, even though $L_1 < L_0$.) It is at least potentially feasible for the labor union to divide the higher wage income (w_1L_1) among all workers, making everybody better off.

We can illustrate the foregoing possibility by means of a concrete example. Suppose that before the union is formed, the industry employs 1000 workers. Each worker works 40 hours per week and earns a wage rate of $10 per hour. The total wage income per week is $400,000 (i.e., $10 × 40 × 1000$), while each individual worker earns $400 (i.e., $10 × 40$). Now let the workers form a union that succeeds in raising the wage rate to $20 per hour. At the higher wage rate, the industry demands only 800 workers. Thus the total wage income rises to $640,000 (i.e., $20 × 40 × 800$). How can all workers share in this success? By sharing the number of hours of work available each week. Essentially, the industry has employment of 32,000 worker-hours per week (i.e., $40 × 800$). Each of the original 1000 workers, then, can work for just 32 hours a week. Instead of the industry employing only 800 workers for 40 hours per week, it can employ 1000 workers for just 32 hours per week. The industry gets all the labor it needs, and each and every worker earns a weekly wage income of $640 (i.e., $20 × 32$). This is reminiscent of the agricultural drama, where the farmers may benefit by producing and supplying less output because of the low elasticity of demand for agricultural products.

The success of the above compensation scheme rests crucially on the assumption that the industry demand for labor is inelastic. When the demand for labor is instead *elastic*, the rise in wages causes a reduction in the total wage income (wL) and the compensation scheme fails. In the end some workers are bound to become worse off. Typically, those workers who retain their jobs earn higher incomes, despite the fact that the total wage income declines.

The reduction in employment that results from the rise in wages is often reflected in the various "featherbedding" policies pursued by the labor unions. The object of such policies is to "make work." Thus labor unions may demand that totally unnecessary work must be done, that work must be done by time-consuming methods, or that unnecessary workers must be hired.

Monopsony in the Labor Market

When the labor market is monopsonistic (or oligopsonistic), the wage increase achieved by a labor union may *expand* both employment and output. Thus the higher wages may be beneficial to both workers and consumers. This possibility is illustrated in Figure 13.5, which reproduces the basic schedules of ARP_L, MRP_L, AE_L, and ME_L of Figure 13.3. For our present discussion, we ignore the schedule of VMP_L. Prior to the formation of the labor union, the monopsonist hires L_0 units of labor (as indicated by the intersection of MRP_L and ME_L at point E) and sets the wage rate at w_0 (as shown by point G on the AE_L schedule).

Suppose now that the workers establish a union that succeeds in setting a wage floor at w_1. Portions JV and JH of the original schedules of AE_L and ME_L, respectively, are now replaced by horizontal line segment w_1V. (Note that the new ME_L schedule jumps discontinuously from V to H.) The new equilibrium quantity of labor is now L_1 (as indicated by point V), which is higher than L_0.

The wage floor at w_1 (determined by the intersection of AE_L and MRP_L at point V) has two important properties: (1) it maximizes employment, and (2) it equates

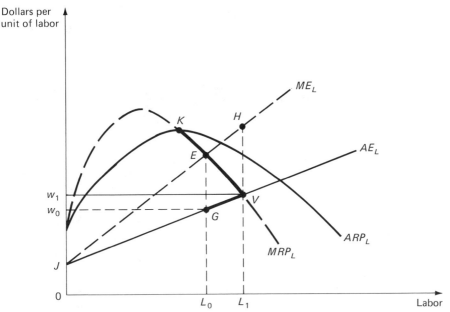

Figure 13.5 The effects of a labor union in a monopsonistic labor market. Prior to the formation of a union, the monopsonist hires L_0 units of labor (determined by intersection E) and sets the wage rate at w_0 (as shown by point G on AE_L). When a labor union sets the wage floor at w_1, portions JV and JH of the original schedules of AE_L and ME_L, respectively, are replaced by horizontal line segment w_1V; and employment rises to L_1, as shown by point V. If we visualize a series of successively higher wage floors starting at w_0, the monopsonist's equilibrium point will first travel from G to V (along AE_L) and then continue from V to K (along MRP_L). The path GVK is heavily drawn for easy identification. Employment is maximized at V, where the wage floor is set at w_1.

the monopsonist's demand for labor (read off the MRP_L curve) to the supply of labor (read off the original AE_L schedule). Property 2 is obvious, because when the wage floor is set at w_1, equilibrium occurs at point V where the schedule of MRP_L and the original schedule of AE_L intersect.

When the wage floor lies between w_0 and w_1, the ME_L schedule makes its upward jump (from a point below the MRP_L schedule to a point above it) at a labor quantity, say L^* (not shown), between L_0 and L_1, and the monopsonist maximizes her profit by hiring the labor quantity L^*. When the wage floor is set above w_1, the MRP_L schedule intersects the new ME_L schedule in the range of the latter's horizontal segment, and again the new equilibrium quantity of labor is smaller than L_1. Accordingly, if we visualize a series of successively higher wage floors starting at w_0, the monopsonist's equilibrium point will first travel from G to V along the heavily drawn segment of the original AE_L schedule, and then it will continue along the heavily drawn segment of the MRP_L schedule, from V to K. It is obvious, then, that employment is maximized at point V, where the wage floor is at w_1 and the monopsonist employs the labor quantity L_1.

We can now see why higher wages may actually benefit not only the workers but also the consumers. As the labor union pushes the wage rate to a level no higher than w_1, the workers benefit because higher employment is forthcoming at the higher wage rate. The consumers also benefit, because the expanded employment implies a larger output and a lower product price.

Keep in mind, however, that if the labor union raises the wage rate above w_1, reverse effects are experienced: Employment declines from its peak (L_1), causing a decline in output and a rise in the product price. The workers who are lucky enough to retain their jobs continue to enjoy even higher benefits, but the laid-off workers and the consumers of the monopsonist's product become worse off.

Note that higher wages benefit both the workers and the consumers only when the monopsonist is actually exerting some positive degree of monopsony power. This happens for wage floors between w_0 and w_1. When the monopsony power is zero, as is the case for wage floors above w_1, that coincidence of self-interests disappears for any further wage increases.

By choosing a wage floor as least as high as w_1, the labor union can reduce monopsony power to zero (i.e., render the marginal expense of labor equal to the wage rate); thus it can completely eliminate monopsonistic exploitation (i.e., restore the equality $MRP_L = w$). However, *the labor union cannot remove any monopolistic exploitation ($VMP_L > w$) that may exist;* because monopolistic exploitation is founded on the divergence between average revenue (AR) and marginal revenue (MR), and the union just cannot remove the inequality $AR > MR$.

Bilateral Bargaining

The most extreme case of imperfect competition in a labor market occurs when there is monopoly on the supply side and monopsony on the demand side. This situation arises when the workers (supply side) are organized into a strong union and the industry (demand side) is a monopoly, as illustrated by a transit union and a city transit authority. Such a market structure is conventionally known as "bilateral monopoly," although a more accurate term might be "monopoly-monopsony."

Bilateral monopoly leads to a multiplicity of possible outcomes that cannot be classified in any simple way. These outcomes depend on the goals and aims of the labor union and the bargaining process itself. Here we consider only the general character of the conflicting interests that are inherent in such a bargaining situation.

Consider again Figure 13.5. The wage rate preferred by the monopsonist is, of course, w_0. What is the wage rate preferred by the labor union? That is not easy to specify, because the various union members do not have a unified common interest analogous to the profit motive of the monopsonist. To be sure, the union will prefer a wage rate at least as high as w_1; because as we explained in the preceding subsection, raising the wage floor up to w_1 benefits all union members (as well as the consumers).

But the labor union may seek a wage rate that is markedly higher than w_1, especially if union policy is strongly influenced by those workers who retain their jobs at the higher wage rate. Alternatively, the labor union may prefer that wage rate that maximizes the total wage earnings of its membership, which corresponds to the point of unit elasticity on the labor demand curve. Furthermore, the formulation of union objectives is also complicated by the desire of the union leadership to remain in office and the militancy of the union members.

Even though we are unable to specify the wage rate that a labor union may prefer, it must by now be clear that there is a conflict of interest between the monopsonist and the union, and that a spontaneous wage agreement between the two parties is highly unlikely. Typically, the underlying conflict of interest is resolved by *bargaining*. The process of negotiation is inevitably a matter of reciprocal demands and threats. The outcome depends on the relative bargaining strength and skill of the employer and the union. Unfortunately, such negotiations do not always lead smoothly to a wage rate that is acceptable to both parties; they often break down into economic warfare (lockout or strike).

*3.6 Selected Empirical Applications

We conclude this chapter with two empirical applications. The first deals with the work-sharing program in California; the second, with the effects of unionism on relative wages and employment in the United States.

Work Sharing in California[6]

During a recession, many corporations are forced to lay off hundreds, perhaps thousands, of workers because of falling sales. Surely such layoffs leave psychological scars that even time cannot heal. The laid-off workers lose their jobs, their wages, and their fringe benefits. Even the corporations are not always pleased with the layoffs. Aside from the cost of rehiring and retraining workers after sales rebound, many companies are also concerned about their image as socially responsible organizations. For instance, during the 1974–1975 recession, Motorola Inc. laid off hundreds of employees at its big Phoenix, Arizona, plant—an action that tarnished its reputation. Since that time Motorola has been determined to maintain a full crew even during business downturns.

Is there a better alternative to massive layoffs? Perhaps work sharing may be the answer. The concept of work sharing has long been used in Europe. Recently, many U.S. corporations also tried it. In the present subsection we restrict our comments to the California program. The latter is the first state work-sharing plan in the United States which also compensates workers for time lost.

Consider the case of Fleetwood Enterprises Inc., the nation's largest manufacturer of recreational vehicles and mobile homes. The recent recession in the late 1970s forced Fleetwood to close down six of its California plants and lay off about 500 workers. But through work sharing, Fleetwood succeeded in saving the jobs of 500 other employees at some nine other plants in California. How did Fleetwood accomplish this triumph? Instead of laying off employees indiscriminately, Fleetwood shortened the workweek at these nine plants from five days to four days, while reducing at the same time weekly wages proportionately. The workers were delighted not only because they retained their jobs, but also because they received regular unemployment benefits (averaging to $22) for the lost day.

Many other corporations had similar successes. For example, during the sluggish winter season of 1979–1980 Odyssey Sail Makers Inc., a small southern California maker of marine equipment, was faced with the unappealing prospect of laying off several of its most skilled work teams. Because the entire marine business was slow at that time, any workers who lost their jobs would certainly have left the industry. Thus breaking up those teams would have been costly not only to the workers, but also to Odyssey. For this reason, Odyssey and its employees were happy to participate in the work-sharing program. Indeed, some of Odyssey's workers were able to earn up to 90 percent of their normal income.

It is interesting to note that the California work-sharing plan did not grow out of public concern for the recession. Rather, it was a direct consequence of Proposition 13, the revolutionary tax-cutting measure enacted in 1978. Worried that the loss of tax revenue due to Proposition 13 would generate massive layoffs of public servants, the legislature pushed through the work-sharing bill in a matter of days. Ironically, few public employees have lost their jobs as a result of Proposition 13, but the work-sharing program has proved to be a blessing to the private sector.

The California work-sharing program is the first state plan that compensates workers for time lost. It is only a stopgap measure whose objective is to provide

[6]This subsection is based on *Dun's Review*, August 1980, pp. 62–65.

Table 13.2 Extent of Union Representation, 1958–1980						
(1)	(2)	(3)	(4)	(5)	(6)	(7)
Workers Represented by Trade Unions (thousands)			Full-Time Equivalent Employees Represented by Trade Unions (percent)			
Sector *a*	Sector *b*	Total	Sector *a*	Sector *b*	Difference	Total
1958	13,701.3	3,217.8	16,919.1	0.606	0.113	0.494	0.331
1959	13,725.5	3,185.3	16,910.8	0.585	0.109	0.477	0.320
1960	13,749.6	3,152.8	16,902.4	0.584	0.104	0.480	0.314
1961	13,478.3	3,160.6	16,638.9	0.587	0.103	0.484	0.311
1962	13,206.9	3,168.3	16,375.2	0.560	0.101	0.459	0.298
1963	13,234.5	3,365.6	16,600.1	0.557	0.105	0.452	0.298
1964	13,262.0	3,562.8	16,824.8	0.550	0.108	0.441	0.295
1965	13,618.4	3,757.0	17,375.4	0.538	0.110	0.428	0.293
1966	13,974.8	3,951.1	17,925.9	0.522	0.111	0.411	0.287
1967	13,901.0	4,791.6	18,692.6	0.514	0.130	0.385	0.292
1968	13,827.3	5,632.0	19,459.3	0.503	0.147	0.355	0.296
1969	13,497.8	5,689.3	19,187.1	0.479	0.144	0.335	0.284
1970	13,168.3	5,746.6	18,914.9	0.483	0.143	0.341	0.280
1971	13,081.6	6,027.6	19,109.2	0.494	0.147	0.348	0.283
1972	12,994.9	6,308.5	19,303.4	0.478	0.148	0.330	0.277
1973	13,315.7	6,669.0	19,984.7	0.466	0.150	0.316	0.274
1974	13,265.7	6,888.7	20,154.4	0.465	0.151	0.314	0.272
1975	11,617.8	7,018.3	18,636.1	0.444	0.153	0.292	0.258
1976	11,963.3	7,372.5	19,335.8	0.442	0.156	0.287	0.260
1977	12,387.4	6,905.7	19,293.1	0.440	0.141	0.299	0.250
1978	12,582.6	7,019.6	19,602.2	0.425	0.137	0.288	0.242
1979	13,382.8	7,642.2	21,025.0	0.436	0.144	0.293	0.251
1980	12,386.9	7,535.4	19,922.3	0.417	0.140	0.277	0.238

Source: Pencavel and Hartsog (1984, p. 196). Permission granted by the University of Chicago Press.

temporary relief to workers and corporations alike during business downturns. A company can participate in the work-sharing program for no more than 20 weeks in a 52-week period. In addition, unionized companies are required to seek union permission to participate.

The cost of California's work-sharing program has been moderate. As of May 1980, the state has disbursed a little more than $825,000 in benefits, a tiny fraction of the robust $2.3 billion unemployment fund and significantly less than what the state of California would have paid in unemployment benefits in the absence of the work-sharing program.

Despite its apparent success, work-sharing faces stiff opposition. For instance, the AFL-CIO argues that work sharing constitutes a threat to the seniority system. In addition, the AFL-CIO argues, unscrupulous employers may attempt to squeeze into four days what is normally five days' work in order to take advantage of the reduced payroll. Furthermore, the National Association of Manufacturers claims that work-sharing uses funds taken away from healthy companies to subsidize inefficient producers.

It is still too early to know how robust work sharing can be to all the criticisms advanced against it. All we can say at the present time is that work sharing is a promising idea that has worked well in California so far.

The Effects of Unionism on Relative Wages and Employment in the United States, 1920–1980[7]

John Pencavel and Catherine E. Hartsog (1984) have recently reexamined the effects of trade unions both on relative wages and relative worker-hours worked in the United States for the period 1920–1980. As in an earlier study by H. Gregg Lewis (1963, 1964), they divided the U.S. economy into two sectors, called *a* and *b*. Sector *a* includes the communications, construction, manufacturing, mining, public utilities, and transportation industries; sector *b* consists of the remaining industries except government work relief and the U.S. military. Table 13.2 shows the estimates of the thousands of workers represented by labor unions during the 1958–1980 period. Columns (1) and (2) give the total union representation in sectors *a* and *b*, respectively; and column (3) presents the sum of columns (1) and (2), that is, the total union representation in the entire economy. Columns (4), (5), and (7) show the percentage of full-time equivalent employees represented by labor unions in sector *a*, sector *b*, and the entire economy, respectively. Finally, column (6) gives the difference between columns (4) and (5), that is, the arithmetic difference in the unionization proportions in the two sectors.

Some conclusions are obvious from Table 13.2. First, the unmistakable negative trend in the series of column (4) illustrates the well-known decline of unionism in "old" industries, such as automobiles and steel. Second, column (5) indicates a slight growth of unionism in sector *b* (reflecting primarily an expansion of unionism in government). As a result of these trends in columns (4) and (5), the unionism difference between the two sectors [column (6)] narrowed considerably, falling from about 50 percent in 1958 to about 28 percent (almost half) in 1980. However, as revealed by column (7), the overall unionism in the entire U.S. economy declined from about 33 percent in 1958 to a little less than 24 percent in 1980.

Figure 13.6 The logarithm of relative wages (ln W), the logarithm of relative labor-hours worked (ln E), and the sectoral difference in unionization (P). [From Pencavel and Hartsog (1984), p. 197).] Permission granted by The University of Chicago Press.

---

[7]This subsection is based on Pencavel and Hartsog (1984).

As is evident from Figure 13.6, the hourly compensation in sector a (where unionism was declining) relative to that in sector b (where unionism was growing slightly) traces a U shape during the 1958–1980 period, declining from 1.43 in 1958 to 1.29 in 1970 and then rising to 1.37 in 1980. Note that the hourly compensation data include not only wages and salaries, but also bonuses, commissions, tips, payments in kind, employer contributions to pension and health plans, and compensation for injuries. However, they are not adjusted for changes in relative labor force composition (except for shifts of employment among large industry aggregates); thus they perhaps exaggerate the impact of unionism on relative wages.

Pencavel and Hartsog conclude that for most of the 1920–1980 period there is strong evidence of a positive impact of unionism on the average wage of union workers relative to the average wage of nonunion workers, even though the magnitude of this impact was not uniform throughout the period. However, they are not satisfied with the apparently negative effect of unionism on relative worker-hours worked. They admit (p. 217) that their "estimates are disturbingly sensitive to small changes in the specification of the estimating equation."

SUMMARY

1. To maximize her long-run profit, a monopolist must adjust the employment of factors so that each factor's MRP equals the factor's price (rental).

2. Some properties of the three value-product schedules (ARP_L, MRP_L, and VMP_L) of a monopolist are: (a) all three schedules have the same vertical-axis intercept; (b) maximum ARP_L occurs at a lower labor quantity than does APP_L; (c) VMP_L lies above MRP_L always, because $AR > MR$; (d) VMP_L lies above, below, or intersects ARP_L according to whether MPP_L lies above, below, or intersects APP_L; and (e) ARP_L rises, declines, or attains a maximum according to whether $MRP_L > ARP_L$, $MRP_L < ARP_L$, or $MRP_L = ARP_L$, respectively.

3. The monopolist's short-run demand curve for labor consists of two disconnected segments: (a) for $w >$ maximum ARP_L, it coincides with the vertical axis; and (b) for $w <$ maximum ARP_L, it follows the MRP_L schedule. When $w =$ maximum ARP_L, there is a two-point indeterminacy.

4. The monopolist's equilibrium VMP_L exceeds the wage rate (which equals MRP_L). The difference $VMP_L - MRP_L$, whose magnitude depends on the elasticity of demand for the monopolist's product, is called monopolistic exploitation by J. Robinson.

5. Because the labor supply curve facing a monopsonist is upward sloping, she can cause a fall in the wage rate by buying less labor

(monopsony power). A monopsonist's marginal expense of labor exceeds the average expense of labor (or wage rate).

6. The cardinal rule for *every* profit-maximizing producer is to expand the employment of each variable input until its MRP equals its marginal expense ($MRP = ME$).

7. When $ARP_L < w$, the monopsonist cannot cover her total variable cost; thus she suspends production.

8. At a monopsonistic equilibrium, $MRP_L > w$. The difference $MRP_L - w$, due to monopsony power, is what J. Robinson calls monopsonistic exploitation.

9. At any monopsonistic equilibrium, the monopsonist's demand for labor exceeds the supply of labor (sellers' market).

10. To minimize total cost, a monopsonist should set the marginal rate of technical substitution (given by the slope of an isoquant) equal to the ratio of marginal expense of inputs (given by the slope of a nonlinear isocost curve), not the ratio of factor prices.

11. The deviation between a factor's actual price and its "just" price is a measure of exploitation. Economic analysis, however, cannot identify a just factor price. The latter depends on ethical judgments.

12. According to Marx, labor is exploited when $w < ARP_L$. The Pigou–Robinson concept of exploitation (which is a logical implication of Clark's concept of distributive justice) applies to any situation in which the *VMP* of a factor exceeds that factor's price. Both the Marxian and the Pigou–Robinson concepts are objectionable.

13. When a labor union succeeds in raising the wage rate in a competitive labor market, total employment falls. If labor demand is inelastic, total wage income rises, and all workers can benefit by sharing the lower employment level. If labor demand is elastic, total wage income falls, and at least some workers become worse off.

14. A wage increase achieved by a labor union in a monopsonistic (or oligopsonistic) labor market may *expand* both employment and output, thus benefiting both workers and consumers.

15. A labor union may eliminate monopsonistic exploitation, but it cannot remove monopolistic exploitation.

16. In the case of bilateral monopoly ("monopoly-monopsony") there is a conflict between the monopsonist and the union. The conflict is usually resolved by bargaining.

QUESTIONS

1. A monopolist combines labor (variable input) with a fixed factor to produce output. In the following table you are given information as to how the monopolist's output (Q), price (AR), and marginal revenue (MR) behave as the employment of labor (L) increases from 1 unit to 8 units. The data for AR and MR come from a linear demand function ($p = 100 - Q$). The monopolist's total fixed cost is $1000.

L	Q	AR	MR
1	10	$90	$80
2	19	81	62
3	27	73	46
4	34	66	32
5	40	60	20
6	45	55	10
7	49	51	2
8	52	48	−4

(a) Determine the monopolist's demand curve for labor.

(b) Assume that the wage rate is $50. What is the monopolist's profit-maximizing employment of labor? Determine also the monopolist's output, elasticity of demand, total profit, and total monopolistic exploitation.

(c) Graph your results.

2. Return to the scenario of Question 1 and assume that the monopolist also happens to be a monopsonist in the labor market. The following table summarizes the information relating to the supply of labor facing the monopolist-monopsonist.

L	Wage Rate
1	$10
2	11
3	12
4	13
5	14
6	15
7	16
8	17

(a) Determine the profit-maximizing quantity of labor.

(b) Determine the maximized profit, the wage rate, output, total monopolistic exploitation, and total monopsonistic exploitation.

(c) Graph your results.

3. I can buy factors V_1 and V_2 at given factor prices w_1 and w_2, respectively. By a well-behaved homogeneous production function these factors produce output Q which I can sell along a downward-sloping demand curve. Starting from a profit-maximizing position, w_2 rises. What happens to the profit-maximizing levels of output (Q), its price, and the employment levels of V_1 and V_2?

4. A monopolist employs three factors (V_1, V_2, and V_3) and produces under constant returns to scale a certain homogeneous product. All factor rentals are determined in perfectly competitive factor markets. These rentals are $10, $5, and $20 for V_1, V_2, and V_3, respectively. At the current equilibrium of the monopolist, the marginal cost of the product is $50, the elasticity of demand is -3.0, and the monopolist sells 1000 units of output.

  (a) What is the price of the product?
  (b) What is the total profit of the monopolist?
  (c) What are the marginal physical products of V_1, V_2, and V_3?
  (d) Is any factor "exploited" by the monopolist? In what sense?

(*Hint:* The marginal cost is constant.)

5. (a) When is a factor said to be exploited?
  (b) What is monopolistic exploitation? Monopsonistic exploitation?
  (c) What is the Marxian view of exploitation?
  (d) What criticism can you offer against any concept of exploitation?

6. "If people desire a variety of products and nonconstant returns to scale prevail, the competitive group equilibrium at the bottom of the U is no longer realistic nor for that matter particularly optimal. With easy entry there would not even be enough revenue to pay hired factors their full value of marginal products, and the hiring factor will get no reward (beyond labor wages and interest on capital) for having helped provide variety. Everyone is exploited except the consumer, who must be benefiting or he would not be doing voluntarily what he is doing." Comment critically, explaining each part.

7. Show graphically that unlike a perfect competitor, a monopolist or a monopsonist can be in equilibrium with increasing average or marginal physical product of labor (variable factor).

8. A profit-maximizing firm's demand for labor is given by the equation

$$MRP_L = 200 - 4L$$

where MRP_L is the marginal revenue product of labor. The supply curve for labor facing the firm has the form

$$w = 10 + 3L$$

  (a) Determine the equilibrium values of L, MRP_L, and w.
  (b) Suppose that at the equilibrium specified in part (a), the elasticity of demand (in absolute terms) for the firm's product is 3, and the marginal physical product of labor is 62. Determine the equilibrium price, marginal revenue, total monopolistic exploitation, and total monopsonistic exploitation.
  (c) Suppose that the equilibrium is disturbed by the creation of a labor union. What value of w should the union bargain for in order to maximize employment?

9. A monopolist maximizes her profit by employing 1000 workers. At the current equilibrium, the marginal physical product of labor is 5, Lerner's degree of monopoly is 0.20, and the price of the monopolist's product is \$10. Determine the prevailing monopolistic exploitation.

*10. A monopolist-monopsonist maximizes her profit by employing 1000 workers. At the current equilibrium, the wage rate is $w = \$10$, the marginal physical product of labor is $MPP_L = 5$, the elasticity of supply of labor is $\eta_L = +2$, and the elasticity of demand for the monopolist's product is $e = -4$. Determine the price of the monopolist's product, total monopolistic exploitation, and total monopsonistic exploitation. Can the formation of a labor union benefit all workers?

FURTHER READING

Bloom, G. F., and H. R. Northrup (1973). *Economics of Labor Relations,* 7th ed. Richard D. Irwin, Inc., Homewood, Ill.

Cartter, A. M. (1959). *Theory of Wages and Employment.* Richard D. Irwin, Inc., Homewood, Ill.

Henderson, J. M., and R. E. Quandt (1980). *Microeconomic Theory: A Mathematical Approach,* 3rd ed. McGraw-Hill Book Company, New York, pp. 190–192, 212–213, and 222–226.

Hicks, J. R. (1932). *The Theory of Wages.* Macmillan & Company Ltd., London.

Lewis, H. G. (1963). *Unionism and Relative Wages in the United States: An Empirical Inquiry.* The University of Chicago Press, Chicago.

Lewis, H. G. (1964). "Relative Employment Effects of Unionism," *Proceedings of the Sixteenth Annual Winter Meeting of the Industrial Relations Research Association,* 1964.

Pencavel, J., and C. E. Hartsog (1984). "A Reconsideration of the Effects of Unionism on Relative Wages and Employment in the United States, 1920–1980," *Journal of Labor Economics,* Vol. 2, pp. 193–232.

Pigou, A. C. (1932). *The Economics of Welfare,* 4th ed. Macmillan & Company Ltd., London.

Robinson, J. (1933). *The Economics of Imperfect Competition.* Macmillan & Company Ltd., London.

Rottenberg, S. (1956). "The Baseball Player's Labor Market," *Journal of Political Economy,* Vol. 64 (June), pp. 242–258.

PART SIX

General Equilibrium and Welfare Economics

CHAPTER
14

General Equilibrium

In the first five parts of this book, we employed a method of analysis known as *partial equilibrium*. Mainly developed by the British economist Alfred Marshall, partial equilibrium analysis seeks to explain the equilibrium of an isolated market, ignoring the rest of the economic system; that is, it seeks to explain only a *part* of the economy. Recall that in drawing supply and demand curves for a particular commodity or factor, we assumed that the prices of all other commodities and factors remained constant, presumably at their respective equilibrium levels; hence we ignored any interactions between the "isolated" market and other markets.

But interactions do exist because markets are interrelated. We noted this fact as early as in Chapter 2 in relation to our discussion of substitutes and complements. For instance, as we explained in Section 2.3, when the price of pork (a beef substitute) falls, the market demand curve for beef shifts to the left because consumers tend to substitute pork for beef. Similarly, when the price of gasoline (an automobile complement) rises, the market demand for large automobiles shifts to the left, as the events of the 1970s reminded us. Nevertheless, the presence of market interactions was nowhere felt as strongly as in the theory of income distribution discussed in Chapters 12 and 13.

Partial equilibrium analysis does provide insights into the functioning of our price system, and when the ignored market interrelationships happen to be quantitatively unimportant, it also leads to conclusions that have practical usefulness. But partial equilibrium analysis is inadequate for the study of the whole economic system. The reader should resist the feeling that one can analyze the entire economy by applying partial equilibrium analysis to each of its parts (or markets) because markets are interrelated. To determine equilibrium in all markets simultaneously, economists use *general equilibrium analysis,* the principal architect of which is Leon Walras. Partial equilibrium analysis is an important first step in the analysis of general equilibrium.

General equilibrium analysis is the subject matter of this part of the book. Because of its inherent complexity and mathematical character, we shall confine our discussion to a few relatively simple cases so that we can show with a minimum amount of effort how the various pieces of the economic puzzle fit together. This chapter is divided into two parts. Part A deals with the general equilibrium of exchange, and Part B studies the problem of general equilibrium of production and consumption in a Robinson Crusoe economy. Chapter 15 develops the two-sector model and demonstrates the existence of general competitive equilibrium. Chapter 16 explores the issues of welfare economics. Finally, Chapter 17 provides a simplified introduction to capital theory.

PART A. GENERAL EQUILIBRIUM OF EXCHANGE

We begin our investigation of general equilibrium with the simple case of *pure exchange*. In this model the activity of production is completely ignored. Instead, all persons are assumed to be endowed with fixed amounts of various consumption commodities. Each person starts with the same endowment at the beginning of each period (week, month, or year). It may be helpful to think either of farmers endowed with already harvested crops, or of recipients of "care packages." Are these people content merely to consume their respective endowments, or are they willing to exchange commodities with one another? If they do wish to trade, how are the equilibrium prices and quantities determined? These are the crucial questions that we analyze in this part of the chapter.

14.1 The Fundamental Principle of Exchange

Why do people engage in voluntary exchanges (or trades)? The answer is simple: because they benefit from them. For instance, when a person purchases a book, he reveals that he prefers the book to the money he exchanges for it; that is, he becomes better off with the purchase of the book. Similarly, the seller of the book also reveals by her action that she prefers the money to the book. Thus the transaction benefits both the seller and the buyer of the book; that is, the exchange is *mutually beneficial*.

If a proposed exchange makes one of the parties better off at the expense of the other party, the injured person will simply refuse to trade; hence the exchange will not materialize. When an exchange does take place, the strong presumption is that both people are better off with the trade, because each party had the option of refusing the transaction but did not. We therefore conclude that voluntary exchange is mutually beneficial. In this book we refer to this important proposition as the *fundamental principle of exchange*.

Note that an exchange is mutually beneficial only when it is voluntary; that is, when there is no compulsion (or force) present. When I surrender my wallet to a robber who is holding his gun at my head, I most certainly become worse off. But this is *not* a "voluntary" exchange. I only agree to the "exchange" because the consequences of refusing it are dismal. In this case I simply act to minimize my losses.

The fundamental principle of exchange also presupposes the absence of fraud, but also mistake. For instance, if I purchase a bad watch from a man in the street who deliberately deceives me, I will be worse off. Similarly, if during a short trip to Italy I accidentally purchase a pair of shoes that do not fit me but I discover my mistake after I come back to the United States, I will again be worse off because I can no longer return the shoes.

Even though it is simple and obvious, the fundamental principle of exchange is not always understood. We often hear of "unscrupulous" lenders ("loan sharks") who charge "exorbitant" interest rates to "poor" consumers. Workers often resent their "low wages" and complain that their employers "exploit" them. When a price ceiling leads to the development of a black market, the sellers are often accused of "taking advantage" of "desperate" consumers. In all such cases, it is widely believed that some people (lenders, employers, and business managers) benefit "at the expense" of their customers or employees. This is not true. In a voluntary exchange, there are no losers; *all* parties benefit. Some people, of course, benefit more than others, but they all reap positive benefits. If they did not, they would not have chosen to trade.

14.2 The Edgeworth Box Diagram

To gain further insight into the fundamental principle of exchange, we develop in this section an important tool: the *Edgeworth box diagram*.[1]

Construction of the Box Diagram

Consider the simple case of an economy consisting of just two people, Adam and Beth. At the beginning of each time period, each of these two people happens to be endowed with a "care package" containing fixed amounts of two commodities, X and Y. This information is summarized in Figure 14.1. Panel (a) shows the situation of Adam, whose initial endowment (x_a^0, y_a^0) is indicated by point E_a; and panel (b) describes the position of Beth, whose initial endowment (x_b^0, y_b^0) coincides with point E_b. Note that these initial endowments place Adam and Beth on indifference curves I_a^0 and I_b^0, respectively.

To make any progress in our investigation, we must somehow combine the information contained in the two separate panels of Figure 14.1. Imagine that Beth's diagram is drawn on a separate piece of paper so that we can freely move it around as we please. Superimpose it on Adam's diagram, so that the points of initial endowments (E_a and E_b) coincide, calling the "common" endowment point E. Place a pin at E, holding points E_a and E_b together at all times, and then turn Beth's diagram around the pin by 180°, as shown in Figure 14.2. The resultant rectangle 0_aM0_bN is the Edgeworth box. The width (0_aM) of this box measures the fixed quantity of X available to the entire economy (i.e., $x_a^0 + x_b^0$); the height (0_aN) of the box measures the total quantity of Y (i.e., $y_a^0 + y_b^0$).

Every point in the Edgeworth box (or its boundary) corresponds to a specific allocation of the economy's total endowment between the two people. For instance, point E gives the initial endowment of X and Y of both Adam (measured from 0_a) and Beth (measured from 0_b). Similarly, point F allocates the quantities x_a^1, y_a^1 (measured from 0_a) to Adam, and the residual quantities x_b^1, y_b^1 (measured from 0_b) to Beth. Moreover, the movement from point E to point F represents an exchange of commodities between the two people: Adam gives Beth $y_a^0 - y_a^1$ units of commodity Y in exchange for $x_a^1 - x_a^0$ units of commodity X.

Points outside the box are irrelevant because they represent unfeasible allocations. For instance, points C and D allocate to Adam more than the total quantities of commodities X and Y, respectively, available to the entire economy; hence points C and D are not feasible.

Finally, note that through every point in the Edgeworth box there pass two indifference curves showing the levels of satisfaction of Adam and Beth. For in-

[1]Edgeworth (1881, especially pp. 21, 28–29, and 34–38) was the originator of the box-diagram idea. The diagram itself was first used by Bowley (1924, p. 5), even though Edgeworth's diagram (1881, p. 28, Fig. 1) has all the necessary ingredients. For this reason, this useful geometric device is often called the *Edgeworth–Bowley box diagram*.

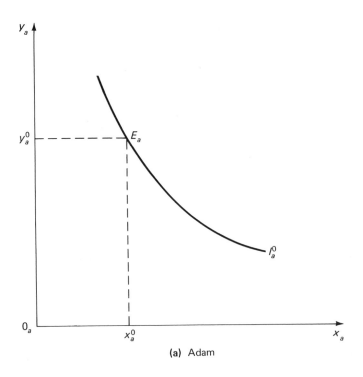

(a) Adam

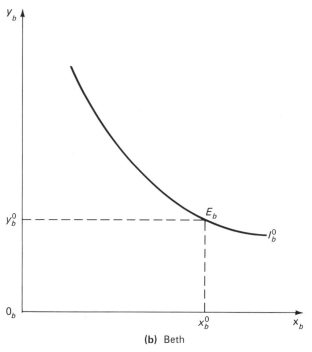

(b) Beth

Figure 14.1 The initial endowments. The initial endowments of Adam and Beth are given by the coordinates of points E_a in panel (a) and E_b in panel (b), respectively. These endowments, which are repeated at the beginning of every time period, place Adam and Beth on indifference curves I_a^0 and I_b^0, respectively.

438

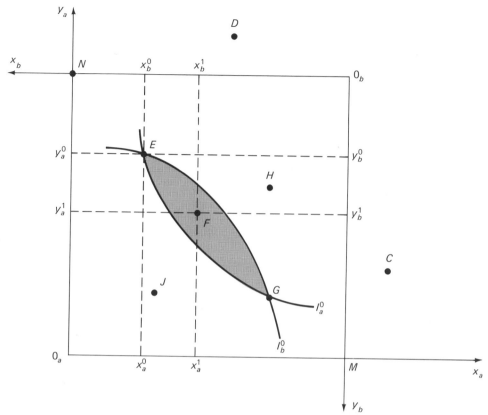

Figure 14.2 The Edgeworth box diagram. Beth's diagram is turned around by 180° and superimposed on Adam's diagram so that the points of initial endowments coincide, as shown by E. Rectangle $0_a M 0_b N$ is the Edgeworth box. The width ($0_a M$) and height ($0_a N$) of this box measure the total amounts of X and Y, respectively, available to the entire economy. Point F allocates x_a^1, y_a^1 (measured from 0_a) to Adam, and the residuals x_b^1, y_b^1 (measured from 0_b) to Beth. The movement from E to F represents an exchange: Adam gives Beth $y_a^0 - y_a^1$ in exchange for $x_a^1 - x_a^0$. Only allocations lying inside the football-shaped area bounded by I_a^0 and I_b^0 are preferred to E by both Adam and Beth.

stance, indifference curves I_a^0 and I_b^0 pass through point E, and the same indifference curves also happen to pass through point G. But while Adam's indifference curves, as illustrated by I_a^0, have the appearance we are accustomed to from Chapter 3, Beth's indifference curves are turned around and upside down, as shown by I_b^0.

The Existence of Mutually Beneficial Exchanges

Is there any reason to believe that Adam and Beth will participate in some voluntary exchange? That depends on whether there exist potential allocations that are preferred to the initial endowment point by both Adam and Beth. In the example of Figure 14.2, all allocations lying inside the football-shaped shaded area bounded by indifference curves I_a^0 and I_b^0 are "superior" to the initial endowment point E, in the sense that they are preferred to E by both Adam and Beth. Thus all allocations lying above and to the right of indifference curve I_a^0, such as F and H, are preferred to E by Adam, while all allocations lying below and to the left of I_b^0, such as F and J, are preferred to E by Beth; hence any allocation, such as F, lying in the shaded area bounded by I_a^0 and I_b^0 is simultaneously preferred by both Adam and Beth. The presumption, then, is that Adam and Beth will recognize their potential gain and voluntarily engage in some mutually beneficial exchange. For instance, they may agree to move from the initial endowment point (E) to point F.

What is the *raison d'être* for the existence of allocations that are superior (i.e., preferred by both Adam and Beth) to the initial endowment point? *The disparity between the marginal rates of substitution of X for Y (MRS_{xy}) of Adam and Beth at the initial endowment point.*[2] In the example of Figure 14.2, Adam's marginal rate of substitution (MRS_{xy}^a) at E is higher than Beth's (MRS_{xy}^b) because I_a^0 is steeper than I_b^0 at E. For concreteness, assume that $MRS_{xy}^a = 5$ and $MRS_{xy}^b = 3$. Roughly, this means that (starting at E) Adam can exchange as much as 5 units of Y for 1 extra unit of X without becoming worse off; and Beth can exchange 1 unit of X for as little as 3 units of Y without becoming worse off. Hence if Adam actually gives to Beth 4 units of Y (or some other number between 3 and 5) in exchange for 1 unit of X, they will both become better off.

We therefore conclude that the inequality $MRS_{xy}^a > MRS_{xy}^b$ means that on the margin, X is less valuable to Beth than to Adam and Y is less valuable to Adam than to Beth; hence a basis for a mutually beneficial exchange exists.

The Contract Curve and the Core

Suppose now that Adam and Beth agree to move from E to F (Figure 14.2). Will they stop there, or will they have an incentive to trade further? That depends on the relationship between their marginal rates of substitution of X for Y at F. If these marginal rates are different (i.e., if the two indifference curves passing through F intersect at F), both parties can benefit from further exchange, but if they are the same (i.e., if the two indifference curves are tangent at F), no further dealing can be mutually beneficial.

In general, exchange equilibrium can occur only at points of tangency between Adam's and Beth's indifference curves, that is, points where $MRS_{xy}^a = MRS_{xy}^b$. Such tangencies preclude the existence of football-shaped areas of mutual benefits; hence they rule out the possibility of voluntary exchanges. The locus of all such tangencies is called the *contract curve*. This is illustrated in Figure 14.3 by dashed line $0_aVZFWU0_b$.

Note that at no point on the contract curve is it possible to make one person better off without making the other worse off. For instance, proceeding from W, Adam could be brought to a higher indifference curve, say I_a^4, but only at the cost of pushing Beth to a lower indifference curve. Similarly, from W again, Beth can be placed on a higher indifference curve, say I_b^3, but at the cost of forcing Adam to a lower indifference curve. Thus any point on the contract curve is a point of rest in exchange.

Given the initial endowment point, we narrow the range of potential exchange equilibria even further. For instance, if the initial endowments are indicated by point E (Figure 14.3), we can expect the general equilibrium of exchange to occur somewhere along that portion of the contract curve lying between points Z and W. This is so because, as we saw, the final equilibrium point must satisfy two conditions: (1) it must lie in the football-shaped area bounded by indifference curves I_a^2 and I_b^2, and (2) it must occur on the contract curve.

The curve ZW is called the *core* of the economy with respect to initial endowment point E. *The core is thus the locus of all potential exchange equilibria.*

---

[2]The discussion in the text assumes implicitly that indifference curves are smoothly continuous, without kinks.

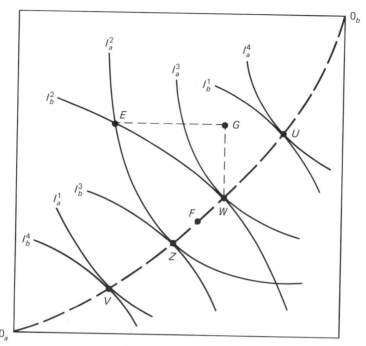

Figure 14.3 The contract curve versus the core. Exchange equilibrium can occur only at points of tangency between Adam's and Beth's indifference curves, such as V, Z, W, and U. The locus of all such tangencies is called the *contract curve*, as shown by dashed line $0_a VZFWU0_b$. If the initial endowments are given by E, exchange equilibrium can occur only along the portion ZW (known as the core) of the contract curve.

In the case of a two-person economy, the exact equilibrium point reached by the two traders cannot be determined. The final outcome depends crucially on the bargaining skills of the two parties. If Beth is naive and reacts passively to Adam's subtle bargaining, equilibrium may occur at W (or very close to it). For instance, Adam could bluff that his "last" offer is WG units of Y in exchange for EG units of X, and that Beth can take it or leave it. In that case, if Beth accepts Adam's offer, equilibrium will occur at W where Adam's benefit is maximized. Of course, Beth may very well ignore Adam's "last" offer, making instead a "last" offer of her own; and so on. Hence equilibrium may occur at any point of the core. This conclusion illustrates the well-known indeterminacy of bilateral monopoly.

14.3 Competitive Equilibrium[3]

In real-world markets, we rarely observe buyers and sellers bargaining over the terms of exchange. The reason is simple: In a typical market, there are many small buyers and many small sellers, and no individual buyer or seller has any control over prices. Each person acts as a price taker; that is, each person accepts prices as given and purchases or sells whatever quantities he wishes to trade at those prices. For instance, a housewife will be disappointed if she expects a grocery-store manager to let her have a loaf of bread below the going rate, because the store manager will simply refuse and wait for the next customer. Similarly, a storekeeper cannot hope

---

[3]This section can be read together with the Appendix to Chapter 14.

to sell his eggs at prices that are higher than the market price, because he will then lose all his customers to his competitors. As we already know, in competitive markets prices are determined by the impersonal forces of supply and demand. In this section we show how general competitive equilibrium is attained in a two-commodity exchange economy.

The Budget Line of a Typical Trader

Before we study the general equilibrium of a multiperson exchange economy, we must explain the behavior of a typical person, say Adam. We begin with Adam's budget line.

Suppose that Adam is initially endowed with x_0 units of commodity X and y_0 units of Y, as shown in Figure 14.4 by point E. For any money prices, p_x and p_y, Adam's money income (I) is equal to the value of his commodity holdings:

$$I = p_x x_0 + p_y y_0 \tag{14.1}$$

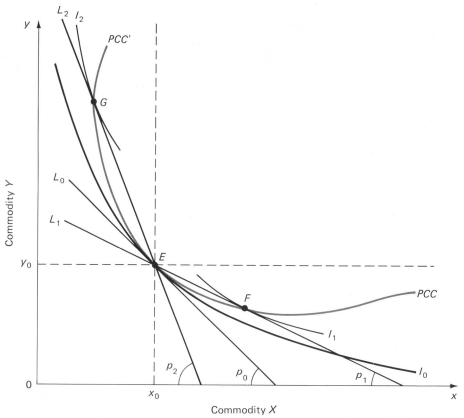

Figure 14.4 The price consumption curve. Adam's budget line always passes through initial endowment point E and has a slope equal to the price ratio ($p \equiv p_x/p_y$), as shown by L_0, L_1, and L_2. When p equals the MRS_{xy} at E, as shown by L_0, Adam consumes his initial endowment. With budget lines L_1 and L_2 Adam consumes at F and G, respectively. Adam's price consumption curve (gray lines PCC and PCC') is the locus of all conceivable equilibria, such as E, F, and G, and lies above I_0 except at E.

Accordingly, Adam's budget equation has the form

$$I = p_x x_0 + p_y y_0 = p_x x + p_y y \tag{14.2}$$

where x and y are the quantities of X and Y, respectively, to be chosen by Adam.

Graphically, equation (14.2) corresponds to a straight line whose absolute slope equals the *ratio* of commodity prices p_x/p_y and *passes through Adam's endowment point (E)*, as shown in Figure 14.4 by the three illustrative lines L_1, L_0, and L_2. We already know why the absolute slope of the budget line equals the price ratio.[4] To verify that the budget line always passes through the endowment point (E) irrespective of prices, observe that when we set $x = x_0$ and $y = y_0$, equation (14.2) becomes an identity. The commonsense explanation of this proposition is simple: If Adam's income is defined to be equal to the value of his endowment, as in equation (14.1), Adam must always have just enough income to "purchase" his initial endowment; hence the initial endowment point must always lie on Adam's budget line, irrespective of the level of the commodity prices.

It is now clear that Adam's budget line, and thus his economic behavior, is perfectly determined when only the *price ratio* p_x/p_y is known. The absolute money prices p_x, p_y are not important. Indeed, our objective in this section is to determine the equilibrium price ratio, not the individual money prices. For this reason, we adopt the symbol p to represent the price ratio p_x/p_y.

The price ratio (p) has a very important meaning: It is the *relative price* of commodity X in terms of commodity Y. That is, p gives the number of units of Y that exchange for 1 unit of X in the marketplace (in the same way that the money price p_x gives the number of dollars that exchange for 1 unit of X). Commodity Y, in terms of which we express the relative prices of other commodities, is called the *numéraire* (or standard of value).

The Price Consumption Curve Again

The economic behavior of Adam is conveniently summarized by his price consumption curve (*PCC*), illustrated in Figure 14.4. When the market price ratio is equal to Adam's marginal rate of substitution at E, as shown by the slope (p_0) of budget line L_0, Adam's best option is to consume his initial endowment. However, when the market price ratio is different from p_0, as shown by budget lines L_1 and L_2, Adam can become better off by selling part of his endowment of one commodity and purchasing with the sale proceeds more of the second commodity (i.e., by engaging in exchange).

For instance, with budget line L_1 Adam would consume bundle F; hence he would exchange Y for X, as indicated by the movement from E to F. If the price ratio increased to p_2 as shown by budget line L_2, Adam's consumption equilibrium would move to G, where L_2 is tangent to indifference curve I_2; hence he would exchange X for Y, as shown by the movement from E to G.

Adam's price consumption curve, shown by gray lines *PCC* and *PCC'*, is the locus of all conceivable consumption equilibrium points (such as E, F, and G). Note that all consumption equilibrium points, except the initial endowment point (E), lie *above* indifference curve I_0 passing through E. This must be so because Adam will not voluntarily participate in any exchange unless he is thereby made better off.

---

[4]See Section 4.1, in particular equation (4.2).

The Existence of Competitive Equilibrium

We can now use the Edgeworth box to illustrate the existence of the general competitive equilibrium of exchange. Assume that the many people in the economy are divided equally into two large groups. Each member of the first group is identical to our old friend Adam with respect to tastes and initial endowments. Similarly, each member of the second group is identical to Beth with respect to tastes and initial endowments. Because in any general equilibrium state all persons face the same relative prices, all Adams (i.e., all members of the first group) must finish with exactly the same baskets of commodities X and Y; and similarly all Beths (i.e., all members of the second group) must also finish with the same bundles of X and Y.[5] Because of this, the general competitive equilibrium of exchange can be conveniently reduced to the competitive equilibrium of a miniature economy consisting of just one Adam and one Beth (i.e., a single representative citizen of each group), as illustrated in Figure 14.5.

The initial endowments are given by point E, which places Adam on indifference curve I_a^0 and Beth on I_b^0 (as in Figure 14.2). General competitive equilibrium occurs at the intersection (F) of Adam's and Beth's price consumption curves (PCC_a and PCC_b, respectively). When the price ratio is p_0, as shown by budget line L_0, both Adam and Beth choose allocation F, because F lies on both price consumption curves. (Note that budget line L_0 is necessarily *common to both parties*.) Thus at p_0 supply equals demand in both markets simultaneously. As before, the movement from E to F is essentially accomplished by an appropriate exchange between Adam and Beth.

The general competitive equilibrium of exchange (point F) necessarily occurs on the contract curve. The reason is simple. Because F lies on PCC_a, budget line L_0 is necessarily tangent to Adam's indifference curve (not drawn) passing through F. But F lies also on PCC_b; hence budget line L_0 is also tangent to Beth's indifference curve (not drawn) passing through F. Accordingly, the two indifference curves passing through F have exactly the same slope at F; that is, they are tangent at F, or point F lies on the contract curve.

How can we be sure that the two price consumption curves intersect at some point? That is, how do we know that general competitive equilibrium exists? First recall that PCC_a lies above and to the right of indifference curve I_a^0, and PCC_b lies below and to the left of I_b^0; hence any conceivable intersection of PCC_a and PCC_b must occur in the football-shaped area bounded by I_a^0 and I_b^0. Now consider the two limiting budget lines L_1 and L_2 associated with price ratios p_1 and p_2, respectively. When $p = p_2$, Adam's consumption equilibrium occurs somewhere on L_2 between E and H, as illustrated by point J; and when $p = p_1$, Adam reaches equilibrium on L_1 at a point that necessarily lies to the right of Z, as shown by R.[6] Surely, points J and R lie on PCC_a as shown. Since J and R are separated by the contract curve, it follows that a continuously drawn PCC_a from J to R *must* intersect the contract curve (at least once) between H and Z (i.e., at the core), as shown by F. (Note that the segment of PCC_a from J to R must lie between budget lines L_1 and L_2.) In a similar fashion we can establish the fact that a pair of points, such as K and M, separated by the contract curve, lie on PCC_b. Hence PCC_b must also intersect the contract curve (at least once) between H and Z. On the basis of the argument of the previous paragraph, PCC_a and PCC_b necessarily intersect the contract curve

---

[5]This proposition is known as the *parity theorem.*

[6]Budget line L_2 lies above I_a^0 only along the segment EH. Hence Adam's consumption equilibrium must occur on EH. Similarly, Adam must choose a point on budget line L_1 to the right of Z, because L_1 intersects I_a^2 at Z from left to right. Hence Adam becomes better off as he travels along L_1 from Z toward R.

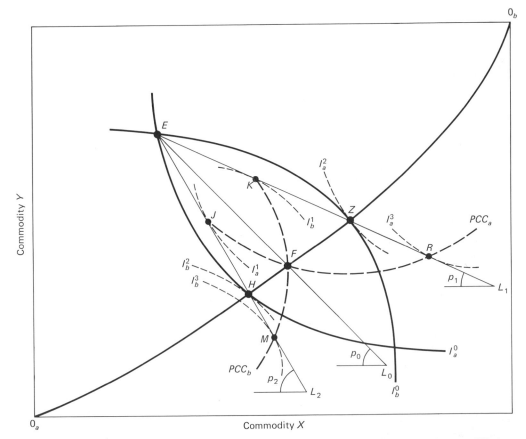

Figure 14.5 The existence of competitive equilibrium. General competitive equilibrium occurs at F, where PCC_a and PCC_b intersect. When $p = p_0$, as shown by budget line L_0, both persons choose allocation F, and thus supply equals demand in both markets simultaneously. Note that allocation F belongs to the core.

along segment HZ at exactly the same point(s). We therefore conclude that general competitive equilibrium exists; and moreover, it coincides with some allocation that belongs to the core.

Stability of Competitive Equilibrium

Suppose that the economy is not at the general competitive equilibrium described above. Will there be any forces that will automatically bring the economy back to equilibrium? In other words, is the general competitive equilibrium of exchange stable? A complete answer to this question lies beyond the scope of this book. What we show below is that a unique equilibrium similar to that of Figure 14.5 can be expected to be stable.

Consider Figure 14.6 which gives only the endowment point (E) and the relevant portions of the price-consumption curves of Adam and Beth. As before, general competitive equilibrium occurs at F where PCC_a and PCC_b intersect. The equilibrium price ratio is p_0, as indicated by budget line L_0 passing through F.

Suppose that the current price ratio is p_2, as shown by budget line L_2. Obviously, $p_2 > p_0$. At p_2 Adam chooses bundle V (measured from 0_a) and Beth chooses bundle S (measured from 0_b); thus there exists an excess supply of X, shown by horizontal

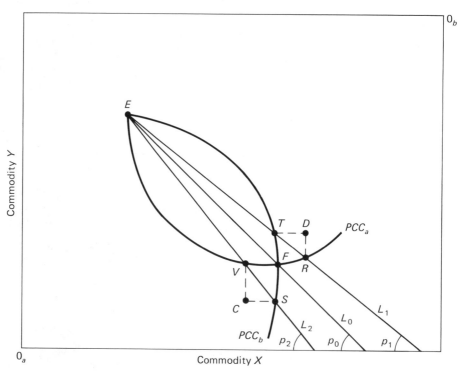

Figure 14.6 The stability of competitive equilibrium. Equilibrium occurs at the intersection (F) of PCC_a and PCC_b. When the price ratio is p_2, as shown by budget line L_2, there emerges an excess supply of X (equal to CS) and an excess demand for Y (equal to CV), causing the price ratio to fall; hence the budget line (L_2) will rotate counterclockwise through E until equilibrium is established at F. If the price ratio is p_1, as shown by L_1, the excess demand for X (equal to TD) and the excess supply of Y (equal to RD) will cause the price ratio to rise; thus the budget line (L_1) will rotate clockwise through E until equilibrium is again attained at F.

distance CS, and an excess demand for Y, indicated by vertical distance CV, as the reader should verify. It is, then, reasonable to assume that the money price of $X(p_x)$ will tend to fall while the money price of Y (p_y) will tend to rise, and *both* of these tendencies will cause the price ratio p_x/p_y to *fall*. As the price ratio falls, the common budget line will rotate through the initial endowment point E in the counterclockwise direction and move closer and closer to budget line L_0. When the price ratio becomes equal to p_0, the rotating budget line will coincide with L_0 and general competitive equilibrium will be attained.

When the current price ratio is lower than p_0, there is a tendency for it to rise. For instance, assume that the price ratio is p_1, as shown by budget line L_1. At this low price ratio, Adam prefers bundle R (measured from 0_a) and Beth prefers bundle T (measured from 0_b). As the reader can show, there exists now an excess demand for X equal to horizontal distance TD, and an excess supply of Y equal to vertical distance RD. Accordingly, there exists a tendency for p_x to rise and a tendency for p_y to fall, and both of these tendencies will cause the price ratio p_x/p_y to rise. As this happens, the common budget line (L_1) will rotate through E in the clockwise direction until it coincides with L_0. At that point, general competitive equilibrium will be attained.

It is now clear that the increase in the number of traders removes the indeterminacy of bilateral monopoly.[7] As Adam Smith noted over two centuries ago, the pursuit of self-interest by individual members of an economy does not lead to chaos, but to a mutually beneficial social order, that is, a stable general competitive equilibrium. This is an admirable result.

PART B. GENERAL EQUILIBRIUM OF PRODUCTION AND CONSUMPTION

The distinguishing characteristic of an exchange economy, discussed in Part A, is the absence of production. That is, at the beginning of each period, each person is miraculously endowed with an initial collection of commodities (initial endowment), and the economic problem is how to redistribute these commodities among the various persons. In the real world, however, commodities do not come "from the heavens" like the manna of the children of Israel. As we pointed out in Chapter 6, practically all commodities come into existence through the process of production. Producers first use the services of factors of production to produce commodities, which are then distributed among the consumers. The purpose of this part of the chapter is to bring production into focus and initiate the discussion of the important problem of allocation of factors of production to alternative uses. We begin in Section 14.4 with the simplest possible world: a one-person economy (or Robinson Crusoe economy). As it turns out, most concepts and propositions developed within the context of a one-person economy are also valid for more complicated economies. Chapter 15 develops the two-sector model of general equilibrium—a model that finds useful applications in many areas of economics, such as the theory of distribution, the theory of growth, and the theory of international trade.

14.4 A Robinson Crusoe Economy

Consider a man shipwrecked on a tiny island that is completely uninhabited. To survive, the marooned person must produce food by cultivating the available amount of land. Our Robinson Crusoe has to decide how to divide his time between leisure and the production of food.

The Production Function of Food

Figure 14.7 gives Robinson's production function of food in the form of a total-product curve (OS), because land is fixed.[8] We assume that unless land is cultivated, the output of food is zero; hence the total product curve starts at the origin. When Robinson applies any positive amount of labor to the available land, total output is positive. Moreover, we assume that the output of food is an increasing function of the amount of labor, but because the amount of land is fixed, the marginal physical product of labor (given by the slope of the total product curve) is diminishing (i.e.,

---

[7]Exceptions do exist. The two price consumption curves may intersect each other many times, leading to multiple equilibria. Indeed, the multiplicity of equilibrium may degenerate into the phenomenon known as *neutral equilibrium,* which arises when the price consumption curves coincide over an entire region of the contract curve. These pathological cases are ignored in the text.

[8]The reader may wish to review Chapter 6, especially Section 6.3, before reading Section 14.4.

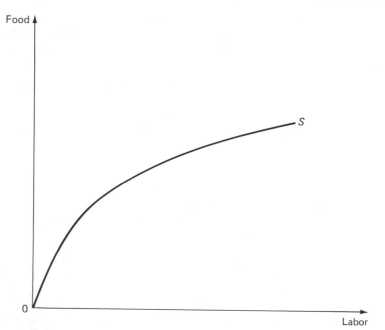

Figure 14.7 Robinson's production function of food. Because land is fixed, the production function takes the form of a total-product curve, as shown by 0S. The output of food is an increasing function of the amount of labor, but as labor increases, the law of diminishing returns causes the marginal physical product of labor to fall, as shown by the curvature of 0S.

the law of diminishing returns holds), as illustrated by the concavity of the total product curve.

The Production-Possibilities Frontier of Robinson Crusoe

We now combine the production function of food with Robinson's fixed amount of time (i.e., 24 hours per day) to obtain the various alternative combinations of food and leisure available for consumption. This is shown in Figure 14.8.

The fixed amount of time available to Robinson is given by horizontal distance 00′, which also corresponds to maximum leisure time. The total-product curve is now drawn with 180° rotation, starting at 0′. Curve 0′V, viewed with respect to 0 as origin, is Robinson's *production-possibilities frontier* (or *transformation curve*). That is, curve 0′V is the locus of all combinations of food and leisure (measured from 0) available to Robinson. For instance, if it were possible for Robinson to work 24 hours per day, the maximum output of food (per period) would be 0V. Similarly, if Robinson worked 0′U per period, the output of food would be UE (or 0M) and he would also enjoy 0U leisure, as shown by point E.

We already know that the (absolute) slope of the total-product curve 0′S at some point, such as E, gives the marginal physical product of labor, as shown in Figure 14.8. This is also true of the production-possibilities frontier, because 0′V is a portion of 0′S. But the latter property is a peculiarity of the current model and does not generalize to more complex economies.

In general, the absolute slope of the production-possibilities frontier, known as the *marginal rate of transformation,* shows the number of units of food that Robinson

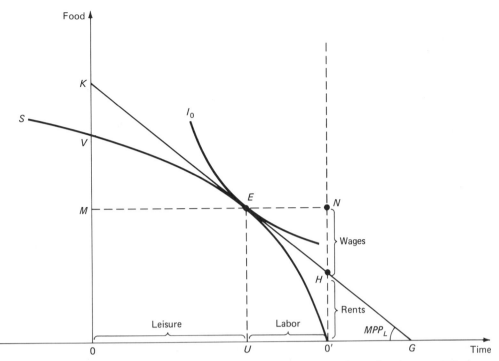

Figure 14.8 Robinson's production-possibilities frontier and production equilibrium.
The fixed amount of time available to Robinson is shown by distance $00'$. The total-product
curve $(0'S)$ is now drawn with $180°$ rotation, starting at $0'$. Curve $0'V$, viewed with respect
to 0 as origin, is Robinson's production-possibilities frontier; its slope (which is equal to
MPP_L) gives the opportunity cost of leisure in terms of food. Robinson's equilibrium occurs
at E where $0'V$ is tangent to indifference curve I_0. The real wage rate (w/p_f) is given by the
slope of $0'V$ at E, and total wages in terms of food are equal to NH. Total rent in terms of
food is equal to $0'H$. Robinson's budget line coincides with $KH0'$.

(or society) must sacrifice for one extra unit of leisure. For instance, starting at E,
Robinson can increase his leisure by one hour by working one hour less than $0'U$.
But then the output of food will decrease. By how much? By the marginal physical
product of labor (MPP_L), which is given by the slope of the production-possibilities
frontier at E. We therefore conclude that the marginal rate of transformation at E
is none other than the *opportunity cost of leisure* (the commodity measured along
the horizontal axis) in terms of food (the commodity measured along the vertical
axis). This is a general concept that is valid for all models.

Production Equilibrium

The production-possibilities frontier $0'V$ is a "menu" of alternative combinations
of leisure and food from which Robinson can choose. To determine Robinson's production equilibrium, we must also introduce his tastes. For this purpose, we superimpose on the production-possibilities frontier Robinson's indifference map, as
illustrated in Figure 14.8 by indifference curve I_0. Evidently, Robinson will choose
the most desirable alternative, that is, bundle E, where the production-possibilities
frontier is tangent to indifference curve I_0. Thus Robinson will enjoy $0U$ leisure and
$0M$ food per period.

The Price System

We can reap more benefits from our Robinson Crusoe economy by introducing prices. For this purpose, we must allow Robinson Crusoe to play two distinct roles: the role of a profit-maximizing producer and the role of a utility-maximizing consumer. In each of these roles, we assume that Robinson acts as a price taker.

As a producer, Robinson hires labor and land and produces food. To maximize profit, he increases his employment of labor until the marginal revenue product of labor ($MRP_L = MR \cdot MPP_L$) equals the wage rate (w). Because he is a price taker, $MR = AR$ = price of food (p_f). Accordingly, the profit-maximization condition becomes

$$p_f \cdot MPP_L = w \tag{14.3}$$

or, dividing both sides by p_f,

$$MPP_L = \frac{w}{p_f} = real \text{ wage rate} \tag{14.4}$$

For instance, if the real wage rate (w/p_f) were equal to the slope of straight-line KG (Figure 14.8), Robinson would hire $0'U$ units of labor, which he would combine with the fixed quantity of land to produce UE (or $0M$) units of food. His total wage bill in terms of food (i.e., wL/p_f) would then be equal to vertical distance NH.[9] The rest of his output (i.e., $0'H$) would be either profit (if the rent for land services were zero) or rent.

Because land is fixed (or inelastically supplied), it earns Ricardian rent. Drawing on our discussion of Chapter 12, especially Section 12.8, we can easily conclude that in the long run all profits will be competed away, and total rent will be equal to the difference between total revenue and total wages; that is, total rent in terms of food (or rT/p_f) will be equal to $0'H$, as shown in Figure 14.8.

As a consumer, Robinson supplies labor and land and earns wages and rents, and he completes the cycle by spending his total income on food. For instance, if the real wage rate (w/p_f) were equal to the slope of line KG and total rents (in terms of food) were equal to $0'H$, Robinson's budget line would coincide with $KH0'$.[10] In that case Robinson would supply $0'U$ units of labor and purchase UE (or $0M$) units of food, and both the factor markets (i.e., the labor market and the land market) and the food market would be in equilibrium. We therefore conclude that the general equilibrium value of the real wage rate coincides with the slope of KG and general equilibrium occurs at point E.

Figure 14.9 shows that the general equilibrium of the Robinson Crusoe economy is stable. General equilibrium occurs again at E. If the real wage rate were below its equilibrium level, as shown by line CD, the Robinson-producer would want to produce at A, but the Robinson-consumer would choose bundle G. In the labor market, demand would exceed supply by horizontal distance MG, and in the food market, supply would exceed demand by vertical distance MA. The excess demand for labor would cause w to rise while the excess supply of food would cause p_f to fall; thus the ratio w/p_f would rise, causing line CD to become steeper. During this process the desired production point would travel along the production-possibilities

---

[9]Note that $w/p_f = MPP_L = NH/EN$. Hence $(w/p_f)0'U = (w/p_f)EN = NH$.

[10]Robinson's budget line must pass through point H, because total rent in terms of food is by assumption equal to $0'H$. The slope of the budget line is necessarily equal to the real wage rate (w/p_f), which is the ratio of the price (w) of the commodity measured on the horizontal axis to the price (p_f) of the commodity measured on the vertical axis.

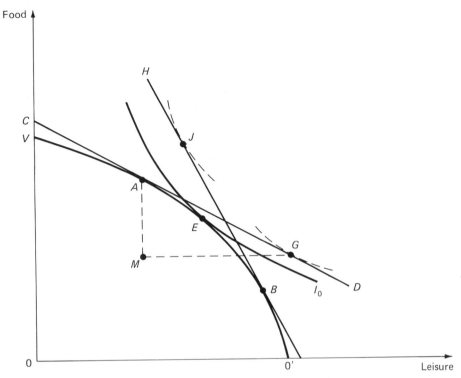

Figure 14.9 Stability of general equilibrium. General competitive equilibrium occurs at *E*. If the real wage rate were below its equilibrium level, as shown by *CD*, the Robinson-producer would want to produce at *A*, but the Robinson-consumer would choose *G*. The excess demand for labor (*MG*) and the excess supply of food (*MA*) would cause the real wage rate to rise until it was equal to its equilibrium value. If the real wage rate were higher than its equilibrium level, as shown by *HB*, the Robinson-producer would want to produce at *B*, but the Robinson-consumer would choose *J*. The resultant disequilibrium in the markets for labor and food would cause the real wage rate to fall until general equilibrium was attained at *E*.

frontier from *A* to *E*, and the desired consumption point would also follow some path (not shown) from *G* to *E*. When the real wage rate attained its equilibrium value, the desired points for production and consumption would coincide at *E*.

Starting with a real wage rate that is higher than its equilibrium level, as shown by line *HB*, the process would be reversed. The Robinson-producer would want to produce at *B*, but the Robinson-consumer would choose bundle *J*. The resultant disequilibrium in both the labor market and the food market would cause the real wage rate to fall until it became equal to its equilibrium value. We leave the details as an exercise for the interested reader.

14.5 East–West Trade: An Empirical Application

It is generally agreed that international trade between the market-oriented economies of the West and the centrally planned economies of the Soviet bloc is mutually beneficial, because such trade bargains are entered voluntarily on both sides. Yet East–West trade faces many political and economic obstacles. In this section we discuss the difficulties that surround East–West trade; we also give a brief account of the recent Soviet–American wheat deals.

Political Obstacles to East–West Trade

On balance, the East exports raw materials to the West in exchange for new technology and manufactured goods (such as machinery, consumer goods, chemical and building materials, and food). Relative to total world trade, however, East–West trade is much more important to the East than it is to the West.

The political obstacles to East–West trade are deeply rooted into the ideological differences between the two blocs and fluctuate with the general state of international relations. After long, unsuccessful efforts at détente (interrupted by the escalation of the Vietnam War), the visits of President Nixon to China and the USSR in 1972 generated an atmosphere of hope and optimism for improved trade relations between the East and the West. Subsequent developments, however, showed how elusive is the goal of peaceful cooperation between the two superpowers of the world. Concern about Soviet policy toward Jewish emigration, and human rights generally, has led to American restrictions (such as the 1978 cancellation of a computer sale, which the Soviets eventually replaced by a French one) and the continued denial of most-favored-nation status to the USSR and other Eastern countries. Soviet–American relations worsened further following the Soviet invasion of Afghanistan, which prompted the American embargo on exports of grain and high-technology goods.

Some political observers are fearful of any serious dependence on, say, Soviet trade. They point to the USSR's sudden cutting of purchases of Icelandic fish in 1948 and the sales of oil to Israel in 1956, even though the United States also reduced abruptly the Cuban sugar quota in 1960.

In addition, many observers on both sides feel that any transaction benefiting the other side, the Enemy, is harmful to their side. Their recommendation is to further restrict East–West trade even if such trade brings direct economic benefits to their own side.

The political obstacles are formidable, but the potential mutual benefits of East–West trade are also high. One wonders if the world will ever be smart enough to throw away the guns and concentrate on peaceful cooperation and free international trade in the pursuit of economic welfare. Surely, the hope to abolish poverty and disease lies in peaceful cooperation, not in mistrust, treachery, hostility, and guns.

Economic Obstacles to East–West Trade

We now turn to the economic obstacles to East–West trade, which are no less formidable than the political obstacles. In centrally planned economies, prices—the basis on which one shops—are primarily accounting devices. Unlike the prices that exist in market economies, the prices in the Eastern bloc do not reflect opportunity costs; and only to a very limited extent do they serve as signaling devices in the allocation of resources. The latter is instead integrated with the planning mechanism, which seeks to achieve material balances.

For instance, for their own internal purposes, the USSR and other Eastern-bloc countries have kept the prices of consumer goods artificially high and the prices of capital goods artificially low. As a result, foreigners are not allowed to trade freely on the basis of such artificial prices, nor can domestic residents buy and sell freely abroad. If such trade were allowed, it would be inefficient; it would also frustrate the main goals of the planners. For this reason, Eastern-bloc countries conduct their international trade through foreign trade organizations. Nevertheless, the function of these organizations is greatly hampered, among other things, by the fact that they cannot compare foreign prices to domestic prices, because the latter are not equal to opportunity costs.

Because of their emphasis on central planning, the leaders of Eastern-bloc countries view foreign trade as an economic disturbance that interferes with the planning process. Thus their tendency is to leave no room for international trade in the long run. The foreign trade organizations are apparently used as emergency devices by means of which the planners expect to correct through imports any deficiencies that may arise in some sectors, or to get rid of any occasional surpluses through exports. However, the full benefits of international trade can be attained only if it is allowed to become an integral part of planning instead of being used as a residuum.

The planning procedures of Eastern-bloc countries render their currencies inconvertible. This means that foreigners cannot legally hold, for example, rubles and hence are not allowed to spend rubles freely, and similarly, Russians are not free to use their rubles to buy foreign currencies. Such currency restrictions rule out multilateral trade, at least in East–East trade. For instance, if Czechoslovakia sells tractors to the USSR, it cannot use the rubles it receives to pay for imports from Romania. Instead, the Czechs must use their rubles to purchase whatever commodities the Soviet foreign trade organization has to sell. However, multilateral exchanges are still possible in East–West trade, because the latter can be conducted with convertible Western currencies. For instance, the USSR may export natural gas to France in exchange for French francs, and later use the francs to purchase machinery from West Germany. The restriction of multilateral trade reduces the scope of potential benefits from international trade.

Another obstacle to East–West trade is the difficulty that Eastern economies face in expanding their exports fast enough to keep pace with their import needs. This problem is primarily due to the low quality of Eastern exports, particularly consumer goods.

The Soviet–American Wheat Deals

The USSR is the world's largest wheat producer. For instance, in 1980 the USSR produced about 98 million metric tons of wheat, while the United States produced a little over 64 million metric tons. Historically, the USSR has been a major exporter of wheat, but since the early 1970s, the country has turned into a net grain importer due to increased domestic consumption.

Russian grain imports are particularly heavy whenever the weather causes the Soviet crop to be bad. This was the case in 1972 when the Soviets purchased about one-fourth of the U.S. wheat crop. This unprecedented Soviet–American wheat deal disrupted the American economy, and it was later suspected that the Russians had taken advantage of their monopoly of information about Soviet crop conditions. The feeling was that the Soviets, knowing that their own harvest would be very poor, quietly purchased large amounts of grain at low prices. This charge was not justified, however, because the Soviet purchases actually unfolded over several months; and their intended magnitude was known to the U.S. Department of Agriculture and major grain dealers when most contracts were negotiated.

What actually permitted the Soviets to enjoy a continuing bargain on U.S. grain was the perverse and obsolete American policy. To support farm incomes, U.S. agricultural policy restricted the number of acres of land that farmers could use to plant wheat, and this acreage control was allowed to continue even after it became known that it was no longer necessary. In addition, the U.S. Department of Agriculture failed to remove its obsolete subsidy on the export of "surplus" grain even when a surplus no longer existed. As a result, U.S. taxpayers' money was used to assist the Russians to purchase U.S. grain at prices that were much lower than those paid by U.S. consumers.

A few years later, the United States and the USSR negotiated a five-year bilateral grain trade agreement (1977–1981) according to which the USSR was to purchase at least 6 million metric tons of wheat and corn each year, and the United States was to permit purchases up to 8 million metric tons a year, with larger purchases requiring new negotiations.

Following the invasion of Afghanistan, however, the United States imposed on January 5, 1980, an embargo on exports of grain and high technology to the USSR. In addition, the United States tried to persuade other friendly nations to avoid supplying the Soviets with the needed grain. But the Soviets were able after all to find grain from other sources, such as Argentina, Canada, and France. The American farmers also recouped part of their lost Russian sales by exporting wheat to those countries that had increased their sales to the USSR. Indeed, there is evidence that some U.S. grain was shipped to third-party countries and reexported to the USSR. So the U.S. embargo did not really work, and the Soviet troops are still in Afghanistan. President Ronald Reagan lifted the embargo in 1981 and renewed the five-year grain trade agreement in 1983.

SUMMARY

1. To determine equilibrium in all markets simultaneously, economists use general equilibrium analysis. Partial equilibrium analysis is not adequate for this purpose, because markets are interrelated.

2. In a pure exchange economy, production is absent. All people are instead endowed with fixed amounts of various consumption commodities, which they trade among themselves. The same endowments are repeated each period.

3. *Fundamental principle of exchange:* Voluntary exchange is mutually beneficial, with fraud and mistake excluded.

4. The dimensions of the Edgeworth box give the total quantities of the two commodities available to the entire economy. Only points in the box (or its boundary) correspond to feasible allocations.

5. With smoothly continuous indifference curves, the *raison d'être* for the existence of mutually beneficial (superior) allocations is the disparity between the marginal rates of substitution of the two people at the initial endowment point.

6. Exchange equilibrium can occur only along the contract curve (i.e., the locus of tangencies

between the two sets of indifference curves inside the Edgeworth box).

7. The locus of all potential exchange equilibria (the core) is that part of the contract curve which is bounded by the two indifference curves passing through the initial endowment point.

8. In a two-person economy (bilateral monopoly), equilibrium is indeterminate as it depends on the bargaining skills of the two parties.

9. General competitive equilibrium of exchange is illustrated graphically by the intersection (along the contract curve) of the two price-consumption curves, which start at the initial endowment point.

10. Crusoe's production-possibilities frontier (*PPF*), or transformation curve, is the locus of all alternative combinations of food and leisure available to him. The marginal rate of transformation (slope of *PPF*) gives the opportunity cost of leisure in terms of food.

11. Crusoe chooses the most desirable combination of food and leisure, indicated by the tangency of the *PPF* to the highest possible indifference curve. This result is also brought about by a perfectly competitive market system.

QUESTIONS

1. According to a recent article in *The Wall Street Journal* (December 20, 1983, p. 6), the three-year contract between Greyhound and the Amalgamated Transit Union involved approximately a 14.8 percent *cut* in wages and

fringe benefits annually. Greyhound's first-year savings were expected to amount to between $40 million and $60 million.

(a) Is Greyhound exploiting its employees?

(b) Since the new labor contract necessarily

makes all Greyhound employees worse off, how can we say that a voluntary transaction is always mutually beneficial?

2. Two isolated persons with normally shaped indifference curves have positive initial stocks of each of two goods, X and Y. Their tastes and endowments are such that mutually profitable trade is possible, and both indifference maps are known to both persons. Assuming rational self-interest on the part of each person, identify the outcome implied under each of the following conditions, and indicate whether each condition is sufficient for a unique outcome.

(a) The exchange ratio is set at a level that will equate the demand and supply for each good.

(b) Person I specifies on an all-or-none basis the quantities to be traded, and person II accepts the deal that does not actually hurt him.

(c) The two people bargain freely as to the quantities to be traded.

3. A person is endowed with x_0 and y_0 of goods X and Y, respectively.

(a) Show how his willingness to demand or supply X depends on the exchange ratio of X for Y. What can you say about the various possible shapes of this relationship?

(b) What can you say about the various possible effects on that relationship if the initial endowment x_0 is increased to x_0'?

4. Define each of the following concepts:

(a) The core

(b) The contract curve

(c) The set of superior allocations relative to the initial endowment point

(d) General competitive equilibrium

Illustrate these concepts by means of a two-person, two-commodity pure exchange economy. State what relationship, if any, exists among the four concepts listed above.

5. A pure exchange economy consists of two persons, A and B, whose marginal rates of substitution of good X for good Y are given by the following functions:

$$MRS_{xy}^a = \frac{x_a}{y_a}$$

$$MRS_{xy}^b = \frac{x_b}{y_b}$$

where a and b indicate persons A and B, respectively. The total fixed endowment of X is

200 units and the total endowment of Y is 100 units.

(a) Draw the Edgeworth box.

(b) Write an equation for the contract curve with variables x_a and y_a only. Draw the contract curve in the Edgeworth box.

(c) Even without knowing the initial endowments of each person, you can (in the present case) determine the equilibrium price ratio assuming perfectly competitive behavior. Show what that price ratio is. What does it depend on?

(d) For each person, write a budget equation and also an equation for the price consumption curve, assuming that A's initial endowments are 50 units of X and 10 units of Y. Graph your results and determine the implied general competitive equilibrium.

6. Wasteland is a primitive kingdom in which there are only two economic activities: berry picking and rabbit hunting. Labor is the only resource required in each activity, and the total supply of labor is 100 worker-days. The relationship between berry production (B) and labor input is governed by the equation

$$B = L_b^{1/2} \qquad (i)$$

where L_b represents the number of worker-days devoted to berry picking. Similarly, the relationship between the number of rabbits caught (R) and the number of worker-days devoted to rabbit hunting (L_r) is given by

$$R = L_r^2 \qquad (ii)$$

Suppose that workers are equally adept at the two activities and can effortlessly shift from one occupation to the other.

(a) Classify the berry picking and rabbit hunting according to whether they operate under decreasing, constant, or increasing marginal returns to labor.

(b) Define the production-possibilities frontier of Wasteland and exhibit it either numerically or algebraically. Also sketch it graphically.

(c) Describe and illustrate graphically the effect on the production-possibilities frontier of a rabbit disease that changes the productive relationship from that described in equation (ii) to

$$R = \tfrac{1}{2}L_r^2 \qquad (ii)'$$

(d) Suppose that the supply of labor is growing at a constant percentage rate. What will happen to the production-possibilities frontier of Wasteland over the long run? Illustrate your answer by means of a diagram.

7. Return to the primitive kingdom of Question 6 in which the total supply of labor is 100 worker-days. Assume now that the production functions of berry picking and rabbit hunting are as follows:

$$B = 0.10L_b$$
$$R = 0.50L_r$$

(a) Show that both production functions exhibit constant returns to scale.

(b) Determine the equation for the production-possibilities frontier and sketch it graphically. Can you explain why this production frontier is necessarily linear?

(c) Suppose that the output of berries is 3 units. Determine the output of the rabbit-hunting activity and the opportunity cost of rabbits in terms of berries.

(d) Suppose that the wage rate is $10 per worker-day. Determine the long-run equilibrium money prices of berries and rabbits, and the relative price of rabbits (using berries as the *numéraire*).

8. Why must a general competitive equilibrium of exchange lie on the contract curve inside the Edgeworth box diagram always?

9. Explain why partial equilibrium analysis is inappropriate for the study of the entire economy.

10. Suppose that the indifference curves of Adam and Beth have "kinks" (or corners) at the initial endowment point.

(a) Is it still valid to say that the existence of mutually beneficial exchanges rests on the disparity between the marginal rates of substitution of Adam and Beth at the initial endowment point? Explain.

(b) If your answer to part (a) is "no," how should you reformulate the condition for the existence of mutually beneficial exchanges to cover the present case?

FURTHER READING

Bowley, A. L. (1924). *Mathematical Groundwork of Economics.* Clarendon Press, Oxford. Chapter 1.

Edgeworth, F. Y. (1881). *Mathematical Psychics.* C. Kegan Paul and Company, London.

Graham, D. A. (1980). *Microeconomics: The Analysis of Choice.* D. C. Heath and Company, Lexington, Mass. Chapter 6.

Hicks, J. R. (1946). *Value and Capital,* 2nd ed. Oxford University Press, New York. Chapters 4 and 5.

Newman, P. (1965). *The Theory of Exchange.* Prentice-Hall, Inc., Englewood Cliffs, N.J.

CHAPTER 15

The Two-Sector Model

We now leave the simplified world of Robinson Crusoe to explore a more complex economy. Imagine a country that has many citizens. To keep the discussion within manageable proportions, however, assume that this country produces only *two* consumption commodities (say, food and clothing) by means of only *two* homogeneous factors of production (say, labor and land). This two-factor, two-commodity economy is usually called the *two-sector model*.

Evidently, a real-world economy using millions of different inputs to produce millions of commodities is much more complex than the two-sector model. Yet the two-sector model provides considerable insight into the nature of general equilibrium in a perfectly competitive economy. Moreover, understanding how the two-sector model works is by no means an easy task. The purpose of this chapter is to develop systematically the two-sector model and use it to illustrate the essence of general competitive equilibrium.

15.1 The Structure of the Two-Sector Model

In this section we study only the basic structure of the two-sector model and clarify the meaning of its crucial assumptions. In the rest of this chapter we demonstrate how the various elements of the model fit together.

Households and Firms

The basic organizational units in our two-sector model are households and firms. The households play two roles: (1) they are the only *consuming units* in the economy (i.e., the only buyers of food and clothing), and (2) they are also the only *factor-supplying units* (because all factors are owned, at least ultimately, by the members of households). For simplicity, we assume that the quantities of factors supplied by each household, and thus the total quantities of labor and land available to the economy, are fixed and independent of the level of the factor prices.

The firms play also two roles: (1) they are the only *producing units* in the economy (i.e., the only suppliers of food and clothing), and (2) they are the only *factor-demanding units* (because only firms use labor and land to produce food and clothing).[1] The firms are artificial units; they are owned, organized, and operated by entrepreneurs who are themselves members of households. This fact is often missed in public debate over economic policy. Thus some people erroneously argue that the profits of "corporations" can be taxed away without any cost to the "people."

Figure 15.1 describes the basic flows in our two-sector economy. The inner circular flow, running in the counterclockwise direction as indicated by arrows 1 to 4, describes the *real* flow of factor services and commodities. The households supply factor services to the firms, as shown by arrows 1 and 2. The firms use those factor services to produce food and clothing; and then they distribute the finished products to the households, as indicated by arrows 3 and 4, essentially in exchange for the factor services supplied to the firms by the households.

The outer circular flow, consisting of arrows 5 to 8, illustrates a *monetary* flow that runs in the clockwise direction (and thus opposite to the real flow). The monetary flow matches precisely the real flow. When the firms purchase factor services, they pay out wages and rents to the households (factor suppliers), as shown by arrows 5 and 8. These wages and rents form the incomes of the households, as

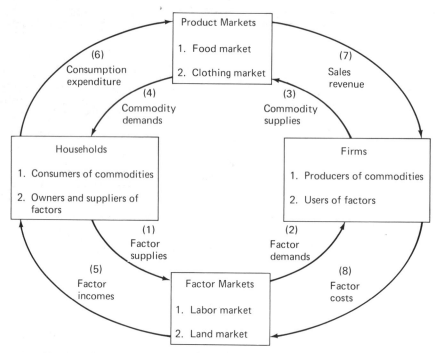

Figure 15.1 Real and monetary flows. The households supply factor services to the firms, as shown by arrows 1 and 2. The firms distribute their outputs of food and clothing to households, as indicated by arrows 3 and 4. The inner circular flow, described by arrows 1 to 4, is called the *real* flow. The outer circular flow, consisting of arrows 5 to 8 and running opposite to the real flow, is called the *monetary* flow. The firms pay wages and rents to the households, as shown by arrows 5 and 8. The households use their incomes to buy food and clothing from the firms, as implied by arrows 6 and 7.

---

[1]The assumption that only the firms can produce commodities rules out the possibility of any production taking place within the household sector, such as cooking, gardening, and shaving.

emphasized by arrow 5. The households use their incomes to purchase food and clothing from the firms, as implied by arrows 6 and 7. The household expenditure on food and clothing becomes the sales revenue of the firms, as noted by arrow 7. Finally, the sales revenue is used by the firms to purchase factor services, and the cycle begins again.

The Industry Production Functions

The two-sector model consists of two perfectly competitive industries: the food industry and the clothing industry. Each industry is, of course, made up of a large number of small firms. Ideally, one would have to study the behavior of each firm separately, which is a rather complicated procedure. To avoid this problem, economists concentrate on the two industries. Thus they postulate one production function for each *industry*. Moreover, each industry production function is assumed to exhibit constant returns to scale. Surely such an aggregation procedure simplifies matters. But is it meaningful or legitimate to bypass the firm and work directly with the industry? The answer is "yes!"

A rigorous proof for the existence of an industry production function which is characterized by constant returns to scale lies beyond the scope of this book.[2] A heuristic argument has already been given in Section 6.7, and the reader is referred to that discussion. (The reader is also advised to review the various properties of constant returns to scale found in Section 6.7.) We conclude that the technology of the two-sector economy can be summarized by two industry production functions that exhibit constant returns to scale.

The Conditions of General Competitive Equilibrium

In our two-sector model there are two product prices, the price of food (p_f) and the price of clothing (p_c), and two factor prices, the wage rate (w) for labor services and the rent, or rental rate (r), for land services. (Even though only relative prices are important, we find it convenient to continue the use of money prices.) General competitive equilibrium occurs for a set of prices $(p_f, p_c, w,$ and $r)$ when the choices of households and firms satisfy the following conditions.

1. *Each household is in equilibrium;* that is, each household purchases the most preferred commodity bundle subject to its budget constraint. A typical household's budget constraint takes the form

$$wL_i + rT_i = p_fF_i + p_cC_i \tag{15.1}$$

   *where L_i and T_i are the amounts of labor and land, respectively, owned by the household, and F_i and C_i are the quantities of food and clothing, respectively, consumed by the household.
2. *Each firm is in equilibrium;* that is, each firm maximizes its profit by hiring the right quantities of labor and land and producing the optimal output.
3. *Each market is in equilibrium;* that is, supply equals demand in each of the four markets of the economy.
4. *In long-run general equilibrium, each firm earns zero profit.* As we know, positive profits attract additional firms into the industry, and this process continues until profits are eliminated. In the presence of losses, sooner or later

[2]A rigorous proof for the existence of an industry production function that is also linear homogeneous can be found in Chacholiades (1978, pp. 96–101 and 118–124).

some firms go out of business, and the exit of firms continues until those that remain active are at least able to break even.

The first three conditions are general in the sense that they must hold in any general equilibrium state, that is, both in the long run and the short run. The last condition (zero profit) holds only in the long run.

15.2 Allocation of Factors Between Industries

How much food and how much clothing the economy actually produces depends not only on the production functions, but also on how the available quantities of labor and land are allocated between the two industries. Obviously, there are many feasible allocations, some efficient, others inefficient. However, not all feasible allocations are consistent with general competitive equilibrium. It is therefore important to identify now all those factor allocations that represent possible competitive equilibrium states.

The Edgeworth Production Box Diagram

The factor allocation problem is very similar to the problem of exchange equilibrium discussed in Section 14.2. For this reason the Edgeworth box is the proper tool to use for the solution of the allocation problem as well. This is done in Figure 15.2.

The dimensions of the box are determined by the total quantities of labor and land available to the economy. Thus $0_c M$ = total quantity of labor, and $0_c N$ = total quantity of land. The factor quantities allocated to the clothing industry are measured from the southwest corner of the box, 0_c, and the quantities allocated to the food industry are measured from the northeast corner, 0_f. Every point in the box (or its boundary) corresponds to a specific factor allocation. For instance, point E allocates the quantities L_c^1, T_c^1 (measured from 0_c) to the production of clothing, and the residual quantities L_f^1, T_f^1 (measured from 0_f) to the production of food. Conversely, every feasible allocation corresponds to a point in the box (or its boundary). Points outside the box represent unfeasible allocations.

Introduce now into the box the isoquant maps of the food and clothing industries. Draw the isoquant map of the clothing industry with respect to the origin 0_c, as illustrated by isoquants 1, 2, 3, and 4, which represent C_1, C_2, C_3, and C_4 units of clothing, respectively. Similarly, draw the isoquant map of the food industry with respect to the origin 0_f, as illustrated by isoquants 1' and 2', which represent F_1 and F_2 units of food, respectively. Note that the isoquants for food are turned upside down, as were Beth's indifference curves in Figures 14.2 and 14.3. Now any point in the box gives not only the quantities of labor and land allocated to the two industries, but also the production levels of food and clothing. For example, at E the clothing industry employs L_c^1 and T_c^1 and produces C_1 units of clothing; and the food industry employs L_f^1 and T_f^1 and produces F_1 units of food.

Efficient Versus Inefficient Factor Allocations

We are now ready to draw an important distinction between efficient versus inefficient factor allocations. Suppose that the economy arbitrarily chooses point E, where the outputs of food and clothing are F_1 and C_1, respectively. Surely, each industry produces the *maximal* quantity of output that it can produce with the specific quantities of labor and land allocated to it. This must be obvious from the

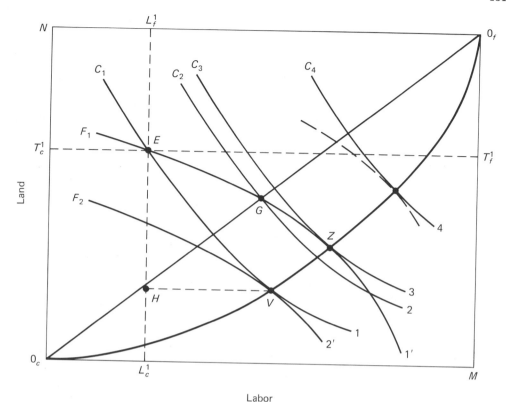

Figure 15.2 The Edgeworth production box diagram. At E the clothing industry employs L_c^1 labor and T_c^1 land (measured from 0_c) and produces C_1 clothing; and the food industry employs L_f^1 labor and T_f^1 land (measured from 0_f) and produces F_1 food. Because isoquants 1 and 1' intersect at E, allocation E is inefficient. Thus the economy could move to Z, where the output of food is still F_1 but the output of clothing rises to C_3; or it could move to V, where the output of food increases to F_2 while the output of clothing remains at C_1. Resources are allocated efficiently at points of tangency, such as V and Z. The locus of all such tangencies, as illustrated by curve 0_cVZ0_f, is called the *contract curve*.

definition of the production function.[3] It, therefore, seems that the only way to increase the output of, say, food (above F_1) is to transfer resources from the clothing industry to the food industry, that is, sacrifice some output of clothing.

Yet the economy can achieve what at first sight appears to be impossible: Starting at E, the economy can reallocate its resources in such a way as to produce more food without giving up any clothing (or produce more clothing without giving up any food). Thus the economy can move from E to V by transferring HE units of land from the clothing industry to the food industry, and HV units of labor from the food industry to the clothing industry. At point V the clothing industry still produces C_1 units of clothing, because point V lies on the same isoquant 1 of the clothing industry as point E. But the food industry produces more food at V than at $E(F_2 > F_1)$. This is indeed a remarkable result, as the economy appears to be

[3]As explained in Section 6.2, the production function incorporates the concept of *engineering efficiency;* that is, the production function gives the *maximal* quantity of output for any specified amounts of labor and land. For instance, when L_c^1, T_c^1 are allocated to the production of cloth, as shown by point E, the maximal quantity of clothing that can be produced is C_1, as indicated by isoquant 1. Thus the underlying assumption is that the engineers of the clothing industry always employ the "best" (optimal) production method available.

producing something out of nothing through a mere reallocation of resources—no worker is working any harder at V than at E!

Alternatively, the economy could move from E to Z. At Z the output of food continues to be F_1 (the same as at E), but the output of clothing *increases* from C_1 to C_3, as Z lies on a higher isoquant for clothing than E.

Resources are said to be allocated *in*efficiently between two industries when the economy (by a mere reallocation of resources) can increase the output of one commodity without reducing the output of the other. Clearly, point E represents an inefficient allocation of labor and land between the food and clothing industries. By an argument similar to the one provided for point E, we can conclude that *any resource allocation which is identified by a point, such as E or G, in the Edgeworth production box where the food and clothing isoquants intersect is inefficient.*

Suppose now that the economy is at a point of tangency between the food and clothing isoquants, such as V or Z. Can the economy, by a mere reallocation of resources, still increase the output of, say, food without sacrificing any clothing? No, this is not possible. Starting at a tangency, any attempt to move to a higher isoquant of one of the industries necessarily brings the economy to a lower isoquant of the other industry. For instance, a movement from Z to any point on isoquant 4 (i.e., an increase in clothing from C_3 to C_4) necessarily puts the food industry on an isoquant that is "lower" (closer to 0_f) than $1'$; hence the output of food falls.

Resources are said to be allocated efficiently (or optimally) when it is not possible to increase the output of one commodity without reducing the output of the other. Efficient allocations are identified by *points of tangency* between the isoquants of the food and clothing industries. The locus of all such tangencies, as illustrated in Figure 15.2 by curve $0_c V Z 0_f$, is again called the *contract curve*.

In summary, resources are allocated efficiently (or optimally) along the contract curve. If the economy is on the contract curve, it is impossible to increase the output of one commodity without reducing the output of the other by a mere reallocation of resources. If the economy is not on the contract curve, however, it is always possible to increase the outputs of both commodities simultaneously by a proper reallocation of resources.

Perfect Competition and Efficiency in Production

In a centrally planned economy, a planning bureau could intentionally allocate resources at some point on the contract curve. How is this accomplished in a free-enterprise system? By perfect competition.

How does perfect competition lead to the efficient allocation of resources? As we saw in Chapter 7, every firm (and thus every industry) minimizes its total cost only when it equalizes its marginal rate of technical substitution of labor for land (MRS_{LT}) to the wage/rent ratio (w/r). That is, the condition for cost minimization is

$$MRS_{LT} = \frac{w}{r} \qquad (15.2)$$

$$(7.2)\,\text{repeated}$$

Equation (15.2) corresponds to the tangency between an isocost line (whose slope is w/r) and an isoquant (whose slope is MRS_{LT}). Accordingly, an industry cannot be in long-run equilibrium unless it operates at a point where equation (15.2) holds. Since factors are homogeneous and factor prices are uniform throughout the economy, both industries must operate at points where their respective marginal rates of technical substitution of labor for land are equal to the *same* wage/rent ratio. Hence, in any long-run competitive equilibrium, the slopes of the food and clothing isoquants must be the same (i.e., the two industries must operate at a point of tangency in the Edgeworth production box) because they are both equal to the same wage/rent ratio.

We therefore conclude that long-run general competitive equilibrium can occur only at points lying on the contract curve. That is, the economy cannot be in long-run general competitive equilibrium unless the allocation of resources is efficient. As Adam Smith would say, in a free-enterprise system millions of diverse individuals, each of whom directly pursues only his or her *own* self-interests, are guided in their actions by an "invisible hand" and ultimately promote the *public* interest.

15.3 Factor Intensities

Under constant returns to scale, the crucial economic variables (such as the average and marginal physical products of labor and land, and the marginal rate of technical substitution) depend only on the proportion in which the industry combines labor and land, not on the absolute factor quantities. For this reason, the labor/land ratios of the food and clothing industries of our two-sector model are very important. In this section we clarify the meaning of factor intensity, which is important in understanding the internal structure of the two-sector model.

The Definition of Factor Intensity

Throughout our discussion of the two-sector model we assume that *clothing is labor intensive relative to food.* What does the term "labor intensive" mean? That *the production of clothing uses more units of labor per unit of land than the production of food.* For instance, suppose that it takes 6 units of labor and 2 units of land to produce 1 unit of clothing, and 8 units of labor and 4 units of land to produce 1 unit of food. Evidently, the production of clothing requires 3 (i.e., 6/2) units of labor, while the production of food requires only 2 (i.e., 8/4), per unit of land; hence clothing is labor-intensive relative to food (6/2 > 8/4).[4]

When clothing is labor intensive relative to food, it is automatically true that *food is land intensive relative to clothing;* that is, the production of food requires more units of land per unit of labor than the production of clothing. For instance, in the example above, food is land intensive relative to clothing because 4/8 > 2/6.

The Factor-Intensity Curves

The ratio (or proportion) in which an industry uses labor and land depends only on the wage/rent ratio. As we explained in Section 7.3, the expansion path of a constant-returns-to-scale production function (drawn for a given wage/rent ratio) is always a straight line through the origin, signifying a fixed labor/land ratio (at all levels of output). When the wage/rent ratio is low, the labor/land ratio is high, and when the wage/rent ratio is high, the labor/land ratio is low. The negative relationship (known as *factor-intensity curve*) between the wage/rent ratio and the labor/land ratio is, of course, due to the law of diminishing marginal rate of technical substitution.

Figure 15.3 illustrates some hypothetical *labor-intensity curves.* Food's labor-intensity curve FF' (in both panels) relates the labor/land ratio of the food industry to the wage/rent ratio (or MRS_{LT}, because $w/r = MRS_{LT}$). Similarly, clothing's labor-intensity curve CC' (in both panels) relates the labor/land ratio of the clothing

---

[4]Do not fall into the trap of arguing that food is labor intensive relative to clothing because each unit of food requires 8 units of labor to clothing's 6. Such a comparison is meaningless, if only because the units of measurement of food and clothing (bushels, yards, etc.) are arbitrary. What is important is the *proportion* in which labor and land are used.

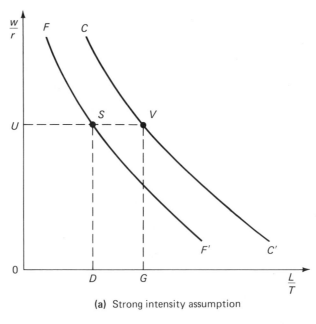

(a) Strong intensity assumption

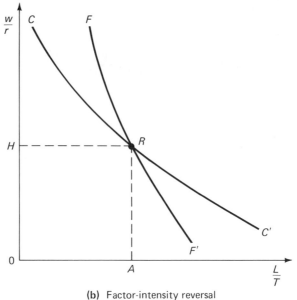

(b) Factor-intensity reversal

Figure 15.3 Labor-intensity curves. Food's labor-intensity curve FF' (in both panels) relates the labor/land ratio of the food industry to the wage/rent ratio. Clothing's labor-intensity curve is shown by CC' in both panels. In panel (a) clothing is labor intensive relative to food for all wage/rent ratios, because CC' lies totally to the right of FF'. In panel (b) a factor-intensity reversal occurs at R, where FF' and CC' intersect. Thus for any wage/rent ratio higher than $0H$, food is labor intensive relative to clothing, and for any wage/rent ratio lower than $0H$, clothing is labor intensive relative to food.

industry to the wage/rent ratio (or MRS_{LT} in the clothing industry). All labor-intensity curves slope downward. Thus as labor becomes relatively cheaper (i.e., as w/r falls), each industry substitutes labor for land, which causes its labor/land ratio to increase.

In panel (a), clothing's labor-intensity curve is drawn totally to the right of food's labor-intensity curve. This means that for *any* wage/rent ratio, the clothing industry uses a higher labor/land ratio (i.e., more units of labor per unit of land) than the food industry. For instance, when the wage/rent ratio is $0U$, the labor/land ratios in the production of clothing and food are $0G$ and $0D$, respectively, with $0G > 0D$. Hence clothing is labor intensive relative to food for all conceivable wage/rent ratios. This state of affairs is often called the *strong intensity assumption*.

In panel (b), however, the two labor-intensity curves intersect at R. If the wage/rent ratio happens to be exactly equal to $0H$, both industries use labor and land in the proportion $0A$; thus food is now just as labor intensive as clothing. But for any wage/rent ratio lower than $0H$, clothing is labor intensive relative to food (because below R curve CC' lies to the right of FF'), and for any wage/rent ratio higher than $0H$, food is labor intensive relative to clothing (because above R curve FF' lies to the right of CC'). Because the relationship between the labor/land ratios of food and clothing is switched at point R, this is known as the case of a *factor-intensity reversal*.

It must be emphasized that factor-intensity reversals cannot be excluded by a priori reasoning. Whether factor-intensity reversals exist or not is an empirical question. However, for our present purposes, we can safely ignore them. As we show below, a factor-intensity reversal cannot be observed in a constant-returns-to-scale, closed economy which is endowed with fixed quantities of labor and land—the case we are presently studying.

Factor Intensity and the Box Diagram

The Edgeworth production box is useful in identifying the labor-intensive commodity. Consider Figure 15.4. If the economy allocates its resources between food and clothing at any point, such as A, that lies *below* the diagonal $0_c 0_f$, then clothing's labor/land ratio (ρ_c^a) is higher than food's (ρ_f^a). If the allocation point lies above and to the left of the diagonal, as shown by point B, then food's labor/land ratio (ρ_f^b) is higher than clothing's (ρ_c^b). Finally, if the allocation point occurs on the diagonal, as shown by point D, both industries use the same labor/land ratio, and the common labor/land ratio coincides with the economy's overall labor/land ratio (ρ).

To verify the proposition above, first note that the overall labor/land ratio (ρ) is given by the slope of the diagonal with respect to the land (or vertical) axis, as shown. At point A, clothing's labor/land ratio (ρ_c^a) coincides with the measure of angle $N0_c A$; and food's labor/land ratio (ρ_f^a), with the measure of $M0_f A$. Obviously, $\rho_c^a > \rho$ and $\rho_f^a < \rho$; hence $\rho_f^a < \rho < \rho_c^a$. At point B, $\rho_c^b < \rho$ and $\rho_f^b > \rho$; hence $\rho_c^b < \rho < \rho_f^b$.

As explained in Section 15.2, long-run competitive equilibrium always occurs on the contract curve. Now we show that under constant returns to scale, the contract curve never crosses the diagonal—it lies on one side of the diagonal, as in Figure 15.2. The reason is simple. Under constant returns to scale, the marginal rate of substitution MRS_{LT} is constant along any straight line through the origin. Hence along the diagonal of the box diagram, the MRS_{LT} of each industry remains constant. If at some point of the diagonal the MRS_{LT} of the food and clothing industries happen to be the same, they must continue to be equal at all points of the diagonal; and in that case, the contract curve coincides with the diagonal. On the other hand, if at some point of the diagonal the MRS_{LT} of the food and clothing industries are different from one another, they must be different at all other points of the diagonal; and in this case the contract curve cannot have any points in common with the diagonal.

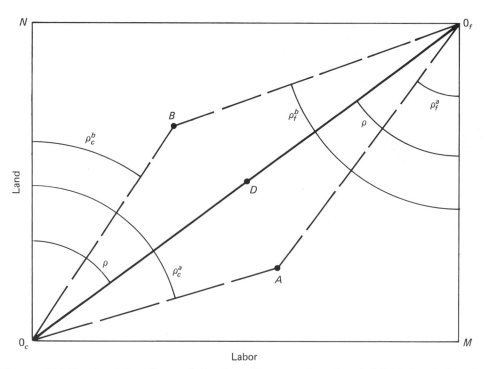

Figure 15.4 Factor intensity and the box diagram. At point *A* (which lies below the diagonal) clothing's labor/land ratio (ρ_c^a) is higher than food's (ρ_f^a). At point *B* (which lies above and to the left of the diagonal) food's labor/land ratio (ρ_f^b) is higher than clothing's (ρ_c^b). At *D* (which lies on the diagonal) the labor/land ratio of both industries is equal to the economy's overall labor/land ratio (ρ).

When the contract curve lies below the diagonal, as in Figure 15.2, clothing is revealed to be labor intensive relative to food at all conceivable long-run competitive equilibria. This will be so whether or not the labor-intensity curves of food and clothing intersect. For the remainder of this chapter we assume that the contract curve lies below the diagonal.

15.4 The Production-Possibilities Frontier

The production-possibilities frontier (or transformation curve) shows the maximum obtainable amount of one commodity for any given amount of the other. As we saw in Section 14.4, it depends on two fundamental data: factor supplies (or endowments) and technology (or industry production functions). The production-possibilities frontier brings the commodity markets into focus. For this reason it is an important tool in the determination of general competitive equilibrium, and we must master it.

From the Contract Curve to the Production-Possibilities Frontier

Our discussion of the Edgeworth production box in Section 15.2 leads to the following important conclusion: *When the economy allocates its resources along the contract curve, it is impossible to increase the output of one commodity without reducing the output of the other commodity.* Hence the contract curve contains all the information necessary for the construction of the production-possibilities frontier. Each point on the contract curve corresponds to a point on the production possibilities frontier, and vice versa.

Figure 15.5 depicts the production-possibilities frontier that is derived from the contract curve of Figure 15.2. Points V, Z, G, and E in Figure 15.5 correspond to the synonymous points in Figure 15.2. Note that only points V and Z lie on the production-possibilities frontier, because only V and Z lie on the contract curve. Points G and E lie *inside* the production-possibilities frontier, because G and E are not on the contract curve.

As we explained in Section 15.2, perfect competition puts the economy on the contract curve. Accordingly, perfect competition must also put the economy on the production-possibilities frontier. In other words, long-run general competitive equilibrium can occur only at points lying on the production-possibilities frontier.

The production-possibilities frontier has two additional properties:

1. It is concave to (or bowed out from) the origin, as shown in Figure 15.5. This property is due to the disparity between the factor intensities of food and clothing, as explained below.
2. Its absolute slope (known as the marginal rate of transformation MRT, or the opportunity cost of food in terms of clothing) is equal to the ratio of the (monetary) marginal costs of food and clothing; that is,

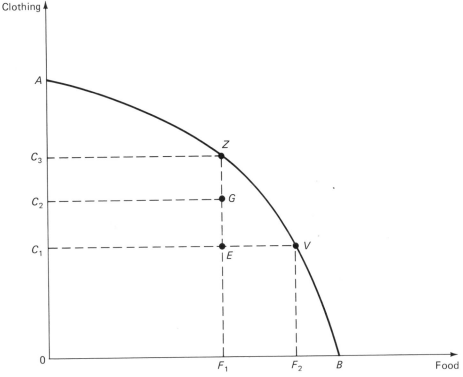

Figure 15.5 The production-possibilities frontier. The production-possibilities frontier AB is derived from the contract curve of Figure 15.2. Points V, Z, G, and E correspond to the synonymous points in Figure 15.2. Only V and Z lie on the production frontier, because only V and Z lie on the contract curve. Points G and E (which are not on the contract curve) lie inside the production frontier.

$$MRT = \frac{MC_f}{MC_c} \qquad (15.3)$$

where MC_f is the marginal cost of food and MC_c the marginal cost of clothing.

We discuss both of these properties below.

The Concavity of the Production-Possibilities Frontier

Consider Figure 15.6, which reproduces the production-possibilities frontier of Figure 15.5 with some additional information. Obviously, at points Z and V (which lie on the frontier) both labor and land are fully employed. First, we wish to show that by allocating resources arbitrarily (as described below), the economy can reach points that lie on dashed straight-line segment VZ, as shown by point M.

For concreteness, assume that the economy is endowed with 5000 workers and 1000 acres of land. At point V, assume that the economy allocates 1800 workers and 200 acres of land to the production of clothing, and the residual factor quantities (i.e., 3200 workers and 800 acres of land) to the production of food. Assume also that at Z the economy allocates 3600 workers and 600 acres of land to clothing, and 1400 workers and 400 acres to food. The reader can easily verify that clothing is indeed labor intensive relative to food at both V and Z (1800/200 > 3200/800 and 3600/600 > 1400/400), and that the labor/land ratios of both industries are higher

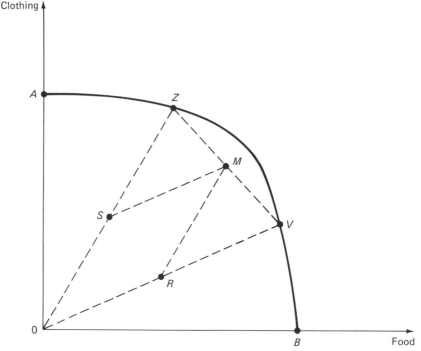

Figure 15.6 The concavity of the production-possibilities frontier. We start at Z and remove 50 percent of all resources employed by each industry. Because of constant returns to scale, the output of each industry is reduced by 50 percent, as shown by point S. Then we allocate the released resources to the two industries in the exact proportions implied by point V so that the outputs of food and clothing are 50 percent of their respective levels at V, as shown by R. Addition of S and R (by means of the parallelogram rule) yields point M.

at V than at Z (1800/200 > 3600/600 and 3200/800 > 1400/400). The reason this should be so is clarified in Section 15.6. For the moment note that at both V and Z labor and land are fully employed.

Start at Z and then remove 50 percent of the totals of labor and land employed by each industry. That is, reduce employment to 1800 workers and 300 acres of land in the clothing industry, and to 700 workers and 200 acres in the food industry. Because of constant returns to scale, such halving of the resource base will cut by exactly 50 percent the output of each industry, as shown by point S, which lies halfway between the origin 0 and Z.

The released resources are exactly 50 percent of the total quantities of labor and land available to the economy. Thus released labor = 1800 + 700 = 2500, and released land = 300 + 200 = 500. Now let the economy allocate these released factor quantities to the two industries in the exact proportions implied by point V. Thus the economy will allocate 900 workers and 100 acres to the clothing industry, and 1600 workers and 400 acres to food (i.e., exactly 50 percent of the total resources employed at V). Again because of constant returns to scale, the resultant outputs of food and clothing will be 50 percent of their respective levels at V, as shown by point R.

We therefore conclude that by the above arbitrary allocation of resources, the economy can produce two commodity bundles, as shown by points S and R. The sum of these two bundles is shown by point M, which lies on dashed straight-line segment VZ.

Other points along VZ can be obtained in a similar fashion; that is, by withdrawing other percentages of the total quantities of labor and land employed by the two industries at Z, reallocating them between the two industries in the exact proportions implied by point V, and finally summing the two resultant commodity bundles.

Note that the production-possibilities frontier between Z and V does *not* coincide with dashed-line segment VZ—it lies beyond it, as shown in Figure 15.6. Why is this so? Because the arbitrary allocations of labor and land between the two industries described above are *inefficient*. Recall that the above procedure requires each industry to simultaneously use *two* methods of production—those implied by points V and Z. However, each point on the contract curve (and thus each point on the production-possibilities frontier) requires each industry to use only one method of production. (The production method used by an industry is identified by that industry's labor/land ratio.) We therefore conclude that the production-possibilities frontier must lie beyond dashed line VS, as shown.

The above argument holds for any pair of arbitrarily chosen points on the production-possibilities frontier—not just V and Z. Accordingly, our argument confirms that the production-possibilities frontier is indeed strictly concave to (or smoothly bowed out from) the origin.

Finally, note that the concavity of the production-possibilities frontier is mainly due to the disparity between the factor intensities of the two industries. If the labor/land ratios of food and clothing were equal at Z, they would also be equal at V, and at all other points of the production-possibilities frontier.[5] Hence the production methods adopted by the food and clothing industries at point Z would be

---

[5]When the labor/land ratios of food and clothing are equal to one another, each industry is necessarily using some percentage of the total quantities of labor and land available to the entire economy. For instance, 10 percent of all labor and land may be allocated to the production of food, and 90 percent to the production of clothing. This means that the economy allocates its resources at some point on the diagonal of the Edgeworth production box. But when one point of the diagonal lies on the contract curve, the entire contract curve coincides with the diagonal, and the labor/land ratios of food and clothing remain equal to one another and to the overall labor/land ratio (given by the slope of the diagonal) of the economy at all points of the production frontier.

exactly the same as the respective methods employed at V, and the "arbitrary" allocations of labor and land between the two industries described above would no longer be inefficient. In this case, the production-possibilities frontier would be linear, passing through points V and Z.

The Marginal Rate of Transformation

The absolute slope of the production-possibilities frontier at some point, such as Z or V, is called the marginal rate of transformation (MRT); it gives the rate at which clothing can be "transformed" into food. Surely, once clothing is produced it cannot be changed into food, but the output of food can be increased by transferring labor and land from the clothing industry to the food industry, that is, by indirectly reducing the output of the clothing industry. For instance, suppose that the absolute slope of the production-possibilities frontier at V is equal to 2. This means that the economy can increases the production of food by 1 extra unit only if it sacrifices 2 units of clothing—a sacrifice that will release from the clothing industry those quantities of labor and land that are necessary for the extra production of food.

The number of units of clothing that the economy must sacrifice for 1 extra unit of food (i.e., the MRT) is also known as *the opportunity cost of food in terms of clothing at the margin* or food's *marginal opportunity cost.* The concavity of the production-possibilities frontier reflects the fact that as the production of food increases (and that of clothing decreases), the marginal opportunity cost of food increases, as shown in Figure 15.7. As the economy moves from A to B and then to C (i.e., as the economy increases its production of food), food's marginal opportunity cost becomes larger and larger, as illustrated by the increasing steepness of the tangents at points A, B, and C.

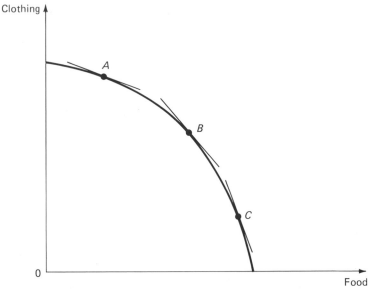

Figure 15.7 Increasing opportunity costs. The concavity of the production-possibilities frontier implies increasing opportunity costs in both industries. As the economy moves from A to B and then to C (i.e., as the economy increases its production of food and decreases its production of clothing), food's marginal opportunity cost (given by the absolute slope of the production frontier) becomes larger and larger, and clothing's marginal opportunity cost (given by the reciprocal of the slope of the production frontier) becomes smaller and smaller, as illustrated by the increasing steepness of the tangents at A, B, and C.

Note that the marginal opportunity cost of clothing in terms of food is merely the *reciprocal* of the marginal opportunity cost of food in terms of clothing. For instance, if the economy must sacrifice 2 units of clothing for 1 extra unit of food (i.e., if the marginal opportunity cost of food is 2 units of clothing), the economy must be able to increase the output of food by just one-half of 1 unit by sacrificing only 1 unit of clothing. If we reverse the last changes, it becomes obvious that the economy can produce 1 extra unit of clothing by giving up only one-half of 1 unit of food (i.e., the marginal opportunity cost of clothing is one-half of 1 unit of food).

When the production-possibilities frontier is concave to the origin, as in Figure 15.7, the clothing industry also experiences increasing opportunity costs. Thus, as the economy moves from C to B and then to A (i.e., as the economy increases the production of clothing), the slope of the production-possibilities frontier becomes smaller and smaller, but the marginal opportunity cost of clothing becomes larger and larger because it is equal to the reciprocal of the (absolute) slope of the frontier.

Turn now to equation (15.3), which states that the marginal rate of transformation is equal to the ratio of the *monetary* marginal costs of food and clothing. We can illustrate its economic content by means of an example. Suppose that at the output levels indicated by point B (Figure 15.7) the marginal cost of food (MC_f) is \$20 and the marginal cost of clothing (MC_c) is \$10. How much clothing will the economy have to sacrifice for 1 extra unit of food? (That is, what is the marginal opportunity cost of food in terms of clothing, or the MRT?) To increase the output of food by 1 unit, the economy must transfer \$20 worth of resources (labor and land) from the clothing industry to the food industry because $MC_f = \$20$. But by withdrawing \$20 worth of resources from the clothing industry, the economy causes the output of clothing to fall by 2 units because $MC_c = \$10$. Thus in order to produce 1 extra unit of food, the economy must give up 2 units of clothing; that is, $MRT = MC_f/MC_c = \$20/\$10 = 2$.

15.5 General Competitive Equilibrium

The preceding sections of this chapter have been devoted primarily to an examination of each of the individual components of the two-sector model. This section illustrates how the various parts of the model fit together, that is, how all commodity and factor markets simultaneously attain equilibrium.

Figure 15.8 depicts the economy's production-possibilities frontier AB in part (a), and the corresponding Edgeworth production box in part (b). We assume that general competitive equilibrium occurs on the production-possibilities frontier at point E, where the economy produces F_0 units of food and C_0 units of clothing. Point E corresponds to point E' in the Edgeworth production box.

From our discussion in Section 15.4, we know that the slope of the production frontier at point E, indicated by the slope of tangent line GH, gives the ratio of the marginal costs of food and clothing [see equation (15.3)]. Furthermore, from our analysis of a perfectly competitive industry we also know that the price of a commodity equals the marginal cost of producing it; that is, $MC_f = p_f$ and $MC_c = p_c$. We therefore conclude that the slope of GH, denoted by p_0, shows the ratio of commodity prices, because $p_0 = MC_f/MC_c = p_f/p_c$.

Turn now to the Edgeworth box and consider point E' (which corresponds to E). At E' the economy allocates L_c^0 units of labor and T_c^0 units of land to the clothing industry, and L_f^0 and T_f^0 to the food industry. This factor allocation places the clothing industry on isoquant 1 (which corresponds to C_0 units of clothing) and the food industry on isoquant 1' (which corresponds to F_0 units of food). As we know from our earlier discussion in this chapter, the common slope of isoquants 1 and 1' at

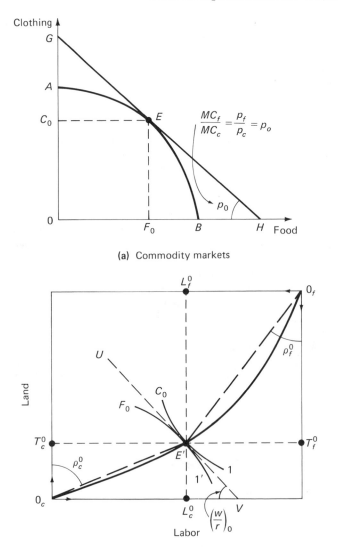

(a) Commodity markets

(b) Factor markets

Figure 15.8 An illustration of general competitive equilibrium. General competitive equilibrium occurs at E on production-possibilities frontier AB in panel (a). The slope (p_0) of tangent line GH gives the ratio of marginal costs, and thus the ratio of prices, of food and clothing as shown. Point E corresponds to point E' on the contract curve, panel (b). The common slope of isoquants 1 and 1' at E', indicated by the slope of dashed tangent line UV, equals the wage/rent ratio, as shown. Further, the labor/land ratios of the food and clothing industries at E' are ρ_f^0 and ρ_c^0, respectively.

E', indicated by the slope of dashed tangent line UV, equals the wage/rent ratio, as shown.[6] But this is not all that we can obtain from the Edgeworth box.

At point E' we also know the labor/land ratios of the food and clothing industries, as shown by ρ_f^0 and ρ_c^0, respectively. Because of constant returns to scale, we know that the marginal physical products of labor and land in the two industries are

[6]See Section 15.2 and specifically equation (15.2).

uniquely determined by the labor/land ratios ρ_f^0 and ρ_c^0. Even though this information is not directly available on our diagram, we know that we can recover it from the industry production functions. Let us assume that the marginal physical products of labor and land, respectively, are equal to MPP_{LF}^0 and MPP_{TF}^0 in the food industry and to MPP_{LC}^0 and MPP_{TC}^0 in the clothing industry.

As we know from our discussion in Chapter 12, under perfect competition profits are maximized when each factor's value of marginal product equals that factor's rental. Consequently, at point E' the following equations hold:

$$w = p_f \cdot MPP_{LF}^0 = p_c \cdot MPP_{LC}^0 \tag{15.4}$$

$$r = p_f \cdot MPP_{TF}^0 = p_c \cdot MPP_{TC}^0 \tag{15.5}$$

Equation (15.4) implies that the real wage rate is equal to MPP_{LF}^0 in terms of food, and to MPP_{LC}^0 in terms of clothing; that is,

$$\frac{w}{p_f} = MPP_{LF}^0 \tag{15.4}'$$

$$\frac{w}{p_c} = MPP_{LC}^0 \tag{15.4}''$$

Similarly, equation (15.5) implies that the real rental rate for land services is equal to MPP_{TF}^0 in terms of food, and to MPP_{TC}^0 in terms of clothing; that is,

$$\frac{r}{p_f} = MPP_{TF}^0 \tag{15.5}'$$

$$\frac{r}{p_c} = MPP_{TC}^0 \tag{15.5}''$$

As we explained earlier, in long-run competitive equilibrium profits are zero. Accordingly, each industry's total revenue equals its total cost. Thus we can formulate the following two equations:

$$wL_f^0 + rT_f^0 = p_f F_0 \tag{15.6}$$

$$wL_c^0 + rT_c^0 = p_c C_0 \tag{15.7}$$

Equation (15.6) sets food's total revenue $(p_f F_0)$ equal to food's total cost $(wL_f^0 + rT_f^0)$, and equation (15.7) does the same for clothing. Adding equations (15.6) and (15.7) together, we get

$$w\overline{L} + r\overline{T} = p_f F_0 + p_c C_0 \tag{15.8}$$

where $\overline{L} = L_f^0 + L_c^0$ and $\overline{T} = T_f^0 + T_c^0$ are the total quantities of labor and land, respectively, available to the economy. Equation (15.8) simply states that the value of all commodities produced $(p_f F_0 + p_c C_0)$ equals the sum of total wages $(w\overline{L})$ plus total rents $(r\overline{T})$ paid out to households for the factor services that the households had offered to the firms.

Now let us consider the behavior of households. We assume that there are m

households which own the total available factor quantities, $\overline{L}$ and $\overline{T}$, in amounts that we may specify as $L_1, L_2, \ldots, L_m$, and $T_1, T_2, \ldots, T_m$. (Some of these factor quantities may be zero, if the particular household happens to own none of that factor.) Now recall the budget equation of the ith household, as given by equation (15.1), and sum over all households to obtain

$$w(L_1 + L_2 + \cdots + L_m) + r(T_1 + T_2 + \cdots + T_m)$$
$$= p_f(F_1 + F_2 + \cdots + F_m) + p_c(C_1 + C_2 + \cdots + C_m)$$

or

$$w\overline{L} + r\overline{T} = p_f F_d + p_c C_d \tag{15.9}$$

where $\overline{L} = L_1 + L_2 + \cdots + L_m$, $\overline{T} = T_1 + T_2 + \cdots + T_m$, $F_d = F_1 + F_2 + \cdots + F_m$ = total quantity of food demanded by all households, and $C_d = C_1 + C_2 + \cdots + C_m$ = total quantity of clothing demanded by all households.

Observe that the left-hand sides of equations (15.8) and (15.9) are equal. Thus their right-hand sides must be equal also; that is,

$$p_f F_0 + p_c C_0 = p_f F_d + p_c C_d \tag{15.10}$$

Equation (15.10) is an identity; that is, it holds always whether or not the economy is in general equilibrium. Its significance springs from the fact that it specifies all alternative combinations of food and clothing, F_d and C_d, that the households think they can purchase; that is, equation (15.10) is the budget equation for all households as a group, and it is illustrated in Figure 15.8 by line GH.[7]

Turn now to the individual household. The budget line of the ith household can be rearranged as follows:

$$\frac{w}{p_c} L_i + \frac{r}{p_c} T_i = \frac{p_f}{p_c} F_i + C_i \tag{15.1'}$$

by merely dividing both sides of equation (15.1) by p_c. Substituting equations (15.4)″ and (15.5)″ into equation (15.1)′ and recalling that $p_f/p_c = p_0$, we obtain

$$MPP^0_{LC} \cdot L_i + MPP^0_{TC} \cdot T_i = p_0 F_i + C_i \tag{15.11}$$

The left-hand side of equation (15.11) is a constant, because all terms are constant. (The sum $MPP^0_{LC} \cdot L_i + MPP^0_{TC} \cdot T_i$ gives the ith household's income in terms of clothing, which we use here as the *numéraire*.) The ith household finally chooses those quantities of food and clothing, say, $\overline{F}_i$ and $\overline{C}_i$, respectively, that maximize its utility subject to budget equation (15.11).

Finally, we assume that the total quantities of food and clothing demanded by all households are equal to the total quantities of food and clothing produced, respectively. That is,

$$F_d = \overline{F}_1 + \overline{F}_2 + \cdots + \overline{F}_m = F_0 \tag{15.12}$$

$$C_d = \overline{C}_1 + \overline{C}_2 + \cdots + \overline{C}_m = C_0 \tag{15.13}$$

[7]The implicit assumption in the text is that the economy produces always on the production-possibilities frontier, so that the factor markets are in equilibrium always.

Thus the households choose collectively commodity bundle E on community budget line GH, and all markets are in equilibrium.

15.6 Comparative Statics

We can gain further insight into the workings of the two-sector model by exploring how the economy responds to external disturbances that disrupt an initial general competitive equilibrium. Because all markets are mutually interdependent, any disturbance in some part of the economy will have repercussions throughout the system.

Return to the general competitive equilibrium described in Section 15.5. For convenience this initial equilibrium is reproduced in Figure 15.9. Suppose now that the household preferences change. In particular, assume that *at the current prices*, households now prefer commodity bundle Q on community budget line GH; that is, they prefer more clothing and less food compared with their initial equilibrium at E. As a result, both commodity markets are thrown out of equilibrium. In the clothing market, where the quantity demanded has increased, there emerges an excess demand, as shown by vertical line segment SQ; and in the food market, where the quantity demanded has decreased, there emerges an excess supply, as indicated by horizontal line segment SE. How does the economy react to this disequilibrium state?

In the short run, the price of clothing (p_c) will rise creating positive profits in the clothing industry, and the price of food will fall generating losses in the food industry. In the long run, the clothing industry will expand, attracting resources away from the declining food industry. In terms of Figure 15.9, panel (a), the economy will attain a new equilibrium on production-possibilities frontier AB at some point between E and A, as illustrated by point Z. Thus compared with the initial equilibrium at E, the economy will be producing more clothing ($C^* > C_0$) and less food ($F^* < F_0$) at the new equilibrium. Furthermore, the relative price of food (p_f/p_c) will be lower at Z than at $E(p_1 < p_0)$, as shown.

The movement along the production-possibilities frontier from E to Z is not as easy as it seems. As explained below, it involves a complete reorganization of the economy: A shift of resources from one industry to the other, a change in the methods of production employed by the two industries, a change in factor prices, a change in the distribution of income among households, and changes in the consumption of food and clothing by every household. As Edgeworth once remarked in a slightly different context, the movement along the production-possibilities frontier is like "the movement of the hand of a clock" which "corresponds to considerable unseen movements of the machinery."

To take a glimpse into the "unseen movements of the machinery," let us take a close look at the Edgeworth production box in panel (b). Points E' and Z' correspond to points E and Z, respectively, on the production-possibilities frontier, and the movement from E' to Z' on the contract curve corresponds to the movement from E to Z on the production frontier.

First note that *the wage/rent ratio is higher at Z' than at E'*, that is, $(w/r)_1 > (w/r)_0$. This is no accident; it is due to the fact that the expanding clothing industry is labor intensive relative to the contracting food industry ($\rho_c > \rho_f$). To see why, suppose that at E' the labor/land ratios of the food and clothing industries are $\rho_f^0 = 2$ and $\rho_c^0 = 3$, respectively. Thus at E' the food industry employs 2 workers, and the clothing industry employs 3 workers, per acre of land. As the food industry contracts, it releases labor and land in the proportion 2:1. But the expanding clothing industry absorbs additional quantities of labor and land in the higher proportion

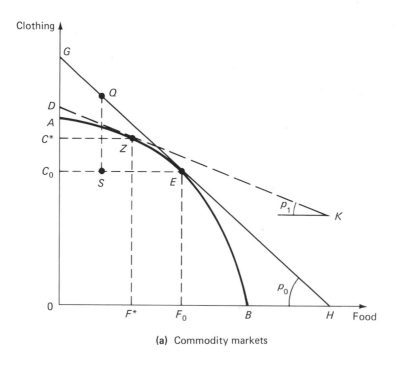

(a) Commodity markets

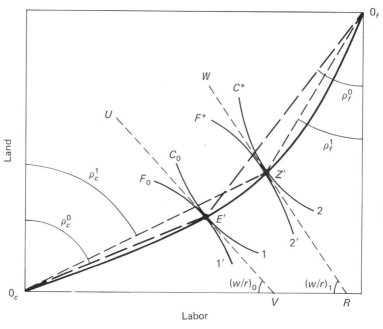

(b) Factor markets

Figure 15.9 The effects of a change in tastes. The initial equilibrium at E, panel (a), is disturbed by a change in tastes: At the initial prices, the households now choose bundle Q on community budget line GH. The excess demand for clothing (SQ) and the excess supply of food (SE) cause the price ratio to fall from p_0 and p_1 as the economy attains a new equilibrium at Z. The movement from E to Z on the production frontier corresponds to the movement from E' to Z' in the Edgeworth production box, panel (b). The wage/rent ratio is higher at Z' than at E', as shown by the slopes of WR and UV. Also both industries are less labor intensive at Z' than at E': $\rho_c^1 < \rho_c^0$ and $\rho_f^1 < \rho_f^0$.

476

3:1. Therefore, for each acre of land released by the food industry and hired by the clothing industry, there is a *shortage of one unit of labor* $(3 - 2 = 1)$. Alternatively, we may say that for every 2 units of labor released by the food industry and hired by the clothing industry, there is a *surplus of one-third of 1 unit of land* $(1 - \frac{2}{3} = \frac{1}{3})$. Consequently, the wage rate will tend to rise and the rent will tend to fall, and both of these tendencies will cause the wage/rent ratio to rise, which confirms the initial proposition.

The higher wage/rent ratio causes in turn both industries to become less labor intensive, because they both tend to substitute the cheaper factor (land) for the more expensive factor (labor). This is also illustrated by the Edgeworth production box. Thus both industries are less labor intensive at Z' than at $E'(\rho_c^1 < \rho_c^0; \rho_f^1 < \rho_f^0)$.

Further, the fact that both industries are less labor intensive at Z' means that as the economy moves from E' to Z', *the marginal physical product of labor rises, and the marginal physical product of land falls, in both industries*. This result, which is a consequence of constant returns to scale, illustrates an important proposition known as the *Stolper–Samuelson theorem*. According to the latter theorem, an increase (decrease) in the relative price of a commodity causes an increase (decrease) in the real reward of the factor used relatively intensively in the production of that commodity.

The rise in the marginal physical product of labor in both industries necessarily makes every household which owns only labor (i.e., every worker) better off. For instance, if $L_i > 0$ and $T_i = 0$, the ith household's budget line becomes

$$L_i = \left(\frac{1}{MPP_{LF}}\right) F_i + \left(\frac{1}{MPP_{LC}}\right) C_i \tag{15.14}$$

To obtain equation (15.14), we merely substitute equations (15.4)' and (15.4)'' as well as $T_i = 0$ into equation (15.1), and then simplify. Hence the intercepts of the household's budget line with the food and clothing axes are equal to $MPP_{LF} \cdot L_i$ and $MPP_{LC} \cdot L_i$, respectively. Therefore, as the marginal physical product of labor increases in both industries, both intercepts of the budget line increase; thus the budget line shifts outward and the household becomes better off.

Similarly, the reduction in the marginal physical product of land in both industries necessarily makes every household which owns only land (i.e., every landlord) worse off. Substituting again equations (15.5)' and (15.5)'' as well as $L_i = 0$ into equation (15.1) and simplifying, we obtain the ith landlord's budget line

$$T_i = \left(\frac{1}{MPP_{TF}}\right) F_i + \left(\frac{1}{MPP_{TC}}\right) C_i \tag{15.15}$$

The intercepts with the food and clothing axes are $MPP_{TF} \cdot T_i$ and $MPP_{TC} \cdot T_i$, respectively, and they both fall as the marginal physical product of land decreases in both industries. Thus the budget line of a typical landlord shifts inward and the landlord becomes worse off.

When a household owns both labor and land $(L_i > 0, T_i > 0)$, we cannot predict exactly how its budget line will shift and whether the household will become better off or worse off. The outcome depends on the specific quantities of labor and land owned by the household as well as the precise changes in the marginal physical products of the two factors. Nevertheless, our discussion shows that as the economy moves from E to Z, the distribution of income changes and each household modifies both the size and the composition of its consumption basket.

SUMMARY

1. Households are the only consuming units, and the only factor-supplying units. The firms are the only producing units and also the only factor-demanding units. The firms are artificial units that are owned, organized, and operated by members of households (entrepreneurs).

2. The firms use the factor services supplied to them by the households to produce goods and services, which they distribute to the households essentially in exchange for their factor services (real flow).

3. When the firms purchase factor services, they pay out wages and rents to the households, who use their incomes to buy goods and services from the firms (monetary flow).

4. It is assumed that the technology of the two-sector model can be summarized by two industry production functions, which exhibit constant returns to scale.

5. General competitive equilibrium occurs when at the prevailing factor prices and commodity prices all households, firms, and markets are in equilibrium. In long-run general equilibrium, each firm earns zero profit.

6. The dimensions of the Edgeworth production box are determined by the total quantities of labor and land available to the economy. Every point in the box (or its boundary) corresponds to a specific factor allocation between the two industries.

7. Resources are allocated efficiently (optimally) when it is not possible to increase the output of one commodity without reducing the output of the other.

8. All efficient resource allocations occur along the contract curve, which is the locus of tangencies between the food and clothing isoquants.

9. Perfect competition leads to the efficient allocation of resources.

10. When clothing's labor-intensity curve (the relationship between w/r and L_c/T_c) lies totally to the right of food's labor-intensity curve, clothing is labor intensive relative to food (i.e., clothing uses more units of labor per unit of land than food) for all wage-rent ratios (strong intensity assumption).

11. When the labor-intensity curves intersect, a factor-intensity reversal occurs; at the intersection, the relationship between the labor/land ratios of food and clothing is switched.

12. In a constant-returns-to-scale, closed economy, factor-intensity reversals cannot be observed.

13. Each point on the contract curve corresponds to a point on the production-possibilities frontier (*PPF*), and *vice versa*. The *PPF* depends on factor supplies and technology only; it is concave to the origin due to the disparity between the factor intensities of food and clothing.

14. The concavity of the *PPF* implies increasing opportunity costs to both industries.

15. The marginal rate of transformation (*MRT*), given by the absolute slope of the *PPF*, equals the ratio of the monetary marginal costs of food and clothing. Under perfect competition, $MRT = p_f/p_c$ (because $p = MC$).

16. A movement along the *PPF* involves a complete reorganization of the economy: a shift of resources from one industry to the other, a change in production methods and factor prices, a change in the functional and personal distribution of income, and changes in the consumption of food and clothing by every household.

17. *Stolper–Samuelson theorem:* An increase (decrease) in the relative price of a commodity causes an increase (decrease) in the real reward of the factor used relatively intensively in its production.

QUESTIONS

1. Labor and land in fixed proportions produce food and clothing. One unit of food requires 3 units of labor and 1 acre of land. The corresponding input requirements for clothing are 1 unit of labor and 1 acre of land. Society is endowed with 20 units of labor and 10 acres of land.

(a) Graph the economy's Edgeworth production box, contract curve, and production-possibilities frontier.

(b) Suppose that the prices of food and clothing are $p_f = \$150$ and $p_c = \$100$, respectively. What are the imputed factor prices of labor and land?

(c) What happens when food becomes very expensive relative to clothing?

(d) What happens when clothing becomes very expensive relative to food?

2. America is endowed with fixed quantities of labor and land and produces, under constant returns to scale, food and clothing. Food is land intensive relative to clothing at all wage/rent ratios. Each citizen owns the same quantities of labor and land. All citizens have the same tastes, summarized by an indifference map with regular convexity. Suppose that an initial general competitive equilibrium is disturbed by what is known as a *neutral invention* in the production of clothing. As a result, each combination of inputs produces 10 percent more clothing after the invention than before. Given sufficient time, America attains a new general equilibrium. Compare the initial and final equilibria and explain how the invention may affect:

(a) The outputs of food and clothing.

(b) The relative price of clothing.

(c) The marginal physical products of labor and land in the food industry.

(d) The well-being of each citizen.

3. An economy is endowed with 400 units of labor and 800 units of land and produces food and clothing. The two industry production functions are identical; they both take the form

$$Q = (10L^{-1/2} + 20T^{-1/2})^{-2}$$

(a) Show that the above production function exhibits constant returns to scale.

(b) Derive the contract curve and the production-possibilities frontier.

(c) Show your results graphically and explain any special features that you may observe.

4. The production functions of food and clothing are:

$$F = L_f^{2/3}T_f^{1/3}$$
$$C = L_c^{3/4}T_c^{1/4}$$

*(a) Show that the marginal physical products of labor in the food and clothing industries are given by

$$MPP_{LF} = \frac{2}{3}\left(\frac{T_f}{L_f}\right)^{1/3}$$
$$MPP_{LC} = \frac{3}{4}\left(\frac{T_c}{L_c}\right)^{1/4}$$

*(b) Similarly, show that the marginal physical products of land are given by

$$MPP_{TF} = \frac{1}{3}\left(\frac{L_f}{T_f}\right)^{2/3}$$
$$MPP_{TC} = \frac{1}{4}\left(\frac{L_c}{T_c}\right)^{3/4}$$

(c) Derive the labor-intensity functions of food and clothing.

(d) Show that clothing is labor intensive relative to food at all wage/rent ratios.

5. (a) Define the production-possibilities frontier.

(b) What relationship exists between the production-possibilities frontier and the contract curve inside the Edgeworth production box?

(c) Explain how perfect competition puts the economy *on* the production-possibilities frontier.

6. What crucial consideration is responsible for the concavity of the production-possibilities frontier? Explain fully.

7. (a) Define the marginal rate of transformation.

(b) Show that the marginal rate of transformation gives the ratio of marginal costs of food and clothing.

8. Explain why in your opinion each of the following statements is true or false.

(a) If in long-run equilibrium the price of a pound of beef is $10 and the price of a pound of chicken is $1, the marginal rate of transformation between beef and chicken must be 10.

(b) If each bushel of wheat requires only a fraction of 1 worker-hour while each Cutlass Supreme requires 100 worker-hours, automobile production can be said to be labor intensive relative to wheat production.

(c) In the presence of a single factor-intensity reversal, the contract curve must intersect the diagonal of the Edgeworth production box once (but only once).

(d) In the two-sector model, the distribution

of income depends on consumer tastes in addition to factor ownership.

(e) The production-possibilities frontier is always concave to the origin.

9. Assume that the U.S. economy is in general equilibrium when a large number of workers migrate from Europe to the United States. Use the two-sector model to answer the following questions.

(a) How does the labor immigration affect the U.S. production-possibilities frontier?

(b) Suppose that as a result of the additional workers, the relative price of food (the land-intensive commodity) increases. Can we say that the influx of new workers harms labor and benefits land?

10. "A movement along the production-possibilities frontier merely means that the output of one commodity goes up as the output of the other commodity goes down. That is all." Do you agree or disagree with this statement? Illustrate your answer graphically.

FURTHER READING

Arrow, K. J., and F. H. Hahn (1971). *General Competitive Analysis.* Holden-Day, Inc., San Francisco.

Chacholiades, M. (1978). *International Trade Theory and Policy.* McGraw-Hill Book Company, New York.

Graham, D. A. (1980). *Microeconomics: The Analysis of Choice.* D. C. Heath and Company, Lexington, Mass. Chapter 7.

Henderson, J. M., and R. E. Quandt (1980). *Microeconomic Theory: A Mathematical Approach,* 3rd ed. McGraw-Hill Book Company, New York. Chapters 9 and 10.

Hicks, J. R. (1946). *Value and Capital,* 2nd ed. Oxford University Press, New York. Chapter 8.

Krauss, M. B., and H. G. Johnson (1974). *General Equilibrium Analysis: A Microeconomic Text.* Aldine Publishing Company, Chicago.

Quirk, J., and R. Saposnik (1968). *Introduction to General Equilibrium Theory and Welfare Economics.* McGraw-Hill Book Company, New York.

Stolper, W. F., and P. A. Samuelson (1941). "Protection and Real Wages," *Review of Economic Studies,* Vol. 9, pp. 50–73. Reprinted in H. S. Ellis and L. A. Metzler (eds.), *Readings in the Theory of International Trade.* Richard D. Irwin, Inc., Homewood, Ill., 1950.

CHAPTER
16

Welfare Economics

Microeconomic theory is divided into two main branches: *positive microeconomic theory* (or *positive economics*) and *welfare microeconomic theory* (or *welfare economics*). Positive economics deals with the problem of how the economic system actually functions, why it produces the results it does, and how changes in the fundamental data of the economy (factor endowments, factor ownership, tastes, and technology) affect the solution of the economic problem. In principle, positive economics is independent of ethical judgments, and its propositions (or theorems) can be tested against the facts of the real world which they purport to explain. So far in this book, most (but not all) of our discussion dealt with problems of positive economics.

Welfare economics, on the other hand, seeks to *evaluate* the performance of the economy as well as the desirability of policy actions that affect the economy.[1] *How well* does the economic system solve the fundamental resource allocation problems of what, how, and for whom? Is a progressive income tax schedule *desirable*? *Should* the government impose a much higher tax on smoking? *Should* the government impose heavy penalties on factories that pollute the air? *Should* the government abolish or expand the food stamp program? *Should* the minimum wage law be repealed? *Should* usury laws (setting maximum interest rates on loans) be repealed? Will the *United States* be *better off* with the breakup of the American Telephone and Telegraph Company? Questions such as these belong to the realm of welfare economics. Positive economic analysis can only help us predict the consequences of policy actions. Whether the situation that is expected to exist after the policy action is better or worse than the original situation (i.e., the situation that exists before any policy action is taken) is a matter that requires the use of an *ethical criterion* for gauging desirability.

The propositions of welfare economics depend crucially on ethical beliefs or value judgments, that is, *subjective* evaluations of alternative situations (or "states of the

[1]Note that welfare economics does not deal only with government welfare programs whose primary objective is to provide assistance to low-income households. Rather welfare economics deals with the *optimal* allocation of resources and the well-being of *all* members of society.

economy").[2] It is therefore important to state explicitly at the outset what sort of ethical beliefs our conclusions depend on. In Section 16.1 we summarize these ethical beliefs. In Section 16.2 we deal with the concept of Pareto optimality and the conditions for economic efficiency. In Section 16.3 we develop the useful concept of the utility-possibility frontier and demonstrate the determination of constrained bliss. In Section 16.4 we provide a formal proof of Adam Smith's "invisible hand" theorem: namely, that perfect competition leads to Pareto optimality. Market imperfections and impediments to Pareto optimality are discussed in Section 16.5. Finally, we conclude in Section 16.6 with a brief statement of the theory of the second best.

16.1 The Social Welfare Function

To decide whether or not a certain policy action is desirable, we must first determine the effect of that action on social welfare. But what is welfare, and how can it be measured? How can we tell whether social welfare increases or decreases with a certain policy action? To answer these questions, we need to make judgments of a purely ethical nature.

Ethical beliefs (or value judgments) are highly subjective. Is it then reasonable to expect any welfare propositions that we may formulate to enjoy general acceptability? Only if the ethical assumptions on which the welfare propositions are based happen to be of a broad and commonly accepted kind. The purpose of this section is to discuss such widely accepted ethical beliefs and formalize them into a social welfare function.

The Bergson–Samuelson Social Welfare Function

The first ethical assumption that seems to be readily acceptable to economists is deeply rooted into the individualistic philosophy of our Western civilization. According to this *individualistic ethic,* only the preferences of the people making up the society are to "count." Thus economists today agree that social welfare is a function of the welfare of each and every citizen. Furthermore, each person's welfare map is identified with that person's indifference map; that is, individual consumers are thought to be the best judges of their own well-being.

Mathematically, we express social welfare (W) as a function of the utility indicators of the people making up the society:

$$W = W (U_1, U_2, \ldots, U_n) \tag{16.1}$$

where $U_i \equiv$ utility indicator of the ith person in the economy. Equation (16.1) is known as the Bergson–Samuelson social welfare function. Note that both the welfare function itself and the individual utility indicators are only ordinally determinable. Thus a switch from one set of cardinal utility indicators to another, as explained in Chapter 3, simply changes the form of the social welfare function so as to leave all social decisions invariant.

The individualistic ethic as formulated above is not universally valid. For in-

---

[2]By a "state of the economy" we mean a specific arrangement of the economy's production and consumption activities. Each state corresponds to a table that shows (1) the precise quantity of each good or service consumed by each person, (2) the quantity of labor supplied by each person, (3) the quantity of each input employed by each firm, and (4) the quantity of each output produced by each firm. For instance, a state of an exchange economy corresponds to a specific point (allocation) in the Edgeworth box. Typically, a policy action (such as the imposition of a tax) will shift the economy from one state to another.

stance, in every society there are many people (such as the very young, the very old, the mentally retarded, and the lunatics) who presumably cannot judge what is good for them. Even sane adults are constrained in their behavior by the rules of law and the canons of religion. Thus it is illegal to drive under the influence of alcohol or to smoke marijuana. Yet economists consider such cases as exceptions.

The Classical Welfare Function

A specific case of the Bergson–Samuelson social welfare function is provided by the classical welfare function. Earlier generations of economists assumed that social welfare was simply the sum of the *cardinal* utilities enjoyed by all members of society. That is, they assumed that equation (16.1) has the form

$$W = U_1 + U_2 + \cdots + U_n \tag{16.2}$$

where W and U_i are cardinal magnitudes.

Furthermore, the object of society was to maximize social welfare (i.e., the aggregate utility). Given the law of diminishing marginal utility, that goal would be achieved only if the marginal utility of income (after taxes) were the same for all people. Making the additional assumption that people are essentially alike in the sense that their cardinal utility functions are similar, these economists concluded that maximization of social welfare could be achieved only by an equalitarian distribution of income. Thus they advocated for the imposition of progressive taxes that would reduce large income inequalities and would bring society closer to the welfare maximum.

Modern economists reject the classical welfare function for two reasons. First, as we saw in Chapter 3, the utility enjoyed by each person is an ordinal concept and cannot be measured cardinally. Second, *interpersonal comparisons* of utility are ruled out as unscientific. We simply cannot add up the utilities of different persons (even if they were cardinally measurable) any more than we can add up society's outputs of different commodities, such as automobiles, computers, dresses, and peanuts.

To appreciate the last point, consider a policy action (say, a transfer of income from one person to another) that makes person A better off, and person B worse off. We cannot say what happens to social welfare unless we find a way to compare the gain of A with the loss of B. Such a comparison, though, requires a judgment of a purely ethical nature and cannot be made objectively. Different ethical observers can, and typically will, pass different judgments.

Aside from the problem of measurability of utility, the classical welfare function incorporates a very specific ethical assumption: that social welfare is the *sum* of the cardinal utilities of people. Thus each person's utility has exactly the same weight in the social welfare function. For instance, the same social significance is attached to a derelict drunkard as to a famous opthalmologist. This ethical assumption is *not* acceptable to many ethical observers. Thus any propositions (such as the equalitarian income distribution and progressive taxation) that follow from it are unacceptable (unless these propositions are verified by other methods).

The Paretian Class of Social Welfare Functions

The Bergson–Samuelson social welfare function, that is, equation (16.1), is intrinsically unscientific—it either summarizes or implies a detailed set of ethical judgments regarding the way in which one person's welfare is to be "added" to another's.[3] But as the preceding discussion of the classical welfare function clearly shows, we should not attempt to specify the social welfare function in detail ourselves. If we did, any welfare propositions following from it would not be generally acceptable—they would be of interest only to those who happened to agree with our detailed ethical assumptions. What we really want to do is to derive propositions that will be true on the basis of widely and commonly accepted ethical beliefs.

Modern economists accept the *Paretian ethic: When one person becomes better off without anyone else becoming worse off, social welfare increases; and conversely, when one person becomes worse off while nobody else becomes better off, social welfare decreases.*[4] Obviously, there is an infinite number of social welfare functions that are consistent with the Paretian ethic. The totality of such functions is usually referred to as the *Paretian class*. Surely, the classical welfare function belongs to the Paretian class. In the remainder of this chapter we shall confine our discussion to all those welfare functions which are members of the Paretian class.

Note that the Paretian class of social welfare functions requires only the very broad ethical judgment that *it is a good thing to make one person better off if nobody else is made worse off*. No statement made on this basis requires the making of any interpersonal comparisons. Accordingly, when some people become better off and others worse off, we are still unable to say (on the basis of the Paretian ethic alone) whether social welfare increases, decreases, or remains the same. This is the price we have to pay for seeking welfare propositions of general acceptability.

16.2 Pareto Optimality

A state of the economy is said to be Pareto optimal (or efficient) if it is not possible, through any feasible reorganization of production and distribution, to make one person better off without making any other(s) worse off. Conversely, a state of the economy is *Pareto nonoptimal* (or inefficient) when it is possible to make one person better off without harming anyone else. Clearly, a social welfare function of the Paretian class cannot be maximized unless the economy happens to be at a Pareto-optimal state. Accordingly, Pareto optimality provides a criterion for economic efficiency which is the foundation of modern welfare economics.

This section discusses the conditions that an economic system must satisfy if it is to be Pareto optimal. These conditions provide general guidelines for the optimal resolution of the three fundamental problems of what, how, and for whom. Our entire discussion is developed within the context of the two-sector model of Chapter 15, and the model of an exchange economy of Chapter 14. For simplicity, we assume that the economy consists of only two persons: Adam and Beth. (Our conclusions generalize easily to the case of many people.)[5]

Pareto Optimality in Exchange

Consider again, as in Section 14.2, an exchange economy consisting of Adam and Beth. Assume that the total quantities of two commodities, say, food and clothing, are given. (These totals of food and clothing may be viewed as the quantities actually

---

[3]The actual construction of a social welfare function is not easy. Majority voting and other mechanisms for making social choices face insurmountable difficulties, as emphasized by the *paradox of majority voting* and the *Arrow impossibility theorem*. On these problems, the interested reader is referred to Arrow (1951).

[4]The Paretian ethic was first formulated by the Italian economist Vilfredo Pareto (1848–1923) [see Pareto (1909)].

[5]The reader may wish to review Chapters 14 and 15 before proceeding with the present analysis.

produced by the economy.) How should the fixed amounts of food and clothing be distributed between Adam and Beth?

Recall that graphically our two-person exchange economy can be represented by an Edgeworth box diagram whose respective sides are equal to the available total quantities of food and clothing. Each point in the box corresponds to a feasible distribution of food and clothing between Adam and Beth (and vice versa). As we explained in Section 14.2, only points lying on the contract curve (i.e., the locus of tangencies) are efficient, or Pareto-optimal. The common characteristic of all such Pareto-optimal points is the equality of the marginal rates of substitution of food for clothing (MRS_{FC}) between the two individuals. That is,

$$MRS^A_{FC} = MRS^B_{FC} \qquad (16.3)$$

where the superscripts A and B stand for Adam and Beth, respectively.

We therefore conclude that equation (16.3) is the primary condition for Pareto optimality in the distribution of commodities between individual consumers. When this equation is satisfied (i.e., when the economy is on the contract curve), it is not possible to make one person better off without making the other worse off, and when it is not satisfied (i.e., when the economy is off the contract curve), it is always possible to make one person better off without making the other worse off.

Note that condition (16.3) does not lead to a single Pareto-optimal allocation. *Any* point on the contract curve is Pareto optimal. Thus the Pareto criterion still leaves a choice to be made among the infinitely many Pareto-optimal allocations. However, the final choice requires interpersonal comparisons, because any movement along the contract curve always makes one person better off and the other worse off. Such interpersonal comparisons, however, presuppose a detailed specification of the social welfare function.

Furthermore, we cannot even conclude that every Pareto-optimal allocation is better than every nonoptimal allocation. For instance, in Figure 16.1, Adam prefers nonoptimal allocation N to optimal allocation P, while Beth prefers P to N. Without an explicit interpersonal comparison of utility, we cannot judge the relative social desirability of allocations P and N.

What we can say is this. We do admit that not every optimal allocation is better than every nonoptimal allocation, but we can always identify some Pareto-optimal allocations that are better than any given nonoptimal allocation. For instance, all Pareto-optimal allocations along segment UV of the contract curve in Figure 16.1 are superior to inefficient allocation N. Thus starting at N, the economy can increase social welfare by moving to a point such as Z.

Pareto Optimality in Production

Consider now the two-sector model of Chapter 15. The economy is endowed with fixed quantities of labor and land and produces food and clothing under constant returns to scale. How should the fixed amounts of labor and land be allocated between the food and clothing industries?

Pareto optimality requires that labor and land are so allocated that society *cannot* increase the output of, say, food without sacrificing any clothing. To see why, suppose that the opposite is true; that is, assume that society can so reallocate inputs as to increase the output of food without sacrificing any clothing. With more food and no less clothing, society can certainly keep all people at least as well off as before, by merely allocating to them the exact amounts that they were consuming when less food was available. That would, of course, leave the extra output of food for further distribution. Any arbitrary distribution of the extra food among consumers would improve the well-being of some people without harming others. Hence more of any

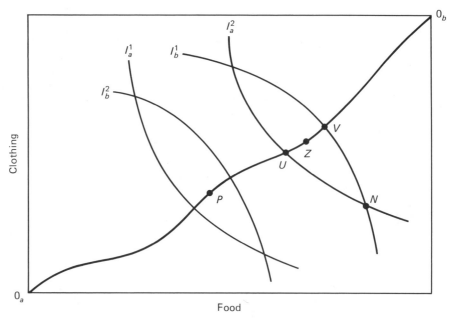

Figure 16.1 Pareto optimality in the distribution of commodities between individuals.
Pareto optimality occurs only along the contract curve 0_a0_b. Note, however, that Adam
prefers nonoptimal allocation N to optimal allocation P, while Beth prefers P to N. To judge
the relative social desirability of P and N, we must make interpersonal comparisons of utility.
But all points along segment UV of the contract curve are Pareto superior to inefficient point
N. Society can increase welfare by moving from N to a point such as Z.

one commodity, the outputs of all other goods and services being constant, is socially
desirable.

Recall again that the factor allocation problem can be represented graphically
by an Edgeworth production box whose dimensions coincide with the fixed quantities
of labor and land available to the economy. Each point in the box corresponds to a
feasible factor allocation. But as we explained in Section 15.2, resources are allocated
optimally only along the contract curve (i.e., the locus of tangencies between the
food and clothing isoquants). At these points, the marginal rates of technical substitution of labor for land (MRS_{LT}) are equal between industries. That is,

$$MRS_{LT}^F = MRS_{LT}^C \tag{16.4}$$

We therefore conclude that equation (16.4) is the primary condition for Pareto
optimality in the allocation of inputs between industries. When equation (16.4) is
satisfied (i.e., when the economy is on the contract curve), it is impossible to increase
the output of one commodity without reducing the output of the other. If equation
(16.4) is not satisfied, however, it is always possible to increase the output of one
commodity without reducing the output of the other by a proper reallocation of
inputs.

The optimal allocation of inputs between industries can also be illustrated in
terms of the production-possibilities frontier, because each point on the production
frontier corresponds to a point on the contract curve, and vice versa. The Pareto-
optimal combinations of food and clothing are represented by points on the production frontier itself. Points lying inside the production frontier are inefficient.
For instance, point N in Figure 16.2 is inefficient (or Pareto *non*optimal) because

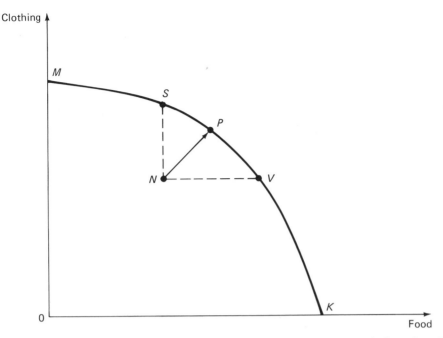

Figure 16.2 Pareto optimality in the allocation of inputs between industries. Only points on production-possibilities frontier *MK* are efficient. Point *N* is inefficient (or Pareto nonoptimal) because society can move to a point such as *P* where more of each output is available.

society can move from *N* to a point such as *P* at which more of each output is available.

Note again that condition (16.4) does not lead to a single Pareto-optimal allocation of inputs between industries; it generally leads to an infinite number of such Pareto optima. Furthermore, not every Pareto-optimal factor allocation is better than every nonoptimal allocation. However, we can always identify some Pareto-optimal allocations that are better than any given nonoptimal allocation. For instance, all output combinations represented by points along segment *SV* of the production frontier of Figure 16.2 are better than the output combination indicated by *N*, which is inefficient (or nonoptimal).

Pareto Optimality in Production cum Exchange

So far we have developed two Pareto-optimality conditions: one for exchange and one for production. Nevertheless, we have conducted our analysis as if exchange and production were two unrelated activities. Surely, this is not true. Pareto optimality requires the economy to also consider combined adjustments in production and exchange. That is, Pareto optimality will prevail in general if it is not possible by any shift in *production cum exchange* to make one person better off without making anybody else worse off. This last condition is met only when *the marginal rate of transformation in production* (i.e., the slope of the production-possibilities frontier at the actual production point) *is equal to the common marginal rate of substitution in consumption;* that is,

$$MRT_{FC} = MRS_{FC} \tag{16.5}$$

where MRT_{FC} is the opportunity cost of food in terms of clothing and MRS_{FC} is the common marginal rate of substitution of Adam and Beth. A Pareto-optimal state is fully described by the three marginal conditions (16.3), (16.4), and (16.5).

What is the rationale behind the optimality rule that the marginal rate of transformation (MRT_{FC}) must be equal to the marginal rate of substitution? Suppose that at the current state of the economy equations (16.3) and (16.4) are satisfied but $MRT_{FC} = 2$ and $MRS_{FC} = 3$. Thus the economy produces on its production-possibilities frontier, and Adam and Beth consume somewhere on their contract curve. The equality $MRT_{FC} = 2$ means that to increase the output of food by 1 unit, the economy must sacrifice 2 units of clothing (since resources must be transferred from clothing to food). Assume that we do just that, so that we have 1 extra unit of food and 2 less units of clothing. Leaving Adam's consumption basket undisturbed, remove 3 units of clothing from Beth's consumption basket and replace them by 1 unit of food (i.e., the extra unit of food produced). Since $MRS_{FC} = 3$, Beth is left indifferent (i.e., she remains on the same indifference curve). What have we achieved? Both Adam and Beth are obviously as well off after this rearrangement as before, *but we are left with one extra unit of clothing.* (We removed $3C$ from Beth's basket and sacrificed only $2C$ for producing 1 extra unit of food.) By allocating this surplus of clothing arbitrarily between Adam and Beth, we can make both of them better off. Hence the original state could not have been Pareto optimal. Such reorganization of production and exchange is not possible when condition (16.5) is satisfied.

The above argument is illustrated in Figure 16.3. The economy produces at E on production-possibilities frontier UV; that is, it produces $0D$ food and $0G$ clothing. Given these totals, construct an Edgeworth exchange box, as shown by $0DEG$. Draw the indifference maps of Adam and Beth in the box, treating points 0 and E as the origins for Adam and Beth, respectively, as illustrated by indifference curves I_a^0 and I_b^0. Assume that point S (the tangency between I_a^0 and I_b^0) corresponds to the initial distribution of the available quantities of food and clothing between Adam and Beth. Note that equations (16.3) and (16.4) are both satisfied in this initial state. However, equation (16.5) is not satisfied, because $MRT_{FC} = 2 < 3 = MRS_{FC}$, as shown by the slopes of lines L_1 and L_2. How can we confirm that Beth can be made better off without harming Adam?

Freeze Adam's consumption at S and redraw Beth's indifference map in its natural state (not upside down), as indicated by the dashed axes through S and indifference curve I_b'. Surely, I_b' (which is drawn with respect S as origin) corresponds to I_b^0 because we know that these two indifference curves have one commodity bundle (shown by vector SE) in common. Since Beth's MRS_{FC} at S exceeds the economy's MRT_{FC} at E, it follows that I_b' must intersect the production frontier at E from above, as shown. Obviously, the economy can shift its production to a point such as J, where Beth consumes on a higher indifference curve than I_b'. Thus Beth can be made better off while Adam remains at S.

Surely, if condition (16.5) were satisfied also, Beth's indifference curve I_b' would be tangent to the production frontier at E. Hence it would not be possible to so reorganize production and exchange as to make one person better off without making the other worse off.[6]

---

[6]For a conclusive proof of the assertion made in the text, we must draw the *Scitovsky social indifference curve* and show that it is tangent to the production frontier at E. However, this elegant approach is beyond the scope of this book. For the definition, derivation and properties of the Scitovsky social indifference curves, the interested reader is referred to Chacholiades (1978, pp. 130–132 and 151–153).

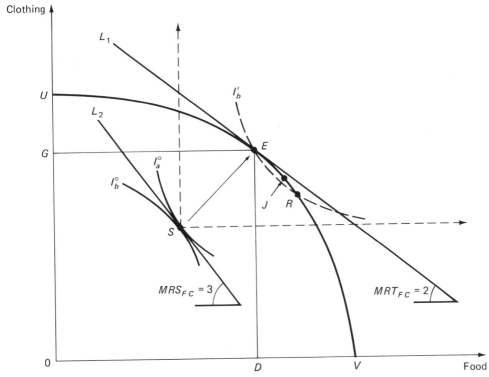

Clothing

Food

Figure 16.3 Pareto optimality for production cum exchange. The economy produces at E on production frontier UV, where $MRT_{FC} = 2$. Construct Edgeworth box $0DEG$ and assume that Adam and Beth consume as S, where $MRS_{FC} = 3$. (0 and E are the origins for Adam and Beth, respectively.) Freeze Adam's consumption at S. Redraw Beth's indifference map in its natural state, as shown by dashed axes through S and indifference curve I_b', which corresponds to I_b°. Since Beth's MRS_{FC} at S is 3 and the MRT_{FC} at E is 2, I_b' intersects the production frontier from above, as shown. The economy can shift its production to a point such as J, where Beth consumes on a higher indifference curve than I_b', while Adam remains at S.

Summary of Pareto-Optimality Conditions

We have discussed the following three important Pareto-optimality conditions:

1. The optimality condition for exchange, that is, equation (16.3).
2. The optimality condition for production, that is, equation (16.4).
3. The optimality condition for production cum exchange, that is, equation (16.5).

The allocation of resources is Pareto optimal only when all three conditions hold simultaneously. Then, and only then, is it not possible to make one person better off without harming others.

16.3 The Utility Frontier and Constrained Bliss

When the three Pareto-optimality conditions are satisfied, it is not possible to so reorganize production and distribution as to increase the utility of one person without decreasing the utility of others. That is, Pareto optimality implies that the utility of, say, Adam is maximized for any given utility level of Beth. This idea can be illustrated by means of a *utility-possibility frontier* (or utility frontier for short)—a concept that is comparable to the production-possibilities frontier. The purpose of this section is to derive the economy's utility frontier, study its properties, and finally use it along with a completely specified social welfare function to determine a point of welfare optimum (or "constrained bliss").

Derivation of the Utility Frontier

Consider Figure 16.4. Panel (a) is similar to Figure 16.3. For the moment concentrate on point E, which lies on production frontier UV. Form the Edgeworth exchange box $0DEG$ as before, and then draw the contract curve, as shown by $0E$. (Recall that points 0 and E are the origins for Adam and Beth, respectively.)

At each point on contract curve $0E$ we can identify the utility levels of Adam and Beth. We can use this information to plot a utility-possibility *curve* in the utility space (U_A, U_B), as shown by dashed downward-sloping curve HF in panel (b). Each point on utility-possibility curve HF corresponds to a point on contract curve $0E$. For instance, points R' and S' on HF correspond to points R and S on $0E$, respectively. The utility-possibility curve HF necessarily slopes downward because, as we move along contract curve $0E$, one consumer becomes better off and the other worse off.

We can repeat the above procedure for each and every point on the production-possibilities frontier. That is, for each point on the production frontier we can construct an Edgeworth exchange box and a contract curve; and then we can use the information on utilities along the contract curve to plot a utility-possibility curve. Hence we can derive an infinite number of such utility-possibility curves as HF. The *outer envelope* of these utility-possibility curves is the economy's utility frontier, which is often called the true (or grand) utility-possibility frontier. The utility frontier (or outer envelope) is shown in panel (b) by solid curve MN.

Note that all points along any utility-possibility curve, such as HF, necessarily satisfy the first two Pareto-optimality conditions, that is, equations (16.3) and (16.4), but they do not necessarily satisfy the last condition, that is, equation (16.5). For instance, point R', which corresponds to point R in panel (a), satisfies all three conditions, but point S' (corresponding to S) satisfies only the first two conditions—it does not satisfy equation (16.5). All points, such as R', which satisfy all three Pareto-optimality conditions lie *on* the utility frontier MN. Those points, such as S', which fail to satisfy equation (16.5) lie *inside* the utility frontier.

The concept of the utility frontier makes clear that there are infinitely many Pareto-optimal states of the economy. Each point on the utility frontier corresponds to a Pareto-optimal state, and each optimal state corresponds to a point on the utility frontier. All points inside the utility frontier correspond to nonoptimal (inefficient) states, and all points outside the utility frontier are unattainable, because of the limitations imposed by the scarcity of resources and technical know-how.

Constrained Bliss

We have just seen that the rules of Pareto optimality do not lead to a single welfare maximum; they lead to a utility frontier. How does society determine *the* socially optimal state? What point on the utility frontier generates maximum social welfare? To answer this question, we need a *completely specified* social welfare function. Without it we cannot determine the bliss point, because this final step requires explicit comparisons of the utility levels of the various members of society. Let us therefore assume that the social welfare function exists and is known to us. Figure 16.5 illustrates the determination of the bliss point.

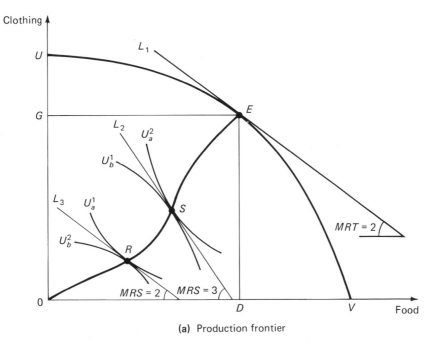

(a) Production frontier

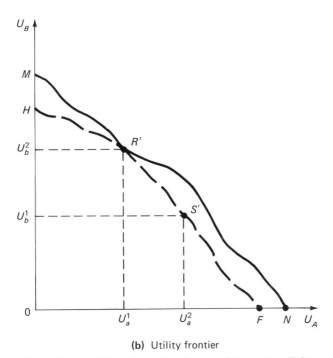

(b) Utility frontier

Figure 16.4 Derivation of the utility frontier. In panel (a) point E lies on production frontier UV. Form Edgeworth box as in Figure 16.3 and draw contract curve $0E$. At each point on $0E$ identify the utility levels of Adam and Beth. Use this information to plot dashed utility-possibility curve HF in panel (b). Points R' and S' on HF correspond to R and S on $0E$, respectively. Derive a utility-possibility curve for each point on the production frontier. The outer envelope of these curves, known as the economy's true utility frontier, is shown in panel (b) by solid curve MN. Point R' lies on MN because corresponding point R satisfies all three Pareto-optimality conditions. Point S' lies inside MN because at corresponding point S $MRT_{FC} \neq MRS_{FC}$.

491

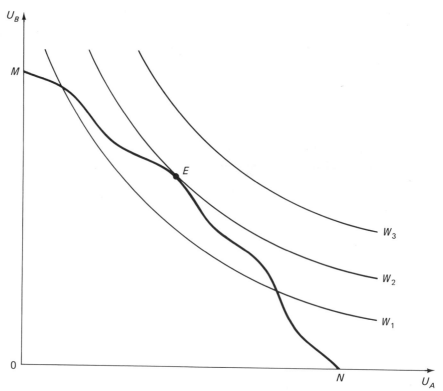

Figure 16.5 Determination of the bliss point. Curve *MN* is the economy's utility frontier
as in Figure 16.4, panel (b). The curves labeled W_1, W_2, and W_3 are three illustrative welfare
contour lines (similar to indifference curves) obtained from a social welfare function. Social
welfare is maximized at *E*, where the utility frontier touches the highest possible contour
line (W_2). However, bliss point *E* is the point of maximum welfare only in relation to the
welfare contour lines drawn. With a different social welfare function, a different point on
MN would be the bliss point.

Curve *MN* is the economy's utility frontier, as in Figure 16.4. The curves labeled
W_1, W_2, and W_3 are three illustrative *welfare contour lines* obtained from the given
social welfare function. Each welfare contour line is the locus of utility combinations
(U_A and U_B) all of which generate the same amount of social welfare. Thus society
is indifferent among the various points lying on a welfare contour line. However,
a higher welfare contour line corresponds to more welfare than a lower one. For
instance, social welfare is higher along W_2 than W_1. Note also that all welfare
contour lines are necessarily downward sloping, because our social welfare function
is assumed to be Paretian.

Social welfare is maximized at point *E*, where the utility frontier touches the
highest possible contour line (W_2) of the social welfare function. With the introduction of a specific social welfare function, the infinity of Pareto-optimal states has
been reduced to a single state indicated by point *E*. This unique point is called the
point of "constrained bliss" (or bliss point); it corresponds to that organization of
production and distribution that leads to the maximum attainable social welfare.

Remember, however, that the bliss point (*E*) is the point of maximum welfare
only in relation to the family of the welfare contour lines drawn (i.e., the given
social welfare function). For a different social welfare function, and thus a different
set of welfare contour lines, another point on the utility frontier would become the
bliss point.

Finally, given the unique bliss point, we can retrace our steps to determine the precise quantities of labor and land allocated to each industry, the precise quantities of food and clothing produced, and the amounts of food and clothing allocated to each consumer—that is, the answers to the three fundamental problems of what, how, and for whom. The details are left as an exercise for the interested reader.

16.4 Perfect Competition and Pareto Optimality

In a socialist state, in which, by assumption, all necessary information regarding technology, tastes, and factor endowments is available to a central planning authority, Pareto optimality can be achieved through centralized decision making based on the solution of an admittedly complex problem of constrained maximization. How is Pareto optimality achieved in a market economy? By perfect competition.

In this section we reintroduce "prices" and "markets" into our analysis. We intend to show that perfect competition leads to Pareto optimality. Indeed, there is an exact correspondence between perfectly competitive prices and Pareto optimality: *Every perfectly competitive equilibrium is Pareto optimal, and every Pareto optimal state is associated with a set of perfectly competitive prices.* Because of this important theorem, one often hears the aphorism that if perfect competition did not exist, it would have to be invented.

Pareto Optimality in Exchange

We already know from our discussion in Section 14.3 that general competitive equilibrium of exchange necessarily occurs on the contract curve; that is, it is Pareto optimal. Here we restate the argument briefly.

Both Adam and Beth face the *same* commodity–price ratio P_F/P_C, where P_F is the price of food and P_C the price of clothing. Adam is in equilibrium as a consumer when his marginal rate of substitution of food for clothing (MRS_{FC}^A) equals the commodity–price ratio; that is,

$$MRS_{FC}^A = \frac{P_F}{P_C} \tag{16.6}$$

Similarly, Beth is in equilibrium when

$$MRS_{FC}^B = \frac{P_F}{P_C} \tag{16.7}$$

Hence

$$MRS_{FC}^A = MRS_{FC}^B \tag{16.8}$$

because both MRS_{FC}^A and MRS_{FC}^B are equal to the same price ratio. We therefore conclude that perfect competition yields Pareto optimality in exchange.

Pareto Optimality in Production

We also know from our discussion in Section 15.2 that general competitive equilibrium can occur only at points lying on the contract curve inside an Edgeworth production box. We again restate the argument briefly.

The wage/rent ratio (w/r) is uniform throughout the economy. The food industry minimizes its costs by employing inputs in quantities such that the marginal rate of substitution of labor for land (MRS_{LT}^F) equals the wage/rent ratio; that is,

$$MRS_{LT}^F = \frac{w}{r} \qquad (16.9)$$

Similarly, the clothing industry minimizes its costs when

$$MRS_{LT}^C = \frac{w}{r} \qquad (16.10)$$

Hence

$$MRS_{LT}^F = MRS_{LT}^C \qquad (16.11)$$

because both MRS_{LT}^F and MRS_{LT}^C are equal to the same wage/rent ratio. We therefore conclude that perfect competition yields Pareto optimality in production.

Pareto Optimality in Production cum Exchange

The proof of the proposition that perfect competition yields Pareto optimality in production cum exchange is also simple. We can demonstrate this by combining the consumer equilibrium conditions, as given by equations (16.6) and (16.7), with the profit-maximizing conditions of the two industries.

To maximize its profit, the food industry produces that output of food where marginal cost (MC_F) equals the price of food; that is,

$$MC_F = P_F \qquad (16.12)$$

Similarly, the clothing industry maximizes its profit when

$$MC_C = P_C \qquad (16.13)$$

Dividing equation (16.12) by (16.13) yields

$$\frac{MC_F}{MC_C} = \frac{P_F}{P_C} \qquad (16.14)$$

Now recall from our discussion in Section 15.4 that the ratio of marginal costs equals the marginal rate of transformation; that is,

$$MRT_{FC} = \frac{MC_F}{MC_C} \qquad (16.15)$$

We also know that

$$MRS_{FC} = \frac{P_F}{P_C} \qquad (16.16)$$

where MRS_{FC} is the common marginal rate of substitution of food for clothing for both Adam and Beth. Hence

$$MRT_{FC} = MRS_{FC} \qquad (16.17)$$

because of equation (16.14).[7] We therefore conclude that perfect competition yields Pareto optimality in production cum exchange also.

Concluding Remarks

The preceding discussion is a formal proof of Adam Smith's "invisible hand" theorem: that in a free-enterprise system millions of diverse individuals, each directly pursuing his or her own self-interests, ultimately promote the public interest, even though the latter is not part of their intention. We conclude this section with three additional observations concerning perfect competition.

1. Perfect competition yields Pareto optimality in the sense that it puts the economy at some point lying on the utility frontier. There is no guarantee that the perfectly competitive equilibrium point coincides with the bliss point, assuming that the latter is known. Many great economists have fallen into the trap of believing that perfect competition necessarily maximizes social welfare. We know now that this need not be so. The equilibrium point attained under perfect competition depends on factor ownership, and to say that perfect competition maximizes social welfare is to assert that the existing factor ownership is somehow socially desirable. To attain the bliss point, the economy may have to redistribute wealth by means of lump-sum transfers (which destroy none of the Pareto-optimality conditions) to secure a movement along the utility frontier from the actual equilibrium point to the bliss point.[8]

2. Adam Smith's "invisible hand" theorem is of relevance not only to the free-enterprise system but also to socialist economies. For instance, Oskar Lange (1904–1965), among others, emphasized in the late 1930s that even socialist states could achieve economic efficiency (Pareto optimality) by means of decentralized decision making while they retain collective ownership of the means of production. Under Lange's scheme, a socialist regime would announce a set of competitive prices and allow individual producers and consumers to make their own choices concerning what inputs to use in the production of each commodity, how much to produce, what to consume, and how much labor to offer and in which occupation. Surely, it would be very difficult and costly to determine a set of competitive prices that would clear all markets—the socialist state might be involved in an adjustment process not unlike the one implied by the law of supply and demand. But the tremendous advantage of Lange's procedure is that there would be no need for the central planners to become ensnarled in the hopelessly complex task of setting targets for each producer or plant.

3. Perfect competition yields Pareto optimality only when the economy is in long-run competitive equilibrium. But in the real world full equilibrium is seldom attained, as the economic system seems to be aiming at a perpetually moving target. Moreover, as we explain below, many of the requirements (such as the absence of monopoly power) for the smooth functioning of a perfectly competitive system do not hold in the real world. For these reasons, in practice one cannot hope for anything better than the crudest approximation to Pareto optimality.

---

[7]Equations (16.14) to (16.16) can be combined as follows:

$$MRT_{FC} = \frac{MC_F}{MC_C} = \frac{P_F}{P_C} = MRS_{FC}$$

[8]Truly lump-sum measures are very hard to devise. On this point, see Graaf (1957, pp. 77–79), and Samuelson (1947, pp. 247–248).

16.5 Anatomy of Market Failure

This section deals with certain pathologies (market imperfections) of the economic system. These market imperfections prevent the attainment of one or more Pareto-optimality conditions and render the allocation of resources inefficient. These impediments to Pareto optimality are usually classified into three groups: *imperfect competition, externalities,* and *public goods.* We give some examples of each below.

Monopoly

In Section 16.4 we assumed that both food and clothing were produced under conditions of perfect competition. We now drop this assumption. Instead, we assume that clothing is produced by a monopoly, while the food industry continues to be competitive.

From our discussion in Chapter 10, we know that a monopolist's marginal revenue (MR) is consistently lower than his average revenue (AR) or price. Because the monopolist's equilibrium is dictated by the equality of marginal cost and marginal revenue, the monopolist's price necessarily exceeds marginal cost. Accordingly, a monopoly in the production of clothing leads to

$$MC_C = MR_C < P_C \tag{16.18}$$

However, in the competitive food industry we continue to have

$$MC_F = MR_F = P_F \tag{16.19}$$

because $MR_F = AR_F \equiv P_F$. Dividing (16.19) by (16.18), we finally obtain

$$MRT_{FC} = \frac{MC_F}{MC_C} = \frac{MR_F}{MR_C} > \frac{P_F}{P_C} = MRS_{FC} \tag{16.20}$$

Therefore, the existence of monopoly in the clothing industry creates a divergence between the marginal rate of transformation and the marginal rate of substitution; that is, monopoly violates the third optimality condition.[9] The above argument is illustrated in Figure 16.6, where for simplicity we assume that there exists only one consumer (Robinson Crusoe) in the economy. The economy reaches equilibrium at point E where indifference curve I_0 *intersects* production-possibilities frontier UV. At E the marginal rate of substitution of food for clothing (indicated by the slope of dashed line L_2) is lower than the marginal rate of transformation (indicated by the slope of line L_1), as suggested by (16.20). Obviously, Pareto optimality requires production and consumption at J, where the production frontier is tangent to dashed indifference curve I_1. But the monopolist produces an output which is smaller than that of an otherwise identical competitive industry and thus equilibrium occurs at a point such as E.

As we anticipated in Chapter 10, the basic misallocation of resources (which is brought about by the inequality $MC_C < P_C$) will persist even if all profit is taxed away from the monopolist by means of a lump-sum tax and redistributed to consumers. Correct policy would be to *subsidize* the production of clothing and thus induce the monopolist to increase her output so that the economy can return to Pareto-optimal point J.

---

[9]When *both* products are produced under monopoly, the third optimality condition is violated only to the extent that the degree of monopoly is different between industries. (Why?)

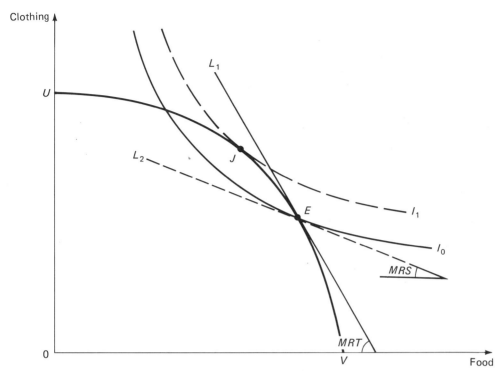

Figure 16.6 The inefficiency of monopoly. Equilibrium occurs at E, where indifference curve I_0 *intersects* production frontier UV. At E the marginal rate of transformation (given by the slope of line L_1) exceeds the marginal rate of substitution (indicated by dashed line L_2) because clothing is produced by a monopoly. Pareto optimality requires production at J, where the production frontier is tangent to dashed indifference curve I_1.

Wage Differentials

Often the price of a factor of production differs between industries. For instance, the wage rate paid by the clothing producers may differ from the wage rate paid by the food producers. The reasons for such a wage differential are many. Some of them are as follows: lack of information, discrimination (age, sex, or race), prestige and humanitarianism, seniority that does not reflect economic superiority, trade union intervention, and minimum wage laws.[10] Wage differentials violate two Pareto-optimality conditions: (16.4) and (16.5). Here we illustrate only how a wage differential leads to an inefficient allocation of inputs between industries.

Suppose that the wage rate is higher in the clothing industry than in the food industry (i.e., $w_f < w_c$) because, say, the clothing industry is unionized while the food industry is not. The rent for the services of land (r), however, is the same for both industries. It follows that

$$\frac{w_f}{r} < \frac{w_c}{r} \tag{16.21}$$

Hence equations (16.9) and (16.10) now lead to

[10]In the field of *economic development,* one often hears the argument that wages may be equal between industry and agriculture but wages in agriculture are equal to the *average* product of labor, while wages in industry are equal to the *marginal* product of labor.

$$MRS^F_{LT} = \frac{w_f}{r} < \frac{w_c}{r} = MRS^C_{LT} \qquad (16.22)$$

That is, the existence of a wage differential creates a divergence between the marginal rates of substitution of labor for land in the food and clothing industries, which prevents the economy from allocating labor and land along the contract curve inside the Edgeworth production box. This is illustrated in Figure 16.7.

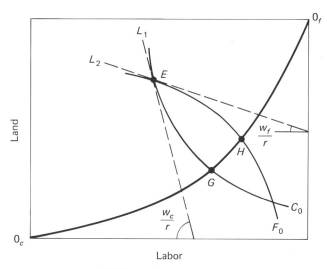

(a) Edgeworth-production box

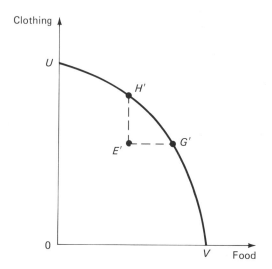

(b) Production-possibilities frontier

Figure 16.7 The inefficiency of wage differentials. Because the wage rate is higher in the clothing industry than in the food industry, resources are allocated at E, panel (a), where isoquants C_0 and F_0 intersect. Point E represents an inefficient allocation of inputs. Compared with E, point G implies more food and no less clothing, and point H suggests more clothing and no less food. Points E', G', and H' in panel (b) correspond to points E, G, and H, respectively. While G' and H' lie on production-possibilities frontier UV, point E' lies *inside* it.

Because of the wage differential, the economy allocates its available quantities of labor and land at point E, panel (a), where isoquants C_0 and F_0 intersect. The marginal rate of substitution of labor for land is lower in the food industry than in the clothing industry, as indicated by the slopes of dashed lines L_1 and L_2. Point E represents an inefficient allocation of inputs. For example, the economy could move to point G, where the output of clothing is the same as at E but the output of food is higher. Alternatively, the economy could move to H, where the output of food is the same but the output of clothing is higher.

Points E', G', and H' in panel (b) correspond to points E, G, and H, respectively, in panel (a). While G' and H' lie on production-possibilities frontier UV, point E' lies inside it. Note that the economy operates inside the production frontier not because some resources are not employed or because workers are lazy and they do not work hard enough, but because of the inefficiency introduced by the wage differential.

Production Externalities

We are familiar with the phenomenon of production externalities from our discussion in Sections 9.5 and 9.6. Recall that externalities (economies and diseconomies) are divided into pecuniary and technological. Presently, we are concerned with the technological species only, because the pecuniary externalities do not really interfere with Pareto optimality. In the presence of technological externalities in production, perfect competition does not lead to Pareto optimality. Technological external economies or diseconomies definitely violate the third Pareto-optimality condition, that is, equation (16.5), and possibly the second as well, that is, equation (16.4). For simplicity, we illustrate below how technological production externalities interfere with Pareto-optimality condition (16.5) only.

In the first instance, technological production externalities create a wedge between *private* and *social* costs. For instance, consider an industry that pollutes the air with smoke—the most common case of a technological external diseconomy. As this industry expands its operations, it imposes a cost on society in general in the form of, say, an increased incidence of upper-respiratory ailments, heart attacks, lung cancer, and so on. Surely, society must withdraw resources from other productive areas in order to clean the environment. Yet the polluting industry does not pay for the damage it does. Thus the industry's private cost is definitely lower than society's cost. For this reason the polluting industry will produce more output than it should, because part of its cost is external to it—it is borne by others. The polluting industry maximizes profit by producing that output where price equals the *private* marginal cost—not the social marginal cost.

The marginal rate of transformation gives the ratio of *social* marginal costs— *not* the ratio of private marginal costs. In the presence of technological externalities, the marginal rate of transformation is *not* equal to the ratio of private marginal costs because of the divergence that exists between private and social costs. The result is a divergence between the marginal rate of transformation and the marginal rate of substitution in consumption.

For example, suppose that the production of clothing generates a technological external diseconomy. Thus the social marginal cost of clothing (SMC_C) exceeds its private marginal cost (PMC_C); that is,

$$SMC_C > PMC_C = P_C \tag{16.23}$$

However, the social marginal cost of food (SMC_F) equals the private marginal cost of food (PMC_F); that is,

$$SMC_F = PMC_F = P_F \tag{16.24}$$

Dividing equation (16.24) by (16.23), we finally obtain

$$MRT_{FC} = \frac{SMC_F}{SMC_C} < \frac{PMC_F}{PMC_C} = \frac{P_F}{P_C} = MRS_{FC} \qquad (16.25)$$

Accordingly, the existence of an external diseconomy in the production of clothing creates a divergence between MRT_{FC} and MRS_{FC}; that is, it violates the third Pareto optimality condition.

A similar analysis holds for external economies. We leave the details as an exercise for the interested reader.

Consumption Externalities

Externalities can also occur in consumption. This happens when a consumer's utility depends not only on the commodities that he or she consumes, but also on the consumption levels of other people. For instance, Adam's desire to "keep up with the Joneses" may have a detrimental effect on Adam's welfare. For instance, if Beth Jones purchases a new Cadillac, Adam may feel he is made worse off. To just maintain his old level of utility, Adam may have to increase his own consumption substantially after Beth's purchase. Because Beth does not pay anything for the welfare loss she inflicts on Adam, Beth's automobile consumption will be excessive (nonoptimal). Pareto optimality would be restored if Beth had to pay Adam a subsidy that was commensurate with Adam's welfare loss.

Alternatively, if Adam derives pleasure from Beth's consumption of, say, housing, the amount of housing consumed by Beth would be suboptimal. Pareto optimality would prevail if Adam paid to Beth a subsidy that was commensurate with the pleasure he got from Beth's housing. We therefore conclude that consumption externalities interfere at least with the condition for Pareto optimality in exchange. Condition (16.3) is no longer valid.

Public Goods

Public goods such as national defense, law and order, flood control, pest control, fireworks displays, and radio and television signals have in common an important property: once produced, they provide benefits to all citizens. No one's utility is reduced because others benefit from public goods. Furthermore, it is not possible to exclude any particular citizen from the benefits of public goods: Your national defense is my national defense, your news bulletin is my news bulletin, your clean air is also mine. For this reason, each person has an incentive not to produce a public good but to wait for others to do so. This is called the *free-rider problem*. Obviously, the free-rider incentive leads to suboptimal production and consumption of public goods. To remedy this situation, governments intervene; through compulsory taxation, they finance the production of public goods.

16.6 The Theory of the Second Best

The preceding section provided a brief survey of market imperfections which prevented the economic system from generating a Pareto-optimal allocation of resources. It is readily admitted that such imperfections (or impediments to Pareto optimality) are always present in any real-world economy. We also hinted to the possibility that such impediments could be neutralized by means of appropriate taxes and subsidies so that full Pareto optimality could be restored. But suppose that some of these impediments cannot be removed. Is it advisable to proceed on a piecemeal basis to correct as many inefficiencies as possible? The answer to this question is provided by the *theory of the second best*, which deals with the study of suboptimal situations, that is, situations in which not all Pareto-optimality conditions are satisfied.[11]

What is the theory of the second best? Its main theorem is simple. Consider an economy that is prevented from fulfilling at least one Pareto optimality condition. Then the other Paretian conditions, although still attainable, are in general no longer desirable. That is, when one Paretian condition cannot be fulfilled and thus maximum social welfare cannot be reached, maximization of *attainable* welfare requires in general the *violation* of the other Paretian conditions.

From the general theorem of second best follows a very important corollary. Consider an economy in a suboptimal situation in which several Paretian conditions are violated (because, say, of the presence of market imperfections). Suppose further that one or more, but not all of the violated conditions were to be fulfilled, as explained in the preceding section. Would social welfare increase? One might be tempted to answer "yes," because such a change would seem to bring the economy closer to Pareto optimality—more optimality conditions would be satisfied. Yet the theory of the second best teaches us that such a conclusion is wrong. The precise effect on social welfare depends on circumstances. When two suboptimal situations are compared, there are no general rules in judging which is better than the other.

Meade (1955, p. 7) offers an illuminating analogy. He imagines a person who wishes to climb to the highest point on a range of hills. Not every step upward helps the person reach the highest summit though. Walking uphill, the person can reach only the summit of the particular hill he happens to be on—not the summit of the highest hill. The person may have to walk downhill first, before she can climb the hill with the highest summit.

SUMMARY

1. Positive economics examines the problem of how the economic system actually works. Welfare economics deals with the question of how the economic system ought to function and studies the desirability of policy actions.

2. According to the individualistic ethic only the preferences of the people making up the society are to count. This idea finds expression in the Bergson–Samuelson social welfare function.

3. The classical welfare function ($W = U_1 + U_2 + \cdots + U_n$) is rejected because (a) utility is not cardinally measurable, (b) interpersonal comparisons of utility are unscientific, and (c) the same weights are indiscriminately assigned to all people.

4. *Paretian ethic:* When one person becomes better off (worse off) without anyone else be-

coming worse off (better off), social welfare increases (decreases).

5. All social welfare functions that are consistent with the Paretian ethic belong to the Paretian class.

6. A state of the economy is said to be Pareto optimal if it is not possible, through any feasible reorganization of production and distribution, to make at least one person better off without making any other(s) worse off.

7. The equality of marginal rates of substitution among people, as illustrated by points on the contract curve, is the primary condition for Pareto optimality in exchange.

8. The equality of the marginal rates of technical substitution between industries is the primary condition for Pareto optimality in production.

---

[11]The beginnings of the theory of the second best can be traced back to Viner (1950). However, the theory was fully developed a few years later by Meade (1955). Shortly after Meade's contribution, Lipsey and Lancaster (1956) restated and generalized the theory.

9. The equality between the marginal rate of transformation and the marginal rate of substitution in consumption is the primary condition for Pareto optimality in production cum exchange.

10. When Pareto optimality exists simultaneously in exchange, production, and production cum exchange, the allocation of resources is Pareto optimal.

11. The Paretian criterion does not lead to a single Pareto optimal allocation, but many, as illustrated by the utility-possibility frontier. Although not every Pareto-optimal allocation is better than every nonoptimal allocation, there always exist Pareto-optimal allocations that are better than any given nonoptimal allocation.

12. Each point on the utility frontier corresponds to a Pareto-optimal state, and each optimal state corresponds to a point on the utility frontier.

13. Assuming that a completely specified social welfare function exists, social welfare is maximized at the bliss point (the tangency of the utility frontier to the highest possible welfare contour line).

14. A movement along the utility frontier can be accomplished by means of lump-sum transfers.

15. Every perfectly competitive equilibrium is Pareto optimal, and every Pareto-optimal state is associated with a set of perfectly competitive prices.

16. Imperfect competition, externalities, and public goods violate Pareto optimality.

17. The existence of monopoly in one industry creates a divergence between the marginal rate of transformation and the marginal rate of substitution in consumption.

18. Wage differentials violate Pareto optimality in production and production cum exchange.

19. Technological external economies or diseconomies in production violate Pareto optimality in production cum exchange and possibly, production as well.

20. Consumption externalities violate Pareto optimality in exchange.

21. Public goods provide benefits to all citizens. Because exclusion is impossible, there arises the free-rider problem, which leads to suboptimal production and consumption of public goods. For this reason the production of public goods is undertaken by governments.

22. *General theorem of the second best:* Even when a single Pareto-optimality condition cannot be fulfilled, the other Paretian conditions, although still attainable, are no longer desirable.

QUESTIONS

1. Writing in 1776, Adam Smith stated that the individual businessman, acting in his own interest, is "led by an invisible hand to promote an end which was no part of his intention."

    (a) What is the "end" that Adam Smith spoke of?

    (b) What is the "invisible hand?"

    (c) Does the invisible hand lead to maximum economic welfare?

2. Explain how Pareto optimality is violated by each of the following:

    (a) Minimum wages

    (b) Oligopoly

    (c) Price supports in agriculture

    (d) Rent controls

    (e) Monopsony

3. Explain why in your opinion each of the following statements is true or false:

    (a) Perfect competition leads to maximum social welfare.

    (b) Economic efficiency is not different from technical efficiency.

    (c) The invisible hand always leads to Pareto optimality.

    (d) The Bergson–Samuelson social welfare function is only ordinally determinable.

    (e) The economy can be on the utility frontier when consumers are free to carry out all the voluntary exchanges they wish.

    (f) Society can move from one point of the utility frontier to another by redistributing wealth by means of inheritance taxes.

4. According to Martin Feldstein (*The Wall Street Journal,* July 8, 1982) the prices of most products in China "are essentially a reflection of the prices that prevailed in 1949 when the

Communist Party came to power. Relative prices were not altered to reflect the radically changing wage rates and labor costs. . . . cost-reducing technological advances haven't resulted in lower product prices."

(a) Explain why in your opinion the Chinese economy may be inefficient.

(b) What Pareto-optimality conditions may be violated?

5. According to *The Wall Street Journal* (April 13, 1983, p. 29), scholarships at most colleges and universities long have gone to the needy or the athletically gifted, but now many schools are awarding scholarships for scholarship.

(a) How will the change in the method of awarding scholarships affect social welfare in the United States?

(b) Would your answer be different if you knew that gifted students are likely to make greater contributions than the less gifted but needy students?

6. You are given the following data:

$$
\begin{aligned}
\text{price of food} &= \$10 \\
\text{price of clothing} &= \$5 \\
\text{marginal cost of food} &= \$8 \\
\text{marginal cost of clothing} &= \$4 \\
\text{wage rate} &= \$20
\end{aligned}
$$

The rent for land services is not known, but it is the same in the food and clothing industries.

(a) Is there Pareto optimality in exchange?

(b) Is there Pareto optimality in production?

(c) Is there Pareto optimality in production cum exchange?

7. Food and clothing are produced by labor alone. Constant returns to scale prevail in both industries. There are no externalities. However, because of a strong labor union in the clothing industry, the wage rate is $20 in the clothing industry and only $5 in the food industry.

(a) What Pareto-optimality conditions are violated?

(b) Explain how the welfare of the workers in the food industry can be improved without reducing the welfare of the workers in the clothing industry. Graph your results.

8. An economy is divided into two sectors: agriculture and industry. Each sector uses labor and land and produces output under constant returns to scale. Perfect competition prevails everywhere. The production of industrial output, though, generates environmental pollution that makes consumers worse off. The marginal cost in agriculture is $10. In industry the *private* marginal cost is $20, but the *social* marginal cost is estimated to be $40.

(a) What Pareto-optimality condition is violated? Be specific. Illustrate your answer both numerically and graphically.

(b) Can you suggest a policy measure that may restore Pareto optimality?

(c) Assuming that you are successful in restoring Pareto optimality, can you be sure that social welfare has improved?

9. In a certain community fishing in a public lake is free. However, crowding reduces each fisherman's technical efficiency and thus raises the *private* marginal cost of fish according to the formula

$$MC = 10 + 0.05Q$$

where MC is the private marginal cost of fish and Q is the industry output (bushels of fish). The demand for fish is given by the function

$$p = 40 - 0.10Q$$

where p is the price of fish.

(a) Determine the equilibrium price and output of fish.

(b) Determine the *social* marginal cost of fish at the equilibrium you reached in (a).

(c) Determine a schedule showing the social marginal cost of fish at alternative levels of industry output.

(d) Determine the optimal output of fish.

(e) What policy measure do you recommend so that output is restored to its optimal level?

*10. An economy is endowed with 200 units of food and 200 units of clothing; it consists of two people, Adam and Beth, whose tastes are identical and in fact are given by the common utility function

$$U = FC$$

where F is the quantity of food and C the quantity of clothing.

(a) Derive the utility-possibility frontier.

(b) How should food and clothing be allocated between Adam and Beth to maximize the *sum* of their utilities?

(c) Alternatively, suppose that social welfare is given by the function

$$W = U_a U_b$$

where the subscripts a and b indicate Adam and Beth, respectively. Determine the allocation of food and clothing that maximizes social welfare.

FURTHER READING

Arrow, K. J. (1951). *Social Choice and Individual Values*. John Wiley & Sons, Inc., New York.

Bator, F. M. (1957). "The Simple Analytics of Welfare Maximization," *American Economic Review*, Vol. 47 (March), pp. 22–59.

Bator, F. M. (1958). "The Anatomy of Market Failure." *The Quarterly Journal of Economics*, Vol. 72 (August), pp. 351–379.

Bergson, A. (1938). "A Reformulation of Certain Aspects of Welfare Economics," *The Quarterly Journal of Economics*, Vol. 52 (February), pp. 310–334.

Chacholiades, M. (1978). *International Trade Theory and Policy*. McGraw-Hill Book Company, New York. Chapters 5, 16, and 20.

Graaf, J. de V. (1957). *Theoretical Welfare Economics*. Cambridge University Press, London.

Henderson, J. M., and R. E. Quandt (1980). *Microeconomic Theory: A Mathematical Approach*, 3rd ed. McGraw-Hill Book Company, New York. Chapter 11.

Lipsey, R. G., and K. Lancaster (1956). "The General Theory of the Second Best," *Review of Economic Studies*, Vol. 24, pp. 11–32.

Little, I. M. D. (1957). *A Critique of Welfare Economics,* 2nd ed. Oxford University Press, London.

Meade, J. E. (1955). *The Theory of International Economic Policy*, Vol. 2: *Trade and Welfare*. Oxford University Press, London.

Pareto, V. (1909). *Manuel d'économie politique*. V. Girard and E. Brière, Paris.

Pigou, A. C. (1932). *The Economics of Welfare*, 4th ed. Macmillan & Company Ltd., London.

Quirk, J., and R. Saposnik (1968). *Introduction to General Equilibrium Theory and Welfare Economics*. McGraw-Hill Book Company, New York. Chapter 4.

Samuelson, P. A. (1947). *Foundations of Economic Analysis*. Harvard University Press, Cambridge, Mass. Chapter 8.

Viner, J. (1950). *The Customs Union Issue*. Carnegie Endowment for International Peace, New York.

CHAPTER
17

Capital and Interest

Chapters 12 and 13 dealt primarily with the determination of the wages of labor and the rent of land. This chapter focuses on capital theory; that is, the study of the nature of capital (and investment) and the return (or yield) of capital, which is traditionally taken to be the *interest rate per annum* (a pure number). The study of capital theory brings us closer to reality, because it takes account of the role of time. An understanding of capital theory is also fundamental to many important areas of economics, such as the theory of economic growth, macroeconomic theory, and the theory of distribution.

Capital theory is one of the most difficult and unsettled parts of economic theory. There are at least three reasons for this. First, capital theory involves some difficult pieces of technical analysis. Second, there is a multitude of different capital models, each of which provides some insights into the problem but never the whole truth. Finally, there are those (i.e., the Marxists and the socialists) who claim that capitalists do not have the "right" to receive interest on the capital they own. In Marx's view, labor produces the entire product and therefore should get it all. The latter view is actually a revolutionary slogan in a crusade to eliminate private property as a source of private income.

In this chapter we content ourselves with the construction of simple models. Our objective is to provide an understanding of the fundamental issues while avoiding most controversial questions. We begin in Section 17.1 with a brief introductory survey of various important concepts and issues of capital theory. We continue in Section 17.2 with the analysis of intertemporal equilibrium in a Robinson Crusoe economy. In Section 17.3 we digress to discuss the simple mathematics of compound interest. We return to the determination of the rate of interest in a market economy in Sections 17.4 and 17.5. The former section deals with the pure consumption model; the latter section extends the analysis to cover productive investment opportunities as well. We conclude in Section 17.6 with a discussion of two widely known investment criteria: the present-value criterion and the internal rate-of-return criterion. The discussion of investment criteria shows clearly how useful the concepts and tools of capital theory can be to the solution of practical problems.

17.1 **Fundamental Concepts of Capital Theory**

Capital theory involves several new concepts and peculiarities which must be made explicit at the outset.

Primary Factors Versus Produced Means of Production

Traditionally, productive inputs are divided into three categories: land, labor (including entrepreneurial or managerial skills), and capital. Land and labor are called *primary* factors of production because their supplies are determined outside the economic system. Thus land is naturally available in fixed supply. As Ricardo put it, rent is a return for the use of the "original and indestructible powers of the soil." Similarly, the supply of labor is determined mainly by social and biological factors rather than economic influences. Capital, on the other hand, is an "intermediate" or "produced" factor of production.

"Capital" consists of all types of capital goods, such as airplanes, buildings, computers, machinery, tools, and trucks. These capital goods are themselves the output of earlier production processes. Capital goods are desired not for themselves but as inputs for further production of goods and services. Thus capital goods are both outputs and inputs; that is, they are *produced means of production.*

Because capital goods are *produced* means of production, they come into existence as a result of deliberate decisions made by producers. Our problem is to find out how these decisions are made.

In addition to being "produced" means of production, capital goods are also intimately and peculiarly connected with time. For instance, the construction of a factory may take several years; and after its completion, the factory may offer productive services for a very long period of time.

The foregoing characteristics of capital goods distinguish "capital" from the other, primary factors of production. These characteristics are also responsible for most of the technical difficulties encountered in capital theory.

The Role of Time

In timeless static theory, discussed so far in this book, the time dimension of economic phenomena is ignored. All economic processes take place within a single time period. Inputs and outputs are synchronous. Firms purchase factor services and produce those outputs that maximize their current profits. Consumers spend their entire current incomes (which they derive from the sale of factor services to the firms) on baskets of consumption commodities that maximize their respective current utilities. In such a timeless static model, there is no need to worry about dating any economic variable. Each economic event reproduces itself every time period. Today is a replica of yesterday, and tomorrow will be a replica of today. This is manifestly untrue.

Capital theory takes account of the role of time. Future events are now allowed to exert their influence on current choices and decisions; conversely, present decisions have a profound effect on the future. Every quantity must now be dated. Cheese today is *not* the same thing as cheese tomorrow. We now recognize that inputs must precede outputs, although cash outlays may or may not precede cash inflows.

We also face up to the fact that firms generally purchase and own their capital goods—they do not just rent them from someone else. Producers must now decide whether or not to acquire new machinery, new equipment, new buildings, and new plants in order to augment their productive capacity in coming years. Producers can no longer afford to make decisions that maximize current profits only. They must try to achieve some intertemporal balance of profits between present and future. As shown in Sections 17.5 and 17.6, producers actually maximize their present *wealth*.

Similarly, consumers should not blindly spend their entire current incomes on current consumption as if there were no tomorrow. Based on their expectations about their future income streams and desires, consumers must seek to achieve a preferred intertemporal balance between present and future consumption.

Uncertainty and Expectations

The trouble with intertemporal choice is that the future is generally unknown. No one has ever devised a crystal ball to read the future. Future events are never known with certainty. Unforeseeable changes always occur. Our calculations of the future are by necessity guesses. In some cases our guesses are chancy, wild, and irrational. In other cases our guesses are based on meticulously collected data and scientific analysis. But irrespective of how they are formed, all guesses suffer from the same drawback: They are uncertain. As Keynes (1936, pp. 102–103) put it, "human decisions affecting the future . . . cannot depend on strict mathematical expectation, since the basis for making such calculations does not exist; and it is our innate urge to activity which makes the wheels go round, our rational selves choosing between the alternatives as best we are able, calculating where we can, but often falling back for our motive on whim or sentiment or chance."

Because of the inherent uncertainty in all our calculations of the future, capital theory is intrinsically difficult. In this chapter we simplify matters by disregarding the problem of uncertainty. Thus we shall assume perfect foresight; that is, we shall assume that all expectations are correct, or treat them *as if* they were correct.

The Productivity of Capital Goods

The ultimate goal of all economic activity is to produce consumption goods and services to satisfy human wants and needs. In principle, this can be accomplished in either one of two ways. The first alternative is a *direct process:* the primary factors, labor and land, are employed in the *direct* production of the desired consumption commodities. The second alternative is an *indirect* (or *roundabout*) *process:* labor and land are first used to produce capital goods, which are then combined with the primary factors for the production of consumption commodities. It is common knowledge that all societies (including primitive societies) prefer the roundabout method of production.

Every roundabout process involves an opportunity cost: Because primary factors are initially diverted from the production of consumption commodities to the production of capital goods, *society suffers a cut in its present consumption.* Consumers must *abstain* from current consumption in order that resources are freed to produce capital goods.

If roundabout processes involve a cost, why are they preferred to direct processes? Why are the primary factors of labor and land ever diverted from the production of consumption commodities to the production of capital goods? Because *roundabout processes* (also known as *capitalistic processes*) *are typically more productive than direct processes.* It is a technological fact that there exist roundabout processes that enable society to increase its future consumption by an amount that is much larger than the current sacrifice of present consumption. Today the per capita income of the industrialized nations of the world is several times higher than the per capita income of the less developed countries of Africa and Asia. This dramatic difference in per capita incomes is largely due to the more extensive use of capital goods, and thus the much higher degree of roundaboutness, in the industrial countries than in the less developed countries.

Time Preference or Impatience

If roundabout methods are so productive, why are nations reluctant to use them more extensively to raise their standards of living? Because their opportunity costs are presumably high.

Whether or not the production of a capital good is economically worthwhile depends on a comparison between its expected future benefits (increase in future consumption) and its present opportunity cost (decrease in present consumption). If the expected increase in future consumption exceeds the reduction in present consumption, the construction of the capital good may be worthwhile. The outcome depends on what economists call the "rate of time preference," or impatience. The latter shows how society rates the desirability of consuming more goods and services today rather than tomorrow—how strongly society prefers present to future satisfactions.

Typically, people dislike postponing consumption. Chocolate today is (allegedly) better than chocolate tomorrow, and people can be induced to wait for their chocolate only if they receive a premium (interest). For instance, I may agree to have my chocolate tomorrow rather than today only if I can have at least 20 percent more chocolate tomorrow than today. That 20 percent premium is my (marginal) rate of time preference.

When society's rate of time preference is very high, few roundabout processes are worthwhile and thus few capital goods come into existence. When the rate of time preference is very low, many roundabout processes become profitable and the degree of roundaboutness is considerable.

Abstinence and Interest

Some classical economists viewed interest (the return of capital) as the reward for "abstinence" (or as Marshall later called it, "waiting"), just as they considered wages as the reward for sweat and psychic disutility. But not everyone agreed. For example, Karl Marx ridiculed the idea that the capitalist suffered from deprivation. In the first place, *the capitalist could not consume his capital* in the physical form in which it was embodied. In addition, the capitalist seemed to draw his income from *current* production just like the worker. More important, the capitalist was generally believed to be able to indulge himself in the consumption of many goods and services that the ordinary worker could not afford.

We should not conclude from this that the classical insight was totally without merit. It made a valid point, namely, that the *creation* of capital necessarily involves abstinence or waiting. Thus it is not the income provided by the use of capital that involves the abstinence. It is rather the production of new capital goods (or the creation of capital) that requires the foresaking of current consumption.

Nevertheless, interest is not paid just for the unpleasant task of abstinence (or waiting) any more than wages are paid for the sweat and psychic disutility experienced by workers. The rate of interest is a relative price; and like any other price, it is determined by both supply and demand considerations. In particular, the rate of interest is determined by the relations of supply and demand for present and future consumption. As Irving Fisher (1867–1947) has taught us, the equilibrium rate of interest is determined by (1) people's *impatience* to consume now rather than in the future (i.e., by people's preferences for present versus future consumption, or the rate of time preference), and (2) *society's opportunity to invest* (i.e., the technical possibilities for turning "present consumption" into "future consumption" by diverting resources from the production of consumption commodities to the production of capital goods). Just as both blades of a scissors are doing the cutting, both factors, impatience and productivity, are needed to determine the equilibrium interest rate. The next section shows how this is done.

17.2 Intertemporal Equilibrium in a Robinson Crusoe Economy

Surprisingly, we can understand most of the fundamental issues of capital theory by studying the simple economy of Robinson Crusoe. Imagine that Crusoe is shipwrecked on a completely uninhabited island and that his only possible source of food is fish—his only consumption commodity. He has no capital equipment (such as nets and fishing rods) because, say, he was unable to salvage anything from the wreck.

At first, the castaway will undoubtedly begin catching fish by hand (direct process). Sooner or later, however, Crusoe will realize that a roundabout process may be more efficient. Rather than working at catching fish (the consumption commodity he really desires), he may digress for a while to produce something entirely different, say, a net (capital good). With the aid of the net, he may be able later to catch more fish per day than otherwise.

Of course, the production of the net requires time—time that could otherwise be spent catching fish. Is the opportunity cost of the net (the foregone fish during the production of the net) worth paying? That depends on two important factors: (1) the expected productivity of the net (i.e., its expected returns or *prospective yield*), and (2) Crusoe's rate of time preference.

Opportunity Cost, Prospective Yield, and Rate of Return

For utmost simplicity, we restrict our discussion of the Robinson Crusoe economy to just two periods (weeks). It may be helpful to think that the castaway will be rescued by the end of the second week.

Suppose that Crusoe can catch 70 fish per week by hand. Using a net, however, he expects to catch 84 fish per week. Crusoe estimates that the construction of the net will require a full day's work spread evenly over the first week, so that the net will be available during the second week only. At the end of the second week, the net will become useless (either because Crusoe will be rescued by then or because the net will fall to pieces). Crusoe's alternative consumption streams are illustrated in Figure 17.1.

Both axes measure fish consumption. But this week's consumption is measured along the horizontal axis and next week's consumption is measured along the vertical axis. Point E represents the option of not building the net. In this case, Robinson can consume 70 fish each week. Point B represents the option of building the net. In this case, this week's consumption falls to 60 fish, because during the first week Crusoe must spend the equivalent of one day's labor to construct the net instead of catching fish. Next week's consumption, however, rises to 84 fish because then Crusoe will be working with the net. Crusoe's problem is to choose between "commodity bundles" E and B.

In principle, Crusoe's problem is not different from the corresponding problem of choosing between two alternative bundles of commodities X and Y within a single period of time. However, in the present analysis of intertemporal choice use is made of a special terminology with which we must become familiar.

The *opportunity cost* of the net is 10 fish this week. If Crusoe constructs the net, he must be ready to accept the resultant cut in this week's consumption, from 70 fish to 60 fish. The *expected returns*—the *prospective yield* of the net—are 14 fish next week. With the assistance of the net, Crusoe expects to be able to increase next week's consumption from 70 fish to 84 fish (i.e., by 14 fish). Whether 14 extra fish next week are a sufficient compensation for the sacrifice of 10 fish this week (i.e., whether the construction of the net is worthwhile) is a matter that must be ultimately resolved on the basis of Crusoes tastes (time preference or impatience).

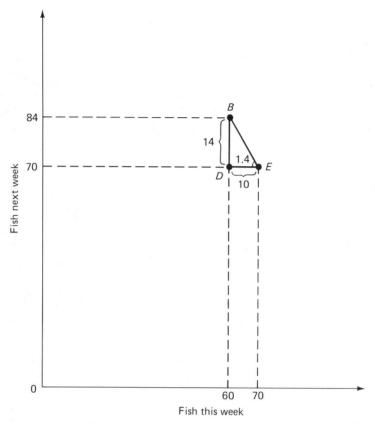

Figure 17.1 Crusoe's alternative consumption streams. This week's consumption is measured along the horizontal axis; next week's consumption, along the vertical axis. If Crusoe catches fish by hand, he can consume 70 fish each week, as shown by point *E*. If he builds a net, this week's consumption will be reduced to 60 fish (because during the first week Crusoe must use part of his time to construct the net instead of catching fish), but next week's consumption will rise to 84 fish, as shown by point *B*. The absolute slope of straight-line segment *EB* is equal to 1 + 0.40, or 1 plus the rate of return.

An important concept relating the opportunity cost of the net with its prospective yield is the *rate of return*. The latter corresponds to the ratio of the *net* return to the opportunity cost. For example, Crusoe sacrifices 10 fish this week (opportunity cost) in order to consume 14 fish next week (*gross return*). Not only will Crusoe recover his cost (10 fish) next week, but he will also get 4 extra fish, or 40 percent (4/10 = 0.40) more, as a *net return* (for the unpleasant task of abstinence). This *net* return expressed as a percentage of the opportunity cost of the capital good (i.e., 40 percent) is known as the *rate of return* (or as Fisher called it, "internal rate of return over cost"). Note that in Figure 17.1, the absolute slope of straight-line segment *EB* is equal to 1 + 0.40, or 1 plus the rate of return.

The Rate of Time Preference and Intertemporal Equilibrium

Figure 17.2 reproduces the information contained in Figure 17.1 together with Crusoe's indifference curves summarizing his preferences between fish this week (present consumption) and fish next week (future consumption). By construction, commodity bundle *B* lies on a higher indifference curve (I_1) than bundle *E*. Accordingly, Crusoe prefers *B* to *E*. This means that Crusoe will choose to build the net. Actually, Figure 17.2 teaches us more.

Suppose that the marginal rate of substitution of fish this week for fish next week at point *E* is equal to 1.10, as given by the (absolute) slope of *FG*, which is tangent to indifference curve I_0 at *E*. What is the meaning of this marginal rate of substitution? It is that Crusoe can be induced to sacrifice 1 fish this week if he is given at least 1.10 (or 10 percent more) fish next week. Thus starting at *E* (which signifies equal consumption in every period), Crusoe exhibits a *bias* toward this week's consumption: *He prefers fish this week than fish next week.* The degree of this bias, or Crusoe's *marginal rate of time preference,* is 10 percent.

Note that Crusoe's bias toward this week's consumption is usually measured along the 45° line, which is the locus of points representing equal consumption in every period. Because of the convexity of the indifference curves (law of diminishing marginal rate of substitution) there are points, such as *H*, where the bias runs toward the opposite direction, that is, next week's consumption. An extreme example may clarify this point. Suppose that Crusoe were able to salvage a few ice creams from the wreck (which is perhaps an impossibility but nevertheless illustrates well

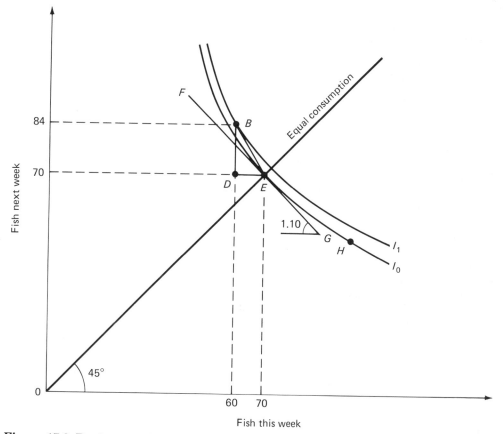

Fish this week

Figure 17.2 Preferences for alternative consumption plans. Points *E* and *B* correspond to the synonymous points of Figure 19.1. Crusoe prefers *B* to *E* because *B* lies on a higher indifference curve (I_1) than *E*. The marginal rate of substitution at *E*, as given by the absolute slope of *FG*, is equal to 1.10, which implies a 10 percent bias toward this week's consumption. That Crusoe chooses to build the net is also seen by the fact that the rate of return (40 percent) exceeds the rate of the time preference (10 percent). Crusoe's saving and investment are given by *DE*.

the point we want to make). Surely, Crusoe would not be able to preserve any ice creams for next week, because that would require a freezer. Would he not, then, be willing to sacrifice two, three, or more ice creams this week for one ice cream next week?

Return again to Figure 17.2. We concluded above that Crusoe will choose to build the net because point B lies on a higher indifference curve than point E. We can express essentially the same idea in terms of the rates of return and time preference. Thus we can say that Crusoe will find it worthwhile to build the net because its rate of return (40 percent) exceeds his rate of time preference. Thus EB is steeper than FG. If Crusoe's rate of time preference at E exceeded the rate of return, FG would be steeper than EB and B would lie on a lower indifference curve than E. In the latter case, Crusoe would not choose to make the net, as he would be better off catching fish by hand.

We therefore conclude that one way Crusoe can determine whether the net is worth making is to compare the rate of return with his rate of time preference. The net is worth making only when its rate of return exceeds Crusoe's rate of time preference. If the two rates are equal, the net is just worth making, and if the rate of return falls short of Crusoe's rate of time preference, the net is not worth making.

Saving, Investment, and the Role of Expectations

The act of abstaining from current consumption is called *saving,* and the act of employing the thereby freed resources to produce capital goods is called *investment.* (More precisely, savings is that part of current income that is not consumed; investment is the increase in the economy's capital stock, or the production of *new* capital goods.) In our Crusoe economy, saving and investment are undertaken by the same person and thus coincide. (In Figure 17.2 both saving and investment are given by horizontal distance DE, which is equal to 10 fish this week.) The only reason Crusoe sacrifices part of this week's consumption (i.e., saves) is because he chooses to build a net (i.e., invest). In a modern society, saving and investment are done by different people and the market system often fails to synchronize their activities. However, this is a macroeconomic problem and we do not pursue it further here.

As Crusoe's investment decision reminds us, the rate of return is always a matter of conjecture. Typically, the opportunity cost of a capital good can be calculated fairly accurately, because it practically occurs in the present. Exceptions do exist, however, as evidenced by the huge cost overruns of nuclear power plants and other facilities with long gestation periods. In all cases, however, the returns anticipated from the capital good necessarily depend on the investor's *expectations* of what the future holds in store, and there is an important difference between what the investor expects to happen and what actually happens. The actual returns obtained from a capital good may be higher or lower than the expected returns. For instance, Crusoe may find out during the second week that with the aid of the net he is actually able to catch only 75 fish per week, not 84 fish as he originally thought. Yet what is relevant to his current choice is what Crusoe expects to happen, not what actually will happen. In the first week, Crusoe makes his decision to produce the net on the basis of his expectation of 84, not 75, fish next week. Surely, if Crusoe knew that he would not even recover the opportunity cost of the net, he would not build it.

Multiple Opportunities to Invest

Finally, we wish to generalize the preceding results by considering the problem of multiple investment opportunities. Even on his uninhabited island, Crusoe may be able to choose among many roundabout methods of production—various types of nets and perhaps other types of capital equipment such as boats. Which round-about method will he choose?

Crusoe's first step is to construct his production-possibilities frontier, giving him the menu of choices between present and future consumption. This is done in Figure 17.3. As before, each conceivable roundabout method of production is represented by a point (commodity bundle), as illustrated by B_1, B_2, B_3, B_4, and V. The production-possibilities frontier coincides with the outer envelope of all these points, as shown by curve VER.

Note that not all roundabout methods are efficient. For instance, the method indicated by point B_4 is inefficient because it is dominated by B_2 and B_3 in both weeks; that is, B_2 and B_3 represent more fish in every time period than B_4. We may imagine that B_4 corresponds to a fancy net that requires several days' labor to

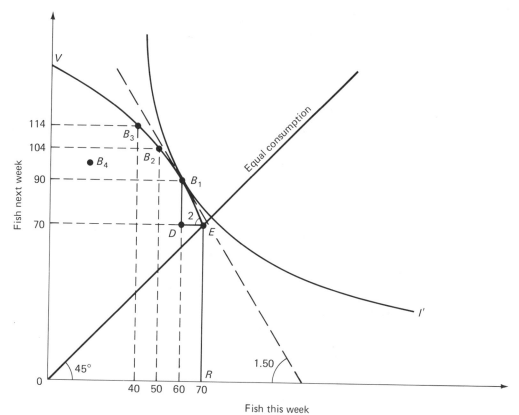

Fish this week

Figure 17.3 The production-possibilities frontier and intertemporal equilibrium. Now there are many roundabout processes. Each is represented by a point, as illustrated by B_1, B_2, B_3, B_4, and V. The outer envelope VER of all these points is the production-possibilities frontier. Only points on the frontier are efficient. B_4 is inefficient because it is dominated by B_2 and B_3 in *both* periods. Starting at E and moving toward V, successive equal sacrifices of 10 fish this week result in diminishing amounts of extra fish next week: 20 extra fish at B_1, 14 more at B_2, and 10 additional fish at B_3. Thus production by roundabout processes is subject to diminishing returns. General equilibrium occurs at B_1, where VER is tangent to I'. At B_1 the marginal rate of transformation (given by the absolute slope of VER) equals the marginal rate of substitution (given by the absolute slope of I'). The latter condition reduces to $\rho = \delta$, where ρ is the marginal rate of return, and δ the marginal rate of time preference.

produce but does not produce more fish next week than some other less laboriously built net, such as the one indicated by B_2.

Only those techniques associated with points, such as B_1, B_2, and B_3, lying on the boundary of the production-possibilities frontier are efficient. None of these efficient techniques dominates any other efficient technique in both periods. For instance, B_1 dominates B_2 in the present period, but B_2 dominates B_1 in the future period.

Note also that production by means of roundabout processes is subject to diminishing returns. Thus starting at E and moving toward V, it is apparent that for successive equal sacrifices of fish this week Crusoe expects to consume decreasing amounts of *extra* fish next week. For example, as this week's consumption is successively reduced by 10 fish, next week's consumption increases first by 20 fish (point B_1), then by 14 fish (point B_2), and finally by 10 fish (point B_3). The numbers 20, 14, and 10 form a declining sequence. This phenomenon is embedded in the concavity of the production-possibilities frontier.

The absolute *slope* of the production-possibilities frontier at any point, such as B_1, is the *marginal rate of transformation of present for future consumption* (MRT_{01}). It shows, *on the margin*, how many extra fish will be made available next week for each fish sacrificed this week. Actually, next week's *gross* return (MRT_{01}) can be split into two parts: (1) the initial opportunity cost (one fish this week) plus (2) the *net* return per fish sacrificed (or the *marginal rate of return* ρ). That is,

$$MRT_{01} = 1 + \rho \tag{17.1}$$

Note that the subscripts 0 and 1 represent the present time period (this week) and the future time period (next week), respectively. This practice will be followed from now on.

As we move on production-possibilities frontier VER from E to V, Crusoe is required to make increasing sacrifices of fish this week. We express this phenomenon by saying that Crusoe's economy experiences *capital deepening*, or becomes progressively *more capitalistic*. In general, capital deepening involves more "capital" per person. This may be illustrated by the case of a woodcutter who switches from an ax to a power chain saw. Presumably, it takes longer to produce a chain saw than an ax, and thus woodcutting becomes more roundabout or capitalistic.[1]

As in Chapter 14, general equilibrium occurs at the point of tangency between Crusoe's production-possibilities frontier and the highest possible indifference curve, as shown by B_1. This means that during the first week Crusoe must digress to produce the capital good associated with B_1. Because of this digression, he will suffer a cut of 10 fish in this week's consumption. (Crusoe's saving and investment are given by horizontal distance DE, as in Figure 17.2.) For this sacrifice he expects to increase next week's consumption by 20 fish.

As mentioned earlier, the absolute slope of an indifference curve at some point, such as the slope of I' at B_1, is the marginal rate of substitution of present consumption for future consumption (MRS_{01}). It shows, on the margin, the (minimum) number of extra fish that must be given to Crusoe next week to induce him to give up one fish this week. But MRS_{01} can be decomposed into 1 (the repayment of the fish sacrificed) plus a *net* reward, the latter being Crusoe's marginal rate of time preference δ. Thus

---

[1]Capital deepening must be distinguished from *capital widening*. When the output of an industry expands through an increase in the number of firms with each new firm duplicating the activities of the original firms, as explained in Section 9.4, there occurs capital widening because the capital/labor ratio remains unchanged. For instance, we can widen the use of capital in the woodcutting process by employing 50 men equipped with axes, instead of 40 men with axes. Each man uses one ax both before and after. Capital deepening would occur if, say, we equipped the original 40 men with power saws instead of axes.

$$MRS_{01} = 1 + \delta \qquad (17.2)$$

The primary condition for intertemporal equilibrium, as implied by the tangency at B_1, takes the form $MRT_{01} = MRS_{01}$; or substituting from equations (17.1) and (17.2) and simplifying,

$$\rho = \delta \qquad (17.3)$$

That is, *Crusoe's optimal intertemporal consumption stream occurs at the point where the marginal rate of return ρ equals the marginal rate of time preference.*

How does a system of prices and markets lead to the solution above? This is an important question. The answer is given in Section 17.5.

17.3 The Simple Mathematics of Compound Interest: Digression

Before we continue with the development of capital theory, we pause to examine the arithmetic of compound interest. This is necessary because capital theory involves streams of expenditures, revenues, and incomes through time, and a dollar today is worth more than the promise of a dollar payable tomorrow.

Future Value

Suppose that $100 are invested at compound interest at the rate of 10 percent per annum. If the interest is added yearly, then at the end of the first year the accumulated amount of dollars will be

$$\$100 + \$100 \times 0.10 = \$100(1 + 0.10) = \$110$$

At the end of two years the amount will accumulate to

$$\$110 + \$110 \times 0.10 = \$110(1 + 0.10) = \$100(1 + 0.10)^2$$

Similarly, at the end of three years, the amount will be $\$100(1 + 0.10)^3$; and so on.

In general, if V_0 is invested at compound interest at the rate of $100i$ percent per annum compounded annually, after n years the accumulated amount will be V_n where

$$V_n = V_0(1 + i)^n \qquad (17.4)$$

Note the influence of the interest rate i on the future value V_n. When i rises, V_n increases. Indeed, when n is large, the increase in V_n is considerable.

As an illustration, assume that $V_0 = \$500$, $i = 0.08$ (or 8 percent), and $n = 15$. Then

$$V_{15} = \$500(1.08)^{15} = \$500 \times 3.1722 = \$1586.08$$

If the interest rate were a little higher, say, $i = 0.10$, the accumulated value would be much greater. Thus

$$V_{15} = \$500(1.10)^{15} = \$500 \times 4.1774 = \$2088.70$$

which is much larger than $1586.08.

Discounting and Present Value

We now reverse the above problem. Suppose that V_1 dollars are available one year from today. What sum of money V_0 must be invested now at compound interest at the rate of $100i$ percent per annum so as to accumulate to V_1 dollars at the end of one year? This sum V_0 is called the *present value* (or *present discounted value*) of V_1. Obviously, V_0 must satisfy the equation

$$V_0(1 + i) = V_1$$

from which we obtain

$$V_0 = \frac{1}{1 + i} V_1 = DV_1$$

where the symbol D, called the *discount factor,* stands for the fraction $1/(1 + i)$.

Similarly, the present value (V_0) of V_2 dollars receivable two years from today must satisfy the equation

$$V_0(1 + i)^2 = V_2$$

from which we get

$$V_0 = \left(\frac{1}{1 + i}\right)^2 = D^2 V_2$$

In general, the present value (V_0) of, say, V_n dollars receivable n years from today must satisfy equation (17.4). Therefore,

$$V_0 = \left(\frac{1}{1 + i}\right)^n V_n = D^n V_n \tag{17.5}$$

When the interest rate i rises, the present value V_0 decreases because V_n is discounted more heavily.

As an illustration, assume that the rate of interest is 6 percent per annum. The present value of \$1000 receivable eight years from today is equal to

$$V_0 = \$1000 \left(\frac{1}{0.06}\right)^8 = \$1000 \times 0.62741 = \$627.41$$

If the interest rate were a little higher, say, 8 percent per annum, the present value would be

$$V_0 = \$1000 \left(\frac{1}{1.08}\right)^8 = \$1000 \times 0.54027 = \$540.27$$

which is much less than \$627.41.

The implication of present value is simple. If an entrepreneur has a claim of $\$V_n$ payable in n years from today, he can sell his claim to a bank (or some other person), not for the full amount of $\$V_n$, but for the present value of $\$V_n$ calculated at the prevailing market rate of interest.

Further Examples of Present Value

Suppose that a firm expects to receive an n-period stream of revenues: R_1 dollars in one year, R_2 dollars in two years, and so on. What is the present value of this stream of revenues? It is that sum of money V which could be invested today at the current rate of interest so as to precisely duplicate the stream of revenues $(R_1, R_2, \ldots, R_n)$ before principal plus accumulated interest are exactly exhausted. This sum of money V is nothing else but the sum of the present values of the elements R_j in the stream of revenues. That is,

$$V = DR_1 + D^2R_2 + \cdots + D^nR_n \qquad (17.6)$$

where, as before, $D \equiv 1/(1 + i)$. Note that after converting each element R_j of the income stream into a present value, their addition is justified. After the translation (or discounting) all sums pertain to exactly the same date, that is, today.

When all the expected receipts (or payments) are equal (i.e., when $R_1 = R_2 = \cdots = R_n = R$), the stream is called an *annuity* and its present value V_a becomes equal to

$$V_a = DR + D^2R + \cdots + D^nR = RD(1 + D + D^2 + \cdots + D^{n-1}) \quad (17.7)$$

The sum $(1 + D + D^2 + \cdots + D^{n-1})$, denoted by S_n, is a geometric series which simplifies to

$$S_n = \frac{1 - D^n}{1 - D} \qquad (17.8)$$

by means of elementary algebra.[2] Accordingly, the present value of the annuity, as given by equation (17.7), reduces to

$$V_a = RDS_n \qquad (17.9)$$

In the special case where the stream of constant payments is expected to continue forever, the annuity is called a *perpetuity*. An example of a perpetuity is the *British consol*. This is a special kind of a bond which is a promise to pay a fixed sum of money (R) to the bearer each year forever. What is the present value V_p of a perpetuity? Assuming that the first payment starts one year from today, we again start with formula (17.9) but allow n to approach infinity. Assuming that $D < 1$, the expression D^n approaches zero, so that equation (17.8) simplifies to

$$S_\infty = \frac{1}{1 - D} \qquad (17.10)$$

---

[2] The proof of equation (17.8) is simple. Assuming that $D \neq 1$, we have

$$
\begin{aligned}
S_n &= 1 + D + D^2 + \cdots + D^{n-1} \\
&= \frac{(1 + D + D^2 + \cdots + D^{n-1})(1 - D)}{1 - D} \\
&= \frac{(1 + D + D^2 + \cdots + D^{n-1}) - (D + D^2 + \cdots + D^n)}{1 - D} \\
&= \frac{1 - D^n}{1 - D}
\end{aligned}
$$

Accordingly, equation (17.9) becomes

$$V_p = \frac{RD}{1 - D} = \frac{R}{i} \tag{17.11}$$

where use was made of the fact that

$$\frac{D}{1 - D} = \frac{1/(1 + i)}{1 - [1/(1 + i)]} = \frac{1}{i} \tag{17.12}$$

As an example of a perpetuity, assume that $R = \$100$ and $i = 0.10$. Then $V_p = \$100/0.10 = \$1000$. This means that $1000 invested today at 10 percent per annum will pay $100 per year forever (starting one year from today).

Finally, there is the case of a *bond*. The latter is a promise to pay R dollars each year for n years plus the face value P of the bond at the end of the n-year period (i.e., upon maturity). The present value of the bond V_b is

$$V_b = (RD + RD^2 + \cdots + RD^n) + PD^n$$
$$= V_a + PD^n = RDS_n + PD^n \tag{17.13}$$

Surely, V_b (the present value of the bond) decreases when the interest rate rises, because the discount factor D becomes smaller.

As an illustration, suppose that a bond with face value $P = \$1000$ promises to pay $R = \$100$ at the end of each year for 20 years plus $1000 (its face value) at the end of the twentieth year. Assume that the interest rate is 5 percent per annum so that $D = 1/1.05 = 0.9524$ and $S_{20} = (1 - 0.9524^{20})/(1 - 0.9524) = 13.0853$. The present value of the bond is

$$V_b = \$100 \times 0.9524 \times 13.0853 + \$1000 \times 0.37689 = \$1623.13$$

If the interest rate were 10 percent, the present value of the bond would be $1000. Thus

$$V_b = \$100 \times \frac{1}{1.10} \times \frac{1 - (1/1.10)^{20}}{1 - (1/1.10)} + \$1000 \left(\frac{1}{1.10}\right)^{20}$$
$$= \$1000[1 - \left(\frac{1}{1.10}\right)^{20}] + \$1000 \left(\frac{1}{1.10}\right)^{20} = \$1000$$

Note that the increase in the interest rate has caused the present value of the bond to drop from $1623.13 to $1000.

17.4 The Rate of Interest in a Market Economy: The Pure Consumption Model

We now turn to the determination of the rate of interest in a market economy. We postulate the existence of a perfectly competitive capital market (or market for loans) in which every person can borrow or lend unlimited amounts at the prevailing rate of interest. The equilibrium rate of interest is determined by competitive supply and demand for loans. In this section and the following one, we analyze both each person's desire to borrow or lend and the determination of the equilibrium rate of interest in terms of a two-period model. As before, we assume that there is only one consumption commodity which we now call Z. In this section we discuss the *pure-consumption model* (also known as the pure borrowing-lending model) in which each person is initially endowed with a *fixed* income stream (so many units of Z this year and so many units of Z next year) and attempts to maximize her intertemporal utility by rearranging the time profile of her consumption by means of borrowing and lending. In Section 17.5 we introduce investment opportunities as well.

The Intertemporal Budget Constraint

For convenience we use the symbols y and c to represent the typical individual's income and consumption, respectively, in terms of units of commodity Z. Because income and consumption must be differentiated by date, we shall also use the subscripts 0 and 1 to represent this year and next year, respectively. For instance, y_1 stands for the units of Z which the typical individual expects to be her income next year. Also, we shall use Z_0 and Z_1 to distinguish between Z this year and Z next year, respectively. As before, the capital letters Z, Z_0, and Z_1 represent commodity *names*; lowercase letters, such as z, z_0, and z_1 represent quantities.

Consider now a person whose fixed income stream is $(\bar{y}_0, \bar{y}_1)$, as shown by point E in Figure 17.4. He could, of course, consume bundle E if he wanted to, but in general he would engage in market exchange in order to exploit the existing market opportunities. Market exchange in this context means either *borrowing* (exchanging some Z_1 for some Z_0, as shown by point B) or *lending* (exchanging some Z_0 for some Z_1, as shown by point L). The terms of such exchanges are determined by the rate of interest. The role of the interest rate can be seen in several alternative ways.

Perhaps the simplest way is to argue that given the interest rate i, one unit of

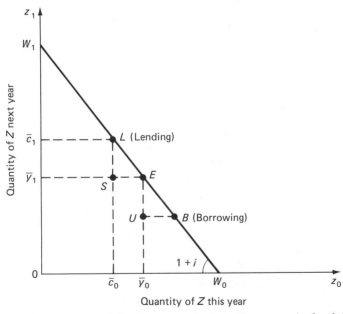

Figure 17.4 The intertemporal budget constraint. The person's fixed income stream $(\bar{y}_0, \bar{y}_1)$ is shown by point E. The intertemporal budget line W_0W_1 passes through E; its absolute slope is $1 + i$. Present wealth is shown by intercept W_0. If the person wishes to consume basket B, he must borrow UB this year and repay (principal plus interest) UE next year. If he wishes to consume basket L, he must lend SE this year and receive (principal plus interest) in exchange SL next year.

Z_0 exchanges for $(1 + i)$ units of Z_1. Accordingly, the person's intertemporal budget line must pass through E and have an absolute slope equal to $1 + i$, as shown by line W_0W_1. This conclusion must be clear from our discussion in Section 14.3.

Another way is to say that the present discounted value of any chosen consumption stream (c_0, c_1) must be equal to the present discounted value of the fixed income stream $(\bar{y}_0, \bar{y}_1)$. This proposition may be expressed algebraically as follows:

$$\bar{y}_0 + D\bar{y}_1 = c_0 + Dc_1 \qquad (17.14)$$

where $D = 1/(1 + i)$. Equation (17.14) is the person's intertemporal budget constraint, as shown by W_0W_1 in Figure 17.4. Its absolute slope is equal to $1/D = 1 + i$. It gives all feasible consumption plans.

The present value of the fixed income stream, $\bar{y}_0 + D\bar{y}_1$, is known as the person's present *wealth*. It shows the maximum quantity of Z_0 that the person could consume this year, as shown by point W_0. The future value of the person's wealth is equal to $(1 + i)\bar{y}_0 + \bar{y}_1$, as shown by point W_1.

It must be obvious from equation (17.14) that the intertemporal budget line W_0W_1 is perfectly determined by the person's *present wealth* (*not* income), which defines its intercept (W_0) with the horizontal axis, and the rate of interest that fixes its slope. In other words, the intertemporal budget line is a "wealth" rather than an income constraint.

Equation (17.14) can also be rearranged as follows:

$$\bar{y}_0 - c_0 = D(c_1 - \bar{y}_1) \qquad (17.14)'$$

Obviously, if $\bar{y}_0 - c_0 > 0$ (which means that the consumer is a *lender* this year), then $c_1 - \bar{y}_1 > 0$ (i.e., next year the individual's consumption c_1 will exceed his income $\bar{y}_1$). This situation is illustrated by point L, where the individual lends $SE = \bar{y}_0 - \bar{c}_0$ this year and receives in exchange $SL = \bar{c}_1 - \bar{y}_1$ next year. The loan proceeds $SL = \bar{c}_1 - \bar{y}_1$ include, of course, the principal (SE) plus interest. The present value of $SL = \bar{c}_1 - \bar{y}_1$, that is, $D(\bar{c}_1 - \bar{y}_1)$, equals the original loan $\bar{y}_0 - \bar{c}_0$. Point B illustrates the case of a *borrower*: The person borrows UB this year and repays UE next year. Again UB is the present value of UE. We therefore conclude that equation (17.14)' means

$$\text{lending} = D \cdot \text{repayment}$$

with the understanding that negative lending is borrowing.

Real Interest Versus Money Interest: Digression

Before proceeding with the intertemporal equilibrium of the individual consumer, we wish to draw a distinction between the *real* rate of interest and the *money* rate of interest. The interest rate we have been using all along in this chapter (save Section 17.3) is known as the real rate of interest. If I lend 1 unit of real consumption today, I will receive $1 + i$ units of real consumption next year. However, the interest rate that every businessperson is most familiar with is the money rate of interest μ. The latter is associated with the borrowing and lending of money. If I borrow \$1 today I shall have to pay \$$(1 + \mu)$ next year. The money rate of interest μ need not be equal to the real rate of interest i.

To discover the relationship between the money interest rate μ and the real interest rate i, we must introduce money prices. Let P_0 and P_1 be the (undiscounted) money prices of Z_0 and Z_1, respectively. (Alternatively, we may take P_0 and P_1 to correspond to the *price levels* of this year and next year, respectively.) Surely, P_0 is known because it is the current price of Z_0. However, P_1 is the price of Z_1 that is *expected* to prevail next year.[3] The price of Z_1 that will actually prevail next year is not known in advance. Thus while I may know what the current price of bread is, I can only guess what its price will be next year. If prices are fairly "stable," P_1 will be the same as P_0; but if prices are changing, P_1 will be higher or lower than P_0. For our purposes, we assume that

$$P_1 = (1 + \alpha)P_0 \tag{17.15}$$

where α is the *expected rate of inflation*.

If I invest P_0 dollars today, my investment will accumulate to $P_0(1 + \mu)$ dollars in one year. In real terms, my P_0 dollars today are equivalent to one unit of Z_0 (delivered now). What amount of Z_1 (delivered next year) do I expect to purchase next year with the accumulated sum of my investment? The quantity

$$\frac{P_0(1 + \mu)}{P_1} = \frac{1 + \mu}{1 + \alpha}$$

where use was made of equation (17.15). Thus we can say that 1 unit of Z_0 today grows to $(1 + \mu)/(1 + \alpha)$ units of Z_1 in one year. What is the real interest rate i? By definition,

$$1 + i = \frac{1 + \mu}{1 + \alpha}$$

or multiplying both sides by $1 + \alpha$ and simplifying,

$$(1 + \alpha)(1 + i) = 1 + \mu$$

or

$$1 + i + \alpha + \alpha i = 1 + \mu$$

or finally,

$$i = \mu - \alpha - \alpha i \tag{17.16}$$

Equation (17.16) shows that the real interest rate i equals the money interest rate μ less the rate of expected inflation α, less the product of α and i.

When the expected rate of inflation α is low (say, below 10 percent) and the real interest rate i is within its normal range (below 10 percent), the cross-product αi is negligible. For instance, when $\alpha = 0.08$ and $i = 0.05$, we have $\alpha i = 0.08 \times 0.05 = 0.004$. Accordingly, we can drop the cross product αi and thus approximate the real interest rate by the formula

$$i \cong \mu - \alpha \tag{17.17}$$

We therefore conclude that *the real interest rate i equals the money interest rate μ less the expected rate of inflation α*.

As Fisher (1930, p. 36) notes, a man who lends \$100 this year in order to obtain \$110 next year is really sacrificing 100 dollars' worth of goods today in the hope

---

[3]Prices P_0 and P_1 are often referred to as "undiscounted" prices in order to emphasize the fact that P_0 is the *current* price of Z_0 (i.e., the price which prevails this year) and P_1 is the *future* price of Z_1 (i.e., the price which a consumer expects to pay next year).

that he will obtain 110 dollars' worth of other goods next year. But because of inflation, one year from now the \$110 will not buy 10 percent more goods than the amount that the \$100 can buy today—they will buy less. In fact, if the rate of inflation is 10 percent, the real interest rate will be zero.

For the remainder of this chapter we assume that the rate of inflation α is zero, so that $i = \mu$.

Individual Intertemporal Equilibrium

Return now to the problem of determining the intertemporal equilibrium of the individual consumer. Figure 17.5 brings together the consumer's intertemporal budget constraint (as developed in Figure 17.4) and indifference map (illustrated by indifference curves I_1, I_2, and I_3). The consumer will obviously choose "consumption basket" L, indicated by the tangency between budget line W_0W_1 and the highest possible indifference curve I_2. Thus point L represents the optimal consumption stream $(\bar{c}_0, \bar{c}_1)$ of the consumer. Surely, L is preferable to the consumer's given income stream $(\bar{y}_0, \bar{y}_1)$ shown by point E, because the latter lies on lower indifference curve I_1. To transform his given income stream $(\bar{y}_0, \bar{y}_1)$ to his optimal consumption stream $(\bar{c}_0, \bar{c}_1)$, the consumer must lend $\bar{y}_0 - \bar{c}_0 = SE$ units of Z_0 this

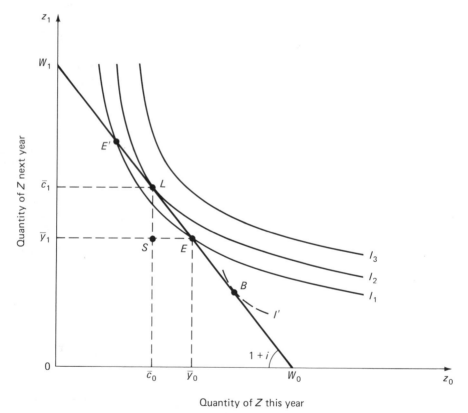

Figure 17.5 Individual intertemporal equilibrium. The consumer chooses consumption stream L, indicated by the tangency between budget line W_0W_1 and the highest possible indifference curve I_2. To transform his given income stream $(\bar{y}_0, \bar{y}_1)$ to his optimal consumption stream $(\bar{c}_0, \bar{c}_1)$ the consumer lends $\bar{y}_0 - \bar{c}_0 = SE$ units of Z_0 this year in exchange for $\bar{c}_1 - \bar{y}_1 = SL$ units of Z_1 next year. Note that the tangency at L also implies equality between the marginal rate of time preference and the interest rate.

year in exchange for $\bar{c}_1 - \bar{y}_1 = SL$ units of Z_1 (including both principal and interest) next year.

Note that the tangency at L implies that the marginal rate of substitution of Z_0 for Z_1, denoted by MRS_{01}, is equal to $1 + i$ (i.e., the absolute slope of W_0W_1). As we already know from Section 17.2, MRS_{01} equals (by definition) one plus the marginal rate of time preference δ; that is,

$$MRS_{01} = 1 + \delta \qquad\qquad (17.18)$$
$$(17.2)\,\text{repeated}$$

Thus the primary condition for individual intertemporal equilibrium reduces to

$$1 + \delta = 1 + i$$
$$(17.19)$$
or
$$\delta = i$$

In other words, the individual consumer adjusts his consumption stream until his marginal rate of time preference δ equals the market rate of interest i.

Whether an individual consumer is a borrower or lender this year depends on two factors: the time profile of his income stream (i.e., the precise location of point E in Figure 17.5) and his preferences (or indifference curves). For instance, if the income stream coincided with point E' (instead of E), the consumer would be a borrower this year, not a lender. Alternatively, if the income stream was given by E but the consumer preferences were different, as shown by dashed indifference curve I', which is tangent to W_0W_1 at B, the consumer would again be a borrower this year instead of being a lender.

Individual Supply and Demand Curves for Loans

Given the indifference map and the fixed income stream, the person's borrowing or lending position is a function of the market rate of interest confronting him. For some values of the interest rate, the person may be a lender; for other values, he may be a borrower. By allowing the rate of interest to assume all conceivable values, we can derive the person's demand curve or supply curve of loans. Graphically, we first rotate the budget line through the endowment point E to derive a price–consumption curve, and then we translate the latter into a demand curve for loans (or a supply curve of loans, as the case may be) in the manner of Sections 4.8 and 14.3. It is not necessary to review in detail the various steps of this procedure.

In the range of interest rates where the person is a net borrower, his demand curve for loans will typically slope downward because the income (or rather wealth) effect of an interest-rate change reinforces the substitution effect. On the contrary, in the range of interest rates where the person is a net lender, his supply curve of loans may be backward bending. In the case of a supplier of a normal commodity, the income and substitution effects work in opposite directions, and the income effect of higher interest rates may be so strong as to outweigh the substitution effect.

More specifically, a rise in the interest rate makes present consumption more expensive in terms of future consumption, and the person (whether a borrower or lender) substitutes future consumption for present consumption. This substitution effect causes the borrower's demand for loans to decrease and the lender's supply of loans to increase. But this is not all. As the interest rate rises a net borrower becomes poorer while a net lender becomes richer. Being poorer, a net borrower tends to consume less now (and in the future) and thus his present demand for loans tends to decrease. This income (or wealth) effect reinforces the substitution effect of a borrower. However, the lender, being richer, tends to consume more now (and

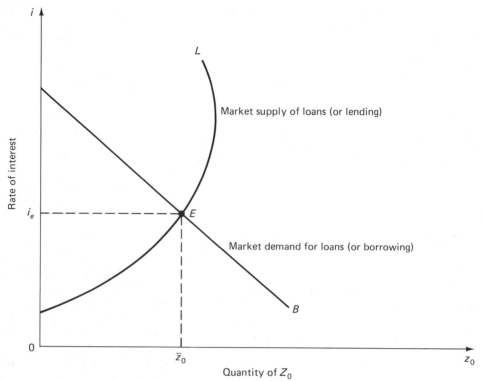

Figure 17.6 Loan market equilibrium. Intertemporal equilibrium occurs at the intersection E of the market supply and demand curves for loans. At the equilibrium interest rate i_e, the borrowers borrow the quantity $\bar{z}_0$ from the lenders. The marginal rates of time preference of all individuals are equal to i_e. At the equilibrium indicated by E, the net saving of the economy is zero: The dissaving done by the borrowers is exactly matched by the saving done by the lenders.

in the future) and has less funds available for lending. Thus the lender's income (or wealth) effect works against the substitution effect, and it is likely that at high interest rates the income effect may predominate, causing the lender's supply curve of loans to bend backward.

Loan Market Equilibrium

How can we determine the intertemporal equilibrium position of the economy? We could use the box-diagram technique of Chapter 14, but that is not necessary. It is simpler to determine the interest rate at which the market demand for loans equals the market supply of loans.[4] This is shown in Figure 17.6.

Along the vertical axis, we measure rates of interest; along the horizontal axis, we measure aggregate quantities of Z_0. The market demand curve for loans, labeled B (for borrowing), represents the horizontal summation of the individual demand curves for loans of all potential borrowers. Similarly, the market supply curve of loans, labeled L (for lending), represents the horizontal summation of the individual supply curves of loans of all potential lenders. Equilibrium occurs at the intersection

[4]Equilibrium in the market for loans (or capital market) means equilibrium in the first time period, of course. However, that also implies equilibrium in the second time period, because of Walras's law. On the latter law, see the Appendix to Chapter 14.

E of the market supply and demand curves. Thus at the equilibrium interest rate i_e the borrowers borrow the quantity $\bar{z}_0$ from the lenders; that is, the borrowers increase, and the lenders decrease, their consumption of Z_0 by the quantity $\bar{z}_0$.

In the equilibrium position portrayed in Figure 17.6, the marginal rates of time preference of all persons in the economy, borrowers and lenders alike, are equal to the equilibrium interest rate. This Pareto-optimality condition is brought about by borrowing and lending in a perfectly competitive loan market.

Note, finally, that in the present pure consumption model borrowing corresponds to *dissaving* (excess of current consumption over current income), and lending corresponds to *saving* (excess of current income over current consumption). Loan market equilibrium, then, means that the dissaving done by the borrowers is exactly matched by the saving done by the lenders. *The net saving of the economy is zero.* Thus the economy as a whole saves nothing and invests nothing; that is, the economy produces no new capital goods. The total available quantity of Z_0 is consumed this year, and the total available quantity of Z_1 is consumed next year. The economy merely reshuffles the available quantity of Z among consumers *within each period.* No amount of Z_0 is allowed to be stored and carried over to the next year. Under such circumstances we cannot even exclude the possibility of a *negative* interest rate. In the next section we drop this unrealistic assumption.

17.5 The Rate of Interest in a Market Economy: Investment Opportunities

In this section we bring together the opportunities provided by the capital market for borrowing and lending as well as the opportunities provided by the available technology for productive investment. As before, we begin with the behavior of the individual and later continue with the determination of the economy's general equilibrium.

The Behavior of the Individual

Curve *VER* in Figure 17.7 represents the individual's production-possibilities frontier, which replaces the fixed income stream (point E in Figure 17.5) of Section 17.4. The person is now confronted not by a single income stream, but by an infinite number of technologically feasible income streams. Each point on *VER* is a possible income stream. Figure 17.7 is very similar to Figure 17.3, but unlike Robinson Crusoe, who would produce and consume at F, our person can also take advantage of the opportunities provided by the existence of a perfectly competitive capital market.

Our person can maximize her intertemporal utility in two steps. First, she must choose an income stream (i.e., a production point on *VER*). This step involves an investment decision. For instance, to attain point F she must invest the equivalent of SE units of commodity Z_0. (Point E represents that income stream which would be available to the person in the absence of any investment.) Second, given the income stream (or investment decision), she must determine her intertemporal budget line and then choose a preferred consumption stream, as in Section 17.4. How is this done?

Which income stream should the person choose? *That income stream which maximizes the person's present wealth.* Given the opportunity for borrowing or lending, the person can always convert the income stream made available by her investment into any consumption stream of equal present value (as explained in Section 17.4). The latter proposition is implied by the person's intertemporal budget line: Every point lying on the latter line corresponds to a consumption stream whose present

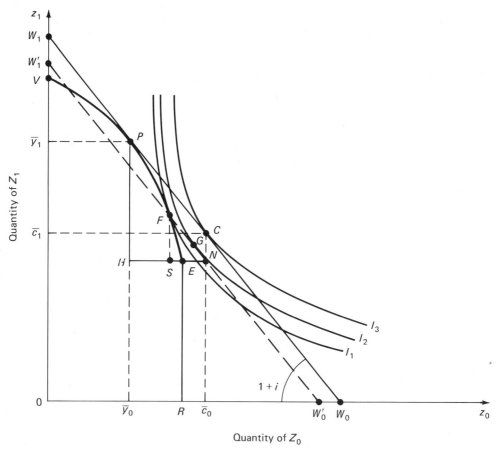

Figure 17.7 *Individual intertemporal equilibrium with opportunities for investment, borrowing and lending.* Production-possibilities frontier *VER* replaces the fixed income stream of Figure 17.5. Each point on *VER* is a feasible income stream. The optimal income stream (or investment plan) is indicated by the tangency *P* between *VER* and highest possible contour line W_0W_1; the latter is known as the consumption-possibilities frontier. The optimal volume of investment is shown by *HE*. The tangency at *P* implies that the marginal rate of return equals the interest rate. The optimal consumption stream is indicated by the tangency *C* between W_0W_1 and I_3, a tangency which implies that the marginal rate of time preference is equal to the interest rate. Distance *EN* shows *dissaving* and *HN* indicates *borrowing*.

value equals the person's present wealth. Now the intertemporal budget line depends on the person's present wealth (which determines its location) and the interest rate (which determines its slope). Choosing that income stream which maximizes present wealth puts the person on the highest possible intertemporal budget line and thus enables her to consume more in every period than otherwise. The choice of the optimal investment plan is illustrated in Figure 17.7.

Parallel straight lines $W_0'W_1'$ and W_0W_1 belong to a family of contour lines whose common absolute slope is equal to $1 + i$ (where i = market rate of interest). Each contour line is the locus of all those combinations of Z_0 and Z_1 that have the same present value (indicated by the intercept of the contour line with the horizontal axis). Each point on production-possibilities frontier *VER* puts the person on one of these contour lines. For instance, point *F* puts her on $W_0'W_1'$. The optimal investment plan corresponds to that point on *VER* which lies on the highest possible contour line. This is illustrated by point *P*, where *VER* is tangent to contour line

W_0W_1. Note that W_0W_1 is higher than $W_0'W_1'$ or any other feasible contour line. For this reason, contour line W_0W_1 becomes the person's *consumption-possibilities frontier*. To attain point P, or income stream $(\bar{y}_0, \bar{y}_1)$, the person must invest the amount shown by horizontal distance HE. The latter amount is her *optimal investment*.

Note that the tangency between production-possibilities frontier VER and consumption-possibilities frontier W_0W_1 at P implies that the marginal rate of transformation of Z_0 for Z_1, denoted by MRT_{01}, equals $1 + i$ (i.e., the absolute slope of W_0W_1). As we already know from Section 17.2,

$$MRT_{01} = 1 + \rho \tag{17.20}$$

where $\rho \equiv$ marginal rate of return. Thus the primary condition for maximizing present wealth (or the optimal investment-decision rule) reduces to

$$MRT_{01} = 1 + \rho = 1 + i$$

or

$$\rho = i \tag{17.21}$$

In other words, present wealth is maximized when the marginal rate of return ρ equals the rate of interest.[5]

Having chosen the optimal income stream (point P), the person must next choose an optimal consumption stream from the menu that is presented by consumption-possibilities frontier W_0W_1. This problem involves borrowing or lending and is not different from the problem of the pure consumption model of Section 17.4. Thus the person will choose consumption stream C, which corresponds to the tangency between W_0W_1 and indifference curve I_3. As before, the tangency at C implies that the marginal rate of time preference δ equals the interest rate i; that is,

$$\delta = i \tag{17.22}$$

Had the person chosen income stream F (as Robinson Crusoe would), her budget line would be given by $W_0'W_1'$ and she would consume at G, which lies on indifference curve I_2. The welfare improvement implied by the movement from F to G is in the nature of a pure *exchange gain*. But the person reaps further gains by exploiting the investment opportunities available to her. By shifting her income stream to P through investment, she finally consumes at C, which lies on I_3. The movement from G to C is in the nature of an *investment gain*.

We therefore conclude that the person chooses income stream P (where $\rho = i$), which involves a volume of *investment* equal to horizontal distance HE. She then chooses consumption stream C (where $\delta = i$), which in the present illustration happens to involve *dissaving* (excess of current consumption over current income without investment), as shown by horizontal distance EN. Finally, the person *borrows* the amount HN in order to finance her investment (HE) in capital goods and her dissaving (EN).

In general, the relationship among investment, saving, and borrowing takes the form

$$\text{investment} = \text{saving} + \text{borrowing} \tag{17.23}$$

---

[5]Equation (17.21) is valid for the two-period model we are studying in this section. It may not be valid for investment opportunities extending over more than two periods (see Section 17.6).

with the understanding that dissaving is negative saving. For a lender, the corresponding equation is

$$\text{investment} + \text{lending} = \text{saving} \qquad (17.24)$$

Loan Market Equilibrium

To determine the intertemporal equilibrium of the economy, we must again derive each person's demand curve or supply curve of loans, aggregate over all persons, and then identify the interest rate at which the market demand for loans equals the market supply of loans, as in Section 17.4 (Figure 17.6). The successive steps in this solution will not be recapitulated here. Two points, however, deserve some discussion.

First, in addition to the substitution and income (or wealth) effects discussed in Section 17.4, there arises now another important effect, which we may call the *investment effect* (or production effect). *As the interest rate rises, each person reduces his volume of investment.* For instance, an increase in the interest rate may induce the person of Figure 17.7 to choose income stream F instead of P, thus reducing her investment from HE to SE. Other things equal, the reduction in the volume of investment tends to reduce the quantity of loans demanded by each borrower and to increase the quantity of loans supplied by each lender. This must be obvious from equations (17.23) and (17.24). Accordingly, *the investment effect works in the same direction as the substitution effect;* and the case becomes stronger for a downward-sloping demand curve for loans and an upward-sloping supply curve of loans, although we still cannot exclude the possibility of a backward-bending supply curve of loans.

Second, summing equations (17.23) and (17.24) together over all persons, we obtain

$$I + \text{total lending} = S + \text{total borrowing} \qquad (17.25)$$

where $I \equiv$ total investment and $S \equiv$ total saving. Equation (17.25) is an identity and holds for all interest rates, not just the equilibrium interest rate. Because the loan-market equilibrium implies that total lending equals total borrowing, it follows from equation (17.25) that the economy's intertemporal equilibrium can also be cast in terms of saving and investment; that is,

$$I(i) = S(i) \qquad (17.26)$$

where the interest rate i is inserted to remind us that both I and S are functions of i.[6]

Perfect Competition and Intertemporal Equilibrium in the Robinson Crusoe Economy

By now it must be clear how the Robinson Crusoe economy of Section 17.2 attains intertemporal equilibrium through a system of prices and markets. As a producer-investor, Crusoe chooses that investment plan which implies a marginal rate of

---

[6]The equilibrium condition $I(i) = S(i)$ was attacked by Keynes (1936), who claimed that saving S is primarily a function of national income. This line of thought is a macroeconomic problem and is not pursued here.

return ρ equal to the market rate of interest i. As a consumer, he chooses that consumption stream which implies that the marginal rate of time preference δ equals the interest rate i. Accordingly, competitive equilibrium requires that the marginal rate of return be equal to the marginal rate of time preference, that is, $\rho = \delta$. Return to Figure 17.3 and confirm that B_1 is the only point along production-possibilities frontier *VER*, which satisfies the equilibrium condition $\rho = \delta$. (Note that for the entire economy, the optimal income stream cannot be different from the optimal consumption stream.)

17.6 Investment Criteria

Despite its inherent difficulties, both technical and ideological, capital theory is an important source of tools and ideas for the solution of practical problems. For instance, corporate executives are constantly concerned with investment decisions. Should I build a new plant? Should I purchase new equipment? Should I scrap my aging machinery? How much should I invest in research and development? In advertising? Such investment projects involve streams of costs and revenues, and the calculations for their desirability are based on the fundamental concepts of capital theory. We will not explore all aspects of the investment decision problem. Our discussion will center around two widely known investment criteria: the present-value criterion and the internal rate-of-return criterion.

The Present-Value Criterion

In the preceding section we explained that the problem of intertemporal maximization of utility can be decomposed into two parts: (1) maximization of wealth (present value of future income stream) subject to the available investment opportunities, and (2) maximization of utility subject to the wealth constraint imposed by the maximum wealth determined in part 1. The essential feature of this two-stage solution is that the determination of the optimal investment plan is entirely independent of the preferences of the individual. Thus the choice of wealth contour line $W_0 W_1$ in Figure 17.7 is independent of the location and shape of indifference curves I_1, I_2, and I_3. For instance, a shift of the indifference map will not affect the choice of production equilibrium at P.

We therefore conclude that given a perfectly competitive capital market, the optimal investment decision is predicated on the maximization of present wealth— an objective that can be pursued either by the person himself or by his agent, such as a corporate executive.

An investment project involves a stream of revenues and costs, that is, a sequence of dated receipts and payments. The present value V of this stream of revenues and costs is the project's present value and can be calculated using the formulas developed in Section 17.3.

The cardinal rule for all investment decisions is to *approve any project whose present discounted value is positive, and reject any project whose present value is negative*. This rule is an immediate consequence of the principle of wealth maximization. Thus the present value of any new project undertaken by a person represents a change in her wealth. If the project's present value is positive, her wealth increases, and if it is negative, her wealth decreases. Since more wealth is better than less, the person must accept the project only if its present value is positive.[7]

---

[7]The discussion in the text implicitly assumes that investment projects are independent on one another— adoption of one does not preclude adoption of another. This assumption is not always valid. For a brief discussion of nonindependent investment alternatives, see Johnson (1973, pp. 151–152).

The Internal Rate-of-Return Criterion

The *internal rate of return* of an investment project (also known as the *marginal efficiency of investment*) is that rate of interest (or return) which would render the present value of the project equal to zero. For instance, suppose that the initial cost of a machine whose working life is just one year is $100. The machine is used to produce a single product. The total output of the machine, expected to be worth $112, will be available at the end of the year, immediately before the machine falls to pieces. The internal rate of return of the machine is 12 percent: $-100 + 112/1.12 = 0$.

This example can be generalized easily. Consider an investment project whose initial cost is C. The project is expected to yield a series of annual returns over an n-year period: R_1 in one year, R_2 in two years, and so on. The internal rate of return ρ is the solution to the equation

$$DR_1 + D^2R_2 + \cdots + D^nR_n - C = 0 \qquad (17.27)$$

where $D = 1/(1 + \rho)$.

Note that equation (17.27) can also be cast in the equivalent form

$$C = DR_1 + D^2R_2 + \cdots + D^nR_n \qquad (17.27)'$$

This means that the internal rate of return can be alternatively defined as that rate of interest which renders the present value of the expected annual returns of the investment project $(DR_1 + D^2R_2 + \cdots + D^nR_n)$ equal to its initial cost C.

The internal rate-of-return criterion asserts that an investment project is profitable, and thus must be undertaken, as long as its internal rate of return ρ exceeds the market interest rate i. The alleged justification for this proposition lies in the casual observation that if an investor can borrow funds at, say, 10 percent per annum, while an investment project is expected to yield, say, 15 percent per annum, the project will be profitable; that is, its future revenues will be more than enough to repay the initial loan with interest, and thus its adoption will raise the investor's present wealth.

Unfortunately, the foregoing proposition is not generally true. To be sure, the proposition is true in two-period models, such as those discussed earlier in this chapter. However, in the presence of investment projects whose expected annual returns extend over more than two periods, the internal rate-of-return criterion does not always yield correct answers. The shortcomings of the rate-of-return criterion are explained below.

Internal Rate-of-Return Difficulties

The mathematical difficulties encountered by the internal rate-of-return criterion are best illustrated by means of concrete examples.

Example 1. Consider an investment project whose initial cost is $C = \$1000$. The project is expected to generate the following income stream in the next two years of its anticipated life: $R_1 = \$2400$ and $R_2 = -\$1430$. Thus in addition to its initial cost, the project generates a loss at the end of its life. This situation is not uncommon to extractive industries, where the landscape may have to be converted back to its natural state at the end of the operation. What is the internal rate of return of the project? Should the project be undertaken if the market rate of interest is alternatively 0, 5, or 20 percent per annum?

To determine the internal rate ρ, we must solve the following equation:

$$V \equiv \frac{2400}{1 + \rho} - \frac{1430}{(1 + \rho)^2} - 1000 = 0 \qquad (17.27a)$$

Multiplying both sides by $(1 + \rho)^2$ and simplifying, we have

$$\rho^2 - 0.4\rho + 0.03 = 0 \qquad (17.28)$$

As the reader can verify, equation (17.28) has *two* solutions: $\rho_1 = 0.10$ and $\rho_2 = 0.30$. Which value of ρ is the internal rate of return? The internal rate-of-return criterion does not provide any hints.

The indeterminacy of the internal rate due to the multiplicity of solutions is not the only problem.[8] Suppose that the market interest rate is 20 percent per annum. Should the investor undertake the project? On the basis of the internal rate-of-return criterion, the investor faces a dilemma. His decision seems to depend on the particular solution of equation (17.28) he chooses to be the internal rate. If he chooses $\rho_2 = 0.30$, the criterion would recommend adoption of the project, but if he chooses $\rho_1 = 0.10$, the project must be rejected. This is a rather confusing state of affairs. A project cannot be at the same time profitable and unprofitable.

One might get the feeling that the investor's difficulties would vanish if the market rate of interest happened to be below 10 percent, say, 5 percent. In this case, the internal rate-of-return criterion would recommend adoption of the project, because the market rate is less than both $\rho_1 = 0.10$ and $\rho_2 = 0.30$. Unfortunately, this recommendation is unwarranted. As it turn's out, the project's present value is *negative* for all interest rates less than 10 percent, and thus the project should be rejected (on the basis of the fundamental present value criterion). For instance, if the interest rate were equal to zero, the project's present value would be $V = 2400 - 1430 - 1000 = -30$.

Figure 17.8 graphs the project's present value V as a function of the interest rate i. Specifically, curve MN is the locus of points that satisfy the following equation:

$$V = \frac{2400}{1 + i} - \frac{1430}{(1 + i)^2} - 1000 \qquad (17.6a)$$

Note that the project's present value is positive only when the interest rate lies between 0.10 and 0.30. Thus when $0.10 < i < 0.30$ the project should be undertaken. Yet for this range of interest rates, the internal rate-of-return criterion does not give an unequivocal answer. Furthermore, when the interest rate drops below 10 percent, the internal rate-of-return criterion wrongly recommends adoption of a project whose present value is *negative*.

This conclusion may appear puzzling. When the interest rate is 20 percent (or 0.20), the project is profitable and must be adopted, but when the interest rate is 5 percent (or *even zero*), the project must be rejected. Is there anything wrong with our calculations? Not a thing. To get to the crux of the matter, it is necessary to calculate the project's stream of receipts and payments at the two alternative interest rates, 20 percent and 5 percent.

Suppose first that the interest rate is 20 percent. We borrow $1000 for the initial cost of the project. (When we invest our own funds, the market rate shows our opportunity cost—the interest we sacrifice by not investing our funds at the market rate.) At the end of the first year, we receive $R_1 = \$2400$, out of which we pay $200 interest on the loan ($1000 \times 0.20 = \$200$). Thus at the end of the first year, we end up with a net cash balance of $2200, which we invest at the market rate of interest. By the end of the second year, our cash balance accumulates to $2200 $\times$

[8]In general, equation (17.27) is an n-degree polynomial and could have as many as n distinct solutions.

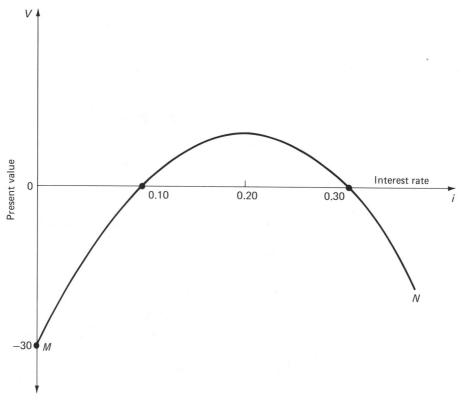

Figure 17.8 Present value as a function of the interest rate. Curve MN gives the present value V of a project as a function of the interest rate i. V is positive, and thus the project should be undertaken, only when $0.10 < i < 0.30$. Paradoxically, when the interest rate falls below 10 percent, the project becomes unprofitable.

1.20 = \$2640. At that time, we must pay R_2 = −\$1430, plus \$200 interest on the initial loan (for the second year), plus the principal of \$1000 (because the loan must now be repaid). Our profit at the end of the project is \$2640 − \$1430 − \$200 − \$1000 = \$10.

Turn now to the case where the interest rate is 5 percent. Again we initially borrow \$1000. At the end of the first year, we receive R_1 = \$2400 out of which we pay only \$50 interest (\$1000 × 0.05 = \$50); thus we are left with a cash balance of \$2350. Surely, we now have more cash at the end of the first year (\$2350 > \$2200), but *we must invest our cash balance at only 5 percent*, not 20 percent as before. By the end of the second year, our cash balance accumulates to only \$2350 × 1.05 = \$2467.50, which is not enough to cover the deficit R_2 = −\$1430, plus interest = \$50, plus principal = \$1000. The project ends up with a *loss* equal to \$2467.50 − \$1430 − \$50 − \$1000 = −\$12.50.

What is the main reason why the project is not profitable when the interest rate is equal to 5 percent? It is the fact that the project's net cash balance at the end of the first year is reinvested at the low market rate of interest (5 percent). Note that if it were feasible to reinvest the net cash balance at $i = \rho_1 = 0.10$, the project would be profitable. Thus by the end of the second year, the net cash balance would accumulate to \$2350 × 1.10 = \$2585, while the total disbursements would be equal to \$1430 + \$50 + \$1000 = \$2480. The positive profit in this last possibility is due to our borrowing at a low interest rate (5 percent) and lending at a high interest rate ($i = \rho_1 = 0.10$).

In general, when the market rate is equal to the internal rate, the present value of the project is zero. If the market rate is allowed to dip below the internal rate, the interest payments on the initial loan will be reduced, and if none of the project's revenues are simultaneously curtailed (which will be the case if the investor continues to earn the internal rate, not the lower market rate, on his excess receipts), the project will show a positive profit. The basic flaw of the internal rate-of-return criterion is its implicit assumption that a positive cash balance can indeed be reinvested at the internal rate, whereas the relevant rate is the market rate of interest. As it turns out, when the market rate is used, the internal rate-of-return criterion reduces to the present-value criterion.

Example 2. Consider now two mutually exclusive projects, A and B. Their respective income streams are as follows:

	C	R_1	R_2
Project A	$ 1,000	$ 2,000	$ −960
Project B	20,000	40,000	−19,800

What is the internal rate of return of each of these two projects? If the market rate of interest is 5 percent, which project should be undertaken?

To determine the internal rate of return of project A, we solve the following equation:

$$1000 = \frac{2000}{1 + \rho_a} - \frac{960}{(1 + \rho_a)^2} \qquad (17.27a)$$

After simplification, we get $\rho_a^2 = 0.04$; thus $\rho_a = \pm 0.2$. The only economically relevant solution is the positive root. Thus project A's internal rate is $\rho_a = 0.20$, or 20 percent.

The corresponding equation for project B is

$$20,000 = \frac{40,000}{1 + \rho_b} - \frac{19,800}{(1 + \rho_b)^2} \qquad (17.27b)$$

which after simplification becomes $\rho_b^2 = 0.01$. Hence $\rho_b = \pm 0.10$. Again only the positive root is relevant. Thus project B's internal rate is $\rho_b = 0.10$, or 10 percent.

Which project should be approved? On the basis of the internal rate-of-return criterion, the presumption is to adopt the project with the higher internal rate. In the present case, this means project A ($\rho_a = 0.20 > 0.10 = \rho_b$). Yet that would be a mistake. Evaluated at the market interest rate ($i = 0.05$), the present values of projects A and B, denoted by V_a and V_b, are

$$V_a = \frac{2000}{1.05} - \frac{960}{1.05^2} - 1000 = 34.01$$

$$V_b = \frac{40,000}{1.05} - \frac{19,800}{1.05^2} - 20,000 = 136.06$$

respectively. Since $V_b > V_a$, the correct decision is to pursue project B, even though its internal rate is less than A's. Remember that the present-value criterion always gives the correct investment signal.

Curves A and B in Figure 17.9 depict the present values of projects A and B, respectively, as functions of the market rate of interest. Note that at low interest rates, $V_b > V_a$.

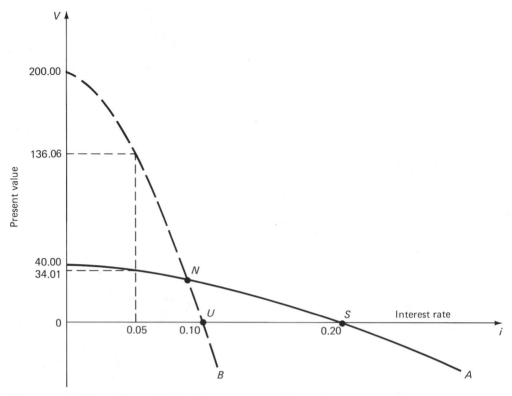

Figure 17.9 *Mutually exclusive investment projects.* Curves *A* and *B* depict the present values of projects *A* and *B*, respectively, as functions of the market interest rate. Both curves are downward sloping and intersect at point *N*. Project *A*'s internal rate is 0.20, as shown by point *S;* project *B*'s internal rate is only 0.10, as given by point *U*. However, when the interest rate is 5 percent, project *B* should be selected because its present value (136.06) exceeds that of *A*'s (34.01).

17.7 Selected Empirical Applications

In this section we first discuss a case study in governmental capital budgeting, namely, Clemson University's stadium improvement, and then present data on capital formation in various OECD countries.

Clemson University's Stadium Improvement[9]

In 1970 the South Carolina General Assembly authorized the Clemson University Board of Trustees to finance and build a 10,000-seat addition to its football stadium. Below we first discuss the data concerning the project's initial cost, expected revenues, and expected operating costs; then we show the project's present value under alternative sets of assumptions.

The stadium's original contract price was $5 million, but construction problems delayed its completion and caused costs to rise. Because a final cost was not available at the time of this calculation, the present value of the project was computed for three alternative amounts of initial construction cost, namely, $5 million, $5.5 million, and $6 million. In addition to the construction costs, the project's initial

[9]This subsection is based on Wiggins (1980).

cost included a total amount of $26,000 for miscellaneous expenses, such as legal fees, and printing and advertizing costs of issuing bonds.

To finance the stadium improvements, in April 1978 the Clemson University Board of Trustees issued $4.25 million bonds which were scheduled to mature serially over the following 20 years. The rest of the project's initial cost ($750,000) came from student and admissions fees. The weighted-average interest rate on the bonds was 5.74887 percent, but for simplicity this figure was rounded to 5.75 percent per annum and used as the appropriate interest rate in calculating the project's present value.

The stream of expected *net* revenues of the stadium improvement coincides with the differences between the stream of annual revenues (expected to be made available by the construction of the 10,000-seat addition) and the stream of additional annual operating costs over the expected life of the stadium, which was taken to be 50 years.

The only significant operating cost was an expected increase in maintenance and cleanup costs of about $500 per game. Based on past experience (5 to 6 games per year), the average number of home games was estimated to be 5.5 per year. Thus the additional operating costs per year were initially set at $2750 (i.e., 5.5 games × $500). But these costs were assumed to grow at an average rate of 5 percent annually.

The expected annual revenues are proportional to the expected sales of tickets per home game. Instead of choosing the most likely figure of ticket sales, however, the present value of the project was calculated for six alternative volumes of expected ticket sales per home game, as shown below in Table 17.1.

Ticket prices were assumed to start at $10, but they were expected to increase by $1 every five years over the stadium's life. Of the $10 ticket price, the University anticipated to receive only $5.33. (The university's share consists of $1 admission fee for the bond funds plus one-half of the remainder, less taxes. The visiting team receives the rest.) This revenue per ticket ($5.33) was allowed to increase every five years in accordance with the assumption that ticket prices were expected to rise by $1 every five years.

In addition to the actual ticket sale revenue, the university was also expected to receive additional revenue from concession, souvenir, and program sales. Based on recent experience, this revenue was estimated to be 6.19 cents per person per game. Thus the total expected revenue per ticket was equal to $5.3919 (i.e., $5.33 + 0.0619).

Assuming 5000 tickets are sold per home game, the total revenue received by

Table 17.1 Present Value of Clemson University's Stadium Addition (thousands of dollars)

Additional Tickets Sold per Game	Initial Cost of Addition		
	$5 million	$5.5 million	$6 million
0	5082	−5582	−6082
1000	−4378	−4878	−5378
2500	−3321	−3821	−4431
5000	−1561	−2061	−2561
7500	− 200	− 300	− 800
10000	+1961	+1461	+ 961

Source: Wiggins (1980, p. 22).

Table 17.2 Gross Fixed Capital Formation as Percentage of GDP

	1961	1962	1963	1964	1965	1966	1967	1968	1969	1970	1971	1972	1973	1974	1975	1976	1977	1978	1979	1980	1981
United States	17.4	17.6	17.9	18.1	18.8	18.6	17.9	18.1	18.2	17.6	18.1	18.7	19.1	18.4	17.0	17.2	18.3	19.5	19.8	18.5	17.9
Japan	32.6	32.9	31.5	31.7	29.9	30.4	32.1	33.2	34.5	35.5	34.3	34.2	36.4	34.8	32.4	31.3	30.5	30.8	32.1	32.0	30.9
Germany	25.2	25.7	25.6	26.6	26.1	25.4	23.1	22.4	23.3	25.5	26.1	25.4	23.9	21.6	20.4	20.2	20.3	20.8	21.9	22.8	22.0
France	21.2	21.4	22.1	22.9	23.3	23.7	23.8	23.3	23.4	23.4	23.6	23.7	23.8	24.3	23.4	23.3	22.3	21.4	21.4	21.6	21.2
United Kingdom	17.3	16.9	16.7	18.3	18.3	18.3	18.8	18.9	18.5	18.6	18.4	18.3	19.5	20.3	19.5	19.0	17.9	18.0	17.9	17.5	15.9
Italy	23.2	23.7	24.0	22.2	19.3	18.8	19.5	20.3	21.0	21.4	20.4	19.8	20.8	22.4	20.6	20.0	19.6	18.7	18.8	19.8	20.3
Canada	20.9	20.5	20.5	22.0	23.5	24.5	23.2	21.5	21.4	20.8	21.8	21.7	22.4	23.0	24.0	23.3	22.7	22.3	22.7	23.1	23.7
Total of countries above	19.8	20.0	20.2	20.7	20.9	20.8	20.5	20.7	21.1	21.3	21.6	22.1	23.0	22.4	21.0	20.8	21.2	22.0	22.3	21.8	21.1
Austria	26.3	25.8	26.1	26.4	27.4	27.9	26.6	25.7	25.1	25.9	27.9	30.2	28.5	28.4	26.7	26.0	26.7	25.6	24.7	25.0	24.9
Belgium	20.7	21.3	20.7	22.4	22.4	22.9	22.9	21.5	21.3	22.7	22.1	21.3	21.4	22.7	22.5	22.1	21.7	21.6	20.6	21.2	17.9
Denmark	23.2	23.1	22.0	24.5	24.1	24.1	24.2	23.4	24.6	24.7	24.2	24.6	24.8	24.0	21.1	23.0	22.1	21.7	20.9	18.3	15.7
Finland	27.0	26.7	24.8	24.6	26.0	26.0	24.6	22.6	23.4	25.9	27.3	27.7	28.7	29.6	31.0	27.7	26.6	23.4	22.8	24.7	24.3
Greece	18.2	20.1	19.2	21.0	21.6	21.7	20.3	23.2	24.6	23.6	25.2	27.8	28.0	22.2	20.8	21.2	23.0	23.9	25.6	23.4	20.9
Iceland	22.7	24.0	27.5	28.3	25.9	27.2	30.6	31.2	24.5	23.8	29.2	27.8	29.4	31.6	32.1	28.6	28.0	25.4	24.5	26.5	25.9
Ireland	16.3	17.9	19.5	20.5	21.4	19.8	20.1	20.9	23.3	22.7	23.6	23.7	25.3	24.7	22.6	24.8	25.9	28.4	31.4	28.9	
Luxembourg	23.2	26.1	29.9	33.5	28.0	26.6	23.3	21.4	21.7	23.5	28.4	28.2	27.4	24.7	27.8	24.5	25.3	23.9	24.6	26.2	23.3
Netherlands	24.8	24.5	23.8	25.5	25.1	26.2	26.3	26.9	24.6	25.8	25.9	23.7	23.1	21.8	20.9	19.3	21.1	21.3	21.0	20.8	19.0
Norway	30.0	29.2	29.5	27.9	28.2	28.7	29.7	26.9	24.3	26.5	29.7	27.7	29.3	30.5	34.2	36.3	37.1	31.8	27.7	24.7	27.2
Portugal	17.6	17.0	18.0	17.3	17.3	19.0	20.2	16.8	17.1	17.6	18.8	20.6	20.3	19.7	19.7	19.0	20.1	20.1	19.1	20.9	
Spain	18.8	19.2	19.4	20.7	21.7	22.0	22.3	22.8	23.2	23.2	21.2	22.2	23.6	24.7	23.3	21.8	21.0	19.9	18.9	19.2	20.1
Sweden	22.6	23.1	24.2	24.6	24.7	24.8	24.8	23.9	23.2	22.5	22.1	22.3	21.9	21.5	21.0	21.2	21.2	19.4	19.8	20.1	19.3
Switzerland	27.4	28.8	30.0	30.7	28.7	27.4	26.0	25.6	25.8	27.5	29.2	29.7	29.4	27.6	24.0	20.6	20.7	21.4	21.8	23.8	24.2
Turkey	15.7	15.1	14.4	14.6	14.6	15.9	16.4	17.3	17.4	18.6	17.0	17.4	17.9	18.6	19.6	23.0	22.4	19.8	21.4	19.3	19.9
Total smaller European countries	22.7	23.0	22.9	23.8	23.9	24.1	23.9	23.5	23.2	23.9	24.1	24.2	24.4	24.1	23.2	22.7	22.8	21.9	21.5	21.4	20.8
Australia	25.0	24.5	24.6	25.9	27.4	27.0	26.2	26.5	26.2	26.0	26.2	24.3	22.9	22.8	23.1	23.1	22.9	22.9	22.3	23.1	24.9
New Zealand	21.9	19.7	20.1	21.4	21.9	21.9	20.3	18.5	19.6	20.8	20.6	22.3	22.6	25.7	27.2	25.0	22.0	20.2	17.8	17.9	20.6
Total smaller countries	23.0	23.0	23.0	24.0	24.3	24.4	24.1	23.8	23.5	24.1	24.3	24.2	24.1	24.0	23.3	22.8	22.8	22.0	21.5	21.6	21.3
Total OECD	20.2	20.3	20.6	21.1	21.3	21.3	20.9	21.1	21.4	21.7	21.9	22.4	23.1	22.6	21.4	21.2	21.5	22.0	22.2	21.8	21.2
Memorandum items																					
OECD Europe	21.9	22.2	22.3	23.0	22.7	22.6	22.3	22.1	22.2	23.0	23.2	23.0	23.1	22.8	21.8	21.5	21.2	20.7	20.8	21.0	20.3
EEC	21.7	21.9	22.0	22.8	22.4	22.2	21.9	21.8	22.1	22.9	23.0	22.6	22.7	22.3	21.1	20.9	20.6	20.4	20.7	20.9	19.8
Total OECD less U.S.	23.1	23.3	23.3	24.1	23.8	23.9	23.9	24.0	24.4	25.3	25.2	25.1	25.8	25.3	24.1	23.7	23.4	23.4	23.5	23.5	23.2

Source: OECD Economic Outlook, December 1982, Table R3, p. 156.

the university per year is approximately equal to $148,277 (i.e., $5.3919 × 5000 tickets × 5.5 home games). Thus the *net* revenue (or cash flow) in the first year is expected to be equal to $145,527 (i.e., $148,277 − $2750). The net revenue in each of the following years is similarly calculated. It must be remembered, however, that the operating costs were assumed to grow at 5 percent per annum, and the ticket prices by $1 every five years.

Table 17.1 summarizes the results of present-value calculations for alternative sets of assumptions. Note that irrespective of which initial cost is used, the present value of the project is positive only when 10,000 tickets are sold for every home game. It is therefore tempting to conclude that the stadium addition will prove to be a good financial investment only if all future home games are sold out completely. This conclusion, however, is predicated on the various assumptions underlying these calculations.

The desirability of the stadium addition may also be influenced by other factors, such as prestige, enhanced ability by the university to attract promising students and athletes, and increased contributions to the university by alumni and friends. These additional factors are not included, of course, in the calculations of Table 17.1.

Fixed Capital Formation in OECD Countries

Table 17.2 gives the gross fixed capital formation as a percentage of gross domestic product (GDP) of the member countries of the Organization for Economic Cooperation and Development (OECD) for the years 1961–1981. Some striking differences between countries are obvious. Consider first the top part of Table 17.2, which lists the larger OECD countries. While in the United States gross fixed capital formation as a percentage of GDP fluctuated between 17 and 19 percent over the entire period, the corresponding figures for Japan were substantially higher—30 to 34 percent.

Germany's fixed capital formation was also relatively higher than that of other large countries (besides Japan) in the 1960s and early 1970s, but has dropped down to the average level of the group (between 21 and 22 percent) since 1974. The United Kingdom's fixed capital formation has been consistently below the average of the large OECD countries.

The middle part of Table 17.2 summarizes the performance of the smaller European OECD countries. The average gross fixed capital formation as a percentage of GDP of this group of countries fluctuated between 23 and 24 percent, but followed a mild downward trend in the late 1970s and early 1980s. Above-average capital formation is observed in several countries, such as Austria, Finland, Iceland, Norway, and Switzerland (but only until 1975). Australia outperformed New Zealand in all years except for the 1974–1976 period.

SUMMARY

1. Land and labor are primary factors—their supplies are determined outside the economic system. Capital is an intermediate (or produced) factor; it is also intimately connected with time.
2. A direct process employs the primary factors in the direct production of consumption commodities. A roundabout (or indirect) process first uses labor and land to produce capital goods, which are later combined with the primary factors for the production of consumption commodities. Roundabout processes are typically more productive than direct processes.
3. Irving Fisher showed that the equilibrium interest rate is determined by the rate of time preference and society's opportunity to invest.
4. Saving is that part of income that is not

consumed; investment is the increase in the economy's capital stock (production of new capital goods). In the Crusoe economy, saving and investment coincide.

5. In the presence of multiple opportunities to invest, a production-possibilities frontier (*PPF*) can be constructed to show the menu of choices between present and future consumption. Only those techniques associated with points lying on the boundary of the *PPF* are efficient. The absolute slope of the *PPF* is the marginal rate of transformation of present for future consumption (MRT_{01}).

6. Crusoe's optimal intertemporal consumption stream occurs where $MRT_{01} = MRS_{01}$, which implies that the marginal rate of return ρ equals the marginal rate of time preference δ.

7. The intertemporal budget line is a wealth constraint, not an income constraint.

8. The real interest rate i equals the money interest rate μ less the expected rate of inflation α.

9. In the pure consumption model, a consumer's intertemporal equilibrium occurs at the tangency between her budget line and the highest possible indifference curve. This tangency implies that $MRS_{01} = 1 + \delta = 1 + i$, or $\delta = i$.

10. Typically, a borrower's demand curve for loans slopes downward, because the income effect reinforces the substitution effect. A lender's supply curve may be backward bending, because in the lender's case the income effect works against the substitution effect.

11. At the market equilibrium indicated by the intersection of the market supply and demand curves for loans, the marginal rates of time preference of all persons, borrowers and lenders alike, are equal to the equilibrium interest rate. This Pareto-optimality condition is brought about by borrowing and lending in a perfectly competitive loan market.

12. In the pure consumption model, the economy saves nothing and invests nothing, and

the equilibrium interest rate may even be negative.

13. In the presence of investment opportunities, the person maximizes his intertemporal utility in two steps. First, he chooses that income stream that maximizes his present wealth—an optimal investment decision which is independent of his preferences and can be executed either by the person himself or his agent. Second, he determines his preferred consumption stream indicated by the tangency between his intertemporal budget line and the highest possible indifference curve.

14. As the interest rate rises, each person reduces her volume of investment. This investment effect works in the same direction as the substitution effect.

15. It is identically true that

$$I + \text{total lending} = S + \text{total borrowing}$$

where I is the total investment and S the total saving. When the loan market is in equilibrium (total lending = total borrowing), then $S = I$.

16. The cardinal rule for all investment decisions is to approve any project whose present discounted value is positive, and reject any project whose present value is negative. This rule, known as the present-value criterion, gives the correct investment signal always.

17. The internal rate of return of an investment project (marginal efficiency of investment) is that rate of interest (return) which renders the present value of the project equal to zero (or makes the present value of the expected annual returns of the project equal to its initial cost).

18. The internal rate-of-return criterion asserts that an investment project is profitable, and thus must be undertaken, if its internal rate of return exceeds the market interest rate. This proposition is not generally true, although it is valid in two-period models.

QUESTIONS

1. Crusoe's preferences between current consumption of fish c_0 and future consumption of fish c_1 are given by the utility function $U = c_0 c_1$. If Crusoe catches fish by hand, he can

consume 100 fish in each period, but if he builds a net, his current consumption will fall to 80 fish and his future consumption will rise to 125 fish.

(a) What is the rate of return of the net?

(b) What is Crusoe's marginal rate of time preference in the absence of the net?

(c) Should Crusoe construct the net? Why or why not?

2. A society's collective preferences between current consumption c_0 and future consumption c_1 are given by the function $U = c_0^{1.1}c_1$. Using labor and land directly, society can maintain its consumption at 1000 units both in the current period and in the future. But there are five mutually exclusive investment projects whose opportunity costs and prospective yields are summarized in the following table.

Project	Opportunity Cost	Prospective Yield
1	100	150
2	200	290
3	300	410
4	400	510
5	500	600

(a) Are any projects inefficient?

(b) Construct the society's intertemporal production-possibilities frontier.

(c) Does this society exhibit any bias toward current consumption? What is the exact degree of this bias?

(d) Which is the optimal investment project for the society?

(e) What will the equilibrium interest rate be, assuming that a perfectly competitive capital market exists?

3. A person's current income is $10,000, and he expects his future income to be $12,000. The price of consumption goods is expected to remain constant at $10. The person's preferences between current consumption c_0 and future consumption c_1 are given by the function $U = c_0^{1.2}c_1$.

(a) Determine the person's intertemporal budget line and equilibrium when the market interest rate takes the following alternative values: 10 percent, 20 percent, 50 percent, and 60 percent.

(b) At what market interest rate does the person's borrowing and lending drop to zero?

(c) Over what range of values of the interest rate is the person a borrower? Over what range is he a lender?

4. Without undertaking any investment projects, Mr. Black's income will remain constant at $10,000 both now and in the future. Nevertheless, by investing $x now he can gain $y in the future, where x and y are related by the function $y = 60x^{1/2}$.

(a) Determine Mr. Black's intertemporal production-possibilities frontier.

(b) Suppose that the interest rate is 20 percent. What is the optimal investment volume for Mr. Black? Does the determination of the optimal investment volume depend on Mr. Black's time preference?

(c) Determine Mr. Black's intertemporal budget line assuming that the interest rate is 20 percent and his investment plan is optimal.

(d) Graph all your results.

5. Return to the scenario of Question 4. Assume that Mr. Black's preferences between current consumption c_0 and future consumption c_1 are given by the function $U = c_0^{1.1}c_1$.

(a) Assuming that the market interest rate is 20 percent, use the budget line you determined in Question 4, part (c), to calculate Mr. Black's optimal consumption stream.

(b) Determine Mr. Black's saving (or dissaving) and borrowing (or lending) in the current period.

(c) Illustrate your results graphically.

6. "Irving Fisher was the first economist who saw clearly that interest is the factor that relates a stream of income (rentals) to the capital value of the source of that stream, and that from that point of view land and labor are 'capital' in the same sense as material capital." Discuss.

***7.** One unit of labor can be expended in planting a tree now. The tree can then grow by itself with no further inputs (other than what nature provides) according to the equation $Q = 100t^{1/2}$, where Q is the quantity of wood and t the time. The harvesting of the timber costs nothing. The price of timber is expected to remain constant at $p = $10.

(a) What is the optimum age at which to harvest the tree if the rate of interest is 10 percent? (*Note:* You may assume that competition among capitalists will enable workers to drive the current wage to the highest possible level, which you should also determine.)

(b) What is the optimum age at which to harvest the tree if the current wage rate is

$100? (*Note:* You may now assume that competition among workers for employment will enable the capitalists to maximize the rate of return on their investment.)

(c) Illustrate all your results graphically.

*8. Return to the scenario of Question 7, but now suppose that there is an ongoing production process in which trees are continually planted and harvested so that the growth function $Q = 100t^{1/2}$ cut off at the optimum age of trees t_0 represents the constant profile of standing trees, and the area under the growth curve from $t = 0$ to $t = t_0$ gives the amount of physical capital that is necessary to enable a sustained unit input of labor to produce a sustained flow of output. The interest rate is 10 percent.

(a) Determine the economy's standing timber (total stock of material capital) at any moment of time.

(b) Determine the value of the stock of capital. How is it related to the stock of material capital?

(c) Suppose that the interest rate falls from 10 percent to 8 percent. Determine the effects on the optimum age of trees, the size of the stock of material capital, and the value of the capital stock. (*Note:* The increase in the stock of material capital is known as the "Ricardo effect" of the interest rate reduction, and the increase in the value of the existing stock is known as the "Wicksell effect.")

(d) Illustrate all your results graphically.

9. There is a stock of 1000 tons of a particular metal in the ground. The metal is widely owned so that each owner acts as a price taker. The demand for the metal in any period t is given by the function

$$D_t = 1550 - 5p_t$$

where D_t is the quantity demanded in period t and p_t the price in period t. For simplicity, assume that the cost of extracting and shipping the metal is zero and that the metal will have no use beyond the second period (i.e., $t = 1, 2$). The interest rate is 10 percent per period.

(a) Explain why the equilibrium price of the metal in the second period must be 10 percent higher than its equilibrium price in the first period.

(b) Determine the equilibrium price of the metal in the two periods.
(*Hint:* Use the relationship $p_2 = 1.10p_1$ together with the requirement that the combined demand for the metal over the two periods must be equal to the total supply.)

(c) How much metal will be sold in each period?

(d) How would a reduction in the interest rate affect p_1, p_2, and the quantities sold in the two periods? Verify your explanation by assuming that the rate of interest falls to 5 percent.

10. An investment project, which has an initial cost of $23,000, is expected to generate the following income stream over the next three years of its anticipated life: $R_1 = \$82,800$, $R_2 = \$-99,130$, and $R_3 = \$39,468$.

(a) Determine the present value of the investment project for the following alternative interest rates per annum: 5 percent, 15 percent, 25 percent, and 35 percent.

(b) What is the internal rate of return of this project?

(c) Should the project be undertaken if the market interest rate is less than 30 percent?

(d) Can you explain why is it that the project may be profitable when the interest rate is high, say, 25 percent, and unprofitable when the interest rate is low, say, 15 percent?

11. In a recent article in *The Wall Street Journal* (July 8, 1982), Martin Feldstein gives his views on China's economy. He states that "Under the old rules, a firm could receive an infusion of new investment funds" at zero interest, which "was consistent with the Marxian view that labor is the source of all value and that capital therefore deserves no reward." Since there are few, if any, consumers who would argue against a low interest rate, why would anyone criticize the Chinese for not charging any interest?

FURTHER READING

Baumol, W. J. (1977). *Economic Theory and Operations Analysis,* 4th ed. Prentice-Hall, Inc., Englewood Cliffs, N.J. Chapters 25 and 26.

Blaug, M. (1962). *Economic Theory in Retrospect.* Richard D. Irwin, Inc., Homewood, Ill. Chapter 12.

Burmeister, E. (1980). *Capital Theory and Dynamics*. Cambridge University Press, New York.

Fisher, I. (1930). *The Theory of Interest,* Reprints of Economic Classics. Augustus M. Kelly, Publishers, New York, 1965.

Harcourt, G. C. (1972). *Some Cambridge Controversies in the Theory of Capital*. Cambridge University Press, New York.

Harcourt, G. C., and N. F. Laing (eds.) (1971). *Capital and Growth,* Penguin Modern Economics Readings. Penguin Books Ltd., Harmondsworth, Middlesex, England.

Henderson, J. M., and R. E. Quandt (1980). *Microeconomic Theory,* 3rd ed. McGraw-Hill Book Company, New York. Chapter 12.

Hicks, J. R. (1946). *Value and Capital,* 2nd ed. Oxford University Press, New York. Parts III and IV.

Hirschleifer, J. (1970). *Investment, Interest and Capital*. Prentice-Hall, Inc., Englewood Cliffs, N.J.

Johnson, H. G. (1973). *The Theory of Income Distribution*. Gray-Mills Publishing Ltd., London. Chapters 11–13.

Keynes, J. M. (1936). *The General Theory of Employment, Interest and Money*. Macmillan & Company Ltd., London.

Solow, R. M. (1965). *Capital Theory and the Rate of Return*. Rand McNally & Company, Chicago.

Wicksell, K. (1934). *Lectures on Political Economy,* Vol. 1. Routledge & Kegan Paul Ltd., London. Part 2.

Wiggins, C. D. (1980). "A Case Study in Governmental Capital Budgeting," *Governmental Finance,* June, pp. 19–22.

Appendixes

Appendix to Chapter 2
The Simple Mathematics of Supply and Demand

This appendix presents the mathematics of supply and demand in three parts. The first part shows how to use equations to determine the equilibrium price and quantity. The second part considers the problem of stability of equilibrium. Finally, the third part explains the simple mathematics of comparative statics—a powerful technique that finds applications in almost all areas of economics.

A2.1 Equilibrium of Supply and Demand[1]

In Chapter 2, we used geometric *curves* to represent the willingness of suppliers to supply alternative quantities at various prices (supply curve), and the willingness of buyers to purchase alternative quantities at various prices (demand curve). Now we wish to represent the same relationships in terms of supply and demand *equations,* and show how to use these equations to determine equilibrium. This is a simple and useful technique that the serious student of economics should master.

The Cournot–Walras–Wicksell Approach[2]

Following the discussion of Chapter 2, we can express both the quantity demanded and the quantity supplied as functions of price, as follows:

$$q = D(p) \quad \text{(demand equation)} \tag{A2.1}$$

$$q = S(p) \quad \text{(supply equation)} \tag{A2.2}$$

In the literature of economics, this formulation of the supply and demand equations is usually referred to as the Cournot–Walras–Wicksell approach.

Equilibrium is specified by the requirement that the quantity demanded, $D(p)$, must be equal to the quantity supplied, $S(p)$. That is,

$$D(p) = S(p) \quad \text{(equilibrium condition)} \tag{A2.3}$$

Equation (A2.3) is referred to as the *equilibrium condition.* The solution of this equation gives the *equilibrium price* (p_e). The equilibrium quantity (q_e) is obtained from either equation (A2.1) or (A2.2) after p_e is substituted for p.

A numerical illustration can make the above procedure clear. Assume the following specific demand and supply equations:

$$q = D(p) = 750 - 25p \quad \text{(demand equation)} \tag{A2.1a}$$

---

[1]This section can be read simultaneously with Section 2.5.

[2]Antoine Augustin Cournot (1801–1877) was a French mathematician and economist; Leon Walras (1834–1910) was a Swiss economist born in France and the champion of general equilibrium theory; and Knut Wicksell (1851–1926) was a Swedish economist.

$$q = S(p) = 300 + 20p \qquad \text{(supply equation)} \qquad \text{(A2.2a)}$$

Substituting equations (A2.1a) and (A2.2a) into (A2.3), we obtain the equilibrium condition

$$750 - 25p = 300 + 20p \qquad \text{(A2.3a)}$$

Solving equation (A2.3a) for p, we get the equilibrium price $p_e = 10$. Finally, substituting the equilibrium price into equations (A2.1a) and (A2.2a), we have the equilibrium quantity $q_e = 750 - 25 \times 10 = 300 + 20 \times 10 = 500$.

The Marshallian Approach

Alfred Marshall followed the alternative procedure of expressing price as a function of quantity. According to the Marshallian definition, the supply and demand equations take the form

$$p = d(q) \qquad \text{(demand equation)} \qquad \text{(A2.4)}$$

$$p = s(q) \qquad \text{(supply equation)} \qquad \text{(A2.5)}$$

where $d(q)$ is the demand price and $s(p)$ the supply price. For this reason, Marshall used the horizontal axis to measure quantity (which, in his system, is the independent variable).

Marshall specifies equilibrium by the requirement that demand price, $d(q)$, must be equal to supply price, $s(p)$; that is,

$$d(q) = s(q) \qquad \text{(equilibrium condition)} \qquad \text{(A2.6)}$$

Equation (A2.6) is the equilibrium condition in the Marshallian system; its root is the equilibrium *quantity* (q_e). To determine the equilibrium price, we substitute q_e for q in either equation (A2.4) or (A2.5).

Whether we specify the demand and supply equations in the manner of Cournot–Walras–Wicksell or in the manner of Marshall, the equilibrium price and quantity are the same. We can illustrate this proposition by pursuing a little further the earlier numerical illustration. Solve each of the equations (A2.1a) and (A2.2a) for p, and rewrite them as follows:

$$p = \frac{750 - q}{25} \qquad \text{(demand equation)} \qquad \text{(A2.4a)}$$

$$p = \frac{q - 300}{20} \qquad \text{(supply equation)} \qquad \text{(A2.5a)}$$

Now solve the equilibrium condition

$$\frac{750 - q}{25} = \frac{q - 300}{20} \qquad \text{(A2.6a)}$$

to obtain the *equilibrium quantity* $q_e = 500$. Finally, substitute the equilibrium quantity in equations (A2.4a) and (A2.5a) to obtain the equilibrium price (p_e):

$$p_e = \frac{750 - 500}{25} = \frac{500 - 300}{20} = 10$$

Thus the equilibrium price and quantity are exactly the same as before. This is as it should be, because equations (A2.4a) and (A2.5a) are mathematically equivalent to equations (A2.1a) and (A2.2a).

A2.2 Stability of Equilibrium[3]

Broadly speaking, we can distinguish between two types of stability: *dynamic* stability and *static* stability. Dynamic stability seeks to explain the changes of prices and quantities as they evolve through time, say, from day to day. This is an ambitious undertaking that lies beyond the scope of this book.

Static stability, on the other hand, involves no explicit framework for determining how price and quantity change through time when the system is out of equilibrium. It merely establishes the *tendencies* that exist when the market is out of equilibrium, and whether these tendencies point toward equilibrium or not. Whenever we deal with stability in this book, we have in mind static stability, unless explicitly stated otherwise.

In the neoclassical writings, there exist two contrasting notions of static stability: the Walrasian and the Marshallian. Even though these two approaches often appear to be contradictory, they refer to quite different economic situations. Thus the Walrasian approach is primarily concerned with the short run, while the Marshallian approach is designed for the long run. Accordingly, we must view the two approaches as essentially complementary—not contradictory. This section elucidates both of these approaches.

The Walrasian Stability Analysis

As explained in Section A2.1, Leon Walras considered the quantities demanded and supplied as functions of price. He then identified a disequilibrium as an inequality between the quantity demanded and the quantity supplied. Finally, he adopted the following postulate: *Price tends to rise (fall) when the quantity demanded, D(p), is greater (smaller) than the quantity supplied, S(p).* In other words, p tends to rise (fall) when the excess demand, $E(p) \equiv D(p) - S(p)$, is positive (negative). Accordingly, an equilibrium is stable when, in the neighborhood of that equilibrium, the slope of the *excess demand curve* is negative. Mathematically, this stability condition is formulated as follows:

$$E'(p_e) \equiv D'(p_e) - S'(p_e) < 0 \qquad (A2.7)$$

where primes indicate a first derivative. Note that all derivatives are evaluated at the equilibrium price, p_e, that is, at that value of p which satisfies equation (A2.3). Obviously, when the demand curve slopes downward [i.e., $D'(p) < 0$] and the supply curve slopes upward [i.e., $S'(p) > 0$], inequality (A2.7) is satisfied, and the equilibrium point is stable.

We can illustrate the Walrasian stability analysis by means of the numerical illustration given earlier [see equations (A2.1a) and (A2.2a)]. The excess demand function is $E(p) \equiv (750 - 25p) - (300 + 20p) = 450 - 45p$, and its derivative is equal to $E'(p) = -45 < 0$. Since $E'(p)$ is negative, the system is stable.

In the above illustration note that the derivative $E'(p)$ is equal to a negative constant (i.e., -45). This means that $E'(p)$ remains constant at all values of p, including the equilibrium price, $p_e = 10$. If the derivative $E'(p)$ were actually some function of p, we would have to substitute the equilibrium price, p_e, to obtain the specific value $E'(p_e)$. It is the specific value $E'(p_e)$ that must be negative for stability.

[3]This section can be read right after Section 2.5.

The Marshallian Stability Analysis

Marshall was primarily concerned with the long-run equilibrium of a perfectly competitive industry. For him, positive profits stimulated an expansion of output; similarly, losses signaled a contraction of output.

To bring into focus the profit-loss mechanism, Marshall identified the *(equilibrium) supply price* of any industry output with the unit cost of producing that output (i.e., the cost that must be just covered by the price if the producers are to continue producing that output). Then he adopted the following postulate: *If at the current output (quantity supplied) the market price (or demand price), d(q), is higher than the supply price, s(q), the output will tend to expand (presumably because of the existence of abnormal profits); and if the market price is lower than the supply price, output will tend to fall (presumably because of the existence of losses).* According to the Marshallian analysis, therefore, an equilibrium is stable if the market price is higher than the supply price for lower outputs, and lower than the supply price for higher outputs.

Consider Figure A2.1. Equilibrium occurs at E where demand curve D intersects supply curve S. The equilibrium price is $10 and the equilibrium quantity is 500 million bushels. Suppose that the producers bring to the market only 400 million bushels. The unit cost of that output is only $5 (see point Y on supply curve S).

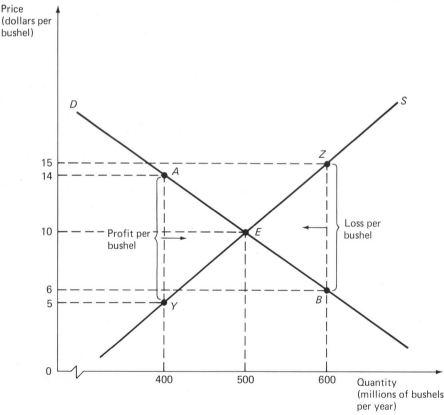

Figure A2.1 The Marshallian stability condition. If the current output is 400 million bushels, the demand price ($14) will exceed the supply price ($5), and the resultant profit ($9 per bushel) will induce producers to expand output. If the current output is, alternatively, 600 million bushels, the supply price ($15) will exceed the demand price ($6), and the resultant loss ($9 per bushel) will convince producers to reduce output. Hence equilibrium point E is stable.

What is the market price (or demand price)? Well, for the current quantity of 400 million bushels, the consumers are willing to pay $14 (see point A on demand curve D). Therefore, the producers are realizing a *profit* of $9 per bushel, which is an inducement to *expand* output. Alternatively, suppose that the producers bring to the market 600 million bushels, which is larger than the equilibrium quantity. The unit cost of this larger output is $15 (point Z), while the market price is only $6 (point B). As a result, the producers will now suffer a *loss* of $9 per bushel, which is a strong inducement to reduce output. We therefore conclude that the equilibrium in Figure A2.1 is stable.

Note the subtle switch in the independent variable. In the Walrasian system, it is the price that is the independent variable. In the Marshallian system, however, it is the *quantity* that assumes the role of the independent variable. Thus the Marshallian analysis begins with a *given current output (quantity)* and uses the supply curve to determine the supply price, and the demand curve to determine the demand price (or market price). Then, on the basis of the relationship between the supply price and the demand price, Marshall determines whether the producers enjoy profits or suffer losses. If the producers enjoy positive profits, they will tend to expand their *output (quantity)*; if they suffer losses, they will tend to reduce their *output (quantity)*. The Walrasian analysis, on the other hand, begins with a *given price* and proceeds to determine the quantity demanded and the quantity supplied. Then, on the basis of the relationship between the quantity demanded and the quantity supplied, Walras determines whether *price* will tend to rise or fall.

Analytically, the Marshallian stability condition takes the form

$$d'(q_e) - s'(q_e) < 0 \qquad (A2.8)$$

Note that both derivatives are evaluated at the equilibrium quantity, q_e, that is, the root of equation (A2.6). Again, when the demand curve slopes downward [i.e., $d'(q) < 0$], and the supply curve slopes upward [i.e., $s'(q) > 0$], inequality (A2.8) is satisfied, and the equilibrium point is stable.

Pursuing a little further the illustration presented earlier by equations (A2.4a) and (A2.5a), we easily show that the equilibrium of that system is stable:

$$d'(q) - s'(q) = -\frac{1}{25} - \frac{1}{20} = -\frac{9}{100} < 0$$

An Apparent Contradiction Between Walras and Marshall

As we have seen, when the demand curve slopes downward and the supply curve slopes upward in the neighborhood of an equilibrium point, that equilibrium is stable according to both the Walrasian and Marshallian stability criteria. However, when the supply curve has negative slope, a mechanical application of these criteria leads to a contradiction; that is, when the system is stable in the Walrasian sense, it is unstable in the Marshallian sense, and vice versa. (The reader is encouraged to draw his own *diagrams* and verify the conclusion.)

Analytically, the contradiction becomes obvious when one notices the following identities:

$$D'(p_e) = \frac{1}{d'(q_e)} \qquad (A2.9)$$

$$S'(p_e) = \frac{1}{s'(q_e)} \qquad (A2.10)$$

For instance, assume that $D'(p_e) < S'(p_e) < 0$. Thus the Walrasian stability condition is satisfied. However, substituting the results summarized by equations (A2.9) and (A2.10), the assumed inequality is equivalent to $1/d'(q_e) < 1/s'(q_e) < 0$, or $0 > d'(q_e) > s'(q_e)$. Thus $d'(q_e) - s'(q_e) > 0$; that is, the Marshallian stability condition is *not* satisfied.

To test his understanding of the above argument, the student should try to prove the opposite. Thus, assume that $s'(q_e) < 0$ and, in addition, inequality (A2.8) is satisfied. Then show that inequality (A2.7) is necessarily violated.

Fortunately, the contradiction between the Walrasian and Marshallian stability conditions is only apparent—it is not real. Thus the Walrasian stability analysis is basically concerned with the short run, while the Marshallian stability analysis deals with the long run. Accordingly, the Walrasian analysis is applicable to cases in which the supply curve is upward sloping, vertical, or backward bending; and the Marshallian analysis is applicable to cases in which the supply curve is upward sloping, horizontal, or forward falling. In the Appendix to Chapter 9 we discuss the truly exceptional case of a long-run supply curve that is backward bending.

A2.3 Comparative Statics[4]

We now turn to the problem of comparative statics. We limit the present discussion to the effects of shifts in demand or supply and the effects of a specific tax. This section is more difficult than Sections A2.1 and A2.2.

General Formulation

In Section A2.1 we explained how to use *equations* to determine the equilibrium price and quantity. That equilibrium, of course, persists for as long as the parameters that lie behind the supply and demand curves remain constant. The method of comparative statics investigates the resultant changes in the equilibrium price and quantity as some parameter changes and the system moves from one equilibrium to another. This investigation ignores the transitional process involved in the adjustment.

Write the demand and supply equations as follows:

$$q = D(p, \alpha) \quad \text{(demand equation)} \tag{A2.11}$$

$$q = S(p, \beta) \quad \text{(supply equation)} \tag{A2.12}$$

The parameter α in the demand equation (A2.11) may represent the price of a related good, income, or tastes. Similarly, the parameter β in the supply equation may represent wages, rents, or the state of the arts. The parameters α and β are usually called *shift parameters,* for reasons that will become apparent below.

In principle, we should have included a shift parameter in each function for each variable held constant. For instance, in the demand function we should have included a shift parameter for the price of each related good. However, our concern is to determine the effects of a change in only one of these parameters on the equilibrium price and quantity. Hence we need to include explicitly just that one parameter.

To solve equations (A2.11) and (A2.12) simultaneously for the equilibrium price, p_e, and the equilibrium quantity, q_e, we must know the initial values of the shift parameters. As the shift parameters change, the equilibrium price and quantity

---

[4]This section can be read simultaneously with Section 2.8.

change as well. Accordingly, *the equilibrium price and quantity may be viewed as functions of the shift parameters*. We can express these relationships mathematically as follows:

$$p_e = p_e(\alpha, \beta) \tag{A2.13}$$

$$q_e = q_e(\alpha, \beta) \tag{A2.14}$$

Equations (A2.13) and (A2.14) show explicitly the strict relationship that exists between the shift parameters, α and β, and the equilibrium price, p_e, and quantity, q_e. Our objective in the rest of this appendix is to clarify this general formulation and study the properties of the functional relationships (A2.13) and (A2.14).

Before proceeding, it is important to note that p_e and q_e, as given by equations (A2.13) and (A2.14), do satisfy equations (A2.11) and (A2.12). Indeed, we can substitute q_e and p_e into equations (A2.11) and (A2.12) to obtain

$$q_e = D[p_e(\alpha, \beta), \alpha] \tag{A2.15}$$

$$q_e = S[p_e(\alpha, \beta), \beta] \tag{A2.16}$$

These equations play a crucial role in the study of comparative statics.

Note that equations (A2.15) and (A2.16) have the same form as equations (A2.11) and (A2.12). Because of this, in the future we may avoid any explicit reference to equations (A2.15) and (A2.16) and work directly with equations (A2.11) and (A2.12), keeping in mind that p and q are the *equilibrium* price and quantity, respectively, and that p and q are functions of the shift parameters.

A Numerical Illustration

Consider the following system of equations:

$$q = D(p, \alpha) = 500 - 40p + \alpha \quad \text{(demand equation)} \tag{A2.11a}$$

$$q = S(p, \alpha) = 20 + 8p + \beta \quad \text{(supply equation)} \tag{A2.12a}$$

Solving these equations simultaneously for the equilibrium price and quantity, we obtain

$$p_e = 10 + \frac{\alpha - \beta}{48} \tag{A2.13a}$$

$$q_e = 100 + \frac{1}{6}\alpha + \frac{5}{6}\beta \tag{A2.14a}$$

Obviously, both p_e and q_e are functions of the shift parameters α and β. Therefore, to determine the precise values of p_e and q_e, we must know the values of α and β; and when either α or β changes, both p_e and q_e change.

Shifts in the Demand Function

Analytically, a horizontal shift (i.e., a shift to the left or to the right) in the demand curve can be represented by a change in the value of the shift parameter α that appears in the demand function. How does a change in α affect p_e and q_e, assuming that all other parameters (and, in particular, β) remain constant? To answer this question, we must differentiate totally equations (A2.15) and (A2.16) with respect to α. We have

$$\frac{\partial q_e}{\partial \alpha} = \frac{\partial D}{\partial p_e} \frac{\partial p_e}{\partial \alpha} + \frac{\partial D}{\partial \alpha} \qquad (A2.17)$$

$$\frac{\partial q_e}{\partial \alpha} = \frac{\partial S}{\partial p_e} \frac{\partial p_e}{\partial \alpha} \qquad (A2.18)$$

Solving these equations for $\partial q_e/\partial \alpha$ and $\partial p_e/\partial \alpha$, we finally obtain

$$\frac{\partial p_e}{\partial \alpha} = \frac{\partial D/\partial \alpha}{(\partial S/\partial p) - (\partial D/\partial p)} \qquad (A2.19)$$

$$\frac{\partial q_e}{\partial \alpha} = \frac{(\partial S/\partial p)(\partial D/\partial \alpha)}{(\partial S/\partial p) - (\partial D/\partial p)} \qquad (A2.20)$$

Equations (A2.19) and (A2.20) are very important; they summarize the results we have been seeking.

A shift in the demand curve to the right is represented by the condition $\partial D/\partial \alpha > 0$. When the demand curve slopes downward (i.e., $\partial D/\partial p < 0$) and the supply curve slopes upward (i.e., $\partial S/\partial p > 0$), it is obvious from equations (A2.19) and (A2.20) that $\partial p_e/\partial \alpha > 0$, and $\partial q_e/\partial \alpha > 0$. In other words, a rightward shift in the demand curve causes both the equilibrium price and the equilibrium quantity to increase. This conclusion actually verifies a similar conclusion that we derived graphically in Chapter 2.

Note that when the Walrasian stability condition [i.e., inequality (A2.7)] is satisfied, the denominator on the right-hand side of equations (A2.19) and (A2.20) is necessarily positive.

As an example, return to the earlier numerical illustration and assume that β remains constant. To determine the effects of a rightward shift in the demand curve, differentiate p_e and q_e, as given by equations (A2.13a) and (A2.14a), with respect to α to obtain

$$\frac{\partial p_e}{\partial \alpha} = \frac{1}{48} > 0$$

$$\frac{\partial q_e}{\partial \alpha} = \frac{1}{6} > 0$$

Shifts in the Supply Function

Similarly, a horizontal shift in the supply curve can be represented by a change in β. What is its effect on p_e and q_e? Again differentiate totally equations (A2.15) and (A2.16) with respect to β, holding α constant, to obtain

$$\frac{\partial q_e}{\partial \beta} = \frac{\partial D}{\partial p_e} \frac{\partial p_e}{\partial \beta} \qquad (A2.21)$$

$$\frac{\partial q_e}{\partial \beta} = \frac{\partial S}{\partial p_e} \frac{\partial p_e}{\partial \beta} + \frac{\partial S}{\partial \beta} \qquad (A2.22)$$

Solving these equations for $\partial q_e / \partial \beta$ and $\partial p_e / \partial \beta$, we finally obtain

$$\frac{\partial p_e}{\partial \beta} = \frac{\partial S / \partial \beta}{(\partial D / \partial p_e) - (\partial S / \partial p_e)} \tag{A2.23}$$

$$\frac{\partial q_e}{\partial \beta} = \frac{(\partial D / \partial p_e)(\partial S / \partial \beta)}{(\partial D / \partial p_e) - (\partial S / \partial p_e)} \tag{A2.24}$$

Equations (A2.23) and (A2.24) give the effects of a shift in the supply curve on the equilibrium price and quantity.

A shift in the supply curve to the right is represented by the condition $\partial S / \partial \beta > 0$. When the demand curve slopes downward (i.e., $\partial D / \partial p < 0$) and the supply curve slopes upward (i.e., $\partial S / \partial p > 0$), it is apparent that $\partial p_e / \partial \beta < 0$ and $\partial q_e / \partial \beta > 0$. In other words, a rightward shift in the supply curve causes the equilibrium price to fall and the equilibrium quantity to increase—a result that verifies the conclusion we reach graphically in Chapter 2.

Again note that when the Walrasian stability condition is satisfied, the denominator on the right-hand side of equations (A2.23) and (A2.24) is necessarily negative.

As an illustration, we pursue a little further the earlier numerical illustration. Thus, differentiating p_e and q_e, as given by equations (A2.13a) and (A2.14a), with respect to β, we obtain

$$\frac{\partial p_e}{\partial \beta} = \frac{-1}{48} < 0 \qquad \frac{\partial q_e}{\partial \beta} = \frac{5}{6} > 0$$

The Effects of a Specific Tax

We now employ the preceding technique to analyze the effects of a specific tax (t) on the price paid by consumers (p_c), the price received by producers (p_p), and the equilibrium quantity.

Equilibrium is now represented by the following system of equations:

$$q = D(p_c) \tag{A2.25}$$

$$q = S(p_p) \tag{A2.26}$$

$$p_c = p_p + t \tag{A2.27}$$

The tax t serves as a parameter. Given t, the three equations (A2.25) to (A2.27) can be solved for the equilibrium values of p_c, p_p, and q. All of these equilibrium values are functions of the parameter t, and they also satisfy equations (A2.25) to (A2.27).

We can simplify matters by solving equation (A2.27) for p_p, and then substituting the result into equation (A2.26) to obtain

$$q = S(p_c - t) \tag{A2.26}'$$

In this way, we reduce the system from three to two equations, (A2.25) and (A2.26)'.

To determine the effects of a change in t on p_c and q, we differentiate totally equations (A2.25) and (A2.26)' to get

$$\frac{dq}{dt} = D' \cdot \frac{dp_c}{dt} \tag{A2.28}$$

$$\frac{dq}{dt} = S' \cdot \left(\frac{dp_c}{dt} - 1\right) \tag{A2.29}$$

(For convenience, we use the symbols D' and S' for the derivatives dD/dp_c and dS/dp_p, respectively.) Solving now equations (A2.28) and (A2.29), we finally obtain

$$\frac{dp_c}{dt} = \frac{S'}{S' - D'} \tag{A2.30}$$

$$\frac{dq}{dt} = \frac{D' \cdot S'}{S' - D'} \tag{A2.31}$$

Equations (A2.30) and (A2.31) give us the effects of a change in t on p_c and q, respectively. To determine the effect on p_p, we must differentiate totally equation (A2.27) with respect to t to obtain

$$\frac{dp_c}{dt} = \frac{dp_p}{dt} + 1 \tag{A2.32}$$

Substituting equation (A2.30) into (A2.32) and then solving for dp_p/dt, we finally get

$$\frac{dp_p}{dt} = \frac{D'}{S' - D'} \tag{A2.33}$$

Equation (A2.33) gives the effect of a change in t on p_p.

When the Walrasian condition is satisfied, the denominator on the right-hand side of equations (A2.30), (A2.31), and (A2.33) is positive. Thus the sign of each of the three important derivatives dp_c/dt, dq/dt, and dp_p/dt depends only on the sign of the expression on the numerator on the right-hand side of each corresponding equation.

When the demand curve slopes downward (i.e., $D' < 0$) and the supply curve slopes upward (i.e., $S' > 0$), it follows from equations (A2.30), (A2.31), and (A2.33) that $dp_c/dt > 0$, $dq/dt < 0$, and $dp_p/dt < 0$, respectively. In other words, an increase in a specific tax causes the price paid by consumers to increase, the equilibrium quantity to decrease, and the price received by producers to decrease.

Appendix to Chapter 3
More Advanced Topics in Consumer Behavior

In this appendix we present some advanced topics in consumer behavior. In particular, in Section A3.1 we deal with some well-known violations of the axioms of consumer behavior, and in Section A3.2 we study several important properties of the ordinal utility function.

A3.1 Violations of the Axioms of Consumer Behavior[1]

In Chapter 3 we derived the consumer's indifference map and established its properties on the basis of the three axioms of consumer behavior enumerated in Section 3.2 plus the assumption of convexity. Unfortunately, the premises of that model could be violated in reality. Here we study briefly the consequences of such violations. In the remainder of the book we return to the basic model of Chapter 3. The student who is not interested in exceptional cases may omit the following discussion.

Thick Indifference Curves

In real life, the typical consumer is unable to distinguish between quantities that differ only by a small amount. For instance, the consumer does not usually distinguish between 1.00005 and 1.00006 gallons of milk (or gasoline). In such cases, *neighboring indifference curves are equally preferable* (or attractive) even though one is a bit "higher" than the other. In economic jargon, this is expressed by saying that indifference curves are "thick," that is, they are no longer curves with zero thickness; rather, they are narrow corridors, violating the axioms of transitivity and nonsatiation as well as the property of nonintersection.

Satiation and Closed Indifference Curves

Suppose that the consumer can become sated with commodities X and Y. In particular, suppose that x_s and y_s are the satiation quantities (or maximal desired quantities) of X and Y, respectively. Quantities larger than x_s and y_s are positive nuisance to the consumer. Under these circumstances, the indifference curves become "closed," as shown in Figure A3.1.

Point B, whose coordinates give the satiation quantities x_s and y_s, is known as the "bliss point" (or saturation point). The indifference curves now take the shape of closed contours around bliss point B. "Inner" indifference curves correspond to "higher" indifference curves; that is, utility (or satisfaction) increases when the consumer moves from an "outer" to an "inner" indifference curve. For instance, utility is higher along $K'L'M'N'$ than along $KLMN$.

The perpendicular lines through B divide the commodity space into four regions. In region I, the consumer is not sated in either commodity, and the indifference curves slope downward with regular convexity. The conventional indifference curves that we studied in Chapter 3 actually correspond to those portions of the "closed" indifference curves that lie in region I.

In regions II and IV the consumer is sated in one of the two commodities, and the indifference curves have *positive* slope. For instance, in region II the consumer desires more of X but less of Y. Hence, for any (unwanted) addition to her overabundant Y, he must be compensated with some extra amount of X; that is, the indifference curve must be upward sloping, as illustrated by the stretch going from K to N (or K' to N'). A similar argument can be made for region IV.

Incidentally, region IV illustrates the indifference map used in *portfolio choice theory*. In selecting the optimal composition of her portfolio, an investor must balance the *mean* asset return (y) against the riskiness (x) of the return. The investor is willing to accept a higher risk but only in exchange for a higher mean asset return.

Finally, in region III the consumer is sated in both commodities. The indifference curves regain their *negative* slope: For any addition to her unwanted X, the consumer must be compensated with a *reduction* in her unwanted Y, as illustrated by the

[1]This section may be read after Section 3.3.

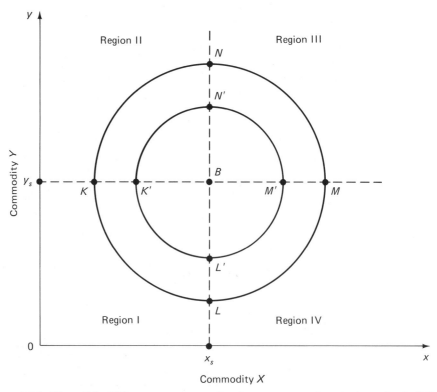

Figure A3.1 *Closed indifference curves.* In the presence of satiation, the indifference curves become "closed" contours around bliss point B. The perpendicular lines through B divide the commodity space into four regions. The conventional indifference curves correspond to those portions of the "closed" curves that lie in region I. In regions II and IV the consumer is sated in one of the two commodities, and the indifference curves have a *positive* slope. In region III the consumer is sated in both commodities, and the indifference curves have a negative slope but the wrong convexity. Utility (or satisfaction) is higher along "inner" indifference curve $K'L'M'N'$ than along "outer" indifference curve $KLMN$.

stretch going from N to M (or N' to M'). However, the indifference curves are no longer convex to the origin.

Lexicographic Ordering

In Chapter 3 we took it for granted that indifference curves do *exist*. Now we wish to offer a counterexample, known as *lexicographic ordering,* for which no such curves exist.

Suppose that commodity X (say, food) is immeasurably more important to the consumer than Y (say, entertainment). Between any two commodity bundles, the consumer always prefers that bundle that has more X, irrespective of the amount of Y contained in each of them. If the two bundles contain the same amount of X, then the consumer prefers that bundle that has more Y. This type of ranking is known as "lexicographic" because it uses a ranking criterion that is similar to that followed in ordering words in a dictionary or "lexicon."

When the ordering is lexicographic there can be no indifference curves because there cannot exist two distinct points indifferent to each other. Consider, for instance, point (or bundle) $A = (x_0, y_0)$ in Figure A3.2. Vertical line L through point

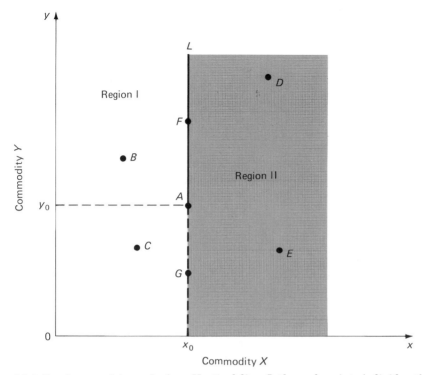

Figure A3.2 Lexicographic ordering. Vertical line L through point A divides the commodity space into two regions. Points in region I, such as B and C, and on vertical line L below A, such as G, are inferior to A. On the other hand, points in shaded region II, such as D and E, and on vertical line L above A, such as F, are superior to A. Hence there are no points that are indifferent to A, and thus no indifference curve can be drawn through A.

A divides the commodity space into two regions. Points in region I, such as B and C, are inferior to A because they contain less X. Similarly, points in shaded region II, such as D and E, are superior to A because they contain more X. Points on vertical line L have the same amount of X. Hence points on L above A, such as F, are superior to A because they contain more Y. Points on L below A, such as G, are inferior to A because they contain less Y. We therefore conclude that there are no points that are indifferent to A; thus no indifference curve can be drawn through A. A similar argument can be applied to each and every point in the commodity space.

In the remainder of this book we ignore the case of lexicographic ordering.

A3.2 The Ordinal Utility Function[2]

As we noted in Section A3.5, we can use an *ordinal* utility function $U = U(x, y)$ to represent the consumer's preference ranking. The following restrictions are usually imposed on this function:

1. The function $U = U(x, y)$ selected must be *consistent with the consumer's preference ranking*.
2. In general, the function $U = U(x, y)$ must be *monotonically increasing*. (This

---

[2]This section may be read after Section 3.5.

restriction is a direct consequence of the axiom of nonsatiation.) Accordingly, the partial derivatives U_x and U_y must be positive.

3. The function $U = U(x, y)$ is *quasiconcave*. This means that the function $U = U(x, y)$ corresponds to (or can be represented by) a family of indifference curves that are convex to the origin.

4. The function $U = U(x, y)$ is *continuous* and *twice differentiable*.

As we noted in Chapter 3, the function $U = U(x, y)$ cannot be uniquely specified. Indeed, any *monotonic transformation* of $U = U(x, y)$ is an acceptable utility function. For instance, the function $V = F(U)$, where $F' \equiv dF/dU > 0$, can describe the consumer's preference ranking as accurately as the original function $U = U(x, y)$.

Note that a "transformation" is equivalent to a replacement of one set of numbers (associated with the family of indifference curves) by another. A "monotonic" transformation implies that a higher number in the old set is always replaced by a higher number in the new set.

Accordingly, *a monotonic transformation of the utility function necessarily leaves the indifference curves unchanged.* (Always remember that the monotonic transformation changes only the numbering of the indifference curves.) As an illustration, consider the function $U = xy$ and the transformation $V = U^2 = (xy)^2$. The indifference curve that corresponds to $U = 5$ is obviously given by the equation $5 = xy$. The same indifference curve corresponds to $V = 25$ and is given by the equation $25 = (xy)^2$, or $5 = xy$.

A consequence of the above conclusion is the important proposition that *the marginal rate of substitution is invariant to a monotonic transformation,* even though marginal utility is not. (This includes the marginal utility of income λ discussed in the Appendix to Chapter 4.) Consider an indifference curve described by the equation

$$\overline{U} = U(x, y) \tag{A3.1}$$

where $\overline{U}$ is a fixed number. Take the total differential of (A3.1) and then solve for $-dy/dx$ to obtain

$$0 = U_x \cdot dx + U_y \cdot dy \tag{A3.2}$$

$$MRS_{xy} = -\frac{dy}{dx} = \frac{U_x}{U_y} \tag{A3.3}$$

Accordingly, *the marginal rate of substitution is equal to the ratio of marginal utilities.*

Consider now the transformation

$$V = F(U) = F[U(x, y)] \tag{A3.4}$$

Set $V = \overline{V}$, take the total differential, and then solve for $-dy/dx$ to obtain

$$0 = F' \cdot U_x \cdot dx + F' \cdot U_y \cdot dy \tag{A3.5}$$

$$MRS_{xy} = -\frac{dy}{dx} = \left(F' \cdot \frac{U_x}{F'} \cdot U_y \right) = \frac{U_x}{U_y} \tag{A3.6}$$

Equation (A3.6) is exactly the same as equation (A3.3), even though the marginal utilities of X and Y changed from U_x and U_y to $F' \cdot U_x$ and $F' \cdot U_y$, respectively.

We therefore conclude that the marginal rate of substitution is independent of the particular ordinal utility function used. (An important implication of this conclusion is that the demand curves are also independent of the particular ordinal utility function we happen to use.)

We can illustrate this result by pursuing a little further the earlier example where $U = xy$ and $V = U^2 = (xy)^2$. Thus we have

$$MRS_{xy} = \frac{U_x}{U_y} = \frac{y}{x} \tag{A3.3a}$$

$$MRS_{xy} = \frac{V_x}{V_y} = \frac{2xy^2}{2x^2y} = \frac{y}{x} \tag{A3.6a}$$

Appendix to Chapter 4
Utility Maximization and the Income and Substitution Effects

This appendix deals with four topics: (1) the first-order conditions for utility maximization, (2) the derivation and properties of the demand curve, (3) the decomposition of the total price effect into an income effect and a substitution effect, and (4) the Marshallian approach to the law of demand.

A4.1 The General Utility Function[1]

The original form of the cardinal utility model suffered from a severe drawback: It rested on the restrictive assumption that the utilities of the various goods were independent of each other and additive. As we saw in Chapter 3, the additive utility function takes the form

$$U = U_x(x) + U_y(y) \tag{A4.1}$$

where $U_x(x)$ is the total utility derived from the consumption of x units of good X, $U_y(y)$ the total utility derived from the consumption of y units of good Y, and U the aggregate utility.

Francis Y. Edgeworth (1845–1926) was the first economist to remove the untenable assumption of independent and additive utility. Thus, in his *Mathematical Psychics*, Edgeworth introduced the general utility function

$$U = U(x, y) \tag{A4.2}$$

Equation (A4.2) postulates that total utility U depends on the quantities x and y of goods X and Y, respectively, consumed per period of time. However, total utility is no longer the *sum* of the independent utilities obtained separately from x and y.

---

[1]This section may be read together with Section 3.4.

A4.2 Utility Maximization and the Demand Functions[2]

Consider now a consumer who spends all of his fixed income (I) on goods X and Y, which are available at the constant prices p_x and p_y, respectively. We summarize this important piece of information by means of the following *budget equation:*

$$I = p_x \cdot x + p_y \cdot y$$

$$(A4.3)$$
$$(4.1)\,\text{repeated}$$

In other words, the consumer's expenditure on the two goods, $p_x \cdot x + p_y \cdot y$, equals (and in general, cannot exceed) his fixed income I.

The object of the consumer is to buy those quantities of goods X and Y (i.e., x and y) that maximize his utility U, as given by equation (A4.2), subject to budget equation (A4.3). For this constrained maximization problem, we use the classical method of *Lagrange multipliers.* (*Note:* To avoid repetition, we employ the general utility function only; the first-order conditions derived below apply to the additive utility function as well.)

Form the *Lagrangian function*

$$Z = U(x,y) + \lambda(I - p_x \cdot x - p_y \cdot y)$$

$$(A4.4)$$

where λ is an undetermined *Lagrange multiplier.* For utility maximization, it is required that the following partial derivatives be zero:

$$\frac{\partial Z}{\partial x} = \frac{\partial U}{\partial x} - \lambda p_x = 0$$

$$(A4.5)$$

$$\frac{\partial Z}{\partial y} = \frac{\partial U}{\partial y} - \lambda p_y = 0$$

$$(A4.6)$$

$$\frac{\partial Z}{\partial \lambda} = I - p_x \cdot x - p_y \cdot y = 0$$

$$(A4.7)$$

Equation (A4.7) coincides with budget equation (A4.3).

Combining equations (A4.5) and (A4.6) and noting that $\partial U/\partial x = MU_x$, $\partial U/\partial y = MU_y$, we obtain the *equimarginal rule:*

$$\frac{MU_x}{p_x} = \frac{MU_y}{p_y} = \lambda$$

$$(A4.8)$$
$$(4.4)\,\text{repeated}$$

As it turns out, the Lagrange multiplier (λ) gives the marginal utility of income, that is, the increase in maximum utility obtained from one additional dollar.

Recall from Section 4.2 that equation (A4.8) may also be cast in the following form:

$$MRS_{xy} = \frac{MU_x}{MU_y} = \frac{p_x}{p_y}$$

$$(A4.8)'$$
$$(4.7)\,\text{repeated}$$

To obtain the optimal values of x and y, we must finally solve equations (A4.3)

[2]This section may be read together with Sections 4.1 and 4.2.

and (A4.8) simultaneously. These optimal quantities are, of course, functions of the commodity prices (p_x and p_y) and the consumer's income (I). Thus, in general, we have

$$x = x(p_x, p_y, I) \tag{A4.9}$$

$$y = y(p_x, p_y, I) \tag{A4.10}$$

Equations (A4.9) and (A4.10) can now be recognized as the consumer's demand functions.

As shown in Chapter 4, demand functions (A4.9) and (A4.10) are homogeneous of degree zero with respect to prices and income. Mathematically, this means that equations (A4.9) and (A4.10) satisfy the following condition:

$$x = x(mp_x, mp_y, mI) \tag{A4.11}$$
$$y = y(mp_x, mp_y, mI)$$

where $m > 0$. In other words, multiplying all prices and income by a positive number leaves the quantities demanded unchanged.

Substituting equations (A4.9) and (A4.10) into the utility function, we have

$$U = U[x(p_x, p_y, I), y(p_x, p_y, I)] = F(p_x, p_y, I) \tag{A4.12}$$

The function $F(p_x, p_y, I)$ is known as the *indirect utility function*. It gives the *maximum* utility attained by the consumer for any given prices and income.

For our purposes it is important to note that in the final analysis, the quantities demanded depend on two elements: (1) the price ratio p_x/p_y (and, therefore, the marginal rate of substitution of X for Y), and (2) the indifference curve (or ordinal utility level U) where equilibrium occurs. Thus we can write the demand functions as follows:

$$x = f\left(\frac{p_x}{p_y}, U\right) \tag{A4.13}$$

$$y = g\left(\frac{p_x}{p_y}, U\right) \tag{A4.14}$$

where U is given by equation (A4.12). Equations (A4.13) and (A4.14) are known as the *compensated demand functions*. Although their rigorous development is postponed until Chapter 5 and the Appendix to Chapter 5, we find it convenient to use them in the present analysis of the income and substitution effects.

A4.3 Numerical Illustrations[3]

In this section we clarify the foregoing procedure by means of two numerical illustrations.

Example 1. Consider the following additive utility function:

$$U = (100x - x^2) + (500y - 6y^2) \tag{A4.1a}$$

[3]This section should be read together with Section A4.2.

Taking partial derivatives with respect to x and y and substituting the results into equation (A4.8), we obtain

$$\frac{100 - 2x}{p_x} = \frac{500 - 12y}{p_y} \tag{A4.8a}$$

Equation (A4.8a) is the first-order condition for utility maximization.

To obtain the demand functions, we must now solve equations (A4.3) and (A4.8a) simultaneously, treating p_x, p_y, and I as parameters. Thus we finally obtain

$$x = \frac{12p_x I - 500p_x p_y + 100p_y^2}{12p_x^2 + 2p_y^2} \tag{A4.9a}$$

$$y = \frac{2p_y I - 100p_x p_y + 100\ p_x^2}{12p_x^2 + 2p_y^2} \tag{A4.10a}$$

To determine the precise values of x and y, we must know the prices and the consumer's income. For instance, assuming that $p_x = p_y = \$1$ and $I = \$45$, we find that $x = 10$ and $y = 35$.

Example 2. Consider the following general utility function:

$$U = xy \tag{A4.2a}$$

Taking partial derivatives with respect to x and y and substituting the results into equation (A4.8), we get

$$\frac{y}{p_x} = \frac{x}{p_y} \tag{A4.8b}$$

Solving equations (A4.3) and (A4.8b) simultaneously (treating p_x, p_y, and I as parameters), we finally obtain the following demand functions:

$$x = \frac{I}{2p_x} \tag{A4.9b}$$

$$y = \frac{I}{2p_y} \tag{A4.10b}$$

A4.4 Decomposition of the Total Price Effect

Assume now that the price of Y and income remain constant. Accordingly, we can ignore them and we can rewrite equations (A4.12) to (A4.14) as follows:

$$U = F(p_x) \tag{A4.12$'$}$$

$$x = f(p_x, U) \tag{A4.13$'$}$$

$$y = g(p_x, U) \tag{A4.14$'$}$$

How does a change in p_x affect the quantities demanded (x and y)?

Total differentiation of x and y, as given by (A4.13)′ and (A4.14)′, with respect to p_x leads to

$$\frac{dx}{dp_x} = \left.\frac{\partial x}{\partial p_x}\right|_{U=\bar{U}} + \frac{\partial x}{\partial U}\frac{dU}{dp_x} \tag{A4.15}$$

$$\frac{dy}{dp_x} = \left.\frac{\partial y}{\partial p_x}\right|_{U=\bar{U}} + \frac{\partial y}{\partial U}\frac{dU}{dp_x} \tag{A4.16}$$

[Note that use was made of equation (A4.12)′ as well.] The right-hand side of equation (A4.15) is the sum of two terms. The first term shows the effect of a change in p_x on x, on the assumption that utility U remains constant. That is, the first term is the substitution effect of the price change. The second term shows the effect of a change in p_x on x through the increase in U ("real income"). That is, the second term is the income effect. A similar interpretation holds for equation (A4.16).

A4.5 Evaluation of the Income Effects

We now wish to derive more workable formulas for the income effects. For this purpose we must evaluate the derivatives $\partial x/\partial U$, $\partial y/\partial U$, and dU/dp_x.

First, consider the derivatives $\partial x/\partial U$ and $\partial y/\partial U$. Rewrite them as follows:

$$\frac{\partial x}{\partial U} = \frac{\partial x}{\partial I}\frac{\partial I}{\partial U} \tag{A4.17}$$

$$\frac{\partial y}{\partial U} = \frac{\partial y}{\partial I}\frac{\partial I}{\partial U} \tag{A4.18}$$

Observe that $\partial U/\partial I \equiv \lambda \equiv$ marginal utility of income. Substituting λ into (A4.17) and (A4.18), we get

$$\frac{\partial x}{\partial U} = \frac{\partial x}{\partial I}\frac{1}{\lambda} \tag{A4.17′}$$

$$\frac{\partial y}{\partial U} = \frac{\partial y}{\partial I}\frac{1}{\lambda} \tag{A4.18′}$$

To evaluate the derivative dU/dp_x, begin by differentiating equation (A4.12) with respect to p_x to obtain

$$\frac{dU}{dp_x} = U_x\frac{dx}{dp_x} + U_y\frac{dy}{dp_x} = \frac{U_x}{p_x}\left(p_x\frac{dx}{dp_x} + p_y\frac{dy}{dp_x}\right) \tag{A4.19}$$

where use was made (in the second step) of equation (A4.8).

Further, differentiate the budget equation ($I = p_x x + p_y y$) with respect to p_x, holding p_y and I constant, to obtain

$$p_x \frac{dx}{dp_x} + p_y \frac{dy}{dp_x} = -x \qquad (A4.20)$$

Now substitute equation (A4.20) into (A4.19), and recall that $U_x/p_x = \lambda = $ marginal utility of income. Accordingly,

$$\frac{dU}{dp_x} = -\lambda x \qquad (A4.21)$$

Finally, substitute equations (A4.17)' and (A4.21) into the second term of the right-hand side of equation (A4.15), and simplify, to obtain

$$\text{own income effect} = \frac{\partial x}{\partial U}\frac{dU}{dp_x} = -x\frac{\partial x}{\partial I} \qquad (A4.22)$$

Also, substitute equations (A4.18)' and (A4.21) into the second term of the right-hand side of equation (A4.16), and simplify, to obtain

$$\text{cross income effect} = \frac{\partial y}{\partial U}\frac{dU}{dp_x} = -x\frac{\partial y}{\partial I} \qquad (A4.23)$$

When commodities X and Y are *normal*, the derivatives $\partial x/\partial I$ and $\partial y/\partial I$ are positive and both income effects are *negative* because $-x < 0$. When X (Y) is an *inferior* commodity, $\partial x/\partial I$ ($\partial y/\partial I$) is negative and the own income effect (cross income effect) is *positive*. Finally, if X (Y) is a neutral commodity, $\partial x/\partial I$ ($\partial y/\partial I$) is zero and so is the income effect.

A4.6 Another Numerical Illustration

Consider again the utility function $U = xy$. As shown in Section A4.3, the first-order condition for utility maximization is

$$\frac{y}{x} = \frac{p_x}{p_y} \qquad \begin{array}{l}(A4.24)\\ (A4.8b)\,\text{repeated}\end{array}$$

The demand functions take the form:

$$x = \frac{I}{2p_x} \qquad \begin{array}{l}(A4.25)\\ (A4.9b)\,\text{repeated}\end{array}$$

$$y = \frac{I}{2p_y} \qquad \begin{array}{l}(A4.26)\\ (A4.10b)\,\text{repeated}\end{array}$$

Note that equations (A4.25) and (A4.26) are homogeneous of degree zero with respect to p_x, p_y, and I. Thus

$$\frac{mI}{2mp_x} = \frac{I}{2p_x} = x \tag{A4.11a}$$
$$\frac{mI}{2mp_y} = \frac{I}{2p_y} = y$$

for $m > 0$.

To get the indirect utility function, we substitute (A4.25) and (A4.26) into $U = xy$. Thus

$$U = \frac{I^2}{4p_x p_y} \tag{A4.12a}$$

Solve (A4.12a) for I to get

$$I = 2\sqrt{p_x p_y U} \tag{A4.27}$$

Substitute (A4.27) into (A4.25) and (A4.26) to obtain

$$x = \frac{\sqrt{U}}{\sqrt{p_x/p_y}} \tag{A4.13a}$$

$$y = \sqrt{U\left(\frac{p_x}{p_y}\right)} \tag{A4.14a}$$

Equations (A4.13a) and (A4.14a) are fundamental because they show how x and y are related to the price ratio p_x/p_y and ordinal utility U.

For the remainder of this section we concentrate on the effect of a change in p_x on x only. The total price effect is given by the *total* derivative of (A4.13a) with respect to p_x, but the substitution effect corresponds to the *partial* derivative of (A4.13a) with respect to p_x, holding U (and p_y) constant. Thus

$$\text{substitution effect} = \left.\frac{\partial x}{\partial p_x}\right|_{U=\overline{U}}$$

$$= -\frac{\sqrt{p_y U}}{2p_x\sqrt{p_x}} = -\frac{x}{2p_x} < 0 \tag{A4.28}$$

Note that the substitution effect is negative.

The own income effect corresponds to the partial derivative of (A4.13a) with respect to U times the derivative of U, as given by (A4.12a), with respect to p_x. In other words,

$$\text{own income effect} = \left(\frac{\partial x}{\partial U}\right)\left(\frac{dU}{dp_x}\right)$$

$$= \left(\frac{\sqrt{p_y}}{2\sqrt{p_x U}}\right)\left(-\frac{4p_y I^2}{16p_x^2 p_y^2}\right)$$

$$= -\frac{U\sqrt{p_y}}{2p_x\sqrt{p_x U}} = -\frac{x}{2p_x} < 0 \qquad (A4.22a)$$

[In the second step, we used equation (A4.12a), and in the third step, equation (A4.13a).] Because the income effect is negative, commodity X is normal.

The total price effect is the sum of the substitution effect and the income effect. Thus

$$\text{total price effect} = -\frac{x}{2p_x} - \frac{x}{2p_x} = -\frac{x}{p_x} < 0 \qquad (A4.15a)$$

Note carefully that the total price effect coincides with the derivative of equation (A4.25) with respect to p_x, as it should be. The reader should repeat the exercise for the effect of a change in p_x on y.

A4.7 Generalization to Many Commodities

The preceding analysis can be extended in a straightforward manner to the case of many commodities. Equations (A4.15) and (A4.16) remain valid in the general case where the consumer purchases n commodities because all other prices, besides p_x, remain constant by assumption. Also, equations (A4.22) and (A4.23) hold for the general case as well. The only insignificant difference is that with more commodities, both the parenthetical expression in equation (A4.19) and the left-hand side of equation (A4.20) will have more terms (one for each commodity), but they will continue to be equal. We leave the details as an exercise for the interested reader.

A4.8 The Substitution Effect

We now wish to show that the *substitution effect is always negative* (Slutsky theorem). For this purpose we follow a *revealed preference approach* that does not require the use of complicated mathematics. (For a direct evaluation of the substitution effect, see the references at the end of Chapter 4.)

It is convenient to work directly with the general case of n commodities: $X_1, X_2, \ldots, X_n$. Suppose that at prices $p_a = (p_1, p_2, \ldots, p_n)$ the consumer purchases the quantities $q_a = (x_1, x_2, \ldots, x_n)$. Suppose, further, that when p_1 changes to $p_1 + dp_1$, with all other prices held constant but with income changed appropriately so as to leave the consumer on the same "indifference hypersurface" (i.e., with the income effect removed), the consumer changes his purchases to the quantities $q_b = (x_1 + dx_1, x_2 + dx_2, \ldots, x_n + dx_n)$. Accordingly, the changes $dx_1, dx_2, \ldots, dx_n$ represent the pure substitution effects of the change in p_1. To prove the Slutsky theorem, we must show that $dp_1 \cdot dx_1 < 0$; that is, we must show that the changes dp_1 and dx_1 have opposite signs.

By construction, the bundles q_a and q_b lie on the same "indifference hypersurface." Because of the assumed strict convexity, each of these bundles is *uniquely* chosen: q_a at p_a, and q_b at $p_b = (p_1 + dp_1, p_2, p_3, \ldots, p_n)$. This means that at p_a only bundle q_a (on the initial hypersurface) is available; that is, any other bundle on the initial hypersurface, including q_b, must cost more than q_a (or q_b lies in the unattainable set). In other words,

$$p_a q_b > p_a q_a \tag{A4.29}$$

[Note that $p_a q_a = p_1 x_1 + p_2 x_2 + \cdots + p_n x_n$, and $p_a q_b = p_1(x_1 + dx_1) + p_2(x_2 + dx_2) + \cdots + p_n(x_n + dx_n)$.]

Similarly, at p_b (when q_b is chosen), q_a is not available; that is, at p_b, q_a costs more than q_b. In other words,

$$p_b q_b < p_b q_a \tag{A4.30}$$

Now subtract (A4.29) from (A4.30) to obtain

$$p_b q_b - p_a q_b < p_b q_a - p_a q_a$$

or

$$(p_b - p_a)q_b < (p_b - p_a)q_a$$

or

$$(p_b - p_a)(q_b - q_a) < 0$$

or

$$dp_1 \cdot dx_1 < 0 \tag{A4.31}$$

[Note that $p_b - p_a = (dp_1, 0, 0, \ldots, 0)$, $q_b - q_a = (dx_1, dx_2, \ldots, dx_n)$, and $(p_b - p_a)(q_b - q_a) = (dp_1 \cdot dx_1 + 0 \cdot dx_2 + \cdots + 0 \cdot dx_n) = dp_1 \cdot dx_1$.] This completes the proof of the Slutsky theorem.

A4.9 Elasticity Conditions

The structure of the model of consumer behavior imposes several restrictions on the price and income elasticities of the consumer's demand functions. The purpose of this section is to summarize these restrictions (or conditions). Note that in this section all price elasticities are given in their natural, algebraic values, not in absolute terms.

The Homogeneity Identity

As pointed out in Section A4.2, the demand function for a commodity, say, X, satisfies the following equation:

$$x = x(p_x, p_y, I) = x(mp_x, mp_y, mI) \tag{A4.32}$$

where $m > 0$. Differentiating equation (A4.32) totally with respect to m, we obtain

$$\frac{dx}{dm} = \frac{\partial x}{\partial p_x} p_x + \frac{\partial x}{\partial p_y} p_y + \frac{\partial x}{\partial I} I$$

Observing that $dx/dm = 0$ and dividing both sides by x, we get the following fundamental identity:

$$e_{xp_x} + e_{xp_y} + e_{xI} = 0 \tag{A4.33}$$

where $e_{xp_x} = (\partial x/\partial p_x)(p_x/x)$, $e_{xp_y} = (\partial x/\partial p_y)(p_y/x)$, and $e_{xI} = (\partial x/\partial I)(I/x)$.

In this book, equation (A4.33) is referred to as the *homogeneity identity*. There is one homogeneity identity for each commodity. In the general case of many commodities, equation (A4.33) has an obvious generalization.

The Price Elasticity Identity

Substitute demand functions (A4.9) and (A4.10) into the budget equation ($p_x \cdot x + p_y \cdot y = I$) to obtain

$$p_x \cdot x(p_x, p_y, I) + p_y \cdot y(p_x, p_y, I) = I \tag{A4.34}$$

Differentiate equation (A4.34) with respect to a price, say, p_x, holding all other prices and money income constant, to get

$$x + p_x \frac{\partial x}{\partial p_x} + p_y \frac{\partial y}{\partial p_x} = 0$$

Rearrange the last equation as follows:

$$x \left(1 + \frac{p_x}{x}\frac{\partial x}{\partial p_x}\right) + \frac{p_y y}{p_x}\left(\frac{p_x}{y}\frac{\partial y}{\partial p_x}\right) = 0$$

Finally, multiply both sides by p_x/I to obtain the *price elasticity identity*:

$$s_x(1 + e_{xp_x}) + s_y e_{yp_x} = 0 \tag{A4.35}$$

where $s_x = (p_x \cdot x/I)$ = share of income spent on X, $s_y = (p_y \cdot y/I)$ = share of income spent on Y, and $e_{yp_x} = (\partial y/\partial p_x)(p_x/y)$.

In Section 4.8 we studied a relationship between the elasticities e_{xp_x} and e_{yp_x} in relation to the shape of the price consumption curve. Equation (A4.35) provides a rigorous foundation for that relationship. Solve equation (A4.35) for e_{yp_x} to obtain

$$e_{yp_x} = -\frac{s_x}{s_y}(1 + e_{xp_x}) \tag{A4.35}'$$

It must now be clear that when the demand for commodity X is elastic ($e_{xp_x} < -1$), inelastic ($-1 < e_{xp_x} < 0$), or unit elastic ($e_{xp_x} = -1$), a reduction in p_x causes the demand for Y to fall ($e_{yp_x} > 0$), rise ($e_{yp_x} < 0$), or remain the same ($e_{yp_x} = 0$), respectively. Equation (A4.35) has an obvious generalization in the presence of many commodities.

The Income Elasticity Identity

Return now to equation (A4.34) and differentiate it with respect to I, holding all prices constant, to obtain

$$p_x \cdot \frac{\partial x}{\partial I} + p_y \frac{\partial y}{\partial I} = 1$$

Rearrange this equation as follows:

$$p_x \frac{x}{I}\left(\frac{I}{x}\frac{\partial x}{\partial I}\right) + p_y \frac{y}{I}\left(\frac{I}{y}\frac{\partial y}{\partial I}\right) = 1$$

or

$$s_x e_{xI} + s_y e_{yI} = 1 \tag{A4.36}$$

where $e_{yI} = (I/y)(\partial y/\partial I)$. Equation (A4.36) is known as the *income elasticity identity;* it generalizes easily to the case of many commodities.

The Slutsky Equations

In the same way that we can decompose the total price effect into a substitution effect and an income effect, we can also decompose the price elasticity into a *compensated price elasticity* (ϵ) based on the substitution effect and an *income elasticity* based on the income effect. Substitute equation (A4.22) into equation (A4.15) to obtain

$$\frac{dx}{dp_x} = \left.\frac{\partial x}{\partial p_x}\right|_{U=\bar{U}} - x\frac{dx}{dI} \tag{A4.37}$$

Multiply both sides of equation (A4.37) by p_x/x and rearrange it as follows:

$$\frac{p_x}{x}\frac{dx}{dp_x} = \left.\frac{p_x}{x}\frac{\partial x}{\partial p_x}\right|_{U=\bar{U}} - \frac{p_x}{x}x\left(\frac{x}{I}\right)\left(\frac{I}{x}\frac{dx}{dI}\right)$$

This equation reduces to

$$e_{xp_x} = \epsilon_{xp_x} - s_x e_{xI} \tag{A4.38}$$

where

$$\epsilon_{xp_x} = \left.\frac{p_x}{x}\frac{\partial x}{\partial p_x}\right|_{U=\bar{U}} = \text{compensated price elasticity}$$

There is an identity like (A4.38) for each commodity. By switching the roles of commodities X and Y (and thus the subscripts x and y) in the calculations above, we immediately derive the corresponding identity for commodity Y:

$$e_{yp_y} = \epsilon_{yp_y} - s_y e_{yI} \tag{A4.39}$$

where

$$\epsilon_{yp_y} = \frac{p_y}{y} \frac{\partial y}{\partial p_y}\bigg|_{U=\overline{U}}$$

We can also derive similar identities for the cross elasticities e_{xp_y} and e_{yp_x}. Substitute equation (A4.23) into equation (A4.16) to obtain

$$\frac{dy}{dp_x} = \frac{\partial y}{\partial p_x}\bigg|_{U=\overline{U}} - x\frac{dy}{dI}$$

Multiplying both sides of the last equation by p_x/y and rearranging, we finally get

$$e_{yp_x} = \epsilon_{yp_x} - s_x e_{yI} \tag{A4.40}$$

where

$$\epsilon_{yp_x} = \frac{p_x}{x} \frac{\partial y}{\partial p_y}\bigg|_{U=\overline{U}}$$

By symmetry, we also have

$$e_{xp_y} = \epsilon_{xp_y} - s_y e_{xI} \tag{A4.41}$$

where

$$\epsilon_{xp_y} = \frac{p_y}{x} \frac{\partial x}{\partial p_y}\bigg|_{U=\overline{U}}$$

In this book we refer to equations (A4.38) to (A4.41) as the *Slutsky identities*. These identities remain valid for the general case of many commodities.

The Symmetry of the Substitution Effect

We finally wish to make explicit an important property of the substitution effect that is not at all obvious from the graphical analysis of Chapter 4. This property, known as the *symmetry of the substitution effect*, takes the form

$$s_x \epsilon_{xp_y} = s_y \epsilon_{yp_x} \tag{A4.42}$$

Equation (A4.42) is equivalent to

$$\left.\frac{\partial x}{\partial p_y}\right|_{U=\overline{U}} = \left.\frac{\partial y}{\partial p_x}\right|_{U=\overline{U}} \tag{A4.43}$$

To obtain (A4.43) from (A4.42), merely substitute the definitions of s_x, s_y, ϵ_{xp_y}, and ϵ_{yp_x} into (A4.42) and simplify.

To prove identity (A4.42), we make use of the various identities we developed in this section. The proof is straightforward:

$$s_y \epsilon_{yp_x} = s_y(e_{yp_x} + s_x e_{yI}) \qquad\qquad\qquad\qquad \text{[by identity (A4.40)]}$$

$$= s_y e_{yp_x} + s_x (1 - s_x e_{xI}) \qquad\qquad\qquad \text{[by identity (A4.36)]}$$

$$= -s_x(1 + e_{xp_x}) + s_x(1 - s_x e_{xI}) \qquad\qquad \text{[by identity (A4.35)]}$$

$$= -s_x(1 - e_{xp_y} - e_{xI}) + s_x(1 - s_x e_{xI}) \qquad \text{[by identity (A4.33)]}$$

$$= s_x[e_{xp_y} + (1 - s_x)e_{xI}] \qquad\qquad\qquad \text{(by simplification and regrouping)}$$

$$= s_x(e_{xp_y} + s_y e_{xI}) \qquad\qquad\qquad\qquad \text{(because } s_x + s_y = 1\text{)}$$

$$= s_x \epsilon_{xp_y} \qquad\qquad\qquad\qquad\qquad\qquad \text{[by identity (A4.41)]}$$

This completes the proof of identity (A4.42).

A4.10 **The Marshallian Approach to the Law of Demand**

Marshall was virtually the first economist after Walras to derive the consumer's demand curve from the utility function. Marshall's approach is deceptively simple. Indeed, the subtlety of the Marshallian approach has caused a lot of controversy in the economic literature. Today the general belief is that Marshall neglected the unreliable income effect.

Marshall uses very effectively the concept of *marginal utility of money* (or income). This is the increase in total utility that results from the addition of one extra "dollar" to the consumer's income (or total expenditure). Marshall then argues correctly that the consumer maximizes his utility by increasing his purchases of any good up to the point where the marginal utility of the good is equal to its price times the marginal utility of money. Accordingly, in equilibrium the marginal utilities of the commodities bought by the consumer must be proportional to their prices, with the marginal utility of money being the common factor of proportionality.

For instance, in the case of two goods, X and Y, the consumer's purchases satisfy the following conditions:

$$MU_x = p_x \cdot \lambda \tag{A4.44}$$

$$MU_y = p_y \cdot \lambda \tag{A4.45}$$

where λ is the marginal utility of money. Note that these equations follow from equation (A4.8).

To establish the law of demand for some commodity, say X, *Marshall assumes that the marginal utility of money is constant.* He knows that his procedure is not entirely correct, but he justifies it by saying that the expenditure on any one good, such as tea, is only a small part of the consumer's total expenditure; and any change in the marginal utility of money is of a second order of magnitude, and, therefore, can be neglected.

The assumption of a constant marginal utility of money essentially means that *Marshall ignored the income effect.* We can see this as follows. Assume that $p_x =$ \$2 and that the consumer purchases 10 units of X. If we further assume that the constant marginal utility of money is 4 utils, we can infer that the marginal utility of the tenth unit of X is equal to 8 utils (i.e., $MU_x = \lambda \cdot p_x = 4 \cdot 2 = 8$). Suppose now that the consumer's income increases either because of a pay increase or because of the "income bonus" made available by a reduction in the price of X. Will the consumer increase his purchases of X? As long as the marginal utility of money remains constant at 4 utils, he will not. Thus, if both λ and p_x remain constant, the consumer must continue to consume the same amount of X because the marginal utility of X must continue to be equal to 8 utils (i.e., $\lambda \cdot p_x = 4 \cdot 2 = 8$).

Finally, turn to the part of Marshall's argument where he establishes the law of demand. For this purpose he concentrates on a single commodity, say, X. Given the price of X, say, p_x^0, and the marginal utility of money (λ), the consumer purchases a certain amount of X, say, x_0, such that the marginal utility of the last unit of X, say, MU_{x_0}, is equal to the marginal utility of money times the price of X; that is, $MU_{x_0} = \lambda \cdot p_x^0$. Suppose now that the price of X falls from p_x^0 to p_x^1. How will the consumer change his consumption of X?

Immediately after the reduction in the price of X, the consumer faces the inequality $MU_{x_0} > \lambda \cdot p_x^1$ because the marginal utility of money remains constant by assumption. Accordingly, the initial volume of purchases (i.e., x_0) is no longer optimal. To restore optimality, the consumer must adjust his purchases of X. In particular, *because of the law of diminishing marginal utility,* the consumer must *increase* his purchases of X. Indeed, he must continue to increase his purchases of X until the marginal utility of X becomes equal to the lower value $\lambda \cdot p_x^1$. Suppose that this happens at the larger quantity x_1, so that $MU_{x_1} = \lambda \cdot p_x^1$. We therefore conclude that as the price of X falls, the consumer increases his volume of purchases of X (i.e., $x_1 > x_0$).

In summary, the constancy of the marginal utility of money means that commodity X is *neutral.* As we know, the *income effect of a neutral commodity is zero.* Consequently, Marshall ingeniously removed the unreliable income effect and showed that the demand curve must slope downward because of the systematic and predictable substitution effect.

Appendix to Chapter 5
Compensated Demand Functions, Complementarity, and the Neumann–Morgenstern Theorem

This appendix deals with three topics: (1) the formal derivation of compensated demand functions (Section A5.1), (2) the various definitions of complementarity (Section A5.2), and (3) the Neumann–Morgenstern theorem (Section A5.3).

A5.1 **Compensated Demand Functions**[1]

Formally, we can obtain the compensated demand function that corresponds to a fixed level of ordinal utility, say $\overline{U}$, by merely *minimizing* the consumer's expenditure on commodities X and Y subject to the constraint that utility is at the fixed level $\overline{U}$. In other words, we must minimize $p_x \cdot x + p_y \cdot y$, subject to $U(x, y) = \overline{U}$.

Form the Lagrangian function

$$Z = p_x \cdot x + p_y \cdot y + \gamma[\overline{U} - U(x, y)] \tag{A5.1}$$

where γ is an undetermined Lagrange multiplier. For expenditure minimization, it is required that the following partial derivatives be zero:

$$\frac{\partial Z}{\partial x} = p_x - \gamma \frac{\partial U}{\partial x} = 0 \tag{A5.2}$$

$$\frac{\partial Z}{\partial y} = p_y - \gamma \frac{\partial U}{\partial y} = 0 \tag{A5.3}$$

$$\frac{\partial Z}{\partial \gamma} = \overline{U} - U(x, y) = 0 \tag{A5.4}$$

Equation (A5.4) coincides, of course, with the constraint $U(x, y) = \overline{U}$.

Combining equations (A5.2) and (A5.3), we obtain

$$MRS_{xy} = \frac{\partial U/\partial x}{\partial U/\partial y} = \frac{p_x}{p_y} \tag{A5.5}$$

which is identical to the first-order utility-maximization condition.

To obtain the compensated demand functions for X and Y, we must solve equations (A5.4) and (A5.5) simultaneously, as shown below. Thus, in general, we have

$$x = x\left(\frac{p_x}{p_y}, \overline{U}\right) \tag{A5.6}$$

$$y = y\left(\frac{p_y}{p_x}, \overline{U}\right) \tag{A5.7}$$

Equations (A5.6) and (A5.7) are the compensated demand equations. They are homogeneous of degree zero with respect to prices (only).

Example. Consider the utility function $U = x \cdot y$. Suppose that we wish to derive the compensated demand curves corresponding to the fixed utility level $\overline{U} = 100$. Accordingly, equation (A5.4) now takes the form

$$x \cdot y = 100 \tag{A5.4a}$$

Similarly, by taking the partial derivatives of the utility function $U = x \cdot y$ and substituting the results into equation (A5.5), we obtain

---

[1]This section may be read together with Section 5.2.

$$\frac{y}{x} = \frac{p_x}{p_y} \tag{A5.5a}$$

Finally, solving equations (A5.4a) and (A5.5a) simultaneously for x and y, while treating p_x and p_y as parameters, we obtain the following compensated demand functions:

$$x = 10 \cdot \sqrt{\frac{p_y}{p_x}} \tag{A5.6a}$$

$$y = 10 \cdot \sqrt{\frac{p_x}{p_y}} \tag{A5.7a}$$

Accordingly, both x and y depend on the price ratio p_x/p_y only; that is, equations (A5.6a) and (A5.7a) are homogeneous of degree zero with respect to p_x and p_y.

A5.2 Complementarity[2]

As we saw in Section 2.3, two commodities that basically satisfy the same need, and one can be *substituted* for the other, are called *substitutes*. For instance, the consumer can eat *either* beef *or* fish, or she can drink *either* coffee *or* tea. Thus beef and fish are substitutes, and so are coffee and tea.

On the other hand, two commodities that tend to be used *jointly* in the satisfaction of some need are called *complements*. For instance, the consumer uses coffee *and* sugar, or tennis rackets *and* tennis balls, *together*. Accordingly, coffee and sugar are complements, and so are tennis rackets and tennis balls.

Below we review briefly three alternative definitions of substitutability and complementarity that attempt to make the foregoing ideas rigorous.

The Cross-Elasticities Definition

The cross-elasticities definition is the one we used in Section 2.3. According to this definition, two commodities are said to be *substitutes* when an increase in the price of one causes the quantity demanded of the other to go up. On the other hand, if a rise in the price of one causes the quantity demanded of the other to decrease, the two commodities are said to be *complements*. Finally, when a rise in the price of one has no effect on the quantity demanded of the other, the two commodities are said to be *independent*.

The cross-elasticities definition of complementarity and substitutability, often called the *gross* definition to emphasize that the *income effect* is not eliminated, suffers from a severe drawback: It can be *asymmetric*. For instance, consider two commodities, X and Y, only. Suppose that at the current prices, the demand for X is relatively *inelastic,* while the demand for Y is relatively *elastic.* A rise in the price of X causes total expenditure on X to go up, implying a *reduction* in the quantity demanded of Y. On this showing, we must classify X and Y as "complements." However, a rise in the price of Y (whose demand is relatively elastic) causes total expenditure on Y to fall, implying an *increase* in the quantity demanded of X. Hence we must now conclude that X and Y are "substitutes."

The above argument actually points to another drawback of the cross-elasticities

---

[2]This section may be read after Section 5.2.

definition. This second drawback concerns the arbitrary influence of the elasticity of demand. Thus when the price of a commodity, say X, goes up, the consumer increases or decreases his expenditure on X (and thus he decreases or increases his expenditure on all other commodities) according to whether the demand for X is inelastic or elastic, respectively. Consequently, when the demand for X is inelastic, at least some other commodities *must be* complements of X, and when the demand for X is elastic, at least some other commodities must be substitutes of X. Surely, this kind of complementarity or substitutability is rather arbitrary.

The Hicksian Definition

The cross-elasticity definition focuses on the *total effect* of a price change, which includes both the substitution effect and the income effect. As we saw in Chapter 4, however, the income effect is unreliable and could interfere with the classification of commodities into complements and substitutes. For instance, a significant drop in the price of beef might induce a consumer to increase his consumption of both beef *and* fish, because of the increase in real income. As a result, we may erroneously classify beef and fish as complements.

The Hicksian definition focuses instead on the substitution effect only. Hicks continues to use the cross-elasticity criterion, but after he replaces the ordinary demand functions by the corresponding income-compensated demand functions.

A drawback of the Hicksian definition is that it exhibits a bias toward substitutability. For instance, when there are two commodities only, they *must* be substitutes. Similarly, when there are many commodities, there must always be substitutes, while no such requirement exists for complements. Nevertheless, the Hicksian definition is symmetrical (when X is a substitute of Y, then Y must be a substitute of X also) because of the fundamental symmetry of the substitution effect.

To emphasize the basic difference between the Hicksian definition and the cross-elasticities definition, economists often use the terms *gross* substitutes (or complements) versus *net* substitutes (or complements). The word "gross" means that the income effect is *not* removed, and the classification is based on the *total* price effect. Similarly, the word "net" means that the income effect is removed, and the classification is based on the substitution effect only.

The Pareto–Edgeworth–Fisher Definition

The Pareto–Edgeworth–Fisher definition of complementarity and substitutability is based on the existence of a cardinal utility function. Its motivation can be seen from the following example. When I increase my consumption of (black) coffee only by just one cup, my utility increases by, say, ΔU_c. Alternatively, when I increase my consumption of sugar only by one teaspoon, my utility increases by, say, ΔU_s. But when I increase simultaneously my consumption of coffee by one cup and my consumption of sugar by one teaspoon, my utility increases by, say, ΔU_{cs}. As it turns out, $\Delta U_{cs} > \Delta U_c + \Delta U_s$, for I do like my coffee sweet. Because the benefit of coffee and sugar together is larger than the sum of their separate benefits, I call coffee and sugar complements.

When I perform the above experiment with coffee and tea, however, I find out that the benefit from both together is definitely smaller than the sum of their separate benefits. For this reason, I regard coffee and tea as substitutes.

The Pareto–Edgeworth–Fisher definition formalizes the above ideas as follows. Consider two commodities, X and Y. When an increase in the consumption of one raises the marginal utility of the other, that is, when $\partial^2 U/\partial x\, \partial y = \partial^2 U/\partial y\, \partial x > 0$, then X and Y are complements. On the other hand, when an increase in the consumption of one lowers the marginal utility of the other, that is, when $\partial^2 U/\partial x\, \partial y =$

$\partial^2 U/\partial y \, \partial x < 0$, then X and Y are substitutes. Finally, if an increase in the consumption of one leaves the marginal utility of the other unchanged, that is, if

$$\frac{\partial^2 U}{\partial x \, \partial y} = \frac{\partial^2 U}{\partial y \, \partial x} = 0$$

then X and Y are independent.

Even though the Pareto–Edgeworth–Fisher definition is symmetrical, it suffers from a most severe drawback: It does not always remain invariant under a monotonic transformation of the utility function. For instance, suppose that $U = U(x, y)$, and $V = V(U)$, where $dV/dU > 0$. The marginal utility of X is given by

$$\frac{\partial V}{\partial x} = \frac{dV}{dU} \frac{\partial U}{\partial x} \tag{A5.8}$$

Taking the partial derivative of (A5.8) with respect to y, we obtain

$$\frac{\partial^2 V}{\partial x \, \partial y} = \frac{\partial^2 V}{\partial y \, \partial x} = \frac{dV}{dU} \cdot \frac{\partial^2 U}{\partial x \, \partial y} + \frac{d^2 V}{dU^2} \cdot \frac{\partial U}{\partial x} \cdot \frac{\partial U}{\partial y} \tag{A5.9}$$

It is evident that by a proper choice of the arbitrary term d^2V/dU^2, the sign of $\partial^2 V/\partial x \, \partial y$ can be made to differ from that of $\partial^2 U/\partial x \, \partial y$. Only in the special case of a linear transformation, that is, when $V = a + bU$, and thus $\partial^2 V/\partial U^2 = 0$, can we be sure that the sign of the cross partial derivative $\partial^2 U/\partial x \, \partial y$ remains invariant to a change in the utility function.

A5.3 The Neumann–Morgenstern Theorem[3]

We now turn to the basic Neumann–Morgenstern theorem on expected utility. To facilitate our discussion, we shall use the symbol $L_i = (\Pi_i, A, B)$ to indicate a lottery ticket, L_i, which offers prize A with probability Π_i, and prize B with probability $1 - \Pi_i$, where $0 \le \Pi_i \le 1$.

The Axioms of the Neumann–Morgenstern Theory

The Neumann–Morgenstern theory is based on the following six axioms (or assumptions):

1. *Axiom of comparison:* For any two alternative prizes, say A and B, the consumer must be able to compare them and state unequivocally one, and only one, of the following results: (a) he prefers A to B, (b) he prefers B to A, or (c) he is indifferent between A and B.
2. *Axiom of transitivity:* If the consumer prefers A to B and B to C, he must also prefer A to C. The same relationship holds also for indifference.
3. *Axiom of continuity:* Assume that the consumer prefers A to B and B to C. Then there must exist some probability Π, $0 < \Pi < 1$, such that the consumer is indifferent between having B with certainty and lottery ticket $L = (\Pi, A, C)$.
4. *Axiom of independence:* Assume that the consumer is indifferent between A

---

[3]This section may be read together with Section 5.6.

and B. Then he must also be indifferent between lottery tickets $L_1 = (\Pi, A, C)$ and $L_2 = (\Pi, B, C)$, where C is any alternative and Π is any probability. On the other hand, if he prefers A to B, he must also prefer L_1 to L_2, for any probability Π.

5. *Axiom of unequal probabilities:* Assume again that the consumer prefers A to B. Then he also prefers lottery ticket $L_1 = (\Pi_1, A, B)$ to lottery ticket $L_2 = (\Pi_2, A, B)$ if, and only if, $\Pi_1 > \Pi_2$.

6. *Axiom of compound lotteries:* Consider two simple lottery tickets: $L_a = (\Pi_a, A, B)$ and $L_b = (\Pi_b, A, B)$. Form the compound lottery $L_1 = (\Pi_1, L_a, L_b)$, *in which the prizes are the simple lottery tickets L_a and L_b.* Then the consumer is indifferent between the compound lottery ticket, $L_1 = (\Pi_1, L_a, L_b)$, and a simple lottery ticket, $L_2 = (\Pi, A, B)$, provided that $\Pi = \Pi_1 \cdot \Pi_a + (1 - \Pi_1) \cdot \Pi_b$, where the expression $\Pi_1 \cdot \Pi_a + (1 - \Pi_1) \cdot \Pi_b$ gives the probability of winning A in the compound lottery ticket $L_1 = (\Pi_1, L_a, L_b)$.[4]

The Expected Utility Theorem

Let $U(\cdot)$ be a utility function that is consistent with the preceding six axioms. Define the *expected utility* of the lottery ticket $L = (\Pi, A, B)$ as follows:

$$\text{expected utility of } L \equiv E[U(L)] = \Pi \cdot U(A) + (1 - \Pi) \cdot U(B) \quad \text{(A5.10)}$$

We are now ready to formulate and prove the Neumann–Morgenstern theorem.

Theorem. *Given any two lottery tickets, $L_1 = (\Pi_1, A, B)$ and $L_2 = (\Pi_2, C, D)$, the expected utility of L_1 is higher than the expected utility of L_2 if, and only if, L_1 is preferred to L_2.*

Proof. Let M represent the most preferred prize for the consumer and W the least preferred prize (or *worst* prize). By the axiom of continuity, there exists some probability Π_a, $0 < \Pi_a < 1$, such that the consumer is indifferent between having prize A with certainty and lottery ticket $L_a = (\Pi_a, M, W)$. Similarly, the consumer is indifferent between prize B and lottery ticket $L_b = (\Pi_b, M, W)$, between prize C and lottery ticket $L_c = (\Pi_c, M, W)$, and finally between prize D and lottery ticket $L_d = (\Pi_d, M, W)$.

Further, by the axiom of compound lotteries, the consumer is indifferent between lottery ticket L_1 and compound lottery ticket $L_1^* = (\Pi_1^*, M, W)$, where $\Pi_1^* = \Pi_1 \cdot \Pi_a + (1 - \Pi_1) \cdot \Pi_b$. Similarly, the consumer is indifferent between lottery ticket L_2 and compound lottery ticket $L_2^* = (\Pi_2^*, M, W)$, where $\Pi_2^* = \Pi_2 \cdot \Pi_c + (1 - \Pi_2) \cdot \Pi_d$.

By the axiom of unequal probability, the consumer prefers lottery ticket L_1^* to L_2^*, if and only if $\Pi_1^* > \Pi_2^*$.

---

[4]The holder of the compound lottery ticket $L_1 = (\Pi_1, L_a, L_b)$ will eventually win either A or B. To determine the final outcome, there must be two drawings. In the first drawing, the ticket holder can win either L_a with probability Π_1, or L_b with probability $(1 - \Pi_1)$. Whether he wins L_a or L_b in the first drawing, there will be a second drawing in which he can win either A or B. In particular, if he wins L_a in the first drawing, he will have the chance of winning A in the second drawing with probability Π_a. On the other hand, if he wins L_b in the first drawing, he will have the chance of winning A in the second drawing with probability Π_b. Accordingly, the probability of winning A through L_a is simply the product of $\Pi_1 \cdot \Pi_a$, while the probability of winning A through L_b is given by the product $(1 - \Pi_1) \cdot \Pi_b$. We therefore conclude that the probability of winning A either through L_a or through L_b is equal to the sum $\Pi_1 \cdot \Pi_a + (1 - \Pi_1) \cdot \Pi_b$.

The expected utility of L_1 must be equal to the expected utility of L_1^* because L_1 is indifferent to L_1^*.[5] Accordingly,

$$E[U(L_1)] = E[U(L_1^*)] = \Pi_1^* \cdot U(M) + (1 - \Pi_1^*) \cdot U(W) \qquad (A5.11)$$

Similarly,

$$E[U(L_2)] = E[U(L_2^*)] = \Pi_2^* \cdot U(M) + (1 - \Pi_2^*) \cdot U(W) \qquad (A5.12)$$

because L_2 is indifferent to L_2^*. Since $U(M) > U(W)$ by assumption, it follows that the inequality $\Pi_1^* > \Pi_2^*$ is equivalent to $E[U(L_1)] > E[U(L_2)]$. In particular, when we arbitrarily set $U(M) = 1$, $U(W) = 0$ (the utility index is arbitrary with respect to origin and scale), we obtain $E[U(L_1)] = \Pi_1^*$ and $E[U(L_2)] = \Pi_2^*$ which establishes the theorem. Q.E.D.

As we mentioned in Chapter 5, the significance of the expected utility theorem is that the behavior of the consumer under uncertainty can be analyzed in terms of the maximization of expected utility.

Linear Transformations of the Neumann–Morgenstern Utility Index

As pointed out in Chapter 5, expected utility rankings are invariant to *increasing linear tranformations*. This proposition is easily proved.

Consider two lottery tickets, $L_1 = (\Pi_1, A_1, B_1)$ and $L_2 = (\Pi_2, A_2, B_2)$. Assume that the consumer prefers L_1 to L_2. Thus the expected utility of L_1 must be higher than the expected utility of L_2; that is,

$$E[U(L_1)] > E[U(L_2)] \qquad (A5.13)$$

Now define a new utility index, V, as follows:

$$V = a + bU \qquad (A5.14)$$

where a and b are constants and $b > 0$.

The expected utility of L_1 in terms of the new index (V) is given by

$$E[V(L_1)] = E[a + b \cdot U(L_1)] = a + b \cdot E[U(L_1)] \qquad (A5.15)$$

Similarly, the expected utility of L_2 in terms of V is given by

$$E[V(L_2)] = E[a + b \cdot U(L_2)] = a + b \cdot E[U(L_2)] \qquad (A5.16)$$

Given inequality (A5.13) and remembering that $b > 0$, we find that

$$E[V(L_1)] > E[V(L_2)] \qquad (A5.17)$$

---

[5]More directly,

$$
\begin{aligned}
E[U(L_1)] &= \Pi_1 \cdot U(A) + (1 - \Pi_1) \cdot U(B) \\
&= \Pi_1 \cdot U(L_a) + (1 - \Pi_1) \cdot U(L_b) \\
&= \Pi_1 \cdot [\Pi_a \cdot U(M) + (1 - \Pi_a) \cdot U(W)] + (1 - \Pi_1)[\Pi_b \cdot U(M) + (1 - \Pi_b) \cdot U(W)] \\
&= [\Pi_1 \cdot \Pi_a + (1 - \Pi_1) \cdot \Pi_b] \cdot U(M) + [\Pi_1(1 - \Pi_a) + (1 - \Pi_1)(1 - \Pi_b)] \cdot U(W) \\
&= \Pi_1^* \cdot U(M) + (1 - \Pi_1^*) \cdot U(W) \\
&= E[U(L_1^*)]
\end{aligned}
$$

Inequality (A5.17) shows that expected utility rankings are invariant under increasing linear transformations.

Appendix to Chapter 6
Linear Homogeneous Production Functions[1]

This appendix deals exclusively with linear homogeneous production functions. These are production functions that are characterized by constant returns to scale.

Definition

Suppose that output Q is a function of labor L and land T only. Write the production function as follows:

$$Q = f(L, T) \tag{A6.1}$$

This production function is linear homogeneous (or homogeneous of the first degree) if, and only if, it satisfies the equation

$$mQ = f(mL, mT) \tag{A6.2}$$

where m is any positive real number. Equation (A6.2) merely says that if we multiply all inputs by a positive number (m), output Q is also multiplied by the same number (m), which in effect is the definition of constant returns to scale.

An Example: The Cobb–Douglas Production Function

We can illustrate the definition of linear homogeneous production functions, and also explain how equation (A6.2) should be applied, by means of an example. For this purpose, we choose the Cobb–Douglas production function, which has the following form:

$$Q = AL^{\alpha}T^{\beta} \tag{A6.1a}$$

where A, α, and β are all positive constants.

The Cobb–Douglas production function exhibits constant returns to scale when

$$\alpha + \beta = 1 \tag{A6.3}$$

To prove this proposition, we must show that equation (A6.1a) satisfies equation (A6.2), assuming that (A6.3) is true. Accordingly,

$$f(mL, mT) = A(mL)^{\alpha}(mT)^{\beta} = m^{\alpha+\beta}AL^{\alpha}T^{\beta} \tag{A6.4}$$
$$= m(AL^{\alpha}T^{\beta}) = mQ$$

When $\alpha + \beta > 1$, the Cobb–Douglas production function exhibits increasing returns to scale; and when $\alpha + \beta < 1$, it shows decreasing returns to scale.

---

[1]This appendix may be read together with Section 6.7.

Properties

A linear homogeneous production function has the following important properties.

1. *The average physical product (APP) of either input depends only on the proportion in which the inputs are used—not their absolute quantities.*

Proof: Setting $m = 1/L$ in equation (A6.2), we obtain

$$APP_L \equiv \frac{Q}{L} = f\left(1, \frac{T}{L}\right) = g\left(\frac{T}{L}\right) \tag{A6.5}$$

Alternatively, setting $m = 1/T$ in equation (A6.2), we obtain

$$APP_T \equiv \frac{Q}{T} = f\left(\frac{L}{T}, 1\right) = h\left(\frac{L}{T}\right) \tag{A6.6}$$

In the case of the Cobb–Douglas production function, the average physical products, APP_L and APP_T, are

$$APP_L = \frac{Q}{L} = \frac{AL^\alpha T^\beta}{L} = A\frac{T^\beta}{L^{1-\alpha}} = A\left(\frac{T}{L}\right)^\beta \tag{A6.5a}$$

$$APP_T = \frac{Q}{T} = \frac{AL^\alpha T^\beta}{T} = A\frac{L^\alpha}{T^{1-\beta}} = A\left(\frac{L}{T}\right)^\alpha \tag{A6.6a}$$

where use has been made of equations (A6.1a) and (A6.3).

2. *The marginal physical product (MPP) of either input depends only on the proportion in which the inputs are used—not their absolute quantities.*

Proof: The marginal physical product of labor (MPP_L) is given by the partial derivative of total output Q with respect to L, with T remaining constant. Rewrite equation (A6.5) as follows:

$$Q = L \cdot g\left(\frac{T}{L}\right) \tag{A6.7}$$

[Equation (A6.7) is equivalent to equation (A6.1).] Taking the partial of Q with respect to L, we obtain

$$MPP_L = \frac{\partial Q}{\partial L} = g\left(\frac{T}{L}\right) - \frac{T}{L}g'\left(\frac{T}{L}\right) = \Phi\left(\frac{T}{L}\right) \tag{A6.8}$$

where the prime indicates differentiation.

Similarly, the marginal physical product of land (MPP_T) is given by the partial derivative of total output Q with respect to T. Thus, differentiating equation (A6.7) with respect to T, we get

$$MPP_T = \frac{\partial Q}{\partial T} = g'\left(\frac{T}{L}\right) \tag{A6.9}$$

We can again illustrate proposition 2 by means of the Cobb–Douglas production function. Thus, differentiating equation (A6.1a) with respect to L, and alternatively with respect to T, we get

$$MPP_L = \frac{\partial Q}{\partial L} = \alpha A L^{\alpha-1} T^\beta = \alpha A \left(\frac{T}{L}\right)^\beta \tag{A6.8a}$$

$$MPP_T = \frac{\partial Q}{\partial T} = \beta A L^\alpha T^{\beta-1} = \beta A \left(\frac{L}{T}\right)^\alpha \tag{A6.9a}$$

where use was made of equation (A6.3).

3. *The marginal rate of technical substitution depends on the proportion in which the inputs are used—not their absolute quantities.*

Proof: Substituting equations (A6.8) and (A6.9) into equation (6.5), we have

$$MRS_{LT} = \frac{MPP_L}{MPP_T} = \frac{\Phi(T/L)}{g'(T/L)} = F\left(\frac{T}{L}\right) \tag{A6.10}$$

As an example consider again the Cobb–Douglas production function. Substituting equations (A6.8a) and (A6.9a) into (6.5), we obtain

$$MRS_{LT} = \frac{MPP_L}{MPP_T} = \frac{\alpha A(T/L)^\beta}{\beta A(L/T)^\alpha} = \frac{\alpha}{\beta}\frac{T^{\alpha+\beta}}{L^{\alpha+\beta}} = \frac{\alpha}{\beta}\frac{T}{L} \tag{A6.10a}$$

where use was made of equation (A6.3).

4. *Given the equation of a single isoquant, the whole isoquant map can be constructed without any further information.*

Proof: The equation for an isoquant is obtained by setting Q equal to a fixed number (representing the number of units produced) in equation (A6.1). Suppose that we are given the equation for the unit isoquant, which is actually obtained from equation (A6.1) by setting $Q = 1$. Thus we have

$$1 = f(L, T) \tag{A6.11}$$

Equation (A6.11) satisfies, of course, equation (A6.2). Accordingly, for any positive real number m, we also have

$$m = f(mL, mT) = f(L^*, T^*) \tag{A6.12}$$

Equation (A6.12) actually tells us how we can combine $L^* \equiv mL$ units of labor with $T^* \equiv mT$ units of land to produce m units of output. Allowing m to vary from zero to infinity, we can thus obtain the equation for each and every isoquant.

As an example, suppose that we are given the equation for the unit isoquant of a Cobb–Douglas production function, as follows:

$$1 = 200L^{0.7}T^{0.3} \qquad\qquad\text{(A6.11a)}$$

Equation (A6.11a) was actually obtained from (A6.1a) by setting $Q = 1$, $A = 200$, $\alpha = 0.7$, and $\beta = 0.3$. To get the equation for the isoquant corresponding to, say, 73 units of output, substitute the values $L = L^*/73$ and $T = T^*/73$ into (A6.11a):

$$1 = 200 \left(\frac{L^*}{73}\right)^{0.7} \left(\frac{T^*}{73}\right)^{0.3} \qquad\qquad\text{(A6.12a)}$$

Other equations corresponding to different isoquants can be constructed in a similar fashion.

5. *(Euler's theorem): Total output Q equals the marginal physical product of labor (MPP$_L$) multiplied by the quantity of labor (L) plus the marginal physical product of land (MPP$_T$) multiplied by the quantity of land (T).*

$$Q = L \cdot MPP_L + T \cdot MPP_T \qquad\qquad\begin{array}{c}\text{(A6.13)}\\ \text{(6.7) repeated}\end{array}$$

Proof: Substituting equations (A6.8) and (A6.9) into the right-hand side of equation (A6.13) and simplifying, we obtain

$$L \cdot MPP_L + T \cdot MPP_T = L \left[g\!\left(\frac{T}{L}\right) - \frac{T}{L}g'\!\left(\frac{T}{L}\right) \right] + Tg'\!\left(\frac{T}{L}\right)$$
$$= Lg\!\left(\frac{T}{L}\right) = Q \qquad\qquad\text{(A6.14)}$$

where in the last step use was made of equation (A6.7).

In terms of the Cobb–Douglas production function, equation (A6.14) takes the form

$$L \cdot MPP_L + T \cdot MPP_T = L\alpha A\!\left(\frac{T}{L}\right)^{\beta} + T\beta A\!\left(\frac{L}{T}\right)^{\alpha}$$
$$= \alpha AL^{1-\beta}T^{\beta} + \beta AL^{\alpha}T^{1-\alpha}$$
$$= AL^{\alpha}T^{\beta} = Q \qquad\qquad\text{(A6.14a)}$$

where use was made of equations (A6.1a), (A6.3), (A6.8a) and (A6.9a).

6. *When the isoquants are convex to the origin, the marginal physical products of labor and land are diminishing; that is, when the law of diminishing marginal rate of technical substitution holds, the law of diminishing returns also holds.*

Proof: The marginal physical product of labor is diminishing when the partial derivative of equation (A6.8) with respect to L is negative; that is,

$$\frac{\partial MPP_L}{\partial L} = -\frac{T}{L^2}g' + \frac{T}{L^2}g' + \frac{T^2}{L^3}g'' = \frac{T^2}{L^3}g'' < 0 \qquad\qquad\text{(A6.15)}$$

where the independent variable T/L has been omitted for simplicity.

Similarly, the marginal physical product of land is diminishing when the partial derivative of equation (A6.9) with respect to T is negative; that is,

$$\frac{\partial MPP_T}{\partial T} = \frac{1}{L} g'' < 0 \tag{A6.16}$$

Since T and L are positive numbers, it is apparent that inequalities (A6.15) and (A6.16) hold if, and only if,

$$g'' < 0 \tag{A6.17}$$

The validity of inequality (A6.17) is guaranteed by the law of diminishing marginal rate of technical substitution. To see this, rewrite equation (A6.10) as follows:

$$MRS_{LT} = \frac{MPP_L}{MPP_T} = \frac{g - (T/L) g'}{g'} = \frac{g}{g'} - \frac{T}{L} \tag{A6.10}'$$

where use was made of equation (A6.8). The law of diminishing marginal rate of technical substitution requires that the derivative of (A6.10)$'$ with respect to T/L is *positive*; that is,

$$\frac{\partial MRS_{LT}}{\partial (T/L)} > 0 \tag{A6.18}$$

Taking the derivative of (A6.10)$'$ with respect to T/L, we obtain

$$\frac{\partial MRS_{LT}}{\partial (T/L)} = \frac{(g')^2 - gg''}{(g')^2} - 1 = -\frac{g}{(g')^2} g'' > 0 \tag{A6.19}$$

Now recall that $g = APP_L > 0$. In addition, $g' = MPP_T > 0$, because of our concern with the "economic" region of production. Accordingly, inequality (A6.19) is equivalent to the inequality $-g'' > 0$, which is the same inequality as (A6.17). This completes the proof of proposition 6.

We can illustrate the above proposition by means of the Cobb–Douglas production function. Thus, differentiating equation (A6.8a) with respect to L, we get

$$\frac{\partial MPP_L}{\partial L} = -\frac{\alpha \beta A T^\beta}{L^{1+\beta}} < 0 \tag{A6.15a}$$

Similarly, differentiating equation (A6.9a) with respect to T, we obtain

$$\frac{\partial MPP_T}{\partial T} = -\frac{\alpha \beta A L^\alpha}{T^{1+\alpha}} < 0 \tag{A6.16a}$$

Finally, the marginal rate of technical substitution is diminishing because

$$\frac{\partial MRS_{LT}}{\partial (T/L)} = \frac{\alpha}{\beta} > 0 \tag{A6.19a}$$

Equation (A6.19a) is obtained by differentiating equation (A6.10a) with respect to T/L.

Constant Returns to Scale and Convexity of Isoquants

We must emphasize that the assumption of constant returns to scale does not guarantee that the isoquants will be convex to the origin. Convexity is an additional assumption. We can verify the truth of this assertion by a counterexample of a linear homogeneous production function that has isoquants that are *concave* to the origin.

Consider the "Pythagorean" production function

$$Q = \sqrt{L^2 + T^2} \tag{A6.20}$$

As the reader should know, equation (A6.20) can be represented by a circle in the LT-plane with *center* at the origin and *radius* equal to Q. Considering Q as a parameter, equation (A6.20) generates a whole "family" of circles around the origin. The quarter circles lying in the first quadrant actually form the isoquant map. Obviously, such isoquants are *concave* to the origin, exhibiting *increasing* marginal rate of technical substitution.

The Pythagorean production function is linear homogeneous because it satisfies equation (A6.2). Thus

$$\sqrt{(mL)^2 + (mT)^2} = \sqrt{m^2(L^2 + T^2)} = m\sqrt{L^2 + T^2} = mQ$$

The Symmetry of the Stages of Production

As we mentioned in Section 6.3, one input's first stage of production coincides with the other input's third stage of production. We now wish to prove this important proposition rigorously.

Rewrite equation (A6.13) as follows:

$$MPP_T = \frac{1}{T}(Q - L \cdot MPP_L) = \frac{L}{T}\frac{Q}{L} - \left(\frac{L}{T}\right)MPP_L$$
$$= \frac{L}{T}(APP_L - MPP_L) \tag{A6.21}$$

Alternatively,

$$MPP_T = \frac{1}{T}(Q - L \cdot MPP_L) = APP_T - \left(\frac{L}{T}\right)MPP_L$$

or

$$APP_T - MPP_T = \left(\frac{L}{T}\right)MPP_L \tag{A6.22}$$

Consider now labor's first stage of production, where $MPP_L > APP_L > 0$. It is evident from equation (A6.21) that $MPP_T < 0$, because $APP_L - MPP_L < 0$. Conversely, when $MPP_T < 0$ (i.e., when production occurs in land's third stage), it follows from equation (A6.21) that $APP_L - MPP_L < 0$, or $MPP_L > APP_L$. In other words, labor's first stage of production ($MPP_L > APP_L > 0$) coincides with land's third stage ($MPP_T < 0$).

Similarly, land's first stage of production ($MPP_T > APP_T > 0$) coincides with labor's third stage ($MPP_L < 0$). This should be obvious from equation (A6.22).

Finally, we can easily show that labor's second stage of production ($APP_L > MPP_L > 0$) coincides with land's second stage ($APP_T > MPP_T > 0$). Thus when $APP_L > MPP_L > 0$, it follows from equation (A6.21) that $MPP_T > 0$; in addition, APP_T must be larger than MPP_T because $MPP_L > 0$ [see equation (A6.22)]. Conversely, when $APP_T > MPP_T > 0$, it follows from equation (A6.22) that $MPP_L > 0$; in addition, $APP_L > MPP_L$ because $MPP_T > 0$ [see equation (A6.21)]. The proof is now complete.

Appendix to Chapter 7
The Mathematics of Cost Curves

This appendix deals with the following three topics: (1) the mathematics of cost minimization and output maximization; (2) the mathematical procedure for deriving the firm's expansion path and cost functions, and also the relationship between the average cost and marginal cost; and (3) the formal proof of the proposition that the shape of the long-run average-cost curve (and by implication, the shape of the long-run total-cost curve) reflects the nature of the underlying returns to scale.

A7.1 Cost Minimization[1]

Consider a firm that uses labor (L) and land (T) to produce output (Q) according to the production function

$$Q = f(L, T) \tag{A7.1}$$

If the firm wishes to produce a given output, say, $\overline{Q}$, it must choose a labor–land combination that satisfies the equation

$$\overline{Q} = f(L, T) \tag{A7.2}$$

This is required, of course, by the existing technology. In general, there are many labor–land combinations that satisfy equation (A7.2), as illustrated by the corresponding isoquant. Which combination should the firm choose? That combination that *minimizes* total cost (C), given by the equation

$$C = wL + rT \tag{A7.3}$$

where w is the wage rate and r the rent. Accordingly, the object of the firm is to minimize its total cost as given by equation (A7.3), subject to equation (A7.2).

Form the *Lagrangian function*

$$Z = wL + rT + \lambda[\overline{Q} - f(L, T)] \tag{A7.4}$$

where λ is an undetermined *Lagrange multiplier*. For total-cost minimization, it is necessary that the following partial derivatives of Z be zero:

[1]This section may be read together with the subsection entitled "Cost Minimization" of Section 7.2.

$$\frac{\partial Z}{\partial L} = w - \lambda f_L = 0 \tag{A7.5}$$

$$\frac{\partial Z}{\partial T} = r - \lambda f_T = 0 \tag{A7.6}$$

$$\frac{\partial Z}{\partial \lambda} = \overline{Q} - f(L, T) = 0 \tag{A7.7}$$

where f_L and f_T are the partial derivatives of $f(L, T)$ with respect to L and T, respectively. (Note that $f_L \equiv$ marginal physical product of labor and $f_T \equiv$ marginal physical product of land.) Equation (A7.7) is exactly the same as equation (A7.2).

Combining equations (A7.5) and (A7.6), we obtain the following important cost-minimization condition:

$$\frac{w}{r} = \frac{f_L}{f_T} \equiv MRS_{LT} \tag{A7.8}$$

That is, total cost is minimized when the wage/rent ratio (slope of isocost line) equals the ratio of marginal physical products (slope of isoquant)—the familiar tangency condition between the given isoquant and the lowest possible isocost line.

Alternatively, equations (A7.5) and (A7.6) can be rearranged as follows:

$$\frac{w}{f_L} = \frac{r}{f_T} = \lambda \equiv MC_L \tag{A7.9}$$

It is now apparent that the Lagrange multiplier (λ) is the long-run marginal cost (MC_L).

A7.2 Output Maximization[2]

Suppose now that the firm wishes to spend a fixed sum of money, say, $\overline{C}$, on labor and land. Evidently, the firm can purchase any labor–land combination that satisfies the equation

$$\overline{C} = wL + rT \tag{A7.10}$$

Which combination should the firm choose? That combination that *maximizes* total output, given by equation (A7.1). Accordingly, the firm must now maximize Q, as given by equation (A7.1), subject to equation (A7.10). This problem of constrained output maximization is dual to the foregoing problem of constrained cost minimization.

Form again the Lagrangian function

$$\Phi = f(L, T) + \mu(\overline{C} - wL - rT) \tag{A7.11}$$

where μ is an undetermined Lagrange multiplier. To maximize total output, it is necessary that the following partial derivatives of Φ be set equal to zero:

[2]This section may be read together with the subsection entitled "Output Maximization" of Section 7.2.

$$\frac{\partial \Phi}{\partial L} = f_L - \mu w = 0 \tag{A7.12}$$

$$\frac{\partial \Phi}{\partial T} = f_T - \mu r = 0 \tag{A7.13}$$

$$\frac{\partial \Phi}{\partial \mu} = \overline{C} - wL - rT = 0 \tag{A7.14}$$

Equation (A7.14) coincides again with the initial constraint, that is, equation (A7.10).

It is evident that equations (A7.12) and (A7.13) can be combined to generate equation (A7.8), which is the cost-minimization condition. Accordingly, *the condition for output maximization is the same as the condition for cost minimization,* as expected.

Nevertheless, the interpretation of μ is different from the interpretation of λ. In particular, equations (A7.12) and (A7.13) can be rearranged as follows:

$$\mu = \frac{f_L}{w} = \frac{f_T}{r} \tag{A7.15}$$

Comparing equation (A7.15) to equation (A7.9), it becomes apparent that μ is the reciprocal of λ. As explained in Chapter 7, the ratios f_L/w and f_T/r, and thus μ, correspond to the extra output per dollar spent on labor and land, respectively. Indeed, equation (A7.15) implies that the firm maximizes output when it can no longer increase it by transferring dollars from one factor to the other.

A7.3 The Expansion Path and Related Cost Curves[3]

In this section we deal with the derivation of the firm's expansion path and cost curves and study the relationship between average cost and marginal cost.

The Expansion Path

By definition, the firm's expansion path is the locus of optimal input combinations, that is, labor–land combinations that satisfy the cost-minimization condition, as given by equation (A7.8), for each and every level of output. Accordingly, equation (A7.8) is "the" equation for the firm's expansion path.

The Long-Run Total-Cost Function

The long-run total-cost function is a relationship between the long-run total cost and total output. Formally, we can derive it from three equations that we already know: the production function [i.e., equation (A7.1)], the isocost equation [i.e., equation (A7.3)], and the cost-minimization condition [i.e., equation (A7.8)]. This is a system of three equations in four unknowns: Q, C, L, and T. Accordingly, we can use two equations to eliminate L and T. The remaining equation is a relationship between Q and C, and we may write it as follows:

---

[3]This section may be read together with Sections 7.3 and 7.4.

$$C = C(Q) \tag{A7.16}$$

Equation (A7.16) is the long-run total-cost function.

A Numerical Illustration

The above procedure can best be clarified by means of a numerical example. Consider the following Cobb–Douglas production function:

$$Q = 100L^{0.8}T^{0.2} \tag{A7.1a}$$

Taking partial derivatives with respect to L and T, and substituting the results into equation (A7.8), we obtain

$$\frac{w}{r} = \frac{0.8 \times 100 \times L^{-0.2}T^{0.2}}{0.2 \times 100 \times L^{0.8}T^{-0.8}} = \frac{4T}{L} \tag{A7.8a}$$

Solving (A7.8a) for L, we obtain

$$L = \frac{4rT}{w} \tag{A7.8a}'$$

Substituting the value of L, as given by equation (A7.8a)' into equations (A7.1a) and (A7.3), and simplifying, we get

$$Q = 100\left(\frac{4r}{w}\right)^{0.8} T \tag{A7.1a}'$$

$$C = 5rT \tag{A7.3}'$$

Finally, solving equation (A7.1a)' for T and then substituting the result into equation (A7.3)', we have

$$C = \frac{r^{0.2}w^{0.8}}{20 \times 4^{0.8}} Q \tag{A7.16a}$$

Because the production function is homogeneous of the first degree, both the expansion path, as given by equation (A7.8a), and the total-cost function, as given by equation (A7.16a), are linear.

The Relationship Between Average and Marginal Cost

As we explained in Chapter 7, when the average-cost curve is downward sloping, the corresponding marginal-cost curve lies below it; when the average-cost curve is upward sloping, the marginal lies above it; and when the average is at its minimum ("stationary" point), the marginal is equal to it.

We can prove the above important relationship as follows. By definition,

$$AC = \frac{C}{Q} \tag{A7.17}$$

The slope of the average-cost curve is given by the derivative of AC with respect to Q. Thus

$$\frac{dAC}{dQ} = \frac{Q\,(dC/dQ) - C}{Q^2} = \frac{1}{Q}\left(\frac{dC}{dQ} - \frac{C}{Q}\right)$$

$$= \frac{1}{Q}\,(MC - AC) \tag{A7.18}$$

where $MC = dC/dQ = $ marginal cost.

It is evident from equation (A7.18) that the slope of the average-cost curve is positive when $MC > AC$, it is negative when $MC < AC$, and it is zero when $MC = AC$. This completes the proof of the proposition.

The above proof was intentionally cast in general terms. In particular, it covers (1) the relationship between the long-run marginal-cost curve (MC_L) and the long-run average-cost curve (AC_L), (2) the relationship between the short-run marginal-cost curve (MC_s) and the short-run average-cost curve (AC_s), and (3) the relationship between the short-run marginal-cost curve and the average-variable-cost curve (AVC).

A7.4 Average Cost and Returns to Scale[4]

The shape of the long-run average-cost curve (and by implication, the shape of the long-run total-cost curve) reflects the nature of the underlying returns to scale. In particular, the slope of the long-run average-cost curve is negative, zero, or positive according to whether the production function exhibits increasing, constant, or decreasing returns to scale, respectively. We now wish to provide a rigorous proof of this important proposition.

To establish the above proposition, it is only necessary to show that (1) when returns to scale are increasing, the long-run marginal cost is less than the long-run average cost ($MC < AC$); (2) when returns to scale are constant, $MC = AC$; and (3) when returns to scale are decreasing, $MC > AC$.

Consider the average cost of production as given by the following equation:

$$AC = \frac{wL + rT}{Q} \tag{A7.19}$$

In the long run, the cost-minimization condition is satisfied. Solving equation (A7.8) for r, substituting the result into equation (A7.19), and simplifying, we get

$$AC = \frac{w}{f_L}\,\frac{L \cdot f_L + T \cdot f_T}{Q} \tag{A7.20}$$

Now observe that the ratio w/f_L is the long-run marginal cost [see equation (A7.9)]. Dividing both sides of (A7.20) by MC, we finally obtain

$$\frac{AC}{MC} = \frac{L \cdot f_L + T \cdot f_T}{Q} \tag{A7.21}$$

Equation (A7.21) shows that, in general, the ratio of the long-run average cost to the marginal cost equals the ratio of the sum $L \cdot f_L + T \cdot f_T$ to total output Q. The expression $L \cdot f_L + T \cdot f_T$ gives the total payments to labor and land when each factor is paid its marginal physical product. As we saw in Chapter 6 (especially, in its appendix), when the production function exhibits constant returns to scale, total output Q equals $L \cdot f_L + T \cdot f_T$. Accordingly, in this case, $AC = MC$, as is required.

[4]This section may be read together with Section 7.5.

What we must also show is that increasing returns to scale imply $L \cdot f_L + T \cdot f_T > Q$, which means that $AC > MC$. Similarly, decreasing returns to scale imply $L \cdot f_L + T \cdot f_T < Q$, which means that $AC < MC$.

Consider the total differential of the production function:

$$dQ = f_L \cdot dL + f_T \cdot dT \qquad (A7.22)$$

Assume that $dL = mL$ and $dT = mT$, where m is a "small" positive number. In the presence of increasing returns to scale, we must also have $dQ > mQ$. Substituting these relationships into equation (A7.22), we have

$$mQ < dQ = f_L mL + f_T mT$$

or dividing through by m,

$$Q < Lf_L + Tf_T \qquad (A7.23)$$

Obviously, when returns to scale are decreasing, $dQ < mQ$ and

$$Q > Lf_L + Tf_T \qquad (A7.24)$$

Inequalities (A7.23) and (A7.24) complete the proof of the proposition.

Appendix to Chapter 8
The Revenue Functions[1]

Suppose that the demand function for the firm's product has the form

$$p = f(q) \qquad (A8.1)$$

where q is the quantity and $f(q)$ the demand price (or average revenue). Total revenue (R) is then given by the function

$$R = f(q)q \qquad (A8.2)$$

The marginal-revenue function is given by the derivative of R, as given by equation (A8.2), with respect to q:

$$MR = \frac{dR}{dq} = AR + q\,\frac{dp}{dq} \qquad (A8.3)$$

where $AR = p = f(q)$ and $dp/dq = f'(q) < 0$. Equation (A8.3) has a significant interpretation. In effect, it says that marginal revenue (MR) equals average revenue (AR) *minus* a "correction factor" which is equal to the absolute value of the term $q(dp/dq)$. The meaning of this "correction factor" was made clear in Section 8.2. To increase its output, the firm must reduce its price at a rate indicated by the derivative dp/dq per extra unit of quantity sold. Accordingly, the rate at which total revenue increases per extra unit of output sold is equal to average revenue *minus the rate at which the firm "loses" revenue on the "original" units,* that is, $q(dp/dq)$.

[1]This appendix may be read together with Section 8.2.

It is evident from equation (A8.3) that marginal revenue is lower than average revenue except in two special cases: (1) when $q = 0$, which graphically corresponds to the price-axis intercept of the demand curve [as illustrated by point Z in Figure 8.1, panel (a)]; and (2) when $dp/dq = 0$, which occurs in the case of a horizontal demand curve [as illustrated in Figure 8.3, panel (a) by the demand curve facing a perfectly competitive firm].

Equation (A8.3) may be rearranged as follows:

$$MR = AR\left(1 + \frac{q}{p}\frac{dp}{dq}\right) = AR\left(1 - \frac{1}{|e|}\right) \tag{A8.4}$$

where use was made of the definitions $p = AR$ and $|e| = -(dq/dp)(p/q)$. Finally, solving equation (A8.4) for $|e|$, we obtain

$$|e| = \frac{AR}{AR - MR} \tag{A8.5}$$

As an example, consider the special case of a straight-line demand curve given by the linear function

$$AR = p = a - bq \tag{A8.1a}$$

where $a > 0$ and $b > 0$. Then the total-revenue function and the marginal-revenue function become

$$R = pq = aq - bq^2 \tag{A8.2a}$$

$$MR = \frac{dR}{dq} = a - 2bq \tag{A8.3a}$$

Accordingly, the marginal-revenue curve is also a straight line because equation (A8.3a) is linear. Further, the marginal-revenue curve has the same vertical-axis intercept as the average-revenue curve. Thus, at $q = 0$, we have $AR = MR = a$. Finally, the marginal-revenue curve has exactly twice the slope of the average-revenue curve ($-2b$ as compared with $-b$). Because of this, the marginal-revenue curve bisects the distances from the vertical axis to the average-revenue curve, as explained in Section 8.2. For instance, the horizontal-axis intercept of the average-revenue curve (where $AR = p = 0$) occurs at $q = a/b$, while the horizontal-axis intercept of the marginal-revenue curve (where $MR = 0$) is at $q = a/2b$, which is just half of $q = a/b$.

Appendix to Chapter 9
The Backward-Bending Industry Supply Curve[1]

In this appendix we wish to consider the rare possibility of a backward-bending long-run industry-supply curve. Such a curve reflects the influence of an underlying external diseconomy, usually of the technological species, that is extremely strong.

[1]This appendix may be read together with Section 9.5.

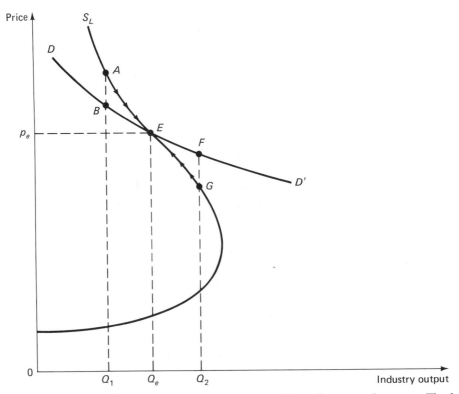

Figure A9.1 Marshallian stability with a backward-bending supply curve. The long-run equilibrium indicated by point E is stable, even though the demand curve (DD') is flatter than the "negatively sloped" supply curve (S_L). When the industry output is higher than the equilibrium output (Q_e) as shown by Q_2, the demand price (indicated by F) exceeds the supply price (indicated by G) and producers *attempt to increase* their output. However, because of the underlying extreme external diseconomy, this effort actually results in a lower total output—the industry moves from G toward E, as shown by the arrows. On the other hand, at a lower output than Q_e, such as Q_1, the supply price (indicated by A) exceeds the demand price (indicated by B) and producers *attempt to reduce* their output. But again because of the external diseconomy, the result is an increase in total output, and the industry travels from A toward E as shown by the arrows.

The most frequently cited example of this phenomenon is the excessive drilling of oil wells into a common underground pool. As drillers intensify their efforts to increase their individual outputs in response to increases in the price of oil brought about by rightward shifts in oil demand, it is not inconceivable that beyond a certain point the total oil output may decline (presumably because the multiplication of wells in a single oil field tends to reduce the pressure in each well). In the region where the oil output falls as the price of oil rises, the supply curve of the oil industry is necessarily backward bending. We should also add, however, that the discovery of new oil fields works against such a tendency, converting an otherwise backward-bending supply curve into a positively sloped one.

In the present case of a backward-bending long-run industry-supply curve, great care must be exercised in the application of the Marshallian test for stability (discussed in Chapter 2).[2] For instance, a mechanical application of the Marshallian stability analysis to the equilibrium portrayed in Figure A9.1 will invariably lead

[2] The current analysis is due to my former teacher, Robert L. Bishop.

to the wrong conclusion—namely, that it is unstable, whereas in fact, it is quite stable. Thus for outputs immediately higher than the equilibrium output (Q_e), such as Q_2, demand price (indicated by point F) exceeds supply price (indicated by point G), and industry output would tend to expand and thus move away from Q_e. On the other hand, for outputs immediately lower than Q_e, such as Q_1, supply price (indicated by point A) exceeds demand price (indicated by point B), and industry output would tend to fall and thus move away from Q_e again.

However, the Marshallian stability analysis should not be applied in such a mechanical fashion. Thus at an output such as Q_2 the existing positive profits will indeed induce the producers to *attempt* to increase their output; but because of the underlying extreme external diseconomy, such an effort will actually result in a lower total output—the industry will be moving from G to E, as indicated by the arrows. On the other hand, at an output such as Q_1 the existing losses will convince firms to *attempt* to curtail their production; but again the actual change in output will be the opposite of the intended change because of the undoing of some of the adverse effects of the underlying external diseconomy. Thus the industry will now be moving from A toward E, as indicated by the arrows.

We must therefore conclude that the long-run equilibrium portrayed in Figure A9.1 by the intersection of the industry supply and demand curves at point E is stable.

Appendix to Chapter 10
The Mathematics of Profit Maximization[1]

In this appendix we study the algebraic formulation of the problem of profit maximization. The functions of total revenue (R) and total cost (C) may be written, respectively, as $R = R(q)$ and $C = V(q) + F$, where q is the output, $V(q)$ the total variable cost as a function of q, and F the total fixed cost.

We intentionally write the total-cost function as $C = V(q) + F$ because we wish to formulate the equilibrium conditions in the most general way. As we pointed out in Chapters 9 and 10, long run is the special case where $F = 0$. In any short run, $F > 0$.

Also, we write the total-revenue function in the most general form, because at this stage we do not wish to draw a distinction between a perfectly competitive firm and a monopolistic firm.

Given the functions of total revenue and total cost, we formulate the total-profit function (π) as follows:

$$\pi = \pi(q) = R(q) - V(q) - F \tag{A10.1}$$

Thus total profit is given by the net difference between the functions of total revenue (R) and total cost (C).

All maximum and minimum values of the total profit function $\pi(q)$ occur where its first derivative is zero

$$\frac{d\pi}{dq} = \frac{dR}{dq} - \frac{dV}{dq} = 0 \tag{A10.2}$$

---

[1]This appendix can be read together with Section 10.1.

Recalling that dR/dq = marginal revenue and dV/dq = marginal cost, it is evident that equation (A10.2) corresponds to the marginal equality $MR = MC$.

Because F is a constant, its derivative with respect to q is zero and does not appear in equation (A10.2). This is true whether $F = 0$ (long run) or $F > 0$ (short run).

Equation (A10.2) is only the first-order condition for a profit maximum. By itself, this condition establishes only some "stationary" value of the total-profit function, which might be a minimum rather than a maximum. To ensure a maximum, we also need a second-order condition: namely, that in the neighborhood of the equilibrium output, that is, the value of q that satisfies equation (A10.2), the total-profit curve must be *concave*. In conjunction with the first-order condition, the second-order condition requires the total-profit curve to have positive slope to the left of its peak and negative slope to the right.

Analytically, the second-order condition is expressed in terms of the algebraic sign of the *second derivative* of the total-profit function:

$$\frac{d^2\pi}{dq^2} = \frac{d^2R}{dq^2} - \frac{d^2V}{dq^2} < 0 \qquad\qquad (A10.3)$$

In other words, the second-order condition requires the second derivative of the total-profit function to be *negative*.

The second derivative d^2R/dq^2 is the derivative of the first derivative dR/dq; that is, d^2R/dq^2 is the derivative of marginal revenue. Similarly, the second derivative d^2V/dq^2 is the derivative of marginal cost (dV/dq). Accordingly, inequality (A10.3) is equivalent to the requirement that the marginal-cost curve intersects the marginal-revenue curve from below.

For example, for a downward-sloping MR curve, the second derivative d^2R/dq^2 must be *negative* (meaning that marginal revenue is declining). If the MC curve is upward sloping, the second derivative d^2V/dq^2 must be *positive*, which guarantees that inequality (A10.3) is satisfied. On the other hand, if the MC curve is also downward sloping, d^2V/dq^2 will be negative, and inequality (A10.3) will be satisfied if, and only if, $d^2R/dq^2 < d^2V/dq^2$, that is, if the MR curve is more steeply downward sloping than the MC curve.

As we explained in Chapters 9 and 10, there is also a third condition, namely, that $R(q) \geq V(q)$. However, this condition does not follow from calculus.

We can illuminate the foregoing principles by means of a numerical illustration. Suppose that the functions of total revenue and total cost are $R = 350q - q^2$ and $C = q^3 - 241q^2 + 4850q + 10,000$, respectively. Then the total-profit function becomes

$$\pi = R - C = -q^3 + 240q^2 - 4500q - 10,000 \qquad (A10.1a)$$

The first-order condition for a profit maximum takes the form

$$\begin{aligned}\frac{d\pi}{dq} &= -3q^2 + 480q - 4500 \\ &= -3(q - 10)(q - 150) = 0 \end{aligned} \qquad (A10.2a)$$

Obviously, the roots of equation (A10.2a) are two: $q_1 = 10$ and $q_2 = 150$. To determine the value of q where profit is at a maximum, we consider the sign of the second derivative:

$$\frac{d^2\pi}{dq^2} = -6q + 480$$

for $q = 10$ and $q = 150$. Since $d^2\pi/dq^2 = -6 \times 10 + 480 = +420 > 0$ when $q = 10$, and $d^2\pi/dq^2 = -6 \times 150 + 480 = -420 < 0$ when $q = 150$, we conclude that the profit-maximizing output must be 150. Indeed, the total profit at this output is

$$\pi = -(150)^3 + 240 \times (150)^2 - 4500 \times 150 - 10,000 = 1,340,000$$

We can pursue the above illustration a little further in order to determine the equilibrium price, the elasticity of demand, marginal cost, and marginal revenue. By definition, average revenue $= R/q = 350 - q$. Thus, at $q = 150$, $AR = 350 - 150 = 200$. Further, $MR = dR/dq = 350 - 2q$, which at $q = 150$ becomes $MR = 50$. Accordingly, the elasticity of demand at the profit-maximizing output must be $|e| = AR/(AR - MR) = 200/(200 - 50) = 200/150 = 4/3 > 1$. Finally, marginal cost is given by $MC = dC/dq = 3q^2 - 482q + 4850$, which at $q = 150$ becomes $MC = 50$ (which is the same as $MR = 50$).

Appendix to Chapter 11
Conjectural Variations and Sophisticated Behavior

In this appendix we refine and extend our discussion of oligopolistic markets. We begin in Section A11.1 with a general formulation of the pure duopoly problem, introducing formally the concepts of conjectural variations and duopolistic inter-dependence. In Section A11.2 we illustrate the concepts developed in Section A11.1 by reconsidering the Cournot solution. We continue in Section A11.3 with a sophisticated model of duopoly, first analyzed by the German economist Heinrich von Stackelberg (1905–1946). Finally, we conclude in Section A11.4 with some comments on differentiated products.

A11.1 Conjectural Variations[1]

Consider a duopoly market in which firms A and B sell a homogeneous product at the same market price (p). The market price is a function of the aggregate quantity sold:

$$p = d(q_a + q_b) \tag{A11.1}$$

where q_a and q_b are the output levels of A and B, respectively. By assumption, the market demand curve, as given by equation (A11.1), is negatively sloped; that is, $d' < 0$.

Firm A's total revenue (R_a) is given by

$$R_a = q_a p = q_a d(q_a + q_b) = R_a(q_a, q_b) \tag{A11.2}$$

Similarly, firm B's total revenue (R_b) is given by

$$R_b = q_b p = q_b d(q_a + q_b) = R_b(q_a, q_b) \tag{A11.3}$$

The profits of firms A and B (π_a and π_b, respectively) are

---

[1]This section can be read together with Section 11.7.

$$\pi_a = R_a(q_a, q_b) - C_a(q_a) \tag{A11.4}$$

$$\pi_b = R_b(q_a, q_b) - C_b(q_b) \tag{A11.5}$$

where $C_a(q_a) = A$'s total cost function and $C_b(q_b) = B$'s total cost function. Equations (A11.4) and (A11.5) are the profit functions of the two firms.

To determine the profit-maximizing output of firm A, we set the derivative of π_a with respect to q_a equal to zero:

$$\frac{\partial \pi_a}{\partial q_a} = \frac{\partial R_a}{\partial q_a} + \frac{\partial R_a}{\partial q_b}\frac{dq_b}{dq_a} - \frac{dC_a}{dq_a} = 0 \tag{A11.6}$$

Similarly, profit maximization by firm B requires

$$\frac{\partial \pi_b}{\partial q_b} = \frac{\partial R_b}{\partial q_b} + \frac{\partial R_b}{\partial q_a}\frac{dq_a}{dq_b} - \frac{dC_b}{dq_b} = 0 \tag{A11.7}$$

To solve equations (A11.6) and (A11.7) for q_a and q_b, we need to know the values (or functional forms) of dq_b/dq_a and dq_a/dq_b, which are known as *conjectural variations*. The derivative dq_b/dq_a represents firm A's expectation (conjecture) of how firm B will respond to a change in q_a; and the derivative dq_a/dq_b corresponds to firm B's conjecture about the response of firm A to a change in q_b. These conjectural variations are *ex ante* concepts and need not be equal to their *ex post* values. The existence of a multitude of oligopoly models reflects the fact that many alternative values can be assigned to the conjectural variations.

A11.2 The Cournot Duopoly Model Again[2]

Cournot solved the duopoly problem by assuming that the conjectural variations are zero, that is, $dq_b/dq_a = dq_a/dq_b = 0$. For convenience, Cournot also assumed zero costs; that is, $C_a = C_b = 0$, and, therefore, $dC_a/dq_a = dC_b/dq_b = 0$. Introducing these simplifications into equations (A11.6) and (A11.7), we obtain

$$\frac{\partial \pi_a}{\partial q_a} = \frac{\partial R_a}{\partial q_a} = 0 \tag{A11.6$'$}$$

$$\frac{\partial \pi_b}{\partial q_b} = \frac{\partial R_b}{\partial q_b} = 0 \tag{A11.7$'$}$$

Assume that demand function (A11.1) has the linear form

$$p = 100 - \frac{5}{24}(q_a + q_b) \tag{A11.1a}$$

[Equation (A11.1a) corresponds to the linear demand curve of Figure 11.4.] Then equations (A11.2) and (A11.3) become

$$R_a = 100q_a - \frac{5}{24}(q_a^2 + q_a q_b) \tag{A11.2a}$$

[2]This section can be read together with Section 11.7.

$$R_b = 100q_b - \frac{5}{24}(q_aq_b + q_b^2) \qquad \text{(A11.3a)}$$

Differentiating R_a with respect to q_a (treating q_b as a parameter) and R_b with respect to q_b (treating q_a as a parameter), we obtain the *reaction functions*

$$\frac{\partial \pi_a}{\partial q_a} = 100 - \frac{5}{24}(2q_a + q_b) = 0 \qquad \text{(A11.6a)}'$$

$$\frac{\partial \pi_b}{\partial q_b} = 100 - \frac{5}{24}(q_a + 2q_b) = 0 \qquad \text{(A11.7a)}'$$

Solving (A11.6a)' for q_a, and (A11.7a)' for q_b, we finally obtain

$$q_a = \frac{480 - q_b}{2} \qquad \text{(A11.8)}$$

$$q_b = \frac{480 - q_a}{2} \qquad \text{(A11.9)}$$

Equations (A11.8) and (A11.9) are exactly the same as equations (11.1) and (11.2), respectively, of Chapter 11.

The Cournot equilibrium corresponds to the simultaneous solution of equations (A11.8) and (A11.9), which yields the following results: $q_a = q_b = 160$, $p = 100 - (5/24)(160 + 160) = 100/3$, $\pi_a = \pi_b = 16{,}000/3$, and $\pi = \pi_a + \pi_b = 32{,}000/3$.

A11.3 The Stackelberg Model

The models of Cournot, Bertrand, and Edgeworth assume that the duopolists behave naively; that is, the duopolists ignore the inevitable interdependence of their market decisions. Stackelberg, on the other hand, developed an interesting model in which either duopolist may behave in a sophisticated manner, in the sense of taking into consideration his rival's naive reactions.

Stackelberg states that each seller can be either a *follower* or a *leader*. A follower behaves more or less like a Cournot seller; that is, a follower takes his rival's quantity as given and adjusts his own output to maximize his profit. Mathematically, this means that a follower obeys his reaction function. A leader takes advantage of the fact that his rival is a follower. This means that a leader maximizes his profit subject to the reaction function of his rival.

Since one or the other duopolist may play the role of a leader, the Stackelberg model yields two alternative solutions, known as "Stackelberg equilibria." As the following analysis shows, a duopolist normally reaps a greater profit as a leader than as a follower. For this reason, Stackelberg argued that both duopolists would have an incentive to be leaders, and that a struggle would ensue between the duopolists, known as "Stackelberg warfare." The Cournot solution corresponds to the special case in which both duopolists are followers, with the added proviso that each seller expects the other to be a follower.

We can illustrate Stackelberg's analysis by pursuing a little further the Cournot model of Section A11.2. Suppose that firm A acts as a leader, and firm B acts as a follower. Firm B follows its reaction function (A11.9). Firm A maximizes its total revenue (and also profit because $C_a = 0$), as given by equation (A11.2a) subject to B's reaction function (A11.9). Substituting (A11.9) into (A11.2a) and simplifying, we obtain

$$R_a = 50q_a - \frac{5}{48}q_a^2 \qquad\qquad (A11.10)$$

Maximization of R_a (and π_a) requires

$$\frac{dR_a}{dq_a} = 50 - \frac{5}{24}q_a = 0$$

which yields

$$q_a = 240 \qquad\qquad (A11.11)$$

We now substitute firm A's optimal leadership output ($q_a = 240$) into B's reaction function (A11.9) to obtain B's equilibrium output: $q_b = 120$. Substituting the equilibrium values of q_a and q_b into demand function (A11.1a), we get the equilibrium price: $p = \$25$. Accordingly, the profits of firms A and B are $\pi_a = \$25 \times 240 = \$6000$ and $\pi_b = \$25 \times 120 = \$3000$.

Suppose now that firm A acts as a follower, and firm B acts as a leader. Now firm A follows its reaction function (A11.8), and firm B maximizes its total revenue (and profit), as given by equation (A11.3a), subject to A's reaction function (A11.8). Again we substitute (A11.8) into (A11.3a) and simplify to obtain

$$R_b = 50q_b - \frac{5}{48}q_b^2 \qquad\qquad (A11.12)$$

Maximization of R_b (and π_b) requires

$$\frac{dR_b}{dq_b} = 50 - \frac{5}{24}q_b = 0$$

which yields

$$q_b = 240 \qquad\qquad (A11.13)$$

Substituting B's optimal leadership output ($q_b = 240$) into equation (A11.8), we obtain A's equilibrium output: $q_a = 120$. Given q_a and q_b, we use demand function (A11.1a) to determine the equilibrium price: $p = \$25$. The profits of the two firms now are $\pi_a = \$25 \times 120 = \$3000$ and $\pi_b = \$25 \times 240 = \$6000$.

Table A11.1 The Stackelberg Model
Firm A's Policy

		Leader		Follower	
Firm B's Policy	**Leader**	(Stackelberg warfare) $\pi_a = 0$ $q_a = 240$ $p = 0$	$\pi_b = 0$ $q_b = 240$	$\pi_a = \$3000$ $q_a = 120$ $p = \$25$	$\pi_b = \$6000$ $q_b = 240$
	Follower	$\pi_a = \$6000$ $q_a = 240$ $p = \$25$	$\pi_b = \$3000$ $q_b = 120$	(Cournot solution) $\pi_a = \pi_b = \dfrac{\$16,000}{3}$ $q_a = q_b = 160$ $p = \dfrac{\$100}{3}$	

If both firms produced their optimal leadership outputs simultaneously (i.e., $q_a = 240$ and $q_b = 240$), the price would drop to zero: $p = 100 - (5/24)(240 + 240) = 0$. In this case each firm would earn zero profit.

The above results are summarized in Table A11.1. It is apparent that it is advantageous to each firm separately to act as a leader, but only on the assumption that the rival firm acts as a follower. The leader–leader behavior is disastrous to both.

A11.4 Differentiated Oligopoly

In the presence of product differentiation, each individual seller faces his own distinct demand curve. The quantity demanded, however, depends not only on the price of the individual seller but also on the price of his rivals and each firm's level of advertising expenditures. For the duopoly case, instead of a single market demand equation (A11.1), we now have two equations

$$p_a = d_a(q_a, q_b, S_a, S_b) \qquad\qquad \text{(A11.14)}$$

$$p_b = d_b(q_a, q_b, S_a, S_b) \qquad\qquad \text{(A11.15)}$$

where p_a is the price of A's product, p_b the price of B's product, S_a is A's advertising expenditures, and S_b is B's advertising expenditures. [Demand functions (A11.14) and (A11.15) are given in inverse form, as was demand function (A11.1).] Even though we do not wish to pursue this idea any further, it must be clear that the pure duopoly models, such as those of Cournot and Stackelberg, can be easily modified to take into account product differentiation. For this purpose we must replace demand equation (A11.1) with demand equations (A11.14) and (A11.15). Note that in the present formulation, each duopolist must choose not only his optimal quantity, but also the optimal level of his advertising expenditure.

Appendix to Chapter 12
The Laws of Derived Demand

In this appendix we deal with three topics: (1) the elasticity of substitution and the distribution of income (Section A12.1), (2) the determinants of the elasticity of the long-run demand for labor by a perfectly competitive industry (Section A12.2), and (3) the "adding-up" problem (Section A12.3).

A12.1 The Elasticity of Substitution Again[1]

Throughout this section we assume constant returns to scale. For this reason we carry out our discussion in terms of the unit coefficients of production and the unit isoquant. We begin with a precise relationship between the elasticity of substitution and the ratio of relative income shares of labor and capital. Then we present several variations of the formula of the elasticity of substitution that are useful in the discussion of Section A12.2.

[1]This section can be read together with Section 12.9.

The Elasticity of Substitution and the Relative Shares

Recall the definitions of the relative shares of labor (s) and capital ($1 - s$):

$$s = \frac{wL}{pq} = \frac{w}{p}\, a_L \tag{A12.1}$$

$$1 - s = \frac{rK}{pq} = \frac{r}{p}\, a_K \tag{A12.2}$$

where $a_L = L/q =$ unit labor coefficient, and $a_K = K/q =$ unit capital coefficient. Divide labor's relative share by capital's relative share to obtain

$$\lambda \equiv \frac{s}{1 - s} = \frac{w}{r}\frac{a_L}{a_K} = \phi \cdot \rho \tag{A12.3}$$

where $\phi = w/r$ and $\rho = L/K = a_L/a_K$. Because $\phi = MRS_{LK}$ and MRS_{LK} is a function of ρ, we may view ϕ as a function of ρ; that is, $\phi = \phi(\rho)$. Evidently, λ increases (decreases) when s increases (decreases), and vice versa. How does λ (or s) behave as ρ changes?

Differentiating λ, as defined by equation (A12.3), with respect to ρ, we get

$$\frac{d\lambda}{d\rho} = \phi + \rho\frac{d\phi}{d\rho} = \phi\left(1 + \frac{\rho}{\phi}\frac{d\phi}{d\rho}\right) = \phi\left(1 - \frac{1}{\sigma}\right)$$
$$= \phi\left(\frac{1}{\sigma}\right)(\sigma - 1) \tag{A12.4}$$

Consequently, the derivative $d\lambda/d\rho$ is positive, zero, or negative according to whether σ is greater than, equal to, or less than unity. For instance, if labor grows while the stock of capital remains constant (i.e., if ρ increases), labor's relative share will increase (and capital's relative share will fall) if the elasticity of substitution is greater than unity.

The Cobb–Douglas Production Function

The elasticity of substitution of the Cobb-Douglas production function ($q = L^\alpha K^{1-\alpha}$) is unity. Indeed, the Cobb–Douglas production function is the only production function with an elasticity of substitution equal to 1.

Recall from the Appendix to Chapter 6, especially equation (A6.10a), that the marginal rate of substitution of labor for capital ($MRS_{LK} = \phi$) of a Cobb–Douglas production function is given by the function

$$MRS_{LK} = \frac{\alpha}{1 - \alpha}\frac{1}{\rho} \qquad (0 < \alpha < 1) \tag{A12.5}$$

or

$$\rho = \frac{\alpha}{1 - \alpha}\frac{1}{\phi} \tag{A12.5}'$$

Accordingly,

$$\frac{d\rho}{d\phi} = \frac{\alpha}{1-\alpha}\left(-\frac{1}{\phi^2}\right) = -\left(\frac{\alpha}{1-\alpha}\frac{1}{\phi}\right)\frac{1}{\phi} = -\frac{\rho}{\phi}$$

and

$$\sigma = -\frac{d\rho}{d\phi}\frac{\phi}{\rho} = \frac{\rho}{\phi}\frac{\phi}{\rho} = 1$$

To confirm the above result, we also consider labor's relative share, which must be constant. Thus

$$MPP_L = \frac{\partial q}{\partial L} = \alpha\left(\frac{K}{L}\right)^{1-\alpha} \quad \text{and} \quad s = \frac{MPP_L \cdot L}{Q} = \frac{\alpha(K/L)^{1-\alpha}L}{L^\alpha K^{1-\alpha}} = \alpha$$

Surely, capital's relative share $1 - s$ is equal to $1 - \alpha$, and $\lambda = \alpha/1 - \alpha$. We therefore conclude that labor's relative share always remains constant and equal to the parameter α irrespective of the value of the labor/capital ratio (ρ).

Some Refinements of the Elasticity of Substitution

Consider the following rearrangement of the elasticity of substitution:

$$\sigma = -\frac{d\rho}{d\phi}\frac{\phi}{\rho} = -\frac{d(a_L/a_K)}{d(w/r)}\frac{(w/r)}{(a_L/a_K)}$$

Expand the differentials $d(a_L/a_K)$, $d(w/r)$ to obtain

$$\sigma = -\frac{(a_K da_L - a_L da_K)/a_K^2}{(rdw - wdr)/r^2}\frac{w/r}{a_L/a_K} = \frac{(da_K/a_K) - (da_L/a_L)}{(dw/w) - (dr/r)}$$

or

$$\sigma = \frac{a_K^* - a_L^*}{w^* - r^*} \tag{A12.6}$$

where $a_K^* = da_K/a_K$ = percentage change of a_K, $a_L^* = da_L/a_L$ = percentage change of a_L, $w^* = dw/w$ = percentage change of w, and $r^* = dr/r$ = percentage change of r.

Now a_K^* and a_L^* are not independent of each other. To see this, consider the unit isoquant defined by the function

$$f(a_L, a_K) = 1 \tag{A12.7}$$

Take the total differential of equation (A12.7):

$$f_L da_L + f_K da_K = 0 \tag{A12.8}$$

where $f_L = MPP_L$ and $f_K = MPP_K$. Recall the first-order conditions for profit maximization ($f_L = w/p$, $f_K = r/p$), and substitute into equation (A12.8) to obtain

$$\frac{w}{p}\,da_L + \frac{r}{p}\,da_K = 0$$

or

$$\frac{wa_L}{p}\frac{da_L}{a_L} + \frac{ra_K}{p}\frac{da_K}{a_K} = 0$$

or

$$sa_L^* + (1 - s)a_K^* = 0 \qquad\qquad\qquad (A12.9)$$

Equation (A12.9) shows that the weighted average of a_L^* and a_K^* with weights s and $1 - s$, respectively, equals zero.

Solving equation (A12.9) for a_L^* and substituting the result into equation (A12.6), we obtain (after some obvious rearrangement)

$$s\sigma = \frac{a_K^*}{w^* - r^*} \qquad\qquad\qquad (A12.10)$$

Alternatively, solving equation (A12.9) for a_K^* and substituting the result into equation (A12.6), we get

$$(1 - s)\sigma = \frac{a_L^*}{w^* - r^*} \qquad\qquad\qquad (A12.11)$$

A12.2 The Elasticity of Demand for Labor[2]

We now turn to a perfectly competitive industry that uses labor (L) and capital (K) and produces a final product under constant returns to scale. We wish to study the determinants of the elasticity of demand for labor.

The System of Equations

For any given wage rate (w), the equilibrium of the perfectly competitive industry is determined by the following system of equations:

$$L = q(p) \cdot a_L\left(\frac{w}{r}\right) \qquad \text{(demand for labor)} \qquad (A12.12)$$

$$p = wa_L\left(\frac{w}{r}\right) + ra_K\left(\frac{w}{r}\right) \qquad \text{(product price} = AC_L) \qquad (A12.13)$$

$$K(r) = q(p)a_K\left(\frac{w}{r}\right) \qquad \text{(supply of } K = \text{demand for } K) \qquad (A12.14)$$

---

[2]This section can be read together with Section 12.6.

where $q(p)$ is the demand function for final product and $K(r)$ the supply of capital to the industry. The unit coefficients a_L and a_K are functions of w/r because they are always selected by the tangency of an isocost line (whose absolute slope equals w/r) and the unit isoquant. Equation (A12.12) defines the quantity of labor demanded (L) by the product $q \cdot a_L$. Equation (A12.13) sets the price of the final product (p) equal to its average cost of production, which is a reflection of the fact that competition eliminates profits. Finally, equation (A12.14) sets the supply of capital $K(r)$ facing the industry equal to the quantity of capital required to produce q units of final output. The supply of capital is a function of r, and the demand for the final product $q(p)$ is a function of p.

Equations (A12.12) to (A12.14) form a system of three equations in three unknowns: L, p, and r. For any given w, these equations can be solved, in principle, for the equilibrium values of L, p, and r.

Comparative Statics

We now wish to determine how the equilibrium value of L behaves as w changes. To accomplish this, we must differentiate totally equations (A12.12) to (A12.14) with respect to w.

As it turns out, it is more interesting to put the results in elasticity form. Thus we immediately introduce the following elasticities:

$$e = \frac{dq}{dp}\frac{p}{q} = \text{elasticity of demand for final product}$$

$$e_{pw} = \frac{w}{p}\frac{dp}{dw} = \text{elasticity of } p \text{ with respect to } w$$

$$e_{rw} = \frac{w}{r}\frac{dr}{dw} = \text{elasticity of } r \text{ with respect to } w \qquad \text{(A12.15)}$$

$$e_L = \frac{w}{L}\frac{dL}{dw} = \text{elasticity of demand for labor}$$

$$e_K = \frac{dK}{dr}\frac{r}{K} = \text{supply elasticity of capital}$$

Differentiating equation (A12.12) with respect to w, we get

$$\frac{dL}{dw} = \frac{dq}{dp}\frac{dp}{dw}a_L + q\frac{da_L}{d(w/r)}\frac{d(w/r)}{dw}$$

where the arguments of a_L and q are eliminated for simplicity. Substituting from (A12.15), we obtain

$$\frac{L}{w}e_L = \left(\frac{q}{p}e\right)\left(\frac{p}{w}e_{pw}\right)a_L + q\frac{da_L}{dw}$$

or (multiplying both sides by w/L and simplifying)

$$e_L = ee_{pw} + \frac{w}{dw}\frac{da_L}{a_L} = ee_{pw} + \frac{a_L^*}{w^*}$$

Solving equation (A12.11) for a_L^* and substituting the result into the preceding equation, we have

or

$$e_L = ee_{pw} - (1-s)\sigma\left(1 - \frac{r^*}{w^*}\right)$$

$$e_L = ee_{pw} + (1-s)\sigma e_{rw} - (1-s)\sigma \qquad (A12.16)$$

because $r^*/w^* = e_{rw}$.

Next differentiate equation (A12.13) with respect to w to obtain

$$\frac{dp}{dw} = a_L + \left(w\frac{da_L}{dw} + r\frac{da_K}{dw}\right) + a_K\frac{dr}{dw}$$

The expression in parentheses equals zero because of the cost minimization condition

$$MRS_{LK} = -\frac{da_K}{da_L} = \frac{w}{r} \qquad \text{or} \qquad rda_K + wda_L = 0$$

Hence

$$\frac{dp}{dw} = a_L + a_K\frac{dr}{dw}$$

or substituting from equation (A12.15),

$$\frac{p}{w}e_{pw} = a_L + a_K\frac{r}{w}e_{rw}$$

Multiplying both sides by w/p, we finally get

or

$$e_{pw} = \frac{wa_L}{p} + \frac{ra_K}{p}e_{rw}$$

$$e_{pw} = s + (1-s)e_{rw} \qquad (A12.17)$$

We finally differentiate equation (A12.14) with respect to w:

$$\frac{dK}{dr}\frac{dr}{dw} = \frac{dq}{dp}\frac{dp}{dw}a_K + q\frac{da_K}{dw}$$

Substituting from (A12.15), we have

$$\left(\frac{K}{r}e_K\right)\left(\frac{r}{w}e_{rw}\right) = \left(\frac{q}{p}e\right)\left(\frac{p}{w}e_{pw}\right)a_K + q\frac{da_K}{dw}$$

Multiplying both sides by w/K and simplifying, we get

$$e_K e_{rw} = ee_{pw} + \frac{da_K}{a_K}\frac{w}{dw}$$

or

$$e_K e_{rw} = ee_{pw} + \frac{a_K^*}{w^*}$$

Finally, solving equation (A12.10) for a_K^* and substituting the result in the last equation, we obtain

$$e_K e_{rw} = ee_{pw} + s\sigma\left(1 - \frac{r^*}{w^*}\right)$$

or

$$e_K e_{rw} = ee_{pw} - s\sigma e_{rw} + s\sigma$$

or

$$ee_{pw} - (e_K + s\sigma)e_{rw} = -s\sigma \qquad (A12.18)$$

Equations (A12.16) to (A12.18) are very important. We can solve them simultaneously to obtain e_L, e_{rw}, and e_{pw} as functions of the important parameters s, σ, e, and e_K.

A Special Case: $e_K = \infty$

Before considering the general case, it is interesting to determine the elasticity of demand for labor in the special case where the supply of capital facing the industry under consideration is perfectly elastic ($e_K = \infty$). That is, we assume that the industry is a price taker in the market for capital services.

In this case, r is a constant, which means that $r^* = 0$ and $e_{rw} = r^*/w^* = 0$. Therefore, equation (A12.17) reduces to $e_{pw} = s$, and equation (A12.16) to

$$e_L = se - (1 - s)\sigma < 0 \qquad (A12.19)$$

(because $e_{rw} = 0$ and $e_{pw} = s$).

Equation (A12.19) says something important: When $e_K = \infty$, the elasticity of demand for labor (e_L) is a weighted average of the elasticity of demand for the final product (e) and the negative of the elasticity of substitution ($-\sigma$), with weights s and $(1 - s)$, respectively.

In the case of the Cobb–Douglas production function ($q = L^\alpha K^{1-\alpha}$), equation (A12.19) reduces to $e_L = \alpha e - (1 - \alpha) < 0$ because $s = \alpha$ and $\sigma = 1$.

The General Case: $0 < e_K < \infty$

In the general case ($0 < e_K < \infty$), we must solve equations (A12.16) to (A12.18) for e_L, e_{pw}, and e_{rw}. First, we rewrite equations (A12.16) to (A12.18) in matrix form:

$$\begin{bmatrix} 1 & -e & -(1-s)\sigma \\ 0 & -1 & (1-s) \\ 0 & e & -(e_K + s\sigma) \end{bmatrix} \begin{bmatrix} e_L \\ e_{pw} \\ e_{rw} \end{bmatrix} = \begin{bmatrix} -(1-s)\sigma \\ -s \\ -s\sigma \end{bmatrix} \qquad (A12.20)$$

The determinant of this system is $\Delta = (e_K + s\sigma) - (1 - s)e > 0$. Solving by means of Cramer's rule (or otherwise), we have

$$
e_L = \frac{1}{\Delta}
\begin{bmatrix}
-(1 - s)\sigma & -e & -(1 - s)\sigma \\
-s & -1 & (1 - s) \\
-s\sigma & e & -(e_K + s\sigma)
\end{bmatrix}
$$

$$
= \frac{1}{\Delta}\left[-(1 - s)\sigma(e_K + s\sigma) + s\sigma e(1 - s) + (1 - s)s\sigma e \right.
$$

$$
\left. + (1 - s)s\sigma^2 + (1 - s)^2\sigma e + (e_K + s\sigma)se \right]
$$

$$
= \frac{1}{\Delta}\left[se_K(\sigma + e) + \sigma(e - e_K) \right]
$$

or

$$
e_L = \frac{\sigma e + e_K[se - (1 - s)\sigma]}{[s\sigma - (1 - s)e] + e_K} < 0 \tag{A12.21}
$$

Equation (A12.21) coincides with equation (5) given by Hicks (1964, p. 374). We return below to the interpretation of equation (A12.21).

Further,

$$
e_{pw} = \frac{1}{\Delta}
\begin{bmatrix}
1 & -(1 - s)\sigma & -(1 - s)\sigma \\
0 & -s & (1 - s) \\
0 & -s\sigma & -(e_K + s\sigma)
\end{bmatrix}
$$

$$
= \frac{1}{\Delta}\left[s(e_K + s\sigma) + (1 - s)s\sigma \right]
$$

or

$$
e_{pw} = \frac{s(e_K + \sigma)}{\Delta} > 0 \tag{A12.22}
$$

and

$$
e_{rw} = \frac{1}{\Delta}
\begin{bmatrix}
1 & -e & -(1 - s)\sigma \\
0 & -1 & -s \\
0 & e & -s\sigma
\end{bmatrix}
$$

$$
= \frac{1}{\Delta}(s\sigma + se)
$$

or

$$
e_{rw} = \frac{s(\sigma + e)}{\Delta} \tag{A12.23}
$$

Note that $e_L < 0$ and $e_{pw} > 0$. When w falls, the industry employs more labor, but the price of the final product falls (which means that q increases).

The sign of e_{rw} is indeterminate. Whether r increases or decreases as w falls depends on what the industry does with the quantity of capital. If K increases, r increases also, but if K falls, r decreases. What determines whether K increases or decreases? For this purpose we must distinguish between a substitution effect and an output effect.

First note that as w falls, w/r falls also. Thus differentiating (w/r) with respect to w, we have

$$\frac{d(w/r)}{dw} = \frac{r - w(dr/dw)}{r^2} = \frac{1}{r}(1 - e_{rw})$$

Substituting (A12.23) and the definition of Δ and simplifying, we get

$$\frac{d(w/r)}{dw} = \frac{1}{r\Delta}[\Delta - s(\sigma + e)] = \frac{1}{\Delta}(e_K - e) > 0 \qquad (A12.24)$$

Accordingly, as w falls, w/r falls also and leads to a substitution of labor for capital along the initial isoquant. This *substitution effect* is captured by σ and tends to reduce K and r. But this is not all.

Because $e_{pw} > 0$ and thus p falls as w falls, the industry output (q) necessarily increases (because the quantity demanded is higher). The increased output leads to an increase in K (and L). This is the *output effect*; it is captured by e and works against the substitution effect. When the output effect outweighs the substitution effect, K and r increase $(e_{rw} < 0)$, but when the substitution effect outweighs the output effect, K and r fall $(e_{rw} > 0)$.

Note that in the case of labor, the substitution and output effects reinforce each other, causing L to unequivocally increase as w falls.

Another Special Case: $e_K = 0$

The special case where the supply of capital facing our industry is perfectly inelastic (vertical) is also interesting. To obtain the elasticity of demand for labor in this case, we merely set $e_K = 0$ in equation (A12.21). We have

$$e_L = \frac{\sigma e}{s\sigma - (1 - s)e} \qquad (A12.25)$$

or (taking the reciprocals of both sides)

$$\frac{1}{e_L} = s\left(\frac{1}{e}\right) - (1 - s)\left(\frac{1}{\sigma}\right) \qquad (A12.25)'$$

That is, the same relationship which holds among e_L, e, and σ in the first special case $(e_K = \infty)$ now holds among their reciprocals: The reciprocal of e_L is a weighted average of the reciprocals of e and σ, with weights s and $(1 - s)$, respectively.

The Determinants of the Elasticity of Demand for Labor

We now turn to equation (A12.21) to study the influence of each of the four parameters $(\sigma, s, e_K, \text{ and } e)$. The rules we are about to establish are often called the *laws of derived demand*.

Taking the partial derivatives of e_L as given by (A12.21) with respect to each of the four parameters and simplifying, we get

$$\frac{\partial e_L}{\partial \sigma} = -(1 - s)\frac{(e - e_K)^2}{\Delta^2} < 0 \tag{A12.26}$$

$$\frac{\partial e_L}{\partial s} = \frac{(e + \sigma)(e_K - e)(e_K + \sigma)}{\Delta^2} \tag{A12.27}$$

$$\frac{\partial e_L}{\partial e_K} = -s(1 - s)\frac{(e + \sigma)^2}{\Delta^2} < 0 \tag{A12.28}$$

$$\frac{\partial e_L}{\partial e} = s\frac{(\sigma + e_K)^2}{\Delta} > 0 \tag{A12.29}$$

We now summarize the laws of derived demand as formulated by Marshall and later amended by Hicks:

1. *The demand for a factor of production is more elastic the larger the elasticity of substitution.* This rule follows from equation (A12.26) because $\partial e_L/\partial\sigma < 0$. Thus the higher is σ, the smaller is e_L or the higher is $|e_L|$.
2. *Provided that the elasticity of demand for the final product (in absolute terms) exceeds the elasticity of substitution (i.e., $e + \sigma < 0$), the demand for a factor of production is more elastic the larger the share of that factor in the total cost of the final product.* This rule follows from equation (A12.27). If $e + \sigma < 0$, $\partial e_L/\partial s < 0$; and the larger is s, the smaller is e_L or the greater is $|e_L|$. (*Note:* Marshall's formulation of this rule ignored the condition $e + \sigma < 0$. The error was later detected by Hicks.)
3. *The demand for a factor of production is more elastic the more elastic is the supply of other cooperant factors.* This rule follows from equation (A12.28). Because $\partial e_L/\partial e_K < 0$, the greater is e_K, the smaller is e_L or the greater is $|e_L|$.
4. *The demand for a factor of production is more elastic the greater the elasticity of demand for the final product.* This rule follows from equation (A12.29) since $\partial e_L/\partial e > 0$. Thus the smaller is e (i.e., the more elastic the demand for the final product), the smaller is e_L (i.e., the more elastic is the demand for labor).

An Illustration

Suppose that the industry production function takes the form $q = L^{1/2}K^{1/2}$, so that $s = \frac{1}{2}$. Dividing both sides by q, we obtain the equation of the unit isoquant

$$1 = \frac{L^{1/2}K^{1/2}}{q} = \left(\frac{L}{q}\right)^{1/2}\left(\frac{K}{q}\right)^{1/2}$$

or

$$a_L^{1/2}a_K^{1/2} = 1$$

Taking the square of each side, we finally have

$$a_K = \frac{1}{a_L} \tag{A12.7a}$$

For cost minimization, it is necessary that

$$MRS_{LK} = -\frac{da_K}{da_L} = \frac{w}{r} \quad \text{or} \quad \frac{1}{a_L^2} = \frac{w}{r}$$

Solving for a_L, we get

$$a_L = \sqrt{\frac{r}{w}}$$

Substituting into (A12.7a), we also get

$$a_K = \sqrt{\frac{w}{r}}$$

Thus both unit coefficients (a_L and a_K) are functions of w/r.

Suppose further that the demand for the final product and the supply of capital are, respectively, given by the functions

$$q = \frac{100}{p^2}$$
$$K = 5r$$

Accordingly, $e = -2$ and $e_K = +1$, as the reader can easily verify.

Now write the three equations that describe the equilibrium of the industry as follows:

$$L = q \cdot a_L = \frac{100}{p^2} \sqrt{\frac{r}{w}} \tag{A12.12a}$$

$$p = wa_L + ra_K = w \sqrt{\frac{r}{w}} + r \sqrt{\frac{w}{r}}$$

or

$$p = 2 \sqrt{rw} \tag{A12.13a}$$

$$K = qa_K$$

or

$$5r = \frac{100}{p^2} \sqrt{\frac{w}{r}}$$

or

$$p^2 = 20 \sqrt{\frac{w}{r^3}} \tag{A12.14a}$$

Substituting p as given by (A12.13a) into (A12.12a) and (A12.14a) and simplifying, we get

$$L = \frac{25}{w\sqrt{rw}}$$

(A12.12a)′

$$r = \left(\frac{25}{w}\right)^{1/5}$$

(A12.14a)′

Substituting (A12.14a)′ into (A12.12a)′ and simplifying, we finally obtain

$$L = \frac{25^{9/10}}{w^{7/5}}$$

(A12.12a)″

Accordingly, $e_L = -\frac{7}{5}$, as the reader should verify. Incidentally, we obtain the same answer by setting $\sigma = 1$, $s = \frac{1}{2}$, $e = -2$, and $e_K = 1$ in equation (A12.21).

We can also use equation (A12.14a)′ to determine $e_{rw} = -\frac{1}{5}$. Again we obtain the same answer from equation (A12.23).

Finally, substitute r as given by equation (A12.14a)′ into (A12.13a) and simplify to get

$$p = 2 \times 25^{1/10} \times w^{2/5}$$

from which we easily calculate $e_{pw} = \frac{2}{5}$. This result, of course, coincides with the answer that we can get directly from equation (A12.22).

A12.3 The Adding-Up Problem[3]

As the marginal productivity theory of income distribution was gaining acceptance, a logical problem arose—a problem that actually threatened to shake its very foundations. If each factor is paid the value of its marginal physical product, what guarantees that total output is always just exhausted by the factor incomes so determined? Is it not possible for the total payment to factors to either exceed or fall short of total output? It seems that the marginal productivity theory cannot be valid unless we are able to show that the sum of the distributive factor shares *add up* to exactly the total output—that there is neither surplus nor deficit left at the end. This problem is known as the *adding-up problem* or the *exhaustion-of-the-product problem*.

An early solution to the adding-up problem was provided by Philip Henry Wicksteed (1844–1927) in terms of the assumption of constant returns to scale. As we already know from Section 6.7, when the production function is characterized by constant returns to scale (linear homogeneous), Euler's theorem ensures that total output is exactly exhausted by the distributive shares of all inputs. Because of this, it was mistakenly assumed that all production functions are linear homogeneous.

The fundamental solution to the adding-up problem was subsequently furnished by John R. Hicks and Paul A. Samuelson. The fundamental point is that the solution to the adding-up problem depends crucially on the market conditions of perfect competition, not the properties of the production function. As we explained in Chapter 9, the free entry and exit of competing firms ensures the absence of both profits and losses. If the logic of the factor-employment choice implies that factors are paid according to the marginal productivity principle, and the logic of perfect competition

---

[3]This section can be read together with Section 12.9.

implies zero profits, it follows that each perfectly competitive firm must choose that method of production which satisfies both requirements.

Mathematically, the zero-profit condition implies that the value of total output (pq) equals the total cost of production $(wL + rK)$; that is,

$$pq = wL + rK \tag{A12.30}$$

Further, the marginal productivity principle of factor employment necessitates that

$$w = p \cdot MPP_L$$
$$r = p \cdot MPP_K \tag{A12.31}$$

Substituting (A12.31) into (A12.30) and solving for q, we finally obtain

$$q = L \cdot MPP_L + K \cdot MPP_K \tag{A12.32}$$

In other words, under perfect competition the marginal productivity payments must exactly exhaust the product.

Note that unlike equation (6.7), equation (A12.32) is established without the assumption of constant returns to scale and the use of Euler's theorem.

The above argument can also be cast in terms of the standard price and cost-curve analysis of the equilibrium of the perfectly competitive firm discussed in Chapter 9. When all competitive firms have the same cost curves (or rather the same minimum average cost), competition ensures that each active firm will be producing at the minimum point of its average-cost curve, where *returns to scale are locally constant.* Thus the requirements of the adding-up problem are fulfilled.

When the competitive firms have different cost curves, all intramarginal producers will enjoy positive profits. These profits, of course, represent the excess of price over marginal productivity payments to the employed factors. At the same time, however, these profits can be regarded as rents accruing to whatever factors of production (such as scarce managerial talent and superior technology) enable these firms to earn these profits. Under competitive conditions, these rents can be viewed as marginal productivity payments to the relevant factors, as explained in Section 12.8. (For instance, these factors could be rented out to other firms for the same prices as their rents.) Including these rents in the total costs of the intramarginal firms has the effect of shifting their U-shaped average-cost curves sufficiently upward as to make them tangent to the price line ($AR = MR$). We therefore conclude that the case of dissimilar cost curves is not any different from the case of identical cost curves.

Appendix to Chapter 13
The Generalized Conditions for Profit Maximization[1]

In this appendix we provide a general formulation of the problem of profit maximization. The reader may recall that in the Appendix to Chapter 10, we analyzed the problem of profit maximization in terms of the functions of total revenue and

[1]This appendix can be read together with Sections 13.1 and 13.2.

total cost. That approach presupposes a cost-minimization process by means of which the firm obtains the total cost function from the production function and the factor supply functions. Here no such assumption is made, because cost minimization is now conceived as an integral part of profit maximization.

Suppose that we are given the demand function for the firm's product, the production function, and the factor supply functions as follows:

$$
\begin{array}{lll}
p = d(q) & \text{(demand function)} & \\
q = f(L, T) & \text{(production function)} & \text{(A13.1)} \\
w = g(L) & \text{(labor supply function)} & \\
r = h(T) & \text{(land supply function)} &
\end{array}
$$

The firm's generalized profit function (π) takes the form

$$
\pi = \pi(L, T) = R(q) - [E_L(L) + E_T(T)] \tag{A13.2}
$$

where $R(q) = qd(q) = qp$ = total revenue, $E_L(L) = wL = Lg(L)$ = total expense on labor, and $E_T(T) = rT = Th(T)$ = total expense on land.

Which are the independent variables (or policy variables) in equation (A13.2)? The factor quantities L (labor) and T (land). This is a fundamental difference from equation (A10.1), where the independent variable is q (output). In our present formulation q is itself a function of the crucial variables L and T, as indicated by the production function.

To maximize total profit (π), the entrepreneur must adjust both factors so that the partial derivatives $\partial\pi/\partial L$, $\partial\pi/\partial T$ are zero:

$$
\frac{\partial\pi}{\partial L} = \frac{dR}{dq}\frac{\partial q}{\partial L} - \frac{dE_L}{dL} = 0 \tag{A13.3}
$$

$$
\frac{\partial\pi}{\partial T} = \frac{dR}{dq}\frac{\partial q}{\partial T} - \frac{dE_T}{dT} = 0 \tag{A13.4}
$$

Now observe that $dR/dq = MR \equiv$ marginal revenue, $\partial q/\partial L = MPP_L \equiv$ marginal physical product of labor, $\partial q/\partial T = MPP_T \equiv$ marginal physical product of land, $dE_L/dL = ME_L \equiv$ marginal expense of labor, and $dE_T/dT = ME_T \equiv$ marginal expense of land. Accordingly, equations (A13.3) and (A13.4) take the form

$$
MRP_L = MR \cdot MPP_L = ME_L \tag{A13.3$'$}
$$
$$
\text{(13.7) repeated}
$$

$$
MRP_T = MR \cdot MPP_T = ME_T \tag{A13.4$'$}
$$
$$
\text{(13.8) repeated}
$$

Before going any further, note that we can combine equations (A14.3)$'$ and (A14.4)$'$, as in Section 13.2, to obtain the general rule for cost minimization:

$$
MRS_{LT} = \frac{MPP_L}{MPP_T} = \frac{ME_L}{ME_T} \tag{A13.5}
$$
$$
\text{(13.10 repeated)}
$$

To gain further insight into the implications of equations (A13.3)$'$ and (A13.4)$'$, we introduce three important elasticities: (1) the supply elasticity of labor $\eta_L = (dL/dw)(w/L)$, (2) the supply elasticity of land $\eta_T = (dT/dr)(r/T)$, and (3) the elasticity of demand for the firm's product (in absolute terms) $|e| = -(dq/dp)(p/q)$.

We also recall from the Appendix to Chapter 8 the following important relationship among MR, AR, and $|e|$:

$$MR = AR\left(1 - \frac{1}{|e|}\right)$$

(A13.6)

(A8.4) repeated

Given equation (A13.6), the left-hand sides of equations (A13.3)′ and (A13.4)′ become

$$MRP_L = MR \cdot MPP_L = AR \cdot MPP_L\left(1 - \frac{1}{|e|}\right) = VMP_L\left(1 - \frac{1}{|e|}\right)$$ (A13.7)

$$MRP_T = MR \cdot MPP_T = AR \cdot MPP_T\left(1 - \frac{1}{|e|}\right) = VMP_T\left(1 - \frac{1}{|e|}\right)$$ (A13.8)

Further, differentiating $E_L(L)$ and $E_T(T)$ with respect to L and T, respectively, and making use of the definitions of η_L and η_T, we obtain

$$ME_L = g(L) + Lg'(L) = w\left(1 + \frac{1}{\eta_L}\right)$$

(A13.9)

$$ME_T = h(T) + Th'(T) = r\left(1 + \frac{1}{\eta_T}\right)$$

(A13.10)

where $g'(L) = dw/dL$ and $h'(T) = dr/dT$. When the factor markets are perfectly competitive, the derivatives $g'(L)$ and $h'(T)$ are zero, but in the presence of monopsony power, $g'(L) > 0$ and $h'(T) > 0$.

Substituting the results of equations (A13.7) to (A13.10) into equations (A13.3)′ and (A13.4)′, we finally obtain

$$VMP_L\left(1 - \frac{1}{|e|}\right) = w\left(1 + \frac{1}{\eta_L}\right)$$

(A13.11)

$$VMP_T\left(1 - \frac{1}{|e|}\right) = r\left(1 + \frac{1}{\eta_T}\right)$$

(A13.12)

It is obvious from equations (A13.11) and (A13.12) that the wage rate (w) cannot be equal to the value of the marginal physical product of labor (VMP_L) unless the elasticities $|e|$ and η_L are infinite; similarly, the rent for land services (r) cannot be equal to the value of the marginal physical product of land (VMP_T) unless the elasticities $|e|$ and η_T are infinite. That is, each factor receives the value of its marginal physical product only when perfect competition prevails in all markets.

The term $(1 - 1/|e|)$ in equations (A13.11) and (A13.12) is a measure of monopolistic exploitation; that is, the term $(1 - 1/|e|)$ drives a wedge between an input's value of marginal product and its marginal revenue product, as shown by equation (A13.7). For instance, if at the firm's static equilibrium $|e| = 2$, the degree of monopolistic exploitation is equal to 50 percent; that is, $1 - \frac{1}{2} = 0.50$. Note that the same degree of monopolistic exploitation applies to all factors.

The terms $(1 + 1/\eta_L)$ and $(1 + 1/\eta_T)$ are measures of monopsonistic exploitation of labor and land, respectively. Thus the term $(1 + 1/\eta_L)$ drives a wedge between the marginal revenue product of labor (which is equal to ME_L) and the wage rate, and the term $(1 + 1/\eta_T)$ is a wedge between MRP_T and r. The degree of monopsonistic exploitation of labor is not in general equal to the degree of monoposonistic exploitation of land. The two become equal only when $\eta_L = \eta_T$.

As an illustration, suppose that $|e| = 3$, $\eta_L = 5$, and $VMP_L = \$90$. The degree of monopolistic exploitation is $\frac{2}{3}$ (i.e., $1 - \frac{1}{3} = \frac{2}{3}$). This means that $MRP_L = \frac{2}{3}VMP_L = \frac{2}{3}\$90 = \$60$. Further, the degree of monopsonistic exploitation of labor is $\frac{6}{5}$ (i.e., $1 + \frac{1}{5} = \frac{6}{5}$), which means that $MRP_L = \frac{6}{5}w$, or $w = \frac{5}{6}\$60 = \$50$. Accordingly, the total divergence between w and VMP_L (i.e., $\$90 - \$50 = \$40$) is divided into monopolistic exploitation equal to $\$30$ (i.e., $\$90 - \$60 = \$30$) plus monopsonistic exploitation equal to $\$10$ (i.e., $\$60 = \$50 = \$10$).

Appendix to Chapter 14
The Equations of General Equilibrium of Exchange[1]

In this appendix we present the system of equations of general competitive equilibrium of exchange. As in the text, we limit our discussion to an economy of two commodities only. However, the analysis can be extended in a straightforward manner to the case of many commodities, but we leave the details of such a generalization as an exercise for the interested reader.

Initial Endowments

Consider an economy of m consumers who bring to the market various quantities of two commodities, X and Y. Let $\bar{x}_i$ and $\bar{y}_i$ denote the initial endowment of the ith consumer. The total quantities of X and Y originally brought to the market by all consumers together are

$$\bar{x} = \bar{x}_1 + \bar{x}_2 + \cdots + \bar{x}_m \tag{A14.1}$$

$$\bar{y} = \bar{y}_1 + \bar{y}_2 + \cdots + \bar{y}_m \tag{A14.2}$$

Budget Equations

For any prices p_x and p_y of commodities X and Y, respectively, the budget equation of the ith consumer takes the form

$$p_x x_i + p_y y_i = p_x \bar{x}_i + p_y \bar{y}_i \tag{A14.3}$$
$$\text{(14.2) repeated}$$

Equation (A14.3) states that the value of the quantities x_i and y_i of X and Y, respectively, purchased by the consumer must be equal to the value of her initial endowment.

Equation (A14.3) can also be cast in the form

$$p_x(x_i - \bar{x}_i) + p_y(y_i - \bar{y}_i) = 0 \tag{A14.3$'$}$$

which is more convenient for our subsequent discussion.

[1]This appendix can be read together with Section 14.3.

Summing the budget equations of all consumers together, we have

$$p_x(x - \bar{x}) + p_y(y - \bar{y}) = 0 \tag{A14.4}$$

where $\bar{x}$ and $\bar{y}$ are defined by equations (A14.1) and (A14.2), respectively, and

$$x = x_1 + x_2 + \cdots + x_m \tag{A14.5}$$

$$y = y_1 + y_2 + \cdots + y_m \tag{A14.6}$$

Thus x and y are the total quantities of X and Y, respectively, purchased by all consumers together. The significance of equation (A14.4) will become clear below. For now note that equation (A14.4) is an identity; that is, it must necessarily hold for all conceivable prices, not just the equilibrium prices.

Demand Functions

The preferences of the ith consumer are summarized by a utility function of the form

$$U_i = U_i(x_i, y_i) \tag{A14.7}$$

The ith consumer chooses those quantities of X and Y that maximize her utility function (A14.7) subject to her budget equation (A14.3)′. For this constrained maximization problem, we again use the method of *Lagrange multipliers*.

Form the *Lagrangian function*

$$Z_i = U_i(x_i, y_i) - \lambda[p_x(x_i - \bar{x}_i) + p_y(y_i - \bar{y}_i)] \tag{A14.8}$$

where λ is an undetermined Lagrange multiplier. For utility maximization, it is required that the following partial derivatives be zero:

$$\frac{\partial Z_i}{\partial x_i} = \frac{\partial U_i}{\partial x_i} - \lambda p_x = 0 \tag{A14.9}$$
$$\text{(A4.5) repeated}$$

$$\frac{\partial Z_i}{\partial y_i} = \frac{\partial U_i}{\partial y_i} - \lambda p_y = 0 \tag{A14.10}$$
$$\text{(A4.6) repeated}$$

$$\frac{\partial Z_i}{\partial \lambda} = -p_x(x_i - \bar{x}_i) - p_y(y_i - \bar{y}_i) = 0 \tag{A14.11}$$

Equation (A14.11) is the same as budget equation (A14.3)′, while (A14.9) and (A14.10) correspond to equations (A4.5) and (A4.6), respectively. Accordingly, the first-order condition for utility maximization takes again the form

$$MRS_{xy} = \frac{\partial U_i/\partial x_i}{\partial U_i/\partial y_i} = \frac{p_x}{p_y} \tag{A14.12}$$
$$\text{(A4.8)′ repeated}$$

Solving equations (A14.3) and (A14.12) simultaneously, we finally obtain the following demand functions:

$$x_i = x_i(p_x, p_y) \tag{A14.13}$$

$$y_i = y_i(p_x, p_y) \tag{A14.14}$$

As we know, these demand functions are homogeneous of degree zero with respect to prices p_x and p_y; that is, multiplying all prices by any positive number leaves the quantities demanded unchanged.

To obtain the market demand functions, we merely sum demand equations (A14.13) and (A14.4) over all consumers. We have

$$x = x(p_x, p_y) = \sum_{i=1}^{m} x_i(p_x, p_y) \tag{A14.15}$$

$$y = y(p_x, p_y) = \sum_{i=1}^{m} y_i(p_x, p_y) \tag{A14.16}$$

The market demand functions are also homogeneous of degree zero with respect to prices p_x and p_y.

General Equilibrium

General competitive equilibrium exists when the prices are such that the market demand for every commodity equals the market supply. That is,

$$x(p_x, p_y) = \bar{x} \tag{A14.17}$$

$$y(p_x, p_y) = \bar{y} \tag{A14.18}$$

Thus we have one equation for each commodity.

As we explained in Chapter 14, one commodity (say Y) has to be taken as the *numéraire* (standard of value). Accordingly, we set $p_y = 1$, so only p_x remains to be determined.[2] Since there are two equations and only one unknown, the question arises as to whether the system is overdetermined and whether equations (A14.17) and (A14.18) may give rise to inconsistent solutions.

As it turns out, equations (A14.17) and (A14.18) are not independent. When one of them is satisfied, the other is necessarily satisfied as well. This follows from identity (A14.4). Surely if $x - \bar{x} = 0$, that is, if equation (A14.17) is satisfied, identity (A14.4) reduces to $p_y(y - \bar{y}) = 0$ or $y - \bar{y} = 0$, which means that equation

---

[2]Because the demand functions are homogeneous of degree zero in prices, they can be cast in the form

$$x = x\left(\frac{p_x}{p_y}, 1\right) \tag{A14.15$'$}$$

$$y = y\left(\frac{p_x}{p_y}, 1\right) \tag{A14.16$'$}$$

by merely multiplying all prices in (A14.15) and (A14.16) by the positive number $1/p_y$. Accordingly, there is only one unknown to be determined: the price ratio p_x/p_y, which reduces to p_x when we arbitrarily set $p_y = 1$.

(A14.18) must also be satisfied. Similarly, when $y - \bar{y} = 0$, the market for X must also be in equilibrium. This conclusion illustrates a general proposition known as *Walras's law: In a system of n markets, when (n − 1) markets are in equilibrium, then by necessity the last market is in equilibrium also.*

An Illustration

Consider an economy that consists of two persons, A and B. Person A is endowed with 40 units of X and 160 units of Y, so his budget line takes the form

$$40p_x + 160p_y = p_x x_a + p_y y_a \qquad \text{(A14.3a)}$$

Similarly, person B is endowed with 60 units of X and 40 units of Y, and her budget line is

$$60p_x + 40p_y = p_x x_b + p_y y_b \qquad \text{(A14.3b)}$$

The utility functions of A and B are

$$U_a = x_a y_a \qquad \text{(A14.7a)}$$

$$U_b = x_b y_b \qquad \text{(A14.7b)}$$

Therefore, the first-order conditions for utility maximization by A and B, respectively, are

$$\frac{y_a}{x_a} = \frac{p_x}{p_y} \qquad \text{(A14.12a)}$$

$$\frac{y_b}{x_b} = \frac{p_x}{p_y} \qquad \text{(A14.12b)}$$

Solving (A14.3a) and (A14.12a) simultaneously, we get, after simplification, the demand functions of person A:

$$x_a = \frac{40p_x + 160p_y}{2p_x} \qquad \text{(A14.13a)}$$

$$y_a = \frac{40p_x + 160p_y}{2p_y} \qquad \text{(A14.14a)}$$

Similarly, solving (A14.3b) and (A14.12b) simultaneously we obtain person B's demand functions:

$$x_b = \frac{60p_x + 40p_y}{2p_x} \qquad \text{(A14.13b)}$$

$$y_b = \frac{60p_x + 40p_y}{2p_y} \qquad \text{(A14.14b)}$$

The market demand functions are

$$x = x_a + x_b = \frac{100p_x + 200p_y}{2p_x} \qquad\qquad\text{(A14.15a)}$$

$$y = y_a + y_b = \frac{100p_x + 200p_y}{2p_y} \qquad\qquad\text{(A14.16a)}$$

Thus the market equilibrium conditions become

$$\frac{100p_x + 200p_y}{2p_x} = 100 \qquad\qquad\text{(A14.17a)}$$

$$\frac{100p_x + 200p_y}{2p_y} = 200 \qquad\qquad\text{(A14.18a)}$$

The solution to each of the last two equations is $p_x = 2p_y$ or $p_x/p_y = 2$.

Given the equilibrium price ratio, we can now return to demand functions (A14.13a), (A14.14a), (A14.13b), and (A14.14b) to determine the quantities finally consumed by each person. Thus we have $x_a = 60$, $y_a = 120$, $x_b = 40$, and $y_b = 80$. Since person A's initial endowment was $\bar{x}_a = 40$ and $\bar{y}_a = 160$, it follows that A bought 20 units of X (i.e., $x_a - \bar{x}_a = 60 - 40 = 20$) and sold 40 units of Y (i.e., $\bar{y}_a - y_a = 160 - 120 = 40$). Similarly, B's initial endowment was $\bar{x}_b = 60$ and $\bar{y}_b = 40$; hence she sold 20 units of X (i.e., $\bar{x}_b - x_b = 60 - 40 = 20$) and bought 40 units of Y (i.e., $y_b - \bar{y}_b = 80 - 40 = 40$).

NAME INDEX

SUBJECT INDEX